Blessed Beyond Measure

RANDALL J. BREWER

BLESSED BEYOND MEASURE

CONTENTS

INTRODUCTION

The challenge of Christianity is that believers live in two worlds at the same time, the physical world and the spiritual world. In Paul's letter to the Ephesians, he shows the believer the difference between the two and how to live in both realms. Many Christians, most really, are not aware of the blessings they possess in Christ and Paul wrote this letter to enlighten their understanding. It's not true that all the blessings of God are reserved for heaven. No, God wants His will and His blessings to be in full manifestation on earth just as it is in heaven. Jesus is the source of all these riches and in Him all blessings flow. In Christ, believers have access to all that He is and all that He has. Paul wants you to comprehend how big and how rich God is. His resources never run out which means your heavenly account is forever overflowing.

This is a letter of encouragement as Paul talks about the deep, spiritual wealth of knowing Christ. He explains that God is both rich and generous, that He's ready and willing to share all spiritual blessings with those He calls His own. There is power available to you that can impact the world as you seek to fulfill the will of God for your life. As you read the words of the apostle, you'll gain insight and revelation. You'll have a better perspective of the divine gifts you can lay hold of and operate in as you apprehend who you are in Christ and what you possess in Him. Obadiah 1:17 says, "But on Mount Zion there shall be deliverance, and there shall be holiness; The house of Judah shall possess their possessions." Through Paul, God is telling you to possess all that belongs to you.

This epistle is the pinnacle of theological doctrine of the Christian faith. There is a sustained loftiness in its teaching which has been deeply praised and prized by Bible commentators down through the centuries. Charles Spurgeon said, "Whoever would see Christianity in one treatise, let him read, mark, learn, and inwardly digest the epistle to the Ephesians." This letter was written to explain some of the great themes and doctrines of Christianity as Paul deals with a wide range of moral and ethical behaviors. He explains that there must be a unity between what you believe and how you behave in front of others. His words contain the power of reconciliation that allow you to both talk the talk and walk the walk. Your obligation as a believer is to live a life characterized by unity, holiness, love, wisdom, and perseverance.

Many scholars consider this book the Grand Canyon of the New Testament for it covers in great detail the depth and breadth and height of God's plan for those who belong to Him. It tells how people everywhere are to begin a new life in Christ with new standards and new relationships. Paul seeks to give people a clearer view of God and a better understanding of the church and its central purpose in God's plan for man. God didn't just save you to get you into heaven, He saved you to put you in a brand new family. He gave you brothers and sisters from every culture and background. He emphasizes the need for unity in the family of God, holiness in life, and one's responsibilities at home and at work. Like a skilled physician, Paul mends back together the broken bones of separation and division in the church as he brings a clarity of being united together as one in Christ.

British minister Martyn Lloyd-Jones said, "If Romans is the purest expression of the gospel, as Martin Luther said, then Ephesians is the most sublime and majestic expression of the gospel." Perhaps more than any other book in the Bible, Paul's letter to the Ephesians tells of the wealth of the believer, the walk of the believer, and the warfare of the believer. In this letter Paul looks at salvation and redemption from the vantage point of heavenly places. It's where the gospel message appears in its most noble form, where it transcends greatness and is exalted above mere human comprehension. Paul teaches you how to grow, how to walk, and how to fight. The central theme of this epistle is that you've been made worthy, now you must walk worthy. For sure, that is what Christianity is all about.

It is Paul's plan and purpose to help believers become more aware of their position in Christ and to motivate them to draw upon His power and His blessings in daily living. This epistle will revolutionize your life as it teaches you how rich you are in Christ and how to use those riches. Paul talks about the "riches of His grace" (1:7), the "unsearchable riches of Christ" (3:8), and the "riches of His glory" (3:16). It is Paul's desire that once you read this letter you'll "be filled with all the fullness of God" (3:19), "the fullness of Christ" (4:13), and "be filled with the Spirit" (5:18). Yes, the glorious fullness of the Father, the Son, and the Holy Spirit is at your disposal and is yours to enjoy when you comprehend who you are in Christ. The first three chapters of Ephesians tell you what those riches are and in this book we will go into great detail to show you how these eternal riches can be yours.

C. S. Lewis wrote, "It would seem that our Lord finds our desires not too strong but too weak. We are half-hearted creatures, fooling about with drinking, sex, and ambition, when infinite joy is offered us. Like an ignorant child who wants to go on making mud pies in the slum because he cannot imagine what is meant by the offer of a holiday at the sea. We are far too easily pleased." These are the type of people Paul wrote the book of Ephesians to. He doesn't want you to be satisfied with the worldly "mud pies" of fortune and fame. No, there are eternal riches and spiritual blessings in Christ that far exceed the wealth of this world, and Paul tells you what they are. As you read and study this epistle you will grow spiritually and be transformed in the way you look at life. Truly, you'll never be the same.

| 1 |

"THE WILL OF GOD"

Walking the walk. That should be the goal of every believer. Paul knows that as he sits down and pens a letter to the saints at Ephesus. He wastes no time but right away plunges into the midst of great and profound truth. He writes, "Paul, an apostle of Jesus Christ by the will of God" (Eph. 1:1). It is the tendency of most people to regard these introductions as formal and non-important. They think these salutations are for the most part unnecessary, something you can skip over as you hurry on to the main message of the epistle. People want to get to the heart of the message and get impatient with all the preliminaries and introductions. They think these opening words are nice and polite but have nothing to do with spiritual doctrine. How wrong they are! If some verses are not worth reading, then God would not have had them put in the Bible. All scripture is important and must never be considered irrelevant. Found in the opening remarks of each epistle is truth that is essential to your walk with the Lord.

Nothing Paul says is formal and great attention and consideration must be given to every word he writes. The ink isn't even dry yet and Paul tells you the most important thing in all the universe. Everything you say and everything you do must be according to the will of God. He says he's an apostle because God planned it that way. It was the will of God for his life. He was an ambassador of Christ, a man set apart by

God. What is an apostle? The Friberg Greek Lexicon says an apostle is a messenger of God who has the special task of founding and establishing churches. Apostles are "called and sent by Christ to have the spiritual authority, character, gifts and abilities to successfully reach and establish people in kingdom truth and order, especially through founding and overseeing local churches." The role of the apostle includes the duties of preaching the gospel (1 Cor. 1:17), teaching and praying (Acts 6:4), the working of miracles (2 Cor. 12:12), and the building up of leaders in the church (Acts 14:23).

Paul was not called to be an apostle by man but by God Himself. Man can't ordain anybody. They can only approve of what has already been ordained. The truth be told, there are thousands of people standing behind a pulpit today who have not been ordained by God but rather by men. At the same time, there are many ordained by God who are not standing behind a pulpit, a place they rightfully belong. God had prepared Paul all his life to be an apostle, a man sent to the Gentiles with a message that they could be grafted into God's holy family along with the Jews. Are there apostles today? Many teach that all the apostles died off in the first century. This is not true. Eph. 4:13 says there will be apostles "till we all come to the unity of the faith and the knowledge of the Son of God, to a perfect man, to the measure of the stature of the fullness of Christ." This has not happened yet so yes, there are still apostles today, along with prophets, evangelists, pastors, and teachers (vs. 11).

Paul was not a self-proclaimed apostle but he says God made him one. He said in 1 Cor. 15:10, "But by the grace of God I am what I am, and His grace toward me was not in vain." Paul says he is what he is by the will of God. Can you say the same thing? Are you doing the will of God in your life? Jesus said in Matt. 12:50, "For whoever does the will of My Father in heaven is My brothers and sisters and mother." Being a Christian is the affirmation of the lordship of Christ. That means He has something to say about all the things you do with your life. It's the will of God that should direct every step you take. Prov. 16:9 says, "A man's heart plans his way, but the Lord directs his steps." Freely and intentionally you are to submit your will to the will of God. Jesus set the example when He said continually that He came to do the will of the Father who sent Him. In the Garden of Gethsemane He prayed to the Father, saying, "Not My will, but Yours, be done" (Luke 22:42). Jesus submitted to the will of the Father and so should you.

The key to your success is the will of God. It should excite you that God has a plan and a purpose for your life. You weren't created by accident and His will for you was established in your mother's womb and has never changed. David said in Ps. 139:16 (NLT), "You saw me before I was born. Every day of my life was recorded in Your book. Every moment was laid out before a single day had passed." The Message Bible says, "All the stages of my life were spread out before You, the days of my life all prepared before I'd even lived one day." God thought through every detail of your life before you were even born. In fact, these plans came into existence before the foundation of the world (Eph. 1:4). In other words, God has been waiting a long time for you to be born so He can reveal His power and His glory through you. It should be your highest desire to know the perfect will of God for your life. He has so much in store for you but you've got to step into His will to experience it.

What is the will of God? It's that which God approves of and determines to bring about. It concerns God's choices of what to do and what not to do. John MacArthur said, "The distinguishing mark of a Christian is a preoccupation and a centering of his life on the will of God." Doing the will of God from the heart (Eph. 6:16) is the foundation to the Christian life. Unless you desire to do the will of God, it is questionable if you are even a Christian at all. Without seeking divine direction from above, you're in essence saying you don't need God in your life. When people have what they want and need, they really don't give God's will for their life much thought. The world today is in chaos because people think they don't need God. Life is serious business and this is why you must live in submission to the will of God. He is a holy God who knows everything and He always has your best interests at heart. All you have to do is yield your will to His will. He will not turn a deaf ear to you if you go to Him in reverence and sincerity.

How do you know what God wants you to do? Ask Him. David said in Ps. 143:10, "Teach me to do Your will, for You are my God; Your Spirit is good. Lead me in the land of uprightness." God did not allow you to be born so you could grow up and do anything you want to do. That wasn't His plan. Sad to say, many people never go to God and ask Him what His plan is for their life. 1 Peter 42 (NLT) says, "You won't spend the rest of your lives chasing your own desires, but you will be anxious to do the will of God." Becoming a Christian brings with it the desire to know the Father's will. The Message Bible says, "Then you'll be able to live out your days free to pursue what God wants instead of being tyrannized by what you want." Everything you do must be framed in the context of the will of God. Ask Him what His will is about everything that concerns you. Ask Him how to spend your time and money. Ask Him who your friends should be and who to marry, where you should go to church and where you should work.

In Col. 4:12 Paul said Epaphras was "always laboring fervently for you in prayer, that you may stand perfect and complete in all the will of God." The Message Bible says, "He's been tireless in his prayers for you, praying that you'll stand firm, mature and confident in everything God wants you to do." God has a purpose, a plan, and a desire for everybody. It cannot be denied that the safest place to be is in the center of the will of God. Still, a lot of people don't seek God's will because they're afraid He'll want them to do something they don't want to do. They act as if God wants to make their life miserable. He doesn't. Eccl. 5:20 says, "For he will not dwell unduly on the days of his life, because God keeps him busy with the joy of his heart." The

Message Bible says, "Yes, we should make the most of what God gives, both the bounty and the capacity to enjoy it, accepting what's given and delighting in the work. It's God's gift! God deals out joy in the present, the now."

Think about it. You enjoying your life is the will of God. His will for your life is not a heavy, strenuous burden that you must bear. If you don't like what you're doing, whether in the kingdom or in the natural world, then it's probable you are not in the will of God. Jesus said, "For My yoke is easy and My burden is light" (Matt. 11:30). Know for certain that His will for your life will harmonize with the way He's wired you. It fits perfectly with your personality and with your gifts and desires. You need to believe that you are who you are because God made you that way. It is no accident where you're currently at in life, what your personality is like, what your interests are, and how you relate to people. The Bible says you are "fearfully and wonderfully made" (Ps. 139:14) and nothing about you is orchestrated by God haphazardly. Who you are and what you are, along with the experiences you've gone through, have been arranged by God in order for you to have a specific impact upon specific people eternally.

The very essence of the Christian life is to do the will of God, to be obedient to what God wants, desires, and requires. 1 John 2:6 says, "He who says he abides in Him ought himself also to walk just as He walked." Jesus always walked in submission to the will of God, and so should you. When you step into whatever He's created you for, realize that your calling is as high and holy and important as any apostle, pastor, or missionary. God is no respecter of persons "for there is no partiality with God" (Rom. 2:11). The NLT says, "For God does not show favoritism." The good news is that God will reveal His will to you when you have a compelling desire to know and do the will of God. This desire comes from the deep love you have for Him, a holy appreciation for all He has done in you and for you. You seek His will as a form of worship, out of a pursuit to bring glory and honor to His holy Name. Your response to His will for your life will have an affect on your peace and joy, and on your usefulness now and forever.

Jesus said, "Behold, I have come to do Your will, O God" (Heb. 10:7). Jesus was born to do the will of God and so were you. You can know what that will is but first you will have to fulfill the one requirement God has in order for His will to be revealed. Rom. 12:1 is one of the most powerful verses in the Bible about knowing the will of God. Paul writes, "I beseech you therefore, brethren, by the mercies of God, that you present your bodies a living sacrifice, holy, acceptable to God, which is your reasonable service." This verse is saying as long as you have your own will, you can never learn the will of God. Willfully you need to surrender the plans you have for your own life so you can hear what God has to say. This is so vitally important that Paul is beseeching you to do it. The word "beseech" means 'to urge; plead; exhort; pray; to earnestly beg.' This is a military term and Paul is saying you need to conquer your flesh and to wage warfare against your own will.

To know the will of God, you've got to present yourself to Him as a living sacrifice. The Greek word for "present" means 'to place at one's disposal; to surrender; to present as a special offering to God; to fully dedicate with no intention of ever taking back again.' You must be willing to do anything and everything God asks you to do. Paul is saying that before you can learn the will of God, it is of paramount importance that you lay aside your own will and become a servant of God. In Greek the word "servant" is described as 'one completely surrendered to the will of his master; to help, assist, and fulfill his master's wants and dreams to the exclusion of all else; one whose will is completely swallowed up in the will of another,' If you're a servant of God, you're literally saying your will has been swallowed up in the will of God. You've forfeited your own rights and plans and are now living exclusively to do the will of God above everything else.

Jesus said in Matt. 16:25, "For whoever desires to save his life will lose it, and whoever loses his life for My sake will find it." According to Jesus, if you hang onto your own will, you will lose your life. But if you will surrender your will to His will, if you'll walk the walk of a servant, you'll have life and have it more abundantly. Paul tells you what to do next in Rom. 12:2, "And do not be conformed to this world, but be transformed by the renewing of your mind, that you may prove what is that good and acceptable and perfect will of God." You can't let yourself think like the world thinks. Their morals change from one day to the next. One minute they're up, the next minute they're down. People who follow the fluctuating tides of thinking in the world system are being manipulated to change their views from one moment to the next. Their beliefs shift with the ever-changing thoughts of the world and by the most recently accepted norms brought about by Hollywood and the rest of social media.

Thankfully, the Word of God never changes. If you'll faithfully read the Bible every day, your thinking will be transformed and your mind will be renewed. The word "renewed" means 'the act of making new again; to put back into its original condition before it was spoiled; to renovate; a complete renewal or restoration.' It takes a commitment on your part to get your mind renewed. It takes time, it takes energy, and it takes an investment. The good news is that once your mind is renewed, you'll be able to easily grasp things which previously were hard for you to see and understand. In other words, if you'll give God your mind, He'll give you His will, a will that is good, acceptable, and perfect. The good will of God is beneficial and profitable and His acceptable will is absolutely wonderful, exceedingly pleasing and pleasurable. His perfect will denotes spiritual maturity, a picture of a person transitioning from being youthful and immature to being full-grown and mature, a person living in accordance to the will of God.

God will reveal His will to you in a clear and concise way when you want Him to. For sure, God's will is not a secret. It is not an elusive thing, a foggy mystery. Don't trust your own intuition to discover what the will of God is for your life. Go to Him confident that He'll reveal it to you. One of the great benefits of the Christian life is hearing God speak to you personally. Jesus said, "My sheep hear My voice, and I know them, and they follow Me" (John 10:27). If you're going to walk the walk, you're going to have to hear God when He speaks to you. Have confidence that He'll reveal to you every step you should take in order to fulfill His plan and purpose for your life. It will help to understand that God has two wills which you must seek to fulfill. There is the general will of God as found in the Bible which applies to everybody. Then there is the specific will of God which pertains to you personally concerning the decisions you have to make in regard to the circumstances you go through on a daily basis.

Both the general will of God and the specific will of God are important. The problem is you can't put the cart before the horse. People want to hear the specific will of God without reading the Bible regularly in order to hear the general will of God. They want to know who to marry, what house to buy, and what job offer to accept. It's a good thing to seek God concerning these personal matters but not at the exclusion of not reading your Bible and seeking the general will of God. If you want to know the specific will of God for your life, first and foremost start by reading the Word of God. The Bible gives universal direction for every person and is a reliable indicator of the general will of God. The Bible reveals it is God's will for you to be saved and delivered from sin, judgment, and hell (1 Tim. 2:4). It is also God's will for every person to be filled with the Holy Spirit, to be guided by the direction He gives (Eph. 5:17,18). It is also God's will for you to prosper and be in good health even as your soul prospers (3 John 2).

As you read your Bible and meditate on the scriptures, the specific will of God will be revealed to you. He will take what you read and make it personal to your life. Something that has special meaning will jump off the page at you and will stir you up on the inside. Before long you'll say, "This is for me. This is the answer I've been look-ing for." You also need to learn the importance and value of hearing God speak, so much so that you'll spend time alone with Him daily so that He'll have the opportunity to speak. Don't quickly jump out of your chair once you've finished reading your Bible. No, get still be-fore Him. You must slow down and be quiet long enough in order to hear Him speak. His voice isn't loud and intimidating. No, it's soft and gentle. He speaks in a whisper, in a still small voice inside your heart (1 Kings 19:11,12). God's voice is always loving. It's the sweetest, most tender voice you'll ever hear even when He's correcting you. By all means, learn the power of a whisper from above.

You honor God when you get still in His presence. You're telling Him that what He has to say is important to you. As you draw near to God, He will draw near to you (James 4:8) and will reveal to you His plan and purpose for your life. Prepare a time and a place to meet with Him. Jesus did. He set an appointment to meet with His Father. Mark 1:35 says, "Now in the morning, having risen a long while be-fore daylight, He went out and departed to a solitary place; and there He prayed." You make appointments to see your doctor and dentist, set an appointment to meet with God. Set a time when you're at your best, when you're the most attentive. Select a place where you won't be disturbed by others, a place where it's just you and God. This is im-portant because God comes to a prepared atmosphere (Ex. 19:10,11). if you want to hear God, you must prepare to hear God. Worship Him by telling Him how great He is and how much He means to you. When you do this you're creating an atmosphere in which His will can be revealed.

Last but not least, Ps. 46:10 says, "Be still, and know that I am God." Since God speaks in a whisper, you must be quiet and still in order to hear Him. God is a true gentleman and He won't interrupt you if you're talking all the time. Some people may not know He is God be-cause they don't get still before Him. They either talk too much or else they're too busy working and don't take time to be quiet in God's presence. The word "still" is a translation of the Hebrew word "rapa" and means 'to slacken, let down, or cease.' The phrase "be still" means 'to stop frantic activity, to let down, and to be still.' Before you can know He is God, before you can hear His voice and know what His will is, you first have to be still and listen. If you'll do that, as hard as it may be for some people to do, you'll hear God speak. Make time for God and He'll make time for you. Yes, He does want to speak to you. He wants to give you direction for your life but you must give Him the opportunity to do so.

It should make you shout for joy knowing that you can know with certainty the will of God. He has an explicit plan for your life and He wants you to know what that plan is. Go to Him and He'll share it with you clearly and in great detail. Then, when you start walking out that plan, when you walk the walk, you'll have great success in whatever you do. To help you find and remain on the path God wants you to be on, there are concrete signs that will confirm that your life is lined up perfectly with the will of God for your life. 2 Cor. 13:1 says, "By the mouth of two or three witnesses, let every word be established." This principle also includes knowing the will of God for your life, the purpose He planned and mapped out before the foundation of the world. God will confirm His will to you through two or three witnesses. This confirmation may come from reading your Bible, your pastor, or your circumstances. These signs will come so you'll have a firm foundation to stand on.

It goes without saying that you'll always be on safe ground when you read and obey the Bible. The God who is leading you is the same God who inspired the Bible to be written. Know with certainty that God will never tell you to do something contrary to His Word. For example, God will never tell you to leave your spouse to go marry another person. Adultery is contrary to the teaching of scripture, as is lying, stealing, and being disrespectful to those in authority. God makes no exceptions to what is already written in the Bible. Also, if you're a child of God, you have a right to be led by the Spirit of God (Rom. 8:14). If you'll listen, the Holy Spirit will lead you and bring confirmation to what the will of God is for your life. The word "led" means 'to lead, often depicted by animals being led by a rope tied around their necks.' The owner would tug on the rope and the animal would follow wherever their owner led them. Likewise, the Holy Spirit will tug on your heart. You have to pay close attention or else you'll miss it.

Ps. 37:4 says, "Delight yourself in the Lord, and He shall give you the desires of your heart." Many times God's will is revealed simply by the desires in your heart. God will put desires inside of you and you need to listen so you'll know what they are. Maybe you have a desire to sing or to work with children or the elderly. There is something burning inside of you. What your heart longs for is God's will exploding inside of you. Ps. 20:4 says, "May He grant you according to your heart's desire, and fulfill all your purpose." Another way God confirms His will to you is through the counsel of seasoned, spiritually mature leaders. These leaders may be your pastor or an elder at your church. It may be the person who's been mentoring you since you gave your life to Christ. They know you well and can help you discern what you should or shouldn't do. Many times they can see things you can't see and may have a clearer picture of what's taking place. Have an open heart for God may speak to you through them.

Another way God brings confirmation regarding His will is through the opportunities that come your way. Paul wrote in 1 Cor. 16:9, "For a great and effective door has opened to me." Pay attention to doors that get opened and doors that get closed. More times than not, many doors will close before the right door opens. That's just the reality of life. Never be discouraged by a door that closes. That just means the right door will open somewhere down the line. Remember, some doors only God can open. Finally, the words of Rom. 14:23 cannot be ignored. "For whatever is not of faith is sin." When God is leading you to do something, it will usually require you to increase your faith. This means you'll have to believe for His will to come to pass. It required faith for the children of Israel to cross through the Red Sea on dry ground and it required faith for David to kill Goliath. Ask yourself, "Does this require faith?" If so, you are in the will of God and there is nothing more glorious than that.

| 2 |

"GLOW IN THE DARK"

The book of Ephesians can be considered a type of survival guide as Paul shares the most important and essential things you must know and do in order to walk the walk of a believer. It teaches you how to survive in horrible places and how to thrive during hostile times. Ephesus was one of the greatest cities in the ancient world and half a million people lived there. It was the capital city of the then Roman province of Asia and its name meant "the desired one." It was the third largest city in the Roman Empire, second only to Rome and Alexandria. In the city was a huge amphitheater, library, and university. It was a port city along the trade route between Europe and Asia and all the merchant traders and all their money flowed through Ephesus. It was a melting pot of different cultures and religions. Throughout the city were several temples built for all the different gods they worshiped, chief among them was the multi-breasted Diana. The temple of Diana was so huge that it was one of the seven wonders of the ancient world.

Diana was the fertility goddess and prostitution was used to finance the activities that went on at the temple. Every night over a thousand men and women went out into the city raising money for their god. This pagan city was so multi-cultured that it created a very hostile environment for a Christian to live in. In the midst of all this, Paul writes a letter to the believers who lived there. It was written around

62 A.D., approximately one year before his death. He begins by saying he is an apostle by the will of God. He then states to whom this letter is written, "To the saints who are in Ephesus, and faithful in Christ Jesus" (Eph. 1:1). Next to the book of Revelation, the word "saint" appears in the book of Ephesians more than any other book in the New Testament. Paul doesn't even get to the heart of his message to the church without first giving an extraordinary description and definition of what it means to be a Christian. He says a Christian is a saint, they are faithful, and they are in Christ Jesus.

What does it mean to be a saint? Some religions vote on who can be called a saint. To them, the requirements of sainthood is that you must be dead for many years and have two or more miracles accredited to your name. They then tell you to pray to these saints and worship them, a practice that is paganistic in nature. Paul, however, is not writing to dead people but to living, breathing believers who are alive and well. What he's saying is that every Christian is a saint in the eyes of God. You can't be a Christian without being a saint which means you've been cleansed inwardly from the pollution of sin and the guilt that goes with it. A saint has been washed and sanitized from that which causes separation from God, from the contamination that affects spirit, soul, and body. 1 Peter 2:9 says, "But you are a chosen generation, a royal priesthood, a holy nation, His own special people, that you may proclaim the praises of Him who called you out of darkness into His marvelous light."

A Christian is a saint who has been delivered from this present evil age (Gal. 1:4). Never be afraid or ashamed of making such a claim about yourself, that you are a saint in the family of God. If you're a believer, you've been separated from the world, set apart by God to do His will on the earth. Jesus said, "They are not of the world, just as I am not of the world" (John 17:16). Being a saint means you've been marked by the blood of Jesus and called out for a specific purpose. This means you're not supposed to live like everybody else. Like a lamp on a stand or a city on a hill, you shine bright and stand out from the rest of the world. In other words, you glow in the dark. A radical change has happened inside of you and this affects your conversations and your behavior. No longer do you go to church on Sunday and live like the devil on Monday. You're a saint and you talk like one and act like one. When you walk the walk of a saint separated by God, your actions will always back up what you believe.

The Christian is a saint. He is also one who is faithful. In Greek the word means "to be trustworthy" and is the characteristic of the person who is reliable, steadfast, and unwavering. God needs people of strong character, saints He can trust to fulfill His will on the earth, people like Hananiah who "was a faithful man and feared God more than many" (Neh. 7:2). Webster's Dictionary defines "faithful" as 'maintaining allegiance; constant; loyal; marked by or showing a strong sense of duty or responsibility.' It implies a steadfast loyalty to a person or a thing to which one is bound by an oath or obligation. The world is full of alluring distractions clamoring for your time and attention. Fleshly pleasures have a way of tempting you to spend all your time and energy seeking after self-satisfaction. This is why Jesus warns that the way of salvation is narrow and difficult, requiring much discipline to remain faithful to the cause of Christ and His will for your life.

In order to be a faithful servant of Jesus Christ, there must be a willingness to give up all carnal desires so you can hold true to the path God has laid out for you to walk on. Faithfulness hinges upon what you value as important, coupled together with commitment. God expects you to be faithful and true, to do something with the abilities and opportunities He gives you. In the parable of the talents, the master said to the two servants who brought increase to what was given them, "Well done, good and faithful servant; you were faithful over a few things, I will make you ruler over many things. Enter into the joy of the Lord" (Matt. 25:21,23). God always rewards faithfulness so be careful to keep and honor what you've been entrusted with. Live in such a way that you can be trusted to do what you say you're going to do. Don't say one thing and do something else. No, talk the talk and walk the walk. Be faithful and keep your word. Do it with all your heart, mind, soul, and strength.

A Christian is not only one who believes in Christ but is one who, in a real sense, is "in Christ." Jesus said, "I am the vine, you are the branches" (John 15:5). That means you are in Him and He is in you. When Jesus was crucified, you were crucified with Him. When He died, you died with Him. When He arose from the dead, you arose with Him (Eph. 2:5,6). Col. 3:3 says, "For you died, and your life is hidden with Christ in God." To be "in Christ" means you've accepted His sacrifice on the cross as payment for your sins. God no longer sees your imperfections, He sees in you the righteousness of His own Son (Eph. 2:13). Only "in Christ" is the debt of sin cancelled, relationship with God restored, and eternity received (John 20:31). Gal. 3:27 says, "For as many of you as were baptized into Christ have put on Christ." This means you've been identified with Christ. You've left your old sinful nature behind and are now fully embracing the new life in Christ.

Rom. 6:11 says, "Count yourselves dead to sin but alive to God in Christ Jesus." To be "in Christ" is to be radically transformed. Paul said, "If anyone is in Christ, he is a new creation; old things have passed away; behold, all things become new." When you are in Christ Jesus, He becomes a living reality to you. He is the source of the abundant life flowing out of you and it shows in everything you say and do. In Him is the strength and power to confront life and all the trials that come with it. To be "in Christ" brings personal fulfillment as a human being. The questions "Who am I?" and "Why am I here?" are answered when you are "in Christ." Jesus said, "I am the bread of life. He who comes to Me shall never hunger, and he who believes in Me shall never thirst" (John 6:35). Being "in Christ" satisfies every hunger and quenches every thirst. The word "Christian" occurs only three times in the Bible but the expression "in Christ," "in the Lord," and "in Him" occur 164 times in the letters of Paul alone.

The primary need of the church in these last days is to have a working knowledge of what it means to be a Christian. The early church, even while small in number, had a deep and lasting impact on the pagan world they lived in because of their quality of life and the power they possessed as a Christian. They knew who they were in Christ and they knew how to walk the walk. If the believers in this present age knew what they knew and did what they did, the world today would be a much better place. This is why it is vitally important that all Christians examine themselves to see if their lives have the same moral standard as those in the early church. 2 Cor. 13:5 (MSG) says, "Test yourselves to make sure you are solid in the faith. Don't drift along taking everything for granted. Give yourself regular checkups." Believers are to examine their motives, their actions, their words, and the current condition of their hearts. By doing this you will bring spiritual health and wholeness to your walk with God.

Knowing you're in Christ and He lives inside of you should promote sanctification and sound moral living. If your life shows no evidence that you're separated from the world, then one will wonder if you are a Christian at all. 1 Cor. 9:27 (NLT) says, "I discipline my body like an athlete, training it to do what it should. Otherwise, I fear that after preaching to others I myself might be disqualified." If you don't regularly examine yourself, you run the risk of becoming disqualified. In Greek this word means 'not standing the test; rejected' and it suggests being 'unacceptable, disapproved, unworthy, worthless, cast away.' The word is illustrated in Rom. 1:28, "And even as they did not like to retain God in their knowledge, God gave them over to a debased mind, to do those things which are not fitting." Consider also Titus 1:16, "They profess to know God, but in works they deny Him, being abominable, disobedient, and disqualified for every good work."

The Message Bible says, "They're real creeps, disobedient good-for-nothings."

A person who is disqualified is cut off from God being unfit and unworthy of His presence in their lives. This is the worst thing that can happen to a born again believer and God's Word clearly shows it can happen (Heb. 6:4-6;10:26-31). Regular self-examination is a proven way to make sure it doesn't happen to you. Lam. 3:40 says, "Let us search out and examine our ways, and turn back to the Lord." Self-examination is necessary so you can correct yourself on a regular basis to make sure your words and actions are bringing glory to God. It's what keeps you honest with yourself and with Him. It gives you the assurance that you're walking the walk of who God called you to be. Many problems come as a result of a life not examined. Gal. 6:3,4 says, "For if anyone thinks of himself to be something when he is nothing, he deceives himself. But let each one examine his own work, and then he will have rejoicing in himself alone, and not in another."

A lack of self-examination can lead to ongoing self-deception. If you're not careful, you can easily be deceived, to think you're more ethical than you really are. One of the devil's favorite traps is to whisper sweet but false assurances in your ear. He'll make you think everything is okay when it really isn't. An example of people who were deceived is found in Matt. 7:21-23, "Not everyone who says to Me, 'Lord, Lord,' shall enter the kingdom of heaven, but he who does the will of My Father in heaven. Many will say to Me in that day, 'Lord, Lord, have we not prophesied in Your name, cast out demons in Your name, and done many wonders in Your name?' And then I will declare to them, 'I never knew you; depart from Me, you who practice lawlessness.'" It's a dangerous thing to lie to yourself. 1 John 1:8 says, "If we say that we have no sin, we deceive ourselves, and the truth is not in us." Truly, it's self-examination that allows you to combat the spiritual deception that is in the world.

You need to stop and realize the magnitude of the relationship you have with God. Never, never take this relationship for granted for it puts you under an obligation to live every second of your life as a faithful representative of the Lord Jesus Christ. In other words, what you say and do are to show people what God is like. You're an ambassador for Christ and this is why Prov. 4:23 says, "Keep your heart with all diligence, for out of it spring the issues of life." Your heart is the storehouse of your character so with humility examine yourself and ask God to reveal to you those things which don't line up with His will. When you do that, you're working out your own salvation with fear and trembling (Phil. 2:12). The words "work out" is the Greek word "katergazesthai" and has the idea of bringing to completion. Paul is saying, "Don't stop half-way; go on until the work of salvation is fully achieved in you." You need to work out what God is working in you.

It is so important that you understand you can't be passive in spiritual matters. You're a faithful saint in Christ Jesus and you need to be aggressive in your walk with Him. Phil. 2:12,13 (NLT) says, "Work hard to show the results of your salvation, obeying God with deep reverence and fear. For God is working in you, giving you the desire and the power to do what pleases Him." Christianity is more than a decision to make Jesus your Savior, it's also a determination to make Him your Lord and Master. If you don't do that, you'll fall into the snare of self-deception. You'll be a hearer only and not a doer of the Word of God. It is a deception when people say, "Let go and let God." They're saying you don't have to do anything as you step back and watch God do everything. This is unbiblical because the Bible says you have to work out your own salvation with fear and trembling. It is a dangerous thing to leave all the work up to God. Without your co-operation, even He is helpless to help you.

When Paul says to work out your own salvation, he's not writing to unbelievers telling them how to get to heaven. You can't earn your salvation by doing a lot of good works. No, he's writing to believers telling them how to walk the walk. As a Christian, there must be evidence in your daily life that you are working out your own salvation. Walking the walk is a journey of continual progress. This means you must press on day after day until your life mirrors that of the Lord Jesus Christ. Allow Him to be your example of how to conduct your life. After all, you are a saint in Him. Allow Him to inspire you and give you the motivation to keep going forward during hard times. So important is this that nineteen times in the four gospels Jesus said, "Follow Me." After washing the feet of the disciples, Jesus said, "If I then, your Lord and Teacher, have washed your feet, you also ought to wash one another's feet. For I have given you an example, that you should do as I have done to you" (John 13:14,15).

The Greek word for "work" is "energein" and is where the word "energy" comes from. It takes energy to walk the walk and grow as a believer. Working out your own salvation means you must "maintain constant energy and effort to finish the task." You can't let go and let God. You've got to get in the race of life and run with all your heart and soul. Christian evangelist George Muller said in the nineteenth century, "The believer must finish, must carry to conclusion, must apply to its fullest consequences what is already given by God in principle. He must work out what God in His grace has worked in." Notice also that it is your own salvation that must be worked out. Sometimes people show great concern for the work of God in others and not enough of His work in themselves. Don't be like Peter who was always concerned about God's plan for everybody else (John 21:21). Jesus reprimanded him for being this way, saying, "If I will that he remain till I come, what is that to you? You follow Me" (vs. 22).

Working out your own salvation is not accidental, it's intentional. It happens when you have a desire to live at a higher level. So great is your desire to be a faithful saint in Christ Jesus that you do it with fear and trembling. This is not the fearful trembling of a guilty sinner, a fear that causes you to hide from God. No, it's the joyful trembling of an encounter with the glory of God. It's what drives you to daily seek Him out, knowing that without His help you can't effectively face life and the hardships that go with it. It also comes from a horror of grieving God. When you love someone, you're not afraid of what they'll do to you, you're afraid of what you might do to them. You need to have a tender conscience toward God with fear and trembling. English theologian J.B. Lightfoot says it's "a nervous and trembling anxiety to do right." God notices those who reverentially are in awe of Him. He said in Is. 66:2, "But on this one I will look: On him who is poor out of a contrite spirit, and who trembles at My word."

Why do you work out your own salvation? So you can glow in the dark. Phil. 2:14,15 says, "Do all things without murmuring and disputing, that you may become blameless and harmless, children of God without fault in the midst of a crooked and perverse generation, among whom you shine as lights in the world." You need to walk the walk of a glowing Christian, shining bright in a dark, murky world. Dan. 12:3 (NIV) says, "Those who are wise will shine like the brightness of the heavens, and those who lead many to righteousness, like the stars for ever and ever." The world is watching you and this is why you can't do the same things they are doing. You can't blend in with them but need to stand out from among them. The world today is crooked and perverse. It's morally twisted and spiritually deformed, a place where people are unable to support the weight of all the hardships life brings. Be different enough so that people appreciate that difference, so much so that the light in you can lead them out of darkness.

Jesus asked in Matt. 17:17, "O faithless and perverse generation, how long shall I be with you? How long shall I bear with you?" The world isn't getting brighter; it's getting darker and darker. The FBI reports that a murder takes place every thirty-five minutes, a rape every six minutes, a burglary every fourteen seconds. These numbers are horrific and shocking, all the more reason for you to glow in the dark. Matt. 9:36 says, "But when He saw the multitudes, He was moved with compassion for them, because they were weary and scattered, like sheep having no shepherd." You need to see people the same way. Don't judge and criticize them for their sinful ways but be a light to them, a beacon that shows them which path to follow. The word "light" refers to the continual glow of a shining star at night. The darker the world gets, the brighter your light can shine. Don't curse the darkness but turn on the light that reflects the radiance and glory of God.

Jesus said in Matt. 5:16, "Let your light so shine before men, that they may see your good works and glorify your Father in heaven." To be effective, light has to be seen. In other words, you have to be around people who are in darkness. If you only shine at church, you're not doing the world any good. A flashlight doesn't do much good in the sunlight, it's only effective in dark places. Light reveals what darkness hides, so you need to be careful when you share your faith with unbelievers. John 3:20 says, "For everyone practicing evil hates the light and does not come to the light, lest his deeds should be exposed." Don't be obnoxious and never point a finger in somebody's face telling them they're going to hell. People will get uncomfortable when their sin and darkness is exposed and, if you're not careful, they may run away from the message you're trying to share with them. Always remember that light does more than just expose darkness, it also shows the way out of darkness.

Matt. 5:14 says, "You are the light of the world." The Message Bible says, "You're here to be light, bringing out the God-colors in the world. God is not a secret to be kept. We're going public with this, as public as a city on a hill. If I make you light-bearers, you don't think I'm going to hide you under a bucket, do you? I'm putting you on a light stand. Now that I've put you there on a hilltop, on a light stand - shine!" (vs. 14,15). In order to glow in the dark, you must work out your own salvation with fear and trembling. If you'll do that, if you'll go to Jesus and grow in Him, you'll be a reflection of Him just light the moon reflects the light of the sun. When you walk the walk of a glowing believer, you carry the light-giving gospel message into the night. Phil. 2:16 (NLT) says you need to "hold firmly to the word of life." This means you need to have a good grip on the truth of the gospel. Not only are you to know the gospel, you must also glow in the dark and show the gospel. What you exemplify by your life must be amplified by your words and actions.

| 3 |

"NOT OF THIS WORLD"

E phesus was an evil pagan city and the church that was there was a light shining in the darkness. The believers faithfully followed the command of 2 Cor. 6:17 that says, "Come out from among them and be separate, says the Lord." They were in the city but they weren't of the city. Indeed, they were not of this world. Nowhere in Paul's writings is any mention of compromise on the part of the saints at Ephesus. In fact, God said to the Ephesian church in Rev. 2:2, "I know your works, your labor, your patience, and that you cannot bear those who are evil." He continues in vs. 3, "You have persevered and have patience, and have labored for My name's sake and have not become weary." It was a working church and the people were motivated and strong in the Lord. One reason for this is they had great leadership. Paul once spent three years at Ephesus where he helped establish the church in its midst. He told the elders of the church, "For I have not shunned to declare to you the whole counsel of God" (Acts 20:27).

The temptation to fall by the wayside was there but still the church thrived in a city polluted with fleshly pleasures and horrific sin. Paul was able to equip this church with spiritual truths and get them grounded in the Word. It was an effective church because he had given them the whole truth about God's salvation and His plan and purpose for their lives. His counsel to them continues here in this epistle, written while under house arrest in Rome. He ends his salutation to these saints by sharing with them the benefits they and believers everywhere should be enjoying because they are born again. He says in Eph. 1:2, "Grace to you and peace from God our Father and the Lord Jesus Christ." It was the custom of ancient cultures to greet one another by saying, "Peace be with you." Here, as in his other church epistles, Paul goes well beyond that and says "Grace to you" first. This greeting is much bigger, wider, and more profound than the formal salutations with which men used to greet one another.

Not one time in the Bible does Paul ever say "God bless you." It's always grace and peace, grace and peace, grace and peace. Paul doesn't use these words loosely and thoughtlessly. This is not some kind of formula he says automatically. No, these heartfelt words are charged with profound meaning. They're very sincere, intense, and full of dynamic power and energy. As he wishes grace and peace to all saints, he is desiring that they experience fully all the extreme riches that are to be found in the gospel of the Lord Jesus Christ. This greeting contains some of the greatest truths of the Christian faith. When you read your Bible, it is of the utmost importance that you look at every word and find out what it means. Quite often people read their Bible so fast that important words like "grace" and "peace" are overlooked without the reader understanding fully what God is saying to them. They're more concerned with the fact that they've read the Bible for the day without comprehending what it was they read.

It is at the very beginning of this letter, in Paul's greeting to the saints, that he plunges you into the depths of the most powerful truths and deep-rooted doctrines that is to be found anywhere in all the Bible. He arouses and stimulates your attention. He whets your appetite so you'll know what he's going to develop at greater lengths throughout his letter. This second verse is the overture to the entire epistle. Indeed, there are probably no two words more important to your Christian faith than "grace" and "peace." These two words are always coupled together, and grace is always listed first. Grace is the beginning of your faith, and peace is the end of your faith. You can never experience God's peace in your life until you first experience His grace. It's the fountain, the ever-flowing spring from which all blessings flow. It's the solid foundation that supports everything on top of it. Grace is the origin and source of everything good in the Christian life which ultimately leads to peace with both God and man.

Grace is a glorious and amazing word, one of the most beautiful words in any language. American statesman Frederick Douglass once said, "Grace, it is a charming sound, harmonious to my ear." It means "unmerited favor." It's favor you don't deserve, condescending love and kindness flowing down from the throne of God into your life. Rom. 5:8 says, "But God demonstrates His own love toward us, in that while we were still sinners, Christ died for us." God gives grace to undeserving sinners for the purpose of salvation, to those who walk in darkness and have no desire to follow His plan for their life. Grace is God's riches at Christ's expense. He lived and died so that you may have life, and have it more abundantly (John 10:10). You must believe and give your consent to be loved by God even when you are unworthy to receive that love. God knows you're not perfect so stop pretending you are. Expect to be blessed even though you don't deserve it. Grace is freely given by God but it must be received by you.

Peace comes when you realize how much God loves you, proven by His grace that is poured out in your life. Rom. 5:1 (NLT) says, "Therefore, since we have been made right in God's sight by faith, we have peace with God because of what Jesus Christ has done for us" Peace is much more than the absence of conflict and it doesn't just mean rest and quiet. It's the presence of a restored relationship. The word "peace" is the Hebrew word "shalom" and it means 'to reconcile that which was broken; to join; to bring back together that which was estranged.' The word "peace" refers to the union that comes after a separation. When people come together after a quarrel and discord, they make peace and shake hands. There is a union between the two parties, a reconciliation. The idea of peace is described in Eph. 2:4,5 (NLT), "But God is so rich in mercy, and He loved us so much, that even though we were dead because of our sins, He gave us life when He raised Christ from the dead."

Grace and peace. The beginning and the end. Why does Paul say this is what he wishes for those saints who are faithful in Christ Jesus? Because it contains the whole meaning of Christian doctrine. He's saying more than anything else, you need the grace of God that leads to peace. People desperately need grace because of what they have become as the result of the fall of man in the Garden of Eden. Eph. 2:1-3 says all people were dead in trespasses and sins and were by nature children of wrath. The Message Bible says, "You filled your lungs with polluted unbelief, and then exhaled disobedience." Without salvation people are alienated from God because of sin. And because they are at war with God, they are also at war within themselves. Man is in a state of internal conflict and they don't understand why. They want to do things they know on the inside they shouldn't do. A battle rages on the inside of him. He cries out, "Wretched man that I am! Who will deliver me from this body of death?" (Rom. 7:24).

Scripture teaches that man was made by God in such a way that he can only be at peace with himself if, and only if, he is at peace with God. For this reason, God put inside of man something he can't get rid of. It's called a conscience. He may think he can do whatever he wants and he happy with it, but he can't. His conscience won't let him enjoy the sin he willfully commits. Misery goes with him wherever he goes and there is nothing he can do about it. There is an internal warfare taking place inside of him seeking for his attention. These people don't realize that man was never created to set up his own rules with which to live by. People are not gods but they seek to act like one just the same. They don't understand that this is the reason for the war and confusion taking place inside of them. They know nothing about peace and this puts them at war with everybody else. Those they argue and fight with want to be gods also and this is where conflicts and quarrels come from.

Because of sin, everybody becomes self-centered. They become ego-maniacs, obsessively consumed with what they want with no regard to the needs and desires of others. This is why James 3:16 says, "For where envy and self-seeking exist, confusion and every evil thing will be there." Sin puts people in a state of war, discord, and unhappiness. Their disobedience to God makes them wretched and is the cause of the disunity they have with other people. Without God, people have a hatred for correction. They think they're right and nobody can tell them differently. What do they need God's laws for when they can make up their own laws? He is a fool who does not listen to wise counsel. He deserves to be punished and rightfully so. It's at this point where the marvelous message of the grace of God comes in. It's utterly unmerited and entirely undeserved. When man deserves to be blotted out of existence, God looks upon him and says, "Grace to you and peace."

If you want to measure grace, you must measure the depths of sin. Unless you understand the meaning of sin and its consequences, you'll never fully comprehend the magnitude of the grace of God. Not only will grace give you peace with God, it also gives you peace with yourself. It's a peace that passes all understanding (Phil. 4:7) and it enables you to have a clear conscience. You'll be able to look in the mirror and say, "All is well." You're a new creature in Christ and you now have a bright future. The grace of God will also give you peace with other people. This doesn't mean everybody is going to like you. What changes is how you view them. You now look at others with a heart of love and passion rather than hate and resentment. Your enemies now become people you can pray for. Jesus said in Matt. 5:44, "But I say to you, love your enemies, bless those who curse you, do good to those who hate you, and pray for those who spitefully use you and persecute you."

Paul says this grace and peace comes to you from the Father and the Lord Jesus Christ. Receiving this grace will change your whole conception of God. When you were a sinner, He was God. But now, as a recipient of grace, He has become your Father. Notice also that all the blessings of God come to you through the Lord Jesus Christ. Who is Jesus? He is the Lord! This was the same word the Jews used in the Old Testament for God. It means "Jehovah," the greatest name of all. Jesus is equal to the Father through and through. Jesus is God just like the Father is God (John 1:1). He was also a man. He was given the name Jesus at His birth in Bethlehem. The Son of God became the Son of man so that the sons of man can become sons of God. Through grace, the Father of Jesus has now become your Father. He is also Christ, the Messiah, the Anointed One. He was sent by God the Father to the earth and received the anointing and the power to be both King and Deliverer. Indeed, He is the Lord Jesus Christ.

What should your response be to being blessed with God's grace and peace? Praise, of course. Eph. 1:3 says, "Blessed be the God and Father of our Lord Jesus Christ, who has blessed us with every spiritual blessing in the heavenly places in Christ." This is a glorious, staggering statement Paul makes. Several times he states the entire gospel message in a single verse, where he says the same thing in different ways. This is one of those times. Without a doubt, this verse is the foundation on which the rest of the epistle stands on. God is the blessed One and He loves to bless His people. Notice the order in which Paul writes this verse. He tells you to praise God before you ask Him for the blessings He has provided for your enjoyment and benefit. You can't be so self-centered that all you think about is how God can bless you. The most miserable of all believers are those who only think of themselves and the blessings they can receive. The way to be blessed is not to run to the blessings, but to the source of the blessings.

Paul is saying the more you worship God, the more you'll enjoy His blessings. Jesus said the same thing in Matt. 6:33. "But seek first the kingdom of God and His righteousness, and all these things will be added to you." Paul began his letter telling the people who they are and what they are. He then tells them about the blessings available to them as Christians. He wants them to understand the priceless blessings that come from God, the blessings of grace and peace. It is his desire that all saints get the most out of their spiritual heritage and to enjoy life as they should, all to the praise and glory of God. The blessings of God can pay off your past debts, your present liabilities, and all your future needs. He forgives all your sins and He then places the righteousness of Jesus Christ inside of you. Like the saints of Ephesus, you are to live a godly life in an ungodly world. The problem today is a lot of Christians struggle because they don't know about all the blessings God has bestowed upon them.

The highest calling on your life is to become the person God called you to be. In order to live a full, productive, and effective life you must lay hold of what God has given you and know how to utilize those blessings in your life. Paul wants "the eyes of your understanding" to be enlightened (Eph. 1:18). He knows that the more you understand the blessings of God, the more you'll experience them and live a good, productive life. Understanding your redemption and who you are in Christ always lead to praise. Paul said, "Blessed be the God and Father of our Lord Jesus Christ." These words are a burst of praise and acclamation and thanksgiving. Daily you need to praise God and thank Him for who He is and all He has done. He has given you His grace and peace and these blessings always lead to praise. Giving God worship and praise is the starting point of any conversation you have with Him. The real measure of your spirituality and your knowledge of God is the extent to which you give Him praise and thanksgiving.

Rev. 4:11 says, "You are worthy, O Lord, to receive glory and honor and power." God is glorified when you walk the walk of a praising Christian. Phil. 4:4 says, "Rejoice in the Lord always. Again I will say, rejoice!" Paul wrote these words while in prison. In spite of his hardships, he was still able to praise his Lord. The Message Bible says, "Celebrate God all day, every day. I mean, revel in Him!" How prominent is worship and thanksgiving in your life? How often do you burst out giving praise to God? There is more to this than saying superficially the words, "Praise the Lord." No, true praise is heartfelt, coming from the depths of your inner being. It's when you can't contain yourself. Giving God praise and adoration is what separates you from the rest of the world. Sinners have no hope and are continually miserable and unhappy. They curse and grumble and complain. They have nothing good to say about anything because they're too preoccupied with their own wants and needs.

If you're going to walk the walk, you'll always give recognition to the Father for His glory, honor, and goodness. Charles Spurgeon said, "He has blessed us, therefore we will bless Him. If you think little of what God has done for you, you will do very little for Him. But if you have a great notion of His great mercy to you, you will be greatly grateful to your gracious God." Notice also that Paul says God "has blessed us." That's past tense. He's already blessed you. When you got born again, you were instantly made spiritually rich. So many times Christians ask God for things He's already given them. They want more of God's love but Rom. 5:5 says, "The love of God has been poured out in our hearts by the Holy Spirit who was given to us." How about peace? You already have it. Jesus said in John 14:27, "Peace I leave with you, My peace I give to you." Consider also 2 Peter 1:3, "His divine power has given us all things that pertain to life and godliness."

God is a good God. He is a kind, loving, gracious Father and He has already blessed you with all the love, peace, joy (John 15:11), and power (Phil. 4:13) you'll ever need. You need to take hold of these blessings and start using them in your life. Special attention needs to be given when Paul says these are spiritual blessings in the heavenly places. Just like you, these blessings are in the world but they are not of this world. Charles Spurgeon said, "Our thanks are due to God for all temporal blessings; they are more than we deserve. But our thanks ought to go to God in thunders of hallelujahs for spiritual blessings. A new heart is better than a new coat. To feed on Christ is better than to have the best earthly food. To be an heir of God is better than being the heir of the greatest nobleman. To have God for our portion is blessed, infinitely more blessed than to own broad acres of land. God hath blessed us with spiritual blessings; they are priceless in value."

The blessings of God are infinite, well beyond one's ability to number. Paul, however, lists several of them here in the first chapter of Ephesians. He's going to tell how you've been adopted into God's holy family, forgiven and redeemed. He'll reveal that you've been sealed by the Holy Spirit and have obtained an inheritance from on high. The list goes on and on. All these blessings are the key benefits of a relationship with God through Jesus Christ. The word "blessing" comes from the Greek word translated "eulogy" and means 'to speak well of.' God has spoken good things over you, all for your benefit. In the Old Testament most of the blessings came in a material, temporal, external form. It was determined if a man was blessed by God by the number of cattle, goats, and sheep he had, and by how much land he owned. They were earthly blessings which you could see with the natural eye. In the New Testament, the blessings of God are beyond sight for they are in heavenly places. In other words, they are not of this world.

Heb. 11:13 says believers are "strangers and pilgrims on the earth" and Phil. 3:20 goes on to say, "For our citizenship is in heaven." You are not of this world but that does not mean you can't enjoy the marks of God's handiwork here on the earth, those things which are a reflection of Him. Ps. 19:1 (NIV) says, 'The heavens declare the glory of God; the skies proclaim the work of His hands." This is not a denial of physical blessings for God "gives us richly all things to enjoy" (1 Tim. 6:17). What Paul is saying is that the blessings you enjoy originate in heavenly places. In other words, you need to thank God for your weekly paycheck and not your employer. You need to thank God for your healing and not the doctor who gives you medicine to take. You can enjoy the good things in the world but don't set your affections on them. 1 John 2:15 says, "Do not love the world or the things in the world. If anyone loves the world, the love of the Father is not in him."

Col. 3:2 says, "Set your mind on things above, not on things on the earth." Don't despise the world but never forget that because of sin it is a fallen world. You need to look at the world differently than the unbeliever. To them, this world is their home. You, on the other hand, and not of this world. You "look not at the things which are seen, but at the things which are not seen; for the things which are seen are temporal; but the things which are not seen are eternal" (2 Cor. 4:18 NIV). The phrase "in heavenly places" appears five times in this epistle and no where else in the New Testament. J. B. Lightfoot said, "The heaven of what the apostle here speaks is not some remote locality. It's not some future abode. It is the heaven which lies within and about the Christian." If you are in Christ, heaven is not something you look forward to in the future, it is something that is a part of you right now, something you can experience with every breath you take.

Finally, Paul makes it clear in Eph. 1:3 that it is "in Christ" that all these blessings come. This is why in the first three verses of this epistle Paul mentions the Jesus Christ four times. He is the exclusive channel through which the blessings of the Father flow. Apart from Jesus, there is nothing. John 1:16 (NLT) says, "From His abundance we have all received one gracious blessing after another." The Message Bible says, "We all live off His generous bounty, gift after gift after gift." Paul said in Col. 2:9, "For in Him dwells all the fullness of the Godhead bodily." These blessings are spiritual which means they come by way of the Holy Spirit. The blessings come from the Father, through Jesus Christ, via the Holy Spirit. It's the Holy Spirit who delivers the blessings to you. Not only that, He brings to you and fills you up with the life of Christ Himself and all the blessings that go with such a life. This is why 1 John 4:17 says, "As He is, so are we in this world."

| 4 |

"THE TUNNEL OF TIME"

God has blessed you richly and abundantly because He wants you to rest in His goodness. Paul speaks of many spiritual blessings here in the first chapter of Ephesians. God is using him to give you a glimpse of salvation from His point of view. It should come as no surprise that the first blessing mentioned is the foundation for all spiritual blessings. Eph. 1:4 (NLT) says, "Even before He made the world, God loved us and chose us in Christ to be holy and without fault in His eyes." The Greek word for "chose" means 'to choose for oneself.' Think about it. Before God created the world, He looked down the tunnel of time and chose you to be His own. Before there were mountains and oceans and stars in the night sky, before God said, "Let there be light," you were on His mind. There has never been a moment in all eternity when God didn't know about you or care about you. You've been loved since before the beginning of time, so much so that God chose you before you chose Him (John 15:16).

Why did God choose you to be one of His children? He chose you because He loves you (Deut. 7:7,8) and there is no other reason than that. Don't try to understand this. Just accept it and receive it. His love is unconditional and there is nothing you can do to deserve it. Charles Spurgeon once said tongue in cheek, "I have no question that God chose me, because I am quite sure that if God had not chosen me, I never would have chosen Him. And I'm sure He chose me before I was born, or else He never would have chosen me afterward. And He must have elected me for reasons unknown to me for I could never find a reason in myself why He should have looked upon me with such special love." All people are looking for unconditional love. They need it, they crave it. Yet, because of their fleshly nature, they're suspicious of it. Human love is not unconditional although many people think it is. All it takes is one sour argument with someone for them to be proven wrong.

You don't have to earn or understand God's love, all you have to do is receive it. Don't wrestle with the concept of unconditional love, just lay back and rest in that love and believe God loves you because He loves you. People ask, "How do I know if I've been chosen?" Charles Spurgeon said, "Accept Christ and you'll know." He used to pray, "God, save the elect and then elect some more." When you gave your life to Jesus, you confirmed beyond a shadow of a doubt that you were chosen to be born again, to be a child of God. Acts 13:48 says, "And as many as had been appointed to eternal life believed." The Message Bible says, "All who were marked out for real life put their trust in God - they honored God's Word by receiving that life." What about free will? If God has already chosen you, is free will an illusion that nobody has? No! God never violates your free will. This means you'll always have a choice to make. You either respond to God's plan or you don't.

The doctrine of election has caused great controversy in the church down through the ages. Like robots, do people involuntary respond to what God is ordaining for their lives? People have asked, "If God has chosen us, then why does it matter what we do? Why did God choose some and not others? Why would God create somebody who He knows is going to hell?" These are good questions that need to be asked and answered. First of all, it needs to be established that it is not God's will that any should perish (2 Peter 3:9) and spend eternity in darkness where there is weeping and gnashing of teeth (Luke

13:28). Jesus died on the cross for everybody and Rom. 10:13 says, "For whoever calls upon the name of the Lord shall be saved." Calvinists, unfortunately, teach that man does not have a free will. You're either chosen or you're not. They say Jesus died for some people but not all. That's foolish because the words "free will" is found seventeen times in the Bible. It is foolish to teach that man does not have a free will.

God chose you before time began but that does not relieve you of your responsibility to choose Him. Both parties in a love relationship must have the opportunity to choose that love. Without the freedom of choice, there is no love. Thankfully, God takes the first step. Jesus declared in John 6:44, "No one can come to Me unless the Father who sent Me draws him." The Message Bible says, "He draws people to Me - that's the only way they'll ever come." The word "draw" has the idea of a hungry man desperately being drawn to food to satisfy his hunger. God draws you in by creating an emptiness inside of you that only He can fill. Matt. 5:6 says, "Blessed are those who hunger and thirst for righteousness, for they shall be filled." Hunger and thirst represent the desperate longing for God in one's life. God knows the hunger you're craving is for a relationship with Him so in His grace and mercy He draws you in. Your ultimate responsibility is to respond to that pulling on your heart.

By drawing you in, God is seeking to change your desires. It is necessary that He do this because, if left to yourself, you will seek to be a god over your own life. Rom. 3:10,11 says, "There is none righteous, no, not one; There is none who understands; There is none who seek after God." God draws you in because you won't come to Him otherwise. Matt. 22:14 says, "For many are called, but few are chosen." Who gets chosen? Those who with free will respond to the call. God gives everybody a chance to get saved. The first thing God gave Adam and Eve was free will, the freedom of choice between right and wrong. Your eternal destiny is determined by what choice you make. It's all about free will. Every person has a free will with which they can choose Him or reject Him. Because God is all knowing, He can look down the tunnel of time and know who will and will not respond to Him. God knowing how you will choose never robs you of free will and the ability to make whatever choices you want to make.

Does God predestine some people to go to hell? Absolutely not! People don't go to hell because God didn't choose them, they go because they rejected Him and the salvation He freely offered. Sinners can't complain that God hasn't chosen them when they don't want to be chosen in the first place. God gives everybody a chance to get saved. Each person has a free will to get saved or remain lost forever. God is sovereign, man is responsible. Just invite Him into your life and you'll discover He has chosen you. Rev. 3:5 implies that every person's name is written in the Book of Life. It's only when a person rejects Christ and dies that their name is blotted out of the Book of Life. God chooses everybody to be saved and He doesn't add your name to this book when you get born again. No, your name was always there and will remain there unless you die without receiving Jesus as your Lord and Savior. Rev. 20:15 says, "And anyone not found written in the Book of Life was cast into the lake of fire."

God chose you in Christ but what has He chosen you for? He has chosen you to "be holy and without blame before Him in love" (vs. 4). You are chosen not only for salvation, but for holiness. God's grace and sovereignty does not diminish your responsibility for personal holiness and sanctification. The proof of election is not perfection, it's separation from sin. There must be a willingness and a desire inside of you to do the right thing. It's what motivates you to walk a holy walk, to be "pure and upright" (Job 8:6) before Him. In other words, God chose you based on what He knew you would become. This is another of Paul's summaries of the entire gospel message. God's will for all His people in Christ is to remove and rectify completely the effects of sin brought about by the fall of man, to undo the disastrous event that took place in the Garden of Eden. 1 John 1:5 says, "God is light, and in Him is no darkness at all." God's plan for your life and destiny is to be like Him, holy and without blame in love.

Martyn Lloyd-Jones said, "Holiness is ultimately the essential attribute of God." It should come as no surprise to you that God says, "Be holy, for I am holy" (1 Peter 1:16). Holiness refers to internal purity while being without blame or blemish refers to an outward condition. It's like a sacrificial lamb that is without spot or wrinkle (Eph. 5:27). God wants you to be pure, perfect on the inside and perfect on the outside. That is true holiness. He wants you to flow in perfect harmony and wholeness according to the way you were designed to live before the foundation of the world. It's a life where everything about you works together for a common good, both inside and outside. Your outer actions are to be an expression and a testimony of the transformation and regeneration that has taken place inside your heart. So important is this that Heb. 12:14 says without holiness "no one will see the Lord." The Message Bible says "you'll never get so much as a glimpse of God."

Long ago God decided to adopt you into His holy family through Jesus Christ. Eph. 1:5,6 says "having predestined us to adoption as sons by Christ Jesus to Himself, according to the good pleasure of His will, to the praise of the glory of His grace, by which He has made us accepted in the Beloved." This is one of the mightiest and most glorious statements in all the Bible. Paul is bringing you face-to-face with the most magnificent blessing you'll ever encounter in all your life, the chance to be a child of God. In the Bible, the word "blessed" is a very rich word. It means you have every joy and every benefit that your heart and soul needs and longs for. Without a doubt, the greatest blessing of all is that God chose and predestined you to be adopted into His family. The word "predestined" means 'predesign, to know in advance.' God looks through the tunnel of time and sees the end from the beginning (Is. 46:10). He then chooses what He predestined to happen.

Rom. 8:29 says, "For whom He foreknew, He also predestined to be conformed to the image of His Son." It's a predestination that leads to a transformation in your life. It is vitally important and essential that you understand the call to holiness comes before the adoption as sons and daughters. Indeed, without holiness there is no adoption. This is why you were predestined to be holy and without blame before Him in love. Acts 4:28 (NLT) says, "But everything they did was determined beforehand according to Your will." God wants you to have a pure heart and to be pure in your words and actions. He predestined you to become more and more like Jesus every day. Remember, you're to be blameless children of God, "without fault in the midst of a crooked and perverse generation" (Phil. 2:15). The work of God in your life should change the things you say and do, along with the way you think. If your lifestyle and the choices you make don't change, then one will wonder if you're even saved to begin with.

Paul will soon share that you've been forgiven of your sins and sealed by the Holy Spirit of promise, both great blessings in and of themselves. Still, being adopted into God's family is the pinnacle of all blessings. Truly, there is nothing higher than that for adoption is what salvation is all about. John Piper once said, "Adoption is greater than the universe. It is above the universe and existed before the universe. In fact, adoption is the purpose of the universe." Paul writes in Rom. 8:15, "For you did not receive the spirit of bondage again to fear, but you received the Spirit of adoption by which we cry out, 'Abba, Father.'" God's amazing, unhindered, and unrestricted love is being poured out on you. You're His adopted child and He's your "Daddy," your "Papa." You can rush into the presence of God without fear because the Spirit of adoption has made you sons and daughters in God's holy family. The gift of sonship is the highest privilege in all the universe because you can now stand before God with His stamp of approval upon you.

You don't have to long for the approval of God, you're already accepted by Him. The word "accepted" is the Greek word "charitoo" and it means 'highly favored; full of grace.' Through adoption, God is making a holy family who will be able to demonstrate His glory to the world in which they live. Jesus prayed to the Father for all believers in John 17:20-26. He said in vs. 23, "I in them, and You in Me; that they may be made perfect in one, and that the world may know that You have sent Me, and have loved them as You have loved Me." Isn't that amazing? God the Father loves you as much as He loves Jesus. John Stott wrote, "When people ask us the speculative question why God went ahead with the creation when He knew that it would be followed by the fall, one answer we can tentatively give is that He destined us for a higher dignity that even creation would bestow on us." In other words, this high position of being adopted into the family of God gives believers something in Jesus that Adam never had.

Paul refers to the urgency and importance of adoption when he writes in 2 Cor. 6:17,18, "Come out from among them and be separate, says the Lord. Do not touch what is unclean, and I will receive you. I will be a Father to you, and you shall be My sons and daughters, says the Lord Almighty." Paul is the only writer in the New Testament who uses the term "adoption." He borrowed this word from Roman law because the Jews knew nothing about adoption at all. It had no part in their legal system while the Romans practiced adoption all the time. In ancient times, the purpose of adoption was not to rescue a child from off the street. Typically what happened is a childless rich man would adopt an older male, a teenager or a person in their early twenties, so they could carry on his name and inherit his estate. Being adopted means you were deliberately chosen by the person adopting you. An adopted son would become the apple of his father's eye and the joy of his father's heart, even more so than that given to a naturally born son.

Most of those who got adopted under Roman law were male because it was to them that the estate would pass. A male was chosen because of his superior ability to represent the family name and to manage the family's future. Adoption gave this young man the name, the title, and the rights of his new father. Also, all his past debts were cancelled. Whatever obligations he had would be met by the father, wiped away as if they never existed. It's as if the son was reborn on the day he got adopted. He instantly became as wealthy as his new father, having access to whatever belonged to him. Whatever the father has now belongs to the son whose responsibility is to carry on and honor his father's name. The word "adoption" means 'the placing as an adult son.' It's a term that emphasizes relationship, standing and rank, and distinction, along with all the benefits and privileges of such a position. This is why Jesus came to live and die on the earth, that you "might receive the adoption as sons" (Gal. 4:5).

God wasn't content just having you as His creation so He predestined you to be a son or a daughter in His holy family. It cannot be denied that adoption is the highest expression of God's love. 1 John 1:3 says, "Behold what manner of love the Father has bestowed on us, that we should be called children of God." You were not an accident. God chose you to be in His family before the foundation of the world. From eternity past it was His intention to adopt you as one of His own. When Jesus willingly died on the cross, when He poured Himself out and shed His blood, He was being the good and faithful elder Brother that you desperately need so that God could be your good and faithful Father. God, the great almighty King of the universe, is now your Father and His name is upon you (Rev. 3:12). A child always bears the name of his father. As a child of God, you bear the name of God because you are a member of His family. This makes your adoption by God deeply personal. When adopted by God, your status changes forever.

Adoption doesn't happen naturally. Just because you were born doesn't automatically put you into God's family. No, it's a choice you make. It happens at salvation, the moment you surrender your life to Jesus and ask Him to be your Lord and Savior. If you are born again, you've been adopted into God's family and are now heirs of God and joint heirs with Christ. Rom. 8:16,17 (NLT) says, "For His Spirit joins with our spirit to affirm we are God's children. And since we are His children, we are His heirs. In fact, together with Christ we are heirs of God's glory." The Message Bible says, "God's Spirit touches our spirits and confirms who we really are." The term "heirs of God" emphasizes your relationship with God the Father. The Greek word for "heirs" refers to 'those who receive their allotted possessions by right of sonship.' Because God has made you one of His children (John 1:12), you now have full rights to receive His inheritance. You are now a beneficiary of all that belongs to Him (Col. 3:24).

As an adopted child of God, you have "an inheritance incorruptible and undefiled and that does not fade away; reserved in heaven for you" (1 Peter 1:4). In the Old Testament, the word "inheritance" was used in reference to the Promised Land, the land which God had given His people "for an inheritance to possess" (Deut. 15:4). The Christian inheritance, however, is even greater than the land flowing with milk and honey. It is incorruptible which means it is "unravaged by any invading army." God's grace and peace have been poured out on you and no enemy can come in and ravage and destroy your life. Your inheritance is undefiled and cannot be "polluted with impious impurity." Your sins have been wiped away which means you have a purity which the sins of the world cannot infect. Your inheritance is also unfading. William Barclay says, "But the Christian is lifted into a world where there is no change and decay and where His peace and joy are untouched by the chances and the changes of life."

As a joint heir with Jesus, all that belongs to Him now belongs to you. Christ gives you His glory (John 17:22), His riches (2 Cor. 8:9), and all things (Heb. 1:2) that pertain to life and godliness (2 Peter 1:3). All these blessings are truly wonderful, but the greatest inheritance is God Himself. Ps. 16:5,6 says, "Lord, You alone are my inheritance, my cup of blessing. You guard all that is mine. The land you have given me is a pleasant land. What a wonderful inheritance!" The Message Bible says, "My choice is You, God, first and only. And now I find I'm Your choice! You set me up with a house and yard. And then You made me Your heir!" How awesome it is to be able to call God your very own Father! Ps. 73:25,26 says, "Whom have I in heaven but You? And there is none upon the earth that I desire besides You. My flesh and my heart fail; But God is the strength of my heart and my portion forever." Because God is your portion, you now have an inheritance which is incorruptible, undefiled, and which can never fade away.

Some people will say, "This is too good to be true." The good news is that it is true. You are loved in the same manner, the same passion, and with the same intensity as the Father loves Jesus. The truth be told, it's impossible for the Father to love you any less. Yes, He loves you with as much consistency, joy, and power as He loves His Son, Jesus. Because of Christ's death on the cross, the Father loves you as if you never sinned. God put Christ's perfection into your heavenly account. You may not be worthy in and of yourself, but you are accepted in the Beloved. Because of that, there is a tidal wave of emotion that surges from the Father's heart toward you as His adopted child. When you got born again, the Father welcomed you with outstretched arms into His family with a love that is so powerful and intense that words alone cannot describe it. His Spirit bears witness with your spirit that you are an adopted child of God. He gives you an internal confidence that all is well.

What does this adoption mean to your everyday life? Rom. 8:14 says, "For as many as are led by the Spirit of God, these are the sons of God." The first mark of an adopted child of God is they are led by the Holy Spirit. He directs you internally for He has taken up residence in your heart. He leads by inclination by changing your longings and desires, by shifting your interests and affections. This is truly miraculous. It's what happens when you partake of the divine nature of God. The Holy Spirit stirs your heart so that you'll love what God loves and hate what God hates. This is a way of life, an invisible miracle. The Holy Spirit will lead you from glory to glory (2 Cor. 3:18). He'll teach you line upon line, precept upon precept (Is. 28:10). David prayed in Ps. 143:10, "Teach me to do Your will, for You are My God; Your Spirit is good. Lead me in the land of uprightness." The Message Bible says, "Teach me how to live to please You, because You're my God. Lead me by Your blessed Spirit into clear and level pastureland."

When you walk the walk of an adopted child of God, many wonderful blessings will come your way. First and foremost, you have access to the throne room of God. This means you can go into His presence at any time. Ps. 100:14 says, "Enter into His gates with thanksgiving, and into His courts with praise." Also, adoption means you have an inheritance. Everybody who has been born again receive all the riches that belong to Jesus. In addition to that, adoption means you have security. Married couples get divorced and bosses at work fire their employees. Thankfully, parents will always be parents over their children. After all, children cannot divorce their parents. God says, "I will never leave you or forsake you" (Heb. 13:5). Finally, adoption means you have a new identity. God gives you His name. You are in His holy family, and He looks at you and says, "You are Mine!" This is what the book of Ephesians is all about. It explains your new identity and tells you who you are in Christ.

| 5 |

"ONCE AND FOR ALL"

God is so amazing. He is a God who is able to do exceedingly abundantly above all that you could ask or think (Eph. 3:20). Who wouldn't want to serve a God like that? He loved you before the beginning of time and He chose you to be adopted into His family, to be His own special child, to be His personal friend. He predestined you to be holy and without blame in love. He chose you to live spiritually fruitful lives, to live a life that would honor Him. You are here to fulfill a divine purpose yet so many people waste their lives on this earth in the pursuit of nothingness. They pursue fortune and fame and say, "Let's eat, drink, and be merry for tomorrow we die." Unfortunately, some of these people will die sooner than expected with nothing to show for the life they lived. They may be mourned for a short while but before long it will be as if they never existed at all. They made no positive impact in the world they lived in and soon their memory will fade away like the going down of the sun.

People ask all the time, "Why am I here? Why do I exist? What is the meaning of life?" In a poll that was taken, 61% of the people said the purpose of life is enjoyment and personal fulfillment. Really? That's the purpose of life? People go out searching for happiness and in the process they waste their lives. They never find what they're looking for in the pursuit of worldly pleasures. What they don't realize is that the world doesn't revolve around them and neither does the world owe them anything. Also, 50% of all Christians polled said the same thing. To them, the purpose of life was enjoyment and self-satisfaction. What does Jesus say about all this? He said in Matt. 6:33, "But seek first the kingdom of God and His righteousness, and all these things shall be added to you." Don't seek happiness, seek God. Put Him first and He'll take care of everything else. C. S. Lewis wrote, "Aim at heaven and you will get earth thrown in; aim at earth and you will get neither."

Paul is in the opening moments of his letter to the saints at Ephesus and it doesn't take him long to answer the question, "Why am I here?" He lists many of the blessings bestowed on the born again believer. He then says in vs. 6,12,14 that all these blessings are "to the praise of His glory." In other words, you exist to bring glory to God. Is. 43:7 says, "Everyone who is called by My name, whom I have created for My glory; I have formed him, yes, I have made him." Do everything for the glory of God. When you go to work, do it for the glory of God. When you wash the dishes and mow the lawn, do it for the glory of God. Remember, people are watching you. This is why Matt. 5:16 says, "Let your light so shine before men, that they may see your good works and glorify your Father in heaven." Sometimes the best sermons are those without words. This is why you need to walk the walk. It's true, actions speak louder than words. It's been said, "Preach the gospel and, when necessary, use words."

1 Cor. 10:31 says, "Therefore, whether you eat or drink, or whatever you do, do all to the glory of God." The Message Bible says, "Do everything that way, heartily and freely to God's glory." Paul is telling you to praise God at all times, when things are going good for you and when things are not so good. Job was a man who praised and honored God during hard times. When struck with calamity, Job 1:20 says, "Then Job arose and tore his robe and shaved his head, and he fell to the ground and worshiped." You also need to praise God in bad times. It's sad but true that some people only praise God when their

bills are paid and when they walk in good health. They have no problem praising Him when the birds sing, when the sky is blue, and when all the lights are green. One problem these people have is they run the risk of forgetting God when everything is going good for them. Prov. 30:9 (MSG) gives the warning, "If I'm too full, I might get independent, saying, 'God? Who needs Him?'"

Ps. 103:2 says, "Let all that I am praise the Lord; may I never forget the good things He does for me." Perhaps these words were on the mind of Paul as he writes the opening remarks of this epistle. It's as if he's rewriting the words of Ps. 66:5, "Come and see the works of God; He is awesome in His doing toward the sons of men." Paul wants you to know and see all the wonderful things God has done for you. He began this wonderful letter by saying you were chosen by the Father. He now shares how you've been redeemed by the Son. "In Him we have redemption through His blood, the forgiveness of sins, according to the riches of His grace" (Eph. 1:7). The work of salvation was conceived by the Father. He purposed it, planned it, and set it in motion. It was also His good will and intention that this plan would come to pass through the work of His Son, Jesus Christ. The obstacle of sin had to be removed before man could be reconciled to God. This was the purpose Jesus came to live and die on the earth.

The Message Bible says, "Because of the sacrifice of the Messiah, His blood poured out on the altar of the cross, we're a free people - free of penalties and punishments chalked up by all our misdeeds. And not just barely free, either. Abundantly free!" Almost all religions seek for the forgiveness of sins. The problem is most of them say that before forgiveness can come, you must first suffer for what you did wrong. You must work and do penance before you can be forgiven. They say forgiveness is earned and not freely given. The good news for the believer is that Jesus did all the work for you. He didn't come to teach man how to save himself by giving him something to do. No, He came to do something for you. He came to do the saving Himself. He suffered, He shed His blood, He died. It's through His sacrifice on the cross that one is forgiven of all their sins. 2 Cor. 5:19 (NLT) says, "For God was in Christ, reconciling the world to Himself, no longer counting people's sins against them."

There is no possible redemption outside of Jesus and His redeeming blood. It is in Him and Him alone that you have salvation and it's all based on what He did on your behalf. Acts 4:12 says, "Nor is there salvation in any other, for there is no other name under heaven given among men by which we must be saved." Redemption always implies a price being paid for the freedom that is purchased. The Greek word "lootruo" means 'to liberate on the receipt of a ransom.' It also means 'to buy out of the slave market.' In that day, every huge city had a slave market. It is estimated that throughout the Roman Empire at the time of this writing there were approximately sixty-million slaves who, sad to say, were bought and sold like cattle. A rich person, if he so desired, could pay a huge sum of money to the owner of the slave, thus purchasing the slave's freedom. The slave would then be redeemed and considered no more a slave. He would be as free as everyone else not a slave.

What Paul is saying here is that people who are not born again are in the spiritual slave market. He said in Rom. 6:20, "You were slaves of sin." Jesus said the same thing in John 8:34, "Most assuredly, I say to you, whoever commits sin is a slave of sin." In the New Testament, over and over again sin is associated with slavery and slavery is associated with poverty. You were once impoverished, poor in your sin. You were a slave to your flesh, an enemy of God (James 4:4). Thankfully, the work of Christ on the cross delivered you out of the sin-filled slave market once and for all. Redemption accomplishes a full release from the shackles of sin. Notice also that Jesus did not redeem you by His sinless life or by His perfect moral example. No, He redeemed you by His blood when He died in your place. Charles Spurgeon said,

"Observe, it is not redemption through His power, it is through His blood. It is not redemption through His love, it is through His blood."

At the last supper, Jesus said, "For this is My blood of the new covenant, which is shed for many for the remission of sins" (Matt. 26:28). In the Bible, salvation is always by blood. Heb. 9:22 says, "And according to the law almost all things are purged with blood, and without shedding of blood there is no remission." The blood of Jesus was innocent, without spot or blemish" (Heb. 9:14), and He shed it on the cross for you "according to the riches of His grace." This is why Eph. 2:8 says, "For by grace you have been saved through faith." It is through the grace of God that redemption brings with it the promise of the forgiveness of sins. Through redemption you are freed from the penalty of sin and, one day in the not too distant future, will be literally removed from the presence of sin. Theologian William Mac-Donald said, "If we can measure the riches of God's grace, then we can measure how fully He has forgiven us. His grace is infinite! So is His forgiveness!"

Martyn Lloyd-Jones said, "God created humanity to live in perfect harmony and fellowship with Himself. Since God is holy and perfect, this fellowship required holiness and perfection on the part of humanity as well. When Adam and Eve disobeyed God by eating of the forbidden fruit, their fellowship with God was broken. Humanity's nature then became so corrupted by sin that man was no longer capable of having fellowship with God. Therefore, the initiative for restoring that fellowship fell entirely upon God. He did this by sending Jesus to become a human being, all the while retaining His deity. Jesus lived a life of perfect fellowship and obedience toward God of which mankind had become incapable. He then endured on behalf of all humanity the death and separation from God that all mankind deserved. He then arose three days later to live eternally proving that fellowship between God and man had once again been made possible."

If you've given your life to Christ, there is no reason whatsoever why you should ever be haunted by anything you've done in the past. If you have guilt and shame over your past, you are operating outside the riches of His grace and are not cashing in on this spiritual blessing. Indeed, God is rich in grace and mercy. Rom. 4:7,8 says, "Blessed are those whose lawless deeds are forgiven, and whose sins are covered; Blessed is the man to whom the Lord shall not impute sin." With the forgiveness of sins came a restoration to divine favor and, more than that, the imputation of Christ's righteousness is given to those who believe. Paul is saying that God accepts Christ's death as full payment for your sin. Heb. 8:12 says, "For I will be merciful to their unrighteousness, and their sin and their lawless deeds I will remember no more." God looks at your sin-stained life and says, "Paid in full." Rejoice for all your sins are forgiven, past, present, and future.

Consider for a moment all that God has done for you. He chose you, adopted you, and accepted you in the Beloved. He has redeemed you in Christ and forgiven your sins. Jesus paid for your soul and if you are saved, you belong to Him. All of this was according to the riches of His grace "that He lavished on us in all wisdom and insight" (Eph. 1:8 NET). In Greek, the word "lavished" describes a flower blossom while it is in bloom. Paul is saying God's grace and His forgiveness will explode in your life. It's over-the-top and is abundant beyond all boundaries. God remembers your sinful past no more and you should do the same. He wants to have fellowship with you and share all His wealth with you. You are rich in Him and as an adopted child of God, no matter where you are in your spiritual journey, you can immediately make withdrawals from the Father's wealth. God is pouring on the blessings here and, if all this weren't enough, there is still more to come.

Eph. 1:8 (NLT) says, "He has showered His kindness on us, along with all wisdom and understanding." The Greek word for "wisdom" is "sofia" and is where the word "sophisticated" comes from. Real wisdom in Christ brings understanding of ultimate things and ultimate issues. It causes you to pause and reflect on things that pertain to God. This wisdom is so wonderful and amazing that it defies logic. There are some people who are intellectually smart yet they fall short in the area of common sense. Why is that? It's because they lack prudence and understanding, practical insight into the most important matters of daily living, as well as the deep things of God. Wisdom and understanding together combine to produce discernment in the life of the believer. Wisdom gives you information about the things of God and understanding shows you how to apply it to your life. You may not have a college degree but you can have wisdom and understanding in Christ.

William MacDonald said, "His desire is that we should have intelligence and insight into His plans for the church and for the universe. And so He has taken us into His confidence, as it were, and has revealed to us the great goal toward which all history is moving." This means that God has graciously and wonderfully revealed His plans and purposes to you. Paul wants you to know that God has a plan for your life, a divine purpose and an intended will for what you should do with your life. Plans are important for they reveal to you what the finished product will look like. Plans give you direction so you don't have to make things up as you go along. The problem is, many people approach life not knowing what they're doing or where they're going. They have no plan for their life and falsely believe things randomly happens and unfold haphazardly as life goes along. This is not how life for the believer is supposed to be. God has a plan for all creation, and He has a plan and a purpose for you.

Eph. 1:9,10 (ESV) says, "Making known to us the mystery of His will, according to His purpose, which He set forth in Christ as a plan for the fullness of time." In Greek the word "mystery" means 'that which is hidden.' God's will is hidden from those who don't believe for they don't have a clue as to what life is all about. All they want to do is party and have a good time. This world is falling apart and it all began in the Garden of Eden. In Gen. 3 man became separated from God and in Gen. 4:8, when Cain killed Abel, man became separated from man. It's all been downhill ever since. The world is getting darker and darker by the day and it's not going to get any better this side of the Second Coming of Christ. Even people in the church don't understand this so they've lost their sense of urgency here in the last days. Fortunately, to those who believe and are aware of what's going on, the will of God has been revealed because they are in His inner circle.

The NLT says, "God has now revealed to us His mysterious plan regarding Christ, a plan to fulfill His own good pleasure." God has a plan that will eventually and ultimately reach its fulfillment. He has an agenda that will one day come to a glorious climax. He knows where history is going and what the end of all things will be. Is. 46:10 says He knows the end from the beginning. The truth is, all of history is part of God's plan and He wants you to be secure in His plan for you. History is not what William Shakespeare said through his character Macbeth, "It is a tale told by an idiot, full of sound and fury, signifying nothing." Macbeth feels that life is absurd and that nothing has any purpose and meaning. A lot of people feel the same way, not realizing that God has a purpose and a grand design for everyone and everything. You didn't just accidentally get born. No, your birth was a part of God's plan and He now wants you to respond to that plan.

God has a plan and purpose for everything He has created. This means He has a plan and purpose for you. It is so important that you realize this for without a plan there will be a sense of nothingness to life. Life with no meaning is a wasted life. It's like the brief flame of a candle that flickers as it is about to burn out. Macbeth realized he had wasted so much of his brief life and it had all been proven meaningless in the end. Because there is a plan, everything you say and do means something. For the believer, there is no meaninglessness of life. Your destiny is "to be conformed to the image of His Son" (Rom. 8:29). God predestined you to live a life of holiness, to talk like Jesus talked and to walk like Jesus walked. Eph. 4:1 says you are "to have a walk worthy of the calling with which you were called." Not only does God have a plan, but He also uses everything in history to fulfill that plan. Eph. 1:11 (NLT) says, "He makes everything work out according to His plan."

Never doubt that God is powerful enough to ensure that His plans will ultimately come to pass. He is forever committed to the finished product, and He is determined to mold and shape things until His vision is accomplished. God has a plan for each person individually and He also has a plan for mankind as a whole. What is that ultimate plan? Eph. 1:10 says "that in the dispensation of the fullness of the times He might gather together in one all things in Christ, both which are in heaven and which are on earth - in Him." The word "dispensation" in Greek means 'household manager; one who manages the affairs of a household.' All the rich people in Ephesus have a well-trusted servant who managed the affairs of their home. What Paul is saying here is that God is managing history and orchestrating the universe. The truth is, history is not running wild with no rhyme or reason to it. God is in control and soon all believers, both in heaven and on earth, will be united with Him forevermore.

William Barclay said, "It so happens that we are living in an age in which men have lost their faith in any purpose for the world. But it is the faith of the Christian that in this world God's purpose is being worked out; and it is the conviction of Paul that one day all things and all men should be one family in Christ. As Paul saw it in his day, that mystery was not even grasped until Jesus came and now it is the great task of the church to work out God's purpose of unity, revealed in Jesus Christ." This unity that God graciously wants and desires is here in part but not totally. Long ago division interrupted God's plan. There was division in heaven when Satan rebelled against God and there was division on earth when Adam sinned in the Garden of

Eden. The two of them no longer wanted to revolve around God, they wanted God to revolve around them. True oneness and unity with God has been fractured because of the division and it is God's ultimate plan to bring all things back together, to create order out of chaos.

Through all the ups and downs of life, you can have an awareness inside of you that the world is not your home, that there is something more beyond this life. Eccl. 3:11 says, "He has put eternity in their hearts." In every human soul there is a God-given awareness that there is something more than this temporary world they live in. There is more to life than what you can see and experience in the here and now. With that awareness comes a hope and a desire that you can one day find a fulfillment not offered by this world. How do you respond to all this? God wants you to embrace His plan, to rest and be secure in His plan, to live every day in the hope of His plan. How you live today is based on what you believe about your future. What you think about your future has more impact on how you live your life than what has happened to you in the past. It's not the past that should shape your life, rather it's the hope of what you're believing in for the future.

There is coming a day when every knee will bow at the name of Jesus and every tongue will confess that Jesus Christ is Lord (Phil. 2:10,11). What a glorious day that will be. In the meantime, never forget that your purpose in all this is to glorify God. Yes, God has a plan and a purpose for your life but the end result of all you do is to glorify Him. That is the ultimate will of God for your life. Glorify Him in everything you say and do, when you talk the talk and walk the walk. As you live your life and all the decisions that go with it, choose that which will most glorify God. He gave you a brain so use it to make quality decisions that will glorify Him. That is your mission in life. If what you do don't glorify God, don't do it. It's as simple as that. Also, don't worry about what other people think about you. Be yourself and glorify God. As you develop and cultivate a lifelong habit of doing that which glorifies God, you will find yourself in the center of God's perfect plan and purpose for your life.

| 6 |

"WORKING ON YOUR BEHALF"

Paul's enthusiasm causes him to keep writing as he passionately pulls back the curtain of spiritual truth and insight. He is giving everybody a panoramic view of God's plan for salvation and many of the great and wonderful spiritual blessings He has poured out on those adopted as His own. As Paul writes his letter to the saints at Ephesus, he is striving to get his readers to realize that this world is not their home. Even Jesus said in John 18:36, "My kingdom is not of this world." Pastor and author A. W. Tozer once commented on this, saying, "The church is constantly being tempted to accept this world as her home. But if she is wise she will consider that she stands in the valley between the mountain peaks of eternity past and eternity to come. The past is gone forever and the present is passing as swift as the shadow on the sundial of Ahaz. Even if the earth should continue for a million years not one of us could stay to enjoy it. We do well to think of the long tomorrow."

Most Christians don't think enough about eternity, the long tomorrow, so Paul endeavors to help you catch a glimpse of the future hope you have in Christ. Eph. 1:11 says, "In whom also we have obtained an inheritance, being predestined according to the purpose of Him who works all things according to the counsel of His will." Here is a promise from God that is wonderful, incredible, and very exciting. Even as you read these words, Jesus is in heaven preparing a place for you to dwell eternally where you'll enjoy the inheritance you have graciously received (John 14:2). Yes, God is right now working on your behalf. G. Campbell Morgan said, "Our God is a God who not only wills; He works; and He works according to His will. The word 'counsel' stands for deliberate planning and arranging, in which the ways and means of carrying out the will are considered and provided for." Everything begins and originates with God. He meditated and deliberated with Himself and then made His plans according to an eternal purpose.

You are who you are because God predetermined it according to His divine purpose. This purpose which God conceived was not suggested to Him by anybody else. The purpose for your life, along with the complete plan of salvation, from beginning to end, came exclusively from God without being influenced by anyone or anything at anytime. God thought of you in the eternal counsel of His own will. It should make you feel special knowing God made no plans without first seeing you in it. You are in the heart and mind of God now because you were there in eternity past. This is a comforting thought because this is the full assurance and guarantee of your future. It is God who put you where you're now at, and He who began a good work in you will complete it in Christ (Phil. 1:6). The Message Bible says, "There has never been the slightest doubt in my mind that the God who started this great work in you would keep at it and bring it to a flourishing finish on the very day Christ Jesus appears."

Rest assured, what God starts, God finishes. Paul said He works all things according to the counsel of His own will. In Greek the word "works" means 'energy.' Whatever God plans, He energizes. He gives it the power and energy to accomplish His will and purpose. God is all powerful and a thought in His mind is energized into reality. How awesome is that? Rom. 4:21 says, "What He had promised He was also able to perform." You are in Christ and you have obtained an inheritance that is beyond your wildest imagination. This inheritance is profound and limitless for it includes every promise God ever made. 2 Peter 1:4 (NLT) says, "And because of His glory and excellence, He has given us great and precious promises. These are the promises that enable you to share His divine nature and escape the world's corruption caused by human desires." God is in the business of giving and whenever He makes a promise, it's for you. 2 Cor. 1:20 says, "For all the promises of God in Him are Yes and in Him Amen."

Paul says you have obtained this inheritance. That's past tense. You received it the moment you got born again. God redeemed you in order to give you an inheritance, an eternal blessing so great that it baffles your imagination and your understanding. One day soon you will see the Triune God face-to-face. Matt. 5:8 says, "Blessed are the pure in heart, for they shall see God." Since you'll be free from sin, you will see God and all His glory unveiled in all its fullness. The Greek word for "see" is "horao" and it denotes a 'future, continuous reality.' In heaven you'll see God continually as you have perfect and unbroken fellowship with Him. Rev. 22:3,4 says, "The throne of God and of the Lamb shall be in it, and His servants shall serve Him. They shall see His face, and His name shall be on their foreheads." John MacArthur said, "Heaven will provide us with that privilege - an undiminished, unwearied sight of His infinite glory and beauty, bringing us infinite and eternal delight."

You'll have a new home in heaven. Jesus said, "In My Father's house are many mansions, if it were not so, I would have told you" (John 14:2). You'll live in "everlasting habitations" (Luke 16:9) more glorious than anything seen on planet Earth. Ever since Jesus ascended into heaven two thousand years ago, He's been working on your behalf to prepare a dwelling place for you to live in and enjoy once you get there. Everything waiting for you in heaven will be elegant and majestic. Jesus assures you that He is preparing a custom made dwelling place designed specifically for you. He knows you so well that this place will be tailor made just for you, based on all those things that bring you the most joy and happiness. Your eternal home will be a gorgeous place with special treasures throughout. It will be a place filled with delightful splendor and dazzling ecstasy. Jesus said in John 14:3, "And if I go to prepare a place for you, I will come again and receive you to Myself; that where I am, there you may be also."

Never forget that you'll also have a new body once you get to heaven. Phil. 3:21 says, "He will take our weak mortal bodies and change them into glorious bodies like His own, using the same power with which He will bring everything under His control." Yes, this glorified, upgraded, and renewed body is for every citizen of heaven. The Message Bible says, "He'll make us beautiful and whole with the same powerful skill by which He is putting everything as it should be, under and around Him." 1 Cor. 15:49 says you'll have a body just like the resurrected body of Jesus. 1 John 3:2 confirms this saying, "But we know that when He is revealed, we shall be like Him, for we shall see Him as He is." This new body is characterized by strength (1 Cor. 15:43) and immortality (vs. 53). They'll be incorruptible (vs. 53) possessing the glory of Christ Himself. A plaque near the tomb of Benjamin Franklin says his now dead body "will appear once more in a new and more elegant edition corrected and improved by the Author."

1 Cor. 2:9 (NLT) says, "No eye has seen, or ear has heard, and no mind has imagined what God has prepared for those who love Him." It may be hard to imagine this but the Bible says in heaven some people will rule and reign with Christ" (Rev. 20:6). 1 Cor. 6:2 says they will judge the world and vs. 3 says they will judge angels. The nature of this judgment is rulership and not condemnation. It is the Lord who will condemn all who are lost (Rev. 20:11), humans and angels alike. In the parable of the talents, the reward of the faithful is found in Matt. 25:23, "Well done, good and faithful servant; you have been faithful over a few things, I will make you ruler over many things." Faithfulness in small things will allow believers in heaven to rule over many things, including angels. Sad to say, those believers who weren't good

and faithful on the earth will be the ones ruled over by those who were. Yes, they'll be in heaven but they'll be ruled over for all eternity after God wipes away every tear from their eyes (Rev. 7:17).

If you want to rule and reign with Christ once you get to heaven, Col. 3:23,24 tells you what you must do here on the earth, "And whatever you do, do it heartily, as to the Lord and not to men, knowing that from the Lord you will receive the reward of the inheritance; for you serve the Lord your God." The Message Bible says, "Do your best. Work from the heart for your real Master, for God, confident that you'll get paid in full when you come into your inheritance." Yes, there are many blessings for you to enjoy here on the earth but your true inheritance is reserved in heaven for you. Be like Abraham who waited confidently "for the city which has foundations, whose builder and maker is God" (Heb. 11:10). John Calvin wrote about this inheritance, "We do not have the full enjoyment of it at present. We walk in hope, and we do not see the thing as if it were present, but we see it by faith. We have something for which to give praise even in the midst of all our temptation. Therefore, we should rejoice, mourn, grieve, give thinks, be content, wait."

God said in Rev. 21:5, "Behold, I make all things new." This means the splendor of your inheritance and the magnificent intensity of it all will never fade away or diminish. While everything on earth is falling apart because of rust and decay, your inheritance in heaven is imperishable. Jesus said in Matt. 6:20, "Lay up for yourselves treasures in heaven, where neither moth nor rust destroys and where thieves do not break in and steal." Just as Christ is holy, blameless, pure, and seated above the heavens (Heb. 7:26), so also is your inheritance, the sum total of all God has promised you in salvation. No earthly corruption or weakness can touch what God has graciously given (Rev. 21:27). David wrote in Ps. 16:6 (NIV), "Surely I have a delightful inheritance." You can say the same thing. This inheritance is yours so "do not look at the things which are seen, but at the things which are not seen. For the things which are seen are temporary, but the things which are not seen are eternal" (2 Cor. 4:18).

In heaven everything will be made new. It will be a place where God and man will dwell together for all eternity. Rev. 21:4 says, "There shall be no more death, nor sorrow, nor crying; and there shall be no more pain, for the former things have passed away." When you understand what's waiting for you in heaven, you'll be able to endure whatever comes your way in this life. 2 Cor. 4:17 says, "For our light and momentary troubles are achieving for us an eternal glory that far outweighs them all." You can give God glory even during hard times because you have His personal guarantee that you will receive all He has promised. This is why you must forever be heavenly-minded. Phil. 3:20 (NLT) says, "But we are citizens of heaven, where the Lord Jesus Christ lives. And we are eagerly waiting for Him to return as our Savior." Heaven is your true home and you need to live with the end in mind. Pursue heaven and walk the type of walk that proves to others you are not of this world but are a citizen of heaven.

This verse can be paraphrased, "We have our home in heaven, and here on earth we are a colony of heaven's citizens." In today's world, if you want to move and become a citizen of another country, you must first take an oath pledging your allegiance to that country. By doing so, you become a foreigner to the country you once lived in, as well as every other country. Likewise, when you become citizens of heaven, you become foreigners on this earth. William Barclay said, "You must never forget that you are a citizen of heaven; and your conduct must match your citizenship." Don't allow your journey to heaven to be derailed by taking your eyes off your true home, by focusing exclusively on the here and now. Paul wrote about those who do this in Phil. 3:19, "They are headed for destruction. Their god is their appetite, they brag about shameful things, and they think only about their life here on earth." Don't be this way. Never forget that you've been made for more.

C. S. Lewis wrote, "Creatures are not born with desires unless satisfaction for those desires exists. If I find in myself a desire which no experience in this world can satisfy, the most probable explanation is that I was made for another world." At all times think aggressively about heaven. Set your mind on things above, not on things on this earth (Col. 3:2). Do this morning, noon, and night. Warren Wiersbe said, "For the Christian, heaven isn't simply a destination. It is a motivation." Clergyman E. M. Bounds said over a century ago, "Heaven ought to draw us and engage us. Heaven ought to so fill our hearts and hands, our conversation, our character, and our features that all would see that we are foreigners and strangers to this world. The very atmosphere of this world should be chilling to us and noxious. Its sun eclipsed and its companionship dull and insipid. Heaven is our native land and it is home to us. Death to us is not the dying hour but the birth hour."

Philosopher Blaire Pascal said, "All men seek happiness. This is without exception. Whatever different means they employ, they all tend to this end." If all men seek happiness, why don't they seek it where it can be found? True happiness is found only in the Person of Jesus Christ, and in the place where He is now working on your behalf, a place called heaven. American theologian Jonathan Edwards said in the 18th century, "It becomes us to spend this life only as a journey toward heaven, to which we should subordinate all other concerns of life. Why should we labor for or set our hearts on anything else but that which is our proper end and true happiness?" In his early twenties he made a special resolution that he would forever be committed to. He wrote, "I resolve to endeavor to obtain for myself as much happiness in the other world as possible." You also need to be heavenly minded at all times. Live every day with the end in mind. This world is not your home so stop living like it is.

Paul wrote in Phil. 3:14 (NLT), "I press on to reach the end of the race and receive the heavenly prize for which God, through Christ Jesus, is calling us." The Message Bible says, "I'm off and running, and I'm not turning back." He said earlier in Phil. 1:21, "For to me, to live is Christ, and to die is gain." Heaven was real to Paul and it needs to be real to you also. Why? Because if you don't know where you're going, more times than not, your steps will take you in the opposite direction of where you need to go. They'll take you farther and farther away from your destination. Make going to heaven the constant and ultimate attraction in your life. Read the scriptures and get a clear understanding of your final destination. When you walk the walk of a heavenly-minded believer, you can have the confidence that your steps are taking you in the right direction. This will bring joy and clarity to your life knowing you've got a reason to get up every morning. After all, how bad can life be if you know you're going to heaven?

In the midst of his suffering, Job cried out in a burst of faith. He said in Job 19:25,26, "But as for me, I know that my Redeemer lives, and that He will stand upon the earth at last on the earth. And after my body has decayed, yet in my body I will see God! I will see Him for myself. Yes, I will see Him with my own eyes. I am overwhelmed at the thought!" How overwhelmed are you at the thought of going to heaven? There is coming a day when God will subdue all things to Himself. Wake up knowing this could be the day when He'll come to change and transform your earthly body into a heavenly one. This could be the day when you will go live in your new home in heaven prepared for you by Jesus Himself. This could be the day when, for the rest of all eternity, there will be no more war, hunger, death, or broken relationships. Remind yourself often that heaven is your true home. Enjoy earth but your eyes and heart ultimately need to be in heaven, the place where the blessings of God are eternal.

Eph. 1:11 says all believers have obtained an inheritance but did you know that God is the recipient of a glorious inheritance also? The English Revised Version says, "In whom also we were made a heritage." God's people are by grace made to be His saints, His elect, His holy ones. And then, if that weren't enough, they are viewed by God as His inheritance. Eph. 1:18 talks about "the riches of the glory of His inheritance in the saints." In other words, your inheritance is Christ and His inheritance is you. Did you know you were created by God to be a gift given to Jesus? Yes, you are the Father's gift to the Son. In John 17:9 Jesus prayed "for those whom You have given Me." He treasures you immensely and you are the apple of His eye. You belong to God as beloved sons and daughters. So much does God love you that He chose you, adopted you, and redeemed you. He forgave all your sins in order to draw you close to Him forever and ever as His own child.

Deut. 32:9 says, "For the Lord's portion is His people." Ps. 2:8 then says, "Ask of Me, and I will give You the nation for Your inheritance, and the ends of the earth for Your possession." It is almost beyond belief that God, who owns everything in the universe, is thrilled to have you as His inheritance. Think about it. God is hungry for something that only you and other believers can satisfy. He is hungry for fellowship with people He can call His own. He enjoys spending quality time with those who love Him. He is richly rewarded with their sinless lives, and He'll delight in having fellowship with them forever and ever. He is thrilled at the thought of spending eternity with you. Ps. 149:4 says, "For the Lord takes pleasure in His people; He will beautify the humble with salvation." Yes, Jesus died so that your sins may be forgiven. But beyond that, He also died to purchase you for Himself. You are His inheritance. You have an inheritance in Christ because you are the heritage of Christ.

Deut. 4:20 says, "But the Lord has taken you and brought you out of the iron furnace, out of Egypt, to be His people, His inheritance, as you are this day." God took Israel to be His inheritance, likewise, Christ takes all believers to be His inheritance. Truly, you are the reason He shed His blood. Heb. 12:2 (NLT) says, "Because of the joy awaiting Him, He endured the cross, disregarding its shame." What was this joy? It was the joy and hope of being given a people who would become His inheritance. Jesus looked forward with joy to the people He would save. He is the Good Shepherd and He willingly gave His life to save His sheep (John 10:11). Crucifixion was a gruesome, tortuous death and it included public humiliation and shame. Jesus was ridiculed as He hung on the cross and was mocked by those who were there. But because He knew you would one day be His inheritance, He endured the shame and opened not His mouth to His accusers. This He did so you could be with Him forever.

If you want to walk a walk that pleases God, be heavenly minded at all times. If you want to be different from the rest of the world, you've got to change the way you think. You've had an encounter with Jesus so the lens through which you view life has changed. You no longer live the way you used to live. You now set your mind on heavenly things and not earthly things. You now see things from God's point of view, from His perspective. This causes you to prioritize where you put your affections, those things that matter most to you. Make going to heaven the constant and ultimate attraction in your life. Don't listen to those people who say you're so heavenly minded that you're no earthly good. Nothing could be farther from the truth. It's being heavenly minded that makes you earthly good. It's what causes you to help those in need and to love your neighbor as you love yourself. The truth is, you'll be no earthly good until you are heavenly minded. The more you think about heaven, the better you'll do on the earth.

Col. 3:1 says, "If then you were raised with Christ, seek those things which are above, where Christ is, sitting at the right hand of God." This is not a suggestion. It's a command and you must do it earnestly and intentionally at all times. On purpose be heavenly minded by setting your mind on things above. The NLT says, "Set your sights on the realities of heaven, where Christ sits in the place of honor at God's right hand." Since Jesus is in heaven, you become heavenly minded when you fix your attention and your thoughts on Him. This is the heart of the gospel, the essence of what it means to be a Christian. The Message Bible says, "Don't shuffle along, eyes to the ground, absorbed with the things right in front of you. Look up and be alert to what is going on around Christ - that's where the action is." Being heavenly minded is seeing Jesus and seeing yourself in Him. He is your inheritance, and you are His. When you grasp the reality of this, never again will you stoop to the low level of worldly thinking.

"NOTHING BUT THE TRUTH"

Before the foundation of the world in eternity past, you were cho-sen by God to be His inheritance. Yes, before time began, God decreed and fixed His heart upon having you for Himself. Why did He do this? Arthur W. Pink said in 1952, "What need has God for us? How can we possibly enrich Him? Does He not have everything - wis-dom, power, graces, and glory? All true, yet there is something that He needs, yes, needs, namely, vessels. Just as the sun needs the earth to shine upon, so God needs vessels to fill, vessels through which His glory may be reflected, vessels on which the riches of His grace may be lavished." God's purpose is to glorify Himself in human vessels, namely, you. This is why you were created in the first place. You live to glorify God. The blessings you bountifully receive abound to His great glory. John Stott said, "Everything we have and are in Christ both comes from God and returns to God. It begins in His will and ends in His glory. For this is where everything begins and ends."

God has an unwavering commitment to His own glory. Everything He does is to heighten the intensity with which His people praise Him for His glory. He made you His inheritance and He gets the glory for it. When God uses you in the kingdom, He gets the glory. When you walk the walk, He gets the glory. Everything is to the praise and glory of God. Of course, it goes without saying that nothing brings God more glory than when a lost sinner repents of their sin and gives their life to Jesus. Luke 15:7 says, "There will be more joy in heaven over one sinner who repents than over ninety-nine just persons who need no repentance." If you are born again, Christ is in you and you are in Him. How did this happen? How does anybody come to be in Christ? First and foremost, it is the work of God who "works all things according to the counsel of His will" (Eph. 1:11). Without His love, mercy, and compassion, nobody would be a Christian. It's all His work, predetermined since before the foundation of the world (vs. 4).

Eph. 2:10 says, "For we are His workmanship, created in Christ Jesus." This verse prevents people from claiming their own righteousness, from taking credit for who they are and boasting for what they have become. It's all done by God but how does He do this? How does He bring salvation to pass? The answer is found in Eph. 1:13, "In Him you also trusted, after you heard the word of truth, the gospel of your salvation; in whom also, having believed, you were sealed with the Holy Spirit of promise." God's sovereignty is real and it works. However, it does not exclude human cooperation. The ones chosen to be saved are those who heard the word of truth, they believed what they heard, which was the gospel of their salvation, and they trusted in the one person the word was referring to, Jesus Christ. The word "heard" means you take what you're hearing with thought and consideration. You contemplate and exercise your God-given facilities. Then, and only then, you respond to what you heard.

God gives each person a measure of faith (Rom. 12:3) with which to be saved but first you must give consideration to the gospel message you've heard. You have to hear the message before you can believe it. Rom. 10:17 says, "Faith comes by hearing, and hearing by the word of God." Paul says there is a particular truth through which people receive their salvation. He said the word of truth is the gospel of your salvation. This truth is the greatest good news you will ever know because it points you to the Lord Jesus Christ. This news reveals who He is and all He has done. That alone, and nothing else, is the good news. Nobody can become a Christian apart from this word of truth. People need to hear the truth, the whole truth, and nothing but the truth. This is why Paul told Timothy, "Preach the word! Be ready in season and out of season. Convince, rebuke, exhort, with all longsuffering and teaching" (2 Tim. 4;2). The Message Bible says, "Proclaim the Message with intensity."

Paul said in Acts 20:27, "For I have not shunned to declare to you the whole counsel of God." The word of truth is desperately needed because there are religious cults in the world that seek to make people feel good and happy about themselves as they encourage them to go about doing good deeds. Being kind to others is an acceptable practice but the argument against these cults is they don't present to their followers the word of truth concerning Jesus Christ. They make people feel good without telling them how to get saved and how to work out their own salvation with fear and trembling (Phil. 2:12). The truth is, people don't need to learn how to feel good, they need to learn how to be delivered from the wrath to come. You can't be a Christian without having a conviction of sin, without realizing you are guilty before God. "For all have sinned and fall short of the glory of God" (Rom. 3:23). By nature, all people are sinners and under the wrath of God and in danger of eternal judgment.

The word of truth is the good news that teaches you that Jesus Christ bore the wrath of God for you. 2 Cor. 5:18 says, "Now all things are of God, who has reconciled us to Himself through Jesus Christ." Vs. 21 says, "For He made Him who knew no sin to be sin for us, that we might become the righteousness of God in Him." God gave the world a fresh start by offering forgiveness of sins (MSG). Eph. 2:1 says, "And you he made alive, who were dead in trespasses and sins." Do you understand and realize everything God has done for you through Christ even when "you were mired in that old stagnant life of sin" (MSG)? Hopefully you do because the word of truth is the foundation for your salvation. 1 Tim. 2:4 says God "desires all men to be saved and to come to the knowledge of the word of truth." Do you have a knowledge of the word of truth? Do you know what you believe and why? Can you give a reason for the hope that is within you (1 Peter 3:15)? Let's hope so because your salvation depends on it.

Hearing the word of truth and believing it causes you to trust Him "who called you out of darkness into His marvelous light" (1 Peter 2:9). One of the greatest ways to honor someone is to trust them. Since God is committed to His own honor above all things, He is therefore committed to those who trust Him. He desires all His people to feel secure in His love and in His power even when the world is crumbling around them. So much in life is unstable. This includes your family, your health, your job, and the world you live in. Millions have been devastated because their marriage that at one time was made in heaven is now over. They're hurt and lonely as they ask how such a thing could have happened. Unfortunately, their pain causes them to wonder if God will walk out on them and abandon the relationship they have with Him. This fear of God leaving generates a sense of insecurity and a lack of confidence and hope. People ask themselves, "Why bother getting saved?"

There are believers who sometimes have this same sense of insecurity for it seems their walk with God is on shaky ground. It is no secret that when you swore your allegiance to Jesus Christ, you signed up for a life of tribulation, distress, and persecution. Rom. 8:36 says, "For Your sake we are killed all day long; We are accounted as sheep for the slaughter." Thankfully, God understands how desperately people need assurance in their lives, assurance of His love and His commitment to them, assurance that He will never leave or forsake them. This firm assurance that people need and crave will ultimately be based on God's Word, His promises, and His character. It's based on the Father's love and care, on Christ's death and resurrection, and on the Holy Spirit's presence in your life. This is why Paul said, "Having believed, you were sealed with the Holy Spirit of promise." You give God your faith in His Son, He then seals you with the Holy Spirit. You give God something, He gives you something.

All the Godhead participates in the salvation and destiny of each and every believer. Your salvation was planned by the Father, purchased by the Son, and is now preserved by the Holy Spirit. Nobody can believe in the Lord Jesus Christ without the Holy Spirit. 1 Cor. 12:3 says, "No one can say that Jesus is Lord except by the Holy Spirit." It's the Holy Spirit who convicts you of sin and points you to Jesus. It's the Holy Spirit who changes your heart (Ezek. 36:26,27) and who transforms a sinner into a saint (John 3:5,6). The word of truth, applied by the Holy Spirit, gives a person the means by which salvation comes. English poet William Cowper wrote a hymn in 1779 which opens with these words, "The Spirit breathes upon the Word, and brings the truth to sight." The Holy Spirit opens your heart so you can receive the word of truth. Martyn Lloyd-Jones said, "It is the Spirit who gives us the faculty of belief. It is the Spirit who gives us this new principle of life that makes all things possible."

All born again followers of Jesus have the Holy Spirit. 1 Cor. 3:16 says, "Do you not know that you are the temple of God and that the Spirit of God dwells in you?" As a result of the operation of the Spirit in your life, you are called upon to hear the Word, believe the Word, and trust the Word. Nobody believes the gospel against their own will for God won't make you do anything. He'll lead you to repentance and He'll lead you to believe by the operation of the Holy Spirit. God draws you in but you must respond to His call on your life. When you do, when you surrender your life to God, He steps in and seals you with the Holy Spirit of promise. When you got born again, God the Father commissioned the Holy Spirit to enter your life and to make you secure forever. To be sealed is to be verified as God's child. Notice, however, this sealing does not come before you believed. There are those who demand some kind of assurance from God before they believe, treating Him as if He can't be trusted.

In the New Testament, the word "sealed" is used three different ways. In Matt. 27:66, the tomb of Jesus was secured by sealing it and putting guards around it. Also, in Rev. 20:3, God throws Satan into a pit and seals it so he can't escape. The Holy Spirit also seals shut, meaning He seals in faith and seals out unbelief. Rom. 4:11 says that Abraham's circumcision is called the sign and seal of the righteousness he had by faith. A second meaning of sealing is that it is a sign of authenticity. You are sealed with the Holy Spirit as a sign of divine reality, a sign that you're an authentic believer of the Lord Jesus Christ. A third meaning is found in Rev. 7:3 where the seal of God is put on the forehead of God's servants to protect them from the wrath coming upon the world. The Holy Spirit is God's seal upon your life. He protects you from the evil forces that doesn't dare enter a person bearing the mark of God's seal. This is done so you'll feel safe and secure in His love and power.

The Greek word for "sealed" is "sphragizo" and it means 'to set a seal upon; to mark with a seal; to stamp with a signet or private mark for security and preservation.' It's a term that speaks of ownership and protection. In ancient times, seals were widely used whenever security from molestation was important, such as sealing bottles of wine, jars of oil, and bales of merchandise. Ephesus was a port city and all the material goods that passed through there had a seal on it. It was like a modern day barcode and was the equivalent of a written signature. A small amount of wax would be put on the product to be shipped out and the owner would take a ring with his own private mark on it and make an impression on the wax. The wax would then dry and harden with the owner's seal on it. The seal would guarantee the product's safe passage across the sea to wherever it was going. Ownership and security. That was the purpose of the seal.

Since God does all things for the praise of His glory, He takes decisive steps to secure for Himself the magnification of His glory forever. How? He seals all believers with the Holy Spirit which guarantees they'll come to their inheritance, praising Him forever. Eph. 4:30 says "you were sealed for the day of redemption." God sends the Holy Spirit as a preserving seal to lock in your faith, as an authenticating seal to validate your sonship, and as a protecting seal to keep out destructive forces. By doing so, He is putting His stamp of ownership on you. He is claiming you as His own adopted child. He is guaranteeing you safe passage across the storms and rough seas of this world into His eternal kingdom where your inheritance awaits. English pastor F. B. Meyer said, "For sealing there are needed the softened wax, the imprint of the beloved face, and the steady pressure. Would that the Spirit might impress the face of our dear Lord on our softened hearts, that they may keep it forevermore!"

Jesus also was sealed for John 6:27 says, "God the Father has set His seal on Him." Being sealed conveys authority and authenticity and is a mark and sign of ownership. It's like a brand that is put on cattle where the rancher puts his mark on the animal. How and when was Jesus sealed? At His baptism when the Holy Spirit descended on Him like a dove (John 1:32), when the Father spoke from heaven saying, "This is My beloved Son, in whom I am well pleased" (Matt. 3:17). Jesus was sealed with the Holy Spirit of promise, just like you. This made it plain and clear that Jesus was indeed the Son of God. He was now able to say, "God has sealed Me and given Me His authority. He established My ministry and anointed Me to be the Messiah." After you heard, believed, and trusted in the word of truth, you were then authenticated and established as a child of God and as a joint heir with Jesus. You believed the gospel of your salvation and immediately you were sealed.

It's believing the word of truth that makes you a child of God, it's the sealing of the Holy Spirit that authenticates that fact. You can't be a believer without being sealed with the Holy Spirit. Only believers are sealed, nobody else. Rom. 8:16 says, 'The Spirit Himself bears witness with our spirit that we are the spirit of God." Here is a clarity of assurance that is heavenly and divine. In your heart, you know that you know you are a child of God. You've tasted the "hidden manna" (Rev. 2:17) and your emotions are kindled and brought to greater heights than they've ever been before. Just as the manna that fell from heaven sustained and strengthened the Israelites as they wandered in the wilderness for forty years, so does Jesus sustain you spiritually as you walk through this life on your way to heaven. Jesus said in John 6:48,51, "I am the bread of life. I am the living bread which came down from heaven. If anyone eats of this bread, he will live forever."

Salvation means you are saved and belong to God. Your relationship with Him is secure because He "has sealed us and given us the Spirit in our hearts as a deposit" (2 Cor. 1:22). It is no accident when you sense the presence of God in your life. That's the Holy Spirit giving you the assurance that you are saved, sealed, and secure in your relationship with God. The Message Bible says, "By His Spirit He has stamped us with His eternal pledge - a sure beginning of what He is destined to complete." Being sealed with the Holy Spirit gives you a foretaste of heaven and is the greatest, most marvelous experience you'll ever have on this earth. This assurance, this sense of security you feel, is an expression of God's love and your response is to glorify Him for all He has done. 1 Peter 1:8 (ESV) says, "Though you have not seen Him, you love Him. Though you do not now see Him, you believe in Him and rejoice with joy that is inexpressible and filled with glory."

The Holy Spirit is Himself the seal, signifying a finished transaction, ownership, and security. Since the Holy Spirit is as much God as the Father and the Son, this means that God sealed you with Himself. The sealing of the Holy Spirit gives the believer the confident and ongoing assurance that they are one of God's children. The Holy Spirit is not simply the symbol of ownership but is God's title deed to your soul. You are God's precious property and this entitles you to the blessings of the Father and the benefits of being joint heirs with Jesus. God gave you the Holy Spirit so you can live and love like you're supposed to. Paul expands on this in Eph. 1:14. He says the Holy Spirit "is the guarantee of our inheritance until the redemption of the purchased possession, to the praise of His glory." The Message Bible says, "This signet from God is the first installment on what's coming, a reminder that we'll get everything God has planned for us, a praising and glorious life."

1 Cor. 6:19,20 (NLT) says, "You do not belong to yourself, for God bought you with a huge price." If you are born again, God calls you His purchased possession. Acts 20:28 tells of "the church of God which He purchased with His own blood." He wanted a relationship with you so much that He sent His only Son to buy you back from the enemy with His own life. Jesus was willing to die to purchase your freedom so that you could belong to God forever. He guaranteed His purchase by sealing you with the Holy Spirit. The word "guarantee" means 'earnest; pledge; down payment.' The Greek word "arrabon" in modern days means 'engagement ring.' An engagement ring is a symbol that promises have been made and that promises will be kept. A guy tells a young lady he loves her and she responds by saying, "Show me the ring. Show me some commitment." In like manner, God has given you the Holy Spirit to be your engagement ring, a sign that He will be committed to you forever.

It is a common practice when you want to purchase something of high value that you make a down payment, a pledge or token that you are serious about purchasing the chosen product. It's a way of signifying serious intent to come back and finalize the purchase. With the down payment comes a promise that future payments will be made. When it comes to salvation, the Holy Spirit is the guarantee, the deposit, of your inheritance. He is given to the believer as the down payment that assures you that God will complete what He began, that all the promises of God will come to fruition because you've been delivered from the penalty of sin. Phil. 1:6 (NLT) says, "And I am certain that God, who began the good work within you, will continue

His work until it is finally finished on the day when Christ Jesus returns." The Message Bible says, "God who started this great work in you would keep at it and bring it to a flourishing finish on the very day Christ Jesus appears."

Take comfort in knowing that God's pledge to you is forever binding. The down payment of the Holy Spirit is a non-refundable deposit. In other words, God will not back out or refuse to make good on His promises. He will see your relationship with Him through to the end, all the way to your final reunion with Him in the glory of heaven. You have the Holy Spirit now and will experience the triune God in complete fullness once you get to heaven. Think about it, if the Holy Spirit is the down payment, can you imagine what your full inheritance will be like? The totality of the wealth of heaven will be yours to richly enjoy for all eternity. 1 Cor. 2:9 says, "Eye has not seen, nor ear heard, nor have entered into the heart of man the things which God has prepared for those who love Him." The Message Bible says, "No one's ever seen or heard anything like this, never so much as imagined anything quite like it." Think about that this week and focus on the fullness of this reality. Set your mind on things above, not on things on the earth.

Life is a struggle when people don't meditate on eternal things. They're downtrodden by the hardships of the nasty here-and-now instead of being lifted up by the blessings of the sweet by-and-by. The proof that these blessings are waiting for you is the down payment of the Holy Spirit. After all, He is the Holy Spirit of promise. Inside of you right now is the assurance of that coming reality. This is why you should live your life with appreciation and the expectation of the blessings that await you a short time from now. What is the purpose for all this? You were chosen by the Father (vs. 3-6), redeemed by the Son (vs. 7-12), and sealed with the Holy Spirit (vs. 13,14) all for the purpose of giving glory to God (vs. 14). God will make known "the riches of His glory on the vessels of mercy, which He had prepared beforehand for glory" (Rom. 9:23). The glory which God shall forever receive shall rise out of His people. Be thankful and rejoice that you are one of them.

| 8 |

"TO KNOW GOD BETTER"

One can imagine the glow on Paul's face as he, with great enthusiasm and eloquence, lays out God's plan of salvation from eternity past to eternity future. He began by sharing how you were chosen by God before the foundation of the world and concludes by telling of the glorious inheritance you'll enjoy in heaven forever and ever. Never have such awe-inspiring thoughts entered the human mind, thoughts so exalted and radiant they're almost hard to grasp. Think about it, God has blessed you with every spiritual blessing in the heavenly places in Christ (Eph. 1:3). The blessings are there for you to have and enjoy. Yes, you can have all you want because they're already yours. One is reminded of what God told Joshua, "Every place on which the sole of your foot treads, I have given it to you" (Josh. 1:3). Wake up each morning determined to step out in faith as you obey God and lay hold of each and every one of His precious and magnificent promises.

Caring for his fellow saints as he does, Paul then writes in Eph. 1:15,16, "Therefore I also, after I heard of your faith in the Lord Jesus and your love for all the saints, do not cease to give thanks for you, making mention of you in my prayers." After talking to the Ephesians about God, Paul now talks to God about the Ephesians. You need to do the same. 1 Peter 2:9 says you are "a royal priesthood" and this is what priests do. They talk to people about God and they talk to God about people. A lack of prayer is probably the greatest spiritual disease in the body of Christ today. You want your spouse and children to change but how often do you pray for them? You tell the sinner they need to get saved but how much time do you spend praying for them? The truth be told, very little or not at all. If you're not willing to pray, then it's best to keep quiet and say nothing. Nobody is praying anymore and people wonder why the world is in the horrible condition it's in today.

Prayer is the pathway that leads to hope and joy and endurance and love. Rom. 12:12 tells you to rejoice in hope, be patient in tribulation, be constant in prayer. In scripture, prayer is the most often commanded spiritual discipline. Over and over again, the Bible calls, commands, and encourages you to pray. In fact, there are 650 different prayers recorded in the Bible, prayers that avail much (James 5:16). You need to be habitual in your prayer life. Make prayer a regular, recurring, and disciplined part of your daily life. Prayer is important just like food and water is important. To function properly, you need it every day. William Barclay said, "We are to persevere in prayer. Is it not the case that there are times in life when we let day add itself to day and week to week, and we never speak to God? When a man ceases to pray, he despoils himself of the strength of Almighty God. No man should be surprised when life collapses if he insists on living it alone."

When V. Raymond Edmon was president of Wheaton College, he often exhorted his students to keep their chins up and their knees down. That is good advice for all to follow. It's an open Bible and a bowed head that creates the atmosphere where God can and will move in your life and in the lives of those you're praying for. Paul knew this to be true, so he wrote in Col. 4:2 (AMP), "Be earnest and unwearied and steadfast in your prayer life, being both alert and intent in your praying with thanksgiving." The Message Bible says, "Pray diligently. Stay alert, with your eyes wide open in gratitude."

Paul is saying you must be devoted to praying persistently, watchfully, and thankfully. The word "devotion" implies a strong attachment, allegiance, and affection for someone or something, in this case prayer and the act of praying. One who is devoted to prayer is continually caring, committed, concerned, loyal, dedicated, steadfast, and true.

These saints at Ephesus are doing well in their walk with the Lord. They have received "the firstfruits of the Spirit" (Rom. 8:23) and the Spirit of God is arousing them from within. Nothing could make Paul happier than to hear of their loyalty to God, their faith in the Lord Jesus Christ, and their love for the brethren. How many people have heard of your faith and your love? Is it noticeable to others? If not, it should be. Jesus said "a tree is known by its fruit" (Matt. 12:33). The church at Ephesus was known for its faith and love. They knew the walk of faith is demonstrated by love (Gal. 5:6). Remove love and faith ceases to do what it was created to do. If your prayers are not getting answered, then you need to check up on yourself and see whether or not you're walking in love. The fact remains, if you're not walking in love, your faith won't work. Faith and love are taught throughout the Bible. Faith in God always leads to love toward others. You can't separate the two.

The same faith that got you born again is needed in everyday life. Daily you are to walk by faith and not by sight. Charles Spurgeon said, "There is the telescope of faith, which you are allowed to use, which will enable you to see much more than you have ever seen as yet." The result of doing that will be an outpouring of love toward your fellow brethren. It's true, a loveless faith is not faith at all. Faith is the expression of one's trust in God whereas love is the evidence of one's proper relationship with others. Jesus said in John 13:35, "By this all men will know you are My disciples, if you have love for one another." This is the agape love of God, love that is unconditional and always sacrificial. It's a love that desires another's highest good. Do you have faith? Then prove it by loving others. 1 John 3:18 (NLT) says, "Dear children, let's not merely say we love each other; let us show the truth by our actions." Words are cheap but actions are priceless.

The saints at Ephesus have got their act together. They're doing what they're supposed to be doing and becoming what they're supposed to become. They're walking the walk as they're supposed to, faithfully going about the Father's business. This good news assured Paul that these saints had indeed taken possession of the spiritual blessings he had just described to them. When he heard of the faith and love of these people, he could do nothing else but give thanks for them. He then prays that the work of God would continue even further in their lives with greater strength and power. Paul understands the power of prayer and its effectiveness. When you pray, you acknowledge you can't do something but God can do all things. Vs. 16 (NLT) says, "I have never stopped thanking God for you. I pray for you constantly." That is the mark of a true shepherd. Paul's deep love and concern for other is shown by his frequent prayers for them (Phil. 1:3; Col. 1:3; 1 Thess 1:2).

Notice that Paul isn't praying for people with problems, he's praying for people doing extremely well. One would think that prayer would not be necessary for people who have experienced all this success. Such is not the case for prayer is also needed for those who are walking the walk fully and completely. Charles Spurgeon said, "Where there was much good, the apostle prayed for more. We all need still further to advance in divine things. To stand still is impossible." Don't stop praying for people just because they're on the mountaintop of success and victory. No, pray for people in the good times as well as in the bad. Another important thing to take note of is that Paul prayed for these people while under house arrest in Rome. He was experiencing hard times yet he prayed for people experiencing good times. He was totally consumed with the care of others in spite of whatever turmoil and struggle he was going through. You, also, need to do the same.

You will also notice that Paul's prayer for the saints at Ephesus isn't very long. It's brief and to the point. Prayers don't have to be long to be effective. Some people pray on and on and never stop talking. Jesus said in Matt. 6:7,8 (NIV), "And when you pray, do not keep on babbling like pagans, for they think they will be heard because of their many words." The Message Bible says, "The world is full of so-called prayer warriors who are prayer-ignorant. They're full of formulas and programs and advice, peddling techniques for getting what you want from God. Don't fall for that nonsense." Martin Luther got it right when he said, "The less you speak, the better you pray." Most important of all is the fact that Paul's prayer focuses on the spiritual well-being of these saints. He doesn't pray for their physical needs but rather for the welfare of their heart and soul, that their spiritual perception would come to full fruition. He knew prayer is most effective when used for spiritual purposes.

Prayer is the breath of every believer. Throughout history great men and women of God have always been people of prayer. Anybody used mightily by God have always spent considerable time on their knees communicating with Him. Paul is showing you the proper way to pray as he gives you the pattern for good effective prayer. When you pray, always give thanks first and then ask for what you need. Make plans to meet with God regularly so you can praise Him for who He is, thank Him for all He has done, and to make your requests known to Him. Paul thanked God for the saints at Ephesus and he then asks "that the God of our Lord Jesus Christ, the Father of glory, may give to you the spirit of wisdom and revelation in the knowledge of Him" (vs.17). The deepest need of every person is to know God better. Not just to know about Him, but to know Him personally and intimately. Jesus prayed in John 17:3, "And this is eternal life, that they may know You, the only true God, and Jesus Christ whom You have sent."

No matter how well you know God and how good your walk with Him is, you should always strive to know Him better. The revelations of who God is and what He is about are endless. As you scale the heights of spiritual maturity, you will realize that when it comes to the knowledge of God, you can climb higher still. For all eternity there will always be more you can learn about Him, more to behold and grasp onto. In order to walk the walk, it is of vital importance that you know God intimately. Why? Because He wants to have an intimate and personal relationship with you. Jesus said in John 6:44, "No one can come to Me unless the Father who sent Me draws him." The Greek word for "draw" is "helkuo" and it means 'to drag,' both literally and figuratively. Clearly, this drawing is a one-sided affair. It is God who draws you to salvation. Yes, you must respond to His drawing, but the drawing itself is all His doing. He initiates the salvation experience and you respond by asking Jesus into your heart.

Why does God draw you to salvation? Because if He didn't, nobody would get saved. Jesus said in John 6:65, "No one can come to me unless it has been granted to him by the Father." The person engulfed in sin has no ability to come to God, nor does he have the desire to. Why? Because his heart is hard and his mind is darkened. So lost is the sinner's heart that he doesn't even realize it. Jer. 17:9 (NLT) says, "The human heart is the most deceitful of all things, and desperately wicked. Who really knows how bad it is?" The Message Bible says, "The heart is hopelessly dark and deceitful, a puzzle that no one can figure out." Therefore, it is only by the gracious drawing of God that one gets saved. And once you are born again, the quest begins to know God better. For that to happen, you need the spirit of wisdom and revelation knowledge of who He is. It's not based on intellectual knowledge. It's when He gives you a divine revelation of who He is.

Most people don't need more knowledge, they need more revelation. Without supernatural revelation from God, all you have is religion. 1 Cor. 2:14 says, "But the natural man does not receive the things of the Spirit of God, for they are foolishness to him; nor can he know them, because they are spiritually discerned." The NLT says, "Only those who are spiritual can understand what the Spirit means." Divine revelation is an unveiling of something hidden. The Greek word "apokalupsis" means 'to remove the cover and expose to open view that which was heretofore not visible, known, or disclosed.' Church leader R. W. Dale said, "The Ephesian Christians had already Divine illumination, or they would not have been Christians at all; but Paul prayed that the Divine Spirit who dwelt in them would make their vision clearer, keener, stronger, that the Divine power and love and greatness might be revealed to them far more fully."

The primary goal of your life is to know God personally (John 17:3), know Him increasingly (Phil. 3:10), and know Him perfectly (1 Cor. 13:9-12). Since you're made in His image, the better you know God, the better you know yourself and other believers. And the better you know Him, the more satisfying your walk with Him will be. Paul is saying here you can't know God better without the help of the Holy Spirit. A relationship with the Holy Spirit is a relationship of revelation. He'll awaken and transform your inner man with wisdom and revelation so you'll get to know God better. Jesus said in John 16:13 that the Holy Spirit "will guide you into all truth." The next time you read your Bible you'll be able to say, "How sweet are Your words to my taste, sweeter than honey to my mouth!" (Ps. 119:103). The Message Bible says, "Your words are so choice, so tasty; I prefer them to the best home cooking." With the help of the Holy Spirit, you'll sense in awe the spiritual beauty of God and the sweetness of His glory.

The knowledge of God is the highest form of knowledge there is. What Paul is saying here is that he wants you to know God the same way God knows you. He prayed in Phil. 3:10, "That I may know Him and the power of His resurrection." Paul wants you to grow and grow in your experiential, intimate, and relational knowledge of God to the point that this knowledge is divine and complete. Knowing God better is the fountain through which everything in life flows. This is why Charles Spurgeon said, "The highest science, the loftiest speculation, the mightiest philosophy which can ever engage the attention of a child of God, is the name, the nature, the person, the work, the doings, and the existence of the great God whom he calls his Father." Bible commentator Henry Alford added to this, saying, "For philosophy comes to man with the message, 'Know thyself,' the Gospel meets him with the far more glorious and fruitful watchword, 'Know thy God.'"

Knowing God intimately gives you the spiritual nourishment to live a rich, full, satisfying life. The problem with a lot of believers is once they get saved, they immediately want God to start giving them things. They want a spouse, a new job, a new car, or a new house. They put material things above knowing God better and this is wrong. When you leave this world, the only thing you're taking with you is your knowledge of God. Everything else will be vaporized in fervent heat (2 Peter 3:10). Truly, the number one, all compassing need in your life is to know God better. Understanding this is vitally important to your spiritual welfare. Paul is saying here what he said in 1 Cor. 12:1 (WEB), "Now concerning spiritual things, brothers, I don't want you to be ignorant." The truth be told, humans are prone to stupidity. Prov. 14:12 says, "There is a way which seems right to a man, but its end is the way of death." Every morning be bold and pray, "God, help me not to be stupid!"

God will help keep you from missing the mark by giving you the spirit of wisdom and revelation in the knowledge of Him. Wisdom and knowledge are related but they're not the same thing. The dictionary defines "wisdom" as 'the ability to discern or judge what is true, right, or lasting.' Knowledge, on the other hand, is 'information gained through experience, reasoning, or acquaintance.' Knowledge can exist without wisdom, but not the other way around. The Greek word for "wisdom" is 'sophia' and is where the word "sophisticated" comes from. Wisdom is knowledge that travels from your brain to your heart from where it affects your daily life. In other words, wisdom acts upon the knowledge you have. For example, knowledge understands the traffic light has turned red, wisdom steps on the brakes. Knowledge sees the quicksand; wisdom walks around it. Knowledge learns the Bible; wisdom obeys it and applies spiritual truths to whatever it is you're going through.

There is a reason God blesses you with wisdom from on high. He wants you to use it to glorify Him and to properly use the knowledge you have of Him. Paul makes it clear that it's "the Father of glory" who gives you this wisdom. Yes, He's the Father to whom all the glory belongs. Jesus ended what is known as "the Lord's prayer" with these words, "For Yours is the kingdom and the power and the glory forever. Amen" (Matt. 6:13). God wants you to have His wisdom and He'll gladly give it to you when your heart is set to receive it. Godly wisdom comes from God and glorifies God. It causes you to see life from God's perspective and it compels you to act accordingly. Solomon received godly wisdom when he asked for it (2 Chron. 1:10,11). You must do the same. To tap into God's wisdom, you must desire it and ask God for it. James 1:5 says, "If any of you lacks wisdom, you should ask God, who gives generously to all without finding fault, and it will be given to you."

The Bible instructs you to seek wisdom above all things. Prov. 4:17 says, "Wisdom is the principal thing; Therefore, get wisdom. And in all your getting, get understanding." The NLT says, "Getting wisdom is the wisest thing you can do! And whatever else you do, develop good judgment." How important is wisdom? Prov. 16:16 says, "How much better it is to get wisdom than gold! And to get understanding is to be chosen rather than silver." The book of Proverbs is devoted entirely to teaching you the wisdom of God. It is full of practical instructions for life, and you need to read and meditate on it daily. You then need to do what it tells you to do. Those who have God's wisdom show it in how they live. James 3:13 says, "Who is wise and understanding among you? Let them show it by their good life, by deeds done in the humility that comes from wisdom." Through wisdom that comes from on high you'll be able to walk the walk consistently with reverence and godly fear.

Paul wanted the saints at Ephesus to have the spirit of wisdom and revelation so they would have a better knowledge of God. Your entire Christian life must be centered around this purpose, to know God better. Unfortunately, many people work for God by the sweat of their brow but they don't know Him. They work to feel better about themselves or to place a false faith in works thinking it will get them into heaven. Matt.7:21-23 tells of people who worked for God but didn't know Him in a meaningful way. They had a form of godliness but denied the power thereof (2 Tim. 3:5). Yes, they did many good works, but it was all in vain because their lives were unchanged as a result of knowing God personally. Bible commentator Charles Ellicott said, "These, by claiming the title of Christian, wearing before men the uniform of Christ, but by their lives dishonoring His name, did the gravest injury to the holy Christian cause." Jesus said to these people, "I never knew you; depart from Me" (vs. 23).

Jesus told the parable of the pearl of great price in Matt. 13:45,46, "Again, the kingdom of heaven is like a merchant seeking beautiful pearls, who, when he had found one pearl of great price, went and sold all that he had and bought it." One interpretation of this parable is that the church is the pearl of great price. By giving His Son to die and shed His blood on the cross, God gave all He had and bought it. Jewelers will tell you there are two things that damage pearls, cosmetics and human perspiration. Your walk with God is damaged when you put on spiritual cosmetics, when you act spiritual at church and act like the devil at home. Even Satan transforms himself into an angel of light (2 Cor. 11:14). Sweat also harms pearls. Working for God without knowing Him first will bring eternal judgment to your life. You're not saved by works, by the things you do. You're saved by grace through faith, not of works lest anyone should boast (Eph. 2:8,9).

| 9 |

"REFLECTION OF GOD'S GLORY"

In the Christian life, information by itself is never enough. You can know all that is humanly possible about God and still live a miserable, unfulfilled life. After all, people forget most of what they've learned anyway. Paul is praying that God will take these truths and make them come alive in your heart which, in turn, will cause you to walk a walk worthy of your calling. Why is a prayer like this even necessary? Because many churches are filled with people who have a lot of knowledge about God but have very little experience with Him. Yes, information is helpful and most times necessary. But knowledge that doesn't lead to transformation is useless. You can read all the books you want about nutrition but if you don't start eating right all that information does you no good. How much more true is this when it comes to the things of God? Christianity is not about having the right answers to life's problems. It goes way beyond that. It's about having a personal relationship with the living God.

Paul prayed that God would give you a spirit of wisdom and revelation so you would know Him better. Added to this is Paul's request that "the eyes of your understanding" would be enlightened (Eph. 1:18). The NLT says, "I pray that your hearts will be flooded with light so that you can understand the wonderful future He has promised those He called." This is a prayer for knowledge and understanding.

Paul is saying you must have a heart that sees spiritual reality. It's what allows you to enjoy the sweetness of divine pleasures in the here-and-now and the inexhaustible joys of heaven for all eternity. Notice that he is not requesting from God material things to be given to the saints at Ephesus. No, his emphasis is on their spiritual perception and what real Christian character is all about. Paul does not ask God to give them what they do not have, but rather prays that God will reveal to them the blessings they already have in Christ.

Ps. 119:18 says, "Open my eyes, that I may see wondrous things from Your law." Only the Holy Spirit can reveal spiritual truth. Is. 11:2 says the Holy Spirit is "the Spirit of wisdom and understanding, the Spirit of counsel and might, the Spirit of knowledge and of the fear of the Lord." This is why you need to look at life with spiritual eyes, eyes that look toward God and all the spiritual blessings that have their source and supply in Christ. English author Os Guinness said, "Faith does not feed on thin air, but on facts." As the Holy Spirit reveals more and more of who God is, as you seek to know Him better, as the spirit of wisdom shows you how to respond to the information He is revealing to you, you grow in that knowledge of Him. The deepest part of your inner being is enlightened and now blessings will come your way that you never imagined. The word "enlightened" means 'to cause something to be fully known by revealing clearly and in great detail.'

The Holy Spirit allows you to perceive divine realities so that the things of God become real to you with vividness and distinction. John Piper said, "The glory of God in His wisdom and revelation is not seen with the physical eye. If the eyes of your heart are not enlightened, you will not see and savor the beauty and sweetness of God's wisdom and revelation. You will not know God." Divine revelation takes place in your inner man so be more aware and become more sensitive to what is taking place inside of you. The Bible teaches that the inner man can see (Ps. 119:18), hear (Matt. 13:9), taste (Ps. 34:8), smell (Phil. 4;18; 2 Cor. 2;14), and touch (Acts 17:27). The heart of a person can be taught things the brain will never know. The heart is the core of one's life, the seat of thoughts and moral judgment, the center of knowledge, understanding, and wisdom. Needed more than intellect is a tender heart sensitive to the things of God.

Not only does God want to get you into heaven, he wants to get heaven into you. For that to happen, you must perceive in your inner man these blessings before you can claim them. The knowledge God wants you to have is that which enters your heart and transforms your life. 1 Cor. 8:2,3 (MSG) says, "Sometimes our humble hearts can help us more than our proud minds. We never really know enough until we recognize that God alone knows it all." The clarity of understanding that Paul is praying for, this deep, internal enlightenment, is clearly the result of the Holy Spirit working in your life. As the light of God's promises grow brighter and brighter, your heart will swell with faith and confidence. You'll enter into sweet fellowship with the Father, the Son, and the Holy Spirit. You're abiding in Jesus and He's abiding in you. Suddenly the realities of the spiritual world become more real to you than your own consciousness.

Paul now breaks down this initial petition to God into three separate requests. He prays "that you may know what is the hope of His calling, what are the riches of the glory of His inheritance in the saints, and what is the exceeding greatness of His power toward us who believe" (vs. 18,19). All the things Paul prays for comes after the quest to know God better. Indeed, that needs to be the top priority of your life. You grow in the blessings of God as you grow in your knowledge of God. Remember, this world is not your home. You're an alien here, a pilgrim passing through a strange place. There's no real substance here for the things of this world are temporal. Here today, gone tomorrow. The only thing that is eternal is the knowledge you have of God. Each and every day you strive to know God better and better. You press in with a hunger and thirst that won't be satisfied until you know all there is to know about God. "As the deer pants for the water brooks, so pants my soul for You, O God" (Ps. 42:1).

Paul wants you to know how valuable you are to God. So much does he want this that he prays that you may know what is the hope of His calling. In the Bible, the word "know" has a much more richer and deeper meaning than just having facts and information and answers. It speaks of intimacy and the bonding between two people closely related. Gen. 4:1 says, "Now Adam knew Eve his wife, and she conceived." In Greek, the word "know" suggests 'fullness of knowledge, absolute knowledge, that which is without a doubt.' When the Holy Spirit opens the spiritual eyes of your heart, you'll readily perceive the infinite importance of knowledge in the Christian's life. It truly is the foundation for walking worthy of your calling. 2 Peter 1:2,3 says, "Grace and peace be multiplied to you in the knowledge of God and of Jesus our Lord. As His divine power has given us all things that pertain to life and godliness, through the knowledge of Him who called us by glory and virtue."

Paul is praying that God will do a mighty work in the hearts of all believers. He doesn't want the saints to just know these truths, he wants them to experience these truths. Ps. 34:8 says, "Taste and see that the Lord is good; blessed is the one who takes refuge in Him." This is the language of knowledge that is experienced, the language of relationship. Once you see and know who God is, when you hear His voice and know His ways, you'll see and know that He is good. For sure, there's a difference between describing how something tastes and actually tasting it. Before information can lead to transformation, it requires divine revelation, it requires God to open the eyes of your understanding. The Spirit searches the deep things of God and He reveals them to you (1 Cor. 2:10). He'll give you a divine understanding of the great and mighty things of God. You'll see yourself lifted high above all your sins and fears and difficulties. You'll see yourself sitting with Him in heavenly places, always safe and triumphant.

It's the Holy Spirit who reveals to you what the hope of His calling is. Hope gives you the assurance of better days ahead, that you're going toward something better than this present life. Hope gives you the strong confidence that what God says will happen will surely come to pass. Heb. 6:19 says, "This hope we have as an anchor of the soul, both sure and steadfast." The Message Bible says hope is "an unbreakable spiritual lifeline, reaching past all appearances right to the very presence of God." Rom. 4:18 says Abraham, "who, contrary to hope, in hope believed." In other words, he was persuaded he had sufficient ground to expect God to make good His promise. He was "fully convinced that what He had promised He was also able to perform" (Rom. 4:21). Paul is praying that, like Abraham, you may know the hope on which rests your expectation of His calling. This hope is so important because what you believe about the future will impact your present life more than what you're experienced in the past.

There comes to every person a call from God and 1 Peter 5:10 tells you what that calling is, "But may the God of all grace, who called us to His eternal glory by Christ Jesus, after you have suffered a while, perfect, establish, strengthen, and settle you." The word "calling" is the Greek word "klesis" and refers to an invitation to a banquet. All people have personally been invited to sit at the King's table. This special invitation is the divine call of God that introduces those who accept His summons to all the wonderful blessings and privileges of the heavenly kingdom. The NLT says, "In His kindness God called you to share in His eternal glory by means of Christ Jesus." How awesome is that! Your calling is to share in God's eternal glory! It's where the very character of God will be lived out in your life fully and completely for all eternity. Flowing out of you will be heavenly love, compassion, goodness, grace, peace, and gentleness. You'll be a mirror-image of God Himself, a reflection of His eternal glory.

C. S. Lewis wrote in his book "Mere Christianity" these words, "If we let Him - for we can prevent Him, if we choose - He will make the feeblest and filthiest of us into a dazzling, radiant, immortal creature, pulsating all through with such energy and joy and wisdom and love as we cannot now imagine, a bright, stainless mirror which reflects back to God perfectly (though, of course, on a smaller scale) His own boundless power and delight and goodness." Do you believe that? Do you hope for this to happen? You should because this is the hope all believers have. Titus 2:13 (NLT) says, "We look forward with hope to that wonderful day when the glory of our great God and Savior, Jesus Christ, will be revealed." It's your duty to cherish such a hope. A Christian's faith in the Lord Jesus and their love for all the saints is crowned by the brightness of this great hope. Faith and love draws back the curtain of eternity and hope gazes into the supernatural glory waiting there.

The hope of His calling is the hope of an immortal and perfect life. As a child of God, you've been chosen before the foundation of the world, predestined to be conformed to the image of His Son, a reflection of God's glory. 2 Thess. 2:14 (NLT) says, "He called you to salvation when we told you the Good News; now you can share in the glory of our Lord Jesus Christ." The Message Bible says, "You get in on the glory of our Master, Jesus Christ." Jon Courson wrote in his commentary, "Throughout scripture, the word 'hope' always refers to that which is coming, to that which is ahead. I'm convinced the single greatest problem carnal Christians have is that they don't know the hope of His calling. They don't know the reality of heaven. Consequently, they constantly strive for material things and are continually caught up in carnal pursuits. They're depressed and discouraged because they don't see the big picture of eternity."

Motivated by the hope of His calling, you should earnestly desire to walk worthy of the calling with which you were called. Bible teacher Warren Wiersbe said, "The hope that belongs to our calling should be a dynamic force in our lives, encouraging us to be pure (1 John 2:28-3:3), obedient (Heb. 13:17), and faithful (Luke 12:42-48). The fact that we shall one day see Christ and be like Him should motivate us to live like Christ today." Christians everywhere need to understand the hope of His calling so they can walk in a worthy manner. 2 Tim. 1:9 says God "has saved us and called us with a holy calling." Heb. 3:1 says the holy brethren are "partakers of a heavenly calling." You've been redeemed by the blood of Jesus and sealed with the Holy Spirit. You've been "called out of darkness into His marvelous light" (1 Peter 2:9) and you've been called to be a reflection of His glory forever and ever (1 Peter 5:10). Act like all this is true and walk the walk. Ps. 119:133 says, "Direct my steps by Your word, and let no iniquity have no dominion over me."

The second thing Paul prays for is that all the saints would know "what are the riches of the glory of His inheritance in the saints" (vs. 18). He wants you to see yourself the way God sees you. Gideon was a frightened peasant but God called him a "mighty man of valor" (Judges 6:12). One of the greatest revelations you can have as a child of God is that you are His purchased possession. You are His inheritance and He considers you a treasure of incomparable worth. You are the apple of His eye and are more valuable to Him than everything in the universe put together. When God looks at you, He feels wealthy. Pastor R. Kent Hughes said, "Think of it, He owns all the heavens and numberless worlds but we are His treasure. The redeemed are worth more than the universe. We ought to be delirious with this truth." It is amazing that God would want or need an inheritance because He owns everything. He owns the cattle on a thousand hills (Ps. 50:10) yet 1 Peter 2:9 says the church is God's "own special people."

The term "riches of His glory" refers to spiritual abundance, the overwhelming preeminent glory of God displayed in the lives of all believers. Bible scholar F. F. Bruce said, "Paul prays here that his readers may appreciate the value which God places on them, His plan to accomplish His eternal purpose through them as the first fruits of the reconciled universe of the future, in order that their lives may be in keeping with the high calling and that they may accept in grateful humility the grace and glory thus lavished on them." You have a bright future ahead of you. For all eternity you will share in Christ's glory. Paul said in Eph. 5:27 that God's aim is 'that He might present to Himself the church, in all her glory, having no spot or wrinkle or any such thing; but that she would be holy and blameless." Paul wants you to get a glimpse of your glorious future so you will walk in the light of it right now. Live daily as citizens of heaven who belong to God.

Finally, Paul prays that you would know "what is the exceeding greatness of His power toward us who believe" (vs. 19). God is powerful! He created the entire universe! He split the Red Sea! He gave sight to the blind! He raised the dead back to life! Paul wants you to know His power, to experience it. David wrote in Ps. 63:2, "So I have looked for You in the sanctuary, to see Your power and Your glory." He's saying, "God, I want to see You do something great!" People often struggle in life because they don't experience God's presence and His power. The truth be told, it is futile to live the Christian life without the power of God. It's what gives you the victory over sin, sickness, and the grave. It changes you from a child of wrath to a child of God, from a nobody to a somebody, from the mortal to the immortal, from the earthly to the heavenly, from the corrupt to the incorrupt, from a sinner to a saint. That's the power of God at work on your behalf and it's working right here, right now.

The Greek word for "power" is 'dunamis" and is where the word "dynamite" comes from. This is the highest power in all the universe. It's the surpassing, unlimited, unimaginable, mighty, explosive, immeasurable power of God and it's working on your behalf if you'll only believe. As you grow in your knowledge of God, as you experience Him in a deeper and more meaningful way, you'll experience His power in a greater way. The NLT says, "This is the same mighty power that raised Christ from the dead and seated Him in the place of honor at God's right hand in the heavenly realms." The Message Bible says this is "endless energy, boundless strength!" Never again do you have to be defeated in this life. Never! It's this power that causes you to "walk in newness of life" (Rom. 6:4) today and forevermore. The Message Bible says, "Each of us is raised into a light-filled world by our Father so that we can see where we're going in our new grace-sovereign country" (Rom. 6:5).

You need to know you serve a God of great power who uses His strength on behalf of those He calls His own. Charles Spurgeon said, "The very same power which raised Christ is waiting to raise the drunkard from His drunkenness, to raise the thief from his dishonesty, to raise the Sadducee from his unbelief, to raise the Pharisee from his self-righteousness." God's power surpasses and goes far beyond all other power. Your walk with God is energized and His mighty power flows in you and through you. The power that works in you is the same mighty power that raised Jesus from the dead. How awesome is that? F. F. Bruce said, "If the death of Christ is the supreme demonstration of the love of God, the resurrection of Christ is the supreme demonstration of His power." The resurrection power that raised up Jesus is the same power that is working in your life. This power propels you from the natural into the supernatural. Warren Wiersbe says Paul "is talking about divine, dynamic, eternal energy available to us!"

There is power available to you and Paul wants you to lay hold of what resurrection power is. It's power that brings dead things back to life. If your marriage is all but dead, God wants to resurrect it. If you are all but dead because of cigarettes, drugs, or any other addiction, God wants to bring you back to life. Stop looking at your problems from the lens of your own ability to solve them. Cast your cares onto the Lord and trust in His power and ability to help you in time of need. Jer. 32:17 says, "Ah, Lord God! Behold, You have made the heavens and the earth by Your great power and outstretched arm. There is nothing too hard for you." The power of God is exceedingly great.

It goes beyond human imagination; beyond anything you can ask or think (Eph. 3:20). How is this power released into your life? The key is to be plugged into the power source. Jesus said in John 15:6, "I am the vine, you are the branches. He who abides in me, and I in him, bears much fruit; for without Me you can do nothing."

Jesus is seated at the right hand of the Father and so are you (Eph. 2:6). Adam Clarke said, "The right hand is the place of friendship, honor, confidence, and authority." The problem in the world today is too many people under-emphasize the power of God and over-emphasize the power of Satan. These people think they live in a demon-possessed world and go around rebuking this and rebuking that. They foolishly try to cast the devil out of every person they see. They cast demons out of their husbands and their wives and their children and especially their in-laws. They even go so far as to cast demons out of their coffee and the sugar they put in it. They don't realize that Satan is a defeated foe, defeated by the power that raised Jesus from the dead, power that is available to you. Trust God and He'll give you power to defeat doubt and discouragement, power to triumph over temptation and sin. He'll also give you resurrection power to live sacrificially so you can love others and serve God continually.

In Christ, you've got all the power you need and then some. There's more than enough to handle whatever it is you're going through. Just look at the empty tomb of Jesus and you'll get a glimpse of all the power that is available to you. The Father raised Jesus and broke the power of sin and death. "And He put all things under His feet, and gave Him to be head over all things to the church, which is His body, the fullness of Him who fills all in all" (Eph. 1:22,23). This great resurrection power placed Jesus above all things. Christ's exaltation over the universe is God's gift to the church. God's power fills the universe with the authority of His crucified and risen Son. Since Jesus is in you, that means you are the embodiment of that fullness. In other words, where He rules, you rule. In the beginning, God created man to inhabit a beautiful creation and to subdue it, enjoy it, and be a reflection of God's glory. Adam failed but in Christ you can do what he was created to do.

| 10 |

"THE SEED OF PERFECTION"

P aul is rejoicing because of the faith and love the saints of Ephesus have on full display. They are truly walking the walk as God intended. So proud is he of these people that he began his letter to them with a song of praise followed by a powerful prayer. He now changes course and begins to preach to them. He summarizes the first three chapters of Romans here in Eph. 2:1-3. In order to fully appreciate where they now are, Paul paints a graphic picture of the tragedy of a life without Christ. He gives a pathetic description of the total depravity of unredeemed humanity. Life is a journey and Paul tells you where you started. What took him three chapters to explain in Romans, he does here in three verses. He begins by saying, "And you He made alive, who were dead in trespasses and sins" (vs. 1). Paul begins this chapter by pointing out man's immeasurable need for divine grace and mercy. You need God's intervention to be made alive. All people, both great and small, are desperately in need of a Savior.

While spiritually dead, there was nothing inside of you that would compel you to do anything for the glory of God. Why is that? Because you were dead to righteousness, dead to holiness, dead to obedience, and dead to faith. Everything you do while not saved is sin. Yes, many unsaved people do good deeds but if it doesn't spring forth from trust in God, if they don't do it to give Him glory, then everything they do is in vain. The Bible says man's righteousness is as filthy rags (Is.

64:6). Nothing sinners do is spiritual. Everything comes from the flesh and all their good deeds are rags and ashes. Paul said in Rom. 14:23, "Whatever is not from faith is sin." Because man cannot save himself, all people are in need of a Savior who can raise the dead, both physically and spiritually. Not only is a Savior needed to forgive your sins, but also to give you spiritual life so that your heart would be inclined to trust and obey Him. Without a Savior you'll have no spiritual inclinations as all. You cannot and will not please Him in any way.

Before Christ, all people were separated from God because of sin. Rom. 3:23 says, "For all have sinned and fall short of the glory of God." People go to church but, it they're not saved, they can be described as a religious sinner. Sad to say, there are many such people in the world today. Most sermons tell people how their lives can be made a little bit better but they never confront the issue of sin. Because of that, people today are too judgmental. They like pointing out the faults and short- comings of others even when they're guilty of doing the same thing. The difference is they're more lenient with themselves than they are with others. They think the problems they're facing is always some- body else's fault, whether it be the boss at work or the slow driver in front of them. In a struggling marriage the husband blames the wife and the wife blames the husband. But here in Eph. 2:1, Paul says they are the ones at fault. As the cartoon character Pogo once said, "We have seen the enemy and he is us."

Not only are you lost in sin, Paul says you are dead in sin. Without a Savior, you will forever be dead in trespasses and sins. Death always brings separation. American theologian Leon J. Wood said, "The most vital part of man's personality - the spirit - is dead to the most important factor in life - God." Because of the sin nature inherited from Adam, every person was born into a state of separation from God. The Bible uses many different pictures to describe the state of the unsaved sinner. He is blind (2 Cor. 4:3,4), a slave to sin (Rom. 6:17). a lover of darkness (John 3:19), sick (Mark 2:17), lost (Luke

15:4), an alien, a stranger, a foreigner (Eph. 2:12,19), a child of wrath (Eph. 2:3), under the power of darkness (Col.1:13). Charles Spurgeon said, "Look back to what you used to be, to the hole of the pit whence you were digged." The word "dead" refers to the spiritual condition of those who are unable to save themselves. People who are not saved are dead and don't even know it.

Everybody, regardless of race or gender, was born a sinner. Yes, even little babies have within them a sin nature that, if not controlled, will lead to a life of crime. In 1926 a task force against crime wrote this about the root cause of why criminals do what they do, "Every baby starts out as a little savage. He is completely selfish and self-centered. He wants what he wants, when he wants it: his bottle, his mother's attention, his playmate's toys, his uncle's watch, or whatever. Deny him these things and he rages with an aggressiveness which would be murderous were he not so helpless. He is dirty, he has no morals, no knowledge, no developed skills. This means that all children are born delinquent. And if permitted to continue in their self-centered world of infancy, given free reign to their impulsive actions to satisfy each want, every child would grow up a criminal, a thief, a killer, a rapist." This may seem a little harsh but it is true nonetheless.

Doing wrong comes naturally to everybody. You're not a sinner because you sin, you sin because you're a sinner. Those not saved are tainted by their sinful nature. There is no good thing within them worthy of God's approval. There is nothing they can do that can live up to the righteous standard of a holy God. Man cannot save himself and this means all people are in desperate need of divine intervention. Without Christ, every human being is on a collision course with divine justice, wrath, and eternal condemnation. All sinners are on the path of total depravity, pulled along by the combined forces of the flesh, the world, and the devil. They violate God's holiness, disobey His commands, reject His authority, defy His will, and ignore His warnings. They are by nature sinners of the worst kind. All are guilty before God (Rom. 3:10-18) for every aspect of the human experience is corrupted by sin. Jesus said in John 8:34, "Most assuredly, I say to you, whoever commits sin is a slave to sin."

Before the salvation experience, Paul says you were dead in trespasses and sins. There are three types of death in the scriptures. The first is physical death which is the separation of the spirit and soul from the body (James 2:26). Then there is spiritual death which is the separation of your spirit from God (Is. 59:2). This may or may not be permanent. Finally, there is what Rev. 2:11 calls the "second death" which is your spirit's permanent separation from God (Rev. 21:8). Spiritual death is probably the most difficult truth in all of scripture for people to believe or accept. Lost sinners are people "having no hope and without God in the world" (Eph. 2:12). They're alive physically yet they don't realize they're dead spiritually. Sin creates a great chasm between God and man. It affects every part of your being, from your words and actions to your emotions and the decisions you make. Sin makes you a slave to your own lusts. It blinds your ability to see clearly, causing you to live in darkness continually.

Let's face it, when you're dead, you're dead. Period. No part of your life is exempt from the debilitation effects of sin. Everybody was born enslaved to sin with the inability to set themselves free. This is why people are in need of a Savior. Christian author Ray Pritchard said, "We are enslaved and we cannot set ourselves free. God says, 'Thou shalt not' but we say 'I shall' and then we hate ourselves afterwards. Why? We are enslaved to sin. Sin masters us, rules us, dominates us. We are a people of high ideals and weak wills, of big dreams and small deeds, high hopes and low living. A person who is lost, blind, separated, dead, and enslaved is truly helpless. He is trapped with no hope within himself. Any help must come from somewhere else." Paul understood this when he wrote in Rom. 7:24," O wretched man that I am! Who will deliver me from this body of death?" The Message Bible says, "I've tried everything and nothing helps. I'm at the end of my rope. Is there no one who can do anything for me?"

Jesus came to save the lost, those dead in trespasses and sins. The Greek word for "trespass" is "paraptoma" and it means 'to cross a line; to go beyond or overstep a limit or boundary.' When you did wrong, you crossed a line, challenging God's boundaries. Committing a trespass is a deliberate action, a willful act of disobedience, a turning away from truth and godliness. It's a deviation from living according to what has been revealed as the right and proper way to live. It conveys the idea of stumbling or falling so as to lose one's footing. When you should have stood tall, you found yourself falling down, falling away from truth and righteousness. Not all people are as evil as they can be but they all fail to measure up to God's high standard of perfection. Non-believers are capable of doing good things but the fact remains, every person not saved is dead in trespasses and sins. They may be good people but they're not good enough because they're not perfect.

A trespass is an outward action caused by willful rebellion. Sin, on the other hand, is an inward condition of sustained corruption. The Greek word for "sin" is "harmatia" and it's an archery term meaning 'to miss the mark; to miss what you were aiming for.' When you sin, you crossed the line and missed the mark. The goal of every believer is to hit the mark of God's righteous standard. Jesus said, "Therefore you shall be perfect, just as your Father in heaven is perfect" (Matt. 5:48). The Amplified Bible says, "You must be perfect, growing into complete maturity of godliness in mind and character, having reached the proper height of virtue and integrity, as your heavenly Father is perfect." The Wuest translation says, "You shall be those who are complete in your character, even as your Father in heaven is complete in His being." Jesus eliminated all human standards of morality and conduct when He spoke these words. God has never had any other standard for man other than perfect holiness.

How good does a person have to be to please God? Jesus said, "As good as God is." You are to always measure yourself not by others but by the Father. He is the standard and His perfection is absolute. Deut. 32:4 says, "He is the Rock, His works are perfect, and all His ways are just. A faithful God who does no wrong, upright and just is He." David wrote in Ps. 18:30, "As for God, His way is perfect. The Lord's word is flawless; He shields all who take refuge in Him." Consider also 1 John 1:5, "God is light, and in Him is no darkness at all." The call to be perfect is what Paul was referring to when he said, "Be imitators of God, as beloved children" (Eph. 5:1). The Message Bible says, "Watch what God does, and then you do it." As children tend to imitate their parents, God's children ought to imitate God and reflect His perfection in the way they live. Dwight Pentecost said, "If one falls the slightest degree short of the standard of God's inviolable, unalterable holiness, he is unacceptable to God."

God is perfect so don't be surprised that perfection is the goal He has set before you. This may be unsettling to a lot of people. They reason God's standard is too high so they refuse to put forth the effort to be like Him. John MacArthur said, "It is folly to think that being imperfect somehow provides us with a legitimate excuse to exempt us from God's perfect standard." The Lord appeared to Abram and said to him, "I am Almighty God; walk before Me, and be blameless." The word "blameless" in Hebrew means 'to be complete; single-hearted; without blame; sincere; wholly devoted to the Lord.' Job 1:1 (DBT) says, "There was a man in the land of Uz, whose name was Job; and that man was perfect and upright, and one that feared God and abstained from evil." It's true, nobody is perfect but followers of Christ are encouraged to seek perfection regardless of how difficult the task may be. Charles Spurgeon said it best, "Though you cannot be perfect, yet you must want to be perfect."

Jesus knew no believer could be sinless and perfect in this life. Nevertheless, this must be the standard and the goal, not for gaining salvation but for living the Christian life. What should you do? Charles Spurgeon gave this exhortation to heaven-bound believers, "Rise out of ordinary manhood. Get beyond what others might expect of you. Have a high standard. Stretch towards the highest conceivable standard, and be not satisfied till you reach it." This is what Paul did continually. He wrote in Phil. 3:12 (NLT), "I don't mean to say that I have already achieved these things or that I have already reached perfection. But I press on to possess that perfection for which Christ Jesus first possessed me." Paul paints a picture of pursuing with earnestness and diligence the goal he set out to fulfill, the goal of being perfect as the Father is perfect. He struggled at times but God said to him in 2 Cor. 12:9, "My grace is sufficient for you, for My power is made perfect in weakness."

The Greek word for "perfect" is "teleios" and means 'to be brought to completion; to attain the intended goal; to be fully accomplished.' If anything has fully attained that for which it was planned, designed, and made, it is perfect. For what purpose did God create you? He said in Gen. 1:26, "Let Us make man in Our image, after Our likeness." You were created to be like God and you must press on to fulfill the standard God set for you. Daily you must "work out your own salvation with fear and trembling" (Phil. 2:12). The NLT says, "Work hard to show the results of your salvation, obeying God with deep reverence and fear." Pastor and teacher Rick Renner said, "This is a word used to describe a child who is graduating from one class into the next class or he reached a point of educational maturity. He was able to think wisely and act on his own behalf. He was able to come to mature conclusions." The word "teleios" includes the idea of being whole and complete and was used to describe full-grown adults.

Paul said in Col. 1:28, "Him we preach, warning every man and teaching every man in all wisdom, that we may present every man perfect in Christ Jesus." He is saying you need to help people grow up, not to be dependent on others all the time but to lead them to a place where they can make godly decisions on their own and to think for themselves and to do what is right. As a person develops, he or she will transition from being youthful and immature to being an individual who is fully grown up and mature, showing a high degree of skill and a special instinctive aptitude or ability for doing something well. Paul used this term only five times in the New Testament and each time he was referring to spiritually mature individuals who are living in accordance with the will of God. The Amplified Bible says, "That we may present every person mature, full-grown, fully initiated, complete, and perfect in Christ." The Message Bible adds to this, saying, "To be mature is to be basic. Christ! No more, no less."

The seed of perfection has been planted inside of you and your responsibility is to allow this seed to grow and develop until it comes to full maturity and finally to perfection. You must choose to do right, all the while asking God for the grace to help you act accordingly. Sin corrupts the power to choose and the power to accomplish. God's grace, however, gives you the motivation and the power to press on and live life as he commands. You're not working for your salvation, you're working out your salvation. The Greek word for "work out" is "katergazomai" and it means 'to engage in an activity involving considerable expenditure of effort.' It means 'to labor; to work out fully and thoroughly' and implies that sanctification and deliverance is a result of persistent work each and every day. Phil. 2:12,13 (NLT) says, "Work hard to show the results of your salvation, obeying God with deep reverence and fear. For God is working in you, giving you the desire and the power to do what pleases Him."

You need to be active and aggressive as you work diligently to live a sanctified life. London minister Thomas Watson said, "There can be no crown without running, no recompense without diligence." This Greek word was used to describe the working of a silver mine with the goal of extracting all of the precious ore. It was also used to describe working in a field with the reaping of a big harvest. God put tremendous potential inside of you by blessing you with "every spiritual blessing in the heavenly places" (Eph. 1:3). Because you have attained the riches of God in Christ, you are to let those riches work themselves out in your life. In short, you are commanded to work out what God works in. By doing that, you'll be living a life that pleases God, a life that conforms to the salvation He has given you. Bible teacher Wil Pounds said, "Work out what God has worked in when you were born again. bring the whole purpose of your salvation to completion. Don't stop short of seeing the fulfillment of your very existence."

Working out your own salvation is an ongoing experience. Make it your life's work to obey this command with the goal of becoming Christlike, of being conformed to His image, to be perfect and complete in all you say and do. As a believer, you have a responsibility to put forth a sincere effort in order to achieve this goal. You can't sit back and do nothing, having a "let go and let God" attitude. No, God moves when you move. The people of Israel had been given the land of Canaan, but they were still commanded to exert effort to possess the land. Paul is commanding a continuous, sustained effort on your part as you bring your salvation fully to its intended goal. William Barclay said, "Don't stop halfway. Go on until the work of salvation is fully wrought in you. No Christian should be satisfied with anything less than the total benefits of the gospel." God has given you a new life in Christ and He desires you to experience this life abundantly (John 10:10). Why be satisfied with a little when you can have an abundance?

Not only are you to work out your own salvation, but Paul also tells you to do it "with fear and trembling." Why would he say this? Charles Spurgeon answers that question, saying, "The fear of God is the cornerstone of all blessedness. We must reverence the ever-blessed God before we can be blessed ourselves." Paul is emphasizing the attitude with which you are to fulfill this command. You need a passion to please the Lord, and this involves humility and vigilance. Only those who fear the Lord will ever walk in His ways. Ps. 128:1 says, "Blessed is everyone who fears the Lord, who walks in His ways." How you think about God will always influence how you act before Him. There should be a fear not of what God might do to you, but of the hurt you may do to Him. A healthy fear of offending or displeasing God will motivate you to do what's right in His eyes. Professor John Murray said, "The fear of God is the soul of godliness." It's not a fear of eternal doom but "a nervous and trembling anxiety to do right" (J. B. Lightfoot).

Working out your salvation is not easy. It takes hard, consistent effort and discipline. Pastor and teacher John MacArthur said, "It involves a lifelong pursuit of holiness that requires following the example of Christ, understanding the love of God, cultivating obedience to the Word of God, appropriating your spiritual resources, and appreciating the serious consequences of sin. Paul said it called for beating our bodies into submission (1 Cor. 9:27) and cleansing ourselves from all filthiness of the flesh, perfecting holiness in the fear of God (2 Cor. 7:1). A high calling like that will mean all will fail at times. But a healthy fear of God will restrain such failure, because it motivates us to pursue godliness above all else." A reverential fear of God produces a sincere desire not to offend and grieve God, but to obey, honor, please, and glorify Him in all things. He described the the fear of the Lord this way, "It is the terror at the thought of a moral breakdown; a loathing of the disqualification such sin might cause."

Paul is saying you must first have a proper heart and mind attitude before you can carry out the action of working out your salvation thoroughly and to completion. Inside of you should be a serious dread of sin and a yearning to do what is right. God said in Jer. 32:40, "And I will make an everlasting covenant with them, that I will not turn away from doing them good; but I will put My fear in their hearts so that they will not depart from Me." Live in such awe of God and His majesty that you shun sin at all costs lest it grieve your Lord. Speaking of righteous fear, God said in Is. 66:2, "But on this one will I look: On him who is poor and of a contrite spirit, and who trembles at My word." If you know God and the greatness of His holiness, you will tremble in His presence. This is something you will never grow out of. Martyn Lloyd-Jones said that fear and trembling are manifested by "a holy vigilance and circumspection. It means that as I work out my salvation, I should realize the tremendous seriousness of what I am doing."

| 11 |

"THE SONS OF DISOBEDIENCE"

Paul's not finished. He continues his quest to get his readers to appreciate where they're now at in Christ by reminding them where they once were. He is writing to believers who were made alive by God's grace and mercy. Though they are now alive, they must never forget where they came from. Eph. 2:1 (MSG) says, "It wasn't so long ago that you were mired in that old stagnant life of sin." Sin is any violation of God's righteous character. It is anything you say or do or think or imagine or plan that does not meet God's holy standard of perfection. Col. 1:21 (NASB) says, "You were formerly alienated and hostile in mind, engaged in evil deeds." Before Christ, all people were dead in trespasses and sins. Trespasses speak of man as a rebel, sins speak of man as a failure. The first time you miss the mark and do something against God, it's a sin. The second time it's a trespass because now you know better. The boundary was set and you willfully crossed over it.

"Wherein in time past you walked according to the course of this world, according to the prince of the power of the air, the spirit that now works in the sons of disobedience" (Eph. 2:2). The Greek word for "walked" is "peripateo" and it means 'to order one's behavior; to follow along a path; to walk about.' Greek scholars suggest this word also means 'to browse; to meander; to follow a winding path; to wander about loosely without a goal or purpose.' These are the people who "go with the flow" of the world system and sing, "Whatever will be, will be." Is. 53:6 (MSG) says, "We're all like sheep who've wandered off and gotten lost. We've all done our own thing, gone our own way." The NLT says, "We have left God's path to follow our own." People today are sinful and self-centered, doing whatever they want at any given moment. One minute they do this and the next moment they change their mind and do that. There's enough confusion and uncertainty in their lives that it will make your head spin.

Augustine said fifteen-hundred years ago, "Our world marches to the drumbeat of three things: money, sex, and power." The same thing can be said today as people follow the course of this world. The Phillips translation says, "You drifted along on the stream of this world's ideas of living, and obeyed its unseen ruler who is still operating in those who do not respond to the truth of God." The Greek word for "course" refers to a weather vane that turns here and there, pointing in whatever direction the wind is blowing. In other words, people don't know if they're coming or going. Ps. 82:5 says, "They do not know, nor do they understand; They walk in darkness; All the foundations of this earth are unstable." People are walking in ignorance and darkness not knowing what's right and what's wrong. Jer. 23:10 says, "For the land is full of adulterers; For because of a curse the land mourns. The pleasant places of the wilderness are dried up, their course of life is evil, and their might is not right."

Before Christ, you were slaves and in bondage to the world system and how the world thinks and acts. You were slaves to the devil and his influence and temptations, and ultimately you were slaves to the passions of your flesh and its sinful nature. The devil is the prince of the power of the air and he seeks to influence the direction the weather vane of the world turns. He does so by keeping men and women focused upon and obsessed with themselves just like he once was (Is. 14:12-15). The truth be told, the world today is a jungle of selfishness. People are so self-absorbed they've become slaves to their wants and desires. Martin Luther said, "The heart of sin is a heart that is perpetually curved in on itself." It's a heart that tries to make you the center of the universe instead of God. Don't forget, Satan tried to do this and he failed. Pastor Timothy Keller said, "Self-centeredness is the hell begun in you that will eventually take you to hell because it will take you toward the person you are becoming like which is Satan."

There is a spiritual battle taking place, a battle between light and darkness. 1 John 5:19 (NLT) says, "We know that we are children of God and that the world around us is under the control of the evil one." The first rule of going into battle is that you must know your enemy inside out. Paul refers to Satan in 2 Cor. 4:4 as "the god of this age" and Jesus called him "the ruler of this world" (John 14:30). It is the devil who is driving the world in its rebellion against God. 2 Cor. 4:4 (NLT) says, "Satan, who is the god of this world, has blinded the minds of those who don't believe. They are unable to see the glorious light of the Good News. They don't understand this message about the glory of Christ, who is the exact likeness of God." The devil wants people to remain in darkness. Some of the worst sins are committed after the sun goes down, adultery being one of them. Here in Ephesians, Paul describes Satan as a prince with power to manifest evil in the world. He controls the ideologies and viewpoints currently in this evil world system.

Satan has a kingdom (Matt. 12:26) and a throne (Rev. 2:13). He is called the "prince of demons" in Matt. 12:24 for he is the chief fallen angel who rules over a vast multitude of other fallen angels who oppose God and His followers. People who were made for the glory of God are being held captive by an alien power. They can't resist him for without Christ they have no power to do so. Kenneth Wuest said, "All their thoughts, words, and deeds are ensphered by sin. Not one of their acts ever gets outside this circle of sin. That is what is meant by total depravity." Paul calls these people the sons of disobedience, "the careless, the rebellious, and the unbelieving, who go against the purposes of God" (AMP). Satan and his demonic hosts dominate, pressure, and control every person who is unsaved. He is the prince of the power of the air. This refers to the atmosphere immediately above the earth's surface. The fiery re-entry of capsules returning from outer space are passing through the domain of Satan.

Paul used the term "third heaven" in 2 Cor. 12:2 and this refers to the dwelling place of God. The "first heaven" is the atmosphere directly above the earth and the "second heaven" is outer space. The lower atmosphere is the main location of Satan's rule. It is notable to note that this is also the location where the final bowl of God's wrath is poured out (Rev. 16:17). Eph. 6:12 speaks of spiritual "wickedness in the heavenly places." Satellite dishes take signals out of the air and people are able to watch the garbage produced by Hollywood. You need to know that everything that comes out of Hollywood is part of an agenda to get you to believe a certain way so you'll follow the course of this world. They make these shows entertaining so you won't know what's really going on, so you won't know what their motive and agenda is. They're trying to get an emotional reaction out of you so they can seduce you into their way of life. Every movie and television show is an attack on the Christian way of life.

Paul said in 1 Tim. 4:1,2 (NLT), "In the last times some will turn away from the true faith; they will follow deceptive spirits and teachings that come from demons. These people are hypocrites and liars, and their consciences are dead." The Message Bible says they "chase after demonic illusions put forth by professional liars." This world is a very wicked place. There are evil, seducing spirits trying to get you to think about fleshly things so you'll spend your life seeking to fulfill those sensual desires that arise because of what you're looking at and thinking about. This is why most new movies have a sex scene in them. They're appealing to your flesh by showing you flesh. The more you see it, the more you get in the flesh and this takes you farther and farther away from God. The world has always been against God and always will be. This is why Hollywood is one of the most evil places on earth. The people there want you to disobey God and walk in the flesh. They care nothing about their eternal destiny, or yours.

There is moral corruption throughout the world and today's culture seeks to get you deeper and deeper into sin by legalizing many of the activities God calls sin. They exploit sensual lusts and desires by legalizing drugs, gambling, abortion, pornography, gay marriages and gay adoptions, and, in some places, prostitution. Many are trapped in "the snare of the devil, after being captured by him to do his will" (2 Tim. 2:25,26). These are the sons of disobedience, those who refuse to believe or be persuaded. It reflects an attitude of willful, perverse disbelief and is manifest as an unwillingness or refusal to comply with the demands of authority. For example, in his sermon that brought about his martyrdom, Stephen called the Jews who were listening to him "stiff-necked and uncircumcised in heart and ears! You always resist the Holy Spirit; as your fathers did, so do you" (Acts 7:51). His words paint a picture of a person who, because of unbelief, cannot be persuaded to do the right thing and remains non-compliant.

Paul said Satan "works" in the sons of disobedience. This means he never rests. 1 Peter 5:8 (NLT) says, "Stay alert! Watch out for your great enemy, the devil. He prowls around like a roaring lion, looking for someone to devour." He approached God in Job 1 and was asked, "From where do you come?" He answered, "From going to and fro on the earth, and from walking back and forth on it" (vs. 7). Satan works around the clock to prevent the Word of God from having any effect on the unbeliever's heart. For example, in the parable of the soils the devil is pictured as a bird that snatches away seed before it can produce life. Matt. 13:19 says, "When any one hears the word of the kingdom and does not understand it, the evil one comes and snatches away what is sown in his heart." The way Satan compounds the hopelessness of people who are dead in sin is to keep them from seeing anything glorious in the gospel of Christ. They are blind to its significance. 1 Cor. 1:18 says, "The message of the cross is foolishness to those who are perishing."

Paul expands on this in 1 Cor. 2:14, "But the natural man does not receive the things of the Spirit of God, for they are foolishness to him; nor can he know them, because they are spiritually discerned." The natural man spoken of here is an educated man at the height of his intellectual power but is devoid of the Spirit of God. He is lost and unsaved, a person in whom the flesh is the ruling principle. Jude 19 says, "These are sensual persons, who cause divisions, not having the Spirit." A natural man is one who's only had one birth. He was born into the natural world and is bound by the natural world. No matter how educated and sophisticated the natural man may be, he still lives in a world of sight and sound and touch. He lives in a tangible world and is totally ignorant of the spiritual realm which transcends all of these physical things. This is why Jesus said to Nicodemus, "That which is born of the flesh is flesh, and that which is born of the Spirit is spirit" (John 3:6).

Kenneth Wuest said the things of God "are investigated in a spiritual realm." When it comes to the things of the Spirit, all your thinking abilities and college degrees will not be sufficient for you to understand the Bible. The natural man can read the Bible and yet fail to understand what it is saying. It's like trying to describe a sunset to a blind man or a symphony to a deaf man. A person like that cannot understand spiritual things for their interests do not go beyond physical life. They reject the message of salvation and refuse to act on it. By contrast, the people of Berea "received the message with great eagerness" (Acts 17:11). Only those who are saved are able to welcome God's truth. The Lord must control, guide, and enlighten your understanding of the scriptures. This only happens when you are born again. Many books can inform but only the Holy Spirit can transform. Spiritual truth can only be seen with spiritual eyes, eyes that have been illuminated by the Spirit of God.

Paul is still painting a picture of who the saints at Ephesus used to be. They were a people who lived to satisfy their selfish selves, a people poured into the mold of worldly thinking. The sons of disobedience were trapped in a delusion, thinking the gospel wasn't true and Christ wasn't real. Their lives were driven by strong desires, impulses, and longings to do that which is outside the will of God. Professor D. Edmond Hiebert said, "Left to himself, instead of gaining mastery over his base desires and steadfastly adhering to the good, the individual so characteristically overcome by his evil cravings, so that they become the dominating force of his life." The sons of disobedience sin willfully for it is their nature to do so. Without hesitation Paul says, "Among whom also we all once conducted ourselves in the lusts of our flesh, fulfilling the desires of the flesh and of the mind, and were by nature children of wrath, just as the others" (Eph. 2:3). Sin dwells within (Rom. 7:17) and the flesh becomes the carrier of sin (Rom. 7:5).

The flesh is the root of man's problems for it is the source of all evil desires. Kenneth Wuest said, "We all ordered our behavior in the sphere of the cravings of our evil nature. We went the limit in sin. The evil nature had full sway." To live by the flesh is to be ruled and controlled by ungodly motives, affections, principles, purposes, words, thoughts, and actions. The flesh has a strong desire to satisfy its appetites so it seeks gratification with great diligence. The flesh says, "If it feels good, do it" with no regard as to whether the deed is good or bad. The person not saved is at the mercy of their flesh. With uncontrolled, reckless abandon they seek to do whatever evil their minds imagine. John Piper said, "The flesh craves the sensation of self-generated power and loves the praise of men. It's the proud and unsubmissive root of depravity in every human heart which exalts itself subtly through proud, self-reliant morality, or flaunts itself blatantly through self-assertive authority - despising immorality."

Paul has identified the three enemies each Christian must face: the world, the flesh, and the devil. The enemy of the Christian is not other believers. Eph. 6:12 says, "For we wrestle not against flesh and blood." Your enemy is the world and everything evil in it. This is why 1 John 2:15 says, "Do not love the world or the things of the world. If anyone loves the world, the love of the Father is not in him." This is a command. Do not love the world! Do not let worldly things engage and control your affections. "Do not court the intimacy and the favor of the unchristian world around you; do not take its customs for your laws, nor adopt its ideals, nor covet its prizes, nor seek fellowship with its life" (author unknown). The world promises you sensual gratification and even this promise it cannot fulfill. Nothing rises higher than its source. The desire for earthly pleasures comes from the world and is limited to the boundaries of the world. In other words, what you see is what you get.

Why shouldn't you love the world? Because the things of this world are not of God. And if you love God, you cannot set your heart on what is not of God. 1 John 2:16 (AMP) says, "For all that is in the world - the lust of the flesh (craving for sensual gratification) and the lust of the eyes (greedy longing of the mind) and the pride of life (assurance in one's own resources or in the stability of earthly things) - these do not come from the Father but are from the world itself." The entire world system is based on man's primitive desires, his greedy ambitions, and the glamour of all that he things splendid. The sons of disobedience are controlled by selfish ambition, pride, and the love of success and flattery. Dr. Thomas L. Constable said, "The lust of the flesh is the desire to do something apart from the will of God. The lust of the eyes is the desire to have something apart from the will of God. The pride of life is the desire to be something apart from the will of

God. The first desire appeals to the body, the second to the soul, and the third to the spirit."

All the flesh wants to do is satisfy its passions and cravings. Bible commentator Robert Jamieson said the lust of the flesh "has its seat and source in our lower animal nature." There's a difference between eating to live and living to eat, a difference between getting much needed rest and being a lazy sluggard, a difference between sex in marriage and fornication outside of it. The sensual desires of a heart not saved perverts and distorts all normal desires. These unethical cravings send people into a relentless pursuit of evil that exceeds the limits of what is good, reasonable, and righteous. The Greek word for "lust" is "epithumia" and it denotes 'the varied cravings of fallen human nature pursued in the interest of self in self-sufficient independence from God.' James 1:14,15 (NLT) says, "Temptation comes from our own desires, which entice us and drag us away. These desires give birth to sinful actions. And when sin is allowed to grow, it gives birth to death."

The fundamental desires of life are good. They're designed to be your servant, not your master. For example, love is patient but lust says "I must have it now!" In Eph. 4:22, Paul says sinful man "grows corrupt according to the deceitful lusts." He's saying that lusts deceive you and lead you astray by promising more than they can deliver and produce. The lust of the flesh causes you to indulge in worldly pleasures that inflame your passions but never satisfy. Not being satisfied drives you deeper and deeper into sin as you seek that which only God can give. The flesh can be called "the beast within" and rightfully so. All evil cravings have its origin in fallen flesh. Submitting to the flesh leads to rebellion and keeps you from being wholly devoted to God. This is why Peter said, "Beloved, I beg you as sojourners and pilgrims, abstain from fleshly lusts which war against the soul" (1 Peter 2:11). Paul said in Rom. 13:14, "But put on the Lord Jesus Christ, and make no provision for the flesh, to fulfill its lusts."

The things of this world are everywhere. They're in every store you go into and on every television commercial you see. They're in the movies, on the radio, on the internet, and on billboards that line the highway. All these avenues of advertisement give you new things to look at and lust after. The cravings of the flesh are always stimulated by what is seen. Satan knows if he can get you to take a look, he can get you to take the bait. Gen. 3:6 says, "The woman saw that the tree was good for food, that it was pleasant to the eyes." Consider also what Achan said in Josh. 7:21, "When I saw among the spoils a beautiful Babylonian garment, two hundred shekels of silver, and a wedge of gold weighing fifty shekels, I coveted them and took them." He said, "I see it. I want it. I'll take it." The eyes are the gateway through which the things of the world inflame ungodly desires. It was through wandering eyes that David fell. 2 Sam. 11:2 says, "And from the roof he saw a woman bathing, and the woman was very beautiful to behold."

2 Cor. 11:14 says Satan is transformed into an angel of light. In other words, he knows how to make bad things look good. He is a deceiver and many have been taken captive by his schemes and trickery. And it all begins with a lustful look in the wrong direction. Churchman Thomas Fuller said in the 17th century, "Our eyes, when gazing on sinful objects, are out of their calling and God's keeping." The eyes serve as the window for fallen flesh. The flesh covets what is seen and takes it for the purpose of sensual gratification. Kenneth Wuest said the lust of the eyes refers to "the passionate cravings of the eyes for satisfaction, these cravings finding their source in the evil nature." Commentator Matthew Henry wrote, "Natural desires are at rest when that which is desired is obtained, but corrupt desires are insatiable. Nature is content with little, grace with less, but lust with nothing." What should you do? Pray the words of Ps. 119:37, "Turn away my eyes from looking at worthless things, and revive me in Your way." Amen.

| 12 |

"THE FIRE OF SIN"

John made it very clear that there is nothing good in this evil, sin-filled world. 1 John 2:16 (NLT) says, "The world offers only a craving for physical pleasure, a craving for everything we see, and pride in our achievements and possessions." The lust of the flesh. The lust of the eyes. The pride of life. Christians have always been, and always will be, lured by these three temptations. The devil will tempt you with the lust of the flesh, things such as sexual gratification, gluttony, alcohol, and drugs. He'll also tempt you with the lust of the eyes, with endless cravings for more and better possessions, for things that ensnare you and hardens your heart to the things of God. Perhaps the most evil temptation of all is the pride of life, the very sin that got Satan kicked out of heaven when he desired to be God (Is. 14:12-15). The arrogant boasting of the pride of life motivates the other two lusts as it seeks to elevate itself above all others and fulfill all personal desires. It's the root cause of strife in families, churches, and nations.

The lust of the flesh and the lust of the eyes refer to the desire to obtain what you do not have. The boastful pride of life refers to sinful pride over what you do have. It is the desire to be better than others so that you can glory in yourself and your accomplishments. Adam Clarke says the pride of life speaks of "hunting after honors, titles, and pedigrees; boasting of ancestry, family connections, great offices, honorable acquaintance, and the like." An example of this is found in what Nebuchadnezzar said in Dan. 4:30, "Is this not Babylon the great, which I myself have built as a royal residence by the might of my power and for the glory of my majesty?" He was a pretentious braggart who used boastful words for the purpose of making a favorable impression on others. The NET comments on the arrogance produced by material possessions, "The person who thinks he has enough wealth and property to protect himself and insure his security has no need for God or anything outside himself."

Pride is one of the first attacks that come against God's people. It gains a foothold in your life when you don't give God the glory for all the good things happening in your life. If you have something and it's good, God put it there. 1 Cor. 15:10 says, "But by the grace of God I am what I am, and His grace toward me was not in vain; but I labored more abundantly than they all, yet not I, but the grace of God which was with me." The Message Bible says, "It was God giving me the work to do, God giving me the energy to do it." Yes, there is work that you have to do but it's God's grace that causes that work to flourish. He gives you the strength to do the work and the wisdom to know what to do. Not recognizing this takes the glory away from God. Pride sets in when you think your skill and intellect earned you all that you have. Don't get prideful when God uses you for it's His anointing that gives you the power to accomplish the task at hand. Gal. 2:20 says, "It is no longer I who live, but Christ lives in me."

Another way people fall into the pit of pride is by relishing the applause of others. Matt. 6:1 (NLT) says, "Watch out! Don't do your good deeds publicly, to be admired by others, for you will lose the reward from your Father in heaven." The Message Bible says, "Be especially careful when you are trying to be good so that you don't make a performance out of it. It might be good theater, but the God who made you won't be applauding." In the book of Daniel, Nebuchadnezzar made a golden image and commanded everybody to worship it. When Daniel's three friends, Shadrach, Meshach, and Abed-Nego refused, Nebuchadnezzar said to them, "If you do not worship, you shall be cast immediately into the midst of a burning fiery furnace. And who is the god who will deliver you from my hand?" (Dan. 3:15). Can you hear the pride in these words? One is reminded of when Satan tempted Jesus in the wilderness. He showed Him the kingdoms of the world and said, "All these things I will give You if you will fall down and worship me" (Matt. 4:9).

Even when you do something with a pure heart and for all the right reasons, be careful because people will still try to give you glory. In Acts 14:6-18, God used Paul and Barnabus to heal a lame man crippled from birth. When the people saw what happened, they raised their voices and said, "The gods have come down to us in the likeness of men!" (vs. 11). Paul and Barnabus wisely rejected this glory as they refused to be seduced by pride. Tearing their clothed they said, "Men, why are you doing these things? We also are men with the same nature as you." They were saying, "Don't worship us, worship God." It's okay to honor someone but only God gets the glory. In the book of Revelation, God sent an angel to show John things which must shortly take place. Rev. 22:8 says, "And when I heard and saw, I fell down to worship before the feet of the angel who showed me these things." The angel responded in vs. 9, "See that you do not do that. For I am your fellow servant, and of those who keep the words of this book. Worship God."

Instead of speaking boastfully, train yourself to speak humbly. Jesus said in Matt. 12:34, "For out of the abundance of the heart the mouth speaks." Yes, people sometimes say stupid and prideful things but that doesn't mean it's in their heart. This verse is saying the things you say all the time, things you say an abundant number of times, is what's in your heart. An abundance of prideful words coming out of your mouth tells you there is pride in your heart. If you don't change, if you don't humble yourself, then know that God will step in and deal with it Himself. Without exception, God always humbles the person who exalts himself. Don't forget, He did kick Lucifer out of heaven because pride was in his heart. Judgment also came upon Nebuchadnezzar because of his prideful boasting. Dan. 4:33 says, "He was driven from men and ate grass like oxen; his body was wet with the dew of heaven till his hair had grown like eagle's feathers and his nails like bird's claws."

People who struggle doing what's right are more times than not stubborn because of pride. Stubbornness is a form of rebellion and rebellion is a form of witchcraft (1 Sam. 15:33). You are not teachable if you're stubborn. You think you're right and everybody else is wrong. Stubbornness is a pride that protects itself from helpful rebuke and criticism. It would rather go down the wrong path than face the pain of admitting it was wrong. The word "stubborn" means 'having or showing dogged determination not to change one's attitude or position on something, especially in spite of good arguments or reasons to do so." Many people get saved but don't turn their will over to God. They believe in Jesus but don't give Him control over their lives. Stubbornness is your strong will turned toward yourself instead of God. Being stubborn is a form of idolatry for it causes you to seek the glory that belongs only to God. King Saul lost his throne because he always wanted to do things his own way. That's stubbornness.

Jer. 5:21 says, "Hear this now, O foolish people, without understanding, who have eyes and see not, and who have ears and hear not." Stubborn people can see things with their eyes but not look at them with their heart. It's the opposite of what happened when Moses saw the burning bush. He said in Ex. 3:3, "I will now turn aside and see this great sight, why the bush does not burn." He saw and he looked. Stubbornness does not do this. It sees and looks away. People see in the Bible where they shouldn't murmur and complain but they don't look at it and murmur and complain anyway. They see in the Bible that their body is the temple of the holy Spirit but they don't look at that verse, choosing to eat lots of potato chips and ice cream. They see it but they don't look at it. In other words, they're stubborn. At the same time, stubborn people hear but they don't listen. They hear the Word of God and it goes in one ear and out the other. They know the truth but don't learn the truth. God is saying, "Don't just hear Me, listen to Me."

Pride opens the door to deception. The only way Satan can get you into bondage is to get you to believe a lie. That's what deception is. It's a lie. Eph. 4:18 says all sinners are "darkened in their understanding, being alienated from the life of God." Pride has kept many people from accepting Jesus Christ as Savior. Admitting sin and acknowledging that in their own strength they can do nothing to inherit eternal life is a constant stumbling block for prideful people. Satan has deceived them into thinking they don't need Jesus and doing good deeds is enough to get them into heaven. These people are mentioned in Is. 43:8 where it talks about blind people who have eyes and deaf people who have ears. Jesus said in Matt. 13:13, "Seeing they do not see, and hearing they do not hear, nor do they understand." Why don't they understand? Because pride has caused them to be deceived. The Message Bible says, "In their present state they can stare till doomsday and not see it, listen till they're blue in the face and not get it."

The phrase "the pride of life" is found only once in the Bible and that's here in 1 John 2:16. What it all boils down to is ego, an obsession with self. The pride of life will make you swell up like a bull frog, to inflate with self-conceit. It will cause you to look down on others, thinking you are something special when you are not. Jesus told a parable of a Pharisee who stood in the temple and prayed, "I thank You, God, that I am not a sinner like everyone else. For I don't cheat, I don't sin, and I don't commit adultery. I'm certainly not like that tax collector!" (Luke 18:11). This religious leader was self-confident as he compared himself to other people and boasted about his lack of outward sin. People do good deeds and this makes them think they're special. They boast saying how religious and spiritual they are. They think God is ready to condemn others but never themselves. They don't realize God doesn't judge on the curve. Jesus went on to say He was not impressed with this man's prayer (vs. 14).

The world system, ruled and controlled by Satan, is founded upon the pride of life. It's having an arrogant, boastful attitude that must be right about everything. It's when you refuse to admit you're ever wrong and that someone else is better than you in a certain area. When people think they're smarter, more successful, and more knowledgeable than anyone else, they're in the devil's grasp. Pride is behavior based and envy driven. It forever tries to elicit envy from others. People want to be more popular than others and better liked. The pride of life has to do with one's desire for praise and worship. It's when you allow your desire for approval from people to become more important than God's approval. The pride of life is a form of idolatry where one considers the grace of God an achievement of their own. They take the things God has provided and rely on them more than God Himself. Instead of praising God for who He is, they foolishly try to make Him who and what they want Him to be.

J. Oswald Sanders said the pride of life is an "ambition to produce spiritual results by unspiritual means." This is what happened with the temptation of Eve in the Garden of Eden. This story clearly shows that the pride of life is linked together with the lust of the flesh and the lust of the eyes. Gen. 3:6 says, "The woman saw that the tree was good for food, that it was pleasant to the eyes, and a tree desirable to make one wise." She perceived the fruit was good for food and this appealed to her appetite. The lust of the flesh is the desire for that which satisfies any of your physical needs. Also, the fruit was pleasing and delightful to the eye. The lust of the eyes is that which you see and desire to own or possess. Finally, she perceived the fruit would make her wise, giving her a wisdom beyond her own. The pride of life is anything that exalts you above where you're supposed to be. It offers you the illusion of God-like qualities which, in turn, cause you to boast in arrogance and pride.

The point being made here is that without Christ, all people are sinners and stand guilty before God. Rom. 3:10-12 (NLT) says, "No one is righteous - not even one. No one is truly wise; no one is seeking God. All have turned away; all have become useless. No one does good, not a single one." Paul paints a picture of the sinner as being dead, diluted, disobedient, defiled, and doomed. Because of the power of sin, all believers at one time "were by nature children of wrath, just as the others" (Eph. 2:3). What this means is that you didn't develop traits that would cause you to become children of wrath. No, all people were born destined to be sinners for they were born with Adam's depraved nature (Rom. 5:12). Children of wrath naturally do things which God hates. They lie, they steal, they cheat, they manipulate. They reject the knowledge of God (Rom. 1:28), they refuse the gospel (1 Cor. 2:14), and by nature are filled with desires that lead to idolatry (Col. 3:5). Sin affects man's standing before God. It places him under the wrath of God.

Adam and Eve at one time were objects of God's love and affection. When they sinned, they became objects of God's wrath. Sin dishonors God and He would be unrighteous if He looked with indifference at the sins of man. Indeed, the wrath of God comes upon the sons of disobedience. John 3:36 says, "The wrath of God abides on him." The Message Bible says, "All he experiences of God is darkness, and an angry darkness at that." Notice that this is present tense. The unbeliever has wrath abiding on him right now at this very moment. He lives continually alienated from God and is subject to God's displeasure and indignation. Jonathan Edwards said, "Their foot shall slide in due time." As you look around, you will see sinners enjoying life to the fullest. They drink, they party, they take drugs and have illicit sex. Satan is deceiving them into thinking all is well because they are in step with the rest of the world. Unfortunately, they don't realize they're headed for eternal judgment for without Christ they are children of wrath.

God's wrath against sin and disobedience is perfectly justified because His plan for mankind is holy and perfect just as He is holy and perfect. The word "wrath" is defined as 'the emotional response to perceived wrong and injustice.' It's often translated as 'anger, indignation, vexation, and irritation.' The Greek word for "wrath" is "orge" and is defined as 'God's holy hatred of sin representing His essential divine antagonism against everything that is evil.' It is derived from the idea of a swelling which eventually bursts and applies to an anger that proceeds from one's settled nature. John MacArthur said, "Orge does not refer to an explosive outburst of temper but to an inner, deep resentment that seethes and smolders, often unnoticed by others. It is therefore an anger that only the Lord and the believer know about." Both humans and God express wrath. God's wrath, however, is holy and always justified. It's a divine response to sin and disobedience directed toward those who don't follow His will.

The wrath of God is a fearsome and terrifying thing. Rom. 1:18 (NLT) says, "But God shows His anger from heaven against all sinful, wicked people who suppress the truth by their wickedness." The Message Bible says, "But God's angry displeasure erupts as acts of human mistrust and wrongdoing and lying accumulate, as people try to put a shroud over truth." God is not timid when He brings forth His judgment. Those who sin willfully and habitually will reap a whirlwind of sorrow and regret. If you play with the fire of sin, you will surely be burned with wrath and indignation. Prov. 24:12 (NLT) says, "He will repay all people as their actions deserve." When this world ends, 2 Thess. 1:7-9 (NLT) says, "He will come with His mighty angels, in flaming fire, bringing judgment on those who don't know God and on those who refuse to obey the Good News of our Lord Jesus. They will be punished with eternal destruction, forever separated from the Lord and from His glorious power."

Those who do not believe in Jesus and receive Him as Savior will be judged on the day of wrath. Zeph. 1:15 says, "That day is a day of wrath, a day of trouble and distress, a day devastation and desolation, a day of darkness and gloominess, a day of clouds and thick darkness." God's wrath is love in action against sin. It is just for it is in direct proportion to man's sinfulness. Rom. 2:5,6 (NLT) says, "But because you are stubborn and refuse to turn from your sin, you are storing up terrible punishment for yourself. For a day of anger is coming, when God's righteous judgment will be revealed. He will judge everyone according to what they have done." God is a holy and just God and His wrath is in perfect accord with His justice. The Message Bible says, "You're not getting by with anything. Every refusal and avoidance of God adds fuel to the fire. The day is coming when it's going to blaze hot and high, God's fiery and righteous judgment. Make no mistake: In the end you get what's coming to you." It doesn't get any plainer than that.

Martyn Lloyd-Jones said, "Wrath is a manifestation of indignation based upon justice." God is a God of love and if His love is rejected, nothing remains but the wrath, justice, and righteousness of God. Gen. 3:24 says, "So He drove out the man; and He placed cherubim at the east of the garden of Eden, and a flaming sword which turned every way, to guard the way to the tree of life." That flaming sword is the sword of God's justice, God's sword of wrath and punishment. The flood at the time of Noah and the story of Sodom and Gomorrah are examples of the righteous wrath of God. He gave man His law and He punished them when they disobeyed it. He punished individuals, He punished nations, and He even punished His own special people. The wrath of God is not an uncontrolled manifestation of anger and rage. J. I. Packer said, "God's wrath in the Bible is never the capricious, self-indulgent, irritable, morally ignoble thing that human anger so often is. It is, instead, a right and necessary reaction to objective moral evil."

The tremendous peril of the wrath of God abides on every ungodly sinner. Ps. 7:11 says, "God is a just judge, and God is angry with the wicked every day." This wrath to come is just and necessary. God has an utter hatred of all evil and He cannot let sin go unpunished. Charles Spurgeon said, "The sluices of the great deep will be pulled up, and the awful torrents will come leaping forth, and will utterly overwhelm all who are exposed to their fury. This wrath to come will in part fall upon man at death, but more fully at the day of judgment, and it will continue to flow over them forever and ever." He also said, "When it does come, it must be something very terrible because divinity enters into the essence of it." Without a doubt, God's wrath is to be feared. Heb. 10:31 says, "It is a fearful thing to fall into the hands of the living God." The Message Bible says, "Nobody's getting by with anything, believe me." If you defy God and reject His plan of salvation, you will pay the price, and what a horrible price it is.

Ps. 94:23 (NLT) says, "God will turn the sins of evil people back on them. He will destroy them for their sins. The Lord our God will destroy them." How awful and awakening are these words! They are written to strike the heart of the sinner with the utmost fear. They're meant to be a warning against willful and presumptuous disobedience against the gospel message and the will of God. Falling into the hands of an angry God can destroy you if you let it. But it can also force you to make the changes you need to become the person God created you to be. Heb. 12:6 says, "The Lord disciplines him whom He loves." This is not a threat, it's a promise. When you turn your back on God and refuse to obey His commands, He will not hesitate to bring you to your knees in humbleness and repentance. Life will get so hard for you that the only thing you can do is fall on your face and beg Him for mercy and forgiveness. Jonah found this out the hard way when he disobeyed God and was swallowed by a whale.

The wrath of God is an expression of His hatred of sin. If you don't understand the wrath of God, you cannot possibly understand the compassion of God and His great love in providing a way of escaping from it. 1 Tim. 1:15 says, "This is a faithful saying and worthy of all acceptance, that Christ Jesus came into the world to save sinners, of whom I am chief." Only those covered by the blood of Jesus can be assured that God's wrath will never fall on them. Rom. 5:9 says, "Since we have been justified by His blood, how much more shall we be saved from God's wrath through Him!" Yes, God provided salvation as a means to gain divine favor and to turn away His wrath from the willful sinner. All this was made possible because God poured His wrath out on Jesus as He hung on that cross in your place. The wrath you deserved caused Jesus to cry out, "My God, My God, why have You forsaken Me?" (Matt. 27:46). Paul said in 1 Thess. 1:10 it is "Jesus who delivers us from the wrath to come." Hallelujah!

| 13 |

"A LIMITED TIME OFFER"

God is a holy God. In heaven the seraphim cry out, "Holy, holy, holy is the Lord of hosts; The whole earth is full of His glory!" (Is. 6:3). Holiness is the defining attribute of God. He is wholly and morally perfect in every way. He is also a just God. The holiness of God demands that sin be punished. He judges sin by a righteous standard, namely His own holy character. The truth be told, God is the sinner's worst nightmare. Not only do they need to be saved from sin, they need to be saved from God. He is sovereign and He determined long ago that sinners will not get away with their sin. Indeed, "the wages of sin is death" (Rom. 6:23). The bad news for the sinner is they can't save themselves even if they wanted to. The good news is they don't have to. God did it all! Paul begins Eph. 2:4 with the greatest two words in all the Bible, "But God..." You were dead in trespasses...but God! You were lost in sin...but God! You were sons of disobedience...but God! You were children of wrath...but God!

The words "But God" is about divine intervention, the sovereign, direct, and unmistakable way God works in human affairs. He intervenes in a variety of ways. He changes circumstances, executes justice, heals sickness, meets needs, provides resources, solves problems, and silences lies. However, His ultimate act of intervention is the salvation of lost sinners. James Montgomery Boise said, "If you understand those two words - 'but God' - they will save your soul." Paul is saying that the sinner's problem has become the sinner's solution. What God required, God supplied. He intervened to save the lost sinner from Himself. Martyn Lloyd-Jones said, "These two words, in and of themselves, in a sense contain the whole gospel." God's love is so great that it extends even to the unlovely, to the sons of disobedience and the children of wrath. Know this, God will always have the last word, not you. Joseph told his brothers, "You meant evil against me, but God meant it for good" (Gen. 50:20).

Sinners give God no reason to love them yet, in the greatness of His love, He loves them anyway. Stop trying to make yourself lovable before God and simply receive His great love while recognizing that you are unworthy of it. Paul said, "But God, who is rich in mercy, because of His great love with which He loves us, even when we were dead in trespasses, made us alive together with Christ (by grace you have been saved)" (Eph. 2:4,5). Yes, God is holy and just but He is also a God of mercy. In fact, Paul says He is rich in mercy. The word "rich" is the Greek word "plousios" and is 'that which exists in a large amount with implications of being very valuable.' It means 'to be filled' and refers to 'having an abundance of earthly possessions that exceeds normal experience.' God is plentifully supplied, over abounding, without measure, very rich and wealthy in regard to His mercy. For sure, God is rich in mercy. Lam. 3:22 says, "Through the Lord's mercies we are not consumed, because His compassions fail not."

Mercy is the outward manifestation of pity. It's the indication of emotion aroused by someone in need and the attempt to relieve that person of their pain and trouble. D. Edmond Hiebert defines "mercy" as 'the self-moved, spontaneous loving kindness of God which causes Him to deal in compassion and tender affection with the miserable and distressed.' God's motive for His divine intervention lies in the endless ocean of His mercy and His great expansive love. J. I. Packer vividly describes God's mercy toward fallen man, "Between us sinners and the thunder clouds of divine wrath stands the cross of our Lord

Jesus." Titus 3:5 (NLT) says, "He saved us, not because of the right-eous things we have done, but because of His mercy. He washed away our sins, giving us a new birth through the Holy Spirit." Mercy is God not giving you what you deserve. It's His kindness and good will toward miserable and afflicted sinners. All of mankind deserves judgment but through the sphere of mercy God offers them eternal salvation.

The world today cannot fill the longings in the heart of man. God planned it that way for true satisfaction is only found in the great invi-tation God extends to guilty sinners. Isaiah 55 tells of a wide ranging, far reaching, and life transforming invitation God makes to a sinful world. In this chapter, God extends a gracious invitation for guilty sinners to get right with Him. Some will say this is too good to be true. In reality, this is an invitation too good not to be true. Stubborn sin had led to the Babylonian captivity and here in Isaiah 55 God of-fers to feed, fulfill, and forgive His people for their rebellion. He is offering the same invitation to people today. There are twelve com-mands in the first seven verses of this chapter. He commands sinners to come to Him, to trust in His promises, and to repent of their sin. Is. 55:1 says, "Ho! Everyone who thirsts, come to the waters; And you who have no money, come, buy and eat. Yes, come, buy wine and milk without money and without price."

Three times in this verse God gives the command to "Come." True satisfaction is only found in God but the sinner must come to Him. You must be spiritually thirsty before you go to God. Why? Because self sufficiency automatically disqualifies you from spiritual benefits. Jesus said in John 7:37,38 (MSG), "If anyone thirsts, let him come to Me and drink. Rivers of living water will brim and spill out of the depths of anyone who believes in Me this way, just as the scripture says." Here in Isaiah 55, God offers food and drink to those who have no money. Matt. 5:3 says, "Blessed are the poor in spirit, for theirs is the kingdom of heaven." To be "poor in spirit" is to recognize your utter bankruptcy before God. No matter what your status in the world is, you are completely helpless spiritually and can do nothing to deliver yourself from the ravages of sin. You must recognize your spiritual poverty before you can come to God in faith to accept His invitation and receive the salvation He lovingly and graciously offers.

God asks in Is. 55:2, "Why do you spend money for what is not bread, and your wages for what does not satisfy?" Vs. 1 says sin robs you of spiritual resources, vs. 2 suggests it also robs you of spiritual discernment. Sin makes fools of everybody. The rich live by their money and the poor live by their labor. The lives of both are wasted by their sin. People spend money on what sin offers only to realize it is not the bread of life. They labor for what sin promises only to find out it does not give them the satisfaction they need and crave. Jesus asked in Mark 8:36, "For what will it profit a man if he gains the whole world and lose his own soul?" Rich sinners wear fancy clothes but their souls are naked before God. What is the solution to this? God says, "Listen diligently to me, and eat what is good" (vs. 2). You must hear, trust, and obey the Word of God to receive the rich outpourings of God's amazing grace. The world doesn't need big houses and fast cars and fancy clothes. It needs the Word of God.

God next commands sinners to trust His promises. Is. 55:3 says, "Incline your ear, and come to Me. Hear, and your soul shall live; and I will make an everlasting covenant with you." Sinners cannot come to God if they do not hear. Those who do hear and come to God will experience a new and abundant life, a life that is satisfying and eternal. God's promise to them is a lifelong guarantee, an everlasting covenant. It's based on God's great love and His amazing grace, not on human accomplishment. This is why you must repent of your sins immediately and completely. Vs. 6 says, "Seek the Lord while He may be found, call upon Him while he is near." People don't realize this but there will come a time when God can't be found. If a person dies a sinner, for them God can't be found. Heb. 9:27 says, "It is appointed for men to die once, but after this the judgment." What should you do? Call upon Him before it's too late. Those who wait until tomorrow to get saved usually die today.

God's divine invitation is a lifetime guarantee but it's a limited time offer. The benefits last forever, the offer does not. Life is short and hell is hot. Eternity is long so don't put off until tomorrow what you should be doing today. Get right with God while you still have the chance to do so. Ps.32:6 (NLT) says, "Therefore, let all the godly pray to You while there is still time, that they may not drown in the flood waters of judgment." The Message Bible says, "Every one of us needs to pray; when all hell breaks loose and the dam bursts we'll be on high ground, untouched." God invites you to come to Him but you must come on His terms. Vs. 6 says sinners should repent immediately, vs. 7 says they must repent completely, "Let the wicked forsake his way, and the unrighteous man his thoughts; Let him return to the Lord, and He will have mercy on him; And to our God, for He will abundantly pardon." Repentance goes beyond feelings of regret and remorse. It's a change of mind that results in a change of behavior.

Once the sin problem has been dealt with, what must you do? Return to the Lord. If and when you sin, you can always come back to God. This is the hope of the gospel. The good news is you don't have to worry how He'll respond. He'll have mercy on you and will abundantly pardon your sins. Is. 55:7 confirms what God said in Is. 1:18, "Come now, and let us reason together. Though your sins are like scarlet, they shall be as white as snow; Though they are red like crimson, they shall be as wool." The remaining verses of Isaiah 55 give you three reasons why you should trust and accept God's great invitation. First of all, you must trust the message of God's Word because of how God thinks. He said in vs. 8, "For My thoughts are not your thoughts, nor are your ways My ways." Canadian composer John Oswald said, "Our understanding must not be the measure of what God can do."

Prov. 3:5 says the same thing, "Trust in the Lord with all your heart, and lean not on your own understanding."

Cast your own thoughts aside. Prov. 3:6 says, "In all your ways acknowledge Him, and He shall direct your paths." God continues speaking in Is. 55:9, "For as the heavens are higher than the earth, so are My ways higher than your ways, and My thoughts than your thoughts." Paul must have had this on his mind when he wrote Eph. 3:20, "Now to Him who is able to do exceedingly abundantly above all that we ask or think, according to the power that works in us." The Message Bible says, "God can do anything, you know - far more than you could ever imagine or guess or request in your wildest dreams." How high are God's ways and thoughts? So high that Rom. 5:8 says, "But God demonstrates His own love toward us, in that while we were still sinners, Christ died for us." You have no right or reason to second guess a God like that. You need to trust Him, obey Him, and praise Him. Ps. 145:3 says, "Great is the Lord, and greatly to be praised; and His greatness is unsearchable."

How can you understand God's thoughts and ways? By how He speaks. Is. 55:10,11 (MSG) says, "Just as rain and snow descend from the skies and don't go back until they've watered the earth, doing their work of making things grow and blossom, producing seed for farmers and food for the hungry, so will the words that come out of My mouth not come back empty-handed. They'll do the work I sent them to do, they'll complete the assignment I gave them." Precipitation from heaven produces transformation on earth. God gives seed to the sower and bread to the eater. Seed is the beginning of bread and bread is the end of seed. In other words, God's got you covered from beginning to end. Scripture is God's Word coming out of God's mouth. It's the unfailing Word of a perfect God. 2 Tim. 3:16,17 (NIV) says, "All scripture is God-breathed and is useful for teaching, rebuking, correcting, and training in righteousness, so that the servant of God may be thoroughly equipped for every good work."

The Message Bible says, "Every part of scripture is God-breathed and useful one way or another - showing us truth, exposing our rebellion, correcting our mistakes, training us to live God's way. Through the Word we are put together and shaped up for the tasks God has for us." The nature, character, and authority of scripture are rooted in the nature, character, and authority of God. His Word will never return to Him without any production. It will surely accomplish and fulfill its divine purpose. Yes, it will succeed in the things for which God sends it. Because of God's sovereign work of deliverance, all of Israel will be led out of Babylonian captivity. Is. 55:12 says, "For you shall go out with joy, and be led out with peace; The mountains and the hills shall break forth into singing before You, and all the trees will clap their hands." You can trust God for how He thinks, for how He speaks, and finally for how He works. His work is so great that nature will join in the celebration.

All of nature is rejoicing. The mountains and hills are bursting with song and all the trees of the forest are exuberant will applause (MSG). God likes singing and clapping. If people don't do it, nature will. The Pharisees told Jesus to rebuke His disciples who were rejoicing and praising God with a loud voice. He answered them saying, "I tell you that if these should keep silent, the stones would immediately cry out" (Luke 19:40). Yes, nature has a voice. The rocks cry out, the mountains sing, and the trees clap their hands. Rom. 8:20,21 (NLT) says, "Against its will, all creation was subjected to God's curse. But with eager hope, the creation looks forward to the day when it will join God's children in glorious freedom from death and decay." Imagine being in heaven watching all of nature praising God right there beside you. What a glorious sight that will be. Is. 55:12 describes how God graciously gives you what you don't deserve. Vs. 13 then tells how God in His mercy holds back what the sinner does deserve.

Is. 55:13 says, "Instead of the thorn shall come up the cypress tree, and instead of the brier shall come up the myrtle tree; And it shall be to the

Lord for a name, for an everlasting sign that shall not be cut off." The ground was cursed when Adam sinned in the garden. He was forced to toil in the midst of thorns and briers. But when God works, death is transformed into life, judgment is transformed into salvation, curses are transformed into faithfulness. Why does God do this? Why does God think the way He thinks, speak the way He speaks, and work the way He works? He does these things to make a name for Himself so no one will take the credit for what He accomplishes. In other words, He gets all the glory, both now and forevermore. Ps. 115:1 (ESV) says, "Not to us, O Lord, not to us, but to Your name give glory, for the sake of Your steadfast love and Your faithfulness!" Oh yes, may the name of the Lord be glorified forever!

Paul reflects on God's grace and mercy when he writes in Rom. 8:1, "There is therefore now no condemnation to those who are in Christ Jesus." Is there any greater verse in all the Bible? Rom. 4:7,8 says, "Blessed are those whose lawless deeds are forgiven, and whose sins are covered; Blessed is the man to whom the Lord shall not impute sin." All are guilty before God but that is not the final verdict for those who are saved and in Christ Jesus. John 8 tells the story of a woman brought before Jesus who was caught in the act of adultery. The law said such a person should be stoned. The religious leaders wanted to know what Jesus had to say about it. He said, "He who is without sin among you, let him throw the first stone" (vs. 7). Being convicted by their conscience, the crowd walked away one by one. Jesus asked the woman, "Where are those accusers of yours? Has no one condemned you" (vs. 10). She said, "No one Lord." Jesus then said, "Neither do I condemn you; go and sin no more" (vs. 11).

The problem in the church today is too many believers act like those religious leaders. They're filled with accusation and condemnation when they're just as guilty as this woman caught in adultery. Rom. 3:23 indicts all of mankind when it says, "For all have sinned and fall short of the glory of God." Yes, all have sinned but faith in the shed blood of Jesus saves you from the guilt and penalty of sin. If you are in Christ Jesus, sin no longer holds any power over you. Rom. 5:18 (NLT) says, "Adam's one sin brings condemnation for everyone, but Christ's one act of righteousness brings a right relationship with God and new life for everyone." Paul is saying the sinner's judgment day is before him while the believer's judgment day is behind him. This is why there is now no condemnation to those who are in Christ Jesus. The word "now" speaks in real time, and the word "no" speaks for all time. Heaven is your hope, but you don't have to wait to get there to have assurance of salvation.

In the Greek language the word "no" speaks of a complete cessation. Never again will you be judged for past sins committed. This is an absolute dismissal of all charges against you. Jesus said in John 5:24, "Most assuredly, I say to you, he who hears My word and believes in Him who sent Me has everlasting life, and shall not come into judgment, but has passed from death into life." If God says there is no condemnation, then you should no longer condemn yourself or others. Rise up and respond to Satan's whispered accusations with bold confidence that through the finished work of Christ on the cross your case is closed. God has found you "not guilty" and because of that there is now no guilt and condemnation to those who are in Christ Jesus. The word "no" means "no"! Yes, there are many reasons for you to be condemned but, thankfully, Rom. 6:23 says, "For the wages of sin is death, but the gift of God is eternal life in Christ Jesus our Lord."

Jesus Christ is the righteous one and by saving faith you are in Him and He is in you. Rom. 8:2 (NLT) says, "And because you belong to Him, the power of the life-giving Spirit has freed you from the power of sin that leads to death." Vs. 1 says there is no divine condemnation in Christ Jesus, vs. 2 says there is spiritual liberation and freedom in Christ Jesus. The word "power" here is a power that controls. Paul is saying the controlling power of the Holy Spirit has set you free from the controlling power of sin and death. Sin corrupts and death consumes but the Holy Spirit is life-giving, life-changing, and life-filling. Rom. 7:24,25 (NLT) says, "Oh, what a miserable person I am! Who will free me from this life that is dominated by sin and death? Thank God! The answer is in Jesus Christ our Lord." This is the testimony of not only Paul but every believer who is in Christ. Jesus said in John 8:36, "Therefore if the Son makes you free, you shall be free indeed."

Like gravity, sin never ceases but it can be overcome. A jet engine can overcome the pull of gravity. In a deeper, higher way, the law of the Spirit of life in Christ Jesus has made you free from the law of sin and death. It was the divine intervention of God that made this happen. Rom. 8:3 (NLT) says, "The law of Moses was unable to save us because of the weakness of our sinful nature. So God did what the law could not do. He sent His own Son in a body like the bodies we sinners have. And in that body God declared an end to sin's control over us by giving His Son as a sacrifice for our sins." God intervened just like He did in Isaiah 55. He did what the law could not do. The law could not save you from guilt and condemnation nor could it set you free from the controlling power of sin. The law exposes sin (Rom. 7:7) but it cannot save you from sin. On the contrary, it stimulates you to sin even more (Rom. 7:8). It's the nature of sin to tempt you to do what you know you're not supposed to do.

Adam and Eve knew they weren't supposed to eat the fruit of the tree of the knowledge of good and evil. It should come as no surprise that this was precisely what the serpent tempted them to do. The problem is not the law; it's the weakness of the flesh to keep the law. Your sinful nature fuels your sinful ways. It's called "iniquity"! There is a spiritual perversion that makes you inclined to do wrong, a sinful virus inside you that programs you to do sinful things. Rom. 7:21-23 (NLT) says, "I have discovered this principle of life - that when I want to do what is right, I inevitably do what is wrong. I love God's law with all my heart. But there is another power within me that is at war with my mind. The power makes me a slave to the sin that is still within me."

This is a reality every person must face. No matter how good you may be, there is always something lacking. The rich young ruler kept all the commandments from his youth, yet Jesus told him, "You still lack one thing" (Luke 18:22).

Personal goodness cannot save you and neither can obeying the Ten Commandments. Thankfully, God intervened by sending His only begotten Son to live and die for you. He did in Christ what you could never do yourself. Eph. 2:1 says, "And you He made alive who were dead in trespasses and sins." Hallelujah! God did not save you so that you could continue in your old ways. He saved you so that He could give you new life. Rom. 8:4 (NLT) says, "He did this so that the just requirement of the law would be fully satisfied for us, who no longer follow our sinful nature but instead follow the Spirit." The goal of your salvation is not merely so you can go to heaven, it's that you may be holy as He is holy. The evidence of conversion is new life, to be those "who do not walk according to the flesh but according to the Spirit." Pastor H. B. Charles Jr. said, "It is the will of God to have the Spirit of God use the Word of God to make the children of God look like the Son of God." It can't be said any better than that.

| 14 |

"TROPHY OF HIS GRACE"

Take just one look at Jesus hanging on the cross and you'll never question the love God has for you. John 15:13 says, "Greater love has no one than this, than to lay down one's life for his friends." Jesus died the death you deserve. He experienced the punishment meant for you. This was God's intervention on your behalf. Oh yes, God's love is amazing indeed. It is a great love, infinite like all of His attributes. It is unconditional and sacrificial. It seeks the highest good in the one who is loved. It is bestowed irrespective of merit to those who are undeserving. It is a love that impels one to sacrifice one's self for the benefit of another. It is the love shown at Calvary. God's love and Christ's death made it possible for you to be saved. 1 John 4:9,10 (NLT) says, "God showed how much He loved us by sending His one and only Son into the world so that we might have eternal life through Him. This is real love - not that we loved God, but that He loved us and sent His Son as a sacrifice to take away our sins."

God's love is an active love. Not only does He tell you He loves you, He shows you He loves you. Yes, He intervened "even when we were dead in trespasses" (Eph. 2:5). There is a death before dying. Because of the sin of Adam, all people were born spiritually dead. Not only does this death mean separation, it also means inability. Dead people can't try harder, they can't do better, they can't change their way, they can't turn over a new leaf. In other words, dead people can't help themselves. This is why there is no place for boasting in your salvation experience. As always, God gets all the glory. Rom. 5:8 says, "But God demonstrates His own love toward us, in that while we were still sinners, Christ died for us." It was mercy that intervened on your behalf. Grace is God's solution to man's sin, mercy is His solution to man's misery. Grace covers the sin, mercy removes the pain. Grace forgives, mercy restores. Grace gives you what you don't deserve, mercy withholds what you do deserve.

C. S. Lewis was asked, "What makes Christianity so unique, so special, so different from all the other faiths out there in the world?" He said, "That's an easy question to answer. One word. Grace." The problem today is that people hear the word "grace" so often that they've lost touch with the full impact of its meaning. For some, grace is nothing more than a well known hymn they occasionally sing on Sunday morning. "Amazing grace, how sweet the sound." They sing about grace but, unfortunately, don't experience it in their lives. The truth be told, it's the grace of God that makes Christianity so great. If these people aren't careful, they can miss out on the grace of God. Heb. 12:15 (NLT) says, "Look after each other so that none of you fails to receive the grace of God. Watch out that no poisonous root of bitterness grows up to trouble you, corrupting many." The Message Bible says, "Keep a sharp eye out for weeds of bitter discontent. A thistle or two gone to seed can ruin a whole garden in no time."

God loved you even when you were spiritually dead. He didn't wait until you were lovable. He loved you even when you were dead in trespasses, providing nothing lovable to Him. Jer. 31:3 says, "I have loved you with an everlasting love. Therefore I have drawn you with lovingkindness." F. B. Meyer said, "He knew what we were, and what we should be, and how much pain and sorrow we should cost Him; but He loves us still." He also said, "He did not love us because we were fair, but to make us so. We cannot understand it, but since He began He will not fail nor be discouraged until He has finished His work." God looked down at the hopeless situation of sinful man and decided to do something about it. You were sleeping the sleep of spiritual death and God woke you up. He made you "alive together with Christ" (Eph. 2:5). The word "alive" means 'raised from the dead.' Dead people can't raise themselves. Someone from the outside must do it. That someone is God.

The Wuest translation of Eph. 2:4,5 says, "But God being wealthy in the sphere of mercy, on account of His great love with which He loved us, and we being dead with respect to our trespasses, hath quickened us together with Christ." Your eternal security is absolute because of your union with Christ. The two of you can't be separated. No one can separate you from Him or Him from you. Your life is intertwined with His. Jesus said in John 15:5, "I am the vine, you are the branches. He who abides in Me, and I in him, bears much fruit; for without Me you can do nothing." You are so united with Christ that His very own Spirit lives in you. This is what happened when you got born again. God made you alive together with Christ. The Father brought Jesus back to life and He did the same thing to you. He intervened and "by grave you have been saved" (vs. 5). The Phillips Bible says, "It is, remember, by grace, and not by achievement that you are saved."

The high price of redemption was paid for by "the grace of our Lord Jesus Christ" (2 Cor. 8:9). Grace is necessary because with forgiveness comes a price that has to be paid. You may forgive someone for denting your car, but a price still has to be paid to fix the damage that's been done. Free grace is never cheap. Although grace is freely given, realize that it cost God everything. It cost Him the life of His only begotten Son. Jesus suffered and died a cruel death so God could express His grace to you in full manifestation. Jesus came and took your place on the cross, receiving upon Himself the penalty of your sin. "For He made Him who knew no sin to be sin for us, that we might become the righteousness of God in Him" (2 Cor. 5:21). John Stott said, "For the essence of sin is man substituting himself for God, while the essence of salvation is God substituting Himself for man." That's what grace is. It's what separates Christianity from all other religions in the world.

On the cross, Jesus put Himself in the place where you were supposed to be. Your sins separated Jesus from the Father as He cried out, "My God, My God, why have You forsaken Me?" (Matt. 27:46). You are saved by grace for Jesus paid the price you could never pay. The word "saved" means 'to rescue one from great peril, to protect, keep alive, preserve life, deliver, heal, be made whole.' Kenneth Wuest said, "By grace you have been saved in past time completely, with the result that you are in a state of salvation which persists through present time." In other words, God's grace saved you in a moment in time and God's grace keeps you saved eternally. By grace you were saved, by grace you are saved, by grace you forever will be saved. The high cost of this grace should help you realize the wickedness of sin and the undeserving state of mankind. Grace was immeasurably costly but is unconditionally freely given to all men. How amazing God's grace is.

What else did God's amazing grace do for you? It "raised us up together, and made us sit together in the heavenly places in Christ Jesus" (Eph. 2:6). This is a spiritual resurrection. Now and forevermore you will be identified with Christ. A Christian is not a person who believes in the resurrection of Christ, they're people who participate in it. When He died, you died. When He was raised up and made alive, you were raised up and made alive with Him. It is so important for you to see yourself as being joined to a living Savior. John Brown said, "Christ rose again but our sins did not; they are buried forever in His grave." This doesn't mean you're immune from temptation or attack. It means you won't be a victim to the devil's evil schemes. You'll overcome him by the blood of the Lamb and the word of your testimony (Rev. 12:11). Don't be like Oscar Wilde who said, "The only way I know of to get rid of temptation is to give in to it." No, resist temptation. When you're tempted, walk away from it. Better yet, run away.

You are a Christian so live up to that name. Stop saying you're fine "under the circumstances." You're seated with Jesus above your circumstances. You have a new place for living, a new arena of existence. You are not of those who dwell on the earth for your citizenship is in heaven (Phil. 3:20). When you got saved, you received eternal life. You are positionally sitting on a seat in heaven looking down on yourself. No matter where you are right now physically, you are spiritually seated in heavenly places in Christ Jesus. The eternal world is more real than the temporal, physical world so start acting like it. In the heavenly places is where your blessings are (Eph. 1:3). It's where godly direction comes from and where all your praise and petitions go. You don't have to live in spiritual defeat. You can grow and have strength you never knew it was possible for you to have. You've been raised up with Christ so rise up and use the power and authority that's been given to you.

Christians are a heavenly people. You live on earth but your citizenship is in heaven. This is why Paul wrote in Col. 3:1,2, "If then you were raised with Christ, seek those things which are above, where Christ is, sitting at the right hand of God. Set your mind on things above, not on things on the earth." How you walk the walk determines where you'll sit. You must continually keep your affections and attention fixed on those things that pertain to your walk with God. You do this through reading the Bible and prayer, as well as through worship and your service unto Him. 1 Tim. 2:8 says, "Therefore I desire that the men pray everywhere, lifting up holy hands, without wrath and doubting." There are some things God will only do if you pray, things He won't do if you don't pray. Prayer moves the hand of God. This is why you need to pray as if it matters. What good is a person who doesn't pray, a person who doesn't know how to talk to God? For sure, a day without prayer is a wasted day.

You can enjoy heaven on earth if you'll keep your heart and mind in heavenly places. Charles Spurgeon once said, "Little faith will bring your soul to heaven; great faith will bring heaven to your soul." Heavenly places encompass the entire supernatural realm of God, His complete domain, and the full extent of His divine operation. Col. 3:3 says, "For you died, and your life is hidden with Christ in God." When you got saved, when you died to your old way of living, God took your heart and soul and put them in heaven with Christ. Paul is saying you are now in heavenly places positionally and eventually will be there with God literally. This world is now a foreign land to you. No longer does it lay claim to your affections and desires. You realize that what this world offers can never satisfy the deepest longings of your heart. This planet is not your home. Heaven is your home and you need to be eagerly watching for Christ's return. Get excited for it could happen any day now.

C. S. Lewis wrote, "A continual looking forward to the eternal world is not (as some modern people think) a form of escapism or wishful thinking, but one of the things a Christian is meant to do. If you read history you will find that the Christians who did the most for the present world were just those who thought most of the next. It is since Christians have largely ceased to think of the other world that they have become so ineffective in this world." God saved you for a purpose that will not be fulfilled until the coming ages. Eph. 2:7 says "that in the ages to come He might show the exceeding riches of His grace in His kindness toward us in Christ Jesus." This is why Jesus can't wait for you to join Him in glory. In heaven, God will shower His unfailing love and kindness upon you forevermore. He'll never stop pouring His grace out on you and will forever continue to unfold its riches to you throughout all eternity. This is why He's really, really looking forward to you coming to heaven.

Think about it. There are exceeding riches of kindness and glory waiting for you. The Message Bible says, "Now God has us right where He wants us, with all the time in this world and the next to shower grace and kindness upon us in Christ Jesus." Christianity is not only about health, wealth, and success in life. It's not about your best life now, it's about true life forever. You are a part of God's eternal publicity program. He's going to put you on display as a trophy of His grace in the ages to come, in "the ages that are coming one upon another." The NLT says, "And so God can always point to us as examples of the incredible wealth of His favor and kindness toward us, as shown in all He has done for us through Christ Jesus." As recipients of His gracious generosity and overwhelming kindness, you'll be on display forever and ever as you bask in the presence of God, enjoying the riches of all His blessings. F. B. Meyer said, "We are the monuments of God's wealth."

Theologian William MacDonald said, "The miracle of transforming grace will be the subject of eternal revelation." The surpassing riches of God's grace are beyond expression, beyond comprehension. The word "surpassing" means 'that which exceeds extraordinary' and the word "exceeding" means 'beyond throwing distance.' God's riches are immeasurable, beyond what you can think or imagine. All the combined wealth of this evil world pales in comparison to the inexhaustible wealth of your Heavenly Father. His kindness is an expression of His abundant grace toward man. It's love in action that you first experienced when you got saved and will continue to experience throughout all eternity. Never will you stop receiving the love, grace, and kindness of God. Bible scholar Harold Hoehner said God will demonstrate the wealth of His amazing grace "in the sphere of that which is His goodness or kindness appropriate to God. It describes the entire work of salvation."

God's generous favor, His abundant grace, will be on display in your life throughout eternity. The KJV Bible Commentary says, "God delights to show great grace throughout the endless ages of eternity. Saints will be concrete demonstrations of the overflowing wealth of His grace." The grace of God is His goodness toward those who don't deserve it, barely recognize it, and hardly appreciate it. All of life is a gift from a gracious God. It produces in you a life of total gratitude as you are overwhelmed by all the love and mercy God has shown you. People are shocked by what the grace of God offers them, as well they should be. Kenneth Wuest said, "Salvation is given to the believing sinner out of the pure generosity of God's heart. The Greek word referred to an action that was beyond the ordinary course of what might be expected, and was therefore commendable. What a description of that which took place at the cross!"

Eph. 2:8,9 says, "For by grace you have been saved through faith, and that not of yourselves; it is the gift of God, not of works, lest anyone should boast." Twice in this chapter Paul says it is by grace that you've been saved. He had to repeat himself for he knew in the hearts of most people was the desire to take some sort of credit for their salvation, namely because of some good works they had performed. For example, some people preach you can't be saved unless you've been baptized in water. Yes, you should obey the command to be water baptized but this is not what saves you. Water baptism is a work you do after you've been born again. It is a symbolic acknowledgement that you died to your old life of sin and have been raised up to a new life in Christ Jesus. All boasting ceases when you realize grace is a gift from God. You're saved by the grace of God through the work Jesus did. Grace starts with God, continues with God, and ends with God.

Grace is God's part, faith is your part. It is "by means of faith you have been saved." Faith is a response to the work God has done in your life. It's the channel through which salvation flows. One is not automatically saved because Jesus died on the cross, one is saved when they put their trust in God's gracious provision. Augustine said, "He who created you without you will not save you without you." In other words, you must do your part. You don't work for your salvation, you receive it by faith. Faith is synonymous with trust, confidence, and belief. It's the conviction of the truth of something. Faith represents a strong conviction that Jesus is the Messiah through whom eternal salvation is obtained and entrance is made into the kingdom of heaven. What's more, the faith you believe with is also "the gift of God." Martin Luther said, "God creates faith in the human heart the same way that He created the world. He found nothing and created something."

Grace is the source, faith is the means, and salvation is the result. William Barclay said, "Many a man knows very well that something is true, but does not change his actions to meet that knowledge. In full-fledged faith, a man hears the Christian message, agrees that it is true, and then casts himself upon it in a life of total yieldedness." Faith brings with it a supernatural longing to obey God in spite of the consequences that follow. It causes you to willfully surrender your will to the will of God, to walk the walk, to follow the path God created you to walk on. You don't work to get saved, you work because you are saved. Professor J. Carl Laney said, "Belief is not a matter of passive opinion, but decisive and obedient action." 2 Tim. 5:21 says you are to be "useful for the Master, prepared for every good work." Also, Titus 3:8 (NLT) says, "All who trust in God will devote themselves to doing good." A. W. Tozer said, "True faith commits us to obedience."

The same grace that saved you is the same grace that motivates you to respond to what God has done in your life. It makes you want to do good works for Him. God planned and designed good works which you are to do for His glory. It's God's work fulfilled through the good things you do. Since it is God's work, never are you to boast in the things God would have you do. The word "boast" means 'to take pride in something; to glory in what one has done; to brag.' Charles Spurgeon said, "We are a boasting people. Man is a poor mass of flesh, and he is largely given to the corruption of pride. He will boast if he can." Grace is a gift and your works is a response to what God has already done for you. Jer. 9:23,24 says, "Let not the wise boast of their wisdom or the strong boast of their strength or the rich boast of their riches; but let the one who boasts boast about this: that they have the

understanding to know Me, that I am the Lord, who exercises kindness, justice and righteousness on earth, for in these I delight."

There is only one thing you are allowed to boast about. Gal. 6:14
(TLB) says, "As for me, God forbid that I should boast about anything
except the cross of our Lord Jesus Christ. Because of that cross, my interest in all the attractive things of this world was killed long ago, and
the world's interest in me is also long dead." Boasting is only appropriate when the purpose is to acknowledge the greatness and glory of
God. Your motive in doing what you do is not to increase your own
reputation but that God might be glorified. Boasting about the good
deeds you do takes away the awareness and recognition of what Christ
did on the cross. David Guzik said, "Paul's heart cared nothing for the
glory that came from fame. He cared nothing for the glory that come
from riches. He cared nothing for the glory that came from status and
power among men. He only cared about the glory of the cross of our
Lord Jesus Christ."

Charles Spurgeon said, "With that 'God forbid,' ("May it never be")
Paul makes a clean sweep of every other ground of boasting, and cast
himself upon the one chosen object of his soul's glorying. And yet, if
you will think of it, Paul had, after the fashion of other men, many
things in which he might have gloried." Many boast in their talents,
their knowledge, their wealth, and their accomplishments. The list
goes on. However, fallen man has no grounds for boasting in the presence of God (1 Cor. 1:29). James 4:16 says, "But now you boast in your
arrogance. All such boasting is evil." Charles Spurgeon then said, "It
is very sad that men should be ruined by their glory; and yet many
are so. To live for personal glory is to be dead while we live." What
really matters is not the external works you do, but whether you've
been changed into a new and different person (2 Cor. 5:17). If your
life isn't different now that you are in Christ, you might want to ponder whether you truly are in Christ.

| 15 |

"A WORK IN PROGRESS"

As Paul writes this second chapter to the saints at Ephesus, he is sharing some of the strongest, most direct, and most powerful verses in the entire Bible. In fact, the entire theology of Christianity hinges upon these pivotal verses. In Vs. 1-7, Paul took you from the lowest of the low to the highest of the high. One moment you were dead in trespasses and sins, the next moment you were seated in heavenly places in Christ Jesus. How amazing is that? What's even more amazing is what Paul said in Rom. 5:8, "But God demonstrates His own love toward us, in that while we were still sinners, Christ died for us." There's those two words again. "But God!" All people are born sinners but God loved man even when He knew they would kill His Son and hang Him on a cross to die. He loved them before they were lovable, while they were still self-centered sinners, mocking Him by the way they lived their lives, when they "were of no use whatever to Him" (MSG).

God rescued you from eternal judgment so you could be the evidence that He is a God of mercy and great love. How were you saved? By grace through faith, not of works lest anyone should boast (vs. 8,9). You need to get off that religious treadmill where you think working for God gets you closer to Him. You don't have to perform for Him like some circus monkey. He's done all the work so now all you have to do is love Him with all your heart and soul. It's all based on grace and not on anything you have done. Cultural Christianity, also known as folklore religion, has a hard time believing this. They think doing good deeds is enough to get them into heaven. They think they're worthy of heaven if they're not as bad as their next door neighbor. To them, getting to the "sweet by-and-by" is all a work-based effort. They say, "This is what I did for God and this is what I deserve from God." This is blasphemy and this verse proves it. The truth be told, hell is full of the nicest people you'll ever meet.

It's a lie of the devil to think doing your best is good enough to win you a free ticket to heaven. Thinking this way is a perversion of God's amazing grace. Another deception of folklore religion is when people think they're okay with God because they go to a certain church. Even crime bosses go to church. They go to church on Sunday and order somebody to be killed on Monday. Are these people saved? Hardly. The sad truth is, nobody in hell will be surprised they are there. They will know they rejected the free gift of salvation. You don't deserve it and you can't earn it. It is the ultimate gift of God. Rom. 11:6 (NLT) says, "And since it is through God's kindness, then it is not by their good works. For in that case, God's grace would not be what it really is - free and undeserved." How are you saved? Wholly and completely by God's grace and only by God's grace. It is the gift of God. The acronym for G-R-A-C-E is "God's Riches At Christ's Expense." No wonder His grace is so amazing.

God gave you eternal life and you should be looking forward to spending all eternity with Him. In the meantime, while you're anxiously waiting for His glorious return, there are things for you to do here. God gave you His amazing grace so you could do an amazing work. Paul wrote in Eph. 2:10, "For we are His workmanship, created in Christ Jesus for good works, which God prepared beforehand that we should walk in them." You are God's workmanship in that He created you according to His own good pleasure and purpose. In the beginning, when God created the heavens and the earth, He spoke everything into existence. For six days God said, "Let there be..." and it became a reality. However, on the sixth day, He did something different. He reached down into the mud and formed a man with His own two hands. He then breathed into man's nostrils the breath of life and man became a living soul (Gen. 2:7). That breath brought life to God's workmanship.

The Greek word for "workmanship" is "poiema" and is where the word "poem" comes from. It is a word used to describe an exquisite masterpiece in which someone expresses himself in a literary form. James Hastings says it's "the expression of truth and beauty in rhythmical form." It's what an artist uses to express his or her mind. It's something they want you to see, a concept they are perceiving in their heart that they want others to understand. Paul is saying you were dead in your sins but God made you alive in Christ Jesus. He didn't stop there for now He is working a process where you are His work of art, His poem, His masterpiece. You are a work in progress. God is trying to reveal His heart and mind to the rest of humanity through the work He's doing in your life. You are His trophy of grace, His inheritance, His evidence to the world that He is love. You're wholly the result of God's creative, redemptive, and sanctifying work, and you belong to Him.

John Phillips said, "Each of our lives is the canvas on which the Master is producing a work of art that will fill the everlasting ages with His praise." If you are saved, you are God's poetic masterpiece. Pastor Rick Renner said, "Paul is saying that on the day you got saved, God put forth His most powerful and creative effort to make you new. Once God was finished making you new, you became a masterpiece, skillfully and artfully created in Christ Jesus. There's nothing cheap about you at all! God's creative, artistic, intelligent genius went into your making." In other words, God turned you into something spectacular! It matters not what people think about you, what they say about you, or what they do to you. In the eyes of God, you are a divine masterpiece. Rick Renner also said, "God took us into His hands and marvelously made us new in Jesus Christ as He released His most powerful creative forces and made us a workmanship that would be worthy to bear His name."

The word "workmanship" refers to more than just the product of creation. It also refers to the degree of skill with which the product is made. That degree of skill imparts value to the thing made. Its value is derived from the talents of the one who designed and produced it. This term puts the emphasis on the Creator rather than the creation. This is why no one can boast in the presence of God. You are His workmanship which means all praise and glory and honor belongs exclusively to Him. The Greek word 'poiema" is found in only one other place in the Bible. Rom. 1:20 says, "Through everything God made, they can clearly see His invisible qualities - His eternal power and divine nature." Ps. 19:1 says, "The heavens declare the glory of God, and the sky above proclaims His handiwork." Rom. 1:20 says the greatness of God is evident in creation, Eph. 2:10 says the greatness of God is also evident in salvation. The two go together.

People who don't believe in God only have to look up and they'll see proof that He exists. The good news is the sun, the moon, and the stars are not God's masterpiece. You are! God made you unique so never compare yourself to someone else. Blessings come when you wake up to the fact that there's a manifold grace of God in your life that is different than anybody else. Instead of trying to be like others, sparkle the way God made you to sparkle. It's okay if you're not like other people. God made you different so accept the way God made you. There is a divine calling on your life to be you, to be the person God made you to be. After all, you are fearfully and wonderfully made (Ps. 139:14). The Message Bible says you were "sculpted from nothing into something." God took you when you were dead in trespasses and sins and made you alive in Christ. When you celebrate who you are, you'll be able to appreciate people for who they are, no matter how different from you they may be.

Pastor Jon Courson said, "He is making you something not only useful but beautiful, something that is poetic." You are the workmanship of God. You are His own special creation, created in His own special image (Gen. 1:7). You need to think of yourself that way, in the content that God shaped you and molded you into the person He wants you to be. All your problems in life come as a result of your failure to realize this great truth about yourself and your position as a child of God. It's why many people struggle with low self-esteem and feelings of inadequacy and insufficiency. What people grew up thinking about themselves falls way short of what God thinks about them. He thinks they're worth dying for and He is writing a story of His grace through their lives. Throughout the New Testament, Christians are constantly being exhorted to rejoice and consider their wonderful destiny. They're told who they are and what they are, being told to lift their head up high and go forward in a triumphant manner.

The first thing you must realize about yourself is that you are His handiwork, a person of His making. In the Bible, great emphasis is given to the fact that Christianity is entirely the result of the activity of God. He is the master workman and the Bible records some of the miraculous things He has done. The very first verse says, "In the beginning God created the heavens and the earth" (Gen. 1:1). From beginning to end, the scriptures tell of the activity of God. It is astounding that people fall into the error of thinking their works have anything to do with salvation, especially when Is. 64:6 says, "But we are all like an unclean thing, and all our righteousness are like filthy rags; We all fade as a leaf, and our iniquities, like the wind, have taken us away." The Message Bible says, "We're all sin-infected, sin-contaminated. Our best efforts are grease-stained rags." They wrongly think it's God's responsibility to respond to what they have done and not the other way around.

The phrase "for we are His workmanship" literally means "for of Him we are a product." The world says you are a product of your environment or a product of your experiences. A lot of believers think that way also. However, the Bible declares that the person who is saved is a product of God. You are the fruit and product of His creative hand. Paul says you were "created in Christ Jesus for good works." To create means to make something out of nothing. When you got saved, you became a new person. 2 Cor. 5:17 (MSG) says, "Anyone united with the Messiah gets a fresh start, is created new. The old life is gone; a new life burgeons!" In other words, God brought into your life something that wasn't there before. That's what it means to be a Christian. 2 Cor. 4:6 (MSG) says, "It started when God said, 'Light up the darkness!' and our lives filled up with light as we saw and understood God in the face of Christ, all bright and beautiful." There is nothing more wonderful than that.

You are not a repaired sinner, you are a new creation in Christ. If you're still what you've always been, you are not saved. At salvation, you received the benefits of Christ's life and the benefits of His death. Not only that, His very life becomes your own. When God looks at you, He doesn't see your past sins and rebellion, He sees His masterpiece. He created you on purpose and with great power. He saw what you would become before He laid the foundation of the earth. Before this universe was made, you were on His mind. David wrote in Ps. 8:4,5, "What is man that You are mindful of him? You have crowned him with glory and honor." You are no accident, a product of cosmic probability. No, you were created on purpose in Christ Jesus. Things of chance happen on their own, things created happen intentionally. Someone with a creative mind dreams of something and then brings it into existence. God is the Creator and you are His creation, His work of art, His masterpiece.

You are no accident but the handiwork of God. He is tired of Christians being preoccupied with how unworthy they are. God made them

His work of art, His poem, and they have the audacity to tell Him they're unworthy. What they're telling Him is they think they have no worth. If they're worthless, then Jesus died in vain. The truth is, you and every other Christian are the most valuable thing God ever created. You are worth the death, burial, and resurrection of the Lord Jesus Christ. Don't say you're worthless, say you're a child of the living God. What you say is what you believe and what you believe is what you will become. Who are you? 1 Peter 2:9 says, "But you are a chosen generation, a royal priesthood, a holy nation, His own special people, that you may proclaim the praises of Him who called you out of darkness into His marvelous light." If you believe that, then you must also believe that God has a purpose for your life, something prepared in advance for you to do.

Every redeemed soul has been sent into the world with a work to do. Pastor Steve Kieloff said, "Works are to salvation what thunder is to lightning, an inevitable result. Just as thunder does not generate lightning, our good deeds will not generate salvation. But on the other hand, just as you can't have lightning without the following thunderclap, you can't experience the transformation of salvation without a change in your attitude and behavior." At Paul's conversion, he asked God two questions. He asked, "Who are You, Lord?" (Acts 9:5). The answer is He's Jesus Christ, the Lord of all who gives new life. The second question was, "Lord, what do You want me to do?" (Acts 9:6). No matter what occupation you have, your real calling is to serve God and reach people. You're here to help make the lives of other people better, to carry the fragrance of Christ wherever you go. God wants you to make your life a masterpiece but you've only got one canvas to work with. Use it wisely.

Good works must flow from your union with Christ by virtue of your faith in Him. A man is not justified by works, but a justified man works. John Calvin said, "It is faith alone that justifies, but faith that justifies can never be alone." Good works are the aim of your salvation and the evidence of your faith. Works never produce salvation but salvation always produce good works. D. L. Moody said, "Every Bible should be bound in shoe leather." God created a path on which you are to walk so that your life would have meaning and significance and purpose. He designed your life so that certain people would cross your path and special doors of opportunity would be opened for you. Gifts and skills and talents will be made available to you. You'll use those things to be a blessing to somebody else. He'll even use your trials and hardships as a testimony to show other people what He can do if they'll only trust in Him.

The proof that you are seated in heavenly places is found in how you walk on earth. Where you're seated governs how you walk. If you're saved, act like it and walk the walk. Time is short and you've got no time to waste in sinful activities and worldly pleasures and empty pursuits and foolish friends. Sin can be fun but the pleasures of sin don't last. Loose living may stimulate you for a while but soon reality sets in. Time is quickly drawing to a close and Ps. 90:12 says, "So teach us to number our days, that we may gain a heart of wisdom." You don't have to live in worry, doubt, and fear. God has planned in advance good works for your life to accomplish. He has designed your life so that you'll have enough time to fulfill everything He wants you to do. Don't worry about dying early. Your life is not in the hands of some drunk driver. Your life is not in the hands of man, your life is in the hands of God. The truth is, you are immortal until you finish what God called you to do.

God put you on this earth to do something so make your life count. Understand that it's what you do that determines the success of your life. You are here to serve God and honor Him. Know also that what God wants you to do was prepared in advance before the foundation of the world. This is how you know your birth was no accident. Before you were conceived, God had a plan and a purpose for your life (Jer. 1:4,5). Scottish pastor William Arnot said, "The simple fact that a Christian is on earth and not in heaven is proof that there is something here for him to do; and if he is not doing it, the neglect shows either that he is not yet a Christian or that he is a Christian who grieves Christ." God's work isn't finished when you receive Christ. On the contrary, it has only just begun. Don't let divine opportunities pass you by. Invest your time and talents wisely. Anybody can talk the talk but it can't stop there. Your talk must be backed up with your walk. Good works must back up good words.

Real fulfillment is to be an instrument through which God works in the world. Allow Him to take charge of your life and walk the walk of a good works believer. Jesus said in Matt.5:16, "Let your light shine before men in such a way that they may see your good works and glorify your Father who is in heaven." Believers are to be known for their consistent and aggressive goodness done out of an unselfish love for God and other people. You don't exist for yourself. You were made to do good works. Just like a potter makes a clay pot to hold water, you are God's workmanship made for the purpose of serving Him by serving people. 1 Cor. 15:58 says, "Always give yourselves fully to the work of the Lord, because you know that your labor in the Lord is not in vain." The NLT says, "Always work enthusiastically for the Lord, for you know nothing you do for the Lord is ever useless." Do what God tells you to do and your influence with reach farther than you ever thought possible.

In your heart should be a fervent, burning desire to be used by God. Titus 2:14 says, "He gave His life to free us from every kind of sin, to cleanse us, and to make us His very own people, totally committed to doing good deeds." Other translations say you need to be "zealous for good works" (NKJV) and "energetic in goodness" (MSG). The word "zealous" means 'totally committed; sold out; dedicated; burning; ablaze; fanatical; fervent; passionate; enthusiastically devoted." Does this describe you? It should. Does God see you as one who is on fire to do good works? The devil needs to shake and tremble every morning when you wake up. Charles Spurgeon said, "We are not only to approve of good works, and speak for good works, but we are to be red-hot for them. We need to be on fire for everything that is right and true. Oh that my Lord's grace would set us on fire in this way! There is plenty of fuel in the church, what is wanted is fire."

Titus 3:1 encourages all born again believers "to be ready for every good work." Readiness implies watchfulness, to be on the tiptoes of expectancy. Live your life in such a way that you'll be able to respond to another person's need without delay or hesitation. God never opens a door that you're not ready to enter. It's doing good deeds on a continual basis that makes you ready to walk through those doors. Titus 3:14 says, "And let our people also learn to maintain good works, to meet urgent needs, that they may not be unfruitful." You don't do just one thing to fulfill your calling. It's an every day walking out the good works that's going to lead you and guide you, to open doors to places of influence, to supernatural opportunities. Acts 9:36 speaks of a disciple named Dorcas. "This woman was full of good works and charitable deeds which she did." She was thoughtful and careful to maintain and continue doing good works. She is an example for all believers to follow.

Rom. 12:21 says, "Do not be overcome by evil, but overcome evil with good." Don't let evil defeat you. Do good works and defeat evil. Do things that are pleasant and pleasing to God. When you do a good work for God, He'll do a good work in you. In other words, good works are working in you. They're building your character. They're making you the person God wants you to be. The good works working in you will help you fulfill your destiny, to walk in your assignment every single day. One of the best things God could ever give you is a strong, fortified life that is living for Him daily and wholeheartedly. Charles Spurgeon said, "Nothing is a good work unless it is done with a good motive." The good works working in you will make you more obedient which in turn triggers the blessings of God. Having a lifestyle of doing good works sets you up for greater things. It's what gives you life and life more abundantly (John 10:10).

| 16 |

"THE CALL TO REMEMBER"

Paul begins his letter to the saints at Ephesus by describing the spiritual blessings God gives to the born-again believer. He reminded them how God has expressed His mercy in saving them on the basis of faith, not perfectionism or performance. He also wanted these saints to grasp and appreciate the eternal glory that awaits them in heaven with Christ. At the start of chapter two, he discussed the sinful past of those who are now members of the family of God. He told how, because of their slavery to their own desires, they were subject to God's condemnation. He goes on to say that because of God's grace and mercy, He sent Jesus to die for their sins and offered salvation to them on the basis of faith. Vs. 1-10 are personal as he tells what it means to be a Christian, vs. 11-22 are interpersonal as he describes what it means to be the church. These two ideas go together for the church is made up of individual believers. If you don't want to go to church, you don't mean what it means to be in Christ.

The church is one of the greatest blessings God has given His people. The problem in today's world is that, for the most part, people live individual lives and are disconnected from those around them. This, in turn, gives them a false sense of independence. They're around others but don't really need them, or so they think. It should come as no surprise that surveys reveal church attendance is rapidly declining from what it was in times past. People are hungry for spiritual experiences but don't want the required commitment that goes with it. In other words, they don't want to get involved. What these people don't understand is that God has chosen to reveal His power primarily through the church. Yes, God works in individual lives but even more so in a body of believers who come together collectively in His name. This is why God wants you to embrace Him and His church. If you want to experience all that God has to offer, you need to be a committed member of a local church.

Many believers have been saved for years and still are not part of a holy family. They need to realize that not only is the church essential to the Christian, the Christian is essential to the church. In order for the church to be what God designed it to be, it needs redeemed, growing, and fruitful Christians. The church is like a huge completed puzzle with each believer being an individual piece. All Christians are individual believers but put together they make up the church of Jesus Christ. The church is the hope of the world. The changes that need to be made on this planet won't come through the government, businesses, or schools. No, real changes come through the church. Why? Because that's where the power is. Unfortunately, this power is disrupted when disunity runs rampant in the church. Division comes among believers because of theological differences and personal preferences. It is a sad but true statement that many in the body of Christ have a hard time getting along with other believers.

The world knows all about discord and disunity. Look around you and you'll see it everywhere. Strife and arguing, quarreling and bitterness, separation and divorce. You see it in homes, in schools, in businesses, in the government, and between nations. It seems as if nobody knows how to get along with those around them. Everywhere you look is conflict, enmity, and division. There was strife in the church at Corinth and Paul said in 1 Cor. 1:10 (NLT), "I appeal to you, dear brothers and sisters, by the authority of our Lord Jesus Christ, to live in harmony with each other. Let there be no divisions in the church.

Rather, be of one mind, united in thought and purpose." He said in 1 Cor. 3:1-4, "You must be carnal because there is division and strife and envy among you." Christians are to be different from the rest of the world. They're supposed to walk a different walk. To win the battle for unity, there had to be a clear statement of what the standard of unity was. This is why Ephesians, in part, was written.

There was a major problem in the early church that Paul addresses here. The major fault-line of division in the church was between the Jews and those Gentile converts who had come out of various pagan religions. At that time, the Jews had a deep-seated resentment toward the Gentiles. The Jews hated them and had no problem or hesitation revealing to them how they felt. It was the worse form of racism that has ever darkened this planet. The first few years of the church age was exclusively made up of Jews. There were no Gentiles in the church until God commissioned Paul to take the gospel message to the non-Jews. The Jews were utterly shocked that this was happening. To them, Gentiles were dogs and "fuel for the fire of the flames of hell." So deep was their prejudice that if they so much as brushed up against a Gentile in passing they would have to be ceremonial cleansed. If you were a Jew, you were considered unclean and defiled by contact and were in need of ritualistic cleansing.

An example of this prejudice is seen in Acts 22. Paul was teaching in the Jewish temple in Jerusalem when suddenly he told them a word he heard from the Lord, "Then He said to me, 'Depart, for I will send you far from here to the Gentiles'" (vs. 21). How did the Jews respond to this? "And they listened to him until this word, and then they raised their voices and said, 'Away with such a fellow from the earth, for he is not fit to live!'" (vs. 22). Disunity is a heartache to God. It was a problem then and it's a problem today. Churches against churches, Christians against Christians. It is the nature of people to build barriers that prevent them from living in peace and harmony with others, especially those who are different than they are. These walls keep people out and enclose certain people in. It is no wonder that Jesus prayed to the Father in John 17:21, asking "that they all may be one, as You, Father, are in Me, and I in You; that they also may be one in Us."

There is no question that originally the Jews were selected to be God's chosen people. He said in Amos 3:2, "Israel only have I known among all the peoples of the earth." God chose the Jewish people unconditionally because it was through the bloodline of Abraham that the Messiah would be born into the world. His intention was that Israel would be a channel through which He could bring blessing to all of mankind. He told Abraham, "In your seed all the nations of the earth shall be blessed, because you have obeyed My voice" (Gen. 22:18). They were to be a missionary people to whom He would reveal His power so the rest of the world would know He was the great and mighty God. Is.43:21 says, "This people I have formed for Myself; They shall declare My praise." Israel was to be a mirror that reflected the glory of God, a channel through which that glory would flow. They were to be the means to an end, the people through whom God reached the world. At first the Jews fulfilled this calling very well.

Deut. 7:6 says, "For you are a holy people to the Lord your God; the Lord your God has chosen you to be a people for Himself, a special treasure above all the peoples on the face of the earth." God wanted the Jewish people to be unique and different so He gave them several laws to follow so they wouldn't fit in with the rest of the world. They were to walk in love, wisdom, and in the power of God. Their whole manner of life was to be different and this would make the world take notice of them. The special privileges God gave the Jews was meant to be a tool to reach the rest of the world. Instead of that happening, it became an excuse for self-glorification and pride. In time, the Jewish people became prejudice and thought themselves to be superior to all other people. They thought they were the only ones who could receive the promises and blessings of God. So overcome with this elitist mentality that they missed the Savior when He did come into the world. They even cried out for Him to be crucified.

What was given as a channel of blessing turned into a point of pride. Instead of having compassion on the Gentiles, the Jews had contempt for them. This is why Jonah ran away when God told him to go preach to the Gentile city of Ninevah. Afterward, when the people of Ninevah repented of their sin, Jonah sat down and said, "God, I can't stand Gentiles getting converted. Kill me." That's how isolated, proud, and carnal the Jews had become. They thought they were the only ones who could be called the people of God. They had twisted the original intention of God and soon had no message to preach anymore. They had a form of godliness but lacked the power thereof. They despised the Gentiles and the Gentiles despised them. There was terrible, antagonistic bitterness and animosity between them, a deep-seated wall of hate so thick that nothing could shatter it. The gulf between them got wider and wider and when Jesus came along it seemed as if no bridge of hope and love could connect the two.

God always had the salvation of the Gentiles in His heart. He said in Is. 57:19, "Peace, peace to him who is far off, and to him that is near." The Jews were called the ones who were near because they lived in close proximity to the temple that was built in Jerusalem. The Gentiles lived beyond the borders of Israel so they were known as the ones who were far off. Deut. 10:17 says God "shows no partiality" and the fact that God is no respecter of persons is an established reality. The Jews should have known this but they rejected their mission to reach out to those that were far off. Jews and Gentiles were equal in God's eyes but they were not equal in the eyes of each other and that had to change. Eph. 2:11-22 discusses the definition of the unity of the church that is at the heart of the will of God. Paul talks about a unity between Jew and Gentile that has no fences, walls, or barriers. But first, before this explanation is given, there is something very important Paul wants the Gentile saints at Ephesus to do.

He said, "Don't forget that you Gentiles used to be outsiders. You were called 'uncircumcised heathens' by the Jews, who were proud of their circumcision, even though it affected only their bodies and not their hearts" (Eph. 2:11 NLT). God wants all believers to remember where they came from, what their lives were like before they got saved. When was the last time you remembered your former state of utter depravity and desperation outside of Christ? To remember means "to call to mind." There are some things you must forever keep in your mind. This is not a suggestion. The call to remember is a divine command. God orders you to remember certain things. There is nothing God desires more from you than obedience for it is the most valuable currency you have to offer in the kingdom of God. Obedience is how you navigate through the maze of whatever this world throws at you. It's what activates the power of God in your life. So, if God says to remember, then obey Him and remember.

The Pulpit Commentary says, "The present is built upon the past, and the memory of the past has much to do with the joys and sorrows of the present, as well as with the hopes and achievements of the future. It is well for believers to remember what they have been in view of their present mercies. Remembrance may thus become a means of grace." Nothing will inspire gratitude more than a look back to the pit from which you came. Eph. 5:8 says, "For you were once darkness, but now you are light in the Lord." To remember where you came from is an essential part of the Christian walk. There are many believers who have lost their fervor and affection for the things of God. They sing with blank expressions on their faces and their hearts no longer break for the lost people among them. They're on the path to lukewarm Christianity and don't even know it. What must they do? Paul tells them right here. God's way to deepen their devotion to Him is to obey the call to remember.

It is of great spiritual benefit to remember the hopeless condition you were once in and would still be in without salvation by grace alone through Jesus Christ. It will be bad for you if you don't remember these things. Eph. 2:12 (NLT) says, "In those days you were living apart from Christ. You were excluded from citizenship among the people of Israel, and you did not know the covenant promises God had made to them." If you're to love God as you should, then you must remember that at one time you were not joined to Christ but cut off from Him in ignorance and unbelief. God said in Ezek. 20:43,44, "And there you shall remember your ways and all your doings with which you were defiled; and you shall loathe yourselves in your own sight because of all the evils that you have committed. Then you shall know that I am the Lord, when I have dealt with you for My name's sake, not according to your wicked ways nor according to your corrupt doings, O house of Israel."

If you're going to be a follower of Jesus Christ, you must learn to both forget and remember. There are some things you must forget. Paul said in Phil. 3:13, "But one thing I do, forgetting those things which are behind and reaching forward to those things which are ahead." You must forget the guilt and grief of the past. Let go of past grudges. Forget about them and press on. Vs. 14 says, "I press toward the goal for the prize of the upward call of God in Christ Jesus." At the same time, there are some things you must remember. Decide on purpose to remember that the shed blood of Jesus cleansed you from all sin. You once were lost but now am found (Luke 15:24). You are to remember the entirety of your hopeless condition apart from the mercy of God found in the Lord's death and resurrection. Remember the time when God was not your God and Jesus was not your Savior, a time when you were storing up wrath for yourself on the day of judgment. Remember that you were lost and utterly without hope.

Moses told the people in Deut. 5:15, "And you shall remember that you were a slave in the land of Egypt, and the Lord your God brought you out of there by a mighty hand and an outstretched arm." Remember all the good things God did for you. Remember the times God gave you strength when you didn't think you'd be able to make it to the end of the day. Remember when God made a way when there didn't seem to be a way out of your situation. Remember that debt He paid off, the time He healed you, that promotion you received, that special someone He brought into your life. James 1:2 says, "Count it all joy when you fall into various trials." Why did he say that? Because the victory you'll soon experience will be what you'll remember in the future. You'll look at what you're currently going through and say, "If God delivered me then, He'll deliver me now." That's the power of remembrance. That past victory will be the fuel that takes you to the next level of glory.

Scottish theologian John Eadie said, "This exercise of memory would deepen their humility, elevate their ideas of divine grace, and invite them to ardent and continual thankfulness." In the Old Testament, the children of Israel had enemies to fight after they were delivered from the bondage of Egypt. Some of these enemies were bigger and stronger than they were. What should they do? God told them in Deut. 7:17,18 (NLT), "Perhaps you will think to yourselves, 'How can we ever conquer these nations that are so much more powerful than we are?' But don't be afraid of them! Just remember what the Lord your God did to Pharaoh and to all the land of Egypt." What did God tell them to do? Remember! When things look impossible, remember what God did in the past. Remember when He turned your mourning into dancing (Ps. 30:11). This will raise the level of your expectancy which, in turn, fuels your faith and allows God to do great things in your life.

If you want to reach your full potential, you have to learn to remember. Why? Because this is what God wants you to do. Ps. 77:11,12 says, "I will remember the works of the Lord; Surely I will remember Your wonders of old. I will meditate on all Your work, and talk of Your deeds." There is a call on your life to intentionally remember all God has done. Joshua 4 is a chapter about remembrance, a chapter where God says there are some things you must never forget. When Joshua and the children of Israel crossed over the Jordan River into the Promised land, God commanded twelve men, one from each tribe, to pick up a huge stone from the dry riverbed. He then said in vs. 7, "And these stones shall be for a memorial to the children of Israel forever." God wanted a pile of rocks to be an everlasting sign to the people so they would remember what He did on this day in their history. Never were they, and all the generations that followed, to forget what He did for them.

Consider what happened at the Last Supper. Jesus had the disciples eat bread and drink wine as a sign of what was about to take place on the cross. As each element was given to the disciples, he said to them, "Do this in remembrance of Me" (1 Cor. 11:24,25). You must intentionally do something to remember, to remind yourself what God has done in your life. Paul wrote in Phil. 3:1, "For me to write the same things to you is not tedious, but for you it is safe." He is repeating himself so they won't forget what he told them. The Message Bible says, "I don't mind repeating what I have written in earlier letters, and I hope you don't mind hearing it again. better safe than sorry - so here goes." 2 Peter 1:12 says the same thing, "Therefore I will not be negligent to remind you always of these things, though you know them, and are established in the present truth." Both Peter and Paul are saying you sometimes have to be reminded of things you already know. Why? So you won't forget them!

One of the greatest enemies of faith is forgetfulness. If you don't remember what God did in the past, you'll have no power for the present. Faith is built on God's faithfulness and the things He's done in the past. David said when he was about to face Goliath, "The Lord who rescued me from the claws of the lion and the bear will rescue me from this Philistine!" (1 Sam. 17:37). David remembered what God did in the past and this helped him gain courage when he faced Goliath. Remembering affects how you feel and how you think and how you act. It was in the past that you learned valuable lessons that shape and mold the decisions you make. It's what taught you how to respond to the challenges you face today. Remembering feeds your hopes and expectations and gives you the confidence to press on in hard times. What happened in the past must be transformed into a present reality. When David remembered being delivered from the lion and bear, he sprang into action and ran toward the giant.

Ps. 77:5,6 says, "I have considered the days of old, the years of ancient times. I call to remembrance my song in the night: I meditate within my heart, and my spirit makes diligent search." What does it mean to remember? It's much more than a casual recalling of something that happened in the past. It goes much deeper than that. The prefix "re" means to repeat something over and over again. It means to ponder, to savor the thought, to think it through, to remember the details, to relive the moment so it won't become a far-distant memory in the back of your mind. Remembering causes you to bring the good things from the past into the present until they come alive in your thinking and memory. Memories stacked one on top of the other shape how you view the world and helps develop the character of who you are. Look at the memorial stones in your life with eyes that see and ears that hear. They're there for a reason. They're signs which give direction, to show you the way to where you want to go.

Recalling the past does you no good if it doesn't change your behavior, if it doesn't raise the level of your faith. In a moment of crisis, many people get caught up in the moment and forget all the times God delivered them in the past. This is why you need to make remembering personal. Josh. 4:6 asks, "What do these stones mean to you?" Be moved by all God has done for you, by how He rescued you when you were drowning in trespasses and sins, how He helped you meet that financial need, how He healed your broken marriage. If you're in a struggle, the best thing you can do is remember, remember, and then remember some more. When you remember what God has done in the past, you're telling Him you want Him to do it again. Pray that God will make your heart soft and sensitive, that He will grant you to be moved by the remembrance of all He has done. This will keep you humble as you love Him more intensely, as you look up and say, "But for the grace of God, there go I."

| 17 |

"THE GOODNESS OF GOD"

Before Paul explains the unity Christ brought to the Jews and Gentiles, he first wants the saints at Ephesus to remember what their lives were like before the goodness of God rescued them from eternal judgment. God wants you to remember the same thing. How should you remember what you once were? You need to let the memory seize you and move you. Imagine the horror of the reality from which you have been saved. Know it, feel it, be gripped by it. An intellectual recollection of past events will be of no spiritual benefit to you if it doesn't move your heart. This is why you need to ponder the realities of your life without Christ, the guilt you carried because of your meaningless existence. Consider the wickedness of hardened sinners, the emotional suffering caused by deep depression and all sorts of abnormalities, the physical suffering of sickness and disease. Look at all the misery in the world and remember that you were once a part of all that.

God is a good God. Don't ever forget that. Ps. 100:5 (TLB) says, "The Lord is always good. He is always loving and kind, and His faithfulness goes on and on to each succeeding generation." Failing to remember God's goodness leads to stress and much difficulty in life. This is why you must never forget how good God is. Remembering His goodness is an important and valuable spiritual exercise. It will keep you humble. You won't be in danger of becoming self-righteous and prideful. It keeps you from boasting in your new condition, in your renewed newness of life. It will make you cherish your forgiveness more as you feel the wonder of the justification of the ungodly by faith. You'll love Christ more intensely and you'll speak of Him often. You won't pray mechanical prayers and you won't blush when it's time to give Him praise. No longer will you sing with a blank face, a face with no expression. You'll be moved to love God with all your heart and soul as words of affection flow out of your mouth.

There is great feeling in Paul's words as he speaks in a forceful, passionate, and intense manner. Why is he stressing this point so vehemently? Because he knows there are severe consequences for not remembering how good God is. You might be tempted to start taking the credit for all the good things God did for you and through you. Prideful ingratitude is one of the worst sins you can ever commit. An example of this is found in Acts 12:21-23, "On a set day Herod put on his royal robe, sat on his throne, and made a speech to them. The people gave him a great ovation, shouting, 'It's the voice of a god, not of a man!' Instantly, an angel of the Lord struck Herod with a sickness, because he accepted the people's worship instead of giving the glory to God. So he was consumed and died." The problem of being a self-made man is they don't worship God nor give Him the credit and glory for all they have achieved. They think they did it all and this puts them on thin ice.

Rom. 1:21 says, "They know God exists but do not give Him the credit for all He's made and they're ungrateful. So their thinking becomes confused and their hearts fill up with darkness. They think they are wise, but they have become fools." People need to realize that ingratitude is one of the roots of atheism. For sure, the slide into unbelief begins with not being grateful for all God has done in your life. In fact, this is one of the signs of the end times. 2 Tim. 3:2 (TLB) says, "As the end approaches, people are going to be self-absorbed, money-hungry, self-promoting, arrogant, profane, rebellious, ungrateful, and having no respect for what is sacred." God wants you to remember the source of your success. 1 Cor. 4:7 says, "What do you have that God hasn't given you? And if all you have is from God, why act as though you are so great, and as though you accomplished it all on your own?" The Message Bible says, "Isn't everything you have and everything you are sheer gifts from God?"

Also, when you forget God's goodness, when you forget how eager He is to bless you, you'll stop asking Him to help you in time of need. He becomes your last resort instead of your first option. You'll foolishly try to help yourself instead of going to God in prayer. You'll stop trusting Him in difficult times not realizing that God only proves His goodness to you when you ask Him to. The Bible says, "You have not because you ask not" (James 4:2). If you remember His goodness, it would be automatic that you go to Him when hard times come. You'll repeat the petition of David recorded in Ps. 69:16 (NIV), "Answer me, O Lord, out of the goodness of Your love; in Your mercy turn to me." You should never try to solve the problem yourself. Let God do it for you. After all, that's what He's there for. Luke 11:13 (NLT) says, "If you, as imperfect parents, know how to give good gifts to your own children, how much more will your heavenly Father give good gifts to those who ask Him?"

Forgetting God's goodness causes you to become pessimistic about the future. You'll lose hope because hope is based on the goodness of God. Ps. 27:13,14 (NASB) says, "I would have despaired unless I had believed that I'd see the goodness of the Lord in the land of the living. Instead, I thought 'Wait for the Lord! Be strong and let your heart take courage! Yes, wait for the Lord!'" The foundation for all hope is the goodness of God. Without God, there is no radical, rational, or logical reason for hope. Ps. 16:1,2 says, "Protect me, God, because I trust in You. You are my Lord! And every good thing I have comes from You!" The more you understand God's goodness, the more hopeful you'll be in life. God said in Jer. 29:11, "For I know the plans I have for you. They are plans for good and not for disaster, to give you a future and a hope." The Message Bible says, "I have it all planned out - plans to take care of you, not abandon you, plans to give you the future you hope for."

Just how good is God? In six short verses, Psalm 23 lists ten different blessings of God's goodness toward you. The first blessing is sustenance as David writes in vs. 1, "The Lord is my shepherd; I shall not want." The NIV says, "I lack nothing" and the NLT says, "I have all that I need." Sheep need a shepherd because they are defenseless animals. They don't run fast so they can't escape from the predators that stalk them. They don't have claws or sharp teeth with which to defend themselves. On top of all that, they're not very smart. They fall off cliffs and wander off and get lost. Left alone they would probably get eaten before the sun goes down. They're not very bright animals so they need a shepherd to watch over them. What does a shepherd do? A shepherd feeds, leads, and meets needs. There is nothing you need that God can't supply. He'll feed you, lead you, and meet all your needs no matter what they may be (Phil. 4:19).

A shepherd also makes sure the sheep get enough rest in order to stay healthy. People today don't know how to relax. They're addicted to adrenaline and don't know how to slow down. Job 20:18 (MSG) says, "They are unable to relax and enjoy anything they've worked for." Why? Because they're too busy getting more things than they actually need and don't take time to rest. Resistance to rest is a sign of immaturity. The truth be told, God considers rest as important as work. This is why David wrote in vs. 2, "He makes me to lie down in green pastures; He leads me beside the still waters." Without rest, you'll be stressed out all the time and won't be good for anything. If you won't do it on your own, God will make you do it. Sometimes the only way God can get you to look up is when you're flat on your back from exhaustion or an illness. Your body wasn't made to handle the physical demands you put on it. You need to relax in the goodness of God.

God will also replenish your strength when you're empty, when you're out of gas and running on fumes. Vs. 3 says, "He restores my soul." Your soul is that part of you that thinks, chooses, and feels. You don't always think straight and often do the things you know you shouldn't do. Your emotions can get severely damaged to the point that you don't even feel anything anymore. They become raw and unresponsive. This is where the Good Shepherd comes in. The GNT says, "He gives me new strength." He'll bless you with resilience which is "the ability to recover from or adjust easily to misfortune or change." He'll give you "beauty for ashes, the oil of joy for the mourning, the garment of praise for the spirit of heaviness" (Is. 61:3). God has a way of turning things around, of bringing good out of bad. Ps. 30:11 (NLT) says, "You have turned my mourning into joyful dancing. You have taken away my clothes of mourning and clothed me with joy."

Rom. 8:28 says, "And we know that all things work together for good to those who love God, to those who are called according to His purpose." This is one of the greatest promises in all the Bible. Anybody can bring good out of good but God specializes in bringing good out of bad. He'll turn your hurts into holiness, your wounds into wisdom, your pain into gain. God uses conflict to build your character. Rom. 8:29 says, "God knew His purpose from the very beginning. He planned in advance that all of us in God's family would become like Jesus, His Son." God is more interested in your character than He is your comfort. This world you're living in is preschool. It's where your character is developed as God prepares you for the next life. In other words, God wants you to grow up before you go to heaven. This is why you need to count it all joy when you fall into various trials (James 1:2). In a trial, ask God, "What are you teaching me? What character trait do I need to develop?"

Another blessing of God's goodness is divine guidance. Nothing stresses you out more than indecision, when you don't know what to do. David continues in vs. 3, saying, "He leads me in paths of right-eousness for His name's sake." Life is a series of choices. You make your choices and then they make you. Every choice has a consequence and many people struggle when an important decision has to be made. They can't decide if they should go this way or that way, if they should do this or do that. They feel like they're being pulled in different di-rections and eventually become double-minded. James 1:8 says, "A double-minded man is unstable in all his ways." In Greek, the word "unstable" means 'staggering like a drunk.' The solution to all this un-certainty is to let God guide you, to let Him tell you what to do. God wants to restore your soul and send you off in the right direction. There are paths of righteousness you need to be on.

The Good Shepherd not only feeds you, He also leads you. Life is a journey and God has given you His Word to be the road map you fol-low. Your conscience is your compass that tells you you're going in the right direction. He's even given you a personal guidance counselor, the Holy Spirit. Being guided by God is proof that you are a member of His family. Rom. 8:14 says, "For as many as are led by the Spirit of God, these are the sons of God." God has good plans for your life and He wants you to know and understand what those plans are. He wants to make sure you're on track with what He wants you to do. To make that happen, He has promised to guide you along the way as you jour-ney down the paths of righteousness. To be led by God, you must first want to be led. It starts with a desire that is craving to hear from God. This isn't a casual longing, a passive request. Get desperate and say, "God, I've got to hear from You!"

You must also be willing to do what God says to do. Be willing to obey before you ask Him for divine guidance. Decide in advance that you'll obey God and follow His instructions. John 7:17 (TEV) says, "Whoever is willing to do what God wants and chooses it will know if what I teach comes from God." Jesus is saying, "Trust Me in ad-vance." People need to realize that most of God's will is already revealed. The principles to live by are found in the Bible from cover to cover. Ps. 119:105 says, "Your Word is a lamp to guide me, and a light to my path." When you open your Bible, God opens His mouth and starts talking to you. Stop listening for a voice from heaven and start looking for a verse. If you're not in the Bible every day, you're in the dark. You're walking through life without a flashlight. As you read the Bible, ask the Holy Spirit to be your guide. He's the author of the Bible and, as your guidance counselor, He'll lead you to verses that pertain to your situation (Ps. 25:9).

Another blessing of God's goodness is confidence. David writes, "Yea, though I walk through the valley of the shadow of death, I will fear no evil; For You are with me" (Ps. 23:4). God is with you no matter what it is you're going through. Yes, He'll forever be by your side even during your darkest days. He is the God of the valleys (1 Kings 20:28), the God of difficult times. You live in a world that is broken and times of darkness, despair, and discouragement happen to everybody. Matt. 5:45 says, "The rain falls on the just and unjust." This means that bad things happen to good people. The truth be told, most of life is not lived on the mountaintop. They give you a great view but most mountain peaks are far and few in between. Know that valleys are inevitable, they're a part of life. 1 Peter 4:12 (TEV) says, " Don't be surprised when you are tested by troubles or painful suffering, as if something unusual happened to you."

Valleys are unpredictable and this is what makes them a problem. More times than not, they come unexpectedly and catch you off guard. One phone call can turn your good day into a bad day. In an instant, everything can change. Still, there is good news. Ps. 34:19 (TLB) says, "The good man does not escape all troubles - he has them too. But the Lord helps him in each and every one." Always remember that you are not alone for God is with you. Together you are walking through the valley. This means your valley experience is only temporary. You don't stay in the valley; you go through it. With God by your side, you can have confidence knowing that the shadow of a dog never bit anybody. A shadow is a figure without substance. They can frighten you, but they can't harm you. There are no shadows without a light. The shadows in your life are the evidence of the presence of light in your life. 1 John 1:5 says, "God is light and in Him is no darkness at all."

Jesus is not the light at the end of the tunnel, He's the light in the tunnel. Stop focusing on your problems and look to the light. If you'll do that, no shadow can harm you. Rest assured, the Good Shepherd will protect you and give you the confidence you need when insecurity sets in. David knew this as he wrote, "Your rod and Your staff, they comfort me" (vs. 4). How can these two sticks bring comfort to your life? It will help to know what they are and what they represent. A rod is a club-like tool not more than two feet long. It's a defensive weapon used against the predators who seek to devour the sheep. The staff, on the other hand, is a long stick with a curved hook on the end of it. Sheep are prone to wander off and the shepherd hooks the staff around their necks and pulls them back to the flock. The staff is a tool to get you out of a bad situation, a tool used for guiding and directing. The rod represents power and authority, the staff represents care and compassion.

Jesus is the Good Shepherd and He wants to give you protection and direction. If you'll bring Him your hurts, He'll show you compassion. Matt. 20:28 says, "I came here not to be served, but to serve others, and to give My life as a ransom for many." Jesus came to show compassion, to serve and to give. If you'll follow Him, He'll bring you comfort by doing whatever it takes to remove your hurt and pain. He'll also be your guide as He leads you in the right direction. John 10:4 (TLB) says, "The Good Shepherd walks ahead of the sheep; and they follow Him, for they recognize His voice." In a cattle drive, you push the cattle forward from the back. On the other hand, a shepherd always leads from the front. He's your model, your mentor, and he always leads by example. The shepherd always goes first and the sheep faithfully follow him. Jesus won't push you through life. He won't force you to do anything. But, as a shepherd, He'll lead the way saying, "Watch how I do it."

As you follow the Good Shepherd, you'll quickly learn that the goodness of God is even found in the midst of your worst battles. Ps. 23:5 says, "You prepare a table before me in the presence of my enemies." God is the host of this banquet and you're the guest of honor. This banquet is on a battlefield when you're under attack. When everybody comes against you, God throws a party for you. People are going to watch you eat with the King because God wants all your enemies to see you being honored. Ps. 5:11 (MSG) says, "You welcome us with open arms when we run for cover to You. Let the party last all night! Stand guard over our celebration." When God's blessings are over you, it doesn't matter what you're going through. Your enemies are powerless to do you harm. Job 36:16 (NCV) says, "God is gently calling you from the jaws of distress to an open place of freedom where He has set your table full of the best food!"

David continues in vs. 5, "You anoint my head with oil." The importance of the anointing is all based on who's doing the anointing. Your drunken neighbor could anoint you king of the universe and it wouldn't have much meaning. In the Bible, olive oil is used to symbolize God's Spirit, His presence, and His blessing on your life. It's an outward sign of an internal process. The "anointing" can be described as "God on flesh doing only what God can do." It's supernatural insight, ability, stamina, authority, and protection that you don't normally have. It's given to empower you to do a job that God has chosen you to do. You are called by Him to do something specific with your life. People who are not happy and unfilled have missed their calling. The good news is that whatever God calls you to do, He'll anoint you and give you the power and ability to do it. Eph. 3:16 (NLT) says, "From His unlimited resources God will give you mighty inner strength through His Holy Spirit."

There are a lot of pressures in life and God wants you to go from overwhelmed to overflowing. David closes out vs. 5 by saying, "My cup runs over." The ICB says, "You give me more than I can hold." Your "cup" is your life and you need to know and believe that God has more than you'll ever need. His resources are unlimited and the result of that is an overflowing life. Jesus said in John 7:37,38 (NLT), "If you are thirsty, come to Me and drink! Everyone who really believes in Me will have rivers of living water flowing out of their lives." Jesus is saying, "If you really depend on Me, your life will be overflowing." Yes, when you trust in and rely on the Good Shepherd, you'll be filled beyond capacity with an endless supply of God's goodness. Your life will overflow. Jesus said in John 10:10 (AMP), "I've come that you may have real life, and enjoy it in abundance - to the fullest, until it overflows!" You're not really living until you know God is good. You're headed for trouble if you don't.

Because your cup is overflowing with the goodness of God, you never need to fear the future. Ps. 23:6 says, "Surely goodness and mercy shall follow me all the days of my life." As the shepherd leads the flock, behind the sheep are two sheepdogs who make sure they don't wander off and get lost. The sheepdogs in your life are God's goodness and God's mercy. They follow you as you follow Jesus, the Good Shepherd. They keep you going in the right direction. Heb. 4:16 (NCV) says, "We can come before God's throne where we can receive mercy and grace to help us when we need it." God's goodness is when God gives you what you don't deserve. Mercy is when God doesn't give you what you do deserve. David ends this psalm on a glorious note. Indeed, he saves the best for last. "And I will dwell in the house of the Lord forever" (vs. 6). He's saying you don't have to fear death for God's glory is waiting for you. Death is not the end, it's a transition from this world to life everlasting. Remember that.

| 18 |

"BOTH JEWS AND GENTILES"

Not only does Paul want the Ephesians to remember the goodness of God, he also wants them to not forget what they were like in the eyes of the Jews. Eph. 2:11 (NLT) says, "Don't forget that you Gentiles used to be outsiders. You were called 'uncircumcised heathen' by the Jews, who were proud of their circumcision, even though if affected only their bodies and not their heart." All of mankind can be divided into two classes of people: the Jew and the Gentile. A Gentile is anyone who is a non-Jew, one who is not a member of the "chosen people." As a religious rite, circumcision was required of all Abraham's descendants as an outward sign of the covenant God made with him (Gen. 17:9-14). Thus, Jews were circumcised and Gentiles were not. Circumcision is the surgical removal of the foreskin of a man's private part. The word literally means "to cut around." If you were circumcised, every day you would be reminded of your covenant with God.

There was hostility between the Jews and Gentiles because of this sign of the covenant. For the Jews, circumcision was a sign of pride. They were more proud of the external operation than anything that was happening in their heart. As far as the Jews were concerned, the Gentiles were outcasts. Not being circumcised was evidence of their estrangement from God. It was a sign of utter rejection. You were cursing someone if you called them uncircumcised. It was a derogatory term of mockery, defamation, and reproach. It was a name of contempt that the Jews flung at the Gentiles and was indicative of the low regard in which they were held. David used this term to belittle Goliath when he asked, "For who is this uncircumcised Philistine, that he should taunt the armies of the living God?" (1 Sam. 17:26). The Jews made this a wall of division that created a gap that could not be bridged. Martyn Lloyd-Jones said, "Any talk of reconciliation seemed monstrous and impossible."

The physical act of circumcision was meant to be an external sign of an internal change of heart, resulting in a love for God. Unfortunately, the Jews were blinded to what this cutting represented. Theologian Charles Hodge said, "To the Jews it expressed a self-righteous abhorrence of the Gentiles as unclean and profane. This feeling on their part arose because they supposed that the mere outward rite of circumcision conveyed holiness and secured God's favor." What these Jews did not grasp onto is that the physical act of circumcision was to be a symbol of man's need for his heart to be cleansed from the disease of sin. This cutting needed to happen internally for the removal of the sin nature inherited from Adam. It is by faith that hearts get circumcised. Moses gave Israel a prophetic promise in Deut. 30:6, "The Lord your God will circumcise your heart and the heart of your descendants, to love the Lord your God with all your heart and with all your soul."

Jeremiah addressed faithless Jews, saying, "Circumcise yourselves to the Lord, and take away the foreskins of your heart, you men of Judah and inhabitants of Jerusalem, lest My fury come forth like fire, and burn so that no one can quench it, because of the evil of your doings" (Jer. 4:4). Paul added to this in Rom. 2:28,29, "For he is not a Jew who is one outwardly, nor is circumcision which is outward in the flesh; but he is a Jew who is one inwardly, and circumcision is that of the heart, in the Spirit." The Message Bible says, "Don't you see? It's not the cut of a knife that makes a Jew. You become a Jew by who you are.

It's the mark of God on your heart, not of a knife on your skin, that makes a Jew." The spiritual circumcision God always desired never transpired in their hearts. This made them just like the unsaved Gentiles. The truth be told, they were as unclean as uncircumcised Gentiles and stood condemned before God.

Before Christ came, the Gentiles were literally cut off from God and separated from the people of God. Paul now mentions five things that were true of the uncircumcised Gentiles. Eph. 2:12 says, "At that time you were without Christ, being aliens from the commonwealth of Israel and strangers from the covenants of promise, having no hope and without God in the world." Paul is reminding them of the deplorable condition they were once in. They were without Christ and had no hope of a Savior and no anticipation of a deliverer. They knew of no atonement for sin and had no assurance of pardon. They were in a state of darkness and condemnation and had no well-founded hope of eternal life. The Messiah was called "the Hope of Israel" (Jer. 14:8), not the Hope of the Gentiles. For them, life was a treadmill and history was going nowhere. John MacArthur said the Gentiles "had no purpose, no plan, and no destiny except the ultimate judgment of God, of which they were unaware."

The Jews lived with the hope and expectation that the Messiah would one day come. The Gentiles, on the other hand, had no expectation of a Messiah to light up their spiritual darkness. No hope or promises were given to them and they knew nothing at all about Him. In regard to the nation of Israel, the Gentiles were aliens who did not belong. They were strangers and foreigners without the rights and privileges of citizenship in the nation of Israel, a nation that was the recipient of God's blessings and the target of His special love. Is. 63:7,8 (NLT) says, "I will tell of the Lord's unfailing love. I will praise the Lord for all He has done. I will rejoice in His great goodness to Israel, which He granted according to His mercy and love. He said, 'They are My very own people. Surely they will not betray Me again.' And He became their Savior." The word "alienated" always implies loss of affection or interest. The Gentiles were cut off from the Jews, living in a state of complete estrangement.

The Gentiles were spiritually homeless, strangers to the covenants of promise. Albert Barnes said in his commentary, "The covenants of promise were those various arrangements which God made with His people, by which He promised them future blessings, and especially by which He promised that the Messiah should come. To be in possession of them was regarded as a high honor and privilege." The Gentiles had not been promised anything by God. He had not promised them blessing, land, or the Messiah. Only the Jews had been promised these things. He promised to bless them, to prosper and multiply them. He promised to redeem them and give them a kingdom over which they would reign. Wayne Barber said, "These covenants were the anchor that pointed to the faithfulness of a God to deliver what He promised. The Gentiles had no anchor. They were sailors on a captainless boat on unchartered seas."

The Gentiles were strangers to all this. They had no promise from God, no guarantees, no security, no nothing. Adding fuel to the fire, the false gods they worshiped were helpless to provide them with any comfort or security. No matter how grand their pagan religion was, it was useless because the gods they worshiped had no power to save them from death and eternal judgment. The only thing the Gentiles could look forward to was condemnation and punishment. Because of this, they were a people "having no hope and without God in the world." A great cloud of hopelessness covered the Gentile world. They had no promises on which they could look forward to a better life. They had no reasonable expectation of improvement in their current condition. To them, hope was nothing more than a temporary illusion. German philosopher Friedrick Nietzsche said hopelessness "is the worst of all evils because it prolongs the torments of man."

The Gentiles had nothing to hope for beyond this world because the promises of God is the only foundation of hope. Those to whom there is no promise have no hope. John MacArthur said, "Hope is a profound blessing that gives meaning and security to life. Living without hope of future joy and enrichment reduces man to a piece of meaningless protoplasm." Job's great anguish and pessimistic outlook can be seen in the words he spoke in Job 7:6, "My days are swifter than a weaver's shuttle, and are spent without hope." The Gentiles were a Godless people. They had no one to cry out to, trust in, love, praise, and serve. They were in bondage, devoid of spiritual freedom. It is interesting to note that although they were separated from Christ, He still had them in His heart. He said in John 10:16, "I have other sheep (Gentiles), which are not of this fold (Jews); I must bring them also, and they shall hear My voice; and they shall become one flock with one shepherd."

For centuries there was a dividing wall between the Jews and Gentiles, an impossible division with unspeakable hatred that has not been matched in all of human history. John MacArthur said, "For many hundreds of years the animosity between Jews and Gentiles has festered and grown. Although they were not always in open conflict, their mutual contempt continued to widen the gulf between them." Then one day a little baby boy was born in Bethlehem and thirty-three years later everything miraculously changed. Paul begins to paint a fresh and glowing contrast to what he had just said. In one verse he's going to explain the entire gospel message. Eph. 2:13 says, "But now in Christ Jesus you who once were far off have been made near by the blood of Christ." The Gentiles are now spiritually and socially united with the Jews. No longer are they alienated but in Christ they are united. Jew and Gentile become one in Him.

This is the glorious message of the gospel. No matter how sinful you've been, no matter what you've done, you have been brought near to God and can have a relationship with Him through Christ. Paul is writing to the Gentile believers in Ephesus and he explains what Christ has done specifically for them in order to sharpen their gratitude and to strengthen their faith. The Message Bible says, "You who were once out of it altogether are in on everything." Peter said in Acts 10:34 after a Gentile named Cornelius got saved, "In truth I perceive that God shows no partiality. But in every nation whoever fears Him and works righteousness is accepted by Him." Faith plus works is the evidence of acceptance with God and it's for everybody in every nation because God is no respecter of persons. The message Paul was writing to the Ephesians is that all believers are one in Christ, both Jew and Gentile. He writes this second chapter in order to help break the barriers down.

Jesus is the meeting point with God for all mankind. Suddenly the gloom is gone. A window is open and light shines in. The Gentiles, even though they were far off, were not forsaken by God for He desires all people to come to repentance and be saved. Never are you to forget the greatness of your salvation. Nothing less than the power of God could have achieved it. The power that made you a Christian is precisely the same power that raised Jesus from the dead. It is truly a supernatural wonder that anybody is a Christian. It's not amazing that many are not Christians, but it is totally astounding that anybody is a Christian at all. Nothing but the power of God in Christ accounts for this, based on the fact that all people were spiritually dead in trespasses and sin. Martyn Lloyd-Jones said, "To measure this power is to measure the depth from what you've been saved from and the height to which you've been exalted."

John Newton wrote in his song "Amazing Grace" these words, "I once was lost, but now I'm found. I was blind, but now I see." But now! Every Christian needs a "But now" testimony. Don't forget what God did and how He did it. You were dead in sin, separated from God, but now there is hope. All is not lost for God is with you. There is an end in sight of despair and darkness and gloom. Those sitting in darkness have seen a great light. God took those who were far off and brought them near. 2 Cor. 4:6 (NLT) says, "For God, who said, 'Let there be light in the darkness,' has made the light shine in our hearts so we could know the glory of God that is seen in the face of Jesus Christ." Only the light of the gospel can penetrate the darkness of unbelief. The word "light" is a common theme in the Bible. It was a metaphor used to represent everything good and valuable. It's usually tied to the idea of knowledge and guidance, when a person is gifted with a revelation from God.

The Message Bible says, "Our lives filled up with light as we saw and understood God in the face of Christ, all bright and beautiful." What this implies is that Christ is the ultimate fulfillment of anything and everything you could ever need or want. The light, knowledge, and glory of your salvation is reflected in the face of Jesus. What makes you a Christian is not a change in your behavior, it's the relationship you have with the Heavenly Father. The change in your moral condition follow being made near by the blood of Christ. 2 Cor. 3:18 (MSG) says, "And so we are transfigured much like the Messiah, our lives gradually becoming brighter and more beautiful as God enters our lives and we become like Him." Those who were far off were made near by the blood of Christ. This is a reference to His death where He suffered and died to pay for your sins. It's sin that creates antagonism, enmity, hate, strife, bitterness, war, and conflict. You remove sin, you have perfect relationships.

When Adam and Eve sinned, they were shut out from the presence of God. But now, in Christ Jesus, the door of access has been opened through which one gains access to the presence of the Father. To be made near means to be brought into spiritual union and intimacy with God. You've been reconciled to Him, restored to His favor. The enmity is removed. The wrath of God is fulfilled and satisfied. Atonement has been made by the blood of Jesus. Pastor Ray Stedman said, "It isn't merely the death of Christ. God emphasizes it. God wants us to think about it, because blood is always a sign of violence. The death of Jesus was a violent death, a bloody, gory, ugly, revolting scene - a man hanging torn and wretched upon a cross, with blood streaming down His sides and running down the cross. God wants us to remember that violent death, because violence is the ultimate result of paganism. It is the final expression of a godless society."

It is only through the shedding of blood that sins can be forgiven (Heb. 9:22). Sin is a loathsome and detestable thing and God demands that blood, and blood alone, be shed for the remission of sins. Why is this so? Because blood is the basis of life. People bleed to death proving that blood is essential for the preservation of life. Lev. 17:11 (NLT) says, "For the life of the body is in the blood. I have given you the blood on the altar to purify you, making you right with the Lord. It is the blood, given in exchange for a life, that makes purification possible." Jesus had to shed His blood because no other blood sacrifice could satisfy the righteous demands of God's holiness and His just hatred of sin. Only the blood of the spotless, sinless Lamb of God could take away the sins of the world and bring men near to God. Jesus said at the Last Supper, "This is My blood of the covenant, which is poured out for many for forgiveness of sins" (Matt. 26:28).

Charles Spurgeon said, "All the repentance in the world cannot blot out the smallest sin for there is no atoning power in repentance. In a sea full of penitential tears, there is not the power or the virtue to wash out one spot of this hideous uncleanness. Without the bloodshedding, there is no remission. Jesus Christ Himself cannot save us apart from His blood. Not the holiness of Jesus, not the life of Jesus, not the death of Jesus, but the blood of Jesus only, for 'apart from the shedding of blood there is no forgiveness.'" Every person who desires a relationship with God must be willing to rely on the merits of that blood. David Guzik said, "Modern (unbelieving, Biblically ignorant) people think sin is forgiven by time, by our good works, by our decent lives, or by simply death. But there is no forgiveness without the shedding of blood, and there is no perfect forgiveness without a perfect sacrifice."

Most people look with revulsion at the fact that blood had to be shed for the remission of sins. They are squeamish and cannot bear the mention of the word "blood." Charles Spurgeon said, "The very horror which the thought of it causes may give you some notion of the terrible nature of sin as God judges it. It is not without a dreadful blood shedding that your dreadful guilt could by any possibility be cleansed." John Phillips said in his commentary, "Those who scorn the shed blood have their eyes blinded both to God's blazing holiness and to the dreadful, radical nature of sin. Sin is a radical and terrible reality that calls for a radical and terrible cure." As gruesome as Christ's death was, you must grasp onto it for now you are able to enjoy all the blessings of God's new covenant with man. Heb. 4:16 says, "Let us therefore come boldly to the throne of grace, that we may obtain mercy and find grace to help in time of need."

Christianity is the religion of free access to God. This unfathomable privilege is awarded to all who have been saved by the blood of Jesus and none are excluded. You're encouraged to go to God and keep going to His throne of grace with no fear or doubt. The word "boldly" means 'in a confident and courageous way; showing a willingness to take risks.' It comes from the Greek word "parresia" and it refers to 'freedom of speech.' It depicts a person who speaks his mind and does it straightforwardly and with great confidence, with a frankness that is very bold. The word doesn't mean you go to God proudly, arrogantly, and with presumption. It means you go to Him with the confident assurance of a child approaching his beloved father. Don't go to Him in apprehensive timidity but with holy courage and reckless abandon, with backbone and a fearless mind, with grit and daring valor. The NASB says you are to "draw near with confidence."

The throne of God is a throne of grace. It's the eternal seat of the sovereign Lord of heaven and earth. Grace does not ignore God's holy justice but rather it operates in the fulfillment of His justice in light of the cross. Because of Jesus, the golden door of the throne room of God has been flung open through which all believers may enter. This should make your own heart leap for joy for now you may approach God with freedom, confidence, and liberty of speech. When you bare your heart to God or request His help, you never have to fear that you are too frank, too bold, too forthright, too honest, too outspoken, or even too blunt. With God, you never need to hesitate or be ashamed to speak whatever it is that's on your heart. After all, He wants to hear exactly what you have to say. At the throne of grace, nothing is to be feared, providing your heart is right with God, trusting alone in the sacrificial blood of Jesus that was shed on the cross.

Theologian Albert Barnes said, "Rejoice that there is a throne of grace. What a world this would be if God sat on a throne of justice only, and if no mercy were ever to be shown to people! Who is there who would not be overwhelmed with despair? There is not a day in our lives in which we do not need pardon; not an hour in which we do not need grace." Thank God that you're able to obtain mercy and find grace when you boldly go to His throne. The word "obtain" means 'to seize or to lay hold of something in order to make it your very own.' The word "find" expresses the idea of a discovery that is made due to an intense investigation, scientific study, or scholarly research. Go to the scriptures and find the blessing you're looking for. Then boldly go to the throne of grace where you'll lay hold of it, take it, and make it your own. God is willing to give you what you need and all you have to do is open your heart and receive it by faith.

| 19 |

"TEAR DOWN THIS WALL"

God alone brings people together. He brought the Jews and Gentiles together as one body, reconciling them to Himself through Christ's death on the cross. All fleshly distinctions - race, gender, nationality - were all nailed to the cross. It wasn't the Lord's teachings or His miracles that brought them together, it was the cross. Jesus said in John 12:32 (NLT), "And when I am lifted up from the earth, I will draw everyone to Myself." This was a prediction that His death would open the door to those who were far off. Yes, God called the Jews to be a separate people for a certain time in history and they had a unique identity. When Jesus walked the earth He deliberately confined His ministry to the Jews. However, every now and then, He gave the indication that something larger, bigger, and greater would happen after He accomplished the work on the cross He was sent to do. It was on the cross that the church was born and the religious identity of the Jews came to an end.

Paul made a remarkable statement in 1 Tim. 3:16 (MSG), "The Christian life is a great mystery, far exceeding our understanding, but some things are clear enough: He appeared in a human body, was proved right by the invisible Spirit, was seen by angels. He was proclaimed among all kinds of people, believed in all over the world, taken up into heavenly glory." The King James Bible said He was "preached among the Gentiles." Paul is saying the gospel message is a proclamation to both Jews and Gentiles and that Judaism, as a religion, is dead. The door to peace with God and one another has been opened by the death, burial, and resurrection of the Lord Jesus Christ. This is the message Paul wanted the Ephesian Christians to lay hold of. This is also the message that needs to be preached today, that "there is no respect of persons with God" (Rom. 2:11). Job 34:19 says, "He is not partial to princes, nor does He regard the rich more than the poor; For they are all the work of His hands."

God is a just God and it is impossible for Him to be anything but impartial. Eph. 6:9 says, "There is no partiality with Him." The word "partiality" literally means 'face taking; a receiving of face.' It pertains to judging someone purely on a superficial level, without a person's true merits, abilities, or character. Thankfully, God doesn't do that. He said in 1 Sam. 16:7, "For the Lord does not see as man sees; for man looks at the outward appearance, but the Lord looks at the heart." In God's eyes, everybody is the same. What's true for the Jews is also true for the Gentiles. The Jews had the law but disobeyed it and were guilty of sin. The Gentiles were ignorant of the law so they also were guilty of sin. Without realizing it, they were both sitting in the same sinking boat. Rom. 3:23 says, "For all have sinned and fall short of the glory of God." Jesus came to save both sinful Jews and sinful Gentiles. Jesus came to unite them together and Paul now explains how this union was accomplished.

Eph. 2:14 says, "For He Himself is our peace, who has made both one, and has broken down the middle wall of division between us." Jesus Christ is the mediator between Jew and Gentile. He is "our bond of unity and harmony. He has broken down, destroyed, abolished the hostile dividing wall between us" (AMP). The peace you enjoy is not just a concept but a person! Paul does not say Christ made peace but that He is peace. Micah 5:4,5 says, "And He shall stand and feed His flock in the strength of the Lord, in the majesty of the name of the Lord His God; And they shall abide, for now He shall be great to the ends of the earth; And this One shall be peace." Wayne Barber said, "Peace is never going to be present until Jesus is in an individual's life. Until a man has received God's grace, he will never know His peace." This is why Paul began this letter to the Ephesians by saying, "Grace to you and peace from God our Father and the Lord Jesus Christ" (Eph. 1:2).

In Is. 9:6, Jesus is called the "Prince of Peace." Not only is He the giver of peace, He is also the one who maintains it. He brings peace in the fullest sense of wholeness, prosperity, and tranquility. The word "peace" is the Greek word "eirene" and means 'to bind or join together what is broken, divided, or separated.' In secular Greek the word described the cessation or absence of war. No longer do the Jews and Gentiles regard each other with hatred and scorn. There's no more separation, no more privileged and unprivileged. A Jew is no longer closer to God than a Gentile. Both are one in Christ, united in position and entitlement. They are no longer Jews and Gentiles, they are Christians. They now worship the same God and have the same Savior. Gal. 3:28 says, "There is neither Jew nor Greek, there is neither slave nor free, there is neither male nor female; for you are all one in Christ Jesus." The Message Bible says, "Among us you are all equal."

Paul said Jesus "has broken down the middle wall of division between us." It's as if Christ received a command from the Father to "Tear down this wall!" There was a literal wall in the temple that separated the outer "Court of the Gentiles" from the inner "Court of the Jews." In the outer court was the city marketplace. It seems the Jews had no problem taking the money of the Gentiles. On this barrier hung a Jewish "No Trespassing" sign that said, "No stranger is to enter within the balustrade round the temple and enclosure. Whoever is caught will be himself responsible for his ensuing death." The Roman government gave the Jews permission to execute any Gentile, even those who were Roman citizens, if they proceeded beyond this barrier. The Jews were deadly serious about this warning to Gentiles to never transgress their barrier. In Acts 21:27-31, the Jews tried to kill Paul because they thought he took a Gentile beyond the barrier and "defiled this holy place" (vs. 28).

Spiritually speaking, as Jesus hung bleeding on the cross, He broke down this dividing wall. God was saying to the Gentiles, "There is now nothing to stop you from gaining access to My presence." God is in the business of tearing down walls. If He can tear down the barrier between the Jews and Gentiles, He can tear down whatever it is that's stopping you from fulfilling your destiny. Give Him those walls and let Him tear them down. For sure, He wants you to experience the fullness of everything He's making available to you. Paul continues in vs. 15 (AMP), "By abolishing in His own crucified flesh the enmity caused by the Law with its decrees and ordinances which He annulled; that He from the two might create in Himself one new man, one new quality of humanity out of the two, so making peace." The Message Bible says, "Instead of continuing with two groups of people separated by centuries of animosity and suspicion, He created a new kind of human being, a fresh start for everybody.'

The Greek word for "abolish" is "katargeo"and literally means 'to reduce to inactivity; to nullify; to render inoperative; to cause something to come to an end.' When Jesus died on the cross, He completely wiped out ceremonial law, the law of commandments contained in ordinances addressing circumcision, ritual feasting, fasting, dressing, and cooking. He did away with all that. The NLT says, "By His death He ended the whole system of Jewish law that excluded the Gentiles. His purpose was to make peace between Jews and Gentiles by creating in Himself one new person from the two groups." It's worth noting that Jesus didn't abolish the moral law, only the ceremonial law. The Jews ate different food and wore different clothes. They had different feasts, different fasts, and different offerings. No wonder they couldn't socialize with Gentiles. All this was the enmity that Christ abolished in His flesh as He hung on the cross. On that day, Judaism was abolished forever.

The word "enmity" means 'hostility, opposition, hatred' and here it refers to the personal and national prejudice and exclusiveness between Jews and Gentiles. The Jews prided themselves in their religious ceremonies that governed their behavior, thinking this made them better than the Gentiles. This was the cause of the hostility between these two groups of people. John Eadie said this enmity was "hatred which rose like a party wall, and kept both races at a distance. Deep hostility lay in their bosoms; the Jews looked down with supercilious contempt upon the Gentiles, and the Gentiles reciprocated and scowled upon the Jews as a haughty and heartless bigot." Jesus came to abolish the enmity contained in the ceremonies of the law. All these ceremonies pointed to Him and, since He was already here, those ceremonies are no longer necessary. With the death of Christ, the law and all its ceremonies are removed from the world as a factor in salvation. In other words, He put religion to death.

What did Jesus do that was so spectacular? He created in Himself one new man from the two, thus making peace. This is a radical, supernatural, and spiritual creation. Paul used the same Greek word in Eph. 2:10 when he said, "For we are His workmanship, created in Christ Jesus for good works." The Greek word "ktizo" means 'to create something out of nothing," such as when God created the entire universe. On the cross, Jesus created a new race of humanity. The Jews didn't become Gentiles and Gentiles didn't become Jews. Together they became Christians and now they both "walk in newness of life" (Rom. 6:4). The word "new" is the Greek word "kainos" and it means 'new in kind or quality; unprecedented; unheard of; something new of which did not exist before; a prototype.' This is something brand new! There's never been anything like it! This is a mystery because the church had never existed before. In fact, there is no mention of the church in the entire Old Testament.

The message here is that both Jews and Gentiles are one in Christ. God has broken down the wall and removed the barrier. Paul calls the church the "new man" because it never existed before. The New Testament church is not a continuation of the Israel of the Old Testament. It is entirely different from anything that has preceded it. Bible commentator William MacDonald said, "It is new that a Gentile should have equal rights and privileges with a Jew. It is new that both Jews and Gentiles should lose their national identities by becoming Christians. It is new that Jews and Gentiles should be fellow members of the body of Christ. It is new that a Jew should have the hope of reigning with Christ instead of being a subject in His kingdom. It is new that a Jew should no longer be under the law. The church is clearly a new creation, with a distinct calling and a distinct destiny, occupying a unique place in the purposes of God."

Notice that God is not making a new world but a new race of people whose citizenship is in heaven (Rom. 10:12). He made the church which is composed of individual new creations in Christ (2 Cor. 5:17). English poet John Oxenham wrote, "In Christ there is no east or west, in Him no south or north, but one great fellowship of love throughout the whole wide world." The barriers that separated the Jews and Gentiles were tore down at the cross and peace was established. The Jew's religion and all their ceremonial observances came to an end as did the Gentile's paganism. All the external things they were doing that separated them from God was put to death on the cross. Jesus removed the cause of their hostility and imparted in them a new spiritual nature. God miraculously raised up a new standard, people filled with the Spirit of God, people who have a divine relationship with God. The cross of Christ is God's answer to racial discrimination, bigotry, and every form of strife between men.

To have peace, all you have to do is die to yourself and allow Jesus Christ to live in you. You must willingly put the totality of yourself on the altar and allow yourself to be consumed by God. Rom. 12:1

says, "I beseech you therefore, brethren, by the mercies of God, that you present your bodies a living sacrifice, holy, acceptable to God, which is your reasonable service." The Message Bible says, "Embracing what God does for you is the best thing you can do for Him." This is how your sin nature gets buried with Christ. You can be raised up in newness of life in Christ and He can become your peace. Col. 3:11 (NLT) says, "Christ is all that matters, and He lives in all of us." His indwelling Spirit guarantees the gradual perfection of all who are called by His name. Col. 3:10 (NLT) says, "Put on your new nature; and be renewed as you learn to know your creator and become like Him." If you'll do that, He will be your peace both vertically with God and horizontally with one another.

Eph. 2:16 (NLT) says, "Together as one body, Christ reconciled both groups to God by means of His death on the cross, and our hostility toward each other was put to death." The Message Bible says, "The cross got us to embrace, and that was the end to the hostility." This is an intensified reconciliation and pictures the total, complete, and full restoration of the relationship between the Jews and Gentiles. Yes, in Christ there is reconciliation where all people come together in wonderful unity. If God can bring together the Jews and Gentiles, He can do the same with you and those you are in conflict with. Just remember, when sin runs rampant, there is discord because sin by definition is selfish. James 4:1 (NLT) says, "What is causing the quarrels and fights among you? Don't they come from the evil desires at war within you?" Where there is selfishness, there can never be peace and harmony. The only place where peace occurs is where self dies. And the only place where self dies is at the cross of Jesus Christ.

It is through the cross that God transforms hostile enemies into close friends. The cross on which Jesus died was an instrument of humiliation and was one of the most dreadful and agonizing means of torture known. The first century historian Josephus called crucifixion the "most wretched of deaths" and it was reserved for those who committed the most heinous of crimes. Death came slowly, sometimes taking several days for the criminal to die. Their death resulted from the accumulation of thirst, hunger, exhaustion, and the traumatic effect of being scourged with a whip. After death, the body was usually left hanging on the cross to decay and become food for the birds in the air. It was viewed as a shameful and dishonorable way to die. Jesus went to the cross for the betterment of all mankind. Through the cross, God killed the enmity, putting an end to the hostility that separated men from each other and from God. Jesus is the bridge that unites all people together.

The lesson to be learned here is very simple. If these two groups of people can come together in Christ and obey His commands concerning unity, certainly the church can do it today. There is now a kingdom of saints where gentiles have the same rights and privileges as the Jews. There can be unity when everybody has the same freedom to grow and improve their lives. Civil unrest happens when everybody don't have the same equal rights. The good news is that in the church, everybody has the same rights and privileges because all people come to God the same way, by the blood of Jesus. Col. 1:20-22 (NLT) says, "And through Him God reconciled everything to Himself. He made peace with everything in heaven and on earth by means of Christ's blood on the cross. This includes you who were once far away from God. You were His enemies, separated from Him by your evil thoughts and actions. Yet now He has reconciled you to Himself through the death of Christ in His physical body."

The war is over. There is now a peace treaty between you and God, a treaty signed with the blood of Jesus. Because of that, Christianity is a gospel of peace. It is peace that binds together what is broken and divided. True peace is oneness. It is not merely the cessation of hostility and the absence of conflict. It means being one, having joy and harmony with one another. Merely agreeing not to fight is not peace for without oneness all previous animosity will surely rise to the surface again. Before long, people will be upset, angry, and emotionally distraught. They won't be able to see straight, their perspective on life will be distorted, everything will be out of focus. In order to live in peace, you must have peace. You don't solve your differences in an effort to have peace. Stop being self-righteous and receive Jesus into your heart. Let Him be your peace and then you can start solving the conflicts around you. When Jesus makes peace, it will be satisfying, permanent, and genuine.

The secret to peace and oneness is found in the person of Jesus Christ. This is why Paul said in 2 Cor. 5:20, "We beseech you on behalf of Christ, be reconciled to God." Man's supreme fundamental need is peace with God. A person consumed by sin is restless and wretched and unhappy throughout his entire being. Why? Because built into wickedness is the impossibility of peace. God said in Is. 57:20.21 (NLT), "But those who still reject Me are like the restless sea, which is never still but continually churns up mud and dirt. There is no peace for the wicked." The sea is always restless because it is continually pulled to and fro by opposing forces. The sea is acted upon by the gravitational pull of the moon and by the magnetic force that is in the heart of the earth. The result of this is that the sea is in constant motion. The wind arises and a mighty, powerful storm takes place doing great damage to people and buildings that are in its path.

The wicked are like the troubled sea that cannot rest. The cause of this is the same explanation as the state of the sea. Man was made by God in paradise and there was no motion or restlessness there. Adam was in communion with God, and his life was a mixture of peace and heavenly bliss. No problems or unhappiness was there. There was no trouble, no anxiety, no tossing of the waves. Man was in a state of innocence and absolute peace and tranquility. There was only one force pulling on the heartstrings of man. God. Unfortunately, man fell when he listened to another power and another force. In listening, he became subject to it. The force of evil consumed him and since that time man's life has been one of restlessness and turmoil. Thankfully, God gave every person a conscience. They've been given a way to know right from wrong, good from evil. They've been given a sense of God and deep inside their heart they know they were meant for something better.

Jesus is the evangelist of peace. Eph. 2:17 says, "And He came and preached peace to you who were afar off and to those who were near." Did you observe the progression here? Eph. 2:14 says Christ is peace, vs. 15 says He made peace, and here it says He preached peace. His message to the world is peace. At His birth the angels appeared in the sky and the first thing they say is, "Glory to God in the highest, and on earth peace, good will toward men!" (Luke 2:14). Almost like an aura around Jesus was the concept of peace. In Luke 10, He sent seventy people out two by two and He said, "But whatever house you enter, first say, 'Peace to this house'" (vs. 5). That was always the message God was offering in Christ. Peace. Peace with Him and peace with one another. The night before His death, Jesus said to the disciples, "Peace I leave with you; My peace I give to you" (John 14:27). He said in John 16:33, "These things I have spoken to you, that in Me you may have peace."

The word "preached" means 'to announce good news, to bring glad tidings.' Preaching is never an argument or a debate. It's simply the announcement of a fact. You can either accept it or reject it, but you can never quarrel with it. Paul is saying Christ "gospelized peace" to both Jews and Gentiles. Jesus began His ministry by quoting Is. 61:1, "The Spirit of the Lord God is upon Me, because the Lord has anointed Me to preach good tidings to the poor; He has sent Me to heal the brokenhearted, to proclaim liberty to the captives, and the opening of the prison to those who are bound." Peace was His personal message after His resurrection. He went to His disciples and stood in the midst of them and said, "Peace be with you" (John 20:19). He said to them again in vs. 21, "Peace to you! As the Father has sent

Me, I also send you." Eight days later, He appeared to them again and said the same thing, "Peace to you!" (vs. 26). With Jesus, peace was always the message.

| 20 |

"ACCESS TO THE FATHER"

Paul is showing the saints at Ephesus the greatness and the glory and the wonder of their position as members of the family of God. He emphasizes the point that they are standing there side-by-side with the Jews, no longer considered outsiders and aliens to the promises of God. He prayed in Eph. 1:18 that the eyes of their understanding would be enlightened. He knew that most of the problems in a believer's life are due to the fact that people fail to realize the great privileges they have being a Christian. Most of your problems, if not all of them, would fall by the wayside if you would rise to the height of your calling in Christ Jesus. So high is your royal position in Christ that your problems aren't worthy of your consideration. This is the theme of every New Testament epistle. Surely, there is nothing more important than to realize your position in Christ. 1 Peter 2:9 (WNT) says, "But you are a chosen race, a priesthood of kingly lineage, a holy nation, a people belonging specially to God."

Paul then makes one of the mightiest and most glorious statements in all the Bible. Eph. 2:18 says, "For through Him we both have access by one Spirit to the Father." This is by far the most stunning thing he could have said to these people. They were once far off but now they have access to the Father. The greatness of this statement is unimaginable. It's the grand climax of all the teachings about Christianity. There's nothing beyond this. When you read this verse, you're standing on the summit of spiritual revelation. You've arrived at the grand plateau and now you're looking with astonishment and amazement at the height to which you have been brought. British minister Martyn Lloyd-Jones said, "The statement of this verse is not only stupendous, it is staggering. The trouble with us is we don't realize the meaning of things like this. Were we to do so, the Christian church would be revolutionized. We would be lost in a sense of wonder, love, and praise."

The word "access" is a beautiful word and it's used only three times in the New Testament, here in Eph. 2:8, in Eph. 3:12, and in Rom. 5:2. The Greek word "prosagage" literally means 'a bringing near.' It describes a continuous and unhindered approach to God. The word was used in ancient times for the person who introduced somebody to the king. You don't come in your own strength, but in the strength of the introducer. Jesus said, "I am the door of the sheep" (John 10:7). He also said in John 14:6, "I am the way, the truth, and the life. No one comes to the Father except through Me." He is the access by whom you can now cry out, "Abba, Father" (Rom. 8:18). The word "Abba" means 'Daddy; Papa.' God is a loving Father who receives you with open arms. The word "access" is also a picture of fellowship and communion. Because of the cross, you can now go to Him with boldness (Heb. 4:16). Never do you have to fear going into the presence of God. Be afraid if you don't.

Through Christ, by one Spirit, you have an introduction to the Father. In the Old Testament, no person ever knew God as Father. As a result of the cross, what was unthinkable with the Jews in ancient times is now available to all who come to Christ by grace through faith. Rom. 5:1,2 says, "Therefore, having been justified by faith, we have peace with God through our Lord Jesus Christ, through whom also we have access by faith into this grace in which we stand, and rejoice in hope of the glory of God." The Message Bible says, "By entering through faith into what God has always wanted to do for us, we have it all together with God because of our Master Jesus. We throw open our doors to God and discover at the same moment that He has already thrown open His door to us. We find ourselves standing where we always hoped we might stand - out in the wide open spaces of God's grace and glory, standing tall and shouting our praise."

1 Peter 3:18 says, "For Christ also suffered once for sins, the just for the unjust, that He might bring us to God." The grand purpose of salvation, its ultimate goal, is to bring you into the presence of God so that you would know Him as your Father. Jesus said in John 17:3, "And this is eternal life, that they may know You, the only true God, and Jesus Christ whom You have sent." Reconciliation is amazing but this is even more amazing. Through Christ, God becomes your Father and you now have access to Him. The friendly relationship with God the Father is now restored whereby you are accepted by Him and have the assurance He is favorably disposed toward you. Are you enjoying this access? Are you taking advantage of it? Do you approach the Father with full assurance of faith? Are you boldly going into His presence? Most of all, are you enjoying your relationship with Him? That's the purpose of salvation. You're here to glorify God and enjoy Him forever.

In this verse you're also brought face-to-face with the mystery of the blessed Holy Trinity. The Father, the Son, and the Holy Spirit are mentioned together in this one verse. Three in one! Eternal in their glory and their holiness and their might. It's a mystery that can't be explained but must be believed. What's more, all three are interested in you and are engaged together on your behalf. Paul explained in chapter one that you were chosen by the Father, redeemed by the Son, and sealed by the Spirit. All three are working in beautiful harmony together, all working toward the same end, that the people of God may have access. This is the most marvelous thing you'll ever hear in time or eternity. The three persons of the Trinity have acted on your behalf so that you may be redeemed and escape eternal judgment. If you would realize this as you ought to, its effect upon your life would be endless. It would change your whole concept of Christianity.

Paul now tells of the overwhelming advantages and privileges that belong to the Gentiles by virtue of Christ's work on the cross. He began by reminding them what they once were, he now tells them what they now have. He sums up their new position in Christ, joyously proclaiming that a complete and permanent change has taken place. Listen carefully because what Paul is about to say applies to you also. "Now therefore, you are no longer strangers and foreigners, but fellow citizens with the saints and members of the household of God" (Eph. 2:19). The Message Bible says, "You're no longer wandering exiles. This kingdom of faith is now your home country. You're no longer strangers or outsiders. You belong here, with as much right to the name Christian as anyone." There are few things more necessary in life than for you to grasp what Paul is saying here. If people understood who they are in Christ, they would know what to do in the midst of all their problems.

Too many people wrestle with terrible anxieties, fears, and hostilities which prevent them from acting as God intended them to. This is why Paul is laboring here to get you to understand and discover the full resources which are available in Christ Jesus. Ray Stedman said, "Please discard the notion many have that this is only magnificent language. It is not merely language; it is reality. Take these words literally and plainly and personally, because this is what will enable us to understand what to do when we get into difficulty, how to handle problems, and how to work out relationships which are strained or broken. It is with these great resources that we can solve these problems." Paul paints three beautiful pictures in this passage that are designed to teach great truths about what it means to be a Christian. All believers have been made one body with no division or separation. His words are designed to instruct you so that his prayer in the first chapter will be answered.

Paul begins by saying "you are no longer strangers and foreigners." The Greek word for "stranger" is "xenos" and it refers to somebody who's an outcast, a person who's wretched, vial, and rotten. A stranger is characterized by not knowing much about the place where he is at. He doesn't know what to do or where to go because he is ignorant of the resources in that particular community, of its advantages and cultural possibilities. Spiritually speaking, the Gentile had no idea about peace and joy and forgiveness. They knew nothing about the capacity to handle their fears and hostilities. They didn't know what to do with their troubles and were utter strangers in knowing how to handle them. They were strangers to the kingdom of God, having a totally depraved nature that made them different, and different in a hostile way. The Jews wanted to keep these people a far distance from them. But no more. They've come to Christ and are no longer strangers and foreigners.

A foreigner is different from a stranger. A stranger is a person on the outside looking in whereas a foreigner is a person you bring into your house as a guest. He may be very familiar with the country in which he lives but he is not a citizen there. He is an alien, living on a passport. He has no birth certificate which makes him a citizen of the land. In a time of crisis, aliens are deported and sent back to their home country. They are not permitted to enter into the full rights of citizens of the land. Paul says when you come to Christ, you are no longer a stranger or foreigner. You're not a wretched outcast who wouldn't be brought into somebody's house nor are you a houseguest with no rights. So what are you? Fellow citizens with the saints and members of the household of God. There are no strangers or houseguests in God's family. You have entered a new kingdom. You've changed your citizenship and are now under another authority.

Being under authority is the first mark of citizenship. This authority regulates certain areas of your life, whether you like it or not. If you step outside the boundary lines which have been set, then this authority can step in and take your freedom away from you. There are two kingdoms in the spiritual world and every person belongs to one of them. There is the kingdom of God and the kingdom of Satan. You will be under the authority of whichever one you choose to follow. You need to realize that the one you submit to will have ultimate dominion over your life. Doesn't it make sense that you surrender your life to God and come under His authority? Consider the words of Jesus in John 10:10, "The thief does not come except to steal, and to kill, and to destroy. I have come that they may have life, and that they may have it more abundantly." When you became a Christian, God "called you out of darkness into His marvelous light" (1 Peter 2:9).

Paul addresses those who have been saved in Phil. 3:20, saying, "For our citizenship is in heaven, from which we also eagerly wait for our Savior, the Lord Jesus Christ." Here on earth, all believers are a colony of heavenly citizens. This planet is not your home, it's not your permanent location. Col. 1:13 says, "He has delivered us from the power of darkness and translated us into the kingdom of the Son of His love." The Message Bible says, "God rescued us from dead-end alleys and dark dungeons. He's set us up in the kingdom of the Son He loves so much." In other words, you've been relocated. Heaven is your true home. It's where you're going once your life on this planet is over. Live every day with your eyes focused totally on that spiritual reality. You're a citizen of heaven on temporary assignment on earth. You live up there but work down here. This is why you have to prioritize the spiritual and eternal things in your life and minimize the natural and temporal.

Always be heavenly-minded. Look forward with eagerness to the day you'll stand face-to-face with your great and mighty Heavenly Father, the loving and caring Lord Jesus Christ, and the always amazing Holy Spirit. Col. 3:2 says, "Set your mind on things above, not on things on the earth." Why should you do this? Because the greater your expectation of heaven, the better your life will be here on earth. Expectation affects behavior. If you want to maximize your time on earth, you must live your life with eternity forever on your mind. You need to have an eternal perspective about life. Paul said in Phil. 3:13,14, "One thing I do, forgetting those things which are behind and reaching forward to those things which are ahead. I press toward the goal for the prize of the upward call of God in Christ Jesus." The Message Bible says, "I'm off and running and I'm not turning back." He's saying if you want to get to tomorrow, you must be heavenly minded and let the pains of yesterday go.

Too many people let their lives be crippled because of what happened in their past. Don't let that happen to you. Your yesterday doesn't have to define your tomorrow. You're a citizen of heaven, not a slave to this earth. Forget about yesterday and press on to the good things which are ahead. Don't be chained to yesterday and don't allow it to stop you from fulfilling your destiny. Your future is not determined by the good, the bad, and the ugly of yesterday. It's determined by the will of God, His plan for your life, and your willingness to submit to that plan. The children of Israel never made it into the Promised Land because they kept looking back to Egypt. They lost sight of where God wanted to take them. They kept looking back and never went anywhere except to the grave. You need to press on in the wilderness until God breaks through and takes you to the Promised Land of spiritual maturity and divine purpose. Press on to a bright future.

Learn from yesterday. Remember where you came from and all the good things God did for you. But, by all means, don't live there. Be heavenly minded and let thoughts of the future consume your thinking. Meditate on all the glorious things God has planned for your life. Place the eternal above the temporal. Make heaven your focus and God's will your purpose. The country in which you belong is not here on earth. You were redeemed for up there while living down here. God expects you to take the things of heaven and bring them down here to the earth. That's your mission in life, your destiny. Jesus prayed, "Thy kingdom come, Thy will be done, on earth as it is in heaven" (Matt. 6:10). These words express the prayerful desire of Jesus to see the Father's kingdom broaden and become increasingly established throughout the world. Have the mindset to recognize God's kingdom purposes and apply yourself with furthering those purposes.

If you are in Christ, you have a citizenship that far outweighs any citizenship on the earth. Paul is saying that Christians are a distinct people, separated from all others. They are in the world but are not of the world. They belong to a different kingdom and are bound together by a common allegiance to a King and His supreme authority and His way of life. They have the same interests and obey the same laws. This, in turn, gives the saints a common allegiance to one another. All believers are citizens of heaven and they need to consistently act like it here on earth. Jesus said, "I am a king but My kingdom is not of this world" (John 18:36,37). Where is His kingdom? Wherever He reigns! He reigns in heaven and on earth and in the hearts of His people. He is your Prophet and your Priest and your King. All who recognize His rule and vow their allegiance to Him are citizens of His eternal kingdom, a kingdom that is going to last forever and ever.

Think about it. You're a citizen of a place whose streets are paved with gold, a place where the glory of God illuminates the entire universe. Rev. 22:5 says, "And there shall be no night there. They need no lamp nor light of the sun, for the Lord God gives them light. And they shall reign forever and ever." In heaven there is no sorrow, no pain, and no more tears. Indeed, heaven is a special place and only those written in the Lamb's Book of Life will be there (Rev. 20:15). This book contains the names of those who have been redeemed by the blood of the Lord Jesus, the names of those who will live with God forever in heaven. The Book of Life is also mentioned in Phil. 4:3, Rev. 3:5, and Rev. 20:12. Rejoice that right now, here on the earth, if you're saved, you're a citizen of heaven. What's more, Paul goes beyond that and says the saints at Ephesus are now members of the household of God.

They're not only fellow citizens, but they're also now family. They're joint-heirs, children of the Father.

Heb. 2:11 (NLT) says, "So now Jesus and the ones He makes holy have the same Father. That is why Jesus is not ashamed to call them His brothers and sisters." The provision and protection of a father is always more intimate and personal than that of a king. A king is concerned about your general welfare whereas a father wants to know all about your intimate problems. Jesus said, 'Do you not know that your heavenly Father knows that you have need of these things? He even knows the number of the hairs on your head" (Luke 12:30; Matt. 10:30). God said in Zech. 2:8, "He who touches you touched the apple of My eye." Can anything be closer than that? Paul is saying, "You are not guests or occasional visitors but permanent dwellers in the house and members of the family, equal in every spiritual way before God." The point is this: if God can accept everybody regardless of social and personal position, then surely you also ought to do the same.

Thirdly, Paul says the Jews and Gentiles are built together as a holy temple. Eph. 2:20-22 (NLT) says, "Together, we are His house, built on the foundation of the apostles and the prophets. And the cornerstone is Christ Jesus Himself. We are carefully joined together in Him, becoming a holy temple for the Lord. Through Him you Gentiles are also being made part of this dwelling where God lives by His Spirit." Paul is stressing the closeness of the members of the very habitation of God, a closeness to one another and to the Lord. In the figure of a building, no separation of stones which make up the walls is possible. Everything is closely joined and knit together. If the stones were separated, the building would crumble. This building becomes the body of Christ, the dwelling place where the Spirit of God lives. The faith and teaching of the apostles and prophets is the foundation the church rests upon. Paul said in 1 Cor. 3:10, "I have laid the foundation, and another builds on it."

The apostles and prophets were themselves not the foundation, but rather they laid the foundation. They taught the world about Jesus, that He was God in the flesh come down to save man from the horror and penalty of sin. The word "apostle" means 'one sent forth by another, often with a special commission to represent another and to accomplish his work.' In a sense, all followers of Christ are called to be apostles. All are to be His ambassadors (2 Cor. 5:8-10), all are to be ones who are sent out (Acts 1:8), and all are to be preachers of the good news (Rom. 10:15). The Greek word "prophetes" means 'one who speaks forth; an advocate.' Prophets speak under divine influence and inspiration, foretelling future events or exhorting, reproving, and admonishing individuals or nations as the interpreter of God's will to men. 2 Peter 1:21 says, "For prophecy never came by the will of man, but holy men of God spoke as they were moved by the Holy Spirit."

Paul describes Jesus as the chief cornerstone on which His church would be built upon. 1 Cor. 2:11 says, "For no other foundation can anyone lay than that which is laid, which is Jesus Christ." The cornerstone was the major stone the builders used in their construction projects. It had to be so large and solid that it could support the rest of the structure. It had to be accurate because the walls were all conformed to the angle of that stone. The cornerstone framed everything, the one thing everything else was adapted. The cornerstone was the support, the connector, and the strength giver. Paul is saying Jesus is to be your standard of measure and alignment. God said in Is. 28:16, "Behold, I lay in Zion a stone for a foundation, a tried stone, a precious cornerstone, a sure foundation." Jesus was chosen by God and precious to Him (1 Peter 2:4). 1 Peter 2:6 calls Jesus "a chief cornerstone, elect, precious, and he who believes on Him will by no means be put to shame."

As the chief cornerstone, Jesus is the sole source of the church's life and growth. Each member has a specific place for which they are exactly suited. When God builds His church, all the pieces fit perfectly. it is solid, cohesive, snug, and firm. Every stone is fitted into its proper place without defect. No stone is out of place, broken, loose, or ill-arranged. The temple is perfect because it has to be. If God is going to build a temple in which He will dwell, then it has to be a perfect temple. For sure, God doesn't dwell in an imperfect place. If you are the temple of God, if He dwells in your heart, then, positionally, you are perfect. 1 Peter 2:5 says you are living stones built together, firmly fitted in exact perfection to be the dwelling place of the Spirit of God. As a member of the household of God, "you are God's building" (1 Cor. 3:9). You are a living stone that is neither broken, marred, or inadequate. Everyone is perfect and fitted together by the Master Builder.

| 21 |

"THE GIFT OF SUFFERING"

T he apostle Paul had a unique, one-of-a-kind calling on his life. God used him to share tremendous insight into divine truths that had not been known by the holy men of old. These truths came under the figure of a mystery, a sacred secret never before revealed until now, secrets about Christ, about the church, about the Spirit of God. 1 Peter 1:10 (NLT) says, "This salvation was something even the prophets wanted to know more about when they prophesied about this gracious salvation prepared for you." There were things they didn't know and couldn't understand. One of those mysteries is that the church would be made up of Jew and Gentile, bond and free, male and female. In the Old Testament, the Jews understood that the Gentiles would be saved, that they would participate in the kingdom. What they didn't understand is that Jew and Gentile would literally be one, that there would be no difference between the two, that they would be equal before God. That was the mystery.

The unity of the church is one of the primary messages of the entire New Testament. It grieves God that the church is fragmented and divisive, how believers fight and quarrel among each other. It grieves Him when they don't "keep the unity of the Spirit in the bond pf peace" (Eph. 4:3). Therefore, it should come as no surprise that Paul goes to such great lengths to emphasize to the saints at Ephesus their place of equality with the Jews in the body of Christ. He wants to be sure these Gentile believers don't take their new found salvation for granted. He wants them to have a good, healthy, and proper appreciation and sense of gratitude for what Jesus did for them on the cross. Paul knows when these truths are grasped, they will pick up their cross and follow Jesus fully and without shame. What he's saying to them will radically impact their conduct to the point they'll be motivated to walk worthy of their new calling in Christ. He knows a bright and exciting future awaits them all.

Paul starts to pray for these Gentile believers in Eph. 3:1 when suddenly a Holy Spirit inspired interruption takes place. It causes him to say, "Wait a minute. I can't pray for you just yet. I'm not sure you understand the mystery." So, in vs. 2-13, he goes back over this whole mystery again. Yes, he did it in chapter 2 and now he's going to do it again here in chapter 3. Why does he repeat himself? Because that's how you learn. Repetition is the mother of learning. Is. 28:10 says, "Precept upon precept, line upon line, here a little, there a little." You can't apply what you don't understand. This is why Rom. 12:2 says your mind has to be renewed. You've got to comprehend it and then you have to walk it out. And so, he's going to go over the mystery once again knowing if they'll understand it, their change of lifestyle would take care of itself. Paul begins his narrative in vs. 1, saying, "For this reason I, Paul, the prisoner of Jesus Christ for you Gentiles."

Paul looks back to what he just told them about their new privileges as a result of their union with Christ. He's referring to the astounding truth which has come to light that Gentiles have been made one body with the Jews in Christ Jesus. After saying this, Paul clearly wants to say something else but he stops, he hesitates. Why did he do this? Why did he suddenly stop and go off on a detour? Why did he interrupt his own prayer? Yes, he wants them to fully understand the mystery that was revealed to him. He was writing in order to help these people, to encourage them in the faith, to establish them, to lead them to the highest heights of this wonderful salvation. It was his concern for others that was his most outstanding trait as a messenger of the gospel. He knew these saints would be troubled that he was a prisoner in Rome so he said in vs. 13, "Therefore I ask that you do not lose heart at my tribulation for you, which is your glory."

Paul doesn't want his pain and suffering to be a stumbling block to these people. It is no secret that people get confused and apprehensive when it comes to the subject of suffering. Why does God allow His own people to go through trial and tribulation? Why do bad things happen to good people? Why do the servants of God suffer for doing the work He called them to do? Why should such a distinguished servant of God like Paul be allowed to suffer like he so often did? He told of the glorious blessings of being members of the family of God and yet here he was a prisoner for the sake of the gospel. Paul often wrote about his sufferings in his writings. He wrote about it in his letter to the Philippians and in his writings to Timothy in particular. Paul knows the concerns of the Ephesians and he doesn't write them a word of comfort. Instead, he tells them how he himself looks at what he's going through. He wants them to see things through his perspective.

Why do good people suffer? First of all, you must have the conviction that God can use bad things for the betterment of His people and the situations they find themselves in. Joseph told his brothers who had sold him into slavery, "You meant evil against me; but God meant it for good, in order to bring it about as it is this day, to save many people alive" (Ge. 50:20). If you will endure hardship, you'll soon find that your suffering will eventually bring forth patience (Heb. 10:36; James 1:3), joy (Ps. 30:5; 126:6), knowledge (Ps. 94:12), and maturity (1 Peter 5;10). Suffering will refine your life and make you a better person (Ps. 66:10-12; Prov. 17:3; 1 Peter 1:6,7). It can be used to glorify God (John 9:1-3; 11:1-4) and it helps to make you more like Jesus (Phil. 3:10). It teaches you to depend on God for all things (2 Cor. 12:1-10). It will also enlarge your ministry toward others (2 Cor. 1:3-7). It has been observed that he who has suffered much speaks many languages.

In the Bible there are four examples of godly men who suffered for the sake of righteousness. Joseph was hated by his brothers (Gen. 37:4,5,8), sold into slavery (Gen. 37:28), was severely tempted (Gen. 39:7), and was imprisoned for a crime he didn't commit (Gen. 39:20). Everybody knows Job suffered greatly. His oxen and donkeys were stolen and his farmhands killed (Job 1:14,15), his sheep and herdsmen were burned by a fire (Job 1:16), his camels were stolen and his servants killed (Job 1:17), his sons and daughters died in a windstorm (Job 1:18,19), and he was covered with boils from head to toe (Job 2:7). What's more, his wife told him to curse God and die (Job 2:9). Jeremiah also suffered, so much so that he is often referred to as "the weeping prophet." He was persecuted by his own family (Jer. 12:6), plotted against by his own hometown (Jer. 11:18-23), rejected and ridiculed by his religious peers (Jer. 20:1-3), and was arrested, beaten, and accused of treason (Jer. 37:11-16).

In the New Testament, who suffered more than the apostle Paul? He was plotted against (Acts 9:23), stoned and left for dead (Acts 14:9), was subject to satanic pressure (1 Thess. 2:18), beaten and jailed (Acts 16:19-24), ridiculed (Acts 17:16-18), and falsely accused (Acts 24:5-9). He endured a number of violent storms at sea (2 Cor. 11:25; Acts 27:14-20), was bitten by a serpent (Acts 28:3,4), and was forsaken by all (2 Tim. 4:10,16). What's interesting about all this is at no time does Paul complain about what he's going through. He doesn't grumble nor does he ask if it's fair what's happening to him. He doesn't say, "That's how life is. You have to take the good with the bad." Also, he wasn't captured by the selfish condition of self-pity. Self-pity exaggerates whatever misfortune that comes your way. It causes you to get lost in yourself as it destroys your life, your relationships, and your walk with God.

Like Paul, there is a divine call on your life and you'll have to wage war against those forces that try to stop you from answering that call. Once this war begins, you'll quickly realize that there is no enemy that is greater or stronger than self-pity. This selfish condition has ruined more lives than sex, drugs, and rock-and-roll put together. It's what causes you to focus on yourself as if you were the center of the universe. The by-product of that is you're not focusing on God and serving others. If you're captured by self-pity, someone else will always be to blame for what you're going through. You'll point an accusing finger at everyone except yourself. Self-pity is destructive by nature. It leads a person to give up or settle for a mediocre Christian experience as it deals a crushing blow to the contentment God would have you enjoy. Thankfully, Paul was unshakable as he refused to buckle under the weight of self-pity.

If you'll read the third chapter of Ephesians carefully, you'll see that Paul is rejoicing in the midst of his tribulations. There's a note of triumphant exaltation in his words, an expression of calm delight. Paul knows his afflictions have promoted the gospel as evidenced by what he said in Phil. 1:12, "But I want you to know, brethren, that the things which happened to me have actually turned out for the furtherance of the gospel." The Message Bible says, "My imprisonment has had the opposite of its intended effect. Instead of being squelched, the Message has actually prospered." In a sense he's saying, "Thank God for the suffering." He told Timothy, "For God has not given us a spirit of fear, but of power and of love and of a sound mind" (2 Tim. 1:7). He then said in 2 Tim. 2:3, "You therefore must endure hardness as a good soldier of Jesus Christ." There was no better man than Paul to give advice about endurance while suffering for the Lord."

The truth be told, Christians should not be taken by surprise when hardships come. Jesus warned in John 16:33, "In the world you will have tribulation." The good news is He followed this warning with a word of encouragement, "But be of good cheer, I have overcome the world." In other words, you can endure by His grace and nobody knew that better than Paul. To endure is more than just continuing to exist. It means "to not be moved by what's happening to you; to continue what you were doing before the suffering began; to remain firm without yielding or giving in though it is difficult." Paul's response to suffering was not to buckle under the weight of his circumstances but to press on and keep proclaiming the gospel message. Heb. 10:38 says, "Now the just shall live by faith; But if anyone draws back, My soul has no pleasure in him." Even Jesus said in Luke 9:62, "No one, having put his hand to the plow, and looking back, is fit for the kingdom of God."

1 Peter 2:14 (MSG) says, "If you're abused because of Christ, count yourself fortunate. It's the Spirit of God and His glory in you that brought you to the notice of others." Why is Paul now a prisoner in Rome? Because he is no longer Saul of Tarsus. He is a changed man. He is now Paul the apostle, sent on a mission to preach the gospel message to non-Jews. He is now "in Christ" and this makes him a "prisoner of Jesus Christ." He wasn't Caesar's captive, he was Christ's captive. In life, perspective is everything. It's how you look at something that matters. Is your cup half empty or half full? Perspective. That's why you count it all joy when you fall into diverse trials (James 1:2). When you're persecuted for righteousness sake, the grace and glory of God rests on you. Paul's chains belonged to Rome but his heart belonged to Christ. He lived for one thing, to serve Jesus. He said in 2 Cor. 5:14, "The love of Christ controls me." He knew Caesar was not in control. Jesus is.

Paul is a prisoner in Rome but he is not bound in his spirit. He's soaring in the heavenlies with Christ proving that one's perspective makes all the difference in the world. Paul was a man on a mission. He was an example of having a single-minded determination to fulfill the call of God on one's life. It will do you well to imitate his zeal as you press on in life to fulfill your destiny. Whatever you do, don't let the fear of persecution cause you to drop the ball and walk away from your calling. The trials that imprison you need not limit God's work in you. It will do you well to realize it is an honor to suffer on behalf of Christ. Phil. 1:29 says, "For to you it has been granted on behalf of Christ, not only to believe in Him, but also to suffer for His sake." The Message Bible says, "And the suffering is as much a gift as the trusting." The NLT says, "For you have been given not only the privilege of trusting in Christ but also the privilege of suffering for Him."

When people think of the blessings of God, they often think of prosperity, good health, and divine favor. Who would ever think that suffering would be a blessing bestowed on you? Surprisingly enough, that is precisely what Paul is saying here. He's saying it was granted on your behalf to suffer for Christ's sake. The Greek word translated "granted" signifies 'a gift of grace; a privilege; a favor.' Paul is saying two things have been graciously bestowed upon the believer: salvation and suffering. People are quick to believe their salvation is attributed to the grace of God, yet they're slow to realize that suffering is also a gift of grace. The disciples had this perspective in Acts 5:41, "So they departed from the presence of the council, rejoicing that they were counted worthy to suffer shame for His name." They knew that suffering was freely bestowed upon them as a gracious gift. Think about it. God loves you so much that He rewards your faithfulness with the gift of suffering. Amazing.

Look at it this way: Faith in Christ is the means of salvation, suffering is the visible sign of salvation. Jesus said in Matt. 10:22, "And you will be hated by all for My name's sake. But he who endures to the end will be saved." Keep in mind the scriptural principle that the cross always precedes the crown. You'll have temporal suffering now but eternal glory in the hereafter (2 Cor. 4:17; Rom. 8:18). 2 Tim. 2:12 (NLT) says, "If we endure hardship, we will reign with Him. If we deny Him, He will deny us." The Message Bible says, "If we stick it out with Him, we'll rule with Him." Notice that the gift of suffering is for Christ's sake. A lot of suffering is self-made, the result of sinful behavior and wrong actions. This is not the quality of suffering Paul is referring to here. When you suffer, ask yourself the question, "For whose sake am I suffering? My own or Christ's?" In other words, don't suffer for the wrong reason.

Paul described in 2 Cor. 8:2 (NLT) the privilege the Macedonia church had in suffering for Christ, "They are being tested by many troubles, and they are very poor. But they are also filled with abundant joy, which has overflowed in rich generosity." The Message Bible says, "Fierce troubles came down on the people of those churches, pushing them to the very limit. The trial exposed their true colors: They were incredibly happy, though desperately poor. The pressure triggered something totally unexpected: an outpouring of pure and generous gifts." Bible commentator John Lightfoot said, "When God has granted one the high privilege of suffering for His Name, it is one of the surest signs that He looks upon you with favor because to suffer for Christ (in the interest of His cause) is a favor granted only to those who believe in Him." Persecution is a believer's privilege. Is it not remarkable that suffering is exalted by Christianity to such a lofty plane?

Sad to say, suffering for Christ's sake is not for everybody. Many people shun suffering like they do the plague. Charles Spurgeon said, "It is not every Christian who receives this mark of honor. There are some believers who have peculiarly tender places in their hearts, and who are wounded and gashed by the unkind remarks of those who love them, not because they love the Lord Jesus Christ." The truth be told, faith and suffering go together. Paul is saying you first believe in Him, and then you suffer for Him. It's the strength of your faith that gives you the endurance to suffer for His Name's sake. Faith is a lifestyle. To "believe in Him" literally means to 'continually believe in Him.' The flame of faith is dynamic. It never ends or fizzles out. This capacity to keep on believing is a gift of grace from God, not something you stir up in your heart. You continue to believe because this privilege has been granted to you by God.

It is a divine privilege to be permitted to believe on Christ because it is by faith that sins are forgiven, that you are reconciled to God, and have hope of heaven. W. E. Vine said Biblical belief is "a firm conviction which produces full acknowledgement of God's revelation of truth (2 Thess. 2:11,12), a personal surrender to the truth (John 1:12), a conduct inspired by and consistent with that surrender (2 Cor. 5:7)." You begin your new life in Christ by faith and then you continue living in the same faith that got you saved. This is how you endure when you are called upon to suffer for His name's sake. You need to understand that suffering for Christ is your spiritual birthright. God not only graciously allowed you to believe in the name of Christ, He has also graciously allowed you to suffer on behalf of Christ. When suffering for Christ is properly understood, it will most certainly become real to you that it is indeed a privilege. Because of all these sufferings, eternity becomes a victorious experience.

What did Jesus say about suffering? He said in Matt. 5:11,12, "Blessed are you when they revile and persecute you, and say all kinds of evil against you falsely for My sake. Rejoice and be exceedingly glad, for great is your reward in heaven, for so they persecuted the prophets who were before you." When you suffer, the Message Bible says "all heaven applauds." The Greek word for "rejoice" is "agalliao" and it means 'jump; gush; leap; spring up.' It means literally to 'jump much; leap for joy; skip and jump with happy excitement; to be exceedingly joyful; overjoyed; and exuberantly happy.' It describes jubilant exaltation, a quality of joy that remains unhindered and unchanged by what happens. It is an exceeding joy, independent of dire circumstances, which is initiated and empowered by the Holy Spirit. It is the joy of the mountain climber who has reached the summit and leaps for joy because the path to the top of the mountain has been conquered.

Learning the truth about suffering prepares you to persevere with praise when persecution comes in its various forms. It will transform you from being a coward to having great courage. The truth be told, suffering is one of the tools God uses to mold His children into vessels that bring glory to His Son (1 Peter 1:6,7). In fact, suffering even perfected the Lord Jesus (Heb. 2:16). You can rejoice because there is grace that comes from your grief, promises you can claim in the midst of your hardships. James 1:2-4 says suffering causes you to grow in Christ and become mature in Him. Suffering helps keep down pride (2 Cor. 12:7) as it weans you from self-reliance (2 Cor. 1:19). Suffering is an evangelistic tool (Phil. 1:12) as it helps you to minister to others (2 Cor. 1:3,4). It increases your eternal reward (Matt. 5:12) and, most of all, it shows you belong to Christ. Phil. 3:10 (NLT) says, "I want to know Christ and experience the mighty power that raised Him from the dead. I want to suffer with Him, sharing in His death."

A willingness to suffer for Christ's sake has been lost in today's Christian church. Believers today are not like the saints of old who considered this the supreme honor of their lives. The early Christians thanked God that at last they'd been accounted worthy to suffer for His name's sake. They praised God as they were dying in the arena, as they were mauled and eaten by hungry lions. The final crown of glory for them was martyrdom. Albert Barnes said in his commentary, "It is a privilege thus to suffer in the cause of Christ, because we then resemble the Lord Jesus, and are united with Him in trials; because we have evidence that we are His, if trials come upon us in His cause; because we are engaged in a good cause, and the privilege of maintaining such a cause is worth much suffering; and because it will be connected with a brighter crown and more exalted honor in heaven." Go to God and allow your suffering to be a tool in His hand.

| 22 |

"THE DAY OF RECKONING"

Paul calls himself the prisoner of Jesus Christ. Whose prisoner are you? Who, or what, is in charge of your life? Are you a fatalist, believing that all events are predetermined and therefore inevitable? If not that, are you a determinist? Do you believe that all events, including human action, are ultimately determined by causes external to the will? Do you believe that people are victims of circumstance? This is how most of the world thinks. Whatever will be, will be. Life determines what happens to you and there is nothing you can do about it. Did Paul feel this way? Not in a million years. He didn't consider himself a prisoner of Caesar, he considered himself a prisoner of Jesus Christ. He had no bitterness or self-pity because of the perspective he had. He's saying that Jesus is in charge of his life, not people or circumstances, and certainly not Rome. Don't get bent out of shape when trials come your way. Have the perspective that God is sovereign and in control of everything in your life.

The first weapon against self-pity is perspective. Sad to say, people betray their belief in Christ by always taking about the hardships they're going through. They think God is almighty and powerful until something bad happens to them. They suddenly begin to live and react contrary to what they were declaring before the storm hit. There's too much negative talk coming out of the mouths of believers. They say Jesus is Lord of their life but all they talk about is their trials and tribulations. The problem is they're listening to the voice of the enemy which is found in the words Pontius Pilate spoke to Jesus in John 19:10, "Do You not know that I have power to crucify You, and power to release You?" He was saying he was in charge, or so he thought. Unfortunately, that's the same voice many people give in to. They then begin to speak about how hard life is and how they're overwhelmed by what's happening to them. These people are prisoners of their circumstances.

Here in Eph. 3:1, Paul is saying Jesus is in charge of his life. With faith and confidence, he boldly proclaimed that he was a prisoner of Jesus Christ. Caesar was not in charge and neither were the guards who watched over him. He knew his Lord had authority even over Rome. This is why Jesus answered Pilate, "You could have no power at all against Me unless it had been given you from above" (John 19:11). The world today wants you to see yourself as a victim of your circumstances, your past, and other people. Resist the world's attempt to pull you under and put your faith in the eternal, almighty God. You're not a victim, you're an overcomer. You're a prisoner of Jesus Christ. You're who you are because of who He is. He is sovereign and in control. Paul knew this and wrote in Rom. 8:37, "Yet in all these things we are more than conquerors through Him who loved us." God is in charge and you are safe in His arms. That's the reality of whatever it is you're going through.

That being said, Paul continues in vs. 2 (BSB), "Surely you have heard of the stewardship of God's grace that was given to me for you." Paul was the custodian of the Gentiles, a steward of God for their benefit. God had entrusted him with great truths and he was under obligation to communicate them to the non-Jews. So important was this calling that Paul said in 1 Cor. 9:16, "Woe is me if I do not preach the gospel." A steward is one who manages something that is not his own. He was a servant to whom a certain responsibility was committed. Certain goods were given to him so that he might give them out to other people. Paul was given the responsibility of having oversight of the grace of God given to the Gentiles. God uses faithful stewards to manage His kingdom. Throughout history, God has used different people, from different backgrounds, using different methods to manage what belongs to Him. This is the purpose of the Spirit-led church.

God has a kingdom and He claims complete ownership over all His creation. Ps. 89:11 says, "The heavens are Yours, the earth also is Yours; The world and all its fullness, You have founded them." Most people think if they're in possession of something, they own it. No, God owns everything. He owns the universe, the world and everything in it. He owns everything and you own nothing. If you'll understand that, you'll be on your way to knowing what life in the kingdom of God is all about. God owns everything and He has chosen human managers to look after and promote the well-being of all that He owns. All of mankind, including you, is God's management crew. Ps. 8:5-8 (MSG) says, "Yet we've so narrowly missed being gods, bright with Eden's dawn light. You put us in charge of Your handcrafted world, repeated to us your Genesis-charge, made us lords of sheep and cattle, even animals out in the wild, birds flying and fish swimming, whales singing in the ocean deeps."

Kingdom stewardship is your earthly responsibility. Ps. 115:16 (MSG) says, "The heaven of heavens is for God, but He put us in charge of the earth." You're here to fill a management position under the sovereign rule of God. Just remember, managers work for the owner, not the other way around. You are the caretaker of God's property in terms of time, talents, and treasures. God is expecting His people to expand what He started in the Garden of Eden. To "be fruitful and multiply" (Gen. 1:28) meant more than having children. It also means to unpack potential that did not previously exist. Gen. 2:15 (BSB) says, "Then the Lord God took the man and placed him in the Garden of Eden to cultivate and keep it." The word "cultivate" means 'to unlock its potential; to unleash what it can do.' It is a sin to not maximize your potential in the sphere of your responsibility, to get out of creation everything creation has the potential to provide for you.

Paul always saw himself as a steward. He said in 1 Cor. 4:1, "Let a man so consider us, as servants of Christ, and stewards of the mysteries of God." You also are a steward. God has committed unto you physical skills and spiritual gifts to be used to advance His kingdom on the earth. He wants those special abilities to be managed properly for the benefit of the unity of the church. 1 Peter 4:10 says, "As each one has received a gift, minister it to one another, as good stewards of the manifold grace of God." Young's Literal says, "God has given gifts to each of you from His great variety of spiritual gifts. Manage them well so that God's generosity can flow through you." Every believer has at least one spiritual gift from God, if not more, and every gift is needed for the church to function properly. These gifts are given so you can make a distinctive contribution to individuals and to the community of faith in order to stimulate their growth and spiritual maturity.

1 Cor. 12:4 (NLT) says, "There are different kinds of spiritual gifts, but the same Spirit is the source of them all." A spiritual gift is a graciously given, supernaturally designed ability granted to every believer. John Piper said, "Gifts are not for a few but for all, and every believer has abilities which the Holy Spirit has given and can use to strengthen others. And it is the supreme joy of life to discover what they are and then pour yourself out to others through these gifts. And you will find them if you really desire to be God's instrument in bringing about faith and joy in other people." Spiritual gifts are not talents, those natural abilities shared by believers and unbelievers alike. A spiritual gift is a divine enablement given supernaturally by the Holy Spirit used in loving concern for the benefit of others. Gal. 6:10 (MSG) says, "Right now, therefore, every time we get the chance, let us work for the benefit of all, starting with the people closest to us in the community of faith."

All of God's children are to be channels through which His grace flows into the life of others. You have been a recipient of God's amazing grace and you share that grace with others through your spiritual gift. Charles Spurgeon said, "God gives much to you that you may give it to others; it is only meant to run through you as through a pipe. You are a steward and, if a steward should receive his lord's goods and keep them for himself, he would be an unfaithful steward." Stewardship is one of the most important themes in all the Bible. It's the proper management of what God has given you for the purpose of bringing Him glory. It started in Genesis when Adam was given the entire world to manage and watch over. Needless to say, he failed in what he had been commissioned to do. The Bible was written to teach you not to turn your head at the very mention of being obedient to God, to not use your talents in rebellion against God rather than in service to Him.

Jesus taught about stewardship in what is known as the Parable of the Talents (Matt. 25:14-30). He began by saying, "For the kingdom of heaven is like a man traveling to a far country, who called his own servants and delivered his goods to them. And to one he gave five talents, to another two, and to another one, to each according to his own ability; and immediately he went on a journey" (vs. 14,15). Here was a wealthy man who entrusted great wealth to three men while he went away on a journey. These three men had been promoted from being a servant to the high position of being a steward. They now had control what was the equivalent of a small fortune and each received a sizable amount based on their ability to manage it. Each man knew the personality and character of their master, knowing he expected them to make good on what he had entrusted to them. Each man now have choices to make regarding what to do with the master's money.

The first thing you learn in this story is that everything you have is given to you by God. James 1:17 says, "Every good gift and every perfect gift is from above, and comes down from the Father of lights." In other words, God owns everything and you own nothing. All that you have - your material goods, your abilities, even your very life - belong to someone else. Do you have any talents? They were given to you by the God of talents. Are you saved? Are you filled with the Holy Spirit? Do you have wealth, influence, and power? Are you a poet, statesman, or a philosopher? If so, whatever your position in life may be and no matter what talents you have, always remember they are not yours. They were lent to you from on high. You are merely holding on to them until the day of reckoning. Charles Spurgeon said, "No man has anything of his own, except his sin. We are but tenants at will. God has put us into His estates, and He has said, 'Occupy till I come' (Luke 19:13)."

The phrase "occupy till I come" means 'Do business! Do it now without delay!' The Greek word "pragma" means 'stay busy; carry on; set in motion; to accomplish.' The idea of this word involves producing good results through great effort and energy. Gal. 6:9 says, "And let us not grow weary while doing good." As a steward, you need to keep busy doing what the Master has entrusted you to do. Be busy for the Lord. Be occupied with the task you've been assigned to do. One is reminded of an army occupying enemy territory. As stewards of Christ, you are to be continually working as "aliens and strangers" (1 Peter 2:11) in this world wherever God has placed you. You work and keep working until the Lord returns to establish His righteous rule over the whole earth. You work with diligence, with a longing desire for His return. The day of reckoning is near, it's closer than you think, and you need to diligently be about the Father's business.

A faithful steward lives for the day he will give the master's goods back to him. This longing will give you the motivation to redeem each day for His glory, making the most of the opportunities that come your way. Go to God and repeat the words of Ps. 90:12, "So teach me to number our days, that we may gain a heart of wisdom." The master expected productivity from these three men. They were to work and stay busy as they watched for his return. Indeed, a watching Christian will be a working Christian. The master was commanding his servants to not only stay busy, but gave them what they needed to accomplish tasks while he was gone. Every believer receives something, but not everyone receives the same amount. They were each given according to their ability, showing that God will not give you something you can't handle. Whatever amount you have, God gives you the ability to take on the responsibility to use it for His glory.

Jesus continues His story, "Then he who received the five talents went and traded with them, and made another five talents. And likewise he who had received two gained two more also. But he who had received one went and dug in the ground, and hid his lord's money" (vs. 16-18). The first two servants went to work immediately for they were ready for the challenge and the responsibility that went with it. Without delay, they traded the talents they'd been given and doubled the master's investment. The third servant, the one with the least ability, had a lack of direction and a lack of purposefulness. What did he do? He turned aside, dug a hole in the ground, and hid the master's money, doing nothing with it. All three servants knew the master's return was sure, even though at times it didn't appear that way. "After a long time the lord of those servants came and settled accounts with them" (vs. 19). For these three servants, the day of reckoning had arrived.

Part of growing up is taking responsibility for the things you say and the things you do. Infants have no personal responsibility whatsoever but, as time goes by and the more they grow up, they are required to take on more and more responsibility. In many ways, the difference between a child and an adult is the willingness to take personal responsibility for their actions. Paul said in 1 Cor. 13:11, "When I became a man, I put the ways of childhood behind me." The Word emphasizes the responsibility of individuals to respond morally to God's revealed truth. He clearly defines right from wrong behavior and His people are expected to do what is right. Cain was warned by God that he would be held accountable for his actions (Gen. 4;7). Achan was held responsible for his sins at Jericho (Josh. 7:14,15) as was Jonah for his decision to run away from the Lord (Jonah 1:7,8). The Bible clearly teaches that all people need to take personal responsibility in all areas of life.

Why is this so important? Because one day you will be called upon to give an account before God for the actions you've committed in your life. The day of reckoning is when a person's position of responsibility is examined by a higher authority. If the reckoning is favorable, great rewards are given out. If not, severe punishment will come to those who didn't do what they were supposed to do. Is. 3:10,11 says, "Say to the righteous that it shall be well with them, for they shall eat the fruit of their doings. Woe to the wicked! It shall be ill with him, for the reword of his hands shall be given him." Yes, the Bible teaches that there will be wonderful blessings for obedience and severe penalties for disobedience. The Master is going to return to settle accounts with how you used the resources He gave you to advance His kingdom on the earth. Choose wisely what you will do with your life. Go to Him in prayer and He'll show you how to maximize your time, talents, and treasures.

In this parable, each servant presents the master with the results of their stewardship, both the financial results and the narrative account of what actions took place. They tell their own story first as the master listens. However, the master will have the final word. Matt. 25:20,21 says, "So he who had received five talents came and brought five other talents, saying, 'Lord, you delivered to me five talents; look, I have gained five more talents besides them.' His lord said to him, 'Well done, good and faithful servant; you were faithful over a few things, I will make you ruler over many things. Enter into the joy of your lord.'" The first servant doubled the talents given to him and the master responded with his approval and great reward. He gave his personal confirmation of the servant's ability, his success, and his faithfulness. The master rewards him with a higher position and more responsibility. He's now going to be entrusted with greater things.

The servant with two talents comes and gives his report. He also doubled what was entrusted to him and receives the same approval and reward as the first servant (vs. 22,23). Just like the talents that were entrusted to them, the reward they received was also according to their ability to handle it. In other words, God won't give you great wealth if you're not able to handle such a huge amount. Money has destroyed many lives so be thankful that God knows what you're capable of handling. Don't complain if you're not rich but be grateful that He doesn't lead you into temptation. Finally, the third servant comes and gives his report. He makes an excuse for his failure and unwisely blames his master for his lack of action. "Then he who had received the one talent came and said, 'Lord, I knew you to be a hard man, reaping where you have not sown, and gathering where you have not scattered seed. And I was afraid, and went and hid your talent in the ground. Look, there you have what is yours'" (vs. 24,25).

What was this servant thinking? He just called his master an inhuman, heartless, over-demanding man who lived off the blood, sweat, and tears of his servants. Because of his harsh opinion, he played it safe and held on to his master's money to be sure the master had something when he returned. Surprisingly, the master doesn't respond to the accusation made against him but instead makes his assessment based on the servant's character. He called him a "wicked and lazy servant" (vs. 26) and that he "ought to have deposited my money with the bankers, and that at my coming I would have received back my own with interest" (vs. 27). The word "wicked" means 'actively evil' and is a word often used to describe Satan. The word "lazy" means 'slothful and irritating' and describes a person who does nothing but cause trouble. The master implies that this servant is also very foolish. Why didn't he put the money in the bank and let the bankers do the work for him?

The master said, "Therefore take the talent from him, and give it to him who has ten talents. For to every one who has, more will be given, and he will have abundance; but from him who does not have, even what he has will be taken away. And cast the unprofitable servant into the outer darkness. There will be weeping and gnashing of teeth" (vs. 28-30). The wicked servant lost his talent, that which gave him the ability to be blessed. He stood and watched his one talent be given to the servant who had ten. Here is a case of the rich getting richer and the poor getting poorer. This is not a parable about social justice and it's not meant to be. Jesus is explaining how things work in the kingdom of God. The blessings of those who are faithful stewards don't add up, they multiply. There's a quantum leap in their riches and spiritual growth. The final judgment finds the wicked servant outside the master's house, sentenced to a destiny of eternal suffering.

You learn from this parable that your view of God will determine the choices you make. If you see Him as "a hard man" with unfair and unrealistic expectations of you, it will cause you to live in fear with unprofitable results. Only those who eagerly look forward to the return of the Master can find the freedom to live with confidence now. For sure, all people will one day give an account for their stewardship, or the lack thereof, of the things that belong to God. With this judgment comes the revelation of who and what they really are. Were they faithful or unfaithful, good stewards or bad? The answer determines their eternal destiny. Some will be glorified with Christ forever and ever, others will be separated from Christ and thrown into utter darkness where there will be weeping and gnashing of teeth. Those who are wicked and lazy will not be included in the circle of the saved. The question to be asked is how well do you manage the talents you've been given?

| 23 |

"THE ROAD TO GREATNESS"

If ever there was an example of a good and faithful servant, it was the apostle Paul. He identified himself as a servant in Acts 27:23 when he talked about "the God to whom I belong and whom I serve." Your identity determines your activity. In order to act like a servant, you have to think like a servant. Ever since Paul was struck down on the road to Damascus, he worked tirelessly to fulfill what he was called to do. He was commissioned by God to bring the gospel message to the non-Jew, thus bringing unity between the Jew and Gentile. A servant thinks in terms of maintaining unity and harmony. They endeavor "to keep the unity of the Spirit in the bond of peace" (Eph. 4:3). You have unity where there is a oneness of purpose. Paul wrote in Phil. 2:2 (NLT), "Then make me truly happy by agreeing wholeheartedly with each other, loving one another, and working together with one mind and purpose." The Message Bible says, "Love each other, be deep-spirited friends."

To have the mindset of a servant, you must always think about serving others. After all, that's what a servant does. A servant sees a need and meets it because they can. Phil. 2:4 says, "Let each of you look out not only for his own interests, but also for the interests of others." The Message Bible says, "Put yourself aside, and help others get ahead. Don't be obsessed with getting your own advantage. Forget yourselves long enough to lend a helping hand." This is supernatural for the world doesn't train you to think this way. All the world thinks about is me, myself, and I. Everybody wants to be a celebrity. They want to be on top of whatever they're involved in. They selfishly seek after fortune and fame and care not who they step over to get it. People want what they want and will do anything to get what they want. They believe they live in a dog-eat-dog world and everything they do is based on what they can get out of it.

Everybody wants to be great. What most people don't know is that greatness in the kingdom of God is measured in a different light. Jesus said in Mark 10:43, "Whoever desires to become great among you shall be your servant." Serving others puts you on the road to greatness. This is why great people seek to serve at all times. If you're seeking greatness in the kingdom of God, then look for opportunities to serve. God has no problem with you wanting to be great. What concerns Him is your attitude about how to become great. People of the world pursue greatness by seeking after power, possessions, prestige, and position. This is the wrong way to achieve greatness. Jesus continued in Mark 10:44,45, "And whoever of you desires to be first shall be slave of all. For even the Son of Man did not come to be served, but to serve, and to give His life a ransom for many." If you want to be first, then you must be serving the most.

Greatness. Humility. Servanthood. These are all synonymous terms because in the kingdom of God they all mean the same thing. Shortly before His death, Jesus set the example by kneeling down in front of His disciples and washed their feet. In love, He even washed the feet of the one He knew would betray Him. Afterward, He sat back down and explained the meaning of what had just taken place. "Do you know what I have done to you? You call Me Teacher and Lord, and you say well, for so I am. If I then, your Lord and Teacher, have washed your feet, you also ought to wash one another's feet. For I have given you an example, that you should do as I have done to you. Most assuredly, I say to you, a servant is not greater than his master, nor is he who is sent greater than he who sent him. If you know these things, happy are you if you do them" (John 13:12-17). The happiest people in the world are those who serve. If you're not happy, you're not serving enough.

Jesus lived His life on the earth giving and sharing, to show you how a godly life is supposed to be lived. There is even a verse in the Bible where Jesus described the type of person He was. He said in Matt. 11:29, "Take My yoke upon you and learn from Me, for I am gentle and lowly in heart." If you want to be like Jesus, the must be "meek and humble" (LSV). In other words, you must become a servant. There is no greater calling in all of life. In fact, it's what you were created for. Paul said in Eph. 2:10, "For we are His workmanship, created in Christ Jesus for good works." You were created for service and saved to be a blessing to others. 2 Tim. 1:9 (TLB) says, "It is God who saved us and chose us for His holy work." God saved you not only so you wouldn't go to hell, He saved you so you could work in His kingdom. Gal. 1:15 (GNB) says, "God, in His grace, chose me even before I was born, and called me to serve Him."

The Lord's command to "take My yoke upon you" is a call to submit your will to His good and acceptable and perfect will (Rom. 12:2). He is telling you to surrender to His lordship, to submit to His rule and authority. Paul said the same thing in Rom. 12:1 where he exhorts all believers to surrender themselves to God as living sacrifices. A farmer would use a yoke to keep his oxen under control, to guide them to perform useful work. If the oxen were not yoked together and harnessed to a plow where their owner directs their energy, then most certainly they would run loose and wild in the field. So important is this that Lam. 3:27 says, "It is good for a man that he bear the yoke in his youth." Unless young people are disciplined and brought under subjection and taught to obey their parents, they are likely to also run wild, rebelling against God and man. Just as oxen are yoked in order to submit to their owner's will, so are you called to yield to Jesus as your King.

Notice that nobody puts this yoke on you. It is something you place upon yourself. When Jesus said "learn from Me," He is telling you to willfully become His disciple, to follow Him and do the same things He did. He served others and you are called to do the same. God wants you to be an active member in His church. Don't be like those who soak up all the benefits of belonging to a local church without giving anything back. This is why Paul said in Eph. 4:1 (NIV), "Live a life worthy of the calling you have received." You can do this if you'll learn from Jesus how to do it. The Greek word for "learn" is "man-thasso" and it means 'to direct one's mind to something and producing an external effect.' It means 'to genuinely understand and accept a teaching, to accept it as true and to apply it to one's life, to acquire a life-long habit.' In Greek culture, the word was used to describe an apprentice who was learning a trade from someone more gifted and talented than they were.

To learn from Christ, you must be teachable like a little child. Children receive with complete submission whatever their teacher tells them. Don't bring your own preconceived ideas to the scriptures and don't take verses out of context making it conform to your way of thinking. No, believe whatever God has spoken and receive it as truth simply on the authority of the speaker. You also need to learn with the diligence of a student, those who have a thirst for knowledge, those who are always in deep thought and employed in laborious investigation. Thus you should be occupied in pursuit of divine knowledge, reading the Word daily, searching for its hidden treasures. You need to meditate upon it day and night, all the while praying over it for divine illumination. Finally, learn with the obedience of a devoted follower of God. Whatever you find to be His will, do it without hesitation and without reserve. Be doers of the Word and not hearers only (James 1:22).

How did Jesus describe Himself? He said He was gentle, meek, and humble. These traits tell you why His yoke is easy and His burden light (Matt. 11:30). He is not harsh and He won't give you a burden that is too great for you to carry. The word "gentle" means 'easy, mild, soft.' The Greek word "praus" describes those who are of a quiet, gentle spirit. The Greeks defined "meekness" as 'power under control.' The Spirit-filled believer is under the control of God's Spirit. This frees you from malice, bitterness, or any desire for revenge. You're to have a gentle spirit which characterizes your relationship with both God and man. William Barclay said, "No man can lead others until he has mastered himself; no man can serve others until he has subjected himself; no man can be in control of others until he has learned to control himself. But the man who gives himself into the complete control of God will gain this meekness which will indeed enable him to inherit the earth."

The Greek word for "humble" is "tapeinos" and it means 'low, not high, not rising far from the ground.' It speaks of one's condition as lowly and described what was considered base, common, unfit, and having little value. It represents a person's proper estimate of himself in relation to God and others. In this sense, Jesus lived a humble life, depending completely on the Father and relating appropriately to all around Him. This, Jesus said, is how you are supposed to be. He also said if you would learn from Him, if you would become gentle, meek, and humble, you "will find rest for your souls" (Matt. 11:29). The word "find" is the Greek word "heurisko" and is where the word "Eureka!" comes from. It means "I have found it!" It was a triumphant cry of joy in discovering or finding something one greatly values. "Eureka!" should be the cry of every weary, heavy laden heart that has discovered the priceless rest found only in the Son of God.

Trusting in Jesus as your loving Savior gives you rest as you place your burdens on Him. He said in Matt. 11:28 (MSG), "Are you tired? Worn out? Burned out on religion? Come to Me. Get away with Me and you'll recover your life. I'll show you how to take a real rest. Walk with Me and work with me - watch how I do it. Learn the un-forced rhythms of grace. I won't lay anything heavy or ill-fitting on you. Keep company with Me and you'll learn to live freely and lightly" (vs. 28-30). The Greek word "anapausis" describes 'an inner tranquil-ity while performing necessary labor.' It's not the cessation of work but rather the restoration of lost strength and inner rest experienced simultaneously in the work. R. Kent Hughes says the rest of God "is a working rest. God's rest is full of active toil. God rests, and in His rest He keeps working." Jesus said in John 5:17, "My Father has been working until now, and I have been working."

Christ's rest is not a rest from work, it's a rest while you work. It's like a river moving calmly and rapidly, in silent majesty and strength. Hasting's Bible Dictionary says this rest is "not the rest of inactivity but of the harmonious working of all the faculties and affections - of will, imagination, heart, and conscience - because each has found in God the ideal sphere for its satisfaction and development." When you receive the rest Jesus provides, you'll jump for joy and shout, "Eureka! I have found it!" In this rest you'll experience the purpose for which you were created. Your work for Him and in Him will be satisfying and of eternal value. You'll wake up each morning looking for ways to be a good and faithful servant. It takes a servant's heart to fulfill your destiny, to walk the walk. When you serve, it's about loving others as God has loved you. It's about adding value to the lives of those around you. It's about kingdom labor and sacrificial giving.

Matt. 5:16 says, "Let your light so shine before men, that they may see your good works and glorify your Father in heaven." A servant al-ways thinks about serving others. You are gifted for service and peo-ple need to see God in the things you do. God put you here to be an influence in the lives of other people, to help make their lives better. Inside of you are strengths, gifts, and abilities waiting to be released. There is something you do that you're very good at, a God-given talent that comes natural to you. God equipped you with great potential and people are waiting for you to use your talents to give them what they so desperately need. Everything God makes is a solution to a problem. Doctors solve health problems, lawyers solve legal problems, and farmers solve food problems. God made you to solve problems also. Your special talent is needed in the body of Christ so don't rob people of what God sent you to give them.

Jesus said in Matt. 20:28 (TLB), "Your attitude must be like My own, for I did not come to be served, but to serve." In other words, you need to have the mindset of a servant. This will not be a problem if you know who you are in Christ. Paul said in 2 Tim. 1:12, "I know whom I have believed." Jesus came to earth in "the form of a servant" (Phil. 2:7) but He never lost sight of His deity. Jesus could serve because He knew who He was. He was God come to earth in the flesh and He was never insecure with His identity. He would never act independently of the Father and often said, "I and My Father are one" (John 10:30). It was no threat to Him to wash the disciples feet or to cry over the people's lack of faith. He shed human tears but flowing out of Him was the power to heal the sick and raise the dead. He knew who He was and you need to know who you are. You're a child of God sent to serve the same way Jesus served.

Contribution is the key to your happiness. It's serving others that makes your life meaningful. 1 Cor. 15:58 (GNB) says, "Keep busy in your work for the Lord since you know that nothing you do in the Lord's service is ever without value." The Message Bible says, "Throw yourselves into the work of the Master, confident that nothing you do for Him is a waste of time or effort." Your church family needs your service. 1 Cor. 12:29 (TLB) says, "All of you together are the one body of Christ and each of you is a separate and necessary part of it." Think like Jesus thinks and have the mindset of a servant. Phil. 2:5 says, "Let this mind be in you which was also in Christ Jesus." Ask not what your church can do for you, ask what you can do for the church. Gal.

5:13 (NLT) says "to serve one another in love." Give your life away. Jesus said in Mark 8:35, "For whoever desires to save his life will lose it, but whoever loses his life for My sake and the gospel's will save it."

You should willingly want to serve God because of the gratitude you have for the compassion He forever shows you. This is what God calls you to be, a willing servant who will do above and beyond what is asked. It is important to note that you are a servant and not a volunteer. The word "volunteer" is a secular word and is found no where in the New Testament. A volunteer focuses on what they do, a servant focuses on what they can do for others. Volunteers focus on what they give, servants focus on what Jesus gave. They serve so Jesus can receive the reward for His suffering. Volunteers keep score, servants make sacrifices. They do what is inconvenient at inconvenient times. They are need sensitive, not time sensitive. Volunteering is about convenience, serving is about commitment. Volunteers want to look good, servants want God to look good. It's not about you being noticed, it's about God being noticed through what you do.

People want to be connected to God but don't want to be committed to Him. They want enough of God to keep the devil away. They want His blessings and favor and everything else that will give them a rich, prosperous life. They're like the people described in 2 Kings 17:33, "They feared the Lord, yet served their own gods." People like this want to be involved but not committed. On the other hand, good and faithful servants, those on the road to greatness, are both committed and available. This is what makes you a good steward of the talents you've been given. You don't hoard and bury your talent like that wicked and lazy servant in the Lord's parable. No, you go to work and take risks. You invest your talents and are constructive with what you've been given. You have faith knowing God won't let you fall when you go out on a limb for Him. Take heart in your work for the Lord, trusting He'll see you through to the very end.

Good stewardship involves a commitment to excellence. Whatever you do for God, do it well, from the most insignificant thing to the most important thing. Every work that needs to be done, both great and small, is important to God and it needs to be important to you also. Don't think too highly of yourself that you won't do some menial tasks that needs to be done. If Jesus washed some smelly feet, you can also. You must be excellent in small things before you can be made ruler over big things. Just remember, everything you do, you're doing for God. Jesus said in Matt. 25:40, "Assuredly, I say to you, inasmuch as you did it to the least of these My brethren, you did it to Me." And, by all means, whatever you do, do it right the first time. Good stewardship involves old fashioned hard work, something people in today's world know little about. Be the best and do your best for the Master. For sure, His return will be sudden and unpredictable (Matt. 24:36).

There are rewards for good stewardship, both in the here and now and in the hereafter. Matt. 6:33 says, "But seek first the kingdom of God and His righteousness, and all these things will be added to you." God has a benefit's package with your name written on it. The first benefit is answered prayer. When God sees you have prioritized the stewardship of your talents for His kingdom, you will experience a quicker response from Him regarding your personal requests. Also, God will "supply all your need according to His riches in glory by Christ Jesus" (Phil. 4:19). When you help meet the needs of others, God in turn will meet your needs. You will also have peace of mind and emotional well-being. Many of your pains have to do with emotional instability. Be a faithful steward and God will calm your chaos. Also, divine guidance will come to you. God will teach you how to be more productive in life by giving you ideas, thoughts, concepts, and so much more.

Good stewards are not only ready but are anxious for the return of their Master. From righteous Abel to the beloved apostle John, those who served with zeal and faith saw the coming of the Lord as a great day, a happy and a blessed day. Why wouldn't they feel this way? Rev. 22:12 says, "And behold, I am coming quickly, and My reward is with Me, to give to everyone according to his work." If that don't make you shout for joy, nothing will. When Paul neared the end of His life, he looked forward to receiving the crown of righteousness that the Lord would award to him (2 Tim. 4:8). He said all who loved and looked forward to the Lord's appearing would also receive the same crown. Other crowns are also promised to faithful believers. James 1:12 speaks of "the crown of life" and 1 Peter 5:4 says, "When the Chief Shepherd appears, you will receive the crown of glory that does not fade away." Indeed, the Master is returning real soon. How good of a steward have you been?

| 24 |

"FROM THE INSIDE OUT"

P aul was on a mission. God had specifically called him to preach the grace of God to the Gentiles. William Barclay said, "It is one of the great facts of the Christian life that we have been given the precious things of Christianity in order to share them with others. It is one of the great warnings of the Christian life that, if we keep them to ourselves, we lose them." The Greek word for "grace" is "charis" and is defined as 'God's unmerited favor and supernatural enablement and empowerment for salvation and for daily sanctification.' Anglican cleric Benjamin Jowett defined "grace" as 'holy love on the move.' Paul was a steward of God's grace, writing in 1 Cor. 4;1, "Let a man so consider us, as servants of Christ and stewards of the mysteries of God." The Message Bible says, "We are guides into God's most sublime secrets." What is the mystery? That Jews and Gentiles are equal heirs in the body of Christ. This was unknown in times past but is now revealed through Paul.

Paul introduced the mystery in chapter one, talked about it in chapter two, and goes into detail about it here in chapter three. Eph. 3:3,4 (NLT) says, "As I briefly wrote earlier, God Himself revealed His mysterious plan to me. As you read what I have written, you will understand my insight into this plan regarding Christ." He's saying, "This mystery is essential and I want you to know and understand my knowledge of it." The Greek word for "knowledge" is "sunesis" and it means 'mental comprehension.' This comes before spiritual application. You can't apply what you don't know. This is why you've got to have a renewed mind. What you understand in your mind is what affects your life. Paul is saying he didn't learn of this mystery from anyone else, nor had he discovered it through his own intelligence. He said this was knowledge he received directly from God. Revelation knowledge is when God transmits knowledge from Himself to your spirit without error.

There are two kinds of knowledge in the world: sense knowledge and revealed knowledge. Sense knowledge is gained through the five physical senses. It comes from what you hear, see, taste, touch, and smell. It's the kind of knowledge gained in school and from life experiences. It is received from the outside in. Revealed knowledge, on the other hand, is revealed to you by the Holy Spirit. This knowledge comes from the inside out. The Greek word for "revelation" is "apokalupsis" and conveys the idea of 'taking the lid off.' It means "to remove the cover and expose to open view that which was heretofore not visible, known, or disclosed; to make manifest or reveal a thing previously secret or unknown." If you have revelation knowledge, the gates of hell will not prevail against you. It's what causes the kingdom of God to be on earth as it is in heaven. It's through revelation knowledge that you receive all things that pertain to life and godliness.

Revelation knowledge is when God reveals something to you about Himself, His will, and His divine providence to the world of human beings. It's when God's words go off inside of you like a long, massive, fireworks display to the point that it has a deep, personal impact on your life. Revelation implies intimacy because you are now exposed to what God is saying to you. It can happen while you're spending time alone with Him, when you're reading your Bible, while you're listening to a sermon at church, when you're reading an anointed book. It can happen in a dream, while you're driving your car, when you're mowing your lawn. It can happen at any time in any place. You're seeking God when suddenly He puts something down inside you. Sometimes it comes by a still, small voice. Other times it's a "knowing" down inside your spirit. You know that you know God revealed something to you. It's a part of you now and nobody can take it away from you.

Revelation knowledge is the very foundation upon which the church of the Lord Jesus Christ is built. It's when God turns the light on and you can see what He wants to reveal to you. It was the rock of revelation knowledge that Jesus was referring to when He said, "On this rock I will build My church" (Matt. 16:18). God will reveal to people that Jesus is Lord, thus causing them to respond and give their lives to Christ. He told Peter in vs. 17, "For flesh and blood has not revealed this to you, but My Father who is in heaven." He then said in vs. 19, "And I will give you the keys of the kingdom of heaven." Those keys are revelation knowledge. They'll open the door to what God wants to reveal to you. Walking in revelation knowledge will strengthen your confidence in the promises of God. It will make your faith solid and cause you to walk by faith and not by sight. It will make you victorious over the devil. You've heard from God and nothing can stop you now.

How important is revelation knowledge? Prov. 29:18 (CSB) says, "Without revelation people run wild, but one who follows divine instruction will be happy." Believers who don't walk in revelation knowledge get restless and walk as people who are blind, always banging into things in the dark. The Message Bible says, "If people can't see what God is doing, they stumble all over themselves; But when they attend to what He reveals, they are most blessed." When you do things out of revelation, there is an excitement to everything you do. For this reason, Paul prayed in Col. 1:9 "that you may be filled with the knowledge of His will in all wisdom and spiritual understanding." God wants you to be filled with divine knowledge, that which comes from the inside out. Other translations say this is a "deep and clear knowledge" (AMP); an ever-growing knowledge" (Barclay); "the advanced and perfect knowledge" (Wuest); "full knowledge" (Young's Literal).

The Greek word for "filled" is "pleroo" and it means 'to be filled to the brim; to make complete; to cause to abound; to furnish or supply liberally; to flood; to take possession of; to ultimately control to the tiniest detail.' Revealed knowledge from the Holy Spirit is exact. It is knowledge that is full and complete. It has to be for it is coming from God Himself. Jesus said in John 16:13, "However, when He, the Spirit of truth, has come, He will guide you into all truth; for He will not speak on His own authority, but whatever He hears He will speak; and He will tell you things to come." Don't starve yourself when it comes to spiritual matters. God wants you filled to the brim with the knowledge of His will for your life. Charles Spurgeon said, "Paul frequently alludes to knowledge and wisdom. He knew that spiritual ignorance is the constant source of error, instability, and sorrow; and therefore he desired that they might be soundly taught in the things of God."

The Message Bible says, "We haven't stopped praying for you, asking God to give you wise minds and spirits attuned to His will, and so acquire a thorough understanding of the ways in which God works." Paul is praying that you'll be satisfied with nothing less than the full limit of the knowledge of God's will. He wants you to obtain divine insight into God's will for your life with a knowledge that is perfect, precise, and much larger and more thorough than sense knowledge. The word "filled" also carries the idea of being fully equipped. It was used to describe a thing that was ready for a voyage. With revelation knowledge, you'll have all you need for the voyage of life. Adam Clarke said, "As the bright shining of the sun in the firmament of heaven fills the whole world with light and heat, so the light of the Sun of righteousness is to illuminate their whole souls, and fill them with Divine splendor, so that they might know the will of God in all wisdom and spiritual understanding."

The primary goal of your life is to know the will of God. Spend time with Him for He has the answers to all you face in life. It is His will you're seeking so stop trying to persuade God to do what you want but try to find out what He wants you to do. Stop trying to get God to listen to you but train yourself to listen to Him. William Barclay said, "It so often happens that when we pray, we are really saying, 'Thy will be changed,' when we ought to be saying 'Thy will be done.' The first object of prayer is not so much to speak to God but to listen to Him." Charles Spurgeon said, "Paul would not have a believer ignorant upon any point. He would have him filled with knowledge, for when a measure is full of wheat there is no room for chaff. True knowledge excludes error. If you have empty spots in your minds unstored with holy teaching, this will be an invitation to the devil to enter in and dwell there. Fill up the soul and so shut out the enemy."

1 Cor. 2:14 says, "But the natural man does not receive the things of the Spirit of God, for they are foolishness to him; nor can he know them, because they are spiritually discerned." The natural man lacks the faculties by which the things of God are known and understood. They seem foolish to him because he lives as if there is nothing beyond this physical life. This is the kind of life common to all animals. Life on this level is without spiritual insight for Satan has blinded the minds of unbelievers (2 Cor. 4:4). Revivalist Vance Havner said, "They have no vision and cannot see through the fog. What the man needs is sight, and spiritual sight only comes through the miracle of the new birth." Jesus said in John 3:3, "I tell you the truth, unless you are born again, you cannot see the kingdom of God." Spiritual truth - revelation knowledge - can only be seen with spiritual eyes that have been illuminated by the Spirit of God. In other words, eyes that see from the inside out.

Kenneth Wuest says the things of God "are investigated in a spiritual realm." The Amplified Bible says "they are spiritually discerned and estimated and appreciated." The word "discern" means 'to judge, distinguish, to examine accurately or carefully from bottom to top, to make careful and exact research.' 1 Cor. 2:12-14 (TPT) says, "For we did not receive the spirit of this world system but the Spirit of God, so that we might come to understand and experience all that grace has lavished upon us. And we articulate these revelations with the words imparted to us by the Spirit and not with the words taught by human wisdom. We join together Spirit-revealed truths with Spirit-revealed words. Someone living on an earthly human level rejects the revelation of God's Spirit, for they make no sense to him. He can't understand the revelation of the Spirit because they are only discovered by the illumination of the Spirit."

The source of spiritual illumination is the Father and the channel is the Holy Spirit. Charles Spurgeon said the Holy Spirit "is a light shining in the midst of us to guide us. And by the light He shows us wondrous things. He teaches us by suggestion, direction, and illumination." To illuminate means to have something brightened with light and made clear to the eyes. It means to be enlightened spiritually, to turn on the light of understanding and divine truth. Ps. 18:28 says, "For You will light my lamp; The Lord my God will enlighten my darkness." 2 Cor. 4:6 says, "For it is God who commanded light to shine out of darkness, who has shone in our hearts to give light of the knowledge of the glory of God in the face of Jesus Christ." The Message Bible says, "Our lives filled up with light as we saw and understood God in the face of Christ, all bright and beautiful." Like the beams of the sun, may the words of God enter the window of your understanding and dispel the darkness of your mind.

Charles Spurgeon said, "God, by His Spirit, brings old truth to the heart, gives new light to our eyes, and causes the Word to exercise new power over us." Through the Holy Spirit, the Word comes forth with power and penetration. He enables you to understand what God is saying so you can apply it to your life. 2 Tim. 2:7 says, "Consider what I say, and may the Lord give you understanding in all things."

If God does not open your eyes, you will not see the wonder of the Word for you are not naturally able to see the beauty of spiritual things. Ask God to illuminate His Word and His will to you and then submit to it. If you'll do that, He will light up every page of the Bible so that each word shines forth like stars. You need to read the Bible daily with spiritual eyes so your heart will be enlightened by the Holy Spirit. English minister Alexander Maclaren said, "He who has the Holy Spirit in his heart and the scriptures in his hands has all he needs."

The first method of God's illumination, the starting point, is a regular study of the Word of God. Ps. 119:130 says, "The unfolding of your words gives light; it gives understanding to the simple." Reading the Bible can and will change your life, especially if you'll allow the Holy Spirit to reveal to your spirit and mind the truths contained within its pages. To receive revelation knowledge, you must read a particular verse of scripture several times. Stop and meditate on it (Josh. 1:8). Read it again and again. Let each word linger in your spirit. The word "meditate" means 'to mutter.' You should be saying what God says about a matter all the time. Talk to yourself. Say what God says. If you'll do that, you'll get stronger spiritually and receive more revelation knowledge than you ordinarily would. Ps. 19:8 (TPT) says, "His teachings make us joyful and radiate His light; His precepts are so pure! The revelation-light of His Word makes my spirit shine radiant."

When you read your Bible, if you want to have one of those "aha!" moments, then be sure to pray the words of Ps. 119:18, "Open my eyes, that I may see wondrous things from Your law." This is a plea for personal understanding. David is asking God to open his eyes to let him perceive and be enlightened on what He is saying. He wanted the glorious wonders of the scriptures to be revealed. Paul prayed in Eph. 1:17,18 that God "may give to you the spirit of wisdom and revelation in the knowledge of Him, the eyes of your understanding being enlightened." As you meditate on a certain scripture, ask God to reveal its meaning to you. Don't ever be afraid to ask God questions. Matt. 7:7,8 (TPT) says, "Ask, and the gift is yours. Seek and you'll discover. Knock, and the door will be opened to you. For every persistent one will get what he asks for. Every persistent seeker will discover what he longs for. And everyone who knocks persistently will one day find an open door."

God has all the answers so ask Him what He wants to reveal to you. Ask Him to shine light on what you've read, to make it real to you. Don't ever feel ashamed because of a lack of understanding. James 1:5 (NLT) says, "If you need wisdom, ask our generous God, and He will give it to you. He will not rebuke you for asking." The TPT says, "He won't see your lack of wisdom as an opportunity to scold you over your failures but He will overwhelm your failures with His generous grace." After you ask Him what a particular scripture means and how to apply it to your life, get quiet and listen for Him to speak to you. Ps. 46:10 says, "Be still, and know that I am God!" It's in those quiet times, in times of stillness, that you'll hear Him giving you the guidance and direction you need. Also, be sure to thank Him for what He says to you. Rejoice for one word from God can change your life forever. When you receive revelation knowledge, your life will never be the same.

As an added bonus, worshiping God will bring forth even more illumination and revelation knowledge. Ps. 25:14 says, "The secret of the Lord is with those who worship Him, and He will show them His covenant." The TPT says, "There's a private place reserved for the lovers of God, where they sit near Him and receive the revelation secrets of His promises." Reverencing God is a fountain of life to all who believe for it provides His people with wise counsel and a place of refuge in times of trouble. Revelation knowledge, the intimate counsel of God, is for those who worship and honor Him so they may know Him personally and understand His ways. Yes, the secret things of the Lord, the plans and purposes of God, have been made known to those who fear Him and worship Him. The more you worship God, the more He will reveal to you the deeper meaning of His covenant promises. Deut. 29:29 says, "The secret things belong unto the Lord our God, but the things which are revealed belong to us and our children forever."

It is important to understand that your spiritual condition greatly influences the process in which this illumination takes place. Vance Havner said, "You might as well try to describe a sunset to a blind man, play music for a deaf man, talk to a dead man, as to discuss the deep things of God with an unconverted sinner." Those not saved cannot understand the deep things of God and neither can the immature believer. Paul said in 1 Cor. 3:1 (NLT), "Dear brothers and sisters, when I was with you I couldn't talk to you as I would to spiritual people. I had to talk as though you were infants in the Christian life." Without a heart for God, revelation knowledge will not come. All His ways are concealed from the prying eyes of unbelievers, false prophets, pagan people, principalities and powers, and those that despise His name. Proper understanding of spiritual truths is dependent on a tender heart that is "humble and contrite of spirit, and which trembles at My word" (Is. 66:2).

It is only to His friends that God imparts these heart-reviving secrets. There are new and exciting realities of Christian knowledge and experience known only by those who worship and reverence God, those who esteem Him greatly and hold Him in highest honor. It is the Lord's loyal followers who are permitted to come into His presence and partake of His counsels in order to receive the guidance they need. Revelation knowledge is the door to abundant life in Christ (John 10:10) as God supernaturally reveals to you the true knowledge of His covenant in all its gracious provisions and glorious manifestations. Albert Barnes said, "Whatever there is in that arrangement to promote the happiness and salvation of His people, He will cause them to understand." This is why your time of fellowship with Him should be sweet and frequent. Listen to His voice, whether He speak by the written Word or by a still small voice inside of you.

Warren Wiersbe said, "As we walk with the Lord in the light of His Word, we develop a close fellowship with Him and better understand His ways." Be like the psalmist who declared, "I rise before dawn and cry for help. I wait for Your word. Oh, how I love Your law! It is my meditation all the day" (Ps. 119:147, 97). What is the purpose of revelation knowledge? Action! Ps. 119:34 says, "Give me understanding, and I shall keep Your law; Indeed, I shall observe it with my whole heart." Illumination always leads to action. This is why James 1:22 says, "But be doers of the word, and not hearers only, deceiving yourselves." The TPT says, "Let His Word become like poetry written and fulfilled by your life." The Holy Spirit enlightens you to hear and understand God's Word. He then takes that knowledge and guides you to apply it to your life, confirming that you are a child of God. Rom. 8:14 says, "For as many as are led by the Spirit of God, they are the sons of God."

| 25 |

"MINISTER OF THE GOSPEL"

In a court of law, the defense attorney will try to discredit the witness for the prosecution in order to nullify his testimony. No matter how accurate and damaging that testimony may be, if the character of the witness is discredited, then his testimony becomes null and void. This is the challenge every messenger of the gospel always faces. The good news of God's amazing grace is undeniable for it is absolutely, unequivocally true. However, the content of the message is always linked to the credibility of the messenger. Without a doubt, the message and the messenger have an intimate relationship with one another. Paul realizes this as he testifies that Gentiles are now fellow citizens with the saints and members of the household of God. He acknowledges and anticipates objection to this message he has been chosen to proclaim, objections that tie the message to the messenger. If what Paul is saying is true, and it most assuredly is, then why is he a prisoner for proclaiming it?

Here in the third chapter of Ephesians, Paul addresses these objections. In vs. 1-6 he writes about the mystery of the gospel, in vs. 7-13 he talks about the messenger of the gospel. Both sections go together. In fact, in these thirteen verses, Paul describes himself three ways. He calls himself the prisoner of Jesus Christ (vs. 1), a steward of God's grace (vs. 2), a minister of the gospel (vs. 7). Paul was under house arrest in Rome because he preached about the mystery. He wrote in

Col. 1:26 (TPT), "There is a divine mystery - a secret surprise that has been concealed from the world for generations, but now it's being revealed, unfolded and manifested for every holy believer to experience." The Message Bible says, "This mystery has been kept in the dark for a long time, but now it's out in the open." Remember, the church wasn't mentioned in the Old Testament. No where did it say that one day the Gentiles would be fellow members of a body in which Jews did not have a privileged position over them.

The inclusion of Gentiles into God's holy family and divine purposes remained mysteriously unclear under the old covenant. None of the prophets of old understood the great truths of the church, Jews and Gentiles united as one body without racial distinction. Still, it was not a secret that God intended to bless the Gentiles for, in the promise to Abraham, He said, "In you all the families of the earth shall be blessed" (Gen. 12:3). Sad to say, the Jews often ignored the promises to the Gentiles through their pride of religion and race. Also, consider the location of the Promised Land. It was no accident that the land flowing with milk and honey was a bridge connecting Europe and Asia with Africa. All the highways of international commerce would pass through Israel, allowing God's chosen people to be a spiritual blessing to all mankind. The book of Acts makes it abundantly clear that Jewish communities around the world formed a natural springboard for global evangelism.

There is no doubt that God had mentioned that others who were not called His people would one day be allowed into His family. Yes, it was alluded to but it had never been as clear as it is now through the teaching of Paul. Eph. 3:5 (TPT) says, "There has never been a generation that has been given the detailed understanding of this glorious and divine mystery until now. He kept it a secret until this generation. God is revealing it only now to His sacred apostles and prophets of the Holy Spirit." The word "revealed" means 'to uncover; to disclose; to make manifest.' The idea is to cause something to be fully known by removing the veil or covering which then exposes to full view what was previously hidden. Paul is saying this mystery had not been known in times past as it has now been revealed. The Message Bible says, "None of our ancestors understood this. Only in our time has it been made clear by God's Spirit through His holy apostles and prophets of this new order."

Upon all believers is the call to holiness, to be holy both in character and conduct. 1 Peter 1:14-16 (TPT) says, "As God's obedient children, never again shape your lives by the desires that you followed when you didn't know better. Instead, shape your lives to become like the Holy One who called you. For scripture says, 'You are to be holy, because I am holy.'" In the Bible, God gives specific instructions and regulations that are to govern your life. This means you are to live by a higher standard than the rest of the world. This is why Paul said in 2 Cor. 6:17 (NLT), "Therefore, come out from among unbelievers, and separate yourselves from them, says the Lord." You've been set apart by God to be exclusively His, to be dedicated to Him, and to manifest holiness of heart and conduct in contrast to the impurity of pagan unbelievers. You've been set aside for sacred use and this is why you need to be living by God's standards, not the world's.

In addition to Paul, this mystery was also revealed by the Spirit to His holy apostles and prophets. An apostle is a person sent forth by another, often with a special commission to represent that person and to accomplish his work. In ancient times, an apostle was the personal representative of the king, functioning as an ambassador with the king's authority to do what needed to be done. In a sense, all followers of Jesus Christ are called to be apostles. All are sent out (Matt. 28:19) and all are called to be His ambassadors. 2 Cor. 520 (TPT) says, "We are ambassadors of the Anointed One who carry the message of Christ to the world, as though God were tenderly pleading with them directly through our lips." A prophet is a person who speaks God's truth to others. The Greek word "propheter" means 'one who speaks forth under divine influence and inspiration.' They were called to exhort, reprove, and admonish individuals or nations as God's ambassadors while also revealing details about the future.

Once again, Paul now makes it very clear what the mystery is that he and these holy men have been sent forth to proclaim. Eph. 3:6 (TPT) says, "Here's the secret! The gospel of grace has made you, non-Jewish believers, into coheirs of His promise through your union with Him. And you have now become members of His body - one with the Anointed One!" Believing Gentiles are now fellow heirs with believing Jews, fellow partakers in the promise of Christ Jesus. Heirs of God are those who receive the blessing that God has for His people. Gal. 3:29 (NLT) says, "And now that you belong to Christ, you are the true children of Abraham. You are his heirs, and God's promise to Abraham belongs to you." Gentiles now share a position of equality with the Jews. They are now "mixed in" with the Jews so that you can't tell the difference between the two. In the eyes of God, they're all one and the same. They are the church, united together in Christ.

This divine secret was foretold by Jesus but not explained by Him. The revelation of this mystery was committed to Paul and in his writings alone is found the doctrine, position, walk, and destiny of the church. He suffered much persecution for this because it was a truth that was difficult for Jews to accept. The basic sin of the ancient world was contempt. The Jews despised the Gentiles as worthless in the sight of God. At worst, they existed only to be annihilated (Is. 60:12), at best they existed to be the slaves of Israel (Is. 45:14). Bible commentator John Phillips said, "The new equality of the Gentiles was a bitter pill for most Jews to swallow. For centuries they had prided themselves as being God's chosen people. They had nurtured a growing contempt for Gentiles and wallowed in religion and sacred snobbery. They had considered themselves to be God's favorites. Now all this superiority was shattered. It turned out that all along God loved the Gentiles just as much as He loved the Jews."

Not a single Jew ever dreamed that God's blessings were for all people. Still, this was the gospel message Paul was sent forth to preach. It was God's will "that the Gentiles should be fellow heirs of the same body, and partakers of His promises in Christ through the gospel" (Eph. 3:6). The word "gospel" means 'good news.' Missionary E. Stanley Jones said, "Religions are man's search for God; the Gospel is God's search for man. There are many religions but one Gospel." Canadian theologian A. B. Simpson added to this, saying the gospel "tells rebellious men that God is reconciled, that justice is satisfied, that sin has been atoned for, that the judgment of the guilty may be revoked, the condemnation of the sinner cancelled, the curse of the Law blotted out, the gates of hell closed, the portals of heaven opened wide, the power of sin subdued, the guilty conscience healed, the broken heart comforted, the sorrow and misery of the fall undone." That is good news.

One thing was certain, this mystery needed a preacher to explain what the mystery was. Rom. 10:14 asks the question, "And how shall they hear without a preacher?" Paul made it clear who that preacher was, saying in Eph. 3:7 (AMP), "Of this gospel I was made a minister by the gift of God's grace given me through the working of His power." Paul did not make himself a minister, God made him one. This is why he said in 1 Cor. 16:10, "But by the grace of God, I am what I am." The word "made" means 'to come into existence.' God brought him into existence to be a minister of the gospel, to explain to the people what the mystery was. This was not an easy task to perform. Paul said in Col. 1:29, "To this end I also labor, striving according to His working which works in me mightily." In Greek, this verse is saying he "worked to the point of exhaustion." The NLT says, "That's why I work and struggle so hard, depending on Christ's mighty power that works within me."

The Greek word for "minister" is "diakonos" and it means 'servant.' A servant, by definition, is one who acts on the commands of another, one who obeys the commands of his master. A servant is someone who always recognizes a higher authority. This Greek word isn't describing a very classy servant, just a common run-of-the-mill servant. In fact, this was the lowest of the servants, one who waits on tables, washes feet, and performs other menial duties. Here, the apostle to the Gentiles, the preacher of the mystery, uses this lowly term to describe himself. He's saying, "I am simply a minister." At best, all those called by God are servants. You'll get in trouble if you don't have the same perspective Paul had. You'll get arrogant and prideful. Prov. 16:18 says, "Pride goes before destruction, and a haughty spirit before a fall." Just remember, a minister is one who serves in the interests and for the benefits of others. He has a task to perform and a calling to fulfill.

Paul also called himself a minister in Rom. 15:15,16, "Because of the grace given to me by God, that I might be a minister of Jesus Christ to the Gentiles, ministering the gospel of God." This time, however, he uses a different Greek word to describe himself. The word used here for "minister" is "leitourgos" and it means 'a worker of the people; a person performing public duties at his own expense; those who render a divinely ordained service.' This word is used referring to angels as God's ministers (Heb. 1:7) and of the priests who ministered in the sanctuary in the temple at Jerusalem (Heb. 8:2). Broadly speaking, being a servant of God makes you a Christian minister. You don't have to be a pastor or stand behind a pulpit to be a minister. If you're a servant of God, you're a minister. Charles Spurgeon said, "Every man should give most attention to that part of the work which the Lord has entrusted him, with the pure motive that God may be glorified thereby."

Here in the third chapter of Ephesians, Paul teaches what it means to be a minister of the gospel of Jesus Christ. He will tell you, in summary, that gospel ministers are just lowly servants bearing good news of amazing grace for lost sinners at all costs. The mystery demands ministers who have a God-given mission. Indeed, the good news is worth sharing. Every person should know what God has done for the world through the works of the Lord Jesus Christ. Paul is a minister of the good news, that God took those who were far off and brought them near by the blood of Christ. How did Paul get to be a minister? He was "made" a minister. He makes it very clear that the ministry chose him, he didn't choose the ministry. Sharing the good news with the Gentiles was not something Paul decided to do on his own. No, he's saying he was made a minister on the road to Damascus (Acts 9). This is why he began this letter saying he was an apostle "by the will of God" (Eph. 1:1).

A calling is something over which you have no say-so. It comes from God, and God alone. You don't decide what your calling is, you discover it. If the choice was yours, you weren't called in the first place. And once the call is given, it can't be taken back. Rom. 11:29 (NLT) says, "For God's gifts and His call can never be withdrawn." The Amplified Bible says, "He never withdraws them once they are given, and He does not change His mind about those to whom He gives His grace or to whom He sends His call." Whatever God calls you to do, obey Him and answer the call. Jonah was called by God but refused to surrender to that call. Instead, he ran the other way (Jonah 1:1-3). He didn't realize that "God's gifts and God's call are under full warranty - never canceled, never rescinded" (MSG). In other words, God won't change His mind about what He has called you to do. You will discover your call by walking closely with the Lord, by practicing obedience, and by offering yourself to Him as a living sacrifice (Rom. 12:1).

Paul makes it very clear that his calling to be a minister of the gospel was "according to the gift of the grace of God given to me by the effective working of His power" (vs. 7). Yes, the manifestation of God's power was most effective. It transformed Saul the persecutor into Paul the beloved apostle to the Gentiles. It turned a hater of the gospel into a lover and proclaimer of the same gospel. This was "dunamis" power characterized by energy and forces that produce results. It was an active, operative power that led to continuous and productive activity or change. The fact that God could save a proud, self-righteous Pharisee and call him to be an apostle was a clear demonstration of the "effective working of His power." Paul was made a minister through grace and power. Grace means he's unworthy, power means he was unable. You must constantly be aware of this because when God uses you, if you're not careful, you might get puffed up with arrogance and pride.

What keeps the power flowing is the humility expressed in vs. 8, "To me, who am less than the least of all the saints, this grace was given, that I should preach among the Gentiles the unsearchable riches of Christ." Being chosen by God to be a minister to the Gentiles produced in Paul a profound wonder and much humility, so much so that he considered himself the least of the least of all the saints. This is not false humility. This is Paul's honest assessment of his own life. He was the worst sinner he knew, saying in Rom. 7:24, "O wretched man that I am! Who will deliver me from this body of death?" The TPT says, "What an agonizing situation I am in! So who has the power to rescue this miserable man from the unwelcome intruder of sin and death?" Paul is teaching a valuable lesson here. A sign that you are maturing in Christ is there will be a greater sensitivity to sin in your life. David didn't run and hide when confronted with his sin with Bathsheba. No, he admitted his sin and asked for mercy.

Ministers of the gospel must always maintain a humble perspective. The fact that God uses you doesn't mean you're better than someone else. Remember, all have sinned and fall short of the glory of God (Rom. 3:23). What it should do is make you love others even more than you already do. If God can save you, if His love and mercy can be poured out into your life, then surely He can save anybody. The point is this, you can't be proud when you're standing next to the cross. Charles Spurgeon said, "While Paul was thankful for his office, his success in it greatly humbled him. The fuller a vessel becomes, the deeper it sinks in the water." Humility is a heart attitude, not merely an outward demeanor. Jesus said in Matt. 5:3, "Blessed are the poor in spirit, for theirs is the kingdom of heaven." Being "poor in spirit" means that only those who admit to an absolute bankruptcy of spiritual worth will inherit eternal life or be considered great in the kingdom (Matt. 20:26,27).

Paul is saying what John the Baptist said in John 3:30, "He must increase, but I must decrease." In fact, in Latin the word "Paulus" means 'little' or 'small.' He is saying, "I am little by name, morally and spiritually more little than the least of all Christians. I am small Paul." He wrote in 1 Tim. 1:15, "Christ Jesus came into the world to save sinners, of whom I am chief." You must remain humble because self-ambition and self-glory gets in the way of God's power. William Barclay said, "We must always remember that our greatness lies not in ourselves but in our task and in our message. The tragic fact is that there are so many who are more concerned with their own prestige than with the prestige of Jesus Christ; and who are more concerned that they should be noticed than that Christ should be seen." With a humble spirit, in Christ you'll become a saint, set apart from that which is secular, profane, and evil. You'll be holy both in character and conduct.

Finally, ministers of the gospel focus on Jesus Christ. Paul was called to preach among the Gentiles the unsearchable riches of Christ, all the truths about Him, and all He means to believers. He is saying, "I've been called to preach the riches. I'm not just here to tell you what God wants you to do, I'm here to tell you what He's already done for you. I'm here to tell you that you've been blessed with all spiritual blessings in the heavenlies in Christ Jesus. I'm here to tell you that you're complete in Him. I'm here to tell you that you have all things that pertain to life and godliness. You're rich, rich, rich!" God is rich and He wants to pass those riches on to you. How rich is God? The Bible says His grace is rich (Eph. 1:7), His goodness and patience is rich (Rom. 2:4),

His mercy is rich (Eph. 2:4), His person is rich (Eph. 3:16), His love is rich (Eph. 3:18,19), His blessings are rich (1 Tim. 6:17), His assurance is rich (Col. 2:2), and His Word is rich (Col. 3:16).

If you're a believer, you are incredibly rich in Christ with blessings that one cannot comprehend fully. Other translations say these are "boundless riches" (NIV), "endless treasures" (NLT), "spiritual wealth that no one can fully understand" (AMP), "blessings that cannot be measured" (CEV), "the unfading, inexhaustible riches of Christ, which are beyond comprehension" (TPT). The Greek word describes something that cannot be fully comprehended or explored. In other words, there is no limit to the riches of Christ. They are past finding out. They are so vast you cannot discover their end. John Eadie said, "The riches of Christ are so vast that the comprehension of its limits and the exhaustion of its contents are alike impossible. Their extent is boundless. The latest periods of time shall find these riches unimpaired, and eternity shall behold the same wealth neither worn by use nor dimmed by age, nor yet diminished by the myriads of its happy participants."

Rev. William Blaikie said in the 19th century, "Two attractive word, 'riches' and 'unsearchable,' conveying the idea of the things that are most precious being infinitely abundant. Usually precious things are rare; their very rarity increases their price; but here that which is most precious is also boundless - riches of compassion and love, of merit, of sanctifying, comforting, and transforming power, all without limit, and capable to satisfy." These words mirror what Paul said in Rom. 11:33 (TPT), "Who could ever wrap their minds around the riches of God, the depths of His wisdom, and the marvel of His perfect knowledge? Who could ever explain the wonder of His decisions or search out the mysterious way He carries out His plan?" Perhaps missionary statesman A. T. Pierson said it best, "There is a boundless continent, a world, a universe of riches, that still lies before you when you have carried your search to the limits of possibility." Amen to that!

| 26 |

"LIGHT OF THE COSMOS"

Paul is sharing with the saints at Ephesus the main qualifications of being a minister of the gospel. They must all have a God-given vision, they must remain humble at all times, and they must forever focus on the Lord Jesus Christ. All these pertain to Paul and he now says in Eph. 3:9 (NLT), "I was chosen to explain to everyone the mysterious plan that God, the Creator of all things, had kept secret from the beginning." God is uniting believing Jews and Gentiles into one body and it was Paul's mission "to bring to light the plan of the mystery" (TLV). Light is the emblem of knowledge. When something hidden is revealed, people say, "I saw the light." Ps, 18:28 says, "For You will light my lamp; The Lord my God will enlighten my darkness." The term "bring to light" means 'to cause something to be fully known by revealing clearly and in great detail; to shed light upon; to illuminate; to enlighten inwardly; to give spiritual apprehension; to make known what is hidden.'

Speaking of Jesus, John 1:9 (NIV) says, "The true light that gives light to everyone was coming into the world." Without Christ, people are incapable of receiving spiritual light because, in and of themselves, they lack the capacity for spiritual things (1 Cor. 2:14). W.E. Vine said, "Believers are called 'sons of light' (Luke 16:8) not merely because they have received a revelation from God, but because in the New Birth they have received the spiritual capacity for it." Charles Spurgeon said, "For Thou wilt light my candle. It will be our own candle, yet God Himself will find the holy fire with which the candle shall burn. Candles which are lit by God the devil cannot blow out. It is said that the poor in Egypt will stint themselves of bread to buy oil for the lamp, so that they may not sit in darkness. We could well afford to part with all earthly comforts if the light of God's love could but constantly gladden our souls."

The concept of the church was new, unique, unprecedented, and was not known before to anyone but God. This mystery was knowledge that couldn't be known except through divine revelation. F. B. Meyer said, "A mystery is a hidden secret. God has many secrets which unfold as the ages are ripe for them, and not before." The word "hidden" means 'to hide away from the common gaze, and therefore secret.' This mystery was formed before the ages of time began and kept secret until the time of Paul. It was he who was sent to enlighten everyone about God's secret plan. 1 Cor. 2:7 (TPT) says, "Instead, we continually speak of this wonderful wisdom that comes from God, hidden before now in a mystery. It is His secret plan, destined before the ages, to bring us into glory." William Barclay said, "Paul here reminds us that the salvation of the Gentiles is not an afterthought of God; the bringing of all men into His love was part of God's eternal design."

Paul is now going to explain the purpose of the mystery. What he's about to say is so profound that it would be hard to believe had it not been written in scripture. Eph. 3:10 (NLT) says, "God's purpose in all this was to use the church to display His wisdom in its rich variety to all the unseen rulers and authorities in the heavenly places." Wow! Think about that! The purpose for which God made the church was so that the angels might know "the manifold wisdom of God" (KJV). Not only was the mystery of redemption preached to a visible audience on earth, it is also being proclaimed to an invisible audience of angelic hosts in the heavenlies. The angels saw the power of God at creation. They saw the wrath of God at Sodom and Gomorrah. They saw the love of God at Calvary. God says they'll see His wisdom in the church. The angels are watching you because God told them to watch the church to see how wise He is.

This verse reveals the grandeur of the mission of the church and its cosmic significance. The truth in this text is so glorious and fantastic that it shines forth on its own merit. Not only are you "the light of the world" (Matt. 5;14), you are also the light of the cosmos with the spectacular mission of revealing the wisdom of God to supernatural beings. Once you become aware of this stupendous privilege and the great magnitude of belonging to Jesus Christ, you'll be able to taste the flavor of eternity and smell the aroma of the spiritual realities around you. As the aroma of God engulfs your very being, you'll see yourself as being a part of God's cosmic plan of the church. This in turn will raise your awareness of your true worth as it fills your heart with passion and excitement. The church is a means to an end, and the end is that God will be glorified. When the angels see the wisdom of God by looking at the church, they'll give Him glory for all He has done.

The one and only purpose of the universe is to give God glory. Your life, your ministry, and your relationship with other believers will cause the very angels of heaven to glorify God. The more you fulfill God's plan for your life, the more God will be glorified in the unlimited praises of the angelic hosts. John MacArthur said, "That God could take diverse male, female, bond, free, Jew, Gentile, and He could melt down all the walls and blend them together in an indivisible oneness. All one with Himself, one with the Father, one with the Son, one with the Spirit, one with other believers, that God could do that kind of miracle of salvation is a wonder beyond wonders of wisdom and causes the angelic host to give Him glory." These angels see the wisdom of God by looking at the church and they give Him glory for all He has done. God is the teacher, the universe is the classroom, the angels are the students, the church is the illustration, and the lesson is wisdom.

Angels are not all-knowing like God is. By looking at you and others in the body of Christ, these heavenly host are being taught something. They're being instructed, they're being given knowledge, they're learning about the manifold wisdom of God. They're learning that Christianity and the salvation that goes with it is the supreme manifestation of the wisdom of God. The Greek word for "manifold" is "polupoikilos" and here in vs. 10 is the only place in the New Testament where this word is found. It means 'many-sided; multi-colored; greatly diversified; abounding in variety.' It is a multi-faceted wisdom that surpasses all previous knowledge. Author Larry Richards said, "Don't put God in a box, or try to squeeze Him into limited categories. God's plans and purposes are multi-faceted, and each facet reflects His complex wisdom and love. The more we glimpse of that complexity, the more we should be moved to worship and to praise."

What is the wisdom of God? Martyn Lloyd-Jones said, "The wisdom of God is that attribute according to which He arranges His purposes and His plans, and brings forth the results that He desires perfectly." God is a God of wisdom and Paul is saying that through the church this attribute of God is being revealed to the principalities and power in the heavenly places in a greater manner than ever before. There is something happening in you that increases the understanding of these mighty beings, the brightest and most glorious angels in the heavenlies. These same angels, who since their creation have been in the presence of God, are staggered and amazed by this glorious mystery that Paul is preaching to the Gentiles. What is taking place in the church is something they never thought of or dreamed of. It surpasses their knowledge, their comprehension, and even their imagination. God's wisdom is inexhaustible as new flashes of truth continually blaze forth.

God's purpose is to make His wisdom known through the church. True wisdom is a divine revelation. You can never understand anything of God unless He reveals it to you. Biblical scholar Harold Hoehner said, "The best wisdom is that which has been revealed by God, for this is the means by which one gains insight into the true nature of God's plan." If you lack knowledge, go to school. If you lack wisdom, get on your knees. Charles Spurgeon said, "Conviction of ignorance is the doorstep to the temple of wisdom." Believers show the wisdom of God to the principalities and powers by being the church that God created. The church is a living organism, composed of living members joined together, through which God works and carries out His plans and purposes. The church is the visible manifestation of God's amazing wise plan to bring great unity out of great diversity and thereby cause all creation to honor Him.

Here in the third chapter of Ephesians is revealed the order in which this divine wisdom is made known. Paul received revelation from God (vs. 1-7) and the church received revelation from Paul (vs. 8,9). The church then makes this revelation known to the angelic hosts in heavenly places (vs. 10). This great spiritual truth, this mysterious plan, has to be taught and communicated by the visible church to its invisible audience so that they understand God's eternal plan for the redemption of mankind. God's wisdom is shown to angels when people from different racial and cultural backgrounds are united together as one in Christ. Steven Cole said, "The overall point that Paul is driving home is to elevate our understanding of the importance of the church in God's eternal purpose. The church is God's vehicle for making known His manifold wisdom, not only on earth, but also to the rulers and authorities in the heavenly places. So we must see how our lives count for eternity."

These words of Paul are remarkably stunning. He is saying you are called for something far greater than your own personal salvation and sanctification. You are called to be the means through which God teaches the universe a valuable lesson. God doesn't use angels to reveal His wisdom to born again believers, He uses the saints to reveal His wisdom to the angelic beings. This is why they are intently looking at you. They are hungry for knowledge, for those lessons God has commissioned you to teach them. Theologian Handley Moule said, "What then have they to learn from us? Ah, they have to learn something which makes them watch us with wonder and with awe. They see in us indeed all our weakness, and all our sin. But they see a nature which, wrecked by itself, was yet made in the image of their God and ours. And they see this God at work upon that wreck to produce results not only wonderful in themselves but doubly wonderful because of the condition."

Each morning when you wake up, be aware that the angels are watching you with eyes wide open. Indeed, they know you far better than you know them. John Stott said, "It is as if a great drama is being enacted. History is the theater, the world is the stage, and the church members in every land are the actors. God Himself has written the play, and He directs and produces it. Act by act, scene by scene, the story continues to unfold. But who are the audience? They are the cosmic intelligences, the principalities and powers in the heavenly places." These angelic beings are instructed by the life you live. This is why your conduct is so important for it is God's intention to teach angels through you. Without a doubt, you need to take this responsibility very seriously. Don't forget, it's these same angels who are given the responsibility to carry souls to heaven at death (Luke 16:22) and they are the reapers of the final harvest (Matt. 13:39-43).

Charles Spurgeon said, "And, lastly, what think some of you, would angels say of your walk and conversation? Well, I suppose you don't care much about them, and yet you should. For who but angels will be the reapers at the last, and who but they shall be the convoy to our spirits across the dark stream? Who but they shall carry our spirit like that of Lazarus into the Father's bosom? Surely we should not despise them." Angels have never personally experienced the wonderful, saving grace of God. Only humanity is the recipient of God's redemptive grace, whereby Christ came to earth as a man and took upon Himself the role of man's Redeemer. Paul elaborates on this in Eph. 3:11,12 (TPT), "This perfectly wise plan was destined from eternal ages and fulfilled completely in our Lord Jesus Christ, so that now we have boldness through Him, and free access as kings before the Father because of our complete confidence in Christ's faithfulness."

What is Paul saying here? He is saying that Christ is the door to God's throne. Everything Paul has been saying to the saints at Ephesus leads inevitably to this particular conclusion. The ultimate purpose of all Christian doctrine is to bring believers to this one verse. Over and above all the glorious benefits and promises in the Bible, this is the grand objective. Indeed, all scripture is designed to bring you into the presence of God and there is nothing greater than that. When you put your faith in Jesus Christ, you can walk into the eternal presence of an eternal God with confidence and boldness. The Greek word for 'boldness" is "parresia" and it means 'freedom of speech.' You have the right to speak openly without fear of retaliation. You need not panic or tremble because the throne of God is a throne of grace. The Message Bible says, "When we trust in Him, we're free to say whatever needs to be said, bold to go wherever we need to go."

The Amplified Bible says, "Our faith gives us sufficient courage to freely and openly approach God through Christ." The word "access" only appears three times in the New Testament (Rom. 5:1,2; Eph. 2:18; Eph. 3:12) and each time it refers to Jesus and what He accomplished for believers. Because of what Jesus did on the cross, you can now stand calmly and fearlessly before God. Contrast this with Adam who ran from the presence of God and hid among the trees of the garden. The Living Bible says you will be "assured of His glad welcome when we come with Christ and trust in Him." Draw near to Him with a heart that beats true unto God. It's the sincerity of your heart that gets God's attention. Like close friends, you fellowship together and enjoy each other's company. There is nothing greater than the deep intimacy of being adopted, welcomed, and affirmed as a child of the living God whose presence you richly and fully enjoy.

There is no doubt that you need to earnestly value and desire the presence of God in your life. Jesus said in John 14:23, "If anyone loves Me, he will keep My word; and My Father will love him, and We will come to him and make Our home with him." In His presence is an overwhelming atmosphere of unconditional, deep, and infinite love. The air is thick with providence, sovereignty, wisdom, and holiness. In His presence is the possibility of miracles, healing, reconciliation, and answers to all your questions. With God, all things are possible for He is able to do exceedingly abundantly more than you can ask or think (Eph. 3:20). Success is guaranteed for in God's presence you cannot fail. All your enemies will be defeated just like David defeated Goliath, Samson defeated the Philistines, and Elijah defeated the prophets of Baal. With God there is victory over sin and death, and everything else the devil throws your way.

Indeed, the presence of God is very, very powerful. Just prior to the crucifixion, close to six hundred soldiers were looking for Jesus so they might arrest Him. When Jesus said, "I am He," John 18:6 says, "They drew back and fell to the ground." The Greek word for "drew back" means 'to wobble; to stagger; to lose one's bearing.' A blast of divine power hit those soldiers so strong they lost their footing. They wobbled, desperately trying to stay on their feet. So much power was in demonstration that they all fell hard to the ground. The Greek word for "fell" is "pipto" and it depicts a person who falls so hard it appears he has fallen dead or has fallen like a corpse. They fell abruptly, and they fell hard. It was as if a bomb was detonated in front of them and there was nothing they could do about it. This was power beyond their wildest imagination. Resistance was futile and all they could do was drop where they stood.

These soldiers were strong warriors. They were well trained and equipped with the finest weapons of the day, weapons needed for serious combat. They were in the presence of deity and the staggering words of Jesus and the power that was released overcame them. They were heavily armed, ready for a skirmish, but with mere words Jesus knocked them flat on the ground. They were paralyzed by His presence, laid low by the power that was released when Jesus said, "I am He." This was the same word God used when He described Himself to Moses in Ex. 3:14, saying, "I AM WHO I AM." In those words, Jesus identified Himself as God in the flesh. This is why Paul told the ancient Athenian, "In Him we live and move and have our being" (Acts 17:28). Just like when God created Adam and Eve, Paul is saying that, because of Jesus, you can now experience the powerful presence of God all the time in a very tangible way.

A lot of believers don't actively think about the presence of God because the visible world around them is constantly screaming for their attention. They don't realize that without God's presence, there is no real distinction between Christian and sinner. In fact, it's His presence in your life that separates you from those not saved. It is exciting to know that God always reveals Himself to His people. Yes, all believers have an open invitation to meet with Him face to face. The Greek word for "presence" is "paniym" and it means 'before the face; front side; in front of; in full view of.' God allows you to see and understand the generous and personal attributes of who He is. Live your life knowing you're always in the presence of God. He is always with you, listening intently to your thoughts and conversations, observing what you do and what you don't do. Knowing this should stop you from doing wrong things as it propels you to do right things.

Paul wants his readers to be so overwhelmed with these glad tidings that they don't have time to be concerned that he is a prisoner in Rome. "Therefore I ask that you do not lose heart at my tribulations for you, which is your glory" (Eph. 3:13). In view of the dignity of his ministry and the wonderful results that flowed from it, Paul encouraged the saints not to be disheartened when they thought of his sufferings. He's saying to them, "Don't worry about me. Just get the message. It's bringing the glory of God into your life." This was a very delicate and touching request, that they would not be distressed by what he was suffering on their behalf. The fact is, Paul's ministry, even in prison, was part of his accomplishing the stewardship of God's grace to the Gentiles. He felt his tribulations was a small price to pay to get the message out. He said in 2 Cor. 12:15 (MSG), "I'd be most happy to empty my pockets, even mortgage my life, for your good."

It is truly amazing that Paul would make this request for most people couldn't endure what he went through. The Greek word for "tribulation" is 'thlipsis" and it refers not to mild discomfort but to great difficulty. It means 'to crush; press together; squash.' It conveys the idea of being squeezed or placed under pressure or crushed beneath a weight. It pictures a person being crushed by intense pressure, difficult circumstances, suffering or trouble pressing upon them from without. Persecution, affliction, distress, opposition, and tribulation all press hard on one's soul. Thankfully, Paul always had an eternal perspective when suffering for the sake of the gospel. He said in Rom. 8:18, "For I consider that the sufferings of this present time are not worthy to be compared with the glory that is to be revealed to us." Hallelujah! It's because of this attitude that he could say in 2 Tim. 4:7, "I have fought the good fight, I have finished the race, I have kept the faith."

Paul always cared for others more than he did himself. This is why he told the people to not lose heart. He was saying don't be discouraged and don't lose your enthusiasm. He said in 1 Cor. 15:58, "Be steadfast, immovable, always abounding in the work of the Lord, knowing that your labor is not in vain in the Lord." The word "immovable" means don't get knocked over by sudden blows. Keep your balance. Stand strong and unshaken when the rains come down and beat against your house. Be like a boulder that can't get washed away. Be like a tree that can't get blown over. Paul is trying to stimulate these peo-ple to not grow weary or tired, to not faint, and to not despair. He doesn't want them to lose their courage, to lose the motivation to ac-complish a valid goal or to continue in a desirable pattern of conduct. He's saying don't become discouraged and don't grow slack. Most of all, never, ever give up. Fight the good fight of faith because it's al-ways too soon to quit.

| 27 |

"POSTURE OF THE HEART"

Do you sometimes feel that God has given you an assignment that you don't have the strength to carry out? It may be in the area of resisting a temptation, of enduring some hardship, or living in obedience. Feeling you don't have the strength that is needed may tempt you to give up, give in, and give way. You're not alone if this is how you feel. The truth be told, too many Christians live weak, frail lives. Rarely do they draw upon the gifts and the power that God has made available to them. Why is this so? They don't understand the inheritance God has given them. Jesus said in Matt. 28:18, "All authority has been given to Me in heaven and on earth." Jesus then turns around and gives this same authority to you. He said in Luke 10:19, "Behold, I give you the authority to trample on serpents and scorpions, and over all the power of the enemy, and nothing shall by any means hurt you." He even said in John 14:13, "If you ask anything in My name, I will do it."

That's power! That's authority! And it's yours for the taking. Even so, there is still a power failure in the lives of most Christians. John MacArthur said, "The divine revelation of God tells us we have all this energy and all this power and yet Christians crank it out on one cylinder, limping and coughing and sputtering and smoking, and nothing really ever seems very dynamic; and the average church is full of a whole pile of spectators who just sort of sit there and watch, and they go out and live a very mediocre Christian life or even less than mediocre." Paul doesn't want the saints at Ephesus to be this way, and he doesn't want you to be this way either. This is why he brings the first half of Ephesians to a close with an incredibly powerful and insightful prayer. This portion of scripture is one of the most magnificent in all the Bible. The tremendous truths contained in this passage are so marvelous they will cause your life to be changed dramatically.

If you pay close attention to the epistles of Paul, you'll quickly realize that he loved to pray. He was always praying for those to whom he writes and for whom he is concerned. The New Testament records almost fifty prayers Paul prayed for the people. He knows it's not enough just to write encouraging letters to the people. He knew the importance and the power of praying these truths into their lives. The recorded prayers in the Bible instruct you as to what God's will is. They also give you inspiration because they let you know the intensity you should have in your life of prayer. It fuels your passion to pray as you ask God to release His power into your life. For the born again believer, prayer is supposed to be like breathing. You do it naturally with little or no thought or concern. Jesus thought it was worthwhile to pray. Mark 1:35 says, "And rising very early in the morning, while it was still dark, He departed and went to a desolate place, and there He prayed."

Why pray? First and foremost, you pray because God commands you to. Phil. 4:6 says, "Be anxious for nothing, but in everything by prayer and supplication, with thanksgiving, let your requests be made known to God." The TPT says, "Don't be pulled in different directions or worried about a thing. Be saturated in prayers throughout each day, offering your faith-filled request before God with overflowing gratitude. Tell Him every detail of your life." Paul is saying here that praying is something you do automatically, all the time. You're commanded to pray for a variety of reasons. For one thing, prayer is a form of serving God and obeying Him (Luke 2:36-38). God intends prayer to be the means of obtaining His solutions to the circumstances you find yourself in. You're to pray when important decisions have to be made (Luke 6:12,13), to overcome demonic barriers (Matt. 17:14-21), and to gain strength to overcome temptation (Matt. 26:41).

In His goodness, God wants you to draw close to Him. The most direct way to do that is through simple, confident praying. When you go to God with specific requests, you have a promise from Him that your prayers are not in vain. Jesus said in Matt. 6:6, "But you, when you pray, go into your room, and when you have shut the door, pray to your Father who is in the secret place; and your Father who sees in secret will reward you openly." Jesus is saying here that simple prayers get big results. You don't need a detailed manual to know how to pray effectively. Children don't need an advanced degree in theology in order to feel confident about approaching their parents with questions and requests. Indeed, prayer is not complicated. It's part of the daily conversation you have with your Heavenly Father. You ask Him for things and you express your gratitude for all the wonderful things He has already done in your life.

Pray simple prayers knowing that prayer should not be seen as a means of getting God to do your will, but rather as a means of getting His will done on earth. Stop thinking you have to tell Him how to handle everything. All you have to do is present the need to Him and leave the results in His very capable hands. He is God, after all. Pray often and with great confidence knowing He hears your prayers and He intends to answer them. 1 John 5:14,15 (NLT) says, "And we are confident that He hears us whenever we ask for anything that pleases Him. And since we know He hears us when we make our requests, we also know that He will give us what we ask for." Paul had great confidence in God's willingness and ability to answer prayer. Not once did Paul hold back from going to God with his prayer requests. He went boldly to the throne of grace because he knew God is the motivator, the initiator, and the force behind all things spiritual.

The Christian experience is about applying God's power to everyday life. Paul makes it clear that you not only need light and knowledge to begin your walk with God, you'll need power to continue. The fact is, you've got inside you all the power you need to walk the walk, to do the job God called you to do. You're in Christ Jesus and you've been blessed with all spiritual blessings in heavenly places. Paul's prayer in chapter one was a prayer for understanding. He wanted the saints at Ephesus to know who they were in Christ and the power that was available to them. He prayed for enlightenment and here in chapter three he prays for enablement. He wants the people to know better and he wants them to do better. He wants them to act like the saints they are. His desire is for them to understand the power and then he wants them to use the power. Paul wants to bring them to the place of maximum power output so that they might begin to do what God's power enables them to do.

Paul is praying that you will live out the truth of who you are in Christ, that you'll comprehend the fact that there is so much more God wants to do in your life than what you're currently experiencing. He knows that with God's power working in your life, you'll be all that He called you to be. This prayer at the end of chapter three is a bridge between the two main messages of Ephesians. The first three chapters is about your wealth in Christ, the last three chapters is about your walk in Christ. He already told you that you're seated in heavenly places. Now he prays that you'll have the power to walk it out on the earth. Before telling you how to walk the walk, he inserts this prayer recorded in Eph. 3:14-21. He prays that God will give you the strength and power to live out the teachings of your faith. Let's face it, you cannot walk the walk in your own strength. The good news is, if you will call on Him, God will give you the strength you need when you need it.

Paul is stirred up. His affections are ablaze for he is going to take you step by step up an awe-inspiring staircase of endeavor, rising constantly, leading you to the fullest experience of Christian vitality. Pay close attention because there is a remarkable sequence described here, a progression of purpose that leads to God's power exploding in your life. As you will see, the ultimate end of Paul's prayer is that God would be glorified. The truth be told, that is the purpose of everything you do. The aim of your life is that God would be glorified in how you think, how you speak, and how you act. Paul prayed a lot for the believers and he always prayed for their spiritual needs, not their physical needs. What he's concerned about here is that they would really know the fullness of the power of God, that they would see released in their lives the power that God can use to do exceedingly abundantly above all they can ask or think.

Paul is calling for God to glorify Himself through what He does in the lives of all believers. Before Paul tells you what to pray, he tells you first the attitude with which you should approach God in prayer. Both are significant because the right content can be nullified if your heart is not right. In other words, you need to pray with the right attitude. You need to pray with both reverence for God and confidence in God. Paul picks up where he left off in vs. 1, saying, "For this reason I bow my knees to the Father of our Lord Jesus Christ, from whom the whole family in heaven and earth is named" (Eph. 3:14,15). Notice the words "For this reason..." This was the same phrase Paul used in vs. 1 of this chapter. After digressing to explain God's eternal purpose in vs. 2-14, that the Gentiles are now fellow citizens in the household of God, Paul resumes the thought of vs. 1 by repeating the same words as he now begins his prayer.

The Phillips Bible says, "When I think of the greatness of this great plan, I fall on my knees before God the Father." In Paul's day, it wasn't customary for the Jews to bow their knees in prayer. They usually prayed standing up with arms outstretched to God. They would only kneel or prostrate themselves before God in times of great distress, times of extreme urgency, or overwhelming need. Ezra 9:5 says, "At

the evening offering I arose from my humiliation, even with my garment and my robe torn, and I fell on my knees and stretched out my
hands to the Lord my God." The Greek word for "bow" is "kampto"
and it means 'to bend or incline some part of the body as a gesture of
respect or devotion.' It suggests an attitude of submission, reverence,
and passion. Here Paul is saying he bows his knees before the Father
not just out of need or urgency or dependence, but also out of wor-
shipful reverence. At all times he wanted to give his Lord and Master
honor and glory.

Ps. 95:6 says, "Come, let us worship and bow down; Let us kneel before the Lord our Maker." When Paul thinks about how sovereign
and gracious God is and all He has done, as he prays he bows his knees
in reverence to God. This verse teaches you the proper posture of
prayer. Never are you to approach God with casual familiarity. He is
the God who created all things by the words of His mouth. He sustains the world by His good pleasure. Come boldly as a small child before a caring father, yet reverential as creatures before their Maker.
An adoring heart should show its awe by prostrating the body and
bending the knee. When the wise men found the Christ child they
"fell down and worshipped Him" (Matt. 2:11). Your adoration for God
is to be humble. You are to pray and worship Him with an attitude of
total and complete reverence. Bowing down shows you count yourself to be as nothing in the presence of the all glorious God.

God said in 2 Chron. 7:14, "If My people, which are called by My
name, shall humble themselves, and pray, and seek My face, and turn
from their wicked ways, then will I hear from heaven, and will forgive
their sin, and will heal their land." Before God even mentions prayer,
you will notice He says first that you must humble yourself. Yes, God
is a loving Father but He's still God. The Bible clearly teaches that God
should be approached with reverence and awe. Humility, along with
faith, lays the groundwork for effective prayer. Without humility, you
might as well be praying to yourself because God is not listening. This

is why you enter into prayer abounding with humility. The position of bowing your knees reminds you of the awesome majesty of the One you address as Father. It also signifies submission to a higher authority. With a spirit of humility you are submitting your will to God's will. Whatever He wants is what you want.

If you're in a situation where you can't physically bow your knees, then make sure your heart is bowed when you approach God. Abraham stood before the Lord when he prayed for Sodom (Gen. 18:22), Solomon stood when he prayed to dedicate the temple (1 Kings 8:22), and David sat before the Lord when he prayed about the future of his kingdom (1 Chron. 17:16). If you can't bow your knees, then bow your soul. It's the posture of the heart that's important, the attitude you have when you pray. It will help to know that prayer has been designed by God to enrich the life of every believer. Even at its most basic level, prayer touches the heart of God. It is through prayer that you are able to enter into intimate fellowship with the King of kings and Lord of lords. Paul said he bowed his knees to the Father. By calling Him Father, Paul is emphasizing the fact that God accepts you when you go to Him in humble prayer.

God is the Father of those who run to the cross and trust in Jesus. Without Christ, you're a guilty sinner separated from God. When clothed with the righteousness of Christ, you have access to God. When you go to Him, you go to a tender, loving, compassionate Father who eagerly waits with anticipation the moment you enter His presence. He is the very epitome of fatherhood. He is the heavenly Father from whom all earthly fatherhood takes its essence and character. Ray Stedman said, "Fatherhood from above evokes concepts of concern and provision and loving guidance and faithful training, of shared pleasures, of occasional firm handling, of increasing communion." In His presence you will be embraced with loving arms along with an eagerness to hear what you have to say. Ps. 66:19 says, "But certainly God has heard me; He has attended to the voice of my prayer." 1 John 5:14 says, "If we ask anything according to His will, He hears us."

God is a Father in an infinite sense, accepting and forgiving and loving and desirous of fulfilling needs and wants. Paul sees God as a loving Father who accepts him, a Father "from whom the whole family in heaven and earth is named" (vs. 15). He is the perfect Father of those now in heaven and those still remaining on the earth. John MacArthur said, "Every family of believers is a part of the one spiritual family of God, in which there are many members but only one Father and one brotherhood." Never should there be any division or disunity in the church for all believers, both Jew and Gentile, are part of one family. Just remember, that Christian who rubs you the wrong way has the same heavenly Father you do. You have no right to judge or reject anybody based on your personal preferences or lofty standards. God has accepted them and you must do the same. Like yourself, they legitimately derive their name from God the Father.

Paul is in jail but he's not praying for himself. He's praying for others, many of whom he don't know personally. Still, he prayed confidently for them even though he didn't know their circumstances. In fact, he didn't need to know what trials they were going through. He was thoroughly convinced that the heart of the matter is the matter of the heart. When he prayed, he didn't pray for deliverance, intervention, or relocation. No, he always prayed about issues of the heart. Every prayer Paul prayed while a prisoner was a prayer for somebody else's spiritual welfare (Phil. 1:9; Col. 1:9). He prayed with spiritual priority, always preoccupied with people's spiritual lives, for their spiritual well-being and development. And because he sees God as a loving Father who gives the best things to His children, Paul prays with an amazing boldness. Pray with reverence for God but also pray with confidence in God. Nothing pleases Him more (Heb. 11:6).

Scholars view this prayer as an ascending stairway of prayer requests. As the verses proceed, the requests get loftier and loftier, higher and higher. Paul doesn't piddle around with puny requests. No, he desires and seeks after the best God has to offer. To start, he wants the saints at Ephesus and you to receive a full manifestation of divine power in your inner man. On bended knees he goes before God and fearlessly asks "that He would grant you, according to the riches of His glory, to be strengthened with might through His Spirit in the inner man" (vs. 16). This is a bold request. Paul is praying that God's power would be richly applied to your spiritual progress. As you yield to the Holy Spirit, you'll be empowered with strength in the inner man. Like dynamite, you'll explode with power and might that will give you victory in your life. It's strength that causes you to conquer Satan, sin, and the world.

This is a prayer for God's power to give you strength in the inner man. It's in the inner man where spiritual renewal takes place. 2 Cor. 4:16 says, "The inner man is being renewed day by day." Through the Holy Spirit, your inner man is getting better, fresher, and more vital. It is increasing, becoming richer and deeper and stronger with each passing day. This world is an evil place and desperately you need God's power at work in your life. Let's face it, you don't have what it takes to be a good Christian, a good spouse, or a good parent on your own. This is why Paul wants you to know and experience God's power at work in your life. There is nothing worse than power that lays dormant and does nothing. The Passion Translation (TPT) says, "And I pray that He would unveil within you the unlimited riches of His glory and favor until supernatural strength floods your innermost being with His divine might and explosive power."

Paul didn't pray for their problems to go away. These saints at Ephesus were in difficult circumstances. They were under the occupation of Rome, there was disease and the constant threat of war and persecution. Paul knew the greatest thing these saints needed was an experience of God's power in their life. If you have the power, you can handle all the trials that come your way. Don't be like those people who go chasing after spiritual experiences. No, seek after God. In His goodness He will, at times, bring an experience into your life. Chasing after experiences cause you to bounce around from one emotional high to the next. But what happens during those dry seasons when those emotional feelings are not there? You'll learn real quickly that an emotional experience by itself don't change you. It's the power of God and His presence that causes change to come in an everlasting, beneficial way. It's the power of God that brings you up to a higher level.

The first step in turning God's power loose in your life is to be strengthened in the inner man by the Holy Spirit. That's the beginning of everything. The idea here is that the Spirit might infuse God's own strength into your inner man. 1 Cor. 12:13 says, "For by one Spirit we were all baptized into one body and have all been made to drink into one Spirit." The Message Bible says, "Each of us is now a part of His resurrection body, refreshed and sustained at one fountain - His Spirit - where we all come to drink." Your spirit was made to drink from the river of the Spirit of life which is in you. Drinking of the Spirit refreshes your spirit just like a drink of water refreshes your body. Do this daily and your spirit will be strengthened so you can begin to live life as God intended. Eph. 5:18 (TPT) says, "Be filled continually with the Holy Spirit." Let the Spirit of God fill you each and every day. Let Him dominate every area of your life.

| 28 |

"RICHES OF HIS GLORY"

As Paul's pen glides across the paper with spiritual relevance, he knows he's about to show the saints at Ephesus how "to have a walk worthy of the calling with which you were called" (Eph. 4:1). He also knows if they're to fulfill their destiny, if they are to walk the walk, then they'll need "to be strengthened with might through His Spirit in the inner man" (Eph. 3:16). Indeed, it takes the power of God to fulfill any heavenly call. John Eadie said, "And this strength is imparted to the inner man by the Spirit's application of those truths which have a special tendency to cheer and sustain. The Spirit gives you the assurance that all grace needed will be fully and cheerfully afforded, and with the hope that the victory shall be ultimately obtained." As you yield to the Holy Spirit, your inner man is strengthened to resist Satan, sin, and temptation. Is there any greater need in a Christian's life than to be made strong with a power outside himself? Certainly not!

God told Paul in 2 Cor. 12:9, "My grace is sufficient for you, for My strength is made perfect in weakness." The TPT says, "My power finds its full expression through your weakness." God is saying, "You're better off when you realize your inabilities. You're better off when you know your own strength is not going to make it and you turn and yield to Me." Paul was convinced of this for he said in the following verse, "For when I am weak, then I am strong" (vs. 10). The

TPT says, "So I'm not defeated by my weakness, but delighted! For when I feel my weakness and endure mistreatment - when I'm surrounded with troubles on every side and face persecution because of my love for Christ - I am made yet stronger. For my weakness became a portal of God's power." Paul said in Phil. 4:13, "I can do all things through Christ who strengthens me." That's confidence. He was in jail yet he was totally yielded to the power of Christ.

Missionary Ruth Paxson said, "God rejoices whenever a child of His comes to the end of himself and acknowledges his own utter impotency, for then God can begin to work. The Holy Spirit who worked for us to implant life now works in us to impart power. The life bestowed by the Spirit through rebirth is to be realized in fullness through renewal." You can't walk the walk without the power of the Holy Spirit strengthening your inner man. This is the ministry of the Holy Spirit, pouring in power to give you spiritual stamina, spiritual vigor, spiritual muscle to approach life victoriously. 2 Cor. 4:16 (TPT) says, "So no wonder we don't give up. For even though our outer person gradually wears out, our inner being is renewed every single day." Without this power all you've got is religion. You'll soon get tired of it all and move on to something else. Don't be like those who have "a form of godliness but deny its power" (2 Tim. 3:5).

The inner man is the issue here. If you're weak on the inside, you'll suffer from frustration, mental strain, as well as emotional and spiritual imbalance. The good news is that when your body begins to show signs of age, the inner man remains remarkably free from the effects of aging. Through the power of the Holy Spirit, your inward man is being renewed day by day. If you are saved, 1 Peter 3:4 says your inner man is incorruptible. The Greek word "aphthartos" refers to 'something that is incapable of suffering the effects of wear, tear, and age.' As you get older, the outer man decays and declines but the inner man accelerates and ascends. You're young at heart and those around you are simply amazed. Your inner man is being strengthened, revitalized, and renewed every day. The sweet fragrance of Christ flows from your heart and through your words and actions. Every morning you get one day older but on the inside you get one day stronger.

Say to yourself, "I'm not getting older, I'm getting stronger and stronger and stronger." In proportion to the decline of the outer man is the renewal of the inner man. And the more you're strengthened in the inner man, the less you're concerned about the declining of the outer man. In order for your inner man to get richer, deeper, and stronger, you must continually yield yourself to the Holy Spirit. Paul warns in 1 Thess. 5:19, "Do not quench the Spirit." The Greek word for "quench" is "sbennymi" and it means 'to extinguish; to put out; to go out.' The word was used to refer to putting out fires, sparks, or the putting out of a lamp (Matt. 25:8). God has granted to believers the ability either to restrict or release what the Holy Spirit does in your personal life. Without the renewing ministry of the Holy Spirit, you won't be able to fight the world, the flesh, or the devil. You've got to be strengthened in your inner man or you can't overcome the enemy.

Pastor Sam Storm said, "The Spirit comes to us as a fire, either to be fanned into full flame and given the freedom to accomplish His will, or to be doused and extinguished by the water of human fear, control, and flawed theology. The Holy Spirit wants to intensify the heat of His presence among us, to inflame our hearts and fill us with the warmth of His indwelling power." The Holy Spirit is a fire dwelling in each believer. He wants to express Himself through your words and actions. When you do what is wrong, when you don't allow the Spirit to be seen in your actions, you suppress or quench the Spirit. Eph. 4:30 says, "Do not grieve the Holy Spirit of God." You grieve the Holy Spirit and stop His holy influence in your life by living like pagans (4:17-19), by lying (4:25), by being angry (4:26,27), by stealing (4:28), by cursing (4:29), by being bitter (4:31), by being unforgiving (4:32), and by being sexually immoral (5:3-5).

When you quench and grieve the Holy Spirit, you cut off your power source. The flow of refreshment will dry up and your inner man will not be strengthened or revitalized. To grieve the Holy Spirit is to act in a sinful manner, whether it be in thought only or in both thought and deed. So what shall you do? Daily yield to the Holy Spirit and conduct your life in the power which He gives. Jesus said in Acts 1:8, "But you shall receive power when the Holy Spirit has come upon you." The TPT says, "You will be seized with power." Your inner man will grow strong as you yield to the Spirit. Gal. 5:6 says, "Walk in the Spirit and you'll not fulfill the lust of the flesh." Walking in the Spirit means to be Spirit-filled, Spirit-conscious, and Spirit-controlled. The simplicity of walking in the Spirit is to yield each and every decision you make to the leading of the Holy Spirit. Every step you take is in the energy and power of the Spirit, yielding yourself to Him at all times.

Eph. 6:10 says, "Be strong in the Lord and in the power of His might." The TPT says it this way, "Be supernaturally infused with strength through your life-union with the Lord Jesus. Stand victorious with the force of His explosive power flowing in and through you." God wants you to be strong and powerful with His strength and His might. So much so that He will strengthen you in the inner man "according to the riches of His glory" (Eph. 3:16). This is a profound, overpowering statement. The word "according" means 'in proportion to one's largeness; not stingily.' God owns the gold in every mine and the cattle on a thousand hills. He meets needs proportionately to His own riches which are infinite. The source of God's bank account is His own riches in glory. The word "glory" refers to God's radiance and splendor, the perfection of His character and activity. God's giving corresponds to the inexhaustible wealth and riches of that glory. He gives as lavishly as only He can.

Eph. 1:17 talked about "the riches of His grace" and Eph. 3:8 mentioned "the unsearchable riches of Christ." Phil. 4:19 says, "My God shall supply all your need according to His riches in glory by Christ."

God is a tender, concerned, loving Father who is deeply involved with you, who wants you to grow, who is concerned about your welfare. This is why He always gives grace and glory "according to" His riches, never "out of" His riches. There is a difference. He doesn't give a portion but a proportion. Charles Spurgeon said, "Your greatest need shall not exceed the liberality of His supplies." The possibilities of God are limitless. He shall supply your need according to those limitless possibilities. The word "riches" is the Greek word "ploutos" and it refers to spiritual abundance and prosperity. God's storehouse will never go bankrupt for He who owns everything and has abundant fullness also has an inexhaustible ability to supply all your needs.

God's resources are infinite, His storehouses are overflowing, His vaults are bottomless. W. E. Vine says God's riches in glory are "in accordance with His infinite and exhaustless fullness. This fullness is in the heavenly sphere, where His attributes and power are in unceasing manifestation, as emanating from His own person. This glory shines into the hearts and lives of His people, expressing to and in them all that centers in Himself." What's being said here is God's glory is God's being. He is His own riches in glory. When God wants to show you His glory, He shows you Himself. He reveals what He is like. The Greek word for "glory" is "doxa" and its basic idea is that of manifestation. The glory of God is the manifestation of His being, His nature, His character, and His acts. Walk outside on a clear night and you will see the glory of God. Ps. 19:1 (NIV) says, "The heavens declare the glory of God; the skies proclaim the works of His hands."

Glory is present in all things that pertain to God, when He is allowed to be seen as He really is. When you are in His presence, there will be glory. When you become the person God intended you to be, there will be glory. When you walk the walk, there will be glory. When you fulfill His purpose for your life, there will be glory. William MacDonald said, "Since the Lord is infinitely rich in glory, let the saints get ready for a deluge! Why should we ask so little of so great a King?"

When someone asked a tremendous favor of Napoleon it was immediately granted because, said Napoleon, "He honored me by the magnitude of his request." There is a reservoir of spiritual riches which
God has given you. Paul is not praying for you to get these riches for
you already have them. Instead, he is praying that you'll be strengthened according to these riches, that you'll let these riches be the source
of your strength as you walk a godly walk.

Remember, this is a petition for empowerment. Paul is saying, "God,
on the basis of the riches of Your glory, I want You to release this
power in the believers." The Greek word "krataioo" means 'to be empowered; to be increased in vigor; to be made strong; to be fortified; to gain the upper hand over; to have energy to resist.' It refers
to strength and might, but especially that which is manifested. Notice
this is a prayer for Christians, not unbelievers. Why is Paul praying
this prayer for people who are already saved? Because it's one thing to
know these things in your mind, another thing to experience them in
your heart. Many people stay at the same level they were at when they
got saved and never move on from that. Yes, Jesus is in their heart
but they're not experiencing the fullness of God in their life. These
people haven't moved on from their salvation experience. There is no
progression in their life, thus they haven't grown in spiritual maturity
(Heb. 5:12-14).

2 Tim. 1:7 (AMP) says, "For God did not give us a spirit of timidity
(of cowardice, of craven and cringing and fawning fear), but He has
given a spirit of power and of love and of calm and well-balanced
mind and discipline and self-control." The TPT says, "For God will
never give you the spirit of fear, but the Holy Spirit who gives you
mighty power, love, and self-control." Speaking of the Holy Spirit,
Wayne Barber says, "You have a divine partner living in you, and He
is in you to strengthen you with power so that you have an ability
that you didn't have before. If you will learn to tap into Him, then
you will begin to lean into the reality of His presence." Every believer

needs abundant strength that will enable them to endure trials, to resist temptation, to perform their duties as a Christian, to glorify God, and to live a life of faith. Let the Spirit of God strengthen you with His mighty power. Then let this power overflow out of you so you'll live life on a higher plane than what you lived before.

The Greek word "krataioo" also means 'to be shown to be strong; to be shown to be mighty.' The idea is to get what is on the inside of you to the outside so that you might be shown to be strong. Paul wants people to look at you and see that you have a divine ability operating inside of you. This spiritual power is the mark of every believer who submits to God's Word and His Spirit. William MacDonald said, "Unlimited strength is at our disposal. Through the enabling of the Holy Spirit, the believer can serve valiantly, endure patiently, suffer triumphantly, and, if need be, die gloriously." The Greek word for "power' is "dunamis" and it means 'divine energy; achieving power; inherit ability.' A stick of dynamite has power but the fuse first has to be lit for the power to be manifested. So it is with God's power. This is why Paul prayed in Eph. 1:19,20 that the saints would be enlightened to the truth that they possess the same "dunamis" power that raised Christ from the dead.

Paul is praying here that you'll be made mighty with power, that you'll have the ability to do that which you couldn't do before, that you'll have the capacity and divine ability to live a life on a higher plane. You'll need this power in order to walk the walk. It's what allows you to live a mature, stable, and wise Christian life in the midst of a crooked and perverse generation. It is always good to remember that Jesus performed His ministry on earth in the power of the Spirit. Acts 10:38 says, "God anointed Jesus of Nazareth with the Holy Spirit and with power." The Spirit of God is the agent in this process of invigoration. It is of utmost importance to understand that God doesn't give you this power so you can use it for selfish purposes. No, He provides His power to accomplish His purposes through you. When your desire is only to serve Him by walking the walk, He is both willing and able to do exceedingly abundantly above all that you ask or think (Eph. 3:20).

This is a magnificent prayer for it's filled with so much potential. The church has been given exceedingly great and precious promises and has become partakers of God's divine nature. Like God, the church is called to perfection and glory, to possess all things that pertain to life and godliness. 2 Peter 1:3 (TPT) says, 'Everything we could ever need for life and godliness has already been deposited in us by His divine power. For all this was lavished upon us through the rich experience of knowing Him who has called us by name and invited us to come to Him through a glorious manifestation of His goodness." For sure, the church of Jesus Christ is a group of special, glorious people. They've been purchased by God through the blood of Jesus, they're forgiven and accepted in the Beloved, and they've been elevated above all the angels. They're sealed with the Holy Spirit, protected by divine love, sustained by divine providence, energized by supernatural power.

Because you're a Christian, you are a part of God's eternal plan and purpose. You have potential that is unlimited and will be fulfilled throughout eternity. Take comfort knowing you are loved by God, indwelt by God, and empowered by God. Your inner man has been strengthened with might by the Holy Spirit. The Spirit is there and the power is there. The result of having a strong inner man is "that Christ may dwell in your hearts through faith" (Eph. 3:17). God's power enables you to sense and enjoy the personal presence of Christ. The Greek word for "dwell" is "katoiksis" and it means 'to settle down and be at home.' It's the idea of total comfort. Jesus wants to settle down and be totally at home in your heart. The Amplified Bible says, "May Christ through your faith actually dwell, settle down, abide, make His permanent home in your hearts." Is Christ comfortable in your heart? Is there anything there that prevents Him from enjoying being with you?

The Lord takes up personal residence in a person at the time of conversion. This is not the subject of Paul's prayer. He's saying it's not a question of Him being in a believer, but rather of His feeling at home there. Inside your heart is the place where He loves to be, just like He enjoyed being in the home of Mary, Martha, and Lazarus. What's in your heat? Is anything there that prevents Christ from feeling comfortable and settling down? John MacArthur said, "It's sad that though the Lord Jesus dwells in the hearts of Christians, in most of them He's unable to rest in comfort because there is so much self, there is so much sin, there's so much lust, so much disobedience." The Holy Spirit strengthens you in the inner man to give you victory over sin. This victory means a pure life, and it is in the pureness of life that Christ can settle down and be at home. When that happens, your fellowship with Him will be rich, sweet, and everlasting.

Just because Jesus lives in you doesn't mean you're making Him feel at home. You must give Him free reign over every area of your life. Pastor Sam Storm says Paul "is praying for the emotional increase or experiential expansion of what is already a theological fact. His desire is that the Lord Jesus, through the Spirit, might exert an ever-increasing and progressively more powerful influence on our lives and in our hearts." Adding to this thought, William MacDonald says, "In effect, the apostle prays that the lordship of Christ might extend to the books we read, the work we do, the food we eat, the money we spend, the words we speak - in short, the minutest details of our lives." Paul is praying that Jesus will feel at home in your heart so you'll come under His full control and blessed domination. Jesus is Lord and, if He's in your heart, then He is the center of your life and exercises His rule over everything you say and do.

When God the Father exalted His Son to be the head over the church, He gave Him the right to be Lord over every Christian. Without Christ dwelling as Lord and Master in your heart, you'll have no alternative but to backslide into the sinful ways of the world. Surprisingly, this verse is the only place in scripture that specifically mentions Christ dwelling in the hearts of His followers. Paul's point here is that Christ should be in permanent residence at the very center of your life. How does this happen? Through faith. Eph. 3:17 (TPT) says, "Then, by constantly using your faith, the life of Christ will be released deep inside you, and the resting place of His love will become the very source and root of your life." Faith is the only way to see the unseeable and know the unknowable. It is only by faith that you perceive His presence in your heart. Faith is to have a continuing trust in God and His holy Word. You must continue to live day by day in faith.

Faith is the channel through which God's grace flows. It is only by faith that you know Him for who He is and all the wonderful things He has done for you. Faith is simply a convicted heart reaching out to receive God's free and unmerited gift of salvation and all the blessings that go with it. William MacDonald said, "We enter into the enjoyment of His indwelling through faith. This involves constant dependence on Him, constant surrender to Him, and constant recognition of His 'at home-ness.' It is through faith that we 'practice His presence,' as Brother Lawrence quaintly put it." Faith means nothing without a willingness to obey God and do as He says. As you trust God and surrender to Him, He makes your heart His home. Faith opens the door and welcomes Him in. When Christ takes up residence in your heart, you'll be able to tap into that power and ability that you wouldn't have if you had not exercised faith in Him.

| 29 |

"A WAY OF LIFE"

With heartfelt openness and sincerity, Paul is making known to you that Christ wants to settle down and be at home in your heart. Jesus said in John 14:23, "If anyone loves Me, he will keep My word; and My Father will love him, and We will come to him and make Our home with him." It's not a question of whether or not He's in your heart, it's a question of is He comfortable there? In many lives He's not comfortable but greatly distressed. Sin always brings discomfort to Christ and for sure it grieves the Holy Spirit. He doesn't want you to take Him to an evil place or expose Him to sin. By doing that, you'll be a constant source of anxiety to Him. Until the Spirit of God controls your life, until you're strengthened and energized by Him, Jesus will not be comfortable in your inner man. He's not at home there. He can't settle down. Inner strength leads to Christ being at home in your heart and this leads to you "being rooted and grounded in love" (Eph. 3:17).

The power of God establishes your life upon the love of God. The result of Christ's unrestricted access to your heart is you'll know love, experience love, give love, receive love, enjoy love. God's love will overwhelm you, humble you, and amaze you. It will change and transform how you think and feel. It will change how you trust people and how you resolve conflict. It determines how you deal with fear, anxiety, and temptation. All this becomes a reality in your life when you're rooted and grounded in God's love. Human reasoning and knowledge does not allow you to tap into this love. It happens when God's power is at work in your life. When it becomes real to you that Christ is dwelling in your heart, His love becomes a source of power to you. No more will you be offended by the bad things people say about you. You survive and thrive when you have roots that go down deep in Jesus, roots that tap into His incredible love for you.

God's strength in your inner man enables you to embrace the love of God. This, in turn, will cause you to be rooted and grounded in love. You must sincerely desire this power. Be desperate for it, be desperate for more of God. Persistently say, "God, I need You. Move in my life. Help me to grasp Your love. Help me to know Your power." This is what Paul is doing here. He's praying for you to experience the power of God. He knows that God desires to fill you up with Himself. He is praying for you to have a deeper experience with God, to be completely taken over by Him. This means God becomes the dominating force in your life, driving you to think and act like Him. This is more than an emotional experience. Real encounters with God's Spirit leads to real change, change that comes from the inside out. This is a lasting change, not a temporary emotional high. God doesn't care how high you jump, He cares how straight you walk when you land.

Paul is saying you won't be able to handle the hardships of life unless you have a solid foundation under you, unless you are rooted and grounded in love. You will have a sense of well-being because you have the assurance that God loves you and has accepted you, that you are dear to Him and precious in His eyes. You find security and love in and through Jesus Christ. If your life is going to be strong, safe, and secure, you need to get your roots deep in the love of God and you've got to build the foundation of your life on the love of God. Remember, it's not your love for Him, it's His love for you. This agape love is the byproduct of Jesus dwelling comfortably in your heart and filling your life with His goodness. He can only do that when your inner man has been strengthened and purified by the Holy Spirit. As the Spirit does His work, Christ settles down and His love dominates your life. Being rooted and grounded in love means you're firmly established in love as a way of life.

Paul uses two metaphors here. Plants are rooted and buildings are grounded. Paul ties them together as beautiful figures of security just like he did in 1 Cor. 3:9, "For we are God's fellow workers. You are God's field, you are God's building." A plant that is rooted is solid and can withstand the storm and stress. The Greek word "rhizoo" literally means 'to cause to take root or be strengthen with roots; to become stable; to render firm; to be firmly established; to be fixed with the focus upon the source of such strength.' Picture in your mind a huge oak tree which must sink its roots deep into the soil if it is to have nourishment and stability. Is. 61:3 says you "will be called oaks of righteousness, the planting of the Lord, that He may be glorified." If you are going to experience the supernatural power of God in your life, there must be depth. In Christ you find life-giving soil. The roots go deeper and deeper into the love He has for you.

Col. 2:7 (TPT) says, "Your spiritual roots go deeply into His life as you are continually infused with strength, encouraged in every way. For you are established in the faith you have absorbed and enriched by your devotion to Him!" Pastor Steven Cole said, "To be rooted in love pictures a sturdy, growing tree that sinks down roots that enable it to withstand drought and fierce storms. A tree is a living, growing organism. Even so, the Christian life is a living, growing relationship with God and with others. God's love is the soil in which it is rooted and it necessarily results in our growth in love for Him and for others. To be grounded in love pictures a solid building, with a foundation that goes deep to the bedrock. It can withstand a flood or an earthquake, because it is built on the rock. This pictures a love for God and for others that is not based on fluctuating feelings or circumstances. Rather, it is solid and steady, undergirding everything else in life."

Love is the soil in which your life must have its roots. It is the rock upon which your faith must ever rest. Paul said in Col. 1:23 that you'll be "grounded and steadfast" if you'll continue in the faith. The TPT says, "If indeed you continue to advance in faith, assured of a firm foundation to grow upon. Never be shaken from the hope of the gospel you have believed in." The Greek word for "grounded" is "themelioo" and it refers to something secure and permanent in itself. It means to be deeply and firmly founded, like a building rising higher and larger. Any architect will tell you that the most important part of any building is the foundation. If you don't go deep, you can't go high. It's the love of God that sustains you during the severe trials of life. 1 Peter 5:10 (TPT) says God "will personally restore you and make you stronger than ever. Yes, He will set you firmly in place and build you up." All this is needed if you are to be successful in walking the walk.

It's the supernatural, agape love of God that you are to be rooted and grounded in. This love is not an emotion, it's an act of selflessness. It is unconditional, sacrificial, and always giving, even to one's enemies. It's when you give with unlimited generosity. William MacDonald said, "To be rooted and grounded in love is to be established in love as a way of life. The life of love is a life of kindness, selflessness, brokenness, and meekness. It is the life of Christ finding expression in the believer." It's this unconditional love that provides the enabling power to love others, the strength that enables you to walk the walk. The benefits of being rooted and grounded in love are limitless. Chief among these blessings is that you "may be able to comprehend with all the saints what is the width and length and depth and height - to know the love of Christ which passes knowledge; that you may be filled with all the fullness of God" (Eph. 3:18,19).

This is not a prayer that you might love Christ more, although you should. Rather, Paul is praying that you might better grasp Christ's immense love for you. Notice that you are not alone in this quest to comprehend the love of God. Paul wants you to grasp and understand this four-dimensional love alongside all the saints, those set apart for a special purpose. Paul is saying you're not to live in isolation but to have a relationship with other believers. Solitary confinement is a trap in which the world lives. People of the world long for privacy, to have parts of their lives that no one sees, areas where no one enters. The price of living this way is loneliness. Yes, the world is full of lonely people and many have committed suicide as a result of this private lifestyle. The Bible teaches in a clear and detailed manner that you are not to live a solitary life. You need to relate to other people, to be open and to share. 2 Cor. 6:13 (TPT) says, "Make room in your hearts for us as we have done for you."

As you connect and associate closely with other believers, you'll begin to lay hold of the breadth and length and height and depth of God's immeasurable love. Eph. 3:18 (TPT) says, "Then you will be empowered to discover what every holy one experiences - the great magnitude of the astonishing love of Christ in all its dimensions. How deeply intimate and far-reaching is His love! How enduring and inclusive it is!" Paul is praying that you'll have the power to lay hold of and comprehend the immensity of Christ's love for you. Asking for power to grasp this love implies that divine enabling is essential. The Young's Literal says, "That ye may be in strength to comprehend" while the Amplified Bible says, "That you may have the power and be strong to apprehend and grasp." The Greek word for "may be able" is "exischuo" and means 'to be in full strength; to be fully able.' This is one of the strongest Greek words for strength and signifies one completely capable of doing or experiencing something.

The Greek word for "comprehend" is "katalambano" and it means literally 'to take eagerly; to seize and thus to make something one's own; to gain control of something through pursuit.' You don't comprehend passively but very aggressively. It means 'to grasp in a violent sense; to lay hold of something; to apprehend; to overtake someone; to wrestle them to the ground.' In this verse, the word means to mentally grasp something, to lay hold of it for yourself. To be able to comprehend means to have the strength to grasp. You literally seize love, grasping every opportunity to love as a personal treasure. The love of God is something you want to seize, something you want to grasp, something you want to cling to. The love of God is the foundation of your life. It's what you want to experience every minute of every day. To live a life that comprehends love is only possible when you're filled with the fullness of the Spirit of God who, in turn, causes Christ to be at home in your inner man.

All of God's power and majesty is in His overwhelming love. Yes, love is a powerful thing and this is why you need strength in the inner man before you can comprehend this love. This is also why you need to be rooted and grounded in love. It is love alone that recognizes and understands love. In other words, in order to comprehend the love of God, you have to experience the love of God. Light attracts light. The more love you have, the more love you'll receive. Matt. 25:29 says, "For to everyone who has, more will be given, and he will have abundance." The TPT says, "For the one who has will be given more, until he overflows with abundance." The most satisfying experience in the world is to be able to comprehend fully the love of Christ which is shed abroad in your heart (Rom. 5:5). To be able to understand the fullness of what that love means is without doubt one of the most wonderful, the most exhilarating experiences a person can ever have.

They say the hardest word to define is love. You can't define it, you can only experience it. Love is a way of life and it is only understood by those who love. You will never know the love of God until you experience it, until the love of God dominates your life. This is why those not saved are not able to comprehend this love. They haven't experienced it. The love of God is a secret love that no outsider knows anything about. Martyn Lloyd-Jones said, "There are things about the love of God you know nothing about. This is why Paul is praying that you'll plunge into the depths of God's ocean of love, a divine love that is there for the taking. He wants you to discover things you have never imagined." Love is something that can be comprehended, something that is seized and personally possessed by all the saints. Living with love is the only way to live, the only way to find true happiness. It's what makes you a kind, merciful, and gentle person.

The love of God is immeasurable, too large to be confined by geometrical measurements. Even so, Paul wants you to experience the love of God in multiple dimensions, to know the unending magnitude of His grace toward you. Going further in the love of God will cause you to deal with others with a greater degree of compassion, to deal more gently with those around you. Sad to say, most people are content to spend their lives in the loneliness and dull plains of this sinful world system and all that characterizes life at its lowest level. There is no greater snare in the believer's life than to know about the love of God yet not experience it personally. Doctrine is good but it's not enough. The purpose of all doctrine is to lead you to a personal relationship with Christ, where you'll know, comprehend, and experience His love every minute of every hour of every day. Love is not a subject to be studied, it's the living proof of a living God. It's something that needs to be experienced.

Love is the parent of all knowledge. Once you experience it, then you can comprehend it. John MacArthur said, "Paul prays that we will have a deep, experiential knowledge of Christ's love, a comprehension of its infiniteness, an expression of that same infiniteness that can only happen because we're rooted and grounded in it, because Christ is at home in us, because we are strong in the inner man, because the Spirit of God is at work there. This is living life at a full throttle." Experience is your only teacher when it comes to the love of God. This is why the Bible says, "Taste and see that the Lord is good" (Ps. 34:8). Paul wants you to know this love by experience and not just in words and doctrine. Charles Spurgeon said, "In this measurement may you and I be skilled. If we know nothing of mathematics, may we be well-trained scholars in this spiritual geometry, and be able to comprehend the breadths and lengths of Jesus' precious love."

Paul is praying that you'll be able to grasp the vastness of God's love. It's as if he is inviting you to look at the limitless sky above and the great depths of the ocean below. F.B. Meyer said, "There will always be as much horizon before us as behind us." Pastor A.T. Pierson said Paul "treats the love of God as a cube, having breadth and length, depth and height. The reason is that the cube in the Bible is treated as a perfection of form. Every side of a cube is a perfect square, and from every angle it presents the same image. Turn it over and it is still a cube - just as high, deep, and broad as it was before." The Holy of Holies was cube-shaped as is the New Jerusalem. Amazingly, so also is the love of God. The measurements that Paul gives emphasize the immensity and vastness of God's love. You can go left or right, forward and backward, or up and down as far as you can, and still you haven't explored all there is to know of God's great love.

What is the width of God's love? It's as wide as Christ's two outstretched arms on the cross. John 3:16 says it is wide enough to reach the whole world and beyond. It encompasses all of humanity, both Jew and Greek. There are no step-children in God's great family. All believers belong to Him and He belongs to them. You can see how wide a river is by noticing how much it covers over. God's love is so wide that it covers over your sin and every circumstance you are going through. It's so wide that all things work out for your good (Rom. 8:28). God's love does not diminish because it is shared with a great multitude. When Jesus fed the five thousand "they did all eat and were filled" (Mark 6:42). So it is with the love of God. All of His love belongs to each recipient of it just as all the sunshine comes to every person. The width of God's love is worldwide, reaching to all those who are willing to receive it. God loves everybody, therefore He loves you.

What is the length of God's love? His love is infinite in nature and the eternal duration of His kindness toward you extends from eternity past to eternity future. Eph. 1:4 says God chose you in Him before the foundation of the world. Eph. 2:7 then says in the ages to come He will show you the exceeding riches of His grace in His kindness toward you through Christ Jesus. Charles Spurgeon said, "Like eternity itself, God's love knows no bounds." God said in Jer. 31:3, "Yes, I have loved you with an everlasting love." The length of God's love covers all those who are on the upward path to glory. It's unending as it passes through the sea of eternity. His love and mercy endures forever, from everlasting to everlasting. His love runs into infinity, far beyond the point where sin ceases to exist. He is gracious and His love out measures all human failures and shortcomings. Charles Spurgeon said, "This love is not only without beginning, but it is without pause. There is never a moment when Jesus ceases to love His people."

What is the depth of God's love? How far is it from the glorious throne in heaven to a little manger in Bethlehem, from the cross of Calvary to the tomb in the garden? That is the depth of God's love. Jesus went from a place forever radiant with glory to the lowly form of a servant. When He walked the earth, His life was filled with sorrows, limitations, rejection, pain, and eventually death by crucifixion. Phil. 2:8 says Christ "humbled Himself and became obedient to the point of death, even the death of the cross." By dying a criminal's death, Jesus became the lowest of the low so He could reach out and bring you into the kingdom. You can't go any deeper than dying on a cross. How deep is His love? Deep enough to reach you when you were dead in trespasses and sin (Eph. 2:1-3). It was deep enough to reach down into the deepest pit and draw you out. There's no hole deep enough that Christ can't reach you there. In fact, He's already there waiting for you in order to pull you out.

The abyss of sin is deep, reeking with corruption. But this loving Jesus goes down, down, down to the pestilent cavern and stretches out a saving hand to all those who would grab onto it. All those times you missed the mark are shallow when compared with the love that goes down beneath all sin, the love that is deeper than all sorrow and misery. No matter how deep the abyss of sin and degradation is, beneath it are the everlasting arms of a loving God. Micah 7:18,19 says, "Who is a God like You, pardoning iniquity and passing over the transgressions of the remnant of His heritage? He does not retain His anger forever, because He delights in mercy. He will again have compassion on us and will subdue our iniquities. You will cast down our sins into the depths of the sea." Your sins and helpless miseries are deep but God's love is deeper. How deep is His love? Deep enough to go down beneath all human necessity, sorrow, suffering, and sin.

What is the height of God's love? It's high enough to bless you with all spiritual blessings in heavenly places (Eph. 1:3), high enough to raise both Jew and Gentile up together to sit in the heavenly places in Christ Jesus (Eph. 2:6). On the summit of every spiritual mountain climbed is the radiant love of God, springing high above you and towering beyond your deepest thoughts. His love gleams like a shining cross on top of some lofty cathedral. The depth of God's love begins at the throne of heaven and goes down to the cross. The height of God's love begins at the cross and goes up to heaven. God sent Jesus to lift you up to Himself, to sit upon the very throne where He now sits. This is the height of God's love. He loves you so much that He'll take you to heaven where you'll rule and reign with Him forever and ever. This is by far the uppermost thing in all the universe. You can't go any higher than that. Taking you there is the pinnacle of God's great love for you.

God's love extends in all directions. It's wide enough to reach every person, long enough to last through all eternity, deep enough to reach the worst sinner, and high enough to take you into the presence of God. That's the love of God, the love you are to build your life upon, the love you are to comprehend and seize every moment of every day. It is God's plan and purpose for you to live, and move, and have your being (Acts 17:28) in the love He has for you. Scottish minister Alexander Maclaren said, "So all of us, islanded on our little individual lives, be in that great ocean of love, all the dimensions of which are immeasurable, and which stretches above, beneath, around, shoreless, tideless, bottomless, endless." Open your heart and let Him in. If Christ dwell in your heart by faith, and if He is comfortable there, you'll be able to comprehend the boudless greatness, the endless duration, and the absolute perfection of the love of God.

| 30 |

"THE FULLNESS OF GOD"

As Paul closes out his prayer for the saints at Ephesus, he makes two final requests of the Heavenly Father. He wants you and believers everywhere "to know the love of Christ which passes knowledge; that you may be filled with all the fullness of God" (Eph. 3:19). The NLT says, "May you experience the love of Christ, though it is too great to understand fully. Then you will be made complete with all the fullness of life and power that comes from God." The first of Paul's two final requests is for you to know the unknowable. The Passion Translation calls it "endless love beyond measurement that transcends our understanding." Sometimes the human mind can't understand spiritual realities. It can surely be experienced but still not be known academically. The word "know" is a personal, intimate, experiential knowledge. Here is where feelings come in full throttle. You can't understand the love of Christ but you can feel it. You are overwhelmed with the sense of love in which He loves you.

This is not a petition that you might love Christ more, but rather that you would be empowered so as to grasp and understand the vast limitless dimensions of Christ's love for you. Paul is praying that you would come to have a relationship with Christ, to intimately know Him through a personal experience with Him. He wants you to experience this magnificent, radical love that is totally consuming and so utterly incomprehensible with mere intellect. The good news is what you can't comprehend in your mind, you can grasp and understand in your inner man. The Holy Spirit living inside of you gives you access to all the answers you'll ever need. 1 Cor. 2:10 says, "But it was to us that God revealed these things by His Spirit. For His Spirit searches out everything and shows us God's deep secrets." The Message Bible says, "The Spirit dives into the depths of God, and brings out what God planned all along." This is why the Holy Spirit can be called "The Great Revealer."

The TPT says, "But God now unveils these profound realities to us by the Spirit. Yes, He has revealed to us His inmost heart and deepest mysteries through the Holy Spirit, who constantly explores all things." The Greek word for "revealed" is "apokalupsis" and it literally means 'to remove the curtain so you can see what's on the other side.' It refers to something that has been hidden for a long time and suddenly it becomes clear and visible to the mind or eye. Rick Renner said, "It is like pulling the curtain out of the way so you can see the scene outside your window. The view was always there for you to enjoy, but the curtain blocked your ability to see the real picture. Once the curtains are drawn apart, you suddenly behold what was previously hidden from your view. The moment you see beyond the curtain for the first time and observe what has been there all along but wasn't evident to you is what the Bible calls a revelation."

Because of the Holy Spirit, ignorance and confusion has permanently been eliminated. He'll reveal to you all things that used to be hidden, things that were at one time unknowable. This is well and good, otherwise it would be impossible to comprehend and fathom Paul's final request "that you may be filled with all the fullness of God." The TPT says you will be "filled to overflowing with the fullness of God." Warren Wiersbe said, "There are four requests in Paul's prayer, but they must be looked on as isolated, individual petitions. These four requests are more like four parts of a telescope. One request leads to the next one, and so on. He prays that the inner man might have spiritual strength which will, in turn, lead to a deeper experience with Christ. This deeper experience will enable them to 'apprehend' (get hold of) God's great love, which will result in their being 'filled with all the fullness of God.' So, then, Paul is praying for strength, depth, apprehension, and fullness."

Paul's prayer to the Father reaches its climax in this final request. You have now reached the top of the mountain. Inside of you is spiritual fullness and perfection. Eph. 3:16 says you can be filled with the Holy Spirit and vs. 17 says you should be filled with Christ. And here, in vs. 19, Paul is saying you can be filled with the fullness of God the Father. Imagine, if you can, that God in all His totality lives in you! He is the eternal God, the almighty God, the creator God, the sustainer God, the great God of the universe! This is so incredible! The God who made it all and fills it all now fills you. God wants you to be full, full, full! Paul said in Eph. 1:23 that the church "is the fullness of Him who fills all in all." In Eph. 4:10 Paul says, "That He might fill all things." Eph. 4:13 says, :That we might come to the stature of the fullness of Christ." Eph. 5:18 says, "That we would be filled with the Spirit." In other words, God doesn't settle for anything less than total fullness.

Martyn Lloyd-Jones said, "There is no more staggering statement in the whole range of scripture than this. To be filled with the fullness of God is the climax to all prayer. There is nothing higher than this. It is the summit of all Christian experiences. Nothing is conceivable beyond this. It is Paul's prayer that all believers partake of this fullness." A sense of awe should overwhelm you knowing that such a thing is possible. There is no higher privilege in all the universe. The perfection of man consists of him being full of God. Paul is praying here for perfection. Jesus said in Matt. 5:48 (NLT), "But you are to be perfect, even as your Father in heaven is perfect." The Message Bible says, "In a word, what I'm saying is, 'Grow up!' You're kingdom subjects. Now live like it. Live out your God-created identity." Theologian Handley Moule said, "The idea is of a vessel connected with an abundant source eternal to itself, and which will be filled up to its capacity, if the connection is complete."

Paul wants you to know the love of Christ in order that you may be filled with the fullness of God. The word "filled" means 'to be filled to the brim; to make complete so as to cause to abound; to furnish liberally.' It also means 'controlled by.' Whatever you're filled with is what controls and dominates you. What are you filled with? What is coming out of your life? Are you filled with the Holy Spirit of God? Paul is praying that you'll be controlled by godliness, that all of God would dominate all of you. You are not filled with the fullness of God unless you let Him take possession of and ultimately control your life. Your obedience to biblical truths deepens and expands your capacity to be filled with the fullness of God. Like an expanding balloon, when you are filled with His fullness you'll begin to love like Him, give like Him, and reach out to others like Him. What a glorious way to live! Surely this is life abundant.

To be filled with all the fullness of God is to find the ultimate experience of life. The true meaning of life is discovered. It is eternal life; it is perfection; it is ultimate satisfaction. Wayne Barber said, "Everything that fills God fills me and controls me and satisfies me. I am living in a realm now that I didn't know was possible. I am loving people I didn't think were lovable. I have put up with people who used to give me a fit. I am handling circumstances like never before." Pastor Ray Stedman adds to this, saying, "It is here that you realize the purpose of your own creation. You were made to be a golden vessel wholly filled and flooded with God Himself. This is when God is in control of your life, enriching you, blessing you, and strengthening you. This is what Paul refers to as being filled with the Spirit. Your faith is strong and vital. You're reaching out to others, ministering to those you come in contact with. You are God's workmanship, created in Christ Jesus for good works."

The Greek word for "fullness" is "pleroma" and it means 'total full-ness; the full measure of something with an emphasis on complete-ness.' Paul wrote in Col. 2:9,10, "For in Him dwells all the fullness of the Godhead bodily; and you are complete in Him." Vs.10 (TPT) says, "And our own completeness is now found in Him. We are com-pletely filled with God as Christ's fullness overflows within us." Paul is praying that you would be filled up with all the fullness that is in God Himself, filled with the perfection of which God Himself is full. You need to comprehend the fact that God's fullness can dwell in your heart and be expressed through your life. The idea of fullness implies total dominance and control. It's when He controls your words, ac-tions, and your will. John MacArthur said, "To think that the Trinity exists within the believer is just staggering, and to realize that when They dominate you, when They fill you, the power flows in such a way that we can't even comprehend it. What a thought!"

God's fullness is His moral perfection as well as His empowering pres-ence. It refers to the grace and mercy and wisdom and knowledge and all those attributes that make up the character of God. There is nothing conceivable beyond the fullness of God. His fullness and per-fection is the standard or level to which you are to be filled. The good news is that if you are born again, in Christ this fullness has taken place. Col. 2:10 says, "You are made full in Him" and John 1:16 says, "Of His fullness have all we received." When you're filled with the fullness of God, flowing out of you will be the fruit of the Spirit which is love, joy, peace, longsuffering, kindness, goodness, faithful-ness, gentleness, and self-control (Gal. 5:22,23). You'll be like Moses who came down off the mountain with his face glowing with the glory of God. God's fullness is an infinite thing and forever and ever He'll pour His presence, His life, and His power into those redeemed saints rescued through the work of Christ.

If God's power is going to work in you, then you have to be filled with His fullness. In order to be filled with His fullness, you need to have the love of Christ dominating your life. This can only happen if Christ is at home in your inner man, when you are controlled by the power of the Holy Spirit. Let the main goal of your life be that God will use you in a mighty way. Let Him release His power through you so that your spiritual victories can cause others to see who He is and what He is like. It's when you're filled with the fullness of God that He'll be able to do anything He wants through you. Paul makes a staggering statement in Eph. 3:20, saying, "Now to Him who is able to do exceedingly abundantly above all that we ask or think, according to the power that works in us." This verse reveals how powerful you are when you follow the pattern that leads to this verse. As powerful as God is, it is you who determines whether or not He'll accomplish anything in you and through you.

God wants to do powerful things in your life but first you have "to be conformed to the image of His Son" (Rom. 8:29). Once that happens, watch the power flow! David said in 2 Sam. 22:33, "God is my strength and power, and He makes my way perfect." This is the God whose will is to live inside of you. Yes, David sinned but when he did he fell on his face and sought God's forgiveness. He knew this was the only way to see God's power work in his life. No wonder he said in Ps. 17:15, "As for me, I will see Your face in righteousness; I shall be satisfied when I awake in Your likeness." Job asked the question, "Who dares contemplate or who can understand the thunders of His full, magnificent power?" (Job 26:14). Yes, God is mighty in strength and mighty in wisdom (Job 36:5). God is great (Job 36:26) and is exalted by His power (Job 36:22). This is the God who wants to fill you, to enable you, to make you powerful so He can do all the good pleasure of His will through you.

The God you serve, the God who loves you exceedingly, is also the God who answers prayer. God changes things, not prayer. It doesn't work because of the words you say, the faith you express, or the promises you claim. You don't learn to pray by studying prayer, you learn by studying the God who answers prayer. This is the theme of what Paul is saying here. You will notice that this prayer is sandwiched between two statements about God (vs. 14,15 and vs. 20,21). The structure of this prayer reminds you that all true prayer is God-centered. You can never pray without the confidence that God is willing to hear and is able to answer prayer. Begin your prayer by proclaiming the greatness of God and conclude your prayer by praising the greatness of God. Too many people say "Amen" too fast. Your prayer shouldn't end after you've given God your list of requests. Prayer should only end after you've given glory and praise to the God who answers prayer.

God has perfect power over the created world and He is fully able to answer your biggest request. God said in Jer. 32:27, "Behold, I am the Lord, the God of all flesh. Is there anything too hard for Me?" The answer is found in Jer. 32:17, "Ah, Lord God! Behold, You have made the heavens and the earth by Your great power and outstretched arm. There is nothing too hard for You." Indeed, He is the God who is able! The word "able" means 'to have the ability to act according to one's will.' It's one thing to have good plans, great expectations, and lofty goals. It's another thing to have the power to accomplish and fulfill your intentions. The Greek word "dunamai" means 'to have power by virtue of inherit ability and resources.' God is powerful and He is continually able to accomplish incredibly great deeds on behalf of those He dwells comfortable. There is never a question about God's divine ability. He has always been able and always will be able. The good news is that He has chosen to be able in you.

God has offered Himself and His ability to each of His children. Eph. 3:20 speaks of the potential of God in every believer's life. Not only is this verse about the power of God, it's a statement about the goodness of God. There is no burden God cannot lift, no door He can't open, no enemy He can't defeat, no need He can't meet, no problem He can't solve, no sickness He can't heal, no sin He can't forgive. This is why God is worthy of your total allegiance, absolute obedience, and unconditional surrender. When you learn that He is able, then, and only then, will you walk in victory. Victory is not when you overcome some hardship, it's when Jesus overcomes you. It's when He indwells you and His Spirit empowers you with His divine power and ability, when you are mastered by His love. That is real victory! The strength you need to do God's will is already residing in your inner man. This is not a promise for the future, it's a present tense reality.

What is God able to do? Exceedingly abundantly above all that you ask or think. Your highest aspirations are not beyond God's exhaustless power to grant. Theologian Benjamin Jowett said, "What I have asked for is as nothing compared to the ability of my God to give. I've asked for a cupful, and the ocean remains. I've asked for a sunbeam, and the sun remains. My best asking falls immeasurably short of my Father's giving. It's beyond all that we can ask." Paul is trying to express something that there were no words to express. He's trying to say that God is able to do more than enough and over and above that. God can do anything and everything and He wants to do more and more beyond anything you have ever asked or dared to think. This ability to give you these things is completely available in the Lord Jesus Christ who dwells comfortably in your inner man. This is why David was able to say in Ps. 23:5, "My cup overflows." He knew the loving kindness of the God he served.

Notice that God does great things "according to the power that works in us." Another way to say this is "according to the power that proves or shows itself at work in us." In Greek, the phrase "according to" means 'in proportion to ones bountifulness.' It's referring to not just a portion but a proportion, that which is proportionate to one's true wealth. God's capacity to meet your needs far exceeds anything you can request in prayer or conceive by way of anticipation. Would you expect anything less from the God who created the entire universe? God's power is a working power and He gives strength when strength is needed. Just remember, His power will meet you at the place of obedience. Willful and habitual sin will cause God's power to lay dormant. It is available but not being used, much like the power stored in a battery. If you've sinned, confess it, forsake it, and move on. When you do that, God's power will be at work in your life fully and completely.

There is no limit to what God can do yet many believers have let unbelief, unconfessed sin, and careless living cut them off from this power. A Christian robbed of power cannot be used by God. Jesus said in John 15:5, "Without Me, you can do nothing." How much this power is released into your life is determined by how much you yield to the Holy Spirit. It is you who determines what God is able to do in your life. Christian missionary Ruth Paxson said, "The limitless power of God is limited by the unwillingness to have it work, or by the unbelief that it can. But in the light of this prayer could there be a greater sin in the life of a saint than to live on the lower level of the carnal when God's provision and power make possible life on the highest plane of the spiritual? Someone has tersely said, 'You have your Bible and your knees; use them.' Let us use them so that these treasures in Christ may become in fullest measure in our lives."

When will God's power and ability manifest in your life? When the Holy Spirit has empowered you, when Christ has indwelt you, when His love has mastered you, and when His fullness has filled you. Until these conditions are met, you might as well skip over this verse because you will never have His ability working in your life. That being said, Paul is now ready to end his prayer as he closes out the first half of his letter to the Ephesians. He does so with a proclamation that is so important it seems as if he saved the best for last. If what he says next is not adhered to, then all your efforts to live the Christian life will be in vain. Imagine Paul clearing his throat and saying, "Drum roll, please." Seconds roll by as you slide to the edge of your seat in eager anticipation of what he'll say next. He pauses a moment waiting for your full attention. When he has it, he says with boldness, "To Him be glory in the church by Christ Jesus throughout all ages, world without end. Amen" (Eph. 3:21).

How fitting it is that the petition of this prayer should glide into praise. Throughout this letter Paul has repeatedly insisted that the end of redemption is the glory of God. To give God glory is an active acknowledgment of who He is and what He has done. Glory is the splendor of moral excellence and God is glorified when He is allowed to be seen as He really is. Pastor H. B. Charles said, "Glory is the sum total of His divine perfection, the crushing weight of His holy character, the blinding light of His divine presence. God is glorious just because of who He is." You eagerly glorify God because of your revelation of who He is. He revealed Himself as the God who is able (vs. 20), you respond by giving Him glory (vs. 21). You can't accept vs. 20 without embracing vs. 21. God is able and He is to receive glory. Why did God save you? Why has He blessed you? Why does He use you? He does none of these things to make your name great, He does them so that He might be glorified!

Before He died, Jesus said, "For this purpose I came to this hour. Father, glorify Your name" (John 12:27,28). Jesus did not die on the cross merely to solve your problems, He died to glorify His Father. That is the reason and purpose for everything. God wants to display His power in the church so that He might be glorified. If the church isn't what it ought to be, if it doesn't reach its full potential, then it diminishes the glory. But when God's power flows through the church, when it becomes an expression of His power and might, then He is fully glorified. The church is the platform of the glory of God in this world. When the world looks at the church, can they see the glory of God? The truth is, the glory of God cannot be in the church unless the church is in Christ Jesus. Paul ends this prayer saying "Amen." So be it. The word means, "Right on, right on, right on!" Paul said God is able! Amen! God answers prayer! Amen! He is worthy of all the glory! Amen! Right on! Right on! Right on!

SUMMARY

As we come to the end of "Blessed Beyond Measure," we are left with a clear and life-changing truth: in Christ, God has already given us every spiritual blessing in heavenly places. Ephesians chapters 1–3 do not describe a distant hope or a future reward, but a present reality for every believer who is in Christ Jesus.

Through these chapters, we have seen that we are chosen before the foundation of the world, lovingly adopted into God's family, and fully accepted in the Beloved. We are redeemed by the blood of Christ, our sins forgiven, and our lives infused with grace that is both immeasurable and inexhaustible. God has not held anything back; He has lavished His favor upon us according to the riches of His grace.

We have also discovered the power of our new position. Though once dead in sin, we have been made alive together with Christ, raised up with Him, and seated with Him in heavenly places. Our identity is no longer shaped by our past, our failures, or our limitations, but by our union with Christ and His finished work. We are God's workmanship - His masterpiece - created for good works prepared in advance for us to walk in.

Ephesians 1–3 reveals the unfolding of God's eternal purpose: the mystery of Christ now made known, where Jew and Gentile alike are brought near, reconciled, and formed into one new man. We are no longer strangers or outsiders, but fellow citizens of God's kingdom and members of His household, being built together as a dwelling place for God by the Spirit.

Finally, we have been strengthened with power in the inner man, rooted and grounded in love, and invited to know the love of Christ that surpasses knowledge - a love so vast it fills us with all the fullness of God. This is not a blessing to be merely studied, but one to be lived, experienced, and trusted daily.

As you close this book, may your heart remain awakened to the riches that are already yours. Walk forward with confidence, gratitude, and faith, knowing that in Christ you are forgiven, empowered, secured, and eternally loved. You are not lacking, not forgotten, and not un-prepared. Through God's grace and purpose revealed in Ephesians 1–3, you are truly - and forever - blessed beyond measure.

www.ingramcontent.com/pod-product-compliance
Lightning Source LLC
Chambersburg PA
CBHW070907130626
46555CB00001B/37

Discerning Christian Witchcraft

AN INTERMEDIATE'S WALK THROUGH THE MYSTIC LIFE

EMYLE D. PRATA, SARA RAZTRESEN

Sveta Lisica

DISCERNING
CHRISTIAN
WITCHCRAFT

An Intermediate's Walk
Through the Mystic Life

EMYLE D. PRATA | SARA RAZTRESEN

Dedication

Mimi Says:

I dedicate this book to the spirits of those who came before me on this journey; the faith healers and yarb women, Grannies and midwives, the teachers and the nurturers, Theclas and Mary Magdalenes, those who were always a little bit witchy, and to every last soul in Appalachia that knows exactly what it means to feel the Spirit come on you.

To those that have loved me through every crash out and moments of spiritual enlightenment, you are why I can stand on my feet and still have my head in the clouds. Especially Sara and Sara, who love and support my autistic brain in different ways (sometimes spa days, sometimes cast iron skillets). To Lina and Hannah, the best part of making this community has been finding your strengths and softness along the way, as we craft something coven-ish together, and lean on one another through tears and screeching. To Savannah, my heart and soul sister—I love you, Sissy. To Josh, who roars when I need to remember who I am. To Amanda the Astro Queen, who is the only astrologer I will ever need and who calls me out because I need it. I love you all with every part of me, because each of you helped this little Piscean queen to dream when my Capricorn stellium made me a little too hard.

To my sweet and precious witchlings, Delilah, Isabel, Maggie, and Brena: Jesus loves you, but Mama loves you more. And a special thank you, Darlin', for calling me Circe, not Cassandra, and seeing me as your equal.

Sara Says:

As cheesy as it may sound, this book is dedicated first and foremost to God: in it is the proof of my works, spurred on by my faith. In the time since I've sworn my pen to Him, I've flourished in both my craft and my understanding, both of which I give Him thanks and praise for.

But this is also dedicated to those who likewise want to seek God: those who came before us, the Saints and theologians and rebels and healers of their days, and those that are here now, all you out here looking for that wisdom you've spent your lives craving, and for those in the future, who will one day look back on this the way we, today, look back on our predecessors. We're here. We're all here, together, in a space where time doesn't exist.

And of course, this book is for all my friends and family who believed in me along the way—especially Mimi, for giving me the pushes I needed, when I needed them, and to Hannah and Lina for being there to listen, and to Fr. Kyle and Mary Rose for their endless support in both learning and shepherding. What a beautiful community we have!

Contents

Introduction

The Mystic and the Witch

I T'S A WARM DAY—ALMOST suffocatingly so. The cloak the Mystic wore to stave off the early morning dew has now made her skin prickle with the beginnings of sweat under the afternoon sun. Summer has been here for what feels like decades now, and the days have grown so long that one finds little time to dream like they used to; winter's long nights are only a murky shadow, a memory. Still, she stands in the light and tips her face up to the sun, as if the warm rays were as tangible as any rain that could come down from the long-banished clouds of spring.

On her arm is a basket, but it isn't laden with food. Rather, it's stuffed with flowers, ones she picked from the field before the forest where her friend lives. In the forest, she knows, are berries and nuts and mushrooms that'll make a fine addition to whatever her friend has prepared for afternoon tea. She's given herself enough time to look for the best specimens in there, and as she leaves the field and walks through the forest, she feels blessed by the shade of the broad-leafed trees.

It's a twisting path to her friend's house: one with no road, only dirt trodden down by years of her and her friend walking along it. The wind rustles the branches and makes the Mystic happy she took her cloak after all; the breeze is sharp and spears her through each thread, as well as rustles her hair about and cools the sweat that gathered at the nape of her neck. She picks her way along knotted roots and mossy boulders; she pauses to observe the occasional squirrel or chipmunk as they eye her basket. That basket is soon to be full of black walnuts and blackberries, which she knows she'll collect absently as she wonders about next steps of spiritual growth. It's been some time since her Lord spoke to her, and despite her frequent bedtime prayers begging for the next steps, the next chapter in her developing piety, she's come up frustratingly empty so far.

The Mystic takes frequent deep breaths of that forest air—so much sweeter and easier on her lungs than the must and dust of her stone home closer to the city. And though she doesn't see it yet, as she pulls morels and chanterelles from their place in the dirt, she trusts that her friend's house lies beyond the beaten path. Just as she knows that, sooner or later, the answer to her prayers will come. It *must* come, she knows, because her Lord doesn't stay quiet forever.

Nor does He give warning as to when He'll speak again.

A ray of sunshine filters through the tree leaves and kisses the Mystic's cheeks. She looks up to find that sun and seeks more of its warmth, but as she watches the light filter through the trees, something happens.

Listen.

The light dazzles her in a way that makes her drop her basket. It blinks, flickers, making it hard to tell if it's the leaves and their shadows that make her vision go dark, or if she's trying to blink the light away. Every flash of light is no longer sunlight through the trees, but a blinding white star, and they dig their bright rays into her head, filling her skull with lightning so painful that it threatens to rip her head in two.

Listen, now.

The Mystic drops her basket. Her legs give out; she falls into the soft grass and lies there clutching her head. This time, her eyes are shut, but the light continues flashing behind her eyelids, and the small, quiet voice she's come to know during these painful moments whispers in her ear.

Tell them all I tell you.

And then comes the flood. Everything from images to smells to sounds, everything from the tickle of wind on her face to the squeeze of damp, musty air in her lungs, they all barrage her in yet another fit of visions, like many she's had before. This story, like many, is a lifetime in itself; the things she witnesses, experiences, they are things that take days, months, to explore. As the pain fades in her head and the images continue to dance, she might almost believe she *is* taking years in this tale that Someone is spinning for her—until she wakes up.

The Mystic's hands are still clutching her head. She cracks her eyes open to see the same grass, the same forest and its beaten path, as she'd been on before the visions. Her basket is still full of the things she foraged, and as the Mystic frantically looks around, she finds the sunlight still filtering through those leaves—though this time, the light doesn't pierce her mind like it did before.

How long has it been?

She doesn't know, but she knows she shouldn't spend another moment mucking about in those woods. The Mystic ignores the last pulses of pain in her head, drags herself up, snatches her basket, and hurries down the path. Whatever that vision was, whatever she was to tell, and to *who,* was a question for her friend. She would know. And if she didn't know, she would know how to find out.

The Witch always knew how to find out.

Discerning Christian Witchcraft

> *While I was begging our Lord today to speak for me, since I knew not what to say nor how to commence this work which obedience has laid upon me, an idea occurred to me which I will explain, and which will serve as a foundation for that I am about to write.* —St. Teresa of Avila, *The Interior Castle*

You wouldn't think it'd be so easy to relate to a Spanish Carmelite nun from the early Renaissance, and yet here we are: Mimi and I, coming back to you all, and like St. Teresa, asking God for the same guidance and grace to deliver the second installment of this series on Christian Witchcraft. Now that the bedrock of this long lost pathway to God has been laid, however, you'll find that this book pivots *hard* in its form and character. Whereas *Discovering Christian Witchcraft* was a book built on the stability of things we can accept as *true*—on scholarship, on facts, on evidence from history and the logical reasoning of the many Biblical scholars and theologians before us—this book takes a turn down a much more fluid, and one might say, a much less *esteemed* and *palatable* road to Truth.

This road is the road of Christian mysticism: the *heart* of Christian Witchcraft, the scaffolding around our understanding of who we are in God's eyes and who God is in, and *beyond,* our minds and hearts.

That's not to say that this entire book is purely based on vibes, though, so don't mistake our meaning here. We couldn't write this book without at least a few (dozen) references to scholars, historians, and theologians. All of that, however, sits underneath plenty of our own personal experience to contextualize what can be very dense, abstract, and difficult mystical theory and its practical application. But it is worth noting that this world of mysticism seems to be out of sorts with a world otherwise focused on *reason* and *evidence,* and as such has often been looked on with suspicion and scorn, especially since the Enlightenment period (from about the 1600s to the 1800s).

Episcopal priest and theologian Mark A. McIntosh, in his book, *Mystical Theology,* spends considerable time discussing this scorn, explaining how at some point, a noticeable schism between *spirituality* and *theology* developed—one in which *theology* was considered the learned, concrete, verifiable, *true* way of engaging with religion, and *spirituality* became something suspicious, wishy-washy, and seemingly based on little more than one's personal experience with no bearing on the larger religious community.[1] (He also notes the convenient timing in which this schism took place: just as women were becoming more religiously and spiritually active in their own theological works and advancements to the understanding of God. Food for thought.) However, that doesn't mean that mysticism doesn't have its place, or that it isn't only good, but *necessary,* to one's religious life. In McIntosh's own words:

> Spirituality grounds theology ever anew in this place of human waiting and speechlessness at the foot of the inestimable speaking of God. It is true that what takes

---

1. Mark A. McIntosh, *Mystical Theology* (Malden: Blackwell Publishers, 1998), 8-9.

place there defies human understanding and would hence seem to defeat the purpose of theology; yet the hope with which spirituality imbues theology enables it to persevere there, to wait not for a clever resolution of its own, but for the 'theology' that God articulates in the resurrection of Jesus of Nazareth from the dead: 'So spirituality—prayer—is, I suggest, that which keeps theology to its proper vocation, that which prevents theology from evading its own real object'... Perhaps we might say simply that spirituality contextualizes theology in the mystery of Jesus' dying and rising which is God's self-disclosure and therefore the matrix of honest theological reflection.[2]

To translate that: spirituality *humbles* theology. *Orients* theology. *Humanizes* theology. Spirituality reminds theology what the point of all this study and talk and thought even is—and it's not just to be correct, or to have the "right" view on God's Law. Mysticism, spirituality, is about acknowledging what we *do not*, and in our limited state, *cannot* know; it's about being vulnerable, open to revelations of God that deny sense or ration or anything else that, according to McIntosh's overview, feminist thinkers have pinned as the result of a "lingering myth of an objective consciousness, which actually hinders both practical and theoretical understanding" in faith.[3]

And this is *terrifying* in a world so hell-bent on getting it "right," and on being "grounded" in this thing called reality–a world obsessed with avoiding the flames of hell, or being a good Christian that follows every little detail of the faith to the letter. One that insists that there is some objective Truth out there, and that (their interpretation of) God is it. Now that you've read *Discovering Christian Witchcraft*, no doubt you're armed with the physical and scholastic tools necessary to stay a bit more sure and stable in the path you're on, no matter what other people might say to you—but as we've said again and again, the first book of this series is only the opening of the door. Or, in the words of St. Teresa, the

---

3. Ibid., 25.

opening of the gate: the gate to the great interior castle, a place where God is nestled deep in the very center, and where we will spend our entire lives trying to navigate, great spiritual maze that it is.

That's why we say to you now, before we go any further: every step you continue to take past that gate will challenge you in ways far outside your comfort zone. You are entering a world that will challenge the very concept of Truth—that will, God willing, break you free from the false security of the binary way of thinking common in so many modern Western Christian denominations these days. You know what we mean: that way of thinking in which all is Black and White, and in which all is True or False, in which all things can be answered with a concrete and definite Yes or No and where every action decisively lands you in either Heaven or Hell. Friend, we tell you now: in this book is where you will learn, through the deep inner workings of Christian Witchcraft, through that dire mystical journey, that such a binary world never existed—that you were never standing on any *bedrock* at all, but in fact on shifting sand, on gravel that'll hold you up until you put too much weight on one foot and slide down into a sinkhole you were trying to avoid.

But don't be afraid. *Discovering Christian Witchcraft* was like a First Day Orientation, and it was the signpost leading up the long and winding road to St. Teresa's work. Now, you must decide to step forward, through that gate, into the murky unknown that is the mystic's journey. Not everyone will be able to handle such a journey—and in fact, many will tell you that not everyone should even *try* if they can avoid this journey—but those who make it to the end of this book will not only have a better understanding of the Mystic path, but also how it, in truth, is the Witch's path, too. After all, the refinement of a Christian Witch's magic arguably takes place in the vulnerability of witnessing God's miracle (and the awe of God Himself).

Sara Says:

I've read a lot of books on mysticism, and a lot of the words of the mystics themselves, and all I can really say is: there's a difference between *reading* and *doing*. For example, you can read all the articles you want about a different country than yours, like France; you can study the language all day long and look at all the pictures you want, but none of that will ever feel the same as standing at the base of the Eiffel tower itself. When you realize the thing you've spent all this time studying, the thing you knew was massive but only ever saw via pictures taken from faraway rooftops, actually is the *tower* it claims to be, it humbles you something nasty. That feeling of being so dwarfed, the incredulity of realizing you are not at home anymore and that all you know and find comfort in is thousands of miles away, the realization that the world itself is so dramatically bigger than you ever really thought about—it hits you all at once.

When it comes to mysticism, I had a lot of the same feelings. It's one thing to read books. In fact, it's important to, because it helps you grab onto that common language that's already been established; it gives you some community and kinship with people who were experiencing such similar stuff as you are now, but centuries earlier. That's valuable. However, when it comes to the mystic journey, there is no simply *reading* about it; you have to *do* it. You have to be *ready* to do it. When I started my Christian Witch journey at the young age of fourteen, I didn't have the maturity, the tools, or the interest in such a thing (I was way more absorbed in the idea of casting spells and making potions), but now, as I get ever closer to thirty years of age, I find myself in a deep, armored cocoon of that mysticism. I am wrapped up in it, swallowed by it—and I know, explicitly, that the *magic,* the actual *witchcraft* part of Christian Witchcraft, is, in fact, simply the *practice* of all the theory and revelation that comes from standing at the foot of this *Tower* of a being we call God.

There is nothing more horrifying than this, in my experience—but given that our God is a God of paradox, there's also nothing that's given me more peace than this. And it's in this peace, this working through all our inner turmoil and calming our inner waters, that we become all the more able to empty ourselves out as Christ did, and to become, as so many mystics have before us, the very hands and feet of God in this physical reality. But I can't give away too much just now, because like a college degree, you can't walk into your first day on campus and immediately take a four hundred level class. You need to start with the fundamentals so that you can keep building this understanding and weaving your experience into it—and now that you've found your footing with the first book, we can keep building that foundation.

Mimi Says:

A long time ago, a little girl was born into two worlds: one of patriarchy and rules, of long-standing tradition and hellfire… but also, one of whimsy and magic, and one of a love and faith in the Divine that cannot be described in any other way except holy. She was always loved through the same dichotomy of a firm fist and endless stories to dream on. When she was small, she always believed she was special, if only because everyone told her she was: precocious and observant, seeing things through the veil and hearing the whispers of the angels. When she told anyone who would hear her what she knew, they praised her for her reverence and reassured that she was truly chosen and loved by God, that she had a calling on her life to love and care for others.

As she grew, however, and the lens of the world helped shape her ideals, she was no longer called special. Her empathy and compassion for all, and her thirst for knowledge and understanding of the world and its many facets of cultures, broke the limits of obedience. Little did she know that obedience was what was honored, not her actual gifts. And yet, she still believed, no matter how much was put on her plate or how many times she was defeated and crushed, that she loved Jesus. More, she still believed in his message. Even when other names, other spirits, would come and find a place in her heart, it always felt like Jesus tucked them in, too. She has always walked the Mystic's path. There were just never words for it until now.

> "Blessed is she who has believed that the Lord would fulfill his promises to her!" —Luke 1:45

There are so many times when you have an "a-ha!" moment as you move through this journey that they all just seem like stepping stones of a single path forward. How often do you stop and look back at the mountain of moments, all shifting together like tectonic plates, that built you into the being you are? That is how mysticism feels. The crushing feeling of being away from God only comes after you notice the ash in your food, the distant memory of smiles from your friends, and how often your mind continues to come back to the glory and majesty of the mystical aspect of the faith.

It sounds so cliché when I say it out loud, but I was born to this. Nurtured under a caring hand, being touched by God to do great things for Him, I used to think that meant I'd be singing in the church or working as a missionary. Do I think Papaw and Mamaw meant my being a mystic? No. But do I think they saw something back then? I do. And it was reinforced, over and over, every time I had a blissful moment of understanding and peace under what I knew as God back then. As I've finished books on mysticism, it strikes me that I have been living this life, with every phase, stripping away the needs of this world to further align with what I've been called to do. And I've been doing it through witchcraft.

This is not what I expected or what I wanted with my life. I had my own grand plans. But being able to surrender, truly surrender to that soul pull to the understanding of the Universe, changes things. My world has been topsy-turvy and my heart has been shattered a hundred times over. And yet, every time I feel the layers pulled away from what I was, I find a new peace in my calling. This is where I bring my own understanding of the journey within the ideas of Invitation (Awakening), Discernment (Purgation), Enjoyment (Illumination), and Commitment (Union), with an emphasis on how it is all a cycle (and not always a direct one). I want to be able to share anecdotes and wisdom with you, so that it's not just a reference to mysticism, but a way to blend being a Christian and a witch. The craft therein has brought me closer to loving and understanding the Holy Spirit, and it has unfolded into this brilliant, soul-nourishing, illusion-crushing, self-realizing experience of being alive in the glory and wonder of it all.

A Note for My Christo-Pagans and Others:

I know that a lot of what I have referenced in God or Spirit may not resonate. A book with scholastic references, mystic intuition, and metaphysical study on a spiritual journey is wont to the opinions and viewpoints of the author.

However.

It is my personal belief that this journey can be accomplished even if you do not follow God. After all, any religion one could think of has some level of mysticism to it, which we'll touch on in a second. Sure, some could argue John 3:27, which says, "...A man can receive nothing, except it be given him from heaven." But does this mean everyone else is excluded?

No. I subscribe to something fairly close to Omnism; all deities exist in the realm of their mythos as a way for Man to find their connection to the Divine, through culture and history. This means that you cannot fake your magic or your calling. Just as some are called by God for this journey, so are others called by Hades, Odin, The Morrigan, Frau Perchta, etc. The way you commune, the acts you dedicate to and the life you live in accordance with the rules of Those you follow, is how you walk this journey of mysticism.

So walk it with your head held high. It's all you can do in a journey as wild as this.

How This Book is Organized

The major arcana in tarot. The cycles of birth, death, and rebirth in nature. St. Teresa's *Interior Castle,* and the seven "mansions" (rooms) therein. The four stages of the Buddhist path to enlightenment. Jewish Kabbalah's Sefirot. Islam's seven stages of spiritual awakening via Sufism. The Western occultist's scavenged and re-tooled Qliphoth. No matter where you look, when you find mystic paths or religions with mystic systems, you will find some kind of map from Point A (mundane existence) to Point B (enlightenment); you will encounter stepping stones, stages, that lead you from one place of understanding to the next. Christian Witchcraft is no different. As we've already said, Christian Witchcraft *is* the Christian mystic journey—only this journey is one that is much more empirical, more deliberate and hands on, and one might even say more honest than the average modern walk through mysticism, precisely because we aren't afraid to call a fig a fig. More than that, we aren't afraid to distill those mystic teachings and secrets into spiritual action via magic (or, in a different lexicon, the orchestrating and channeling down of God's miracles).

When reading books on mysticism, theology, philosophy, and psychology, there's something we had to do, and that was *synthesize* and *structure* this information accordingly. That's why you'll notice that there are four *sections* and seven *chapters* (not including the introduction and conclusion). This organizational structure follows the map of the mystic journey, as outlined by theologians, scholars, and mystics, like St. Teresa of Avila.

Each section follows the overview of the mystic journey, in terms used by scholars like John R. Mabry in his work, *Growing into God*. These terms are *Awakening, Purgation, Illumination,* and *Union*. Then, within each of these sections, we borrow a little from the structure of St. Teresa's *Interior Castle*, fitting each of her seven mansions into these broad topics. As such, you'll notice that before all the more direct and scholarly discussion and explanation of these mansions that Sara and Mimi have to offer, each chapter begins with a continuation of the story you began earlier: one that fully illustrates the allegory St. Teresa uses by painting visceral pictures of the spiritual scene you're stepping into. This is deliberate, as anyone who has read the more metaphorical works of a mystic like St. Teresa knows that while they try for imagery, it does eventually devolve back into the abstract concepts that perhaps one can *understand,* but are still difficult to *feel*. And when things are difficult to *feel,* they're even more difficult to internalize, remember, and implement, in our experience.

That's why we go further than simply *telling* you about what other Saints and scholars say about mysticism, and further than just sharing our own experiences. You're following a story here, one journey of millions: the journey of the Mystic and the Witch, where we paint said story in full, colorful detail in each chapter's beginning narratives. These episodes unspool more of the Mystic's vision and the Witch's analysis, all so that you might know where you are and where you have yet to go in the world of allegory and metaphor—which is arguably *the* language of mysticism to begin with. Employing this language in this way allows us to get more specific and intentional with every step of this inner work, as well as provides the proper containers for the heavy discussions and spiritual exercises to come. Hell, you may very well even use the imagery of the Mystic's visions for your own meditation exercises when (not if, *when*) you find yourself in any of the situations she describes. It may be easier to digest what's happening to you if you decide on that course of action.

To that end, you'll also notice the Witch's analysis uses the symbolism and esoteric study of the Tarot to help divine what steps to take next and how we move forward. The energy represented in the Tarot is pulled through this journey, channeled and studied by the Witch, to exemplify just another way that the mystic journey has come together. Tarot decks used in Mimi's personal journey are the Spirit Keeper's Tarot and Dark Woods Tarot. Both decks have shown layers of understanding and prepared a story of the journey she would take in these years of writing these books. She will be referring to them as SKT and DW in each chapter.

It should be noted, though, that the pathway presented with these "rooms" in the Manor of the Mystic, and in the imagery and flow of the Tarot's Major Arcana, is not a hard and fast roadmap, nor is it something specific to any one denomination of Christianity (as many denominations have their own mystics and exploration of God). In his work, *The Big Book of Christian Mysticism,* Carl McColman says explicitly:

> Every one of us is called to be intimate with God and worship and enjoy him in a way that is unique and personal and can never be repeated by anyone else. What this means, of course, is that no program of mystical development, no game plan for mastering contemplation, no step-by-step process for "becoming a mystic," can ever be written or implemented... there can never be a one-size-fits-all approach to the unfolding of the splendors of mystical Christianity in your life.[4]

---

4. Carl McColman, *The Big Book of Christian Mysticism: The Essential Guide to Contemplative Spirituality* (Hampton Roads Publishing Company, 2010), 125.

One can liken this path to many things, which is why *Discerning Christian Witchcraft* is such a cocktail of metaphors in its construction. One more we might offer you is a comparison of the process of the Mystic (even if done more systematically and near-scientifically under the title of Witch) to the process of navigating a Candyland board. You may find yourself moving several spaces ahead, only to hit a slide and end up falling a ways back, or getting stuck on a certain space when you feel you should be moving forward. Such is the (frustrating, maddening, agonizing) journey of the Mystic, and by extension, the Witch. If you don't believe us, take it from St. Teresa; she, herself, acknowledges that one "must not think of a suite of rooms placed in succession" when talking about these mansions she's explained, "but fix your eyes on the keep, the court inhabited by the King"—by God.[5]

The Adversary Approaches: Your Prosecutor in God's Court

And sometimes, the metaphors this book brings up may very well frighten you. For example, you may find yourself confronted by none other than Satan himself in this journey. In fact, don't look behind you, but here he comes now—looking to test your mettle before you even begin getting into the rest of this book. He's here to see if you're ready to begin not just blindly absorbing, but truly *wrestling with,* the many concepts that'll come up in this book, and you can start right here, with the very concept of Satan as perhaps a Gate-*keeper* to the next chapters. How exciting, no? Perhaps we're mixing too many metaphors into this situation, but as we've already said and will remind you of again and again: *metaphor is the language of mysticism.* Time to get fluent.

Now, pause. Before you become too frightened at the idea of Satan prowling after you and trying to ensnare you in the details of your *own* story, know that reading these words here is your first opportunity for deconstruction, reflection, and re-evaluation of your current beliefs: *who is Satan?* Who is he, really, and what is his purpose in confronting you across these chapters? How could God, our dear and beautiful and

---

5. St. Teresa of Avila, *The Interior Castle or the Mansions,* 3rd ed., edited by Benedict Zimmerman (London: Thomas Baker, 1921), 22.

all knowing, all powerful Lord, allow this *monster* to come near us, test us, torture us, and try to make us crack under the pressure of his spiritual attacks?

Well, let us now ask you to consider that the word Satan is not a name, but a *title,* and that it means not the face of a demon, nor the Great Evil opposing God, but an angel *of* God: the Adversary. Satan comes from the Hebrew term *Ha-Shatan,* meaning *the Adversary,* and according to Rebecca Lesses in her essay, "Supernatural Beings," in *The Jewish Annotated New Testament,* this figure "develops from references in the Tanakh" (a word meaning the Hebrew Bible, or what Christians call the "Old Testament"), "where [Satan] is a member of the divine council, into the enemy of God and all humanity."[6] The concept of Satan as we now have it, therefore, has become the idea of this rebellious and evil creature over time, but earlier on, the appearances of this Satan presented a more "ambiguous figure who is a servant of God."[7] We see hints of this elsewhere, like in the Book of Zechariah, where the prophet Zechariah has a vision of Joshua, a high priest with his own book in the Bible, standing with the angel of the Lord (an advocate), who speaks to the Accuser (a term translated from Ha-Shatan):

> He further showed me Joshua, the high priest, standing before the angel of the Lord, and the Accuser standing at his right to accuse him. But [the angel of] the Lord said to the Accuser, "The Lord rebuke you, O Accuser; may the Lord who has chosen Jerusalem rebuke you! For this is a brand plucked from the fire."[8]

This specific translation, from the *Jewish Study Bible,* has footnotes from the editors that likewise note that the "NJPS [New Jewish Publication Society] correctly translates the Heb 'ha-satan,' as the *Accuser*

---

6. Rebecca Lesses, "Supernatural Beings," in the *Jewish Annotated New Testament* (London: Oxford University Press, 2017), 686.

7. Ibid., 686.

8. Adele Berlin and Marc Zvi Brettler, eds. *Jewish Study Bible* (London: Oxford University Press, 2014), 1240-1241

instead of the common, but erroneous, 'Satan.'"[9] It then directs us to the note on the Book of Job, Chapter 1, verse 6, where again our editors give us some context for the development of this idea of Satan as becoming more like an active enemy. The editors have this to say:

> Like a monarch in court, the Lord in His abode in the sky receives His agents, *the divine beings* (lit. "sons of God"), the angels, periodically to receive their reports and give them assignments... God singles out the Satan ("Adversary"), whose role, He knows, is to "descend [to earth] and lead [people] astray, and then ascend [to heaven] and arouse [the Deity's] wrath" (*b. B. Bat* 16a).[10]

This development, again, is a later development; the fact that this Bible's editors point to this as being of the Persian period when discussing the term Satan in Zechariah suggest this is developed around the time of the exile in Babylon, in which concepts we now recognize (such as an eternal torture world for all evil people, demons opposing the one God and trying to entice people to evil) begin leaking into Judaism.[11]

But from Carson-Newman University comes Associate Professor of Biblical Studies and Associate Dean of the School of Biblical and Theological Studies, Dr. Ryan E. Stokes, who, in his book *The Satan: How God's Executioner Became the Enemy,* gives a much fuller and more extensive overview of the concept of Satan throughout his work. To bring forth a quick summary of his thoughts, condensed from the conclusion:

> The Satan began as a punishing emissary of God, bringing death on those whose actions warranted such treatment. The notion of the Satan as an attacker or execu-

---

9. Ibid., 1240.

10. Ibid., 1497.

11. Excerpt of N.F. Gier's *Theology Bluebook,* Chapter 12, as sourced from the University of Idaho, https://www.webpages.uidaho.edu/ngier/309/zorojud.htm.

tioner would remain part of the tradition through the first century CE and later. Nevertheless, this notion would recede into the background as thinking about the Satan evolved. The Satan came to be regarded more fundamentally as one who created problems for the righteous than as one who troubled the wicked. The Satan became a deceiver, a tester, the enemy of God's people, and eventually even the enemy of God…

…Eventually, the question of the Satan's origin would arise. As long as the Satan was believed to be a functionary of God, there was no real need to account for his existence. As the balance shifted from understanding him as God's agent to regarding him as a superhuman rebel, however, an explanation for this evil figure's existence became more necessary. In order to provide such explanations, theologians created stories of the Satan's primordial fall (e.g., Irenaeus, *Against Heresies* 4.41; 5.24; 2 En. 31:2–6 [recension J]; LAE 12–17).[12]

Despite the efforts of various writers and theologians to maintain human responsibility for their own errors, and despite the conflicting understandings of Satan within the various texts, like the Epistle of Enoch, Zechariah, 1 Chronicles, and other stories where the basic function of Satan is disguised under a different name/character (like Prince Mastema in Jubilees), we eventually found our way here: to a place that leaves us wondering *why* Satan is poking at evildoers in hell if he's supposed to be the apparent enemy of God (per later theological understanding). It's a confusing place, and it seems, according to how Stokes posits it, to be a more Christian place. The idea that Satan is some evil enemy of God that seeks to tempt the righteous into evil is

---

12. Ryan E. Stokes, *The Satan: How God's Executioner Became the Enemy* (Grand Rapids: Wm. B. Eerdmans Publishing Co., 2019), chap. Conclusion.

more specific to Christianity, whereas it's the Jewish Rabbinic idea that Satan is God's employee.[13] Having Satan as an enemy of God also gives an easy out to the problem of evil—so long as one *doesn't,* again, ask why Satan, who apparently is fighting God, would want to punish the evildoers in hell who are helping stir the evils of the world that persecute good people. When we consider the many lenses on this being, and the fact that God Himself is apparently out there pouring all manners of good *and* evil spirits out on people and nations Himself (as Stokes points out in his chapter titled "Demons, Evil Spirits, Fallen Angels, and Human Sin," where, for example, God takes His Holy Spirit away from King Saul in First Samuel and replaces it with "a *rûaḥ rā'â mē'ēt yhwh,* 'evil spirit from the LORD,'"), it seems clear that the thing we call Satan is a bit more complicated than just *that really bad guy flying around causing problems.*[14]

Therefore, in this book, we are choosing to look at Satan less from the lens of these early Christian church fathers, and more from the lens of the Rabbinic teachers, if only because we've found that to much more accurately match our own experience with any concept of "the Satan" vs. the one Christians call Satan as his own independent character. As Adversary, Satan functions less as the little devil with a pitchfork poking you in hell for all eternity and more as the prosecutor in court, who's looking for any possible way to trip you up, make you stutter on the stand, and incriminate yourself before God, the Almighty Judge.

The Adversary is therefore one that tests, provokes, intimidates; in short, he doesn't play fair. We all have a little piece of him sitting within us, too, if we think to the Jungian concept of the shadow that so frequently appears in modern witchcraft discourse: that part of us that holds all the dark and ugly truth of ourselves that we don't want to acknowledge, the center of our own complicated self-curse that may have been passed on through generations. You might read more about Sara's experience with that shadow, and the Adversaries that are dreadfully effective at uncovering it, in Chapter 3—but we recommend you take this one chapter at a time rather than go skipping around.

---

13. Ibid., chap. Conclusion.

14. Ibid., chap. 3.

As we go along in this book, you'll find many moments where the Adversary comes to test you, just as he has so many others who have undertaken this mystical journey and retreated to the familiar, earthly comfort of institutional religion (with or without the presence of the true God) rather than brave the unknown depths of God's infinity that the Mystic must come to brush against. As coal becomes diamond under pressure, so too is this journey one of incredible spiritual pressure, and whether you condense into diamond or crumble into dust entirely depends on whether or not you can walk the path of so many before you: of Job, of St. John of the Cross, of St. Ignatius of Loyola, and so many others.

With all that said and done, you should know this, and know this well: unlike *Discovering Christian Witchcraft,* this book is not simply a resource. It is a *tool,* one we hope you'll come back to again and again for reminders, exercises, and thoughtful questions to consider, and we wish that through this tool, you'll be able to pull back the curtain on the inner machinations of what we call *witchcraft* in the modern era. By developing your spiritual life, walking the mystic path, and learning where the Witch and Mystic align through this task of inner healing and rebuilding, it's our aim to help you empower yourself into knowing not only *how* to engage in the magic, the witchcraft—but *when* and *why,* as well.

So come along. Let us show you what we've learned from books and from experience. Let us guide you, not only as scholars, but as friends and mentors. It won't be an easy journey, we can tell you that right away, but at the very least, it's one you won't have to start alone.

Section 1

Awakening

"Dragged down by the world's passing delights, he wanted to wander away from the right road of salvation into 'the region of unlikeness'... But divine mercy took pity on him, enlightened him in an ineffable way, and through paths both pleasant and difficult drew him along and finally brought him back to the path of truth through love of Wisdom…"

Henry Suso

The Clock of Wisdom

Chapter One

The Gate and the Courtyard

The Mystic and the Witch

*I*T DOESN'T TAKE LONG *until the Witch's house appears through the brush of the forest. It sits under the trees: a wooden hut with an old, shingled roof covered in moss and last year's leaf litter, and with window and doorframes slanted with years upon years of sitting, resting, in this secluded grove. Flower pots full of parsley and basil sit in what spots of sunlight the leaves don't cover, and in the ground are great hedges of rosemary, lavender, thyme, and oregano. A fence peeks out from behind the house, and the gentle clucks of hens breaks the otherwise peaceful, silent air.*

In the doorway, broom in hand, is the Witch. She sweeps a bit of onion scraps and other daily dirt out the house before looking up to see her friend, and her sharp brow shoots up like a flag, hooking her lip up with it into a friendly half-smile. Her hair is bushy, wild, sticking out seven ways from the ribbon that's already coming loose, and her apron is smeared with all matters of water spots and other stains. But her smile doesn't stay up long once she sees the way the Mystic is rushing up to her step.

"Hey, hey!" *She sets her broom against the door frame and opens her arms to the Mystic.* "What's this, now? Why such a face?" *As the Witch takes the Mystic by the shoulders, she looks over her friend's shoulder into the woods and mutters,* "Did you see a bear?"

"No, no, it's—I had the strangest vision, the strangest, and—"

The Witch pauses, then claps her hand on the Mystic's shoulder, hard enough to make her friend flinch. Her smile comes back, in fact grows to a grin, and she waves the Mystic inside.

"I understand. Come, sit. We'll make tea. I have scones baking."

And goodness, does it make the house smell lovely. The door stays open as the Mystic and the Witch sit at the round, chipped dining table in the center of the room; the Witch sets a kettle full of water on the flat iron stove, all while a fire roars underneath it. The kitchen counters wrap around under the window on the far back wall, all the way to the staircase's pantry on the far right wall, and every available surface is covered with something for food or magic or both: roots and herbs and vegetables and tools.

"Sit, sit," *the Witch says as she waves her friend to the table. Before she joins the frazzled Mystic, she goes to the little bookshelf by the door and plucks one of several tarot decks from its dusty corners; she lights a stick of incense for the little sacred space she's assembled on top of it. With her deck in hand, she joins her friend at the table and takes the deck out; she shuffles it, then says,* "Tell me, now. What did you see?"

The Mystic blows a gush of air out of her lungs and wrings her hands. How to begin? How to explain? She has no choice but to start at the start, and perhaps, hopefully, end at the end.

"As I sit, Sister," *she says,* "and as I beg my Lord to me to help me understand the Beginning, let me tell you the strange things I experienced in the far forest."

After my affliction gripped me in the forest, I fell into my vision the way one falls into a deep and clawing dream—but worst of all was that it felt like neither vision nor dream at all. In my vision, it felt like... like I'd already lived an entire life. Like I'd been perhaps put in the body of another, in some strange and distant world, and like all this life I live now, and all I know now, never existed.

When I came to, and I blinked away the bleariness in my eyes, I began my walk in a world of ash, as if I'd always been there–and I had what felt like years of memories already stitched into the very fabric of my being. It was so strange. All my life, it seems, I've lived in a small, grey room. It was filled with grey trinkets: knick-knacks, toys, soft things that had nice shapes or glassy things that shined in the sunlight that came through one small, square window. Outside that window were yet more grey shapes barely peeking through soft, cool, grey mists—the homes of my friends, my family, my colleagues. The biggest, greyest building of all was at the end of this one short road: my church. And once a week, I and those I loved went down that grey road, that sweet mist kissing our flushed cheeks, and then we sat in that church where the pastor preached about all the amazing shades of grey. Then we walked back up that grey road, to our grey home.

I got the sense that once, perhaps as a child, or even a young adult, I might've seen a color. Maybe pink. Maybe yellow. Maybe purple. But it scared me to see it, because in this strange dream world, I seem to have been told all my life that these colors were the signs of corruption, sin, *depravity*—of forces I would do better not to entertain, forces that wanted to trick me and entice me with their bold and immodest hues. So I retreated back to the safe color I'd been seeing all my life, that steely, simple grey—even if, secretly, deep down, I wished for just the smallest touch of that color in my life. Just a touch.

It was so beautiful. That color, it was so pretty. So bold, so *undeniable,* unlike all this grey.

Still, whoever I was in this vision, I was someone that tried to forget it. I was told—by my family? my friends? my colleagues?—that it was better to: that anything outside this grey, and anything outside the *silence* that came with that grey, would lead to damnation—would lead me astray. I buried that hue for years, tried to outright erase the memory of it lest it tempt me and haunt me and torture me; every day, I prayed that I would stay on the steely grey path, as everyone had before me, because that was what was right and good. Until one day, as if *awakened* from a dream, I heard a call come from outside my little grey window.

Maybe it was just my own imagination, that call–or maybe it came to me, in the form of a book or a feeling or a thought or a note of unfamiliar (and unauthorized) music. No matter where it was from, however, it dragged my head up all the same on that fateful day. It snagged my focus and pulled me away from all that was before me in the little grey space of my day to day existence: the long and dreary work and anxiety-inducing demands that frayed my sense of stability, all those bills and calls and e-mails and texts. These were things that, even if I was told were only a small scrap of life, still took up the bulk of my attention (and I felt bad about that, because I knew the largest bit of my life should've belonged to that little grey church down the street; they told me so).

However, I felt it in my soul: this wasn't the way things should be. This wasn't right; this wasn't *true*. Perhaps it was a holdover of my true self, Sister, my true mind creeping into my vision–but in this world, in this life I'd been dropped into and compelled to be happy with, there was nothing else for things *to* be. In fact, the world told me it would make me sinful, selfish, and deluded if I was *not* happy with such things. The world, this strange and uncanny World, told me it would be my soul in the fire, should I ever look for that sparkle of color that I saw that one time instead of content myself on a steady diet of grey.

And yet this call I'd perceived one day, it was stronger than the shouting of this World. This call, this one soft little nudge in my soul, it dragged my head up from other things, too: from the toys, trinkets, and other such little grey oddities that filled my space, from the things that numbed me and helped me forget any such woes I might've had. *Distractions,* that's what they were, and I knew it deep down: these trinkets and other such things were *distractions* from the questions I had that seemingly nobody could answer, diversions from the gaping hole in my heart that countless platitudes and turns of phrases and orders to "just have faith" could not plug. Distractions from that one glimpse of color that I saw so long ago.

This call was one that disrupted my daily rhythm; it took me out of my routine of worrying, working, soothing, and sleeping. In fact, some might say this call woke me up, made it so I couldn't go back to sleep again surrounded by all those toys and trinkets and duties and *distractions.* Made it so I could not bear another day weighed down by all my doubts and worries and woes. It was one that made me look around at all the things I'd gathered that were important to me and made me tilt my head at an angle, until as I looked at them, I began to wonder why they were so important to begin with. After all, they were all so *Goddamn grey,* and I knew I wanted something more: something with a certain hue that I couldn't quite visualize anymore.

Even when I first ignored that call, and I tried to bury that sudden splinter of longing lodged in my heart, I simply couldn't stop hearing it. I couldn't deny that whatever was calling me was something that hooked my attention more than the little odds and ends of the reality that had grown so stale on my tongue, and that had felt so empty in my hands.

So one day, I simply… followed it. The call.

Terrified as I was, I followed this call away from all that I was familiar with, and my decision to do so didn't do *anything* to soothe my fear. After all, even if what I knew was so square, so grey, and so stale, even if the platitudes and sermons and speeches of preachers always seemed to hit my ear so *wrong* ever since that day (despite all my attempts to force it to sound *right*), I stayed so long in that space because it was *safe.* Predictable. Acceptable. There were obvious *rights* and obvious *wrongs,* so clearly and definitively delineated, and even if it felt like wearing a shirt three sizes too small to constrain myself to those things, even if all that grey eventually started to settle on my skin like three years' worth of dust on old shelves, and even if every word I spoke to myself or others began to *taste* just as foul as such dust on my tongue, it seemed to me that wearing a proverbial shirt too small was better than no shirt at all. That coating myself with dust was coating myself with protection, and that I shouldn't wish for something so decadent as a pleasant taste on my tongue, anyway. The grey mist I'd been living in was far, *far* better than the bright and burning hues I was promised if I stepped outside its cold, clammy cover.

Yet there I was, stepping out from that cover anyway—stepping away from my friends, my family, my colleagues, from my grey life and grey home, outside my grey little town and down a path to a place I knew the mist would no longer stretch to. Every step had me asking myself *why* and *what if;* every inch farther from all that was familiar to me made it seem as if some invisible fist was tightening around my heart. I couldn't breathe well, even as the mists began to lift and left crisp air behind. I couldn't hear anything but the crunch of gravel under my shoes, even though I wished another voice would call from behind and give me a reason to turn back. I was *possessed,* it seemed, captured: whatever this was that dragged me away from my safe and predictable place in this world, it would not let me go.

Eventually, after a long time walking, I found the source of this call. I stood before it in terror as much as wonder, in shock as much as intrigue, unable to tease apart where one such sensation ended and the other began. Before me was no person, no musical instrument, nothing; no, before me was a Gate. A massive, towering Gate made not of the same grey concrete I was used to seeing my whole life, but something that shined in the sunlight that sheared down through the clear day: gold. Bright, gleaming yellow gold. And in the middle of it was a lock with that exact color I tried so hard to forget I ever saw: a red as deep and stark as a pinprick of blood.

The Gate creaked, and the lock clicked open, then split in half. Those thin golden bars flared out as the Gate opened, and in doing so, I noticed all the rest of the colors around it: the green grasses, the pink and purple wildflowers that clustered at the Gate's base, the rich brown trunks of old and mighty trees around the sides of the Gate. And then, after all that, the only place to look was ahead—to the white marble, the golden roofs, the green ivy and the fiery red lilies, the huge white fountain spurting glittering blue water, of the grand Courtyard and its Manor beyond that Gate.

Terrified, unsure, and yet suddenly fully aware that ahead of me was everything I'd been seeking, I stepped inside that Courtyard. The Gate did not close behind me, which almost made things worse, because at least then, I could've felt like I was locked into my choice. But there was no such theft of my agency. In fact, I thought I felt a temptation of choice: as I walked into the Courtyard, I felt the openness of that Gate at my back as if it were some Adversary's carving stare, one just *daring* me to turn around and flee.

I didn't turn. Not yet, at least. Already, this simple Courtyard, with all these colors and this open space, this crisp, dry air, these new, strange sights, were so *different* and *wonderful* that it bordered on overwhelming. I mean, the sheer *majesty* of something as trivial as little blades of green grass growing between the cracks of the stone! Such small things, even as small as that, struck me like lightning. Even though that huge Manor loomed over me, I could hardly comprehend it at first just because I became so enraptured with the black and red ants that marched along the stone, and the bright birds of *every* color singing their songs from the green-leafed trees, and the little white and orange fish swimming in the fountain waters, and the little pond skaters that found their way onto the water's surface!

It felt like I could be there forever, learning about every square inch of just this one spot; I felt I'd never get bored or like I'd seen enough. I started to see the things that I was warned about, these *temptations* and *decadences* and whatever else—and I saw that they weren't soul-damning, or even scary. No, these things were incredible, beautiful, rich with the touch of some grand Artist I couldn't even conceive of, and I desperately wanted to amuse myself in that Courtyard for a long, blissful time; the thought of going back to all the grey of my life chafed at my mind.

However, I could feel Someone watching. The Artist, maybe? Certainly not the Adversary I'd felt from the Gate's mouth. Whoever this Someone was, They didn't shoo me out of this place, nor did anyone come from that castle to throw me out and lock the Gate behind me, but I could feel it like I could feel the kiss of the sunlight on my skin: Someone was watching. This was Someone's home, after all; this wasn't my home. I was a guest, even if Some*thing* invited me, and I knew I'd do well to be on my best behavior—even just in this Courtyard.

The Witch listens with the same focus she gives all the Mystic's strange visions. This fills much of their time together: the Mystic's odd visions, the Witch's picking at their pieces as if putting a puzzle together. There's joy in the work of untangling meaning for the Witch, satisfaction in watching it come together. Her mouth pulls into a wry, knowing grin as she cradles her tarot deck in her hands. A soft flutter fills the room as she shuffles, and from the feeling that skitters along her skin, she knows this time-worn handshake between her and

the Divine will unlock the mysteries of the visions the Mystic received. The first card, eager to be seen and its meaning to be heard, falls to the table and spins, until its face beams back at the Witch.

"Mm, I had a feeling. The Fool dances under the sun and skips along the path happily, somehow both unaware of the nearby cliff ledge but fully aware of the call from the Divine." After a pause and a rush of breath, a subtle shift in energy coils around every word the Witch has said so far, almost a spell unto itself as she discerns the truth from the story The Mystic leans in, rapt; she listens to her friend the way she does to her priest, ready to parse the wisdom like wheat from the chaff.

"The Fool unfolds in phases," the Witch continues "It begins in the face of the one who is just starting their initiation, but doesn't know quite where to go, and is only aware of the Gate he must push through. But you've done that before, haven't you?"

Have I? The Mystic blinks, thinking, but the Witch drags her attention back to the cards with the tap of her nail on the card stock.

"Most of us, in our faith, take those precarious steps off of the ledge when that first glimmer of Something appears to us—that call you described. The path begins, as it always has, with blissful ignorance, and perhaps trepidation, too. This is the 'beginning of the journey,' which I think you saw at that Gate you mentioned.

"Even though you have traveled these roads and been in these woods before, every choice to return is another beginning. Your first steps onto this path, even today, initiated a new chapter in your story. Even if you're unsure of where to go, you know you must keep pressing forward." She presses a finger to the card and pushes it towards the Mystic. "It's you: this Fool is you."

"Hey!"

The Witch and the Mystic chuckle, and as the Mystic leans in to listen again, the Witch goes on.

"Anyway, you know you've been here before; your heart and soul sing for something else, something more. This time, the Fool calls for you to search for truth to the deepest parts of yourself. You are worthy to take those steps down that gravelly path once more. Whether coming from the other side of a decision to start fresh, or on the other side of a cycle to begin again, this card represents the energy we take with us to move through the Gate and into the Courtyard. This is where we abandon what we thought we needed and prepare to move forward, with all our curiosity and terror mixed together." The Witch pauses,

and she tears her gaze off the Fool just long enough to pin the Mystic and ask, "Does this, perhaps, sound like a familiar verse from your good Book?"

The Mystic tips her head back and forth, side to side, as if rolling the well-studied verses around her mind like marbles. After long enough, one clicks into place, and she perks up as it rolls off her tongue, out her open mouth:

> *Do not remember the former things, or consider things of old. I am about to make a new thing! Now it springs forth – do you not perceive it? I will make a way in the wilderness and rivers in the desert.*

"From Isaiah, chapter 43, verses 18 and 19," she says matter-of-factly, pleased with herself.

The Witch resists rolling her eyes at her silly friend and that Book she studies so deeply. She smiles instead, nods, and then her hand moves back to the deck and slips the top card between her finger and thumb. The Magician appears as she flips it over, pointing to its counterpart, and the Witch is obliged to slide it to its place on the table beside the Fool.

"Ah," the Witch muses. She tucks into herself, one arm wrapped around her body, the other propped up along her so she can hold her face in her palm. "I see."

The Mystic stares at the young man on the card with his wand and his trinkets. "What?"

"The Fool comes in phases, as I said, and this," the Witch taps the Magician, "is the evolution here. Once applauded for his bravery in taking those steps forward as Fool, the Magician now brings about a realization of inner potential and an awareness of Self. This is where we see examples of As Above, So Below; As Within, So Without. *It is also, in your practice, in your words, the building blocks of your* 'On Earth as it is in Heaven.' *Here is where you find (and build) what you think is Heaven on Earth in this Courtyard you described."*

"Oh." The Mystic studies the Magician further, finding something familiar in the imagery: the chalice, the white lilies of the Mother around the altar table, the robes. "Oh, oh, oh, I see."

"Mm. We find our fellowship here, my friend, brought together by the Divine. We relish the magic within us that had been hidden or discouraged before, by those who would steal it from us."

The Mystic cringes and avoids the Witch's eye; her friend's words touch a raw wound of sympathy, the history heavy as a wet cloak.

For the Witch, however, that wound has long since scabbed with acceptance. She keeps talking, her voice numbing the sting: "Likewise, we're alive with the energy around us and working through the beauty of what we've seen, with this Magician. We might've even patted ourselves on the back for being so bold and taking those steps away from fear and the life of monochrome and basic understanding.

"We begin to see the Divine, to see God within the edges of every leaf, the prism of every dewdrop, and each warm stream of light that falls along our face. But whichever image speaks to you, know that this is the truth of the Magician. Here is where we start to tap into the Divine power in our mortal selves—proof that we all have the Divine Spark within us, and therefore are also human and divine."

That last part rings in the Mystic's head; she'd recognize the words of her Lord and His Son and Spirit anywhere, from any mouth. She curls into herself much like the Witch has, though her teeth find her thumbnail as she considers the implications of the idea.

Noticing this, the Witch presses on. "The Magician brings awareness of one's spiritual gifts," she says, "but with the bluntness and fumbling of a toddler: going headfirst into something just because you know you can, without any real learning or refinement. This boldness, though, can help alchemize your understanding of your self-worth; by leveraging the potential, manifesting it into reality, we are able to fully recognize in ourselves what the Divine sees in us. However, this potential, without taking the time to understand what it is and what we are, can easily turn into something more based in Ego than Spirit. Perhaps that's the danger this vision is trying to show you, and what I'm picking up on now."

The Mystic sat silent for a moment. "Perhaps."

With a small smile, the Witch said, "Come. Let's make tea."

Resting in the Courtyard Past the Gate

The Mystic's story (and the Witch's analysis) may sound, or feel, familiar. It may be a story you've heard from other people that have gone through a rough time with their religious upbringing, or it very well may be *your* story, depending on how you were introduced to Christianity and how your pastors, priests, or family structured your avenues of learning about this religion and its God. No matter what, though, it seems anyone who has picked up the label of Christian Witch specifically knows that feeling of discovering something special: finding a way of existing in the faith that turned the tables on much, if not all, we thought we knew about Christianity and God Himself. That's what brought you to the Gate in the first place, and that's what has you sitting in the Courtyard now (or what St. Teresa calls the first mansion) as you continue to learn the many elements of the Witchcraft portion of this identity we've taken on together.

First, let's discuss this mansion as St. Teresa understands it. This may help you orient yourself and realize where you stand in this spiritual plane: within yourself. As it turns out, the great and beautiful mansions and the whole castle itself that St. Teresa describes aren't some remote location where God lives, nor is He waiting for you to come back to Him in some faraway, magical place; no, the mansions are rooms within *you,* and the castle itself is your very own soul. St. Teresa explains this idea to the nuns set to read these works like so:

> I thought of the soul as resembling a castle, formed of a single diamond or a very transparent crystal, and containing many rooms, just as in heaven there are many mansions. If we reflect, sisters, we shall see that the soul of the just man is but a paradise, in which, God tells us, He takes His delight. What, do you imagine, must that dwelling be in which a King so mighty, so wise, and so pure, containing in Himself all good, can delight to rest? Nothing can be compared to the great beauty and capabilities of a soul; however keen our intellects may be,

they are as unable to comprehend them as to comprehend God, for, as He has told us, He created us in His own image and likeness.[1]

There's something important to glean from this idea of the soul as a crystal, as a *castle*: it means that we are God's own dwelling. We are God's palace, ourselves a living temple, and we were never without God, because He has always been within us, not hiding in some lofty place above the clouds where He judges us in silence. Such has been a common "doctrine of faith," so to speak: this idea of an absent, male God in the sky watching our every move, demanding we do a number of elaborate steps to deserve to even look His way. St. Teresa feels strongly about just the opposite, noting how the King (God) dwells in our very souls, and what a beautiful dwelling it must be, for Someone as esteemed as God to find it fit to rest there!

Moreover, St. Teresa notes that the average person has a dire lack of awareness about the sanctity, beauty, and wonder of the souls God gave us and which He uses to stay near to us. She asks her readers, those nuns:

> Would it not be gross ignorance, my daughters, if, when a man was questioned about his name, or country, or parents, he could not answer? Stupid as this would be, it is unspeakably more foolish to care to learn nothing of our nature except that we possess bodies, and only to realize vaguely that we have souls, because people say so and it is a doctrine of faith. Rarely do we reflect upon what gifts our souls may possess, Who dwells within them, or how extremely precious they are. Therefore we do little to preserve their beauty; all our care is concentrated on our bodies, which are but the coarse setting of the diamond, or the outer walls of the castle.[2]

---

1. St. Teresa, *Interior Castle,* 17.

2. St. Teresa, *Interior Castle,* 17–18.

Think about that picture we gave you earlier: of that grey existence, every single day exactly the same, repeating the steps you were told to repeat because *it is a doctrine of faith* or some other such thing—because that's *what you do,* because that's *how things are,* or some such reason that never satisfied you. Jesus may tell us that we are the light of the world, and that we should raise that light up for all to see rather than hide it under a basket,[3] yet how the light seems to *burn* the eyes of those who want you to keep it hidden for their comfort, huh? If the light you have to bring isn't the right brightness, the right color, the right size, it seems people will sooner tell you that it's a light from the devil[4] than that of your own shining soul, that gem that God Himself carved and polished.

This is where, as we sit in this Courtyard together, we might come to realize that there's more to do than simply learn about the tools and types of witchcraft. Given that witchcraft feels so infinite, with so many traditions and schools of thought to learn from, it's easy to feel like you'll never be done learning. Everything from sigils to kitchen witchcraft to ceremonial ritual to simple cantrips makes it easy to get absorbed in these little details of technique rather than zoom out and see the bigger picture of *why* you're seeking this kind of power to begin with—why you're seeking power at all, *if* you are. In fact, after a lifetime of minimizing, dimming, and concealing your light, the very idea of seeking power you're told you're unworthy of may still feel uncomfortable, and the idea that this Truth you've been called to is actually Truth despite it being so different from what you've heard all your life may still feel so strange to accept.

In this space, known by many who study mysticism as the time of *awakening,* it is exactly as it sounds: people become wholly aware of something more than them, be it by discovery of some new idea or fact, or direct revelation from God Himself. According to Dr. John Mabry, a minister and educator with the United Church of Christ and the Chaplaincy Institute for Arts and Interfaith Ministry respectively (and more), the process of awakening is something of a "minor miracle":

---

3. Matthew 5:14–16

4. 2 Corinthians 11:14

This is the essence of awakening... sometimes dramatic, sometimes subtle, but usually just enough to make us go, 'Whoa! What was that?" and start searching in a direction we might not have gone otherwise.

It is, in a sense, an experience of conversion, but not in the way we normally think about that word. For it is not a conversion to a set of doctrines or beliefs, but a conversion—a transformation, if you will—of one's very perception of Reality...

Awakening is a momentary flash of insight when we are granted a glimpse of the universe as God sees it.[5]

As Witches, the truth is that we, like scientists, have some experience in *seeking* such "minor miracles," in *provoking* or *inducing* such encounters with the Divine through concentrated efforts rather than happenstance. Unlike dear disciple Nathanael that Mabry references from the Gospel of John, who Jesus showed a small miracle to get him to leave his home behind in promise of witnessing greater things, we don't need to be lured out of our mundane existence by such things; we know implicitly that such things are there, and that we, as spiritual folk, have to go discover it. As such, you see what we mean when we say that the Witch (or the Wizard, or the Magus, or the Theurge, or the Occultist) is simply a more scientifically inclined Mystic: one with procedures, with tools, with cross references and book learning, that wishes to find a more systemic and collaborative way of encountering the Divine and invoking those miracles, minor or not.

However, that is us *now,* as folks who have already decided to be Witches. Now, we know that this encounter with the Divine is not

---

5. Mabry, *Growing into God,* 13-14.

passive, not something that just happens to us at random, but something that we can likewise initiate, just as we can be the first to text or call a friend rather than waiting around for them to contact us. Once upon a time, though, we might've still been like Nathanael: told all our lives not to expect more, told all our lives that such miracles and things were not possible (or, at least, not for us to see or experience). Like the Mystic earlier in her former ashy, grey existence, we might've been warned away from all such glimmers of the Divine attempting to contact us—until something happened that wrenched our focus off the long list of spiritual "dos" and "don'ts" forever.

Many mystics of note have had the same disruptive experiences of awakening, in which they were pulled *out* of their daily routine, their daily beliefs, understanding, and existence, and in that period of interruption, realized there was more work to do that they couldn't leave earth for just yet. One such mystic is the famous Julian of Norwich: an English anchoress from the 14th century, whose life we really don't know much about, but whose writings were some of the earliest English writings by a woman that were ever preserved. In fact, we don't even know her real name: *Julian* refers to the St. Julian church she was an anchoress of, and *Norwich* is the town of England the church was located in.[6]

Being an anchoress meant she was essentially built *into* a church, living the rest of her life locked in a small room with little more space than needed to sleep and pray, and with a space in the wall connecting to the church so she might still receive communion and hear the church service. She was expected to live by a strict code of honor, as was outlined in the Middle English text, *Ancrene Riwle:* a code demanding anchoresses "live in confined isolation, in poverty, and under a vow of chastity."[7] However, that didn't mean she never saw people; she had a window where visitors would stop by for spiritual advice and where, according to legend, her pet cat would go in and out.

---

6. "St. Julian of Norwich," *Catholic Online,* accessed Oct 30, 2025, https://www.catholic.org/saints/saint.php?saint_id=4124.

7. Ibid.

For Julian, her experience of interruption (Awakening) was a near-death experience she'd prayed to have at the age of thirty for the sake of purifying her and making it easier for her to love and worship God in fullness afterwards. Through this sickness, she experienced a rather hefty miracle and direct revelation. She'd been convinced that she was about to die, and certainly by reading her account in *Revelation of Divine Love,* anyone else would be convinced of this, too: she lost feeling in her body from the waist down, then in her chest, making her unable to breathe properly, and then her vision went dark—but her suffering, in that moment, disappeared entirely. Afterwards, she asked Jesus to give her the "second wound" of three she outlines in this Revelation (the "wound of very contrition, the wound of kind compassion, and the wound of steadfast longing toward God"). She recounts of her experience thereafter, which we might see as a moment of awakening:

IN this [moment] suddenly I saw the red blood trickle down from under the Garland hot and freshly and right plenteously, as it were in the time of His Passion when the Garland of thorns was pressed on His blessed head who was both God and Man, the same that suffered thus for me. I conceived truly and mightily that it was Himself shewed it me, without any mean.

And in the same Shewing suddenly the Trinity fulfilled my heart most of joy. And so I understood it shall be in heaven without end to all that shall come there. For the Trinity is God: God is the Trinity; the Trinity is our Maker and Keeper, the Trinity is our everlasting love and everlasting joy and bliss, by our Lord Jesus Christ. And this was shewed in the First [Shewing] and in all: for where Jesus appeareth, the blessed Trinity is understood, as to my sight.

And I said: *Benedicite Domine!* [Blessed be the Lord!] This I said for reverence in my meaning, with mighty voice; and full greatly was astonied for wonder and marvel that I had, that He that is so reverend and dreadful will be so homely with a sinful creature living in wretched flesh.

This [Shewing] I took for the time of my temptation,—for methought by the sufferance of God I should be tempted of fiends ere I died. Through this sight of the blessed Passion, with the Godhead that I saw in mine understanding, I knew well that It was strength enough for me, yea, and for all creatures living, against all the fiends of hell and ghostly temptation.

In this [Shewing] He brought our blessed Lady to my understanding. I saw her ghostly, in bodily likeness: a simple maid and a meek, young of age and little waxen above a child, in the stature that she was when she conceived. Also God shewed in part the wisdom and the truth of her soul: wherein I understood the reverent beholding in which she beheld her God and Maker, marvelling with great reverence that He would be born of her that was a simple creature of His making. And this wisdom and truth: knowing the greatness of her Maker and the littleness of herself that was made,—caused her to say full meekly to Gabriel: *Lo me, God's handmaid!* In this sight I understood soothly that she is more than all that God made beneath her in worthiness and grace; for above her is nothing that is made but the blessed [Manhood] Of Christ, as to my sight.

I saw that He is to us everything that is good and comfortable for us: He is our clothing that for love wrappeth
us, claspeth us, and all encloseth us for tender love, that
He may never leave us; being to us all-thing that is good,
as to mine understanding.

Also in this He shewed me a little thing, the quantity
of an hazel-nut, in the palm of my hand; and it was
as round as a ball. I looked thereupon with eye of my
understanding, and thought: *What may this be?* And it was
answered generally thus: It is all that is made. I marvelled
how it might last, for methought it might suddenly have
fallen to naught for little[ness]. And I was answered in my
understanding: *It lasteth, and ever shall [last] for that God
loveth it.* And so All-thing hath the Being by the love of
God.

In this Little Thing I saw three properties. The first is that
God made it, the second is that God loveth it, the third,
that God keepeth it. But what is to me verily the Maker,
the Keeper, and the Lover,—I cannot tell; for till I am
Substantially oned to Him, I may never have full rest nor
very bliss: that is to say, till I be so fastened to Him, that
there is right nought that is made betwixt my God and
me.[8]

The language still holding onto that essence of 14th century English,
doesn't always make for the easiest read, of course, and yet there is
still plenty to glean from this regardless: that Julian came to understand

---

8. St. Julian of Norwich, *Revelations of Divine Love,* translated by Grace Warrack (Grand
Rapids: Christian Classics Ethereal Library, 1901), 5-6, https://www.documentacatholic
aomnia.eu/03d/1343-1398,_Julian._of_Norwich,_Revelations_Of_Divine_Love,_EN.pdf

the same gravity of presence Mother Mary did, that this presence was the great Being which provides us everlasting goodness and comfort and grace, and that *all creation,* every single thing that is in the entire universe, is to God... but the size of a hazelnut in the palm of one's hand. And the reason it hasn't been crushed into hazelnut butter yet is simply because God loves it and wants it to exist. By extension, God loves *us* and wants *us* to exist.

This insight Julian received, along with the fulfillment of her wish for God to strike her down at thirty with illness so as to purify her, put her into the headspace she needed to walk further down the mystic path and likewise teach others to come into that space of understanding just how important God is to the soul. For instance, she notes how people "seek here rest in those things that are so little, wherein is no rest, and know not our God that is All-mighty, All-wise, All-good': plainly, people are so distraught and restless because they keep trying to find peace in earthly things rather than rest themselves in God, who is the "Very Rest," the ultimate refuge for the soul.[9]

Reading this very well may rub you the wrong way, and if it does, we ask you to sit with that feeling and inspect it. *Why* would it make you uncomfortable, to think that God is (not "should be," *is*) the source of all comfort and goodness, not anything else you can find on this earth? Is it because when you think of God, you think of the stuffy platitudes of your time growing up in mainstream Christianity? Or the vague guilt-tripping that pastors and priests would lay on you for not thinking God was better than the other comforts that made up your life (especially if you were still a child at the time)? Is it because the image—the *idol*—of God they'd given you was the mere face of a Man, a concrete *thing* that they spoke of so literally, rather than the cosmic, infinite, ineffable Force that is truly unknowable, and yet truly God?

Because we understand. If this is how you feel, then know that we once felt the same way: turned off by the mention of God or Jesus, seeing only those flat, static images of one specific Father in the Sky. These were images that we, as women, couldn't see ourselves in because the way the systems and powers that be interpreted Him had no room

---

9. Ibid., 6.

for us, despite how they also told us that we were *also* made in His image. Likewise, we don't doubt that many folks who are not white, or not straight, or not cisgender, also had trouble seeing themselves in the warped image of Jesus that became the poster Child for only one very specific demographic in western Christianity.

But this one static image is not God, and if you're here, then you already know this. Whatever folks call this grand, ineffable concept of God now—the Divine, Source, Spirit, Universe, etc.—we know it can't be pinned down to any one image, and that it is therefore very possible that God *is* the grand source of comfort we've been seeking all this time, in this world full of chaos and disaster. In fact, *especially* as Witches, we know this: that all that matters in the world can't be contained in your wallet or in the little pleasures, like good food or a pretty sunset or whatever else that we might've been thinking of whenever the priest or pastor started going on about how *wrong* it was for us to like those things instead of focusing every minute on the Man-God. As Witches, we know by virtue of our own experiences and contact with something Other than us in the spiritual world: there is more to life than these things, and these experiences, in the waking world.

After all, we might enjoy these mundane things, these "real life" experiences, but we also know that to keep trying to find such rest *in* these things would only be a way of avoiding those problems that vex us, since we couldn't dive into them all day and ignore our every other responsibility. To seek comfort in food is to eventually jeopardize your health when you eat just for the sake of eating, and to seek comfort in places like the beach is to never live in the present moment, but to always wish to be away from your problems and avoid the work you know you need to do. When you put your comfort in God, however—God the infinite, God the Force that is woven through the universe, God who dwells *within* you, and is always with you, always cloaking you in His love—then you don't need to go anywhere, consume anything, or have anything to have that peace; it is stitched into the great gem that is your soul, and through this journey, you can learn to navigate that gem, that Castle, that Manor, anytime. You can learn to find your center in that great Force of God, to swaddle yourself in God's love, no matter where you are or how the world around you tries to hassle you.

Let us be clear, though, as we cannot stress this enough: *everyone's journey looks different*. Everyone's Manor looks different, and every one of St. Teresa's mansions we take you through in this book may look exactly like the Mystic describes, or it may look *nothing* like she describes. However, no matter what your path looks like in your mind's eye, or how its challenges manifest to you in your life, you know it's the right path if the fruits it brings match the fruits of the Spirit in Galatians 5:22-23:

> But the fruit of the Spirit is love, joy, peace, forbearance [*patience under provocation*], kindness, goodness, faithfulness, gentleness and self-control. Against such things there is no law.

And trust us when we say cultivating these things is easier said than done, and that it is a *lifelong process*. You will not read this book and be done with the journey, or able to skip this journey. No, if you are truly called to this path, then this book will simply help you *contextualize* the journey; it'll give you a way to understand it. And hopefully, by the way we, Mimi and Sara, share our stories going through our own journeys and bringing in the occasional voices of the Saints before us who went on theirs, you'll be able to recognize those moments where you may already *have* gone through these moments—and what it'll feel like when another such journey through a certain mansion comes through again.

As we sit in this Courtyard together right now, you will hopefully consider not only the root of the Witchcraft part of this identity you now hold, but the Christian part, too—the underbelly of it, the guts of it. But to do so means you have to come to terms with some things in the Courtyard, as well as leave some things behind at the Gate. Be prepared: the sunlight shearing down on you in the Courtyard will only feel so warm and lovely before it'll begin to sting. In fact, the longer you sit in it, the more it'll burn. However, only when the sun has shriveled those last grey scales of your fears up, and when you've gathered the courage to scratch them off and let them become ash that fertilizes the Courtyard ground, will you be ready to move on. Until then, let us pull back the curtain on one of the mechanisms working on you here in this part of your inner journey.

Mimi Says:

At about seven, I distinctly remember sitting in the second row pew, coloring and humming hymns while the preaching was going on, only to be suddenly run through my heart by something that felt white-hot and yet wholly comforting. Folks were up singing and shouting to claim the Glory of God, but I stayed in my seat, quietly sobbing at the love that felt like it was pouring out of the hole that the Holy Spirit just pierced through my chest. I saw kaleidoscopes of colors and wonders, and heard something ethereal above the tongues and translations and banging on the piano. Mamaw was sitting next to me, shouting, "Say it, Lord! Lord, help 'em!" and waving her tissue around. I crawled up beside her, hugged her, and said, "I think God loves me."

The rest of that memory is a blur of hands being laid on me and shouting to the rafters, until it felt like the little church was going to collapse around me from the sheer force of Hallelujahs. Before this, there was always an angel or a spirit or a loved one that sat with me. I would talk to them on the school bus on my way to school. It wasn't really *psychosis* the way you see people shout about now online, nor just a child's imagination, either; it was always someone different, and sometimes, it was someone I didn't know at all. My mama said I always talked about my dream walks (astral projecting) and talked to ghosts, so when I would commune and receive messages, I thought it was normal. This was normal in my family, but only as far as my family. I was told to keep my stories just to church and don't tell anyone else. It was my little light, and it needed to be protected. There was always talk of demons and the devil trying to get to me, but I never knew of evil from the spirit world, only humans. So when that moment came that I can now describe as a moment of Holy Ecstasy, it was like coming into full consciousness and realizing a calling all at the same time.

And for a seven-year-old? That's terrifying. There were times I was asked to tell what I knew, especially at Papaw's knee while he read the Bible, and times when I was just given a pat on the head. The worried looks were kept for when they thought I wasn't looking.

This sort of thing would happen in waves throughout my life. I would have tremendous, sensory-overwhelming experiences, usually when I was somewhere out and talking to God. And, unfortunately, these experiences did lead me to have a 'why can't God fix the bad or hard things in my life?' where I displaced blame. If the awe and wonder of my experiences with God was so powerful, why was I still so helpless? Why did the bad things keep happening?

Obviously, those ecstasy moments became fewer and fewer when I started to doubt and feel jaded over it all; how could I have these incredible moments and then... nothing? The knowledge of such mysteries and magic made me thing that I could do a lot on my own. Finding books on magic was a step I took in high school; I combined a lot of the folk practice with what I learned, and set about "giving myself enough power to do something about it," but even then, I never left the Courtyard. Deconstructing was one of the keys I needed to open the door to the next part, as did decolonizing, and recognizing that the Church itself was not where I was called to be.

This took *years*. It was also not all at once, either. As I pick apart every trial, I can see where I began as Seeker of Truth; like many of us do in our teenage years, I began to "rebel" and look at everything I could to gain a better understanding of what more there is in the world. The internet was still new and most of us gathered in chat rooms and forums. In a rural community, the books on any other religion were relegated to encyclopedic paragraphs in the reference sections. I devoured what I could find, and still went looking for more. There was a single book on witches called *The Witch's Handbook* by Malcolm Bird that was both humorous and non-threatening; however, it got the wheels turning on what things could actually look like. A reference to replacing old ingredients (like worms or flies) turned into spaghetti and raisins. I told my young self, "Self, what if this was serious? What if we could look at things and make them into actual ingredients?"

It wasn't until I got hold of Silver Ravenwolf's *Teen Witch* from a friend at a larger school in the city, and then was gifted Ray Buckland's *Big Blue Book* from an old family friend, that I realized it was all something I *could* do. I would sneak away from my conservative family to read what I could from friends who had "secret books." And finally, due to my obsession with Egyptian Mythology and my insistence on staying hidden in the library for most of my high school career, I was gifted the *Egyptian Book of the Dead* from my school's head librarian as a graduation present. Taoism, Buddhism, Hermeticism, Wicca—these studies built on further understanding of what my path was meant to be, and as I trudged through this path's cycle for over a decade, I understood that this was where I had to roll up my sleeves and do the hard work, not just take what I knew from a book and throw it around like a hefty weight. But it wasn't just the work; it was remaining humble and hopeful, still holding wonder and awe like a child.

I am reminded of Matthew 18:4 here: "Whosoever therefore shall humble himself as this little child, the same is greatest in the kingdom of heaven." A child is like a sponge, absorbing everything and (mostly) dutifully listening to the ways to go. They explore, they learn, and they glean their own beautiful faith through the magic of the Divine that they see in this world.

My fellow Evangelicals will hear the phrase "backsliding Christian" and know full well the weight of guilt that comes crashing along with it. The times I felt like I was a bad Christian, a "backslider," were the times I felt the most lost in my faith—not because I didn't believe in God, but because it felt impossible to follow the influence of the church and leave my compassion and empathy out of it. Not only watching the cruelty happen on the news and in real time with strangers, there were moments where I experienced the shame and hatred of that phrase "no hate like Christian love" for something seemingly benign. A lot of it started in high school: this was post-9/11, and right as we entered the "war on terror," with Bush and his righteous fury stirring the hearts of those around me. All the while, I carried the guilt of my shifting religious beliefs in my heart secretly while publicly de-crying the wages of war and the bigotry barely hidden behind "love thy neighbor." I would go back to church every so often, and usually at the behest of those who wanted something good and stable in my life. The feelings of ecstasy became fewer and fewer, and I had to live with the whispers of *hypocrite* around me.

The tools of shame and guilt and isolation were still at play, and there were times I ran back to the church because I didn't know how to let go of that cycle. I didn't know how to walk on my own under Grace. I honestly thought you had to go to church because where else could you find the joy that was fellowship? Those fellowship halls and dinners and events felt like popularity contests back then, and they feel that way now. It's still ego and the ideal of living by the bible without actually doing more than one or two things.

Even when I tried my best to sit in with progressive churches over the years, it never felt the way it had. For the sea of righteousness I would be submerged in, I was drowning in the discord and lies. After leaving the church and deconstructing as much as I could on my own, I *still* stayed in the Courtyard because I didn't understand how the calling on my life meant action and doing. Every saint and mystic we discuss took steps to move out of the courtyard that is so familiar and into the unknown because they have such faith and love in God. I did not leave the courtyard until I could recognize the ecstasy for what it was and know that I was capable of more. Loving God and Loving others as yourself are radical *acts*, not just thoughts, which meant lifestyle adjustments and re-framing my thoughts in a way that I hadn't allowed them to go before.

Mysticism didn't feel like a big to-do, like the emphasis we put on Tower moments; the smoke did not clear and I wasn't instantly in this life. Romans 12:1 states fairly simply: "Therefore, I urge you, brothers and sisters, in view of God's mercy, to offer your bodies as a living sacrifice, holy and pleasing to God—this is your true and proper worship." I chose to accept and embrace this mystical life, in little pieces, until one day I looked back and said, "Is that what I just lived through—the trials of a Mystic?!"

The idea of being a Mystic showed up in energy when I joined Sara on this path to write *Discovering Christian Witchcraft*. At almost forty years old, I can see the decisions that felt so small at the time shape my path to where I am now, and the path that still lay before me. I am taking my commitment to my journey, understanding, and knowledge as it strengthens me. Sara asked me to write on why I chose to be a mystic, but the answer isn't so easy or clear. I didn't choose it; I embraced the magic that was in me already and let that be my guide. I chose love that was bigger than just my life. I chose to listen and trust and be guided by the Holy Spirit, even if that meant the practice of witchcraft and leaving the church constructs how I did. I didn't know what this was exactly, only that, yeah, it might be different, but it's my calling. It's how I live my most authentic life.

Be prepared as you move on: this may take longer than you think. This journey is not a race, nor a contest. This is building a relationship, from scratch, with God as He has called you. The intimacy that comes from the relationship between yourself and Spirit is one that has to supersede doubt and overcome trauma; this experience is the feeling of being called and wanting to return to them. Recall, if you will, in *Discovering Christian Witchcraft*, where we grazed the topic of being called by other deities; this is answering God's call on you, like someone would answer the call to Hekate or the Mórrígan or Thor. It is the act of knowing, understanding, and experiencing God in a way that would truly be the idea of subservience and devotion. This is a relationship that most see in the liminal spaces but don't fully understand or know how to reach it. By reading *Discovering Christian Witchcraft*, you made it here, and now it's time to decide whether you'll go further or walk back and seek what your soul wants somewhere else.

The Adversary Provokes: Kataphatic Mysticism as Double Edged Sword

Now, before we go any further out of this Courtyard, let us take you aside and remind you of something important, something that'll keep you grounded on your walk to come. There's a term that'll make a lot of things make sense once you know it (and its corresponding term, which we'll come to later): *kataphatic mysticism.*

To put it simply, *kataphatic* (meaning "with saying") mysticism is the type of mysticism that approaches Divinity with, and understands Divinity through, images, tools, and symbols; it insists that "humans *need* metaphor, words, and images in order to approach the great Mystery, because the unmediated Divine is incomprehensible."[10] Through kataphatic mysticism, one comes to frame their understanding of Divinity through positive statements: *God is love, God is mercy, God is the Father, God is...* With an infinite being like God, we can make these statements

---

10. Mabry, *Growing into God,* 5.

quite literally forever (or at least for as long as we can think of things to say about God). It's how mainstream Christianity got so tangled in the first place, as we spoke about earlier: always choosing images to relate to God that serve one demographic (ex. the Father, the Warrior), yet somehow ignoring all the equally important images that make up so huge a Being (ex. the Mother, the Healer). It seems, all too often, that society's most powerful demographics are the ones who get to have *their* slice of God show up the most often. Interesting.

This doesn't mean kataphatic speech is inherently bad, though. It helps us to make an Other of God, as distinct from ourselves, while still knowing that any such distinction doesn't really exist; however, according to many a theologian and philosopher, *like* can only be revealed by *like,* yet can only be God revealed by the opposite of God—in which an Other is necessary to grasp any inkling of God at all.[11] It's this kind of talking about Divinity, through characteristics our minds can comprehend, that according to Mabry cause many mystics to "speak of their relationship with God as a love affair, a marriage of their soul with God's spirit."[12] As you encounter the words of other mystics in this book, and think about ones you already have encountered, like those of St. Teresa in her *interior Castle,* you may notice such romantic, bridal language: this is because the metaphor of marriage itself is a symbol with which we might understand our relation to and experience of the Divine. We can conceptualize it, understand it, and therefore, we can engage with and practice it.

Reading all this, you may very well guess that this is where the heart of witchcraft lies, too: in organizing our rituals or other spells by matching our intentions to objects like crystals, herbs, fruits, vegetables, candle colors, and more. What we're really doing when we choose our items for our ritual is creating *tangible metaphors* for otherwise abstract concepts; we're giving our mind imagery it can anchor these ideas onto, per the symbolism we've come to know through our cultural upbringing.

---

11. Jürgen Moltmann, *The Crucified God* (Minneapolis: Fortress Press, 2015), 30–32.

12. Ibid., 6.

Think of how the color green often makes people think of money, or the element of earth; think about how rabbits are so closely linked with our seasons of fertility, like with the Easter Bunny in spring. Think about how the dove became so unmistakable as a symbol of peace, and how the phrase "extending an olive branch" came to infer reconciliation. None of us live in a vacuum; all of us, by virtue of growing up in community informed by centuries of art, literature, history, and more, will be able to attach specific colors, shapes, animals, flowers, or any other symbols to abstract concepts like *love* or *creativity* or *power* or *wealth,* and this is where not all, but certainly many, of these associations *in* witchcraft come from: our collective cultural memory, from which folk magic and folk remedy are born.

In more mainstream religions, including Christianity, you'll also notice how denominations that honor God through the beauty of their worship spaces focus on art: paintings, sculptures, icons, and the massive, high ceiling, ornate churches themselves. In times before most of the population could read, it was important for churches to have the story of the Gospels displayed in the stained glass windows, so that the laypeople could still understand the story of Christ through art; those huge, towering crucifixes with Christ hanging dead and desolate on them, likewise, portrayed the gravity of His death that simply saying it with words might not have been able to get across for people. It's important for spiritual folk, be they conventional believers of a pre-set religion or self-directed, solitary practitioners of magic, to have something to look at, touch, visualize, and resonate with when they begin working with, and through, these higher and more abstract concepts.

Now, let us be clear about something: there is nothing wrong with using tools in your practice. In fact, there's much to love and enjoy about all the little trinkets and tools and crystals and herbs and whatever else that draws your eye and excites you in your practice. In this Courtyard, the *novelty* of your newfound spiritual path is so great that *everything* looks so shiny and exciting. We might return here to that childlike state of wonder Christ demands of us, settling into the whimsy and sheer joy of rediscovering *ritual.*[13] We might look upon our altars full

---

13. Matthew 18:1-5

of spellwork tools the way a child looks upon their sand castle at the beach, beautifully decorated with rocks and shells, and be satisfied by the *majesty* of magic.

However, what starts as a source of childlike fascination and wonder can just as quickly become a source of anxiety as that old thief called *Comparison* comes to steal all our joy away. When we take a look through the workings of other practitioners, we might notice certain elements of their witchcraft: the grandeur of all the candles burning in their perfectly fixed positions, the gleam of silver trays peeking through otherwise thick layers of herbs and spices, the elaborate grids of crystals and salt covering up the whole floor, the wax-sealed bottles full of all kinds of strange things, and we might think that our own magic is *weaker* for not looking so intense. We might see those spells and compare them to our own cup of tea that we charmed and think we're doing something wrong. We might sigh longingly as we pass those "witchy" shops and wish we could come out with bags full of crystals that, ultimately, will do little more than take up space in one's house.

And so, as the trinkets pile up, and the money flees from your hands, you may find yourself more overwhelmed and wanting than delighted. *I can't do this spell for creativity; I don't have an orange candle!* you might say, or *how will I do this month's money spell if I have no cinnamon to blow through my door?* Just as quickly as these tools motivated and empowered you to act, they can also become your biggest snare and vice. If you begin to focus too much on the things that come from outside you and attribute your power to *them* instead of their true Source, you soon become disconnected from that Source. Kataphatic mysticism is therefore interesting and helpful in many ways, but there comes one important thing that anyone, be they devout Catholic or free-spirit witch, can tell you:

The icon is not actually the Saint. The crystal is not the object of worship.

Thus, ironically, many of these mainstream Christians crowing about how it's "demonic" or "sinful" to use crystals and tarot cards and other such tools actually might be in the ballpark of Truth, even if they don't quite grasp the *why* behind it. It's not as if these things are actually demonic in any way or have little impish creatures hiding in them and waiting to trip us up (and many other mystics like St. Hildegard von Bingen and Meister Eckhart will tell you all about how God's majesty dwells in all His creation), but it *is* that when people get too focused on the tools and not on the God that informed them and speaks through them, we may come away more tangled than we started, as we begin to ignore the power of God, from which our power (and the crystals', herbs', and other such things' power) stems from. In a funny twist of fate, in our search *for* power, we get confused: we *limit* possibility and the power of God, and we lose ourselves to details rather than step back to see the true mechanisms of this thing we call "magic."

If there is any trick of any Enemy or any Adversary, it is this two-fold lie: the first part being that witchcraft *has* to be expensive, tool-based, or otherwise difficult, and the second part being that one can still have incredible power just like they *want* from witchcraft by simply "submitting to Christ" (or, more accurately, outsourcing one's religious and spiritual practice to another's schedule and demands, like in the Evangelical church).

Regarding the first part of this lie, surely the many witchy books that proliferated at the end of the 20th century and in the very early 21st century are partly to blame, with how many inaccessible items they say are *completely necessary* to do certain spells: herbs one would never reasonably find in local stores, crystals sold by boutiques that can rack up quite the cost, deck after deck after deck of tarot cards that collect dust on a shelf, you name it. This issue was only exacerbated as these common witchcraft trinkets became, for some companies, an opportunity to sell yet more products to consumers. The most notable example is the beauty chain, Sephora, which attempted to launch a "'Starter Witch Kit' in collaboration with fragrance company Pinrose," according to religious sociologist Dr. Chris Miller.[14] This starter kit included "tarot cards, white sage, a rose quartz crystal, fragrances, and an instructional guide advising how to 'create and cleanse your ceremony space, charge your crystal, read your tarot card, and anoint your fragrance.'"[15]

Naturally, such an obvious attempt to capitalize on spiritual practice (and the inclusion of items that are now endangered due to overhar-

---

14. Chris Miller, "Sephora's Starter Witch Kit: Identity Construction through Social media Protests of Commodified Religion," *Nova Religio,* vol. 25, no. 3 (2022), 87. https://doi.or g/10.1525/nr.2022.25.3.87.

15. Ibid., 88.

vesting and sacred to indigenous folks, like white sage), led to some serious outrage online, which had the kit cancelled in September of that same year. However, this debacle became an important conversation around commercialization in witchcraft while witches on Twitter (now known by some as X) were out there trying to define and legitimize their spiritual practices. As Miller explains:

> Witches remain divided over commercial-ism. Religious studies scholar Todd LeVasseur argues, for example, that Reverend Billy's Church of Stop Shopping is oriented against "an oppressive capitalist, white supremacist, speciesist system" that exploits "the poor, communities of color, and Earth." Many Witches posting on Twitter denounced Sephora with similar language, aligning themselves with other oppressed communities. However, the counter-promotion on Twitter of "real" Witchcraft stores demonstrated the impossibility of entirely escaping consumerism and highlighted that Modern Witches still integrate commercial consumption into their identities—they simply wish to do so on their own terms.[16]

The rest of Miller's study has quite the fascinating content, as it analyses the way in which "individuals seek to assert exclusive ownership over traditions and practices, and in some cases, side-step their own accusations of appropriation"—a worthy topic that is definitely relevant (as the white sage many specifically Wiccan witches claimed was "theirs" was then challenged by Native American users, sparking a deeper debate in witchy online spaces at the time).[17] As it stands, however, the key fact here can't be ignored: like all things, commercialism has seeped into the cracks of spirituality, convincing people that they *must* buy these trinkets, tools, and other products to bolster their connection and get the results they want out of life–or, in Christian spaces, to act as

---

16. Ibid., 89.

17. Ibid., 90.

public displays of their devotion (see the many Bible pillows, Bible covers, Bible annotating kits, apparel with Bible quotes, and other more traditionally Christian tools like rosaries and jewelry).

In the end, what originally served as reminders, anchor points, or more direct representations of difficult and abstract concepts per the kataphatic approach has, in this heavily commercialized world, become an *overload* of money-siphoning, space-wasting clutter that doesn't really help people at all. This kataphatic, hands-on, and *immersive* experience of spirituality, this beautiful space where one works *with* God instead of just passively waiting for God to drop everything in their lap, becomes corroded into a materialistic, shallow system in which the more things one has—the nicer, prettier, more *aesthetic* things—the stronger a witch is. Add to this the fact that witchcraft is inherently *personal* and *self-directed*, as in, a practice that requires the individual to build their own ethics, beliefs, observances, and other religious structure from the ground up as opposed to relying on the pre-built framework of a church or liturgical calendar, and not only is this path seemingly expensive, but *difficult*, too. Difficult and time consuming and plain *tiring*.

As such, we see here a mighty opportunity to walk out of the Courtyard, out of the Gate, and back to the Mystic's vision of that ashen world: we find ample opportunity to become another face on the internet giving "testimony" as an "ex-witch turned Christian" that decides all of this was always bad because of the challenges such a path poses to a practitioner (whether or not those challenges were the cause of one's own misunderstanding surrounding witchcraft to begin with). For example, take YouTube user lovlovelle9237's testimony, found in a YouTube comment under creator Shane Miller's video, "Pastor Confronts a Witch in Church, Then THIS Happens":

> It's actually SO MUCH easier to walk in the power of God then [sic] witchcraft! It's almost relieving. I've spent easily thousands of dollars on crystals, cards, healers, stones, etc. and it was exhausting! At the end of the day NONE of them truly helped me. God loves me, provides for me, heals me, and has delivered me from many unclean spirits. All I had to do is surrender and for the first

time in my life I can say I'm genuinely happy! My only
regret is not doing it sooner but I just didn't know until I
got attacked by evil spirits. God LITERALLY saved my
life and I pray for those out there to come to repentance
and get FREE!![18]

In this language, we see the two-fold lie in action: the financially
destructive portion, where this individual has spent "thousands" on all
manners of witchy items, and the claim that it is "so much *easier* to
walk in the power of God." In both cases, as happens in the video itself
and in this comment, there is a discussion of *power:* and especially an
argument made that the power one gets from God is *better, easier, more
accessible, more potent,* than any power received through witchcraft. The
people who sought some power to change their life through witchcraft
are heretofore promised *more* power for *less* effort, which, given we
are creatures who take the path of least resistance, is a tempting claim,
and that is the bottom line of this test of the Adversary: are you doing
witchcraft because you want *power?* Because you want things to go
your way, or because you want to force change in the world? And if so,
will you so easily *abandon* this path when promised an easier source of
power? A source that requires less effort, less knowledge, less dedication,
less work?

The Adversary aims to pin you now: do you seek to walk this path
because you wish to sew your heart ever closer to God's, because you
seek Union with Him? Or is your magic for such petty, material things
that it doesn't matter one way or another where you get your power,
so long as you get to reap the shallow rewards of it for the least effort?

Moreover, even if we do approach witchcraft from its most historical
context–the context not of someone who wants to be rich and powerful
by any means necessary, but of the disenfranchised with no other way to
access justice, survival, and protection–then one thing people nowadays
seem to forget is that witchcraft was always about using what you had
available to you for free or at least very cheap, *not* what was expensive

---

18. @lovlovelle9237, June 2025, comment on Miller, "Pastor Confronts a Witch, Then THIS
Happens."

and out of reach. Maybe the witchy books on the shelves tell you that you *must* have mugwort for psychic enhancement, and you live in a place where mugwort doesn't grow. But maybe what you do have easily available is thyme, which you can pick up at the store and which your other books say is *also* good for psychic enhancement. Or maybe you associate anything that reminds you of the moon with this trait, and so when you find the most beautiful, milk-white rock on your walk around your neighborhood, you tuck it in your pocket for future rituals.

What matters in these cases isn't the herb or the stone itself so much as what it means to you when you see it or smell it or taste it (if you're using edible items). What matters is that it anchors your focus, represents these concepts to you and helps you better guide your intentions along as you ask God to let His miracles flow through you and into the world. And, naturally, what matters above all is what you're asking for in the first place, and why. This is another point of opportunity for the Adversary that'll come up later in your mystic journey.

Now, of course, when we look at kataphatic mysticism and consider the tools and items we *do* have available, there is something to be said for them in an animistic sense on top of their value as symbols and metaphors. Many folks will insist that each herb is *fixed* in what it represents: that you can't make cinnamon suddenly a symbol of water and coolness when its properties make it so clearly a warming spice that quickens the blood, or that you can't make an amethyst mean war and aggression when it's so *clearly* energetically aligned for peace and wisdom. In the philosophy of *animism,* which insists that all creation has its own life force or spiritual cognizance, one might argue that each item has its own talents and preferences just like people do.

Folks like Henry Cornelius Agrippa von Netterheim especially might disagree that any item can mean anything (at least, in reference to natural magic), as we see him say quite plainly:

> Whosoever therefore is desirous to study in this Faculty [magic], if he be not skilled in naturall Philosophy, wherein are discovered the qualities of things, and in which are found the occult properties of every Being, and if he be not skilful in the Mathematicks, and in the

Aspects, and Figures of the Stars, upon which depends the sublime virtue, and property of every thing; and if he be not learned in [theology], wherein are manifested those immaterial substances, which [dispense], and minster all things, he cannot be possibly able to understand the rationality of Magick.[19]

In essence: if you don't have a solid grasp of philosophy, math, astrology, and theology, which chart and hold within them the implicit characteristics of everything that makes up *natural* magic, you just won't understand how and why anything is the way it is. A lot of what people take for granted now in witchcraft (like the planetary or elemental alignment of things) actually do get referenced in works like Agrippa's *Three Books of Occult Philosophy;* pick them up and see (between the very stuffy writing style) very similar ideas as you would on any contemporary witchcraft book sitting in places like Barnes & Noble.

With an animistic philosophy, however, we also might consider that, like us, these items *do* have spiritual power. After all, according to a more literal reading vs. poetic reading in various places in the Bible (such as 1 Chronicles 16:33, Psalm 96, Romans 8:19-22, even Luke 19:40), one might say that creation is able to reason and recognize God as their Creator, as well as yearn for Him. As such, rather than credit these things as the source of power, we might understand these specialized creations with their specific natures and talents as something like Saints instead: capable of interceding for us, contributing their prayers and their energy *with* us in ritual, which we all offer up together before God bestows down His blessing, the true power of a Christian Witch's spell or ritual.

However, even Agrippa turned on his heel (in a way) when it came to things like magic. According to Dr. Justin Sledge in his introduction to *Invisibila Dei: A Collection of Hermetic, Mystical, and Anti-Magical Works by Heinrich Cornelius Agrippa,* the private letters (epistles) Agrippa sent to colleagues and other figures outside of his sharp rebukes against

---

19. Henry Cornelius Agrippa von Netterheim, *Three Books of Occult Philosophy,* translated by James Freake, edited by Donald Tyson (USA: Llewellyn Publications, 1992), 4.

society "reveal a central Agrippan theme: that inner divine illumination is the key to true magic, with magic itself serving as a propaedeutic [introduction] to the bliss of of perfect communion with the divine, or *felicitas*."[20] Sledge insists these letters reveal that Agrippa still held tightly to the concepts of magic he professed (despite how a lot of those ideas got him in trouble with ecclesiastic authorities at the time), and that it wasn't so much magic as a whole he rebuked, but the *sophistry* people employed with their more *forced* versions of magic (like mathematical magic) that he had issue with: the deception, the charlatanry, the nonsense people came up with to *appear* holy rather than *be* holy.[21]

Take both sides of this scale, and we find something important to note: God made all things on heaven and earth just so, with their own unique properties and qualities, that the Witch would do well to respect and recruit in her workings–but that also the entire mechanism of magic is, in itself, a way to bring us into the fold of divine experience, to *illumination* (which is thought to come far after awakening, and after purgation). Unlike the charlatans Agrippa decries, that use things like mathematical magic to *mimic* natural magic and deceive people with their supposed power, and unlike the scholars who focus so much on reason that they forget the entire concept of *religious* Truth entirely, the Witch of modern day holds within her two forces at once: that of the Scientist in her books and empirical study of nature and things that God created, and that of the Mystic in her openness to the mind-boggling, inexplicable Truth of God that ration and reason cannot touch–the openness to Truth that all things source their life energy from the creative singularity that is God, and that God is the most direct source of any miracle, magic, or other wonder.

In understanding this, we might thwart the Adversary, at least for now. We come to understand what Sledge summarizes of Agrippa's stance: magic, and all the trinkets and tools and such inherent in that practice, is simply an *introduction*. It is the sandbox in which we learn how to better identify and discern what spirits are coming through, and

---

20. Sledge introducing Agrippa, *Invisibila Dei*, xxi.

21. Ibid., xxii.

how to better contextualize spiritual experiences, through metaphor, tools, anchoring points, and symbol. It is inherently kataphatic, and it works to be the training wheels of spiritual development: just as a child learns how to pedal on a bike, how to use the handles and the brake and ring her little bell, all while the training wheels help keep her from falling and therefore avoiding the process altogether after she gets hurt, so too does magic and kataphatic mysticism give us a structure to abide by, so that we might be introduced to the experience of the Divine in a more controlled box of our making.

However, training wheels on a bike does not mean a child is free from danger on the bike. And symbol, metaphor, tool, and magic circle do not necessarily mean a Witch is free from danger in her contact with the Divine. Like all things, it requires consistent practice to do with any skill, and like all things, it requires vigilance to the world around us—and an eventual removal of the training wheels altogether. That, however, is for another time. For now, in this Courtyard of our soul's Manor, we might simply be happy to ride about this spiritual space at all, to feel the wind of such spiritual freedom and the delight of this exhilarating experience, which no doubt any who have experienced such awakening or such mystical, spiritual, "witchy" practice have the right to enjoy.

Sara Says:

Lest you think we say all this to warn you away from ever buying a single witchy-looking item that makes you happy, let me tell you: I wouldn't have ever had the relationship I have with God now if I didn't play around with all these fun little trinkets and tools and aesthetics, and that's just a fact. When we use the term *sandbox,* when we say *rediscovering the whimsy of a child,* we really do mean it in terms of that imaginative play that constitutes the way children learn about the world and about themselves. Because let's be real: when you're a kid, organized religion, and its requirements to sit quietly in church, is boring as hell.

Magic, on the other hand—that's fun for a kid. Whether we're mixing up a "soup" of ketchup and mustard in a bowl of dirty dish water or mixing some seriously rank blend of herbs that match our witchy intentions, fact is that it's essentially the same thing: mimicry, play. It's not until we learn the ins and outs of cooking or herbalism that our elders have mastered that we actually do something other than waste materials and make a mess; it's not until we are mentally, emotionally, and spiritually developed enough that we can start appreciating the parts of faith that were so "boring" to us as youths. At this point, we can finally "lift the hood" of magic and see the mystical philosophy/theology that's been waiting for us underneath it all.

Naturally, for a kid that couldn't have sat through a chapter of Jürgen Moltmann even if threatened with being grounded for a year, the first stop was this trinket-based understanding of witchcraft. I loved going to the local witchy shops and looking at all the different herbs and stones and books and other such things; my fiance's sibling, also a witch, would take teenage me out to the shops where I would find all kinds of fun little things to use in my (very clumsy, very silly) witchcraft. The box of crystals I have spawned around this time, as did a lot of the other items that are now staples for my altar (some of which were my mom's regular household decorations that I just really liked, such as a big angel statue). It made things fun! It gave me something to look at, and having all the items made the witchcraft feel more *real* at the time.

However, when it comes to items like these, the reality is that a new witch is bound to have way more stuff than she needs, and an experienced witch is likely to make a crazy good spell just with whatever regular items she has lying around. It's like when you go to live alone for the first time and buy food based on what your parents always had growing up, only to realize you don't regularly eat half of what your parents eat. Why bother buying containers of sour cream that just go bad because you only make chili once a month when you could replace it with something you do use regularly, like Greek yogurt? Items in witchcraft are the same: they're fun, they're cool, and they certainly help in the big sit-down rituals, of course, but you have to learn to consolidate and be practical, too.

Eventually—just recently, in fact—I went and gathered up several bags worth of old things I never ended up using in my witchcraft: bottles full of hawthorne berries and special oils, empty bottles "for potions" that stayed empty and dusty, and many other such things that cluttered up my house and made it feel so much smaller than it was. This kind of thing is important for magic, too: throwing out the old things that stagnant energy settles on like dust and cobwebs. Throwing out my years-old herbs and keeping my tools better organized means that the things I *do* still use (like bells, holy water, candles, incense, and the many types of tea I turn into quick potions) didn't limit my magic in any way; it only got me to learn how to better prioritize what I buy and cut the fluff out of my toolkit.

There's naturally more to kataphatic mysticism than just items like statues and rosaries and all that, though: there's also the visualization element. Cheesy as it is, I do love to get my ideas about magic from stories as much as actual books on magical practice, and one thing that's stuck with me is the way magic is described in *Frieren: Beyond Journey's End* (a fantastic anime and manga that I highly recommend). I watched the anime, and in it, they describe magic as a *visual craft:* one where, if you can't imagine a way for your magic to work or a way for your goal to be reached, you just can't do it no matter how skilled a magician you are.

In that way, the trials magicians have to overcome to rank up can be seen as less a test of raw power and skill, and more a test of the limits of one's mind. Kataphatic mysticism asks the same of us: what symbols and language can move us from doubt and uncertainty into faith and confidence? What ways can we think of God that have Him feeling less distant, abstract, and invisible, and more a force we can perceive, and therefore recognize? It's hard to relate to something or someone you can't perceive or understand, and that's why this style of mysticism is so helpful, *especially* for new initiates into Christian faith and witchcraft: because it gives us something to latch onto so that our minds don't get in the way of our souls. From there, we learn to recognize the signs of God's presence after we accept some perception of Him.

The only danger of this is when one forgets that the symbols and language one uses aren't the full picture of God. The mystics who subscribe to kataphatic mysticism, again, they know this: they know that God is more than any one name, title, or idea they can give Him. They just use their images as a starting point, an entryway, a door to the Divine. Keep that in mind yourself, and you might eventually find yourself in a different type of mysticism that we'll get into later. For now, though, know that you aren't wrong for enjoying all the bells and whistles of a modern witchcraft practice; you're simply giving your mind doorways to access the concepts that are sometimes too hard to grasp without something to symbolize it.

Now go and lift your heart up to God, however it is you see Him and understand Him. Tip your face towards that sunlight. Enjoy it while it's warm; embrace the burn on your cheeks and nose and temple. And stay steadfast, even when it stings enough to bring you to tears and sends tracks of mud down your ashen face.

Unto you, it is given to know the mysteries of Heaven. —Mark 4:11

Shadow Work Prompts for the Gate and the Courtyard

- Think back to the beginning of your magical journey. Was it in childhood? Was it teenage years, bucking back against the constraints of religion? Was it as an adult, when you started to piece more and more together? When did you notice this aching pull at every fiber of your being? Write your origin story.

- When you've written out that story, highlight parts that include seeking power, whether it was for self-preservation or getting even. Underline parts where you did things out of spite. Circle parts that were based in fear. You need to be honest with yourself because it will come back to bite you in the ass later if you aren't.

- Pray. Talk to God, Jesus, your Angel, your Saint, etc., about why it is important for you to continue your journey. Are you feeling the pull to go deeper, or are you happy being in the Courtyard? Some people won't move away from this part, and that's okay. If it's not for you, then it isn't. This is not something where you can just "fake it until you make it." If you've never considered what you do or how you align with certain things, now is the time to really dig in and write it out—for yourself and for your future.

- Go back after a week and re-read what you wrote. How do you feel about it? What do you think has changed since you started growing deeper in your magic? What do you *wish* was different? Where do you feel called now?

- What is something in your practice that you decided to just do? Both feet in first, no study, just throw yourself in because it caught your attention? Did it do well? Did it backfire? Did you find out the practice was closed or co-opted, or did you find something relevant to you and your background?

- A lot of this section discussed "awakening," like our senses were lit up, and our world became HD. Have you had that experience? If so, write it down in as much detail as you can remember, and emphasize the date. Have you experienced that sensation since? How do you feel like things have changed?

- When you give a child a crayon for the first time, they're going to put it everywhere except the paper. Sometimes, the markings can be washed off, and sometimes, the marks leave stains. How did you approach this feeling when you started your practice, or started something new? Did you remain shy and reserved? Did you decide to only study and not act out of some fear? Write it out. See where you've grown and where you still struggle.

Chapter Two

The Foyer

The Mystic and the Witch

"BUT THAT WASN'T ALL of my vision," the Mystic says. She sips a cup of tea the Witch made for her, then munches on one of those fresh scones, and she stares at the cards, that Fool and Magician. They're ones she's seen fly out of the Witch's deck before, though this time, those two men on the cards seem to mock her with their carefree faces. She certainly doesn't feel so carefree, what with the images that haunt her. "The vision goes deeper than that."

After the Witch settles back down with her own steaming cup of tea, she plucks the cards off the table and shuffles them back into her deck. "Then tell me more."

The Mystic rubs her eyes, sighs, and does what she's told; she brings herself back to that all-too-vivid scene and tries to find the words to describe what the Holy One showed her.

—◦❖◦—

The Courtyard I'd stumbled upon was beautiful, and I'd spent quite some time in it as I'd mentally organized myself and adjusted to the new scenery: I admired the flowers, I watched the water pour out of the main fountain, I noticed each drop glimmering in the sun and a rainbow refracting through the mist it made. By this point, I'd investigated each and every corner of the Courtyard, to the point that I could chart my own tracks pressed into the fine gravel. The breeze was still sweet, though the birds were chirping a music I was, even after several hours, unfamiliar with.

Hell, I'd even stumbled upon a little free library on the grounds that had some old weathered books—and after flipping through them, sitting on a patch of soft grass that defiantly sprouted up from all that gravel, I discovered so many things that spoke to me in a way that nothing ever spoke to me before! So many secrets about the history of magic, of my faith, of power and the people that kill for it. So many stories of Saints and sinners alike, of magicians and mystics and what-have-you. The knowledge filled my mind as if it were a cup with no bottom, and I knew without having to say it: *this is what I've been looking for.* This knowledge, this *vindication* that the way I've been feeling about the grey life I walked away from wasn't a bad thing after all—it was like someone took a metal cage off my chest and let me breathe properly for the first time.

In that place, I thought I might've found my forever home, out here in Someone's Courtyard. After all, it was *there* that I could *do things:* the plants responded to me and shared their light and talents with me, helping me weave a new reality together. The wind seemed to speak to me as it ruffled my hair and whistled past my ears. The rocks hummed with an energy I was secretly almost afraid of, because even for all my intellectualizing and deconstructing and reconstructing, I still had that thought in the back of my mind: *is this really okay? is this the work of demons, or are the rocks really singing? can I do this? am I allowed to do this?*

Most of all, I was nervous to notice that there was a light *within* me as well: one that felt just as golden and sunny as the sunshine above. It made my palms feel warm and my skin light up with little crackles of electricity. It flowed through me as if my veins were full of honey, and it speared through my feet and anchored me to the ground. It was *me*—I knew it was me, and I also knew that it was what every magician and mystic, every wonder and miracle worker before me once held, too—and yet, still, I shook out my palms sometimes, rubbing them on my pants as if that would make this feeling go away and prove to me it was all in my head.

Because I didn't have power. I knew I didn't. I'd been told again and again and again: I didn't have power. I didn't need power. I... I didn't *deserve* power. Even though I'd already received my vindication, it didn't take long for these thoughts to come and steal my bliss away. Moreover, a power like this came with so many questions that turned the golden embers at my temples into the cold, scraping metal of my deepest fears: *what if I make a mistake and hurt myself? or hurt those around me? what if demons or evil spirits come after me, or I open a portal to something I can't defeat? what if I accidentally invite a trickster spirit or something pretending to be God or Jesus or Mary or—?*

What if this is a test, and the second I use this power, I'm doomed to hell?

I asked myself all these questions and then some. The warmth in my chest became a cold iron ball that sank into my stomach and threatened to anchor me to the spot. My ribs became a tight metal cage once again, and I sank to the ground, huddled against that little library with all its books. All the while, that beautiful golden sun above me seemed to spurn me, too; its shining rays scraped my face to the point that I could feel my skin tighten with the beginnings of sunburn.

This Courtyard was a fine place. But I knew that I can't stay there forever. Once again, I became painfully aware of the eyes of Someone stinging my back. Someone was watching, and perhaps Someone was telling me that it was time to get home. I thought to myself that clearly, if I couldn't handle some time out in the sunshine, in a beautiful space like this, then maybe I never should've left the grey walls I started with. Maybe those really *were* what was best for me, and I'd overstayed my welcome in Someone's home.

So I got up and dusted myself off. I put the books back in the little free library and arranged it as if it had never been touched. With a heavy heart, I squared my shoulders and took the first step towards that Gate, mentally apologizing to Someone as if they could hear my thoughts.

I never should've come here. This isn't where I belong.

However, I didn't even make it past the fountain before I heard a *click* from behind me. My back lit up with prickles; the weight of

Someone's stare was as heavy as if a thick tarp had been laid over my shoulders. It didn't feel uncomfortable, though. It felt solid, almost like a hug, or a hand clasping my shoulder and urging me to turn around. Every thought against it raced across my mind, giving me a thousand reasons why it was bad news to turn around when I knew I belonged elsewhere—and yet I couldn't shake Someone's stare, nor Their presence hovering around me.

So I turned, expecting to see Someone there, but I found No One. No One and Nothing. The Courtyard was virtually untouched. It took me a while, as a result, to see the one thing that changed: the main entrance to the mansion was open. It was open, and it looked like a black square cut out of an otherwise ornate and grand wall; there was nothing there but shadows, nor was there anyone to greet me or beckon me inside. Yet still, I could feel it: Someone calling me, just as They called me to the Gate.

My family would tell me that this is dangerous. My pastor would tell me that this is the Enemy. My congregation would step away from me, as if this experience were contagious, and that they, too, might be lured towards that darkness. But... had they *ever* experienced anything except grey? Had they ever felt this power flowing through them, warm at the cheeks and palms as if one had drunk a cup full of honey wine? Had they *ever* seen flowers so bright, or spoken to the rocks, or had the wind tell them something sweet in its own beautiful, whistling way?

No. And if they never experienced this, then they had no way of knowing if this was really the Enemy or not. Neither did I in this world, of course, but at least I was in the position to go and find out. So I turned around again, and I changed my course: I marched to that open door and, after a moment's hesitation, I crossed the threshold from sunlight to shadow, the way I might've plunged my foot into the water on the beach. Despite the prickling fear at my scalp, I stepped fully inside and felt the cool relief of that shadow on my burning cheeks; I blinked a few times and found my eyes adjusting enough to make out shapes. I half expected the door to shut behind me and lock me in, too—but it never did.

Instead, I found myself standing in a grand Foyer, a carpeted staircase leading up to two separate wings of the Manor. There was another open door to my right with a single light flickering from inside. A big lantern, maybe. The Foyer itself was pretty empty, though its walls were papered in rich red, with veins of gold cutting across them in swirling leaf-and-vine patterns. There were also swords along the wall, with handles encrusted in rubies and blades that seem to glow in certain places, as if they had embers burning from deep within their steel.

But most odd of all was that off to the left side of this Foyer, next to a heavy iron door that had been bolted shut, was what seemed to be a small marble altar, like those in old Catholic churches. There was no relief of any Saint or anything on it, but there was a single candle making the tiniest spot of orange light that glimmered off the swords closest to it and the walls' golden paint. There was also a black basin of water, as well as a glass case holding an ornate golden crozier, one that has a diamond in its hook and seems more like a wizard's staff than anything a bishop would hold. It gleamed even in the low candlelight as if alive—as if begging me to take it. And use it.

For what? I came closer to the altar and peered into the basin. My own face stared back at me, and I realized that the tight skin around my nose and cheeks was explained by the deep crimson hue of sunburn blooming across them. My brows were tightly knit together, creating deep shadows between them. *What should I use it for?*

The cool air cloaked me, but it offered no answer. Someone, however, was waiting for an answer all the same.

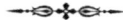

"What is it, this place?" The Mystic's tea is cool by the time she brings it back to her lips. *"What is it that Someone is trying to show me? I don't understand. This is certainly not a place I've been to, or a path I've walked before, in this Manor."*

The Witch's brow shoots up like a sail, and her accompanying half-smile makes the Mystic feel like there's a joke hanging in the air that she can't hear. It makes her search the deepest depths of her mind for what the Witch could possibly be smiling about, but she comes up empty, and she has no choice but to sit and wait with a pout for the next cards to come.

The rhythmic shuffle of the Witch's cards brings three to eventually slip from their resting place and into her hands; the first, a Chariot, being pulled by two fearsome, mythical beasts. The second are a pair, the Emperor and Empress, seemingly stuck together, though whether by force or by fate is uncertain. The Witch looks them over with a slow, quiet nod.

"Time spent in your Courtyard cultivated that childlike wonder; it lends itself, however, to very childlike habits," the Witch mutters. Before the Mystic can complain about her assessment, the Witch glances at her friend and taps her own temple. "Think back to the Magician; we react with emotion, feel deeply, do things without fully knowing the consequences. Now, here, this concept of Free Will is amplified."

Tying the story together takes a little more work, and in doing so, the Witch's gaze becomes soft, almost unfocused, as if she's trying to listen to the voice of the Chariot card itself. The warmth of her cabin and its rich smells and sounds help to ground her against the coldness that comes from understanding. Her fingers trace the outlines of each image on the card, coaxing the creatures forward from the ether.

"This here is a card of action, not reflection. You have spent too long thinking without doing, talking but not taking the steps needed. The choice is yours now, to move forward with maturity and understanding that how you are now is not the way you always should or will be." The Witch's nail taps the Chariot with sharp clicks. "Look again: the Beasts before the carriage could easily overtake the driver and do whatever they want. Yet, they are unchained and stoic before the gleaming carriage. You are being asked—no, demanded to show self-restraint and discipline, and to put away childish reactions that could cause harm to yourself and others."

The Mystic stares at the Chariot, with its Romanesque ruler by those two sphinx-looking creatures. There was quite the holy, wise man who walked this earth once, and in his quest for sharing the truth of his Savior, he said something that reminds the Mystic of all this:

> *When I was a child, I talked like a child, I thought like a child, I reasoned like a child. When I became a man, I put the ways of childhood behind me. For now we see only a reflection as in a mirror; then we shall see face to face. Now I know in part; then I shall know fully, even as I am fully known.*[1]

---

1. 1 Corinthians 13:10–11

It makes enough sense.

As the Witch's gaze begins to focus once more, the Mystic reaches a hand for her dear friend in reassurance. She then takes her teacup to her lips, encouraging her friend to do the same with a nod towards the Witch's tea cup. The tea may be cool now, but it's still zinging from the loose herbs collecting in the bottom of the cup.

The Witch blinks the light back into her eyes and dives into the rest of her thoughts as if she received the exact words she needed from somewhere out of the air. "The understanding and tempering of Free Will versus Discipline will be tested in the next part of your journey, in this Manor you speak of, and is therefore paramount in its mastery," *she says.* "No matter how many times you have come down this path, there will always be something that needs to be settled or released from the Ego, and the action taken to become more."

With a gush of an exhale, the Witch sits back, satisfied. The Chariot's message is properly set with words, which is good—but her creeping gaze settles next on the pair of cards that boldly claim their place on the table: the Emperor and Empress, with their stoic presence, rich robes, and beautiful crimson hues. The words seem to come directly from the air again, settling on the Witch's mind like morning dew, and she pitches into the next portion of what the Divine is communicating to her.

"Once that foundation has been set, you will be asked to lean into the energy of the Emperor and Empress," *the Witch says.* "These cards are two sides of the same coin; they are what the strength within looks like once the discipline has been achieved. They are the boundaries you must cultivate, for yourself and your environment, your community. How can you be called a leader when you do not have discipline over yourself? How can you be called to nurture and encourage creativity when you ignore your own calling?

"Here, my dear, you are birthed into a new way of self-stability and what we think is benevolent control, while still wielding the creative powers within. Spirit is still with you as you walk; however, in spite of ourselves, we've stuffed Divinity into a box as caregiver, as nurturer, as 'good energy' and only ever love and light, all while trying to minimize, to sanitize, that more lawful, strict, and resolute side of Divinity that metes out just punishment. We've done this in an attempt to control that energy while we seek control of ourselves. Hold onto this idea too tight, and we risk losing all we learned. This shifts us into the next part of your path, where we find out what happens when, not if, we try too hard to hold control."

*The Witch scoops the cards back to shuffle them with their kin once more;
she places the deck between her and the Mystic and returns her attention to
the forgotten tea. One glance at her friend, however, tells her that those cards
wouldn't be on the table for too long.*

"*My cards are humming, and your face reads like a novel,*" *the Witch
mutters. "Surely there are more chapters to your vision?*"

*With a sigh, the Mystic puts her tea down and rubs her temple as her head
begins to ache. "There is, yes. There very much is."*

And she is not excited to recount it.

The Choice (and Peril) of the Foyer

Go, go, go—so says the Chariot, the Magician. *Lead and be led*—so says
the Emperor, the Empress. And yet, it's paramount we ask where we're
going every now and then—as well as who is leading us, and what we're
shepherding within ourselves in turn.

Let's think together for a moment. When you see someone going to
the store to buy a new kitchen knife, what do you assume they're going
to buy it for? It's a common kitchen tool, one necessary to break down
big ingredients into smaller things that cook evenly and make delicious
meals for the family, so surely that's the safest bet to assume.

Right?

One could hope. However, we all know that no matter how utilitar-
ian a knife is, there's something about it that can make a person uneasy:
the danger of it, the sharpness of the steel, the cold way it glints. It
is a helpful thing—we use one nearly every day when we make our
meals—and yet there's that tenderness in our hand as we hold it *just so*,
so we don't hurt ourselves. Perhaps a butter knife would make us feel
better, or a plastic knife, even: something with all the shape of a knife,
and at least part of the function.

But a butter knife, a plastic knife, can't cut everything we need a knife
to cut.

Hold on. Let's return to the person we might see buying a knife
for a moment. Consider: the easily accessible, seemingly innocent (yet
somewhat off putting) tool in question is the kind that people could
buy from virtually anywhere without question. No one needs to show

their ID to buy this thing (in certain places), unlike when buying super glue or permanent markers. Yet the stainless steel knife intended for cutting chicken and fish could go from the shelf to an evidence bag very quickly. According to Statista, 1,562 homicides by knife or other cutting instrument were reported in the United States in 2023—which, if one removes handguns and unidentified firearms from the list, does make it *the* most common murder weapon.[2] We'd venture to guess it's for the reasons described: they're cheap, easy to access given just about every kitchen has one, and easily made lethal when used for purposes outside preparing food.

An important thing to note, however, is that a *person's* intended use of the knife doesn't change the moral baseline of the knife. Whether you're cutting up a strip of chicken filet to fry into a delicious meal for you and your family, or hacking apart your worst and most bitter enemy to fit in plastic bags and drop into a lake, the knife is just a knife. There is no intention living in it; there is no inherent good or evil in what is, realistically, just a sharp piece of metal on a stick. It is *you,* and only you, who determines what that knife is used for, and the consequences thereafter.

Witchcraft is no different. At the end of the day, it's nothing more than a tool—or, more specifically, a practice. Just like writers and film-makers across the world have used their craft to advance various agendas, everything from Christian nationalism and racist manifestos to pamphlets for peace and PSAs about social services, so too can witches use their craft to advance a variety of goals: money, fame, power, glamor, love, justice, protection, peace, you name it. Your ethical ceiling is your limit when it comes to what you can do and accomplish, and that's precisely what one must hammer out in this Foyer: your ethics, your morality, your discipline and mastery over your free will, or as we like to call it, your *social philosophy.*

You may be thinking to yourself that such a social philosophy would be easy to develop. After all, we're Christians, aren't we? We already have a moral code pre-established for us! We have a whole handbook

---

2. Statista Research Department, "Murder Victims by Weapon Used in the U.S. 2023," *Statista* (2024), https://www.statista.com/statistics/195325/murder-victims-in-the-us-by-weapon-used/.

called the Bible that tells us the best way to live, per God's own recommendation. This should be a pretty open and shut case, knowing what's right and wrong in this world, and how to act around others. And for the most part, it is!

Until one church condemns homosexuality as sin and perversion while another embraces members of the LGBTQ+ and celebrates the divine union of two people in love.

Until a priest asks for donations to contribute to their church's feeding ministry while a pastor demands donations towards his own home improvements as a way for their congregation to prove their devotion.

Until one man uses St. Paul's letters to justify stripping women of their voice, agency, and autonomy while others point to the women St. Paul recognized as financial supporters, deacons, and even fellow apostles.

It happens with more than just the Bible, too, of course. Even Meister Eckhart, whose writings seem so full of wonder for God's creation and see every creature, no matter how small, as reflecting their Creator, somehow caught the attention of the Nazis and, in their minds, *justified them,* according to Raymond B. Blakney in his translation of Eckhart's works.[3] How? How possibly could a regime built on social hegemony, white supremacy, and state sanctioned genocide ever look to a man writing poems about the divine beauty in caterpillars and think that their philosophies matched in any way? It's a good question, but the answer is so unfortunately simple: because Eckhart wrote more than just those sweet poems, and what he wrote was dense, difficult, intellectual—and entirely up to anyone's interpretation. It's why the Catholic Church tried to eventually stifle his works: because mysticism is all well and good, *as long as it doesn't fall into the wrong hands.*[4]

One could say this of religion entirely, not just mysticism, if we're being honest. In his book, *The Bible Says: What We Get Right (and Wrong) About Scripture's Most Controversial Issues,* Biblical scholar Dan McClellan goes over many a common issue that people debate over

---

3. Raymond B. Blakney, *Meister Eckhart: A Central Source and Inspiration of Dominant Currents in Philosophy and Theology since Aquinas* (New York: Harper & Row, 1941), xv.

4. Ibid., xv.

in the Bible and what the actual data we have about the Bible, its writers, and the sociopolitical context of its time have to say about it. He also does this extensively on his TikTok page and his *Data over Dogma* podcast, one named after his most iconic mottos for his work. He makes Biblical scholarship accessible to the masses in a time where the Bible has become less of a spiritual text and more of a brick to beat people into submission with, and as a result, McClellan's book goes over the main Biblical issues that most people get wrong (either on accident or on purpose to further their rhetorical goals) with the hard, cold, anthropological and archaeological facts. The conclusions he comes away with are what anyone might guess, neatly summed up in the introduction:[5]

> What this all means for the Bible is that we're never just extracting pure and unadulterated meaning. We're always constructing it ourselves. A common metaphor for interpreting the Bible is the notion that the Bible is like a jigsaw puzzle and, to best understand how the pieces fit together, we have to look at the picture on the box. The idea is that the whole Bible and its broader message should guide how we understand the individual pieces.

In essence: everyone has their own *interpretation* of the text based on the words they read. In McClellan's words in his frequent talks on this subject, people *renegotiate* with the text, either reading meaning into it that may have never been there (such as the idea of homosexuality as an actual identity and sexual orientation when that never existed in the time of the Bible's creation),[6] or denying the uncomfortable, prickly parts of the Bible that no one wants to admit happened and would never dare repeat in modern day, like the institutions of slavery or the belief that women were a man's property as wife or daughter. The same

---

5. Dan McClellan, *The Bible Says So: What We Get Right (and Wrong) About Scripture's Most Controversial Issues* (New York: St. Martin's Essentials, 2025), 8.

6. Ibid., 172-173.

exact book has been used to justify and defend about every position one can think of, and so when it comes to defining our *social philosophy*, not just our morality, we have to consider what our relationship is with the world around us and all the people in in it to get a better idea of how we operate in the world. According to the University of Sheffield's School of History, Philosophy, and Digital Humanities, *social philosophy* is something that "scrutinises our social world, and looks at the identities, relations, and power structures within it."[7] It analyzes many different aspects of what we call *society*, and all the things that make it up, like the power dynamics between divisions of people across identity lines (race, sex, sexuality, etc.). In their words:

> [Social philosophy] also encompasses how all of these aspects interact with social structures, both informal ones, such as friendship groups or family structures, and formal ones such as the workplace, or institutions such as marriage. Much social philosophy is done with an eye on how we might change things in order to make our social world better (theorists engaged in anti-racist and feminist philosophy often have this goal in mind).[8]

To that end, we must first define the Christian way and walk—*after* emptying ourselves of what we have been told it is. The Witch told us about action vs. talking, about free will vs. discipline. Unfortunately, wounds like the ones religious trauma creates make it difficult to act from a level-headed place; like threatened or injured animals, it's all too easy for us to seek whatever it is that distracts us from this pain, or vindicates us and gives us reason to pull out our spiritual claws and teeth for perhaps the first time. However, when you come into this Foyer and your eyes adjust to the dark, and you realize the true task before you—one that has nothing to do with crystals and candles and whatever else and everything to do with why you're reaching for them in the

---

7. "Social Philosophy." The University of Sheffield, July 18, 2024. https://www.sheffield.ac .uk/hpdh/research/philosophy/themes/social-philosophy.

8. Ibid.

first place—all that's left is a question that we now pose to you. And we want you to ask yourself honestly: *what drew you to witchcraft?* What does witchcraft give you that you can't find elsewhere? What is it that you really want, holding both this book and this title of Christian Witch?

They're hard questions to ask. The Ego doesn't want us to know this, but we'll say it: it's okay not to know everything. It's okay to look to our God when we're confused and lost, and it's okay to maybe start on a path for less-than-noble reasons and find our truth somewhere along the way. It's okay to admit that while we have free will, yes, we still need Someone to teach us how the hell to use it effectively, with proper boundaries and good spiritual discipline–that God isn't telling us things just to boss us around for fun.

Sometimes—rather, pretty much *all the time*—God snags our attention and asks us these hard questions, makes us look at ourselves and our actions in the big black scrying mirror, because He knows what we need far before we do.

The Adversary Cross-Examines: What Type of Witch Will You Be?

There was a sermon Sara heard that still sticks with her, months later, that we'll share with you now: one about Jesus in the desert. In this sermon, the priest told the congregation about how Jesus was tempted in the desert not by things normal people would be tempted by. Normal people, after all, couldn't very well be tempted to turn a stone into bread or call the angels to save them from dying after they pitched themselves off a cliff, as normal people don't know how to do these things. But Jesus, out there in that desert, hungry, thirsty, and alone, had Satan hounding Him seven ways to Sunday to do these things and ease His suffering.

We know from the Scriptures that Jesus *could* do these things. We remember how He fed thousands of people with but one basket of bread and fish (multiple times!) and how He raised the dead others mourned over, how He cast out spirits of illness that bent old women's backs for eighteen years and healed them of their chronic hemorrhaging with but one touch of His cloak. We know that Jesus displayed incredible acts of power for others, and yet never for Himself—and that was precisely what these tests of Satan were for. They were tests that posed a question: What kind of Messiah Jesus would be? One who uses His power for His own glorification and comfort, or one who uses His power to uplift, heal, and save everyone else, to empower them to be like Him and likewise pay that power forward?

His answer became clear after His tests, and He put it to words for us, too: *For even the Son of Man did not come to be served, but to serve, and to give his life as a ransom for many...*[9] Knowing this, we also have to ask ourselves what kind of Witch we're to be, and *why* we're choosing witchcraft over any other spiritual system to begin with.

To understand why we're taking this plunge into a system that many of us have been told is a highway to hell, we have to not only analyze what we believe, but why we believe them—which means we also have to dig into the very wiring of our brain to figure out what aspects of our past are informing our present. That begins not with doing any prayers or spells, but with taking a hard look at our psyche. In a book written by a formerly Evangelical psychologist, we might find some hints of what ideas have been able to take root in our hearts and how to properly *up*root them. Beginning with *When Religion Hurts You: Healing from Religious Trauma and the Impact of High Control Religion* by Dr. Laura E. Anderson, the foundation of our deepest fears, our most strongly held beliefs, and even the way in which we come to believe things become clear.

If you have any sort of religious trauma, let us first say, genuinely: we are sorry you had to experience such a thing in a place that was supposed to help you grow, thrive, and connect with both the Divine and your fellow humans. What happened to you should not have happened, and it was not your fault, and you did nothing to deserve it. Here, as we step away from Awakening and take the first true steps towards the next phase of mysticism, Purgation, we might begin to clean out these old wounds; we might ask ourselves honestly what it is we're seeking the Mystic's new and strange world full of color for, and what it is that drew us away from this painful world of grey.

---

9. Mark 10:45

Still, there have been so many reasons people pick up the craft, especially when coming from those high control religions, or HCRs, that Dr. Anderson talks about. This pain and anger from years of spiritual abuse and disenfranchisement, as well as such blatantly conditional love from the God we're told apparently loves us *unconditionally,* make it easy to begin grabbing for anything that makes us have our own sense of power and control over our lives. By doing this, however, people more often than not also begin swinging the complete opposite way when it comes to one's morality and ethics. They abandon any notions of communal power or communal ritual, usually out of necessity since witchcraft as a practice has no central organizing structure or socially acceptable public spaces like Christianity does, and this can and often does have the unintended consequence of forcing these people to spend a lot of time alone—thus allowing them to focus on *personal* power that serves them and their sense of individualism first over any sense of social responsibility or public faith. Their newfound spiritual journey therefore takes them away from the toxic Christianity they grew up with, but not necessarily towards anything better, and trying to rely on their own sense of direction as they rebuild their social philosophy just gets them all kinds of mixed up.

It's unfortunate, because while there is something beautiful in every faith, creed, and tradition that can absolutely help people become more centered, stable, and well rounded, the fact is that growing up in such HRCs does two things: breeds an intense fear of the unknown in people, *and* takes away their ability to think critically.[10] In Anderson's words:

> Fundamentalism is a pattern of thinking and relating; it is the belief that a certain person or group of people know the right way to think, act, talk, relate, believe, and engage with the world and that those who do not subscribe to this worldview are lesser than, dangerous, pitied, hard to relate to, or to be avoided. We often see this

---

10. Laura E. Anderson, *When Religion Hurts You: Healing from Religious Trauma and the Impact of High-Control Religion* (Grand Rapids: Brazos Press, 2023), chap. 3, sec. "Why Didn't You Just Leave?"

in various wellness communities, multilevel marketing companies, cults, social media, and lifestyle groups…

An appeal of fundamentalism is the illusion of certainty that it offers; fundamentalism prescribes what is right, good, and true and encourages people to discard critical thinking and curiosity. This means that when new or unfamiliar situations arise, fundamentalist teachings and thinking feel like soft landing pads as they offer concrete answers and steps for how to do things the right way.[11]

What this means is that people who recognize the surface level harm mainstream Christianity causes and get the courage to leave still get stuck in the same behavioral patterns and subconscious habits even after leaving. They don't realize that they have to go deeper than simply abandoning a faith paradigm, all the way down to the very psychological framework created by those beliefs that has been thoroughly grooved into their minds. The fundamentalism of many HCRs, which defines the world in black and white and leaves no room for grey areas or for two things to be true at once, radically stunts a person's ability to approach new information with curiosity and to digest it slowly. It makes it so that people must shove new information in a category of Good or Bad in their minds, and it also becomes so well ingrained that people don't realize just how much their former belief system might impact future beliefs, *even after they believe they've left old views behind.* For example, Anderson talks about purity culture and how, even after leaving something like Evangelical Christianity, people still feel great shame around their bodies, but we see this so frequently in witchcraft, too: the way in which one's Christian values ingrained in them since childhood still arrest their ability to look at witchcraft and magic from a neutral perspective.

---

11. Ibid., chap. 5, sec. "Embodied Fundamentalism."

In our own witchy example, let's think about people's reaction to hexing others. Many witches, Christian or not, insist that only "good magic" is okay: magic that "harms none" (a very Wiccan ideal that, while helpful for many, doesn't translate to all practices of traditional witchcraft). Some will even go as far as to say that someone who does such "evil" practices isn't a "real witch," as if the centuries-old understanding of witchcraft as a specifically malefic practice never existed (and boy, will some actually try to tell you that this is the case: that witches were always just misunderstood, benevolent healers!) If one is coming to witchcraft after leaving an HCR, doing only "good magic" is typically the first step of getting into it, as it helps one justify what they do in a value system very deeply ingrained in them from their religious upbringing. There is a lot of language in witchcraft that warns people away from hexing (like another New Age concept, the Threefold Law, or more vague ideas that someone's "karma" will come back to them) that ironically aligns with a familiar Christian saying that comes from Galatians 6:7-9: *you shall reap what you sow.* It very well could be that this Christian concept, and any lingering fears of consequences, are informing this mindset. After all, even if one says they don't believe in Satan or hell anymore, the reality is that if the subconscious feeling of impending doom or punishment for "bad" actions are still burrowed deep in one's psyche, then the conscious mind will therefore go through all kinds of hoops to rationalize that feeling, which causes the same behavior or convictions regardless of whether one believes their actions will send them to hell or simply come back to haunt them.

On the other hand, you have the way that the people come into witchcraft thinking it's exactly everything Christians fearmongered about: something dark, negative, and lucrative in the way they believe they can use it to get anything they want at any time, as if they've discovered a cheat code for the world. Moreover, they bolster their sense of self as a *powerful, dangerous* person by proudly flaunting the baneful work they do against other practitioners, or constantly find themselves in some "witch war" online. All the reckless hexing for petty reasons, slinging threats and aggression, and gloating about their newfound power, shows an extremely contrarian view of witchcraft that isn't any better than what the Christianity they grew up with told them about it; it's still a one-note view of witchcraft that tells a lot about a person's psyche and understanding of the craft *and themselves*. That latter part, especially, is important: if they truly think witchcraft is bad, and they act in the "bad" way they think they should, that is something that eventually gets internalized into thinking *they* are bad–even if they never say it or want to acknowledge that's how they see themselves.

When we discuss communal vs. personal spirituality in Christianity vs. witchcraft, therefore, it's actually entirely understandable how people end up going with a very individualistic, self-centered practice where one doesn't care about how their workings affect others and where they can do whatever they want and get whatever they want if they're "powerful" enough. One can theorize that this is because they are actually becoming their own spiritual leaders, and in toxic Christian settings, their only role model for spiritual leadership was typically their pastor or youth pastor, which is a problem. More often than not, *those* spiritual leaders were the ones pushing exactly that mindset of "my way or the highway" where, as Anderson details of her own experience, these folks think everyone should walk on eggshells around them and do only what they want while calling it some directive from God. It's all too easy to feel as if, by virtue of one being in charge of their spiritual practice, they now have the *right* to do all those things their spiritual leaders did, even though they really didn't like being on the receiving end of that kind of behavior.

Now, people who eventually pause between these two ideas of Good and Bad witchcraft might ask: *can* Christians do any baneful work, like hexes or curses? And the answer, technically, is yes! Despite how upset some folks may be to hear this (and boy, were some folks *upset* when we first brought this up in *Discovering Christian Witchcraft*), the reality is that there is endless precedent both within the Bible and in apocrypha, as well as in the lives of Saints and Christian laymen alike, that suggest that God has been an active agent in things like curses. Psalm 109 remains the most infamous imprecatory Psalm, and according to Martin Duffy in his book, *Anathema Maranatha: Christianity and the Imprecatory Arts,* when a Saint cursed the absolute hell out of someone to the point of barren fields, flooding rivers, and *death,* people assumed that because a

Saint was the one to initiate such a calamity, that it *had* to have been co-signed by God Himself.[12]

However, that doesn't mean it's open season to do whatever you'd like, nor can you assume every action you make is co-signed by God just because you're His child. While it might seem nice, the idea of being a beacon of God's power here on earth and helping to manifest His miracles on earth, the fact is that not everything that *looks* or *sounds* good *is* good, after all. Not everything that *can* be done *should* be done, nor should we take for granted the ethics that God demands we hold as the bedrock of how we use the power He gives us. It's interesting that St. Paul says it in this way, though, especially after introducing the idea a little differently in 1 Corinthians 10:23:

> "All things are lawful," but not all things are helpful.
> "All things are lawful," but not all things build up.

Whether or not it is *spiritually beneficial* to do these things, and whether or not it helps you grow as a person, is another story entirely. Sometimes, something we are fully within our rights to do will only aggravate a situation further or make all attempts at reconciliation impossible (if that was a goal of yours at some point), because burned bridges are much harder to rebuild than ones that only have a few rotting pieces to replace. And sometimes, we actually have no right to act in the way we want at all: even if we think it's only fair to take an eye for an eye, the Divine reminds us that our idea of serving justice is not necessarily the best way to navigate our problems.

Still, this is difficult to understand to a mind that has been deeply grooved and shaped by fundamentalism. The concept of this grey area, of the Twilight that connects the Light and the Dark, is scary, unsafe. The fact that sometimes, such things in magic are not inherently good or bad, but are taken on a *case by case basis,* is intolerable to a psyche that wants to have safely delineated boundaries around what is acceptable and unacceptable.

---

12. Martin Duffy, *Anathema Maranatha: Christianity and the Imprecatory Arts,* 37.

In the end, whereas people might come to witchcraft because they think it's a middle finger to the HCR they grew up with, or because they want to feel more in control of their life or get nice things for themselves they think religion can't help them get, the reality is that magic isn't really about any of that—not if we're peering behind the curtain to see how occult scientists and magicians have thought about it, anyway. People who come to witchcraft for the aesthetics, or the easy tool to get things or destroy their enemies or any other such reason—people who come with such weak or even fear-based ethics and selfish, shallow reasons for wanting power—quickly realize that if they're serious about this stuff, they won't stay on that line of thinking forever. They'll realize how much work it takes to walk this path.

Because that's what mysticism, and what Christian Witchcraft, *any* witchcraft, is: it's work. Not glamor and glory and fun. Not power to bludgeon people with or feel better than people with. It's *work*. Often ugly, grueling, painful work, work that'll feel like–yes, really–the persecution of demons nipping at your heels. Even St. Antony had to sit among them and experience their torments and temptations, and he did that all alone out there in the desert, constantly being assailed by the lies of demons—*literal* demons, not just trials of the mind. Demons that would threaten him, beat him, transform into beautiful women to tempt him, even demons that manifested as a silver plate just laying on the ground in the middle of the desert to try and incite just a shred of greed into him.[13]

It was St. Athanasius of Alexandria, alive in the 4th century CE and known in his life as the "Father of Orthodoxy,"[14] who wrote an extensive biography of the life of St. Antony, and in this biography, we get many of the desert father's trials laid out to us. In this situation, it wasn't just a case of bad dreams or lonely desert evenings that got to St. Antony, but apparently entire physical beatings that he endured; he was physically beaten so badly by demons that one of his compatriots, who was to bring him bread out there in the desert tombs, carried him

13. St. Athanasius of Alexandria, "Life of St. Antony," New Advent, chap. 11, accessed October 30, 2025, https://www.newadvent.org/fathers/2811.htm

14. Cornelius Clifford, "St. Athanasius," *The Catholic Encyclopedia*, vol. 2 (New York: Robert Appleton Company, 1907), <http://www.newadvent.org/cathen/02035a.htm>.

back to the village where people mourned him because they thought he was dead. And yet he *still* went back, *still* held the determination to sharpen himself spiritually in that desert surrounded by evil spirits, and continued to suffer their assaults.[15] St. Athanasius writes:

> And after he had prayed, he said with a shout, Here am I, Antony; I flee not from your stripes, for even if you inflict more nothing shall separate me (Romans 8:35) from the love of Christ. And then he sang, 'though a camp be set against me, my heart shall not be afraid.' These were the thoughts and words of this ascetic. But the enemy, who hates good, marvelling that after the blows he dared to return, called together his hounds and burst forth, 'You see,' said he, 'that neither by the spirit of lust nor by blows did we stay the man, but that he braves us, let us attack him in another fashion.' But changes of form for evil are easy for the devil, so in the night they made such a din that the whole of that place seemed to be shaken by an earthquake, and the demons as if breaking the four walls of the dwelling seemed to enter through them, coming in the likeness of beasts and creeping things. And the place was on a sudden filled with the forms of lions, bears, leopards, bulls, serpents, asps, scorpions, and wolves, and each of them was moving according to his nature. The lion was roaring, wishing to attack, the bull seeming to toss with its horns, the serpent writhing but unable to approach, and the wolf as it rushed on was restrained; altogether the noises of the apparitions, with their angry ragings, were dreadful. But Antony, stricken and goaded by them, felt bodily pains severer still. He lay watching, however, with unshaken soul, groaning from bodily anguish; but his mind was clear, and as in mockery he said, 'If there had been any power in you, it would have sufficed had one of you come, but since the Lord has

---

15. St. Athanasius, "Life of St. Anthony," chap. 8.

made you weak, you attempt to terrify me by numbers: and a proof of your weakness is that you take the shapes of brute beasts.' And again with boldness he said, 'If you are able, and have received power against me, delay not to attack; but if you are unable, why trouble me in vain? For faith in our Lord is a seal and a wall of safety to us.' So after many attempts they gnashed their teeth upon him, because they were mocking themselves rather than him.

Nor was the Lord then forgetful of Antony's wrestling, but was at hand to help him. So looking up he saw the roof as it were opened, and a ray of light descending to him. The demons suddenly vanished, the pain of his body straightway ceased, and the building was again whole. But Antony feeling the help, and getting his breath again, and being freed from pain, besought the vision which had appeared to him, saying, 'Where were thou? Why did you not appear at the beginning to make my pains to cease?' And a voice came to him, 'Antony, I was here, but I waited to see your fight; wherefore since you have endured, and hast not been worsted, I will ever be a succour to you, and will make your name known everywhere.' Having heard this, Antony arose and prayed, and received such strength that he perceived that he had more power in his body than formerly. And he was then about thirty-five years old.[16]

Unlike the Book of Job, where dear Job gets put through the wringer without his consent and just has to deal with it, St. Antony *elected* to do this. Went back again and again to tough it out and devote himself to the task at hand: becoming closer to God, more rich in his spirit as he grew poorer in his body. And even his body was preserved in the end! Despite

---

16. Ibid., chap. 9–10.

never eating anything but bread and salt and a little water, his body stayed strong, his mind clear, his disposition optimistic and cheerful–a serious miracle.[17] But not a miracle that went unearned, not in the least. As with any monk or other ascetic from any other religion, St. Antony seemed to have transcended the need of material life by sheer devotion, his spirit tempered like a sword in the forge and his body following suit to properly house that spirit.

But again–it was work. Terrible, grueling work that was unglamorous, hard, painful, and bare of any and all material comforts. We certainly aren't going to tell you to pack your bags, take a flight to Arizona, and try and tough it out in the sandstone hills with just a bottle of water, a loaf of bread, and some table salt, as the reality for many such monks was a serious case of mental illness (loneliness, depression, even violent insanity, etc.) that Catherine Nixey charts in *The Darkening Age: The Christian Destruction of the Classical World;* in their attempts to destroy the "tyranny of joy" and model after St. Antony, they did some truly horrendous acts of self-harm and harm even to others.[18] In a way, though, one might think of the path of mysticism to be something similar: a path that not all are called to, that not all can or *should* go on, and yet one that, if you are called, you cannot avoid.

The demons that come for you, the creatures sent by the Adversary to try and trip you up to accuse you later, they can't be avoided. There is some truth in the idea that the closer you try to get to God, the harder these spirits work to undermine your efforts, and the more lax you are, the more easily you stray the path, the less they bother you. It's true, yes, and we see mention of them everywhere, across various mystics' writings. In this modern world, however, they won't come looking like beautiful women while you sit in some tomb in a desert, unwashed and unfed and un-socialized; they'll look like whatever will spur you to anger, to fear, to frustration that has you lashing out like a whip, to whatever will pierce your heart and run you through and make you question if God actually loves you or not. And just like St. Antony, God

---

17. Ibid., chap. 93.

18. Catherine Nixey, *The Darkening Age: The Christian Destruction of the Classical World* (New York: First Mariner Books, 2017), 213–222.

may sit back for a moment and watch, to see if you can properly find out where to rest the blame (the evils of the world) and how to draw down His strength to help you overcome these things.

Sounds bad, doesn't it? Sounds like something that a loving, comforting God would never do. But don't worry; here, in the Foyer, you're not there just yet. As we said: unlike Job, St. Antony *sought* that experience. He felt he needed it because the material world he lived in was no longer good enough for developing his spirit; he had to find himself entirely cut off from it in order to achieve his transcendent state of being. Here in the Foyer, trust, is *not* where you experience the worst of the worst yet, even if you begin to see traces of the foul creatures of the world, the way you see the traces of mice in a kitchen or the damage of termites in a house without seeing the beasts themselves.

For the Mystic and the Witch alike, even if you start just playing with little potions in your kitchen or throwing sparkle dust into your backyard fire pit and whatever other fanciful, cute little things you see people doing online—even if you start with your cute little Bible all color coded just right and wrapped in some cute pink Bible cover, with all your sweet little cross necklaces and pretty little medals and bells and trinkets—you're going to find yourself eventually uninspired by any of those things. You may very well find yourself like St. Antony: knowing that this world, with all its *things* and *items*—its *distractions*—cannot bring you any closer than where you are. This is where you get closer and closer to the Dark Night of the Senses, as it's so called by Mabry. He makes this point:

> This mysticism thing is not safe; it is not something you can do in a controlled fashion. It's kind of an all-or-nothing thing. So maybe you're not ready yet. That's okay. But maybe you are... You may be ready for a lot of change, you may be ready for a little, but the question is, are you ready?[19]

19. Mabry, *Growing into God,* 39.

Many times, that answer is actually *no*. The fact is that here is where, ironically, we find *another* stumbling block that produces both people who walk away from Christianity (the folks who just cannot, refuse to, square why God would allow this) and walk away from witchcraft (because clearly all this suffering was caused by the fact that witchcraft is exactly as evil as everyone always said it was, and the egregore Christ would *never* do this to us). You can tell exactly who hit their limit when all the crystals go in the trash and out comes another of those age-old "ex-witch to Christian" testimonies we see floating around online. The glamor and illusion around what witchcraft is, as so often peddled by the aesthetics and heavy commercialization of the craft we've talked about already, quickly falls apart when people realize that the forces they're encountering are *real* and not often comfortable.

While one might say that the Wiccan Rede applies to Wiccans only, or that "karma" as western mystical folk throw the term around is a serious misapplication of the dharmic concept (both of which are true), the fact of the matter remains that what you put out in the world is something people perceive and respond to, whether you like it or not. As the way Newton's Third Law of Motion phrases it: *for every action, there is an equal and opposite reaction.* In a metaphysical setting, we might understand this to mean that there is resistance, pushback, especially when dealing with people (*every single one of which* has the same ability to develop and project magic as we do).

So the person who slings negativity (in words or spells or what-have-you) with no regard for consequences or constantly bares their teeth at anyone who comes by, be they friend or perceived foe, or the person who tries to contain the neutrality of magic by only follow-ing "love and light" principles (and then still trying to force the world to give them more money, more beauty, more lovers, more glamor, more ease, more comfort, *more, more, more*), eventually, they might run into some issues. Their reasons for becoming a witch and their motivations behind harnessing their power are received, *per*-ceived, and eventually reflected back at them by the forces that be (whether human or Divine) as a question:

Is this all you're here for? Is this all witchcraft is to you: a means to satisfy your own selfish desires, with no thought to the purpose of your being given spiritual gifts in the first place?

Thus begins a great test of the Witch that, when you practice long enough, you cannot escape: the test of Purgation. The test of growth, of deep self reflection and introspection. The taunt and call to go deeper, find deeper, *be* deeper, than the binary thinking and the surface level trinkets and gains that people think witchcraft is for. Many people, when faced with this test, perceive it as a threat: they feel the pressure of the reaction to their magic, understand it as negative or as some kind of punishment since it is inherently uncomfortable (as growth is), and they tuck tail and run back to mainstream western Christianity, which was much more comfortable for them precisely *because* it was far less demanding spiritually, as all the responsibility to make life good is out of their hands and into the Divine's. This is another trap of the Adversary, a test all too often failed, and an indictment of one's reason for why they're a part of *any* religion or practice in the first place.

So, are you scared? And if so, are you ready to face that fear head on? Do you know why you're a Witch? Why you're a Christian? And most importantly, just like Jesus had to decide what type of Messiah He was to be, do you know what type of Witch *you* want to be? Because if you haven't thought about it, don't worry; God's Prosecutor will serve you that question one way or another, and if you're serious about coming into Union with God instead of wading in the pools of your own comfort, you will have to answer it.

Remember, whispers the Adversary, *you can turn back. Go back to your pen. Play with your sweet little toys and pretend that's all there is. Forget any of this ever happened.*

Go on and go home. Walk back out that Foyer door. Out into that Courtyard again. Out that Gate, and back into the world of ashen grey.

(What an easy win.)

Sara Says:

Listen, I've seen a lot of shit. Enough to know I don't want to see anything more, but not enough to think I've seen it all. However, when it comes to this second part of the Manor, and we talk about all those "demons" you might encounter out here as you embark on your spiritual desert journey, I can't help but think I've already seen mention of these creatures before. In fact, I remember them quite clearly when I think back to what I read in St. Teresa of Avila's *Interior Castle:*

> In this part of the castle are found souls which have begun to practise prayer; they realize the importance of their not remaining in the first mansions, yet often lack determination to quit their present condition by avoiding occasions of sin, which is a very perilous state to be in... These souls hear our Lord calling them, for as they approach nearer to where His Majesty dwells He proves a loving Neighbour, though they may still be engaged in the amusements and business, the pleasures and vanities of this world. While in this state we continually fall into sin and rise again, for *the creatures amongst whom we dwell are so venomous, so vicious, and so dangerous,* that it is almost impossible to avoid being tripped up by them. (Emphasis mine.)[20]

Venomous creatures, she says. These are ones that notice that you've picked up on something greater than what material items you try to satisfy yourself with and try to drag you back into the mundane with all kinds of distractions and temptations. That's spiritual continuity right there: the affirmation of mystics across centuries, spanning over a thousand years, who will tell you that the closer you get to God, the harder the world tries to drag you back down to being the spiritually blindfolded, earplugged, and easily led animal it wants you to be.

Makes me think of pigs. How we get them cute and fat, make them nice and happy with all those tasty scraps, just to kill them for good bacon. I've seen a video where a little piggy is getting his back brushed, all nice and cozy, and never sees (or even suspects) the guy just out of sight with a massive axe to cleave his little piggy head from his little piggy shoulders.

(I don't know about you, but I don't wanna become good bacon. I like my head firmly attached to my shoulders, thank you very much.)

---

20. St. Teresa, *Interior Castle*, 26.

Now, if we go back to St. Teresa, listen: when reading the words of a Saint from the 1500s, it's easy to feel disconnected from what she's saying because she's talking about things exactly in that stuffy, churchy way that's become so unpalatable in the modern era. Who the hell is "practicing" prayer, right? What does that even mean? But just as witchcraft is a craft, so too is the art of prayer—and *prayer* goes beyond just rattling off some good turns of phrase in the typical *Hail Mary* or *Glory Be* or what-have-you. More on that later, though; I'm not referencing St. Teresa to talk specifically about prayer just yet.

Rather, I'm referencing this part because of that bit about those *creatures:* those terrible and venomous things lurking around and waiting to drag you out the Gate and back into the hell of our waking world. We can think of this part about "beginning to practice prayer" in a broader context of "beginning to engage with mysticism," in that the person entering this Foyer is one who is finally realizing that there's more to spirituality than just going to church once a week and singing along to gospel music, or doing little Bible camps and retreats (or, for my more Catholic neck of the woods: saying you're Christian and then just kind of fucking off on the whole thing entirely until a funeral or a wedding comes around). People entering this Foyer realize that there is *actually something out there.* They've caught their first glimpse of it in that Courtyard, felt like there's something calling to them, and then they get here… and don't realize that the games have only just begun.

Think of all the incredible things one can learn in the Courtyard: all the spell formats, all the ritual instructions and divination tools, all the many different ways you can use cinnamon in a spell (I mean, damn, it's amazing in a money spell, a love spell, a psychic enhancement spell, and more; it's a wonder spice, I tell you). All these things we can do are glorious! Overwhelming, even! And so very *fun!* So exciting! It's like when you finally start a workout routine and achieve your first push up. The newfound capabilities of your body are so exciting that you can't help but show off a little bit to anyone who'll watch. However, the stronger and more experienced you get, the more pressing the question becomes: *what are you going to do with that strength?*

Like we'd hope someone buying a knife just needs a sharper tool to cut chicken with, the answer we'd hope people would choose about strength is *to defend oneself and others.* However, we know that this isn't the option everyone chooses. Some people choose to get strong for terrible reasons: *to prove oneself better than others, to destroy one's enemies, to intimidate others into submission,* and so on. That's what these creatures are in this Foyer: they're the temptations of the world, and the allure of false power and the intoxicating feeling of superiority that comes from thinking they've got a leg up over others in some way.

Getting to this point, and getting a taste of the contact with the Divine that opens up possibilities you'd never imagine otherwise, puts you face to face with this first test of whether or not you're even capable of handling those possibilities. It tasks you with developing a sense of *responsibility* and a strong *social philosophy* alongside that power, and that's precisely why we started this chapter with such a discussion of power and control, as well as what we *can* do versus what we *should* do. After all, the Witch showed you two types of leadership enmeshed as one: the gentle Empress, whose office it is to nurture and encourage life, to create new things and guide people gently along their way as one might a young child, and her bold husband, the Emperor, who knows that sometimes, laws must be drafted fresh: boundaries must be drawn with a strong hand and proper, non-negotiable sentences given to children who grow up cruel and twisted, if all are to be protected and given dignity.

Now, I can ask you about your social philosophy until you throw this book in the trash, because you either already have your social philosophy penned out or don't have the answers fully formed in your mind yet. Either way, that's fine. Instead, I'll tell you a bit about how I determined *my* social philosophy—and why I call it that instead of morality to begin with. You see, one of the things that irks me the most when I see religious folks talk about non-religious folks is the idea that *morality* comes from religion, and that anyone without religion has no morals. This is patently untrue; anyone who can decide something is *right* or *wrong* has a sense of morality, and it doesn't depend on any one religion. However, morality is also something that, to me, is deeply *individual,* in that it doesn't concern more than the individual person and their ego: what they deem *immoral* they will not do, even if it doesn't hurt others or themselves to do it.

For example: I would consider it against my personal morals to sleep with someone I'm not romantically involved in or committed to. This doesn't mean I think anyone that does choose to do so is a bad person, or that it's inherently harmful to do it to any of the parties involved. It just means it's something I can't square with my personal ethics and boundaries for my body or with what intimacy like that means to me in the first place. So while I don't really care what someone else does and don't judge them for doing whatever they'd like, I likewise would hope for the same courtesy in kind as I do what I like—which is to save that kind of intimacy for a committed partner like my fiancé. It's personal! Doesn't affect others!

It *can* be informed by religion, which mine is, as I do think there's *some* merit to the whole idea of two people becoming "one flesh" in marriage (Matthew 19:5, Mark 10:8), but it also doesn't have to be. Someone who isn't religious might just think no one deserves access to their body unless they're in it for the long haul, which achieves the same end result. Still, it's generally assumed that people under the same religious community (not necessarily the religion itself) will share at least similar morals: things like guidelines around intimacy, modesty, and charity, for example, may all look generally similar in their respective religious communities.

But *social philosophy* is different, and that's something that can radically change among people even of the same religion, even despite a community's best efforts to get everyone on the same page. It's a way to see how we can improve the world around us with what we know of how people organize and define themselves. However, a field of study doesn't just exist for the sake of itself; it exists so that we might make use of it, and that's why you'll see people who subscribe to certain styles of philosophical thinking identify themselves in such a way. You have post-modernists, absurdists, stoics, nihilists, and so on, even though these schools of thought are *schools*: hypothetical systems in which people argue. You can therefore develop, through your own study, a sense of your own personal *social philosophy* that dictates how you deal with the world and the people in it: how you're willing to treat them, how you're willing to be treated, etc.

This is often what people think of when they think of morality in that sense, and of course, this, too, can be guided by religion. After all, Jesus gave us His one commandment:

> As the Father has loved me, so have I loved you. Now
> remain in my love. If you keep my commands, you
> will remain in my love, just as I have kept my Father's
> commands and remain in his love. I have told you this
> so that my joy may be in you and that your joy may
> be complete. My command is this: Love each other as
> I have loved you. Greater love has no one than this:
> to lay down one's life for one's friends. You are my
> friends if you do what I command.[21]

To know how Jesus loved His disciples, one only needs to read the Gospels and see how, time and time again, Jesus coached them, loved them, corrected them when they said or did something wild, healed them and gave them the means to heal, and finally, gave His life for them. Jesus's life is defined by acts of service and the dispensing of wisdom, culminating in one true Law: *Love God, Love One Another* (identified by Jesus as the greatest of all commandments and that which all of God's laws boils down to, as we see in Matthew 22:37-40). This gives the average person at least some kind of scaffolding for developing their social philosophy; having religion thus gives the average person of faith a template for building it. But again, as I'm sure you've noticed, not all people in a religion have the same kind of social philosophy.

You'll have a Christian advising us to love one another, and another Christian piping up, asking, "How do you define love?" (Hint: it's already defined for us in 1 Corinthians 13:4-8.) Or, worse, another Christian will pop up and insist that it's okay to "love the sinner," but never the sin (typically in reference to members of the LGBTQ+ community despite homosexuality not being a sin, and despite the fact that this line never shows up in the entire Bible).

And yes, I did just say that homosexuality is *not* a sin. Of course you'll find many Christians using the Bible to argue just the opposite, but just as many scholars are now discovering an entirely different sociopolitical

---

21. John 15:9-14

context to the typical "clobber verses" that suggest a therefore entirely different issue the Bible was addressing.

Remember what Dr. McClellan said, about how we're always building the meaning of the Bible ourselves?

Yeah.

For every argument *against* the LGBTQ+ community, one can be made *for* them, and context for "clobber verses" drawn out to explain that even *those* verses have nothing to do with the LGBTQ+ community at all, and all from the same source material (the Bible)—hence it's important you pin down what the hell you're in this religion for in the first place.

I had a friend in school who, later in life, joined Catholicism for messy reasons. She was never very directly religious, even though she grew up Catholic with the rest of us in our heavily Italian/Portuguese/Polish community here in Rhode Island. However, she *was* always more conservative, which only got worse as we both got into adulthood: anti-choice, vaguely tolerant of the LGBTQ+ community (but still open to saying homophobic slurs when she thought she could get away with it), longing for a tradwife life with traditional gender roles, and refusing to believe racism still existed because she, a white woman, "didn't see it" anywhere in our not-so-diverse little state. The funny thing is that she used to be into tarot cards and spirituality, manifesting, all that, but the second she read those Bible verses against witchcraft (the very same ones we broke down in *Discovering Christian Witchcraft*), she threw it all out and decided it was all demonic, and she settled into a very comfortable, near traditional Catholic routine (all while her fiancé started telling me I was a minion of Satan and going to hell, which she said nothing against). You can guess how that friendship eventually ended, despite all my efforts to try and get her to understand... *anything* about the world we lived in, spiritually or otherwise.

Still, the point is: from where I was standing, I saw that she chose the religion not because she was interested in the spiritual growth that comes with actually following the Golden Rule ("do unto others as you would have done to you"), but because it was safe, and it seemed to line up with her pre-existing beliefs and goals for her life. Meanwhile, I, raised Catholic and now staunchly Episcopal (so... Catholic without as much of the socially reprehensible bullshit), have the opposite social philosophy despite being a part of the same base religion. I am pro-LGBTQ+ and affirming (and in fact, I am the B in that list of letters, too). More, I'm vehemently pro-choice, and I'm politically left-leaning and continuously going out of my way to learn more about intersectional feminism and politics, which therefore gives me no interest in having children or being a tradwife of any kind. As I said, I'm the polar opposite from my former friend, yet apparently of the same religion. That's the bitch of this whole thing: you can justify *literally any position* with the Bible depending on what you're willing to cut out, add in, contextualize, or de-contextualize, because the Bible is not univocal, and it's been compiled over thousands of years in a different culture and language with a whole different social structure.

As an adult, I found that my social philosophy actually lined up with many other peoples' across *all religious paths:* from Norse and Celtic pagans to Hindus, from demonolaters and Satanists to atheists, from Methodists and Pentecostals to Catholics and Episcopalians, I found people across *all* walks of life and *all* faiths and *all* faith variations who had my social philosophy, which is so simple that, just like Jesus did with the Law, I can define for you in one sentence: *uplift, love, and dignify everyone from the lowest of society upward, and all of society will flourish.* I make my social philosophy not just based on my religion, even though Jesus's summary of the Law is like the great diamond in the center, magnifying and refracting all the light and colors of my mindset off of it. I make it also based on what I know of history, of ethics, of philosophy, of economics, of anthropology and sociology, and with *all* that information, and Jesus as my North Star, I come to that simple, single sentence of a conclusion.

Yet even as I see people from all walks of life and all faiths come to my conclusion and fight for intersectional justice and mutual aid in their communities, I also see the same people from all walks of life come to the opposite conclusion. I've seen neopagans pushing everything from white supremacy to conspiracy theories about Jewish people; I've seen Christians decrying any of the social aid Jesus and His cousin St. John encouraged as Marxism; I've seen demonolaters still afraid of hell while working with the demons that they think would send them there and I've seen atheists still arguing conservative Christian points about why being gay is a sin.

I've certainly been on #witchtok long enough to see people who are totally fine with fleecing their followers of hundreds, if not thousands of dollars; I've seen practitioners who laugh at the Indigenous peoples begging them to stop using critically endangered plants like white sage or to not use the bones of the coyote, going as far as to sic their followers on these voices and harass them off the internet. I've seen people dodge accountability for their actions by inventing entirely new (and completely nonsense) "systems" to initiate hapless and unknowing followers into for yet *more* money. I've seen people think that because they have the power magically, they have the *right* to do whatever they want to anyone they're strong enough to overpower, be it with hexes, love and obsession spells, or whatever else.

Just as my friend became a Christian because she thought the faith already aligned with her pre-existing conservative values, these people become witches *because* they want to have the power over others that they would never have otherwise, and that maybe others have even had over them. The wounds of their religious trauma, the airtight seal of repression religion gave them that witchcraft popped open, make them swing like a pendulum in the totally opposite direction of faith they were once brow-beaten into; like the Magician, they act without knowing the consequences, and like the Chariot, they want to *go:* to reach that place of power after being denied power (namely, agency and autonomy) for so long. They want to return tooth for tooth, fist for fist, eye for eye, even though that's a surefire way to make the whole world go blind—or worse, they just want to bring the fire down on people because they think they can judge who does and doesn't deserve that, and they think mercy is weakness. And be they Christian or Witch, I've watched the fruits of this kind of social philosophy grow, and they are *bitter* and *hard* and *cruel,* and they more often than not lead to a poisoning and burning down of everything they ever tried to build when they hurt enough people in their selfishness.

And that's when both Emperor and Empress come to get you: to smack you down in the court of public opinion, and to rebuild and restore you as you (hopefully) learn better. It's why we're asking you here, just as Mabry did: are you ready? Because listen: getting into Purgation, where we're about to take you, you're going to have to unpack a *whole lot* of shit—and you're going to have to *purge it,* leaving it behind for good. As Meister Eckhart (quoted in Mabry) says: "No container can hold two kinds of liquid. If it is to hold wine, we must necessarily pour out water; it must become empty and void. If, therefore, you are to receive divine joy and God, you must necessarily *pour out the creatures*" (emphasis mine.)[22]

Talk about a cosmic crossover, that a German mystic and philosopher from the 1300s could speak in such similar ways as a Spanish Carmelite nun and mystic from the 1500s. All of this wisdom, you see, is passed down from writing to writing, book to book, experience to experience—and you best believe there's more out there than even what we're showing you here. So much more. To appreciate it, though, one must empty themselves first of all the nonsense you picked up in this world, this era.

Hold on for a second and let me be clear: I'm not special, nor am I perfect. I have rage in my heart at injustice and its perpetrators that make me understand God's destruction of Sodom and Gomorrah as a whole city, no exceptions. I struggle real bad to kick up any empathy or mercy for nations that perpetuate cruelty, even though I logically know that not every citizen in those nations has a choice or agrees with their government. And I certainly didn't become a witch for any bleeding heart reasons; as I said before, I was just an eleven year old that was jazzed to find out magic would be real in any way and wanted to be cool and powerful like any witch or wizard I'd ever seen in any book or movie. It was a stupid reason for getting into a path like this, but it was a reason that got me started, and once I'd gotten started and had to deal with the dissonance of knowing my religion at large condemned it, I started looking at the bigger picture and updated my social philosophy—as well as my own personal limits and boundaries on how, when, why, and for who, I use my magic.

Of course, that doesn't mean my path will look anything like anyone else's, or that I've only stuck to this "love and light" nonsense we see online. I've done all the things that the mainstream church tells you that you should just avoid altogether. I've encountered, spoken to, and worked with demons. I've cast counter-curses and return-to-senders

---

22. Eckhart quoted in Mabry, *Growing into God*, 33.

and bindings. I've skipped church for twelve years straight, then come back for confirmation to continue a spotty every-other-week-(hopefully) attendance. And I've absolutely shaken a proverbial stick at God in drunken rage, only to then tucker out like a kid after a tantrum and cry for His comfort. Through all of it, though, I had God with me and guiding me along, showing me when it was time for mercy (most of the time) and when I should call on Him to make someone answer for injustice (the rest of the time); He showed me when it was time to go after what I wanted (a minority of the time) and when it was wise to sit back and let Him direct me to where I needed to go (the rest of the time). That's exactly what we need to figure out in this Foyer before we take a single step further. It's why this chapter's been so damn long.

So now, one more time, I'll ask you: what are you about? What are your red lines, either in the magical world or the mundane one? And who, what, if anything, helped you define those red lines? And most importantly of all: are you capable of handling the responsibility that comes with the divine power you want to access? Once more: *what kind of Witch do you want to be?*

Because anyone can be a witch (or, as I like to say, a mystic that does arts and crafts). Anyone can be a Christian. Not everyone can, in this sociopolitical climate full of the sins of the "religious" and the scarring of their captive abused, so successfully walk on the knife's edge between the two. Not everyone can recognize what they're signing up for and, like Jesus did in that desert, and again in the garden of Gethsemane, make that choice to commit—to see it all through to the end.

Can you?

Growing Accustomed to the Dark in the Foyer

When you walk into the spiritual Foyer, know that it's going to feel like it would if you walked into one in the real world: suddenly cold, darker, and a little disorienting as your eyes adjust to the lack of light. This is where the first steps of "walking in faith" are going to matter the most, and where it'll be wise to find someone to take your hand and help you through, whether that's a trusted friend who understands your spiritual path, a spiritual mentor or scholar, or a larger spiritual community; those who have been through the mess of this mysticism thing can help you slowly regain your sight as you step deeper and deeper into the dark (and while this book here is a good resource, know it doesn't replace the benefits of growing a spiritual village). You can always turn back and stay in the Courtyard, of course—because no one is saying you *have* to move forward. But if you *want* to move forward, then you'll have to get comfortable with being uncomfortable, and there's no better time to start than now.

The simplicity of the Courtyard is nice, but you feel pulled to go deeper, especially because you might realize that it's awfully lonely sitting there in the dirt by yourself. Can you overcome the fear of taking those steps, though? Can you step out of your comfort zone and into the public spotlight with others? Can you look at yourself and see how you were and how you could be? We are entering the part of the Awakening where your perception of reality will be changed and challenged—where *you* will perhaps encounter uncomfortable things about yourself that you didn't want to think about before, and where you will realize you can't just shrug them off or put them out of sight and out of mind anymore. We will be looking inward, more and more, to sit with our Self and the Divine. When you're sure you want this, then you're ready to take that pretty crozier the Mystic saw in her vision—but only if you can stomach the sight of your own face over that scrying bowl.

And let's be honest for a moment: feeling the pull to go deeper in this supernatural stuff, to have that miraculous experience again, does not mean it's as simple as saying yes and jumping in with both feet; in actuality, the darkness of the Foyer is where most people turn back from fear. They have the full audacity of someone who feels empowered but has no idea what they're doing. And that usually leads to backfiring and messing with things you're nowhere near ready for. (Obviously, this applies to many paths, not just this one.)

Secretly, there's still that cling to ego, where you believe you can handle the drastic change that comes with an awakening. In actuality, most consider it like burnout or mild psychosis, because what could possibly be *so* dramatic, *so* drastic? It's easy to get here and think that all this was demonic all along, and that the Church was right: that you need to run back to Jesus and be "saved" from the very thing He's trying to enlighten you to. Turns out a lot of people don't like the feeling of being convicted, or the fact that witchcraft and mysticism only give you a different *way* to be convicted—a more visceral, undeniable, and mind-consuming way than just feeling a little bad when a Bible verse pops up on your daily social media scroll and reminds you not to lie or be mean to your neighbor.

This mystic work, just like all works of energy and faith, have no room for ego. Ego is scared of the dark; it is scared of the unknown. It is scared of the rumbles and tappings of things that folks condemn as the wiles of demons, when it's really just the trappings of what kept you held back before. And so when you have something like the invitation of the Holy Spirit, the chains still hooked into Ego are going to rattle when you try to pull away from what's comfortable and familiar and towards the Unknown in the Holy Spirit's calling. And just how do you get accustomed to the dark when you're terrified of it? Well, this is where fellowship and prayer comes in; a healthy balance of both will help you overcome the obstacles in this strange new place. It's other people, who can see outside of yourself *and* the things your ego tries to tell you to keep you comfortable, that you can stay accountable as much as productive on the walk forward.

McColman speaks of the importance of community in his book, too, and now, we send you forth on this mission: to find your community, whether online, in the real world, or both. He gives many tips as to what to look for in spiritual communities. like churches, and he insists that anyone who could eschew the inherent communal nature of community "makes about as much sense as trying to become an attorney without going to law school."[23] For McColman, those who just want to know about mysticism without ever engaging in it are free to read these books and then go back to whatever they were doing before with their life, but those who are serious about finding God must turn their face away from the clouds and towards the faces of one another: they must start "getting to know others with a similar hunger for Christ's presence in their lives."[24]

---

23. McColman, *The Big Book of Christian Mysticism*, 136.

24. Ibid., 136.

It doesn't have to be a church that goes against everything you believe reflects God, naturally; no one is asking you to brave the megachurches clawing for your wallets or put yourself at the mercy of those judgemental, performative congregations you might've known growing up. But it does have to be a fellowship of believers, who are part of that Body and therefore united in this mission to spread love and justice and mercy. There are so many ways to achieve this in our modern day, so many communities pushing for the greater good, that you can take your pick of them all—and in fact, you may very well join our faith community, the Ministry of Christ under the Order of Divine Mysticism, which we've created as a proper digital faith community full of learning, fellowship, and spiritual growth! Our Discord community is now here, and with it, a place for folks to find that church-like environment they've been missing (or maybe didn't realize they've been missing).

You need that community, and this is the point in the journey where you realize just how lonely and scary things can get without it. That doesn't mean you need to go hop back into your local church full of strangers that stare at you funny when you try to make small talk, but it does mean you find people who approach Christianity and spirituality and mysticism in similar ways. We're out there, us witchy Christians who get it; we're all online and in smaller spaces in churches, out in the highways and hedges, as it were. The internet is a fascinating place and usually our go-to resource for anything that might be an outlier. Hashtags like #ChristianWitch or #jesuswitch or even #folkmagic can help you find content, people, even guidance on social media when you start getting overwhelmed with where to turn. Moreover, as Christians, we feel we should remind you of something: *the dead aren't dead.* The dead are alive in Christ, and they're watching over you right now, and you can bet your behind that at least one Saint has gone through something similar to what you are. Pray for the intercession of Saints: of the figures you see in those church paintings, or of those in your own family that have passed on. Ask them to help you find who, and what, you need.

And remember: it can be a bit messy in all those Facebook groups and Discord servers, so please use your best judgment and discernment when dealing with new people. If something doesn't feel right, honor that feeling. While we'd love to say that witchy spaces are perfectly safe, the fact is that so long as people are people, there will be room for bad actors just like there are among Christian spaces: room for spiritual co-opting and bypassing, room for ego issues and popularity contests. It's all too common for a social media creator to get swallowed up by the frenzy of their notifications, and for the people forming parasocial bonds with them in the comments to inflate their egos to an unmanageable degree—or for those people in the comments to assume the creator is a commodity available to ask questions at anytime as if their name is Google. Remember: even online, creators and commenters alike are people behind that screen, subject to the same pitfalls as anyone else.

If you need more in-person communities, look at your local pagan space or even non-denominational churches. Facebook or your local metaphysical store may have fliers and group meetings. Ask questions, read books, join in discussions with an open mind and an open heart—or maybe even start your own space, if you really can't find any already built. If something makes you feel guilty or troubled, write it down and bring it to Jesus and the community (if it feels safe to do so, like folks will be receptive). However, just as people form parasocial relationships and get awfully demanding of internet creators, let us note: most of us in these public places, while we do have experience and wisdom, are not therapists. There are usually other things intertwined on an emotional and spiritual level that need multiple hands to assist... *like the hands of a therapist.*

Trust us when we say that doing everything by yourself is a surefire way to end up in a situation where you have no idea what right and wrong even mean anymore, because you have no outside frame of reference to check yourself against. It's times like this where you realize more viscerally than ever that things of this nature, this spiritual journey and all the learning in it, *cannot* be done in a vacuum; like McIntosh once said, there was no mystic *singular* in the early days of the church, but mysticism among the *collective,* a shared experience with the Church as one body.[25] Finding people who get it, especially ones who are on the same walk as you (be they regular Christians or witches or our special

---

25. McIntosh, *Mystical Theology,* 7.

blend of the two), will help you keep your bearings as you move forward on a path where you can't see much ahead.

Sharing community space with people who know what you're going through doesn't mean all your friends are some kind of mind readers, though. On the contrary, you need to be able to step away from yourself, actually communicate, and let people know what's going on, both in life and in your soul. The ones who understand won't mock or shirk your worries. There is no shame in asking for help, or in sharing your experiences to get more clarity and understanding, like the Mystic does with the Witch. Everyone has a unique perspective, and what you might miss on your own, others can help you see–but only if you let them in enough to give them a proper picture in the first place.

Think of a doctor. How can they help you if you don't tell them your symptoms? So many people go undiagnosed and untreated because of shame in medicine–because of toxic doctors with terrible bedside manner, and also because of the shame and judgement people project onto the doctor, who becomes a symbol of the institutional stigma and history of mistreatment people have gone through. But that doesn't mean the solution is to never go to a doctor again, just like the solution to years of religious trauma isn't to avoid any and all kinds of religious fellowship ever again.

Guilt and shame usually have their lingering roots wrapped deep within ourselves; it is with this that we need to move forward with a sense of tenderness. Because in the Foyer, you're at a precipice; you are, essentially, just beginning to take a good, hard look at the very fiber of your being you've been avoiding looking at. It's part of Awakening: to not only realize that there's more to God, but that there's more to *you,* and you've been stifling it. You may have been told to stifle it all along, and it may hurt now to realize how much time you've spent burying your own face under other people's dirt, but you have to dig yourself up now; there is still much to pull up to look at from the roots. Whether you were raised in the church and your whole life revolved around that pulpit or just had core influences from a church or religious sect that was in your life, there are moments and memories that have shaped you in one way or another, and you don't have to seal them away to heal them. In fact, that does the opposite of healing.

A lot of bad things that happen in this world in the name of God is because Man took on the mantle of the Divine and twisted it until they could use the power as they wanted, not how God wanted. And when God tried to meet us as Man, wrapped His Logos in flesh and bone to reach us face to face... we killed that Logos, that Son, that Lamb. Over and over, God's been trying to reach us, and every time, we invent some way to avoid listening or looking deeper–but that stops here, in this Foyer, where there is nothing and no one but your own choices waiting to be made. No one can make them for you, nor tell you how to make them; this is where you square your shoulders and commit to finding out what you don't know rather than sitting comfortably in what you do.

As you walk through your deconstructing (and reconstructing!) of faith, keep this in mind: "The road ahead seems to go backwards," according to the Chinese Taoist Mystic Lao Tzu. There are times it will feel like we go two steps forward and one step back. The idea used in the church would be similar to "backsliding." Take a moment now to let that word, and all those ideas, go. Learning and loving is not linear, and to expect as much takes time away from the outer influences of the world that would say otherwise. Sometimes, we have to step away from the Church as an institution to heal. Sometimes for a while, sometimes forever.

Something that happens when folks step away from the church, and it isn't decompression or deconstruction; in fact, a lot of people who leave the modern construct of Christianity go right into some type of witchcraft. A lot of the elements of empowerment in witchcraft, specifically female-leaning divinity, is appealing for those who have felt detached and silenced in their lives. The harmonious comfort shown on the surface is a sure draw from someone who has left with large wounds inflicted on them in the name of God. In a lot of ways, they use practices like Heathenism and Wicca as a bandage, then simply inflict the same wounds on others under the guise of "you're not doing it right" while still harboring the guilt for how they used to be or their thoughts as they move forward. The only thing that changed was the name called at the altar.

As we deconstruct further, we get to a point where we have to start with a new foundation. To reconstruct on this mystic's path, there is only one thing we know for certain: we have no idea what we're truly doing. And that's the whole point: we don't know what God is doing or what His plans are. We only know what we are doing here, in this time, and want to share that with you on your journey. Deconstructing the frameworks that man put on God will liberate your mind and understanding moving forward. This is, in our opinion, the ultimate point of deconstructing: the crap that needs to be pulled out of us so we can find the faith that's always been in us.

Mimi Says:

Listen, we can talk a good game about connecting yourself to a community to check yourself on your spiritual journey, but let's be honest: even if others are telling you to slow down, or to think twice, a lot of times, we still go off in directions we shouldn't just because we're stubborn and think we know better. Or worse, sometimes we don't listen because we don't want to acknowledge that what we're doing isn't what's right even if it feels good to do it. You can be told a lot of things by a lot of people, but at the end of the day, you have to make the choices—and mistakes—on your own.

I can tell you right now: every time I had a crisis of faith, it wasn't because I thought I was bad or sinful; plainly, my heart's discernment told me to listen, and I didn't. I made the decision to not follow the *clearly* given signs from above, and instead relied solely on myself, which means I got lost. Frequently. My discernment was overruled by the free will I used like a shield against any outside influence, desperate to maintain my autonomy and sense of self no matter what. "I'm gonna do it my way!" I'd shout and stomp, and Spirit would look down with mirth and go, "Oh yeah?"

Cue the chaos that would ensue. I consider this the place where I realized that I was acting a little big for my britches.

The infinite battle of ego and higher self plays out in big and small ways; there's usually a spiritual facepalm moment and I have to stop and check myself. This is where all the journaling and therapy and shadow work comes in—though not everything is so apparent. The darkness of that Foyer comes when you realize that not only do you have the power to do what you will: you also have to face every consequence that comes with your action (or inaction). This can look like a meltdown from spiritual whiplash and psychosis that leaves you unable to think straight or act like *you*. Sometimes, it looks like imposter syndrome and the inability to do what you love because you no longer feel like you can or should. Whatever it looks like, it usually isn't pretty.

But even all the journaling in the world does nothing for moving through this part of the spiritual journey. You have to actually *move*. Use tarot or oracle decks, astrology, consult with others who you trust to double check your divination, or even just a flip through the Bible in those really desperate moments as a signpost for the action that it takes to get through this mess. Refine your craft, your thoughts. Test what you do, don't just write it down and forget. And, above all, be willing to be vulnerable and allow yourself to receive the answer of "no." Discipline is in the consistency of showing up for yourself; The Emperor, declaring strength in stability by actually *doing* something, is the other side of the coin to the Empress, who declares that creativity is the way to feed your soul and continue the momentum of motion.

Like a sword in the fire, everything starts with an idea and an outline, but it can't do anything until you start putting in the work to hammer it out and sharpen it. Back in 2020, I got the same message a *lot* from my guides, such as:

- start a grounding practice

- let your emotions be seen

- create something to speak your truth

And, of course, being in this hard space called *a battle of wills*, I brushed a lot of what was given off. I have ADHD, so how do I do meditation and grounding effectively? And my emotions? Those always get me in trouble. I'm not gonna let those out. Creating something–in *this* economy? Hobbies are expensive, so I'm just going to keep playing video games.

I did not have the discipline to keep going because I did not show up for myself. I let myself down and framed it with excuses. Not only that, but I refused to take action because I was fighting my own demons, who constantly taunted me by asking "why does it matter?" The only way I fixed it was small steps, moving forward a little at a time.

One day, for instance, I tried meditating after having a huge emotional blow up. *Nothing* worked, not a single thing. And instead of throwing away the idea of meditating altogether, like I'd done before, I decided to try something different. And then, when that also didn't work, something else. I banged that proverbial hammer against the sword until the shape started to form. I paid attention to the process and, in my stubbornness, actually committed to it. And while it did take me a long time, and it's something I still struggle with, I did eventually find my own grounding practice. Let me tell you: it makes a *huge* difference in how I approach my craft and my spiritual boundaries.

Prayer and meditation are paramount to a healthy spiritual practice, whether you're on this path or not. In Matthew 6:8, we are shown the way to pray. And where does it put us? In the closet: a place of dark and quiet, so that we can meditate on His word and call out to Him unashamed. This is how we grow accustomed to being in the darkness itself, to being in the quiet. And I know it's hard to be quiet in meditation. Neurodivergence and the societal shaping of our attention spans has given us little reason to simply sit still and be.

This is why you start slowly. Say one prayer, something simple, then close your eyes and just listen. You can do this for one minute, then two, then three, and so on and so forth. I used to participate in this when I would wake up early, with a kiddo still snuggled next to me and the dog snoring at my feet; I would just close my eyes and say thank you, then sit and listen to all the sounds. I can now successfully do ten full minutes of prayer in the dark, after almost four years of trying, failing, and coming back to it. (Praying while falling asleep still counts; don't think it doesn't!)

I didn't understand the purpose of the Chariot for a long time. I believed that the foundations were the study of the fundamentals, and that's all I needed. Except... how could I apply fundamentals of magic and wisdom if I didn't have the foundation of knowing myself? What were my strengths? My weaknesses? My biggest triggers? Why did I want this? Why did I do things a certain way?

The Chariot wasn't necessarily about what type of witch I was going to be, but what kind of *person* I would be with this esoteric knowledge. That's important to figure out, too. After all this talk of community, social philosophy, witchcraft, religion, and everything in between, if you go deep enough, you find out that *that* is what all this is really about, and that at some point, you have to give yourself a long, honest assessment to find out what you're really doing. All the tools and trinkets, all the noise of spiritual leaders and fellows in faith, it can only go so far before you need to just buckle down and get serious about who you are and what you're doing in life. Understanding this made it easier for me to move forward in discipline: teaching myself proper boundaries so I could heal deeper and explore farther, knowing when to hold back and when to dive in, and learning my whole truth until I was able to use my words to speak what I know.

This has been a long chapter, I know. But that's because out here, in the shadows of the Foyer, you gotta know: you're in for a long night, and the faster you adjust, recognizing all those places where you gotta dig deeper in your soul, the faster you can stop dawdling in the dark and get back to walking along your path with courage.

Shadow Work Prompts for the Foyer

- Go back and find some of your favorite Christian songs, like something from Hillsong or Toby Mac. How do you feel when you listen now? Where do you feel it in your body? (Tightness in chest, pit in stomach, heat in neck, etc.)

- A lot of times, we simply thought a rush of dopamine was the same as a spiritual calling. In fact, a lot of evangelic pursuits for such callings can be attributed to speech mannerisms and the beat of live music. We're not saying things were made to manipulate you, but... in some ways, they were. Sit on these things as you work through the deconstruction. How did they influence you when you started to dig into your witchy journey? Did you abandon it all, or did you treat a few things like a guilty pleasure?

- What was the first thing you let go of in your deconstruction journey? Did it help you in your magical walk?

- What do you feel like is still clinging to you? (Or you to it!)

- If you don't think you've had that experience, write down your first experience with faith or God that you can remember. What did it feel like then? What does that faith feel like to you now? What experiences made you stop in awe or wonder?

- What was the reason you first decided to explore witchcraft?

- Another aspect in higher learning of Christianity is to "Walk the Roman Road" to be a better Christian and no longer be childish (which is different than child-like!) in your faith and understanding. We look at verses like Romans 8:28 and see an irony in the study of the modern church: they have outlined the Foyer's struggle. What are some things you've noticed that are parallel in this journey so far with what you learned as a Christian? Come back to this as you dig deeper in the Foyer.

- Go back to Matthew 19:26. Oftentimes, this is abused as a reason for us to do anything we want because we use God's strength to do it. How have you *truly* relied on his strength in moments when you didn't think you had any?

Section 2

Purgation

You were taught, with regard to your former way of life, to put off your old self, which is being corrupted by its deceitful desires; to be made new in the attitude of your minds.

St. Paul

Ephesians 4:22-23

Chapter Three
The Sitting Room

The Mystic and the Witch

S ILENCE SETTLES ON THE *Witch's kitchen like the first snowfall of winter. It's been like this so many times before that the Witch knows what to do in the face of the Mystic's growing agitation; she sips her tea, flexes her fingers, and rolls her shoulders, waiting patiently for the Mystic to find her Holy One's direction.*

Poor thing, *the Witch thinks as the Mystic's lips twist and her brows furrow in her concentration. Whatever is coming next from this vision, it doesn't seem particularly pleasant. The Witch would love to talk about other, simpler things—what vegetables the Mystic is growing with her sisterhood, how the tomcat that always begs for scraps around the abbey is doing—and perhaps they'll get a chance to later, but that snowy silence tells the Witch that there is more that Spirit wants to say, and it will say it, whether either the Mystic or the Witch want it to or not.*

"Okay," *the Mystic finally says. She straightens in her seat and gives her temple one more tender touch before taking a deep breath.* "Here's what else I experienced."

❖

In that moment, I knew. I just *knew*. The crozier was in my hands against all possibility, all reason, and I knew what I was going to use it for. My hands glided along its smooth wood, and the gem within its golden crook gleamed at me, humming with power and light that radiated off of it and warmed my cheeks. It still seemed too good to be true, and I found myself continuously glancing back at its holding case—and the black scrying pool that I nearly lost myself in—wondering how I was worthy enough to be allowed to hold it.

Just as the diamond gleamed and the gold of the crozier shone in its radiance, my heart likewise felt as if it was made of crystal and catching every shred of light. My lungs were full, my cheeks flush with excitement, and all I wanted was to begin *using* this latent power. I promised to myself: *I'll use it for good; I'll use it for justice, mercy, and righteousness! I'll be a sword and a shield, and I'll never compromise on my values!* These sentiments lit up my skin and skittered along my spine; even the dark of this Manor didn't feel so intimidating anymore, once I had this crozier in my hands.

And that's because I knew explicitly: I am holy, and I am also *powerful:* I have not only the energy, but the right to use it, in fascinating spiritual ways. Something still sent a shiver down my back as I realized this, because all my life, I've been told that I am *nothing*, you see: a filthy sinner in desperate need of grace, one who cannot be trusted and therefore should never even *dream* of power. That any power I might actualize from my own hands was *witchcraft* (no offense, my friend), and witchcraft is the very antithesis of the holy, godly, Apostle-like life my community once demanded of me (again, my friend: my apologies). And yet I knew then that two things can be true at once. There, in Someone's Manor, I'd figured it out and saw myself fully in that mirror, and the clarity resting on me was almost too much.

I couldn't stay still. The only open door in the Manor beckoned me closer, and with a warm, tingling thrill skittering along my skin, I rushed for it. My mind was full of all the things I might do with my newfound power, all the new workings I might begin and miracles I might channel down with the Lord my God. Workings for prosperity—for myself and those in need! Workings for mending hearts, for achieving clarity! Workings for opening the mouth only for sweet and helpful words! Yes, I was committed to being so very *good* with the power I'd discovered, and I could not wait to get started. In that room, I was sure, was the next step in understanding more about what to do, how to grow.

Once I crossed the threshold of that room, however, I paused. I wasn't sure what I was expecting, but I knew damn well that it wasn't what I found: a bare, empty room made of nothing but grey brick, with no carpet, no rug, no paintings and certainly no bookshelves stuffed with tomes. All that existed in that room was another closed door, a single rocking chair with a little table beside it, a weathered old prayer book on that table, and a fireplace roaring with life—the source of the bright light that drew me there to begin with.

I went for the next door, thinking maybe this is just a little sitting room or a vestibule or something, but when I jiggled the cold metal handle, I found it locked. So I thought: *maybe this isn't the way I need to go, after all. Maybe another door—*

But as I turned around, the door I'd come in from swung shut on its own with a definitive *click*. I ran for it, desperate to catch it, but I was too slow; it shut, and I jiggled the handle to find that *this* door was locked, too. No amount of beating on the door—either with my fists or the crozier—nor yelling for help, nor fiddling with the lock, did anything.

I was trapped. Worse, it seemed no one was there to hear me call for help. Whoever I'd felt calling me this whole time, that distant Someone—I didn't know where They were, or if They knew that I was trapped. I just knew that I wasn't going anywhere anytime soon, and before that sent me into a panic, I decided to sit in that little rocking chair and keep my crozier safe over my lap; I slid its smooth bar under the rocking chair's arms as if to lock myself in place out of pure spite.

I could've maybe convinced myself that it was comfortable despite there being no cushion on its wooden frame. Snug and supportive, you know? Like the old chairs in the grey place I began my life in. The fire, at least, was warm on my face, and the light kept the shadows away from the edges of my vision. My head turned seemingly on its own, my gaze focusing on that weathered prayer book—the kind I used to see in the grey world I fled from—and my skin crawled at the thought of touching it, never mind opening it.

Still, it called to me, and for all the unease wriggling through my gut like a bowl of earthworms desperate to find the dirt, I began to wonder.

The Witch wipes the crumbs of her own scone off her fingers and washes the last bite down with tea. She remains silent after receiving the next twist of the vision. Save for the snap and crackle of the stove's fire that punctuated their shared breath, there is no sound. No rustling or chirping from without, no ticking or humming from within. The Witch's hands smooth the deck in an arc before her as her wiry hair finally frees itself from her ribbon's slipping hold. She moves two cards from their hidden place, tucked neatly between one another, and flips them. The face of the High Priestess and the angelic visage of Temperance peer back, holding secrets in their own silence.

The Witch sucks her teeth and says, "You're being told to hush and listen now. These cards—they suggest a surrender in Ego, meaning giving up *control, not necessarily gaining more. The previous trial of the last lesson gave us a chance to balance that which is now being tested, and tested you are."*

"What? Why?" The Mystic withers in her seat, her face falling. "What's the test about?"

A moment passes as the Witch considers that, and then she points to the first card. "Right away, we find the energy of the High Priestess. She was once associated with patience and stillness, and with the stark absence of almost everything in this Sitting Room of yours, we find the call from within once more. Here begins the stripping away of things that you may consider distractions—idols, 'evils'—whatever they may have been called before you started this journey, which have still been relevant all this time. Now, you are more aware in the silence, as you are laid bare in your most authentic self.

"But even when it feels as if nothing holds meaning or value in this empty space, we know that Divinity is still here, hiding inside us as the sacred wisdom of the Spirit that dwells within. This is where you make that spiritual awareness and are given a chance to practice grace, compassion, and a connection to yourself and your intuition under the newly acquired skill of discernment. This is the card that represents the vastness of inner work as well, as the potential of the Magician has been refined through alchemizing the energy of the space. You are everything and nothing here. It is a precipice."

The Witch's nail taps against the face of the angel as that knowing sparkle reappears in her eye.

"The demanded balance of discipline and free will takes the form of taking responsibility for our actions, thoughts, and ego. Temperance's energy is also known for frugality and being at peace with the bare minimum; I am reminded of the mystics that came before you, who cast away all of their belongings to follow the call of the Spirit."

The Mystic's face twists a bit further before it smooths like a cloth under a hot iron. With her eyes suddenly alight, she nods and says, *"Like St. Francis! How he gave everything up to live by the words of our Lord!"*

"Precisely. He made do with less than anyone; if he'd been stuck in that Sitting Room you described, I'm sure it wouldn't have mattered to him."

"No, likely not." The Mystic sits back and crosses her arms; her chin burrows into her chest as she turns the idea over in her mind. *"He really did give away every possible thing. Even sold his one weathered Bible to give that money away. Truly a magnificent man."*

The Witch can't help but smile at the Mystic, with all her wonder over men long dead. *"With this energy,"* she continues, pouring once more over her cards, *"we are now forced to reconcile with how we see ourselves as human and how we see ourselves as divine, and the balance therein. I want to say an example of this is deep focused meditation, like those of monks and shamans that follow in the footsteps of those like your St. Francis. Patience, moderation, harmony, 'zen'—all lie on the other side of what was: fear, the unknown, and that inner turmoil such things create. Temperance shows us the energy we transmute and work through to move onto our path and towards a higher echelon of understanding and learning."*

She speaks carefully, as if hoping that would help the Mystic understand a little easier while the poor thing thinks herself dizzy. A lock of hair tumbles from its place and dares to lay a shadow along the Witch's face, but she pays it no mind and moves to put the cards back. Upon taking Temperance, however, the Hermit card peeks itself from the edges. The cards were stuck together this whole time, and the Witch separates them, revealing something more.

"Well, well." She lays the Hermit down on the table. *"An old friend has appeared to teach us something we may not have seen on the surface. Perhaps this is another chance to make the space and time for a true spiritual connection?"*

Both the Witch and the Mystic lean over the table, studying the Hermit and his great stave, his lantern, his identity-concealing cloak. There's a shroud of mystery there, an acceptance of silence and solitude that, even just seeing it, *helps the Mystic unwind the tension from her shoulders. The Witch notices and lets the last note of the Divine roll off her tongue.*

"We see him, almost hidden, holding a stave that looks awfully familiar, doesn't it? Like your crozier in your vision." The Witch traces her nail down that stave. "While this may sometimes be seen as a card of negative energy with isolation, it is instead asking you to now interrogate yourself: what needs to be stripped away? What beliefs need to come loose? It asks that we take part in a vow of mystic silence, to let go of the boastfulness and sit in introspection; it is the rock in the road that the Chariot hits, forcing it to stop and consider how it's been moving down this path. This card's request is a simple one: respect the absence of distraction to truly gain insight, and let yourself be guided by the inner knowledge, understanding, and tempering of your will."

"Hmm." The Mystic tilts her head back and forth as she studies the Hermit. "I understand, I think. Yes, that Sitting Room—I can see the Hermit enjoying himself there. But…"

"But?"

"But there's more to the vision, unfortunately."

The Witch blinks, then huffs a deep sigh. She shuffles her cards back into her deck and taps them down on the table, then says, "Shall we make lunch first, before you tell me more?"

With a graceful glide of her hands, the Witch scoops her cards into a neat pile…save two. They snag on the table's rough surface and stubbornly refuse to go with the rest, as if insisting on their presence being known right then. *The Witch purses her lips.*

"So… there's more to this, then?"

Her words are gentle, as to not raise more alarm for her poor friend, who already froze and fixed her eyes on those two leftover pieces of card stock (as she understood what her deck meant when cards were left behind). An urgent message—a warning, perhaps? The Witch plucks the cards from their place, only to flip them quickly, as one would rip a bandage from a healing wound. The Devil and the Hanged Man stare back at her, meeting her incredulous gaze with brutal defiance.

"My dear Sister," the Witch whispers, "here come two more visitors. A unique pair, to be sure, but I don't think they're here to be intimidating. What do you know of the Devil?"

The Mystic's cheeks pale; her lips tremble. She stares at the cards as if they're speaking a curse into the air, and her brows set hard as she says, "The Devil is the icon of wickedness and evil! Of the Enemy! What reason should any Spirit have to send me such a message like that?"

Only the quirk of the Witch's brow breaks the steel in the Mystic's gaze, and as the Mystic takes a breath, the Witch shakes her head. They both sit down again, and the Witch murmurs, "Mmm, as I thought. You need to hear this, then, and hear it well."

The Mystic folds her arms tight across her chest, her distrust bending her lips into a bitter little scowl. Once settled, the Witch taps her nail to the cards and lets the Divine move her mouth, hopefully in a way the Mystic would accept.

"This is another piece of the test that you are being guided through," she starts. "Don't let the image or the name fool you: The Devil is not a 'bad' card, nor is its energy 'bad.' The struggle mentioned shows how you are being forced into reflection. Take a step back and look at yourself, hard, with no distractions and no facades. You must look at how your habits have actually held you back; your traumas that you cling to—whether from being unhealed or as a crutch, as a sense of identity—the shadow work you refused or ignored, the dark and scary parts that peeked up from unhealed parts of you, you need to address them, and now in your little Sitting Room there, you have nothing to hide behind to ignore it.

"The temptation to take what you have learned and seek the easy way out—going back to when it wasn't such a burden, all this responsibility of Self and your magic—is staring at you. When you bring these things to the light, whether by force and intervention or purposeful focus, you will be able to transmute that energy and move forward with the energy from the High Priestess."

The Witch pauses, hunching as if the heaviness of truth is bearing down on her shoulders.

"The Hanged Man is asking something similar, but still different. How many times have you tried and failed to resist temptations? Look here, at the Hanged Man, showing you the answer to what you desperately seek when the Devil is tempting you. A casual glance shows us someone looking at things upside down, and so you would surmise that you simply need to look at things from a new perspective; in this case, it goes a little deeper. Look again: you have been thrust into an experience that turns your world upside down. It is disorienting, no matter what you do, and you find yourself bound to keep from moving.

"*Think on the silence, the stillness, for that is the point. You must be able to sit and focus in order to regain your senses. At first, this new position almost feels as if you are being punished, doesn't it? Strung up and pulled away from your world, still bound by habits and behaviors that tie you to your worst self. But the longer you sit there, the more you realize that your bindings are things you've earned. They are simply you, and nothing from the outside is holding you back as much as it seems it is, but the Divine itself is slowing the Chariot's forward charge, disrupting your rhythm to force you to stillness and contemplation. There is nothing you can do but endure as the Devil dances in your face and shows you every bit of darkness you fooled yourself into thinking you'd erased from yourself.*

"*There are times when you still feel trapped in the ways of the old, which makes the world feel empty and dull. Take care that the new things you've found do not undo the work you've put in. New habits can just as easily take the place of old ones and still damage you. The suffering exists because you have not yet worked out your own restraints.*"

The Mystic's frown deepens. Her eyes flicked back and forth, from card to card, as if she were reading not their images, but the words of her Good Book. "*The entire book of James speaks on patience in suffering, and reaping the reward thereafter,*" she mutters. "*Is that what this suffering looks like?*"

With a shrug, the Witch says, "*If that's what you wish to see, by all means, see it. The solutions are simple, but they are not always easy. This is not a comfortable path to walk, my dear friend. You have experienced trials to help temper yourself in order to withstand what would've crumpled you before. These cards are speaking of something else—not necessarily calamity and catastrophe, but rather, the bondage of Self and the Divine's attempt to tease you out of them with bindings of Its own. The energy shifts at the end of the lessons of the Hanged Man.*

"*You are able to see the patterns and the ways that no longer serve you, and let them go towards your balance and purpose. Transmuting this energy allows you to see the direction lit by the Hermit and the understanding and balance of Temperance. How will you move forward, my dear Mystic?*"

The Mystic takes in a deep breath and lets it out in a rush. "*Through faith, and not by sight…?*"

Reclaiming the unlikely pair of cards with a soft smile, the Witch tucks them both back into her deck and leaves it in the center of the table as she moves away to prepare lunch.

"There's still more, as you said, to your vision. Let us take a moment to gather our senses and sit with the truths we've heard."

The Dark Night of the Senses and the Dryness of Prayer

When was the last time you prayed? Not cast a spell or pulled tarot or anything, but *prayed?* Talked just to talk, or repeated time-worn prayers that help your whirring mind sit still and get centered? It may be as early as this morning to ground and start your day in a fresh headspace, or it may be a long time ago, back when you were told to do so for the sake of your salvation and, as a result, haven't been able to think of prayer the same way since. Either way, there are moments where, inexplicably, everything seems to feel *off* in our spirituality, and no doubt you've felt them before.

Times where spirituality feels boring. Or like work. Times where connecting with God feels like you're talking to a wall, or when picking yourself up to pray is like fighting to stand up while wearing a vest of bricks. Perhaps even before we all got into this crazy spiritual life, the religious things in life–the Bible, church, prayer, whatever else–felt especially stuffy and boring, like things that only those fanatic, overly devout, performative people claimed to love so much. It certainly felt that way to a certain St. Ignatius–*before* he became a Saint, of course. Though that only goes to show you that truly anyone can become a holy person, no matter where they started.

As Mabry puts it, for St. Ignatius of Loyola, "the church was just part of the furniture": a handsome, rich young soldier didn't really think much about the actual spiritual aspect of it, just the cultural and social aspects that would be necessary for him to sustain his reputation as he progressed in life.[1] All the actual church-going and the devotion those holy folk put on really couldn't have been further from his mind; like many of us in our own lives full of all kinds of ambitions, curiosities, and comforts, the idea of suffering for God or being so wholly devoted to Him just wasn't that attractive.

---

1. Mabry, *Growing into God*, 51.

However, it was during the siege of Paloma in the 1500s that he caught a particularly nasty injury when a cannonball smashed into his leg, and after that, there was no more of his usual lifestyle: no more running around with his friends, no more chasing after women, no more of any such typical fun for a young man of money. He was stuck healing inside, and there was little else to do except read and pray, and "in the emptiness that followed, he began to see what was Real and what wasn't": he began to find value not in his old life, but in the past lives of the Saints he read about, and in prayer.[2]

The emptiness and desolation his paused life held him hostage with was eventually filled with a "spirit of consolation" in God, and while such prayer wasn't miraculously fixing his leg or restoring his old life or any of the things people usually pray for, "it was changing *him,* from the inside out," and it helped St. Ignatius understand what things were truly important to him and what things were really worth living for once all the distractions of his rich boy life were gone.[3] This process of detachment from the world, while not exactly something St. Ignatius chose to do, was one that helped him understand and accept his connection to God, which strengthened his spirit while his body slowly healed and brought a peace and maturity that wouldn't have happened otherwise. That starting detachment set the stage for the purgation of a past life that wasn't actually healthy for his mind, body, heart, or soul.

In some times, as Witches, we may find ourselves like pre-cannon-ball St. Ignatius, bored with spirituality and wanting to think about anything else—but then there are times where *something happens,* something just *clicks,* and then, like post-cannonball St. Ignatius, nothing feels interesting *except* for spirituality. By this point, you may sit there wondering what the point of everything earthly is—especially as you begin getting a taste of gnosis, of those divine secrets, and realize that the world around you just seems all too focused on the *wrong things.* Money, possessions, the approval of your peers—what are any of these things worth? Why should anyone ever bother with these things when

2. Ibid., 52.

3. Ibid., 52.

there's clearly *so much more* out there—things so much bigger than the material world and all its petty worries and trifling vanities?

And yet, even knowing how there's something so much more important out there... it's easy to feel demoralized to the point that even prayer feels empty. Hollow. It's easy for your witchy tools and altars to collect dust, and for your books and studies to go neglected while you vegetate on your phone and doomscroll your time away. Sometimes the world is boring, and then sometimes spirituality is boring, and when both hit at the same time, it seems like everything just tastes and feels as grey as ash all over again, with no point behind it all—because what is all this *for*, if we still find ourselves so small in this big world, and so dwarfed by problems too twisted for anyone to tackle on their own? What's the point of power, if the kind of power we have doesn't really do what we thought it *would* do?

We know. We've been there, too.

In St. Teresa's *Interior Castles,* she describes this portion of the castle as a time where, after passing through the first two rooms and all the trials within (the shock of Divinity's calling, the awareness and battling of the temptations of the world), the people who come to this place are ones who aspire to please God in their works and behaviors. In St. Teresa's view, this is where a deep impatience sets in: we have people who want nothing more than to be God's hands and feet, to advance His will in the world by their just management of their resources and their care for others, leading by example in their gentle and compassionate behavior and their calm state of being. But they're just not there yet.

As such, it is a terrible thing that they can still feel how far away they are from God. They want to find God right away, to hurry to meet Him in the innermost part of the castle (the soul), and yet they still have ways to go, and they still have all this ugliness and disaster in the world to contend with. She describes a "dryness of prayer," the "aridities" of which are torturous and cause many people going through it to complain bitterly, to which she reminds the nuns she writes to that they took up their habit of their own free will, and that rather than doing what they do in search of rewards that God doesn't owe us (since He really doesn't need our works for *His* health, but wants us to do them for our own development), we should remember that every gift we get from God is another measure of our debt to Him.[4]

That might sound rough enough to make you bristle and chafe, the idea that God owes you nothing and that everything you do get is a grace and a mercy, not something you earn, but it's something we implore you to sit on and digest, even if it makes you uncomfortable. After all, in St. Teresa's eyes, it's keeping this mindset, and developing the humility that it spawns, that keeps us grounded and helps us avoid following this path just for the promise of some reward for doing well.

Because think about it: who else goes to church and tithes all their money away and does a whole song and dance, giving away all their time, energy, and autonomy, for the promise of especially *earthly* blessings? Who benefits from a message like that of the Prosperity Gospel mess, which tells you that if you do enough donating, you'll get your donations returned to you manyfold? To go into any kind of spiritual relationship, be it a normal church-going Christian life or the self-directed life of a Witch, with only your own personal, earthly gain as your north star, is to fail before you even begin.

And so, this third mansion, which the Mystic calls the Sitting Room, is a time to really sit with what you've begun to shed; it is a sizeable part of the mystical process of *purgation,* in which we undo all these earthly snares that trick us and lie to us about what it means to gain or receive reward in the first place. It's about detachment, though the problem is that the more you shed, the more you find yourself in this demoralizing space, wondering to yourself, *what's the point? Why bother?* You know there's more than these earthly temptations and trinkets, and you want so badly to progress, but something is blocking you, and you just can't figure out what.

There's an interesting story in Mabry's *Growing into God* that illustrates this feeling, and it's one that has to do with the Merkobah mystics. The word "Merkobah" is Hebrew for "chariot," according to Mabry, and these mystics believed that "by hard word at specific mystical disciplines, they could gain access to" God's chariot, which they believed the Sun symbolized, and "which would carry them into

---

4. St. Teresa, *Interior Castle*, 32–33.

heavens" (think of how the prophet Enoch never died, but was described as being taken directly up to heaven).[5] Mabry, in his section on the Dark Night of the Senses, describes the interesting tale of Rabbi Akiva and the other three men who attempted to storm heaven and see God directly for themselves. They succeeded, but only Rabbi Akiva kept his senses enough to tell of the consequences. In Mabry's summary of the tale, we see what happened to the other men:

> One's mind snapped and he went stark raving mad, spending the rest of his life in restraints in a cell. Another, having accessed the throne room of God, beheld not one God, but two! Upon his return he was exiled as a heretic.

> But the final rabbi is the one we are most concerned with. This rabbi gained entrance to paradise and when he came back, he simply lost all interest in anything else. Food lost its flavor, study seemed empty, worship seemed rote. Even sex caused him to shrug his shoulders and go "eh…" which could not have pleased his wife. Nothing on this earthly plane could in any way compare to the glorious vision he'd beheld, so he simply stopped eating, wasted away, and died.[6]

In this chapter, Mabry speaks extensively about the signs and symptoms of experiencing this *Dark Night of the Senses*. He describes this as a transition from *purgation* to *illumination,* which will come later, and it's because this is a time of *detachment:* of learning not to grasp for some trophy that proves we're doing our spirituality right, as well as learning not to look for ways to fill the void in us that we haven't dealt with our entire lives.

---

5. Mabry, *Growing into God,* 48.

6. Ibid., 49.

More, it's a time of *contemplation,* of acceptance, of learning to do a lot with a little. It's a time when not only are we not finding any (obvious) progress towards the enlightenment we envision for ourselves, but all our other ways of self soothing have been ripped away from us on top of it. Think about this Sitting Room we've started this chapter with: there is *nothing* inside it. Nothing but the fire, four walls, a chair, and a little prayer book.

How long could you sit in a room like this before you started feeling that anxious itch deep under your skin? How long could you sit still with no stimuli—no games, no books, no phone, no work, no school, no friends, no food, no anything—until you began wanting to peel your brain out of your head? How *maddening* is it, knowing that God has given you power via the Breath of Life that created all humanity, has given you the Soul and its crystalline capacity for channeling down and transmuting God's raw, ineffable miracle to this earth, and that you are being asked *not to touch it* for some indescribable amount of time?

Now, here's the thing: yes, Mabry says that this is a transition, and that one has to do some purgation beforehand to get here. It's true in some sense! Realistically, purgation is the process you started in the Courtyard and the Foyer: it's what you did when you really analyzed yourself and picked away all your selfish reasons for getting into your magic like scabs off old wounds. It's what you did when you realized that spells to find a boyfriend or win the lottery or make your high school bully's life miserable maybe *weren't* going to make you any happier than you are now (or even realistically work in the first place in the case of a lottery spell, as you realize that's… not really what magic is *for* or how it works). After all, how could you ask yourself all those hard questions and dive into all these intimidating new things and not begin detaching from the life you knew before? How could you not begin shedding pieces from the old you, like the scales that fell from St. Paul's eyes after being blinded by his encounter with the risen Christ, as you interrogated your own motives and threw all you knew into a new perspective?

However, it's also something you are going to continue doing again and again and again. As Mabry points out, dark nights of the senses like these can come out of nowhere, and like any other part of this

journey, you're not going to go through it only once in your life.[7] It's
not to be confused with clinical mental health issues like depression or
anhedonia or other conditions that make life feel impossible and fruitless
(and please do consult your mental healthcare provider whenever you
feel your mental health is suffering), but it is a notable point in the
mystical journey that we all hit at one time or another.

And it's also yet another invitation to look inward. When everything
is going well for you, only for your legs to be swept out from underneath you, it's a moment not to scramble up and keep running, but to
sit with that pain and really pick it apart. To stop asking for a return to
a life you *thought* you wanted, and instead begin asking yourself what
God wants for your life. This can feel horrible, especially when we're
told that the closer we get to God, the *better* life should be, the shinier
and more perfect. St. Teresa likewise identifies people who run into the
struggle of the third room and notes a certain something about them:

> I HAVE known some, in fact, I may say numerous souls,
> who have reached this state, and for many years lived,
> apparently, a regular and well-ordered life, both of body
> and mind. It would seem that they must have gained the
> mastery over this world, or at least be extremely detached
> from it, yet if His Majesty sends very moderate trials
> they become so disturbed and disheartened as not only
> to astonish but to make me anxious about them. Advice
> is useless; having practised virtue for so long they think
> themselves capable of teaching it, and believe that they
> have abundant reason to feel miserable.

> The only way to help them is to compassionate their
> troubles; indeed, one cannot but feel sorry at seeing peo-
> ple in such an unhappy state. They must not be argued
> with, for they are convinced they suffer only for God's

---

7. Ibid., 50.

sake, and cannot be made to understand they are acting imperfectly, which is a further error in persons so far advanced. No wonder that they should feel these trials for a time, but I think they ought speedily to overcome their concern about such matters. God, wishing His elect to realize their own misery, often temporarily withdraws His favours: no more is needed to prove to us in a very short time what we really are.[8]

Read that again and again. These unhappy people *cannot be told* that they're acting imperfectly—that they're refusing to let the space opening up within them remain empty of expectations, misunderstandings, and desires, even if they try to tell themselves they have none of these things because of how much virtue they've supposedly accumulated. The ego is cruel, and like a parasite, it does what it can to hide its presence from its host as it entrenches itself.

Still, though, does that make you uncomfortable? The idea that God might start to withdraw a bit, the way a parent's hand withdraws from a child's arm as they begin to learn the balance of riding a bike? That in between that sudden perceived space between you and God, there is the opportunity for crash, for wreckage? More, does it make you uneasy to think of handing everything over to God like that, and letting Him draw up a new five year plan for you that looks nothing like your own? Does it scare you, or make you shrink back from God? If so, let us tell you: that's normal. It doesn't make you a bad person. But it *does* mean you have some hard questions to ask yourself, and more importantly, some things to deconstruct.

Yes, deconstruct. There is *much* more to break down and deconstruct than just your old religious beliefs, you know. Much, much more. In the process of deconstruction, you will absolutely end up shredding everything you ever grew up knowing about Jesus—but you'll end up shredding everything you ever thought you knew about yourself, too, and that's something that a lot of books on deconstructing from specifically Evangelical Christianity might not tell you.

8. St. Teresa, *Interior Castle*, 34-35.

In this quiet space of the Sitting Room, where there are no distractions, no comforts, and no outlets for you to dissipate your discomfort, you have no choice but to look it head on and pour it all into that great fire. So let us help you through the process of purging yourself, and baptizing yourself not just in water, but in that great Someone's flame.

What Does it Mean to Properly Deconstruct One's Faith?

"How do I deconstruct without losing my faith? I'm afraid that if I do this, I won't believe in God anymore."

We've heard this question many times in some shape or form, with the biggest block to starting that deconstruction either explicitly stated (like above) or heavily implied to be the fear of losing one's religion, and so it's only natural that we would have to talk about breaking apart our understanding of Religion along with the Self. After all, the faith we grew up with holds a space in our hearts for better or worse, and it's often the very foundational pillar that we were told to build our Self on to begin with. No matter our experiences with it, there's something about it that makes it hard to let go, especially when it's the lynch pin keeping people together for things like the holidays. It's not easy to avoid *Christ*ianity when you meet up for *Christ*mas dinner, you know? But it's at this point that one would do well to remember that old adage: you can't fill a cup that's already full. As such, while we've touched on the ways that HCRs can kneecap people who leave a church but not the behaviors that church taught them, now we actually have to dive deeply into both belief *and* behavior, so we can empty ourselves of the things we were taught and refill ourselves with new (and most importantly, honest and accurate) information to keep moving along our path with.

By the end of this deconstruction process, this could look like anything from shifting to a different interpretation of the same religion and coming to a fresh understanding of many of the concepts that haunted you growing up, to outright leaving the label "Christian" behind because you realize it never quite fit you to start. We can't tell you what'll happen at the end of your own journey; nobody knows except you, and you'll only know by marching forward. It's a risk you'll have to take if you're serious about finding the real God beyond the substanceless sock puppet that modern western Christianity has tried to convince you He is. It's peeling back the many layers of illusions that organized religion has given us that'll help you find your true path forward, as well as help you purge your own Self of habits, behaviors, and patterns of thinking that no longer serve you. This includes habits and ideas around the very *meaning* of deconstruction, too, as we, Sara and Mimi, have seen some… *interesting* interpretations of the word.

The bare idea of deconstruction is touched on in the first book, *Discovering Christian Witchcraft,* alongside a hefty argument for why and how we practice. However, a lot of folks fall into the trap of "take what resonates and feels good, leave what doesn't," when they start dipping their toes into the realm of magic and spirit and energy. People call this convenient practice "discernment," and surely "discernment" is a good tool to have when listening to others talk about faith, sin, devils, angels, God, Satan, magic, prayer, and whatever else you might be investigating in this bold adventure we call Christian Witchcraft.

However.

True deconstruction is like dealing with a broken leg bone. If you don't break it clean, and more, if you don't set it right and put it in a splint, your bone may eventually heal, but it won't heal right; it'll leave you with a limp, the bone all gnarled and fused together in a way that leaves you stiff and in constant, chronic pain for the rest of your life. Ask yourself: what do you have to do if you don't break something cleanly, or if it isn't set right?

Well, sometimes, you might have to re-break it to set it straight, not try to nurse and baby the mangled thing to avoid that extra pain.

Many, *many* people, when they deconstruct, don't end up breaking their old views cleanly *or* setting them back in alignment in reconstruction after. They end up stuck in that Foyer space, wandering around blind and not realizing why they can't see, because they haven't shed any light on the deeply ingrained subconscious factors that their beliefs spring up from. What happens is something of a 180 degree turn: rather than trying to mold themselves to religious and spiritual ideology that hurts them like they did in the church, these folks unwittingly over-correct and run for ideology that makes them *feel good* (but doesn't challenge them) instead. We see this in many places online, and as much as we hate to admit it, sometimes, the more Evangelical types have a point in relation to this stuff. The math might be all wrong, but they do occasionally still get the right answer.

One of those times is in the case of deconstruction, as in *The Deconstruction of Christianity: What it is, Why It's Destructive, and How to Respond* by Alisa Childers and Tim Barnett. While we certainly don't recommend or endorse this book, as it is exactly what you'd expect from a set of Evangelical Christians trying to tell you why deconstruction destroys perfectly "good" faith (and should therefore be avoided like the actual plague so you never even risk walking away from the white-washed tomb they call a church), they do make this one *really* good point that we have to give to them:

> As Christians, we should seek to reject false ideas. We ought to stand against abuse. But we will be unable to discern whether or not a teaching is abusive if we don't have a way to know what is correct in the first place. And we certainly cannot settle these theological disputes without an objective standard to appeal to. This requires the Bible. Deciding theological positions by what one perceives to be helpful vs. harmful, oppressive vs. liberating, or right vs. wrong is an invalid method for doing theology. If we simply follow some type of internal moral compass to determine which beliefs are "harmful," we might inadvertently reject truth in favor of our sensibilities.[9]

Granted, we don't think Childers and Barnett really know what the Bible actually says about things like witchcraft or homosexuality or any of these other hot button topics. In fact, they prove that they wouldn't when, for example, they refer to exclusively anti-LGBTQ+ apologists to help themselves feel better about their belief that modern society's growing acceptance of LGBTQ+ people is some sinful and terrible sign

---

9. Alisa Childers and Tim Barnett, *The Deconstruction of Christianity: What it is, Why it's Destructive, and How to Respond* (Stream: Tyndale Elevate, 2023), 120.

of ungodly times. As one would expect, they also conveniently ignore *pro*-LGBTQ+ apologists like Matthew Vines, author of *God and the Gay Christian,* and they seem to forget that apologetics work in all directions, not just the ones they like. They, too, fall victim to the "take what resonates, leave what doesn't" philosophy, even if they don't realize it.

Unfortunately, we don't have time to get into all of those specifics (but we do recommend Vines' book if you're interested on why being part of the LGBTQ+ community isn't sinful). We just want to be clear here: the fact is that Childers and Barnett could and *did* produce this true statement about requiring source text to inform our theology, even if they ironically stuck that statement in the middle of a barrage of nonsense about why women couldn't be leaders of the church and why Evangelical Christianity doesn't actually have ties to white supremacy. This is, frankly, another simple case of a broken clock still being right twice a day, and that's about it.

After all, let's use the idea of *charity* as an example of how deconstruction could fall apart the way they're talking about. You couldn't exactly "deconstruct" the Biblical command to help the poor and destitute by saying that giving up your hard-won money to some random person doesn't "resonate" with you. It would be very difficult to argue that God would actually be *totally fine* with you hoarding your wealth at the expense of others, especially given one of the few consistent rebukes the Bible makes is a rebuke against greedy people. You might *try* to point to the Book of Job, and how God replaced all of Job's stuff with even more abundance after his trials against Satan were over, or you might point to King David, who was a beloved of God even though he was a king with all kinds of money himself, but when we understand the context of these things, they are weak pieces of evidence that don't outweigh the many pointed, direct, and scathing rebukes of exorbitant wealth that people hoard and never put into a community.

Think of it like being in your literature classes in school again: when the teacher asks you to write a paper about a book you read, like *The Great Gatsby* or *Brave New World,* you can argue anything you want—*so long as you can back it up with the source material.* You might find secondary sources, like high quality scholarly articles and video essays and other books *about* these books that can help you explain your point, too, but you still have to be able to interpret the original books to be able to come to a sound conclusion. This is no different here with the Bible; your deconstruction process should be well reasoned and argued, like a solid paper defending your interpretation of a book you read in school. It should be based in the source text and informed with proper scholarly consideration of the historical and sociopolitical context, which will help you avoid the trap of the ego that tells you to do what is *comfortable* instead of what is *right*. This is what apologetics *should* look like.

So let us tell you something simple now: prosperity gospel is prosperity gospel, no matter if it looks like being promised a mansion for donating to church or being promised divine protection by focusing only on love and light and what "resonates" with your "highest good" (or whatever that means). The mentality that informs problematic things like prosperity gospel is one that acts as a shortcut to spiritual fruits; it's one that lets you cobble bits and pieces together into some Franken-Faith that, if you're not careful, quickly becomes full of parts that don't challenge you to grow anywhere past where you are right now, in this moment. As a result, those "shortcuts" don't actually give you any fruits at all, because they doesn't require you to put in the *work*. Moreover, it is something that actually holds you back from seeing what you are being called to, not something that heals you.

Let's think on some clearer examples. One thing that the modern church has sort of duped us all into believing, at one time or another, is that God will grant the wishes of your heart if you just ask him. Psalm 37:3-4 is a good example of that:

> Trust in the LORD and do good; dwell in the land and cultivate faithfulness. Delight yourself in the LORD, and He will give you the desires of your heart.

Sounds good, right? Just ask and trust that he will give you all that you need, provide everything! What a wonderful and gracious God! Except, they always forget the next part of that verse:

> Commit your way to the LORD; trust in Him, and He will do it.

Even if we just look at *only* this next verse (and we strongly recommend, if you are serious about this mystic path, to read the entire chapter and then come back to it during the last few chapters of this book), we are shown that it isn't just that God gives us what we want, but that we have to trust in Him and commit ourselves to Him. That's a lot more than just asking. A *lot* more than just doing what "feels right."

Thus, your deconstruction journey must be rooted in that desire not for vindication and comfort, but truth—and this means analyzing your own reactions to ideas as much as anything else, as well as deconstructing the very *way* you think, not just *what* you think.

Mimi Says:

Meditating on this has been like trying to explain what it's like going to a lazy river. There is such a rush as you're taken in (which we see in the Courtyard), the first turn or two is fun and a little scary, especially if they have buckets of water to dump on your head (Foyer), and now, finally, you're on the loop itself, and you can sit and relax. In the quiet, we find our nervous system resets after the rush. We're able to clearly look at ourselves without outside influence and see what burdens we carry. We are able to truly just sit and be... and then we realize that we cannot move out of this loop the same way we came in.

The turns start to get boring. The thrill is gone. The peace is gone. The panic sets in as you realize you can't get off, and you are going to go around and around and around the same cycle and never get anywhere. It isn't until you can stay calm long enough to truly focus and take in your entire surroundings that the exit appears, tucked into a corner somewhere that you would've missed if you kept trying to fight against the current and escape with sheer will alone.

The Sitting Room is a place to let your spirit rest. It is a place where you learn to sit with yourself, soothe yourself to remain calm and focused, and can simply be with yourself. A lot of times, when you finally get here, you swear that this is burnout or depression. Your practice feels pointless, you don't find joy in anything, and the way your mind rushes to find even a scrap of something to be entertained and distracted with instead of learning to exist in the silence feels unbearable. It pushes you into doubting yourself, your magic, your relationship with God, all of it, and this feeling that all your spiritual, emotional, and mental senses are *muffled, blocked,* is *why* this is called the Dark Night of the Senses. In many cases, this is where most people want to get off the ride so they can begin seeking their separate thrills again. They haven't overcome the *need* for all that in-your-face spirituality, and the thrill of feeling the Spirit hover near.

Of course, this is not to say that all these spiritual experiences are just something to overcome; *please* seek therapy and treatment from doctors and other professionals alongside your spiritual work! However, part of the Dark Night experiences can be viewed through a psychological lens to help achieve the centering and understanding you need to feel connected again. Shadow work, CBT, Somatic Therapy, these are all things that help you heal the wounds you haven't been dealing with head on and finally move forward. There isn't a doubt that the wounds are still there, some fresh and some still tender scars, but overall, wellness depends on a balance of things from spiritual, emotional, physical, occupational, and social wellness. Something like a break-up or a negative life event can throw you off balance, and what once was a comfort now feels like bland routine and drudgery. This can indicate a number of things and lend itself to the dryness of prayer and the lows of emotion St. Teresa talks about.

It isn't until the spiritual food we know is good for us to eat (be it Communion, our rituals, or any of our normal centering practices with God) start to taste like ash in our mouths that we realize things can't go on this way. Did you feel a tug to do something and deny it? Did you ignore the guidance of the Spirit and intuition somewhere along the way? Did you confuse "deconstruction" for avoiding the things that make you uncomfortable with yourself and your God? We can't say; only you know that. All we know is that when things get *this* dreary, that boring quiet is actually the loudest shout the Holy Spirit can make to knock you off your indulgences and make you say, "now, wait just a second!"

Because while deconstruction is important, it can feel like an endless cycle of tearing things down and reducing your beliefs to nothing more than dust and rubble. And, in fact, it is endless. Useless, even—unless you can calm your mind and spirit and finally acknowledge truths you didn't want to acknowledge. Welcome to the Sitting Room, where there is absolutely nothing to keep your focus off those truths. No doors. No windows. No place to sit. Silence.

You might ask yourself, "Where is God in all this silence?" And we'll tell you: He's there. He's seeing you take the steps you need to let this layer of Ego go, to let this piece of your Shadow self be absorbed and forgiven. This is very similar to the Michaelangelo painting, where Adam is barely reaching his finger out to touch God while He is reaching as far as He can to man—we find our strength to reach back in the depths of the silence, and that silence... hurts. It feels *wrong*. It feels like we've been abandoned, or like we never had any connection to the Divine to begin with. But here, silence is sometimes necessary to teach you your own boundaries for spiritual hygiene. How much of this is still you limping along, doing what you've always done, and expecting God to show up in very obvious ways? To magically fix you up for free so you can make the same mistakes again and end up in the same spot?

You're not in Kansas anymore, you know. You're going to have to learn to get comfortable with being uncomfortable. You're going to have to learn how to sit here and break things down one by one until you are at rock bottom—and that means learning how to deconstruct in a way that *helps*, not hurts, your walk forward.

The Adversary Opens His Case: All That Resonates is Not Gold

What's easier to do: try to walk the narrow path, fall down, and pick yourself up covered in bruises and scratches to keep walking? Or to convince yourself that the ground you landed on is actually the coziest, comfiest place in the world, and that you're perfectly content lying there in the dirt? That you don't need to do more or go any farther?

That you are *enlightened now*, covered in filth that you tell yourself is glitter?

When it comes to deconstruction, the concept of "take what resonates, leave what doesn't" is, like most things, a double-edged sword: to follow this concept healthily leads to one person deciding what religious system, or what denomination of a religious system, actually brings them those "fruits of the spirit" from Galatians we've discussed before. To follow it *unhealthily*, however, is to do what people call "throwing the baby out with the bathwater": creating a messily hacked up carcass of what their former faith once was, which later leads to reforming (or altogether abandoning) their faith on equally rocky premises and definitions. For example, let's take a look at this bit from Childers' and Barnett's investigation of the deconstruction scene, in which they focus on one man, Jake, who left the faith and church after being an ardent member of both for years:

> Specifically, Jake identifies his realization about the true nature of faith as "the biggest piece" of his deconversion to atheism. So what did he discover about faith? Defining the word, he says, "It's believing in something when you don't have all the evidence for it, or you don't know for certain." Jake goes on to add, "Once I realized how much of my faith was based on faith, a flip switched in my brain and . . . I just knew that I didn't want to have to believe things on faith anymore."[10]

Again, we will be patently clear here: this book is one that certainly goes out of its way to paint a less than charitable picture of people who collect themselves under community labels like "ex-vangelical" or who collect their thoughts around hashtags like #deconstruction. However, that doesn't mean that every person who deconstructs, or every person who calls themselves ex-vangelical, is automatically correct in doing what "resonates." This quote is a perfect example of what happens when one "deconstructs" without fully understanding the concepts they're deconstructing in the first place.

Moreover, this isn't our dear Jake's fault, of course. His definition of faith is exactly right: one *does* need to believe, not know irrefutably, that God is there and that this path is true. You cannot prove religion. You cannot logic your way to God. In a highly rational, logic-based world, this is hard to deal with. Yet "spiritual leaders" like Childers and Barnett tell these folks that faith *can* be proven, which exacerbates the feelings of

10. Childers and Barnett, *The Deconstruction of Christianity*, 127.

betrayal when people like Jake find out that's not true and sends them in the completely opposite direction. In the very next bit, Childers and Barnett are using Hebrews 11:1 to justify defining "faith" like so:

> Faith is the assurance of things hoped for, and assurance entails solid reasons to believe something. Think about the last time you were "assured" something was true. It was probably after you examined the reasons to be convinced of its truthfulness. We find assurance only when we have a sufficient amount of evidence.[11]

The problem is, Hebrews 11:1 as they quote it—"Now faith is the *assurance* of things hoped for, the *conviction* of things not seen"—is not always translated so. "Assurance," the word they hinge their ideas on, is also translated sometimes as "confidence" (like in the New International Version). Being *confident* in something, however, is not having irrefutable evidence of something.

Moreover, Hebrews 11 does describe a list of people with faith in the promises of God, like Childers and Barnett say, but they apparently missed the line of Hebrews where St. Paul acknowledges that all these people who had such faith never saw those promises fulfilled; "these were all commended for their faith, yet none of them received what had been promised, since God had planned something better for us so that only together with us would they be made perfect," according to Hebrews 11:39–40. Childers and Barnett also point to Jesus performing miracles in order to prove that He does have the power to forgive sins, thus providing *evidence* for the faith people are to hold afterwards, but how many times does Jesus rebuke those who need evidence to have faith, and bless those who can believe without seeing?

As we know, poor Doubting Thomas has been called that for a reason by generations of Christians to come, and is the perfect example of how Jesus finds those who can believe *without* this evidence all the more blessed in John 20:29. The *Amplified Bible, Classic Edition* (AMPC) actually has a fascinating way of translating this verse that directly

---

11. Ibid., 139.

contradicts the point Childers and Barnett makes, and also reproves dear Jake there, too:

> Jesus said to him, "Because you have seen Me, Thomas, do you now believe (*trust, have faith*)? Blessed and happy and to be envied are those who have never seen Me and yet have believed and adhered to and trusted and relied on Me." (Emphasis ours.)

Again, this is where folks like Jake may have taken a wrong turn to begin with, of no fault their own, by being introduced to a flawed definition of faith. Often, the more Evangelical branches of modern western Christianity will put a hard focus on this idea of their religion being the *objective* truth, something capable of being directly proved with hard evidence the same way any scientific truth might be; this is what creates less-than-honest "scholars" of Christianity who are, in fact, merely apologists trying to find ways to dance around the reality that the Bible's stories (like Adam and Eve, the flood, etc.) are *metaphorical,* not literal.

It's this desperation to have "proof," to have something tangible that can be seen, verified, and most importantly, *not questioned or challenged,* that caught Sara in such a snare trying to write this book about faith and what is unseen to begin with. After all, what we believe becomes the foundation of who we are, no? As such, it follows that if it's not built on solid, stable pillars, then our beliefs—and by extension, our very core, our identities—are no better off than something built in the shifting sands of the desert, especially according to people like Jake or others coming out of this Evangelical understanding of the term.

To build "faith on faith," as Jake puts it, or to build one's beliefs based on *trust* and *hope* in something's existence or promises rather than concrete evidence, is terrifying, and breaking that down often leads people away from their starting religion as they try (and perhaps fail) to cope with the reality of what faith is. But notice that, in this story, neither Jake nor the ones trying to push back against him (Childers and Barnett) seem to have the right idea? Notice how the former is deciding to throw the whole concept away, while the latter are trying to break the bones of Scripture to appease their own fears of believing in something that isn't perfectly provable as objective truth (even when they claim not to be doing this)? Whether "deconstructed" or not, neither party here has an honest understanding of the term, only one that helps them avoid the discomfort of *cognitive dissonance:* the genuine anguish that occurs in the mind when holding two conflicting ideals or facts.

This is only one example of deconstruction gone sideways, of course, but it is a prime example of how *foundational* concepts like how we define faith can get so bungled that it becomes hard to see past what we've been taught, even when we *think* we're walking away from them. If we go from Childers and Barnett to a more pro-deconstruction book, we can see this exact phenomena in action when Karla Kamstra (or Rev. Karla) discusses her experiences as a TikTok creator dealing with the general public in her book, *Deconstructing: Leaving Church, Finding Faith.*

Rev. Karla's platform revolves around her work as an interfaith minister with her own long journey of deconstructing the harmful paradigms of her Southern Baptist upbringing. In her book, she discusses everything from blind obedience to pastors to the expectation to burn oneself out giving free labor to the church to accepting verbal abuse from spiritual leaders. She also discusses the deep fear of leaving her faith community that she eventually overcame—only to be met with deep loneliness and isolation that occurs when no community is left. This book a powerful discussion of the challenging work of *rebuilding* one's faith and spirituality after this collapse of one's otherwise deeply entrenched place in a religious community, and we recommend it if you're looking for more first-hand accounts of these spiritual upheavals and rebirths.

More than just a memoir, though, in this book, Rev. Karla shares stories of folks in her comments of folks who have exited the church and deconstructed, only to sit around with the same harmful ideas or paradigms as the religion they claim to have left. In one example, on a video where Rev. Karla affirms the LGBTQ+ community's right to exist without constant threat of hellfire or damnation, a purported atheist claimed she was lying—that the faith he was taught growing up, and the Bible itself, claimed that being part of the LGBTQ+ community was a sin. In response, Rev. Karla pushed back quite gently, with an interesting result:

> While it's uncommon to receive comments saying that the Bible says being gay is a sin (for the record, it isn't), I found it interesting that someone who identified as an atheist felt the need to state his nonbelief while defending this homophobic interpretation of scripture.

> That is basically what I said to this person, and his response back was even more perplexing. He became very defensive and insulting, insisting that he couldn't care less about the harm it does to the LGBTQIA+ community. He reiterated that if they're gay, they're going to hell because being gay is a sin. He ended one comment with, "The truth is the truth."

A couple paragraphs later, Rev. Karla reflects on this (and other such related moments) with this sentiment:

> While many [people] have said they "deconstructed" from religion, which led to their now identifying as spiritual but not religious, agnostic, or atheist, most of them could not quantify their deconstruction process beyond "leaving the church."[12]

Now, in our own work as TikTok creators and people engaging with the general public in the world of spirituality, we (Mimi and Sara) have seen much of the same pitfalls in spiritual spaces online, especially on #witchtok. This is where the Adversary so easily snags even the most

---

12. Karla Kamstra, *Deconstructing: Leaving Church, Finding Faith* (New York: St. Martin's Essentials, 2024), 49.

well-intentioned person "deconstructing" their faith and traps them in the quicksand of their initial belief systems, even if they think they've found stable rock instead. He does this by diluting the concept of deconstruction, or allowing people to believe that deconstruction in and of itself is some free-for-all of just throwing out any ideas that make us uncomfortable.

All too often, what happens is that people who "left the church" then go and enter a new temple with rules they don't realize are different from what they know. They take all their Christian baggage, and the implicit, more abstract beliefs that stem from it, and try to wholesale apply it to non-Christian faiths as they "convert" to some flavor of paganism or begin practicing something like witchcraft. Worse, just as Christian apologists engage in radical mental gymnastics to support a patently untenable worldview (like the idea that the entire world was only made in 6,000 human years), so too do those who deconstruct do the same mental gymnastics to support radically ahistorical narratives that support a very comfortable space to the ego: the space of the victim.

This sounds harsh. When reading those words, it makes us sound perhaps like Childers and Barnett, whose entire book hits back at what they see as a weak, victim-centered culture where everything someone doesn't like can be easily dismissed with an accusation of some -ism or -phobia lying beneath the surface and where everyone can stay comfortable in their "sinful" lifestyle (or whatever). Of course, that's not at all what we mean. What we mean is that if there's one thing neither Christian apologists nor "deconstructionists" can readily swallow, it's that exact harsh truth: that facts do not illuminate what one *wants* to be true, only what *is* true, and that this goes for *both* Evangelicals and ex-vangelicals. As such, it really is ironic that one of the common phrases many mainstream Christians like to quote is that line from 2 Corinthians (11:14): *And no wonder, for Satan himself masquerades as an angel of light.*

To learn to accept facts and truth, even when uncomfortable and challenging? That is difficult. That hits people deep in their ego, rattles them from their seat of comfort, and breeds a dissonance in people's minds that torments them day in and day out until they find *something*, be it fact *or* fiction, that soothes that cognitive pain. Just like St. Paul's "devil" dresses in beauty and gold and loveliness to deceive people into thinking he's an angel, these narratives masquerade as truth to soothe the egos of the frightened and wounded.

However, the irony here comes from the fact that while there is a worthy warning in this verse, all too often, religious leaders and other members of a church will end up *becoming* the "devil" of this line more often than abating that devil. They'll use this line to sow even *more* doubt and confusion in the hearts of people who are trying to do the right thing (even if it goes against the norms and expectations that Christians are told to abide by), and this is because often, in HCRs (high control religions), a church is built in a pyramid-style hierarchy of power that makes those at the bottom entirely dependent on what the one (or few) at the top have to say. According to Dr. Anderson, going against the grain they set is often seen as one of the gravest sins of all in these "systems built on dynamics of power and control":

> Systems built on dynamics of power and control are abusive at their core. Within these systems is a hierarchy, typically built on patriarchy. At the top of this hierarchy is the leader(s) of the group who determines the roles, rules, and consequences and who—in the realm of high-control religions—is believed to be "called by God." This calling implies that followers will demonstrate submission and that the leader's words will not be questioned. Many systems also preach a message about the devil being actively at work in the world and wanting to tear down spiritual leaders. Many HCRs teach that suffering, being persecuted, and enduring hardships are either God's or the devil's way of testing you. This teaching creates a dynamic of silencing and suspicion as individuals who speak out about the leader(s) are often considered to be gossiping, persecuting the leader, or trying to stir up drama as an act of spiritual warfare. Concerns are dismissed or silenced.[13]

---

13. Anderson, *When Religion Hurts You,* chap. 3, sec. "Religious Abuse and Adverse Religious Experiences."

In environments like this, you're eternally taught to second guess yourself, never trust your own judgement (and especially not the ideas of outsiders), and take every direction from these "called" folk at the top who are just spiritually blessed to know better than you in every single circumstance somehow. No doubt many are familiar with refrains like Jeremiah 17:9 (*the heart is deceitful in all things…*), and it's all the easier to weaponize lines like 2 Corinthians 11:14 as a result. St. Paul's words are used to imply that the average person's judgement is twisted, wrong, corrupt, and unworthy of trust. It's easy to control a people, after all, if they're trained to outsource their intuition and play "Follow the Leader" instead of think for themselves and use their own discernment—and that very *style* of thinking isn't a single belief you can so easily pin down, refute, and cast aside like you can specific facts that you find are disproven by new evidence and discoveries.

When deconstructing, one must go deeper, to the very wiring of their minds and the very way they understand religion and religious text, along with the gods they're about. Many people leaving the evangelical church are at a disadvantage in this regard: folks who grow up with the doctrine known as *Sola Scriptura*, which is found in a lot of Protestant denominations and posits the Bible as the sole infallible source of authority for Christian faith and practice, are raised with a type of faith that's no doubt very sensitive to questions. Far too many people have been told that their faith is weak or that the devil has a hold of them for asking questions; some are even kicked out of Sunday school for their innocent, earnest questions altogether. Seeking knowledge is discouraged; pressing authority is taboo.

However, what these Protestants don't realize is that *Sola Scriptura* is considered a *heresy* in the eyes of the Roman Catholic Church (RCC). Maybe for the Protestants that don't care about what the RCC has to say, they don't care about being called heretics by them, either (and fair enough on that end), but these folks who cling to this doctrine also ignore its complete hypocrisy in logic because of how much and how often the Bible itself has changed and contradicted itself within its own books.

It also voids any prophetic or miraculous input from God, acting as if Revelation was the very last of the holy words God ever deigned to give us and thus rendering the two *thousand* years of Saints, prophets, mystics, and wonder workers that came afterwards as inconsequential at best, or actively deceived and dangerous to other believers at worst. If you see folks preaching on their works and testimony and proof of God, but you get dismissed when you ask about the miracles of Saints (because, according to them, those people were obviously either lying or using some other *false* power and pretending it was holy to lead people astray), then you see where this kind of double thinking leads.

Moreover, this kind of thinking is something that reading new books and getting new ideas alone cannot undo. It goes so far beyond simply replacing one set of surface level, nuanceless (yet nice sounding) "facts" with another from equally unqualified and bunk sources. A great example is the way in which people in HCRs are taught to never question God, to view Him as perfectly and always and forever Good and try, desperately, to rationalize away all the violence and chaos of many Biblical narratives as good and just and deserved, only to eventually leave those HCRs and then do the exact *opposite.* They then see God as a cruel dictator, an evil being hell bent on tyrannical control that has never done anything loving or beneficial, unlike any of the pagan gods and goddesses people often run to after leaving the church.

Ignore the fact that Demeter starved the entire world to get her daughter back from Hades, or that Loki literally ended the world by kickstarting Ragnarok; ignore the Roman poet Ovid's version of Medusa's myth, where Poseidon assaulted Medusa in Athena's temple and Athena punished *Medusa* instead of her uncle for it; ignore the way Izanagi abandoned his dead wife Izanami in the underworld because she'd become a decaying corpse, and she responded by committing to killing a thousand people every day to spite him. They're all *justified* in their actions; they're all still *good,* unlike that evil Christian God and His evil, tyrannical ways.

Suddenly, one god becomes the virtuous, the beautiful, and the fair, while another god becomes a demon set to trick humanity into following it and committing evil. When put like this, what exactly is the difference between an Evangelical that sees Satan behind every corner, waiting to drag them away from the light of God with these "false gods," these fallen angels or demons or what-have-you, and a "deconstructed" person who "sees the truth" about the God they grew up with, and "realizes" Him to be no more than a devil? It's the same exact thought pattern, the same exact story, just with the names of said gods switched around; the surface level idea has been "deconstructed," the perspective flipped, but the way in which one thinks *about* myths, gods, and faiths themselves shows us exactly the same thought process as that of those in their old church community.

We've discussed examples of this in some effect in *Discovering Christian Witchcraft*, like with the argument that Christians "stole" pagan holidays (when it was actually a much more nuanced and interesting process known as *syncretism*), or the idea that the church was burning "witches" (when it was actually just a convenient excuse to get rid of women, Jewish people, and other political adversaries instead). However, the tendency to point to the Christian God as an evil demon always hell bent on killing everyone, or the Church as only ever bringing death and destruction everywhere it went, or Christianity as only ever an institution full of all the –isms and –phobias we can think of, is not a sign of truth-seeking or deconstruction; it is a sign of *wound*. It is a mark of someone who, when boiled down to the bare essence of this behavior, is just doing the same thing they've always been taught to do: point fingers at the perceived "enemy" and demonize everything about them with no nuance or considerations outside the point of view that allows them to hold the position of righteous victim against an evil, toxic assailant.

Does this mean Christianity as an institution has never done anything horrible to any culture, tribe, or other faith? That all Christians have always been the persecuted, loving lambs just out to peacefully spread the good word and nothing more? Or that modern Christianity doesn't provide people with a socially acceptable framework for holding all manners of harmful beliefs that strip innocent people's rights away based on their sexuality or gender or race or anything else? Of course not. To ignore the harm that Christians, the Catholic Church, and Christianity at large have done would be no better than to ignore the good that so many church historians and theologians credit it with; it would be just as ahistorical, just as nuanceless, and just as delusional. And yet, it is this delusion that captures both devout and deconstructed folk alike, because it feeds something more primal than the need for knowledge and truth: the need for *comfort,* and for *vindication.*

The Adversary offers you this comfort like a sweet fruit; he baits you with this vindication and validation every time he offers you a quip you can't cite the source of, a "resonating" belief you can't back up in the spiritual source texts (Bible, apocrypha, etc.), or an idea that you've heard enough people repeat (and therefore are sure must be true to some extent, because why else would people be repeating it?). Every time you reel at a fact that cracks your worldview open, or dig your heels in at an idea that makes you viscerally uncomfortable, or close the book and throw it in the trash for saying something that challenges you, you are not serving the higher mind and soul's need for truth: you are serving the ego's need for self preservation and comfort. Much like the body doesn't go where the mind doesn't push it in training and exercise, the ego will not go where the higher will does not guide it.

When we sit in the comfort of the ego—the belief that we are right, and that everyone else is wrong, or that if the church that hurt us was wrong, then everything the exact opposite of what it ever said *must* be right instead, or any other number of fallacies that people pick up when leaving the church—we stop ourselves from growing. We stop asking the tough questions, we stop grappling with the hard truths, and we stagnate there in our comfort, like an animal in captivity given all the snacks it could need with no reason to move.

That makes us mentally, spiritually, and emotionally weak. When the Adversary gives you this opportunity for weakness, it is to trap you in this Sitting Room: to make you dream a long dream, to think you've reached the end of the line of your growth when you most certainly have *not*. Worse, the Adversary can and *will* prosecute you for this soon enough. When you take this bait, fall for this trap, it soon snowballs into punishments you cannot avoid: like those people St. Teresa mentioned who don't even realize they're acting imperfectly, you may find yourself saddled with hubris that has you mocking or blocking others who push back on your claims. You may experience a disconnect with reality and a sense of anti-intellectualism as you spit on valid sources as "conspiracies," or find yourself wearing rose-colored lenses regarding one situation while taking unforgiving, uncharitable views of another. Worst of all, you may have an inability to see how the *roots* of the beliefs you claimed to deconstruct still inform how you view *new* faiths and ideas, and the prejudices you may not realize you still carry with you.

Ways to avoid this trap are to not only *read*, but to *talk* and *connect* and *explore:* to engage with perspectives outside our own, chart our initial feelings and reactions to these things, show ourselves grace when something triggers us and put it away for later, and to then *actually* come back to it later. Above all, we avoid this trap by being humble enough to recognize when we are not experts in a topic, and to *trust* the experts, the scholars, to enlighten us rather than insist that a little bit of internet searching can match years and years of in-person study and devotion to the field. Rev. Karla explains her approach in her book:

> When I began my deconstruction journey, I knew I no longer wanted to be bound to this theology and entrenched in fear, and I wanted to untangle who I was becoming from the beliefs that held me captive. For me, that meant becoming a voracious reader of scholars and sages to understand the Bible outside the construct of my religious heritage… deconstructing should include a peeling back of indoctrinated beliefs to see them outside the construct of your religious heritage.

> Without this work of deconstructing, there is a risk of holding on to biases and prejudices that will continue to impact how you are showing up in the world. And how we show up in the world is what I believe is one of the most critical elements of spirituality.[14]

There's a reason that, despite religion and spirituality being things science will never be able to "prove" and which we know are largely based on myths of ancient people, there is still such a focus on *truth*. Truth is paramount in a walk with God: the kind of truth that forces us not only to come to terms with the world we live in, but the fracture lines of our own selves, the weaknesses born of that ego's animal desire

---

14. Kamstra, *Deconstructing*, 50–51.

for comfort and safety. Truth provides no quarter, no shelter, to such a beast; truth has no means to seduce us into complacency, because it continues to challenge us to accept it when the lies we tell ourselves are sweeter.

Truth is bitter medicine, but it must be taken. Otherwise, you languish in the same sickness you thought you defeated, like "waking up" from a dream only to find that you're still asleep, still trapped in a surreal world warped by all things that torment you from deep within. You stay on a fruitless journey to nowhere, like a moth, advancing not towards the silver sheen of the moon but the distracting, destructive flame of someone else's candlelight.

What an easy day in court it'll be for your Adversary, if you can't overcome such vice—if you let your wings burn on that fiery, false light.

Sara Says:

Boy, was it funny when I saw folks complaining that we decided to include a chapter on demons in *Discovering Christian Witchcraft*. So, so funny that they thought that "proved" the book was evil or against Christianity or something, all because I tried to tell people to... not be scared of demons and that they can actually be pretty handy partners in deconstruction and spirituality. I understand why these folks would have that knee jerk reaction to the mention of demons in a Christian book, but it had to be done! People had to know that there is a way of engaging with spirituality that does *not* mean living in fear about beings that do not actually operate in the way people think they do.

And you know what? I'll say it again just to ruffle a few more feathers: there is no little red devil with a pitchfork and goat horns waiting to poke you in the back end and torture you into an early grave, okay? Nor are the members of the Ars Goetia, that compendium of seventy-two *Kings* and *Presidents* and *Princes* (and more) of Hell, just waiting around to catch you and ruin your life—not any more than the seventy-two corresponding angels that are matched up to each and every one of them in those medieval occult grimoires.

No, rather, in my time speaking with other people and witnessing other practices, especially occult, demon-centered practices, I came to learn something quite interesting: the demons seem to be helping my friends grow the same spiritual fruits that the Bible says are a sign of the Holy Spirit, just with a radically different method.

Impossible! So might those anti-demon folk say. *Only darkness comes from demons!*

And yet, my friends who work with demons are a delight to be around, and a light to their communities. Not the false light of St. Paul's devil, but a true light, with the love, kindness, forbearance, and more that he advocated for the early Christian communities to foster.

You see, I can measure not the *goodness* of a spirit (because who am I to go throwing these kinds of judgements around on ancient beings?), but rather *how beneficial* a spirit is *to me specifically* by measuring what they give me and what they leave behind in me. As such, in my walk with the demons, I've found that they are adept at clearing one's spiritual fields so that the fruits one actually wants can grow. In fact, if we take a look at Daniel C. Matt's *The Essential Kabbalah. The Heart of Jewish Mysticism,* he says plainly what I've learned from my own experience: "From a more radical perspective, evil originates in divine thought, which eliminates waste before emanating goodness. The demonic is rooted in the divine."[15]

And it makes sense, doesn't it? How can you grow spiritual fruits in a field overtaken by earthly weeds and wild things that get in your way? It was in the experience of the Qliphoth, or "Tree of Death/Knowledge," a medieval occult extrapolation of Jewish Kabbalah's Sefirot, or "Tree of Life," that I realized (with some shock) that the demons I'd grown up being told were so evil and out to kill me were actually just... not interested in coddling me through my own spiritual development.

Just like St. Teresa's *Interior Castle,* we might think of the Qliphoth as something of a mystic initiation pathway, with different steps and lessons to learn; for folks who approach the Divine through the Demonic, this path makes a considerable amount of sense compared to the ways more commonly used in mainstream Christian religious life, like those of the Saints. And if I'm to be candid with you, in my opinion, it's also a system of mystic journeying that, due to how it's presented, much more easily appeals to the *ego* for those who are rubbed wrong

---

15. Daniel C. Matt, *The Essential Kabbalah: The Heart of Jewish Mysticism* (USA: HarperOne, 2009), 6.

by the way modern Christianity explains–often incorrectly–concepts of submission, obedience, faith, and their own human frailty in the face of the Divine.

By that I mean: as it is still a mystic system of initiation, it destroys and liquidates your ego anyway. It's actually something of a cruel trick: the path that promises all this nonsense about "ascension" and "becoming a god rather than submitting to one" still, if one is serious about it, hooks people up to Divinity anyway and makes all the things they might've started the path for seem so dull and meaningless afterwards, like all the enlightened sages over time who realized their food and money and fine dress meant nothing and sold it all to be ascetic monks and Saints instead. In the end, the packaging is different, but the results are practically the same. Whether you willingly walk to the cross with Christ and crucify your ego, or your ego gets goaded into seeking the decadent taste of power like a mouse seeking the peanut butter on a mouse trap, *something* will die by journey's end, and it will leave space for something to be born anew.

Before I say anything else, because I know this will be a point of contention in someone's mind at some point, I should make something very clear: even if the Qliphoth comes from the idea of the Sefirot, is *not* the Sefirot, nor does it any longer qualify as specifically Jewish mysticism to engage in it. To say otherwise would be to say that Christianity itself is still Judaism just because it's built on the foundation of Judaism and Jesus Himself was Jewish. This is obviously false. Christianity comes from Judaism, but it has become a different system entirely and has become accessible to different groups of people as a result. There will always be a conversation about appropriation and misuse of concepts, and the reality is that avoiding any and all traces of Judaism is honestly impossible to avoid if you are a Christian, because our religion is inherently based in the other; like St. Paul says in the metaphor of an olive tree with grafted branches in Romans 11:11-24, we shouldn't spurn the origins of our religion, nor disrespect them, nor take them for granted, because we are supported by that *root*, that founding faith.

Judaism being our root doesn't mean that we are free to practice Judaism wholesale, of course; I will say that the actual Sefirot of bona fide Jewish Kabbalah is *not* our system of climbing up to God, the same way actual Jewish holidays and festivals are *not* our method of religious practice and observance. Even if we have Judaism as our origin, that doesn't mean we need to make "Christian seders" and whatever nonsense when we have our own holidays and traditions by virtue of becoming our own faith. I theorize that people do this because they want their religion to feel more "legitimate" or storied; it's often those specific individual churches who have little to no rich history, cultural syncretisms, and tradition to fall back on, and who succumb to that *Sola Scriptura* doctrine, that are most prone to trying to abide by some warped and misconstrued idea of Jewish tradition than anyone else.

But to give you some much needed context before I talk more about the demons: the Sefirot are ten emanations of God that signal things about His character. In practice, as a map for a mystical journey, I understand them as functioning something like little mini-worlds, like Candyland board spaces, that one hops their way up to eventually reach God at the very top in the sphere called Keter. The Kabbalist initiates through these spheres much the way the demonolater does in the Qliphoth, learning and contemplating the qualities of God along the way (like Geburah, the Severity of God, vs. Chesed, the Mercy of God, ever interlinked and held in perfect balance in the Sefirot).

And *in* Jewish Kabbalah, we also find an interesting theory of the *shells* left over from the creation of these spheres: when these spheres were born, it's believed they burst out of their shells much the way a butterfly might shed a cocoon, and those shells never disappeared; rather, they became all that was discarded and separated from God, and they became their *own* anti-worlds where the forces of evil (namely, demons) made their home. For example, Netzach, meaning *eternity,* is the sphere in the Sefirot about honest victory; it's the sphere in which, alongside Hod (*splendor*), the prophets find their voice and their means to prophesy. Netzach's opposite in the Qliphoth, A'arab Zaraq, is by contrast a sphere of consumption. From my experience and understanding, it's a sphere of winning by any means necessary, of employing scorched earth tactics that destroy everything so one might crown themselves king of the ashes left behind: a very Five of Swords energy, one could say.

It reminds me of the dichotomy we see so often in every other faith, system, or divine metaphor when talking about war: the part of war dedicated to strategy, wisdom, and lawful, honorable action, and the part of war dedicated to bloodlust, chaos, and the fever pitch of bloodshed. Tyr and Odin, Athena and Ares, these and more divine faces come to mind. Even the meanings of tarot can be seen here: Five of Wands right side up is a card of fighting hard, good competition, championship, and reversed, it's a card of dirty, *anything goes* fighting, doing whatever's necessary to choke out the competition. These concepts can be found virtually anywhere, but at the end of the day, the box these lessons come in doesn't change the lessons being learned.

Now, here's the thing: from what I understand of Jewish mysticism (which admittedly isn't a lot), one *does not touch* these Qliphotic shells. Why would they? This is quite literally the refuse of creation, the sewage, everything unholy and *wrong*. It's my understanding that nobody would, or should, go playing with that according to Jewish faith and mysticism, similar to the way Christians will say nobody should worship Satan as an anti-God. Yet there are still Satanists who, rather than let a good archetypal figure go to waste, make use of it in their own religious philosophies no matter what Christianity thinks about them doing that.

The Qliphoth is called the *Sitra Ahra,* the *other side,* and according to Matt, it's what is created when Severity (Geburah) is out of line with love and Mercy (Chesed), becoming a force unbalanced, and therefore one that "lashes out and threatens to destroy life."[16] And yet, long after these ideas were all circulated among Jewish and Christian mystics alike in the middle ages (with Christians often appropriating them for the express concept of trying to get Jewish people to convert to Christianity, unfortunately, so there is more nuance and care to take with this issue than the Christian/Satanist comparison drawn earlier),[17] no doubt somebody looked at those Qliphotic shells and said, "hell yeah, I can probably use these to become my own god and master rather than submit to any other god out there." They then took these off-limits negative husks of Kabbalah (along with a *lot* of other random stuff one

---

16. Matt, *The Essential Kabbalah,* 6.

17. Jewitches, "Kabbalah, Cabala, & Qabalah: Coercion, Appropriation, & the Desecration of Sacred Tradition," Substack, Oct 31 2024, https://jewitches.substack.com/p/kabbalah-ca bala-and-qabalah.

might find in this more modern, hodge-podge thing called Qabalah that the Qliphoth falls under) and made it into their own treasure, basically.

It's not a pretty history by any means, and lots of unsavory characters, like Aleister Crowley, have been mixed into all this, but that means the modern occultist has to be properly informed and culturally sensitive to this stuff rather than write it all off because it makes them uncomfortable. Nonetheless, all of this is why I say: the Qliphoth as a theory specifically came from Kabbalah, but it is not necessarily something you touch in Kabbalistic practice, which is similar to how Christianity came from Judaism, but is not compatible with Judaism whatsoever in its core beliefs, traditions, and practices. One should respect the root of this system and take care not to be a massive antisemite (of which there are unfortunately *many* in occult scenes), but that doesn't mean that one is suddenly going to be a master of Jewish tradition and faith by using the more comparatively modern occult system of mystic journeying like the Qliphoth, nor does it mean someone is Jewish or a Jewish mystic for engaging in it.

Now, to be clear, as we talk about deconstruction, and deconstructing "correctly," as well as sourcing our ideas from legitimate scholarship and religious texts rather than just making stuff up that makes us feel good, I *do* have to also make my own case against my own Adversary there: there is value in Unverified Personal Gnosis (UPG) when it comes to things like this (as, after all, the Saints' visions and writings we now take as a source of insight were once that same UPG), and there is value in being able to look at things from the perspective of those we perceive as opposed to us and hear *their* UPG, too.

I was a Christian Witch for almost ten years before taking the plunge into what the religious and cultural institutions of Christianity deemed *entirely* off limits: demons. What I didn't realize all that time prior was that by negotiating away the warnings against witchcraft as just the mistranslating of words that actually signaled poisoning or deception, I would fall into that "love and light" caveat. That philosophy instantly attached to my practice: that note that witchcraft was okay, so long as it wasn't hurting anyone or "going against God." In fact, it was *because* of finding those mistranslations that this "love and light" approach was so easily reinforced; as much as it's the truth, it also does little to illuminate the full breadth and reach and extent of God, as we've already talked about with our look back to *Anathema Maranatha.*

It also did absolutely nothing to change the *way* I thought about and understood magic, God, or spirituality in general; it didn't make me any less afraid of the dark, spirits, or demons, nor did it make me any more sure of the power God trusted me to use. For all my magic, and for all my lax Catholic upbringing, I still grew up in a culture where Hollywood could and would make a mess of King Paimon's name in *Hereditary* (2018) or where churches insisted there was a devil waiting to eat me around every corner; I still had to fight my parents to allow me to research my craft as they were overcome with fear that I'd get actually, *physically* hurt by some dangerous, otherworldly force they couldn't protect me from.

Worst of all, I still had nightmares where my magic did nothing against the shadows that chased me down. This meant that I still didn't trust in the power God gave me, and therefore, by extension, I didn't really trust God to protect me, either (even if I never would've admitted, or even recognized, such a thing).

At some point, though, we realize we have a choice to live in fear or face our fears. It wasn't until I watched that silly Netflix series, *Lucifer,* that I wondered if maybe the devil I'd grown up thinking was evil and terrible had more to him than what we've been told. I wondered about why someone evil would torture evil men, and I wondered if maybe Lucifer (or Satan or the Devil or whoever) wasn't just a guy out doing their job. Lo and behold, I would come to discover that Rabbinic philosophy of Satan as prosecutor a la the Book of Job later, as well as Stokes' work, but it was by my asking *what if?* that I even allowed myself to consider this "devil" as anything other than, well… *a devil.*

Then I got on #witchtok. I met people, like my dear friend Aziel (@heyaziel), who was gentle and kind despite working with the demons I'd been raised to fear, and who had the same values for justice and knowledge that I, a Christian, had. How could this be possible, if our religions and ideas of Divinity were such polar opposites? Weren't *Satanists* supposed to be selfish, callous, and out for their own goals at the expense of everyone else? Weren't they my enemy as a Christian, and diametrically opposed to everything I valued and was brought up to value? What did it mean, if we apparently valued not opposite things, but the same things—if they got the same comfort, sense of peace, and empowerment to stand against cruelty and injustice from *demons* as I did from my God?

Turns out that separation really *is* the root of all evil. It is through fear of the Other that the evils of division and separation persist: it is when we refuse to listen to those we believe are against us at all that we begin to dehumanize and want to destroy them, leading to the destruction of our own spiritual garden and the rotting of the fruits we should be cultivating from the Holy Spirit. What I discovered in my opening up to people not like me was exactly what we said in the very beginning of this book: that any path that brings the spiritual fruits St. Paul outlined in Galatians is one worth respecting. And if what I knew about the people who followed those demons could be so tragically and terribly wrong, then what about the demons themselves? Was there more to them than I realized?

You already know the answer. In my friendship with Aziel, I found the pathway forward to my brazen exploration of demons: my first conversation with Lucifer in *Where the Gods Left Off*, my follow-up with him that Aziel facilitated, and my foray into the texts and ideologies and philosophies of people who walk the Left Hand Path (so, the people who often identify as Satanists, Luciferians, "demonolaters," etc.). I discovered their beliefs are only "diametrically opposed" to Christianity on the surface, in that they walk the path of the Adversary instead of the Advocate: they expose without hesitation the evils of those who claim to be righteous rather than try to coax them back to righteousness with gentleness and mercy. Moreover, I discovered of their demons something all the more shocking: they teach the same lessons as the angels, just in a much more blunt and indifferent way.

I learned that angels council you, even if roughly, and even if you think yourself unworthy of such grace. They push you to greatness even when you think you can't and provide encouragement when you fall down. And I learned that demons council you, too, but only if you decide, with great resolve, that you're worth their time; they hold up a mirror to the worst parts of yourself the angels want to help you cut away, and if you cannot bear what you see, if you run from it, then you tell them that any time spent on you is wasted, because you're still interested in lying to yourself about who and what you really are. It'd be like a doctor trying to treat a cancer patient that refuses to acknowledge they have cancer: you can't force them to do the treatments, only give them an estimate of how much time they have left.

Angels show you the grace, mercy, and love of God, His holy balm that your soul so desperately seeks. Demons make you stop your pathetic mewling about how worthy (or unworthy) you are, accuse you of being a vain creature either roostering up or fishing for soft pats on your ego, and instead challenge you to *decide* you'll chase God's grace in what feels like rebellion–rebellion not against God, but against the "enemy" that is your doubts and fears, your own shadow.

In fact, let me walk you through a bit more concrete of a description of that shadow we mentioned way back at the start of this book. According to Hans Dieckmann's contribution to *The International Dictionary of Psychoanalysis,* this concept of the shadow per Carl Jung can be expressed as follows:

> In Carl Gustav Jung's analytical psychology, the shadow as a concept comprises everything the conscious personality experiences as negative. In dreams and fantasies the shadow appears with the characteristics of a personality of the same sex as the ego, but in a very different configuration. It is presented as the eternal antagonist of an individual or group, or the dark brother within, who always accompanies one, the way Mephistopheles accompanied Goethe's Faust.

What is especially interesting is the way in which this Shadow Self thwarts us by hiding itself the way a parasite might hide itself in its host, cleverly bypassing the immune system or even convincing its host that it is, itself, part of the original body, the way some parasitic mistletoe does to trees. Dieckmann goes on to say:

> The role of the shadow within is sometimes hidden, and sometimes rejected or repressed, by the conscious ego. In the latter case it is pushed into the unconscious, where, because of its energy, it acts as a complex. People

can, for example, be fully aware that they are avaricious, greedy, or aggressive and still manage to hide these truths from others beneath the mask of the persona. But they can also repress those characteristics. Then they are no longer conscious of them at all, and their moral ego is reestablished.[18]

In short: our shadow is the creature spawned by those very things we don't like to admit about ourselves. Sure, the angels can help you overcome this shadow—*if* you're able to recognize it and acknowledge that it's there. But was it Michael who tested Job, to try and tease out his true motives for loving God with misfortune and chaos?

Or was it (the) Satan?

Think of it this way: imagine your shadow like termites, hiding in the deep, dark moisture of their pulpy caves. They can't survive in heat, in air, and so you'll never see them on the surface; you'll only see the damage they do to houses or the signs of their nests (and therefore their infestation). Not many animals enjoy them, but the ones that do, like aardvarks and anteaters, are especially built to lap them up from their caves or break their nests down until those ugly little creatures are scrambling about the wreckage, soon to be stuck to their predator's tongue or dried out in the punishing rays of the sun.

Demons are masters at teasing out the worst parts of you and bringing them to the surface, where they cannot survive. Whether it's so the demons can go to "eat them up," to destroy them as Azazel has been thought to do when every wayward goat was sent out to him in the desert,[19] or because once exposed, the angels then exorcise those awful things in blinding light and blistering heat, the fact is that if you don't want to acknowledge that they're there, then *you,* whose soul is riddled with termites chewing you up, won't notice until you're dead of their damage. It's easy to look at the flaws you're *ready* to acknowledge and

---

18. Hans Dieckmann, "Shadow (Analytical Psychology)," in *The International Dictionary of Psychoanalysis*, ed. Ayla Michelle Demir (USA: Thomson Gale, Macmillan Reference, 2005), 1596.

19. Leviticus 16:6-10

bear the angels' strict, yet graceful guidance; it is another beast entirely to have this Adversary point his finger at you, accuse you of things that you insist are false, and then *horrify* you as you realize those accusations are true when they appear in discovery.

(Which, if ever you were wondering, is the point of Catholic confession: forcing you to *speak* the worst of yourself out loud, to admit it not only to the priest or to God, but to *yourself.* To leave it there in the confession booth, where it hangs in the air and cannot be avoided. To bring it to the light, where the priest can then offer you a way to exorcise it for good: with repentance and prayer and reconciliation.)

Many people, however, turn away from these flaws and project them out, making them everyone else's fault, as Dieckmann says folks do with their shadow when it goes unintegrated and unrealized.[20] In the case of demons, too, well–aren't they just the most perfect canvas for people to project their flaws onto? One can say they were never lustful, only haunted by Asmodeus. One can, to take Dieckmann's example, reject any notion that they were ever *truly* greedy or aggressive, only oppressed by Mammon or Satan. And it makes sense, doesn't it? When you banish these *demons*, these obviously *external* influences of some antagonistic *Other,* surely the issues will automatically go away, right? Because the issue was never, *ever* actually a part of us, but something planted there by something, some*one* else... *right?*

(The pride that protects our positive self image, or what Jung calls our *persona*, might be the sneakiest, most well hidden termite of them all.)

Again: demons don't cause problems, but they do find them, like poking at a bruise you didn't know you had and bringing your attention to it until you can't deny it anymore. There's an honesty to these "fathers of lies" in that way that is wholly unexpected, yet doesn't carry a drop of the same judgement that one might expect from the divine light of angels. Instead, there's only a completely neutral indifference that, for some, might be even worse. For others, though, that indifference is its own type of grace and mercy, as well as an invitation to begin something like exposure therapy rather than continue to repress what we hate about ourselves.

---

20. Dieckmann, "Shadow," 1596.

But I say all this to make this point: I never would've discovered any of this if I'd never followed the coaxing of the Holy Spirit to truly embrace my enemies as much as my neighbors, or the guidance of Archangel Michael on how to master my fearful, reactive mind. I never would've realized that my enemies *are* my neighbors, and that the only real enemy was my own prejudice—a termite I didn't realize I'd carried despite how much *better* my ego let me think I was to other "ignorant," non-witchy Christians (ha! what hypocrisy on my end.). I never would've been brave enough to speak to those not like me, to listen to them with the earnest wish to understand and see the similarities between us alongside the differences. Never would've realized where my own shadow was still evading me, and where I still had so much room to greet others, to grow, learn, accept, and love. Definitely never would've realized that the term *Morning Star* is applied to two beings: Lucifer (whose name *means* Morning Star) and Jesus, per Revelation 22:16. Never would've known how much Lucifer and the forces of hell actually cross paths and collaborate with Michael and the forces of heaven, both through my direct experiences with them and the continuous discovery of more apocryphal tales about Solomon and the demons.

And you know what? My magic works in my dreams now. But the truth is I don't even need to use it most of the time. The shadows that chased me in my nightmares, when I turned around them and faced them head on, dissipated all on their own, because they were never anyone or anything other than my own fear. I spoke about demons in *Discovering Christian Witchcraft* to offer people the same way out of that fear as I found: the knowledge, and the courage, to approach the most terrifying bogeyman of our society head on and realize they're not all we were taught they were. That they have something to offer us on our journey of spiritual growth, or at the very least, that we don't have to constantly look over our shoulder for them like a mouse watches for the shadow of an owl.

However, if all those who didn't like any neutral mentions of demons in their *Christian* (yet witchy) book want to stay a slave to their fear, and to remain blissfully blind to the hardware our culture installed in their heads, so be it. In the end, though, it isn't losing your faith that you should worry about, whether because you don't believe anymore or because you've somehow convinced yourself that your beliefs invalidate you from the light of God. Rather, it's falling into the traps of the ego that seek comfort over truth, that take the teeth out of God, that strip your understanding of your Christ down to only water, no blood, and that allow you to feel better than others on top of it all, that you should watch out for.

To "deconstruct" this way–holding yourself back from exploring even the scariest things, taking for granted what you "know" is good vs. evil, refusing the scholarship that challenges the worldview you clearly don't want to let go of–is to invite a very unwelcome guest to your doorstep, and here lies another chance to fail your journey of walking towards God. Just like the ex-witches who run back to Christ when things get hard, so too is this hubris, this "Us vs. Them" mentality (in *witchcraft* of all things), this insistence on *only* love and light, another opportunity to yet again be dragged out of the Mystic's Manor. Go ahead and take that opportunity! Be my guest! It'll sure be confusing for you when you find yourself pulled out of that Gate to end up lost, hapless, in the woods beyond it, and it'll suck for you to have to find the painful, thorny way back to begin your journey towards Him all over again.

But it's your prerogative to mess that up and have to learn the hard way, y'know? You've got free will, so go use it. Perhaps I'm like a demon myself now, in that way: like the Adversary, I don't mind leaving you to struggle and suffer in the darkness of the Sitting Room, nor will I pull you out before you're ready just because you say it hurts and you're scared.

Sink or swim. Stagnate or grow. Fear or love. Neither I, nor all the angels of heaven and demons of hell, will twist your arm to get you to past where you are now. Only you decide how deep you go in your deconstruction and how far you progress towards Truth.

Shadow Work Prompts for the Sitting Room

- Look at yourself in the mirror. Yes, a literal mirror. What does the voice say when you look at yourself? Write it down - every bad, awful, good, boring thing that pops into your mind. Whose voice did you hear? How long have you thought of yourself this way? Take time to sit with these, and then write how you think the Holy Spirit sees you. Imagine the warmth of that voice filling you as you rewrite that inner dialogue.

- Spiritual health, emotional health, and mental health all go hand-in-hand. If you neglect the hygiene of one, you will see its repercussions in the others. A big part of our spiritual work is being aware of ourselves. What do you do for your mental health? How do you decompress? What do you do for your emotional health? Do you struggle with expression or pinpointing an emotion, or is it more bottled up til everything explodes?

Chapter Four

The Study

The Mystic and the Witch

*F*OR SOME TIME, THE *Mystic and the Witch work to make something delicious together: a tart, of fresh summer tomatoes and basil from the Witch's garden, as well as boiled eggs, clover honey, and hard, pungent cheese that go well with the walnuts and blackberries the Mystic brought. They work mostly in silence, as the Witch can tell by the Mystic's furrowed brow that she's lost in her work—and in the vision she has yet to finish explaining.*

Once the tart is in the oven, the dishes are mostly washed, and the teapot refreshed with a good, strong brew, the Mystic sets a cutting board of morsels on the table and settles back into her seat. She hugs herself, her face set hard in her determination, and before the Witch can ask her to continue, she opens her mouth.

"Here's what I saw next."

—◦❖◦—

At this point in the vision, my eyes were burning. Each blink felt like sandpaper scraping over their delicate lenses. My tongue was dry, and the only moisture I got was the tang of blood I licked off the cracks in my lips. The fire in the little fireplace had long since burned to embers, and I was left in the dark, the silence as empty as my mind.

You must understand, my friend, how real this all felt at the time, and yet how hazy on my faculties. By this point, I'd long forgotten my way, and forgotten how long I'd even been in this place. When was the last time I saw something other than the four walls of this Sitting Room? I didn't know. I only knew that the shadows were thick enough to begin feeling like a cool embrace, and the one pinpoint of light still burning in those embers suddenly felt like an intrusion in the odd feeling of, somehow, *peace*. Comfort.

Suddenly, it seemed as if maybe there was no start to the darkness and no end to me; it seemed as if all things were melded together. Boundaries between Physical and Ethereal began to blur in such a way that I could almost sense that Someone was there with me: above me, behind me, in front of me, everywhere. They weren't really here… yet at the same time, They were.

Had I gone insane? I asked myself that in this darkness, but surely that didn't make sense. What *did* make sense was that maybe I'd made a mistake coming to this Manor at all: maybe this was where I would die, in this damn box, and maybe I would die with my mind broken after what felt like an eternity of solitary confinement. The thought was suffocating, and the thoughts that flowed after were enough to terrify even the bravest Sister, the most spiritual and wise person.

What if this was a trap? So I thought to myself. *What if I was deceived in coming here? What if my friends and family and pastor(s) were right: that I should've stayed away from all this? What if they* knew *this was going to happen?*

In that moment, I believed I'd never see them again. I'd never taste my favorite bland, grey food again, or see a dull, grey sunset again. If I was really stuck forever in this room, then I knew my throat would soon go dry to match my mouth, and my skin would stick to my muscles, which would begin to atrophy—God almighty, my skin would stretch so tight over my *bones* that it would rip and tear like paper, and my eyes would dry up until they're like the husky skins of garlic—

Suddenly, a great *clang* made me jump. My crozier had become unbalanced; it'd slipped from one side of the rocking chair and landed on the stone. I'd forgotten I was ever holding it. That thing, that damned thing—*why* did I go and pick it up? Why didn't I just leave it and turn around, back out of this creepy, abandoned Manor? What good has it done me now? What power has it really given me?

And yet… the loss of its weight disturbed me. Without it, my hands felt too light, like they'd break off my wrists and drift away, into the fireplace. There was something about that crozier that, once I wasn't holding it, I realized felt more like a walking stick than a weapon: one that guided me as much as it might guard me. With a deep sigh that scraped past my parched throat, I bent over as slow as an elder (and felt my spine pop along the way); I reached down and wrapped my hand around the crozier once more. It was still warm where I'd been holding it all this time.

And then I heard a *click* from behind me. Then another *click*. Light spilled into the room and cast my shadow against the near-dead fireplace. I shot up from my seat, only to have to lean on my crozier as a wave of dizziness knocked me off balance. But when I looked behind me, I saw it: *two* open doors.

One led back out the way I came. There was no light coming from that direction; it was the same as it was before I was trapped in here. I knew that path, though. I could've easily dashed from this room and hurried out to the Foyer, then back into the Courtyard, back out that Gate, and back to that grey world I knew for certain would never do *this* to me. God, even if the greyscape of my old home and community and church felt monotonous, at least it didn't do *this* to me! Never did I have to worry about anything there. So long as I followed the rules (the many, *many* rules) and kept a grateful smile on my face, I was guaranteed all the things I needed: the spiritual food and water required to feel safe.

However, my eye snagged on that next door. Light as thick and golden as honey poured through there, and I couldn't help but think that just a little peek wouldn't hurt. Just *one*. Then I could go in peace.

I shuffled over to the door and poked my head past the frame, half expecting something to jump out at me and eat my face. A wiry apprehension tugged my shoulders up into my ears; I gulped a thick helping of unease down my throat, and it made a tangled yarn ball of my guts. Yet still, I peered past that door, and I found something beautiful as that golden light hit my face: a luxurious rococo chair, one with gold rimming the beautiful cream upholstery that had white lilies and pink roses embroidered all over it.

Behind it was a desk laden with strange tools: incense burners, rosaries, wands made of crystal, little jars of dirt and bones and scraps of cloth, and a few odd things that looked like crystal balls, or even snow-globes. After all, they swirled and swished with some glittery golden stuff the way fake snow might swirl around a little Christmas scene, you know? And I wondered: were they the source of this golden light, maybe? I wasn't sure, but I *was* sure that the dozens and dozens of books littering the rest of the desk, the floor, and the massive bookshelves built into the cream-and-gold walls likely held some interesting ideas.

And you know how I *love* new ideas, my friend. After all that time in the Sitting Room, the very thought of new things to learn had me salivating as if imagining a plate of fresh food, and licking my cracked lips as if anticipating a deep drink of cold water. If the books out in that little library in the Courtyard were already so full of good food for thought, after all, then I could only imagine what was in all of these. They were all there before me, just waiting to be explored, and I could feel the wordless beckoning of Someone inviting me in.

But I needed *real* food and water—didn't I? Even if all the food I've ever eaten in that greyscape tasted like ashes, and all the water was the same temperature and consistency as my own spit, it was better than *nothing*. The Foyer was still open behind me. All I had to do was turn around and walk out to make sure I got what I needed to survive: real food, real water, a real bed, and a real house. Not whatever Manor of madness I'd walked into.

The choice was mine. I knew nobody would stop me from leaving—or from going further in.

All while the Mystic spoke, the Witch sat shuffling her cards. Now that the vision has concluded for the time being, the shuffling becomes a little more erratic, with the deck cut in three ways, shuffled, and cut once more. Her fingers fly along the faded edges to pull the top card from each stack. Death, Justice, and The Hierophant arrive, one by one; the sharp change in energy is reminiscent

of academic halls and commands a presence much like the Emperor before. With eyes heavy-lidded and unfocused, the Witch's smile fades into something softer, born of understanding and wisdom that one receives after meeting again with an old friend.

"You speak of a room full of vast new ideas and bright views, but here stands a stark contrast," she begins. The words flow as easily as water from a stream. "The energy of the Death card greets you with a smile and a hand extended, as if expecting you. As you begin to take in the new, it asks you to leave the old in order to continue on your path. Here, Death is gentle, patient, and implying that something is, indeed, dying: ignorance and bigotry, which die at the foot of knowledge and wisdom. Ah-ah," the Witch says when she notices the Mystic's mouth pop open in preparation for protest, "hush. You have enough humility to know that we all carry a misguided idea or two that needs to be washed out of us."

The Mystic's mouth snaps shut, and her lips purse as she waits for the Witch to continue.

Which she does. "This is the point where the change we've been going through all along this journey becomes more permanent, and we see more of what we need as we are able to discern between the old ways that no longer serve us and the new ways we have learned." Her fingers move to the next card, tracing the outline of the sword held strong and proud. "There is something here about the Sword that Justice carries. Something about the Truth being wielded as a weapon. Do you know that weapon, Mystic?"

A beat passes, then the Mystic goes to take a piece of cheese and says, "You mean the crozier, no?"

"Mm, no. A different one." A shadow passes over the Witch's face. Her nose twitches as she suppresses a scowl at the thoughts that come to her—thoughts of the people she fled from, who took the wings of their Holy Spirit and made them into the hilt of a sharp, merciless sword. "One the men in robes are quick to put to the throats of those outside their institution."

The Mystic's eyes widen, and she sobers. Her hand still hovers over the board of treats, but she puts the cheese down rather than eating it. Such a thought wanes her appetite.

"'Take the helmet of salvation and the sword of the Spirit, which is the word of God,'" she mutters.[1] *Even though she wants to duck her face in shame, she never lets her eyes leave her friend's, whose story she knows well.* "That weapon."

"That weapon, yes."

A thick silence settles over the two women. The Mystic makes no apology for the misfortune of the Witch's past, and the Witch doesn't require her to. No, these women are both bitterly aware that the apology isn't the Mystic's to make—that the tip of the sword once held under the Witch's chin was only one confounding vision and one cleric's suspicion away from finding its place under the Mystic's chin, too.

The Witch plucks a walnut from the board and pops it in her mouth. She washes it down with tea, then clears her throat and lets the words of the Divine find their way out of her mouth again.

"This Sword has been used for cruelty, power, and control. No longer. Justice follows behind, as the standard of deconstruction, decolonization, and de-capitalization. Your beliefs and ideals have come forward and been found wanting. This is where we see the fallacies in things you have listened to before, those crooked sermons from crooked priests, all seeking the coins of peasants with barely enough money to feed themselves.

"Justice asks you to stand firm in the command of the universe: love one another. Justice calls for accountability, not only for your actions, but of those around you, and those that came before. Seek out fairness and call out hypocrisy hiding behind love and peace. This requires no other books, no other learning, no other teaching; you see, with every book and letter and lecture, all these truly holy men and women are driving you back to the only Truth you require to find and express what lies within you. You see what your Lord—"

"—requires of me." *The Mystic's chest presses against the edge of the table as she leans over to study the cards.* "Yes, I see what He requires of me, as the good prophets once said: 'To act justly and love mercy and to walk humbly with [my] God.*[2] *Yes, I see."

The Witch leans back and drapes her arm over the back of her chair. "I wonder what your Savior considers Justice."

---

1. Ephesians 6:17

2. Micah 6:8

"Oh, my Jesus stood up against *the greed and hypocrisy in the religious leaders of His day,"* the Mystic says. *"May I recount a bit of the story to you?"*

The Witch blinks slowly, then nods. "You may."

With a nod and a deep breath, the Mystic speaks each carefully remembered word:

> Then the Lord said to him, "Now then, you Pharisees clean the outside of the cup and dish, but inside you are full of greed and wickedness. You foolish people! Did not the one who made the outside make the inside also? But now as for what is inside you—be generous to the poor, and everything will be clean for you. Woe to you Pharisees, because you give God a tenth of your mint, rue and all other kinds of garden herbs, but you neglect justice and the love of God. You should have practiced the latter without leaving the former undone.

> Woe to you Pharisees, because you love the most important seats in the synagogues and respectful greetings in the marketplaces."[3]

"Mm, yes, that sounds about right from what I know of your Savior," the Witch *says with a nod. She rolls the words around in her head, digesting them in her spirit, and then she looks again to her cards. When looking at the last one, the Witch reaches out and pauses; her fingers twitch over the image on this card. It's as if she's trying to reconcile a stranger's face in a place it normally doesn't appear. As if that, in itself, is some ill omen. After a time, she blows out a sigh and relaxes. "The Hierophant... I once knew this energy as the High Priest," she murmurs. "It is meant to go along with the High Priestess; however, unlike the Emperor and Empress, its message doesn't compliment its feminine counterpart so well. Instead of silence and reflection, this is where you*

---

3. Luke 11:39–43

are called to actively apply what you have learned, and to apply it with respect to tradition and those who have walked this path before you.

"If knowledge is meant to be shared, then you must cultivate it and share Truth with others, just as the sages and Saints of yore have shared it with you. The Hierophant also asks you to look at the old traditions, the old ways, and build new traditions out of their shed skins. It's a time of deconstruction for you, surely, but there are also echoes of syncretism, of seeing the bones beneath the skin. Though beware of spiritual sloth, and of stealing from traditions that are surely not your own; you are not a vulture that needs to go picking about for scraps of spiritual food you didn't do anything to earn. Your voice, as the others who have come before you, will join together in sharing the love and Truth you've found by your own work."

The Witch sits back once more, but before she lets herself be satisfied with her reading, she watches the Mystic—and sure enough, her friend's face purses in thought. After a moment of the Mystic's eyes racing across the cards, she shakes her head.

"That's all well and good, but..."

"But?"

No answer comes from the Mystic—not yet. The Witch picks up her deck, already shuffling, and she waits for her friend to prepare the next part of whatever vision her Lord gave her.

Braving the Study After the Dark Night of the Senses

"How do you know you're actually talking to God? How do you know it's not the enemy trying to deceive you?"

If we had a nickel for every time someone asked us this question, we'd have the funds to disappear into the woods and live the Hermit life for good, seriously.

Is it an understandable question to ask? Yes, of course. You can't go five steps without having some blog post or Christian website telling you that everything that doesn't align with (each individual church's very specific interpretation of) the Bible is actually from "the enemy," Satan, the "devil," or what have you. For example, this article on *iBelieve* by Shakia Clark tells us that three "sneaky" tools used by the enemy (Satan) include *twisting the word of God* (something we've been accused of doing), *planting doubt amongst the truth* (something we've also been accused of doing), and elevating fear (something, ironically, we see others doing when they come into our comment sections telling us we'll burn in hell for "leading people astray").[4] Clark doesn't mince words, either; she says that this here "enemy," this devil, this Satan, "knows our weaknesses, but we have to be bold Christians standing on the truth of God's Word—if God said it, we need to believe it no matter how unqualified we may feel or what we lack."[5] Which, for all intents and purposes, doesn't *sound* like an issue—until you search "LGBTQ" on that same website and see the slew of titles and articles that are *very* anti-LGBTQ.

That's odd, considering the LGBTQ+ community was never spoken about in the Bible, given sexual orientation as we understand it didn't yet exist for these ancient Mesopotamian and Levantine cultures.[6]

You've already begun your deconstruction process by this point, and in this space, the Study we have to do a bit of *reconstruction*: rebuilding our understanding of the Bible (and, by extension, God) brick by brick with a balance of scholarship and meditation. It's the process Rev. Karla calls restoration: the part in which we stand in the aftermath of all our demolishing and deconstructing and begin putting the pieces back together. And it's at this point that our warning against deconstructing only to what "feels good" or what "resonates" is the strongest: because in the world of spirituality and witchcraft, in a digital age where misinformation flourishes, it is of utmost importance that our deconstruction in the Sitting Room, and then our *reconstruction* in the Study, is rooted in fact, sound reasoning, and also, the direction and guidance of the Holy Spirit, which does require some level of discernment.

After all, there *is* something to be said for the idea that one has to walk by *faith,* not sight[7] —and that one has to follow the logic of *God,*

---

4. Shakia Clark, "3 Sneaky Tools of Deception from the Enemy," *iBelieve* (2022), https://www.ibelieve.com/christian-living/3-sneaky-tools-of-deception-from-the-enemy.html.

5. Ibid.

6. McClellan, *The Bible Says,* 172.

7. 2 Corinthians 5:7

not Man.[8] Scholarship in archaeology and anthropology of the original areas the story the Bible takes place in is a beautiful gift given to us by the many passionate people who dedicate their lives to better understanding the cultures and contexts that engaged with God, but so is the work of Saints, of theologians, of philosophers, who put nose to grindstone and really try to *wrestle* with the concepts given to us by this ineffable, infinite God.

Still, there are so many who might look to challenge the cruel remarks of Christians like Clark and set out to read the many books digging deeper into the background of God and His people. They might discover untenable things there, in books like Matthew Vines' *God and the Gay Christian* or like Francesca Stavrakopolou's *God: An Anatomy* or like Bart. D. Ehrman's *Misquoting Jesus*. There are those that, upon learning the truth of God's origins and having the illusion of an infallible and perfect Bible utterly torn apart, ask themselves, "why believe any of it, then? If God isn't who everyone says He is, and maybe wasn't ever trying to be?" But this is where, for all our preaching of learning with right scholarship, we might say clearly: *to hell with thine books.*

Because yes, it's at this point, where we've deconstructed our beliefs and went finding all this scholarship, where we sift through the misconceptions of modern culture and language and find all these citations and records and artifacts the way a defense attorney pours over mountains of evidence, that we begin to wonder: *is this all there is? These concrete things, is this all our faith can be boiled down to?* Perhaps it's true, what these modern Christians say: that you can study yourself out of your faith. And yet, in this place surrounded by facts that shatter the illusion you grew up with, you might find your spirit beginning to grow something of a rebellious edge to it.

Now, past this point, comes the time where the paltry cries of Christians who do not understand the platitudes they repeat might actually shine in your memory, and that's because those old and often misused verses get polished hard enough by your own two hands after hours and hours of reading, searching, learning, and questioning. Here is where you might begin to ask yourself if it really matters if the name we know

---

8. 1 Corinthians 1:25

for God now started as reference to some little war and storm deity from the Levant, or if it matters that Deuteronomy wasn't written by Moses, or whether Moses even existed at all, legendary literary figure that he is. You might wonder, with some frustration, if it matters whether or not the world was literally made 6,000 years ago, in the span of one human week.

So to your budding question, that haunting feeling asking you, *is this it? Is our faith a lie? Is everything just the propaganda of Man?* The answer is, naturally, *of course not.* The feeling of betrayal in all that learning stings us in the Study, yes, but it gives way to a numbness, and to a realization: Man is fallen, always trying desperately to twist the words of the Divine, always failing to fully grasp the infinite edges of Its meaning, and yet Divinity twinkles through all the same, consistent everywhere it matters: in the commands of protection for the poor, in the fiery wrath for their mistreatment at the hands of people pretending holiness, in the one single and shining command to *love, love, love* across all times, places, and peoples—love itself being the necessary cornerstone of all things we do.[9]

This is where we might decide to find something of a *north star* in our guidance towards understanding God, and where we might look again to not just the scholars, but the Saints, who lived through much of the same issues and questions and doubts and fears as we have now. Contrary to those articles on sites like iBelieve, it is very normal and good to have doubts and questions; it is not a sign that you're being manipulated or led astray, but a healthy sign that you take your faith seriously. In moments like this, too, it's all the more important to remember: *you are not the first person to have reached this point.*

In this case, one has to let God—the true God, the Force that exists in all the universe and which is the Source of all life—lead the way in their studies, and show them the direction they must go. This is not an easy undertaking, especially if you're still wondering whether or not the thing you're hearing from is God or something else entirely, per every article and book and podcast and sermon and pastor telling you that the enemy is waiting to gobble you up like a Christmas ham at every

---

9. 1 Corinthians 16:14

opportunity. In fact, this Study we find ourselves in may become more than just a Study; it may become a verifiable Court Room where we argue with God, gather our facts and lay out our arguments, and wait patiently for Him to give some sign or indication that He's heard us and has something to say in response.

But how? You may very well be asking yourself that, as no doubt what's been said so far hasn't given you an exact, easy-to-follow direction on how to develop discernment. *How do we know what it looks like when God responds? How do we know it's God?*

Well, it's simpler than you might think. We've told you already about the fruits of the Spirit St. Paul speaks about in Galatians 5:22-23, but now remember: the one commandment of Jesus is love. Love for one another, love for God, the love on which every law God ever gave hangs like a tapestry.[10] However, many have tried, and many successfully so, to warp the meaning of love. They've gotten lost in the books of their studies, drowned themselves in philosophy until their spirit was a bloated corpse floating down the stinking river of their own vice, and they managed to make abstract and overly complicated the otherwise simple notions of *love* and *empathy*.

Make it simple. Make it so simple that your mind has no need to think of it, and your heart can't bring itself to stir in its selfish notions of who "deserves" grace, mercy, and compassion or not. When all else fails, and you feel you can't trust anything else, neither your heart nor your mind, neither your books nor your Bible, can you trust the fruits you gain from your path? Can you trust the love you hold for your fellow man, and for your God? Do you have faith that your heart is softened towards the weak and helpless, and your spirit ignited in righteous indignation towards those who abuse them, in a wish to correct such injustice?

And did our mention of any kind of anger there just make you hesitate?

No doubt, even the topic of anger is tenuous among many Christians in modern era, and is in itself a fabulous example of how one must consider nuance and question what they think they know. They must not simply take everything at face value without question because "God

---

10. Matthew 22:34-40

said so," and yet they must not make things so complicated that no answer can be found. No one can doubt the faith and conviction these Saints had, or at least not easily, and yet you see in the way they write and speak how concerned they were with being able to eke out the specifics, to understand the reason and logic behind their views on topics like anger.

St. Thomas Aquinas knew that anger had its place, that it did not always lead to the sin of Wrath; he notes that "evil is found in a passion in respect of the passion's quantity, that is in respect of its excess or deficiency," in essence, saying that anger, like a seasoning, needs just the right amount, not too little or too much, "and thus evil may be found in anger, when, to wit, one is angry, more or less than right reason demands. But if one is angry in accordance with right reason, one's anger is deserving of praise."[11] When one's anger pushes them to pursue justice in accordance with the will of God, as God has outlined in His Law, and not go an inch further into inflicting evil on the wrongdoer, St. Thomas Aquinas finds anger to be the very thing that inspires people to act *against* that which harms a community.[12] Thus, we see exactly how the Saints before us, in their consideration and their wisdom, model for us the way we should grapple with these ideas. Wisdom comes not only from the Bible, but those who are also rightly inspired by it and who make their arguments *from* the Bible, like St. Jerome, St. Augustine, and many others.

The Study brings us to this hard work. It brings us to the work that separates chaff from wheat, so to speak: that separates those who are interested in the trinkets and fun of witchcraft but not the theology from those who understand that the theology is the battery of their witchcraft. Let's be clear here: your witchcraft won't ever be much more than the fruitless pretending of a child if you don't ever put the theory and theology and proper learning behind it to give foundation to the workings you attempt or the reason for attempting them. As Mark A. McIntosh discusses in *Mystical Theology*, there can be no true separation

---

11. St. Thomas Aquinas, *The Summa Theologica of St. Thomas Aquinas*, 2nd. ed, (USA: New Advent, 2017), Q158, https://www.newadvent.org/summa/3158.htm.

12. Ibid.

of these things (which, in his book, aren't theology and witchcraft, but theology and *spirituality*—which these days, so many people call witchcraft anyway). They go together, and to try and tear them apart is to cut off one half of the religious brain from itself. In McIntosh's words:

> Put as bluntly as possible, theology without spirituality becomes ever more methodologically refined but unable to know or speak of the very mysteries at the heart of Christianity, and spirituality without theology becomes rootless, easily hijacked by individualistic consumerism… In other words, when a culture has grown used to the divorce between theology and spirituality, between doctrine and prayer, then the mutually critical function of the two breaks down. Neither is in sufficient dialogue with the other to keep it honest. And after a long period of such separation it becomes increasingly difficult to see what is missing in so much of the pale pretenders that pass fairly often for theology and spirituality today.[13]

For McIntosh, the scholarship and the rigorous intellectual understanding of faith is important, yes; scholarly theologians like St. Thomas Aquinas and the like all certainly have their place. However, with the advancement of the Enlightenment, the parts of scholars like St. Thomas—the *mystical* parts, those parts that were just as concerned with direct experience and communion with God as with a scholarly, rational study of Him and His Word—were left behind as silly and superstitious.

What we now call *mysticism* was, then, simply *contemplation,* and it had to do with a combining of experience (mysticism) and knowledge (theology): this was a skill that had to be honed, figuring out how to filter one's experience through the theological, dogmatic truths that our collective Body (the Church) has come to understand and accept. Whereas spirituality brought life to theology, and therefore away from the sophism occult scholars like Henry Cornelius Agrippa von Netterheim raged against, theology brought spirituality a lens it needed to

---

13. McIntosh, *Mystical Theology,* 10.

make *any* sense of what it was experiencing, lest it completely rip itself up by the root and fall prey to those *pale pretenders* McIntosh talks about.

You know those pretenders. To replace *mysticism* with *witchcraft* in this discussion—witchcraft being, as we've said many times, simply a more empirical and experimental approach to the experiences of mysticism—theology is what keeps our witchcraft from becoming a boundless, tradition-lacking, easily commercialized and corrupted distraction from our awareness of the Divine. Theology keeps spirituality/mysticism/witchcraft disciplined, focused, and directed with a solid goal that doesn't get taken up in self-absorbed, comfortable delusions of power and false wisdom, all while spirituality/mysticism/witchcraft do the work of unlocking the physical and mental box theology so often tries to put God in so that He might be better understood (and therefore contained, controlled, and even weaponized). As McIntosh quotes of Spanish Jesuit priest Jon Sobrino:

> It is not enough merely to speak of God. Theology must allow God to speak. Theology must move the human being to speak with God... in order to do this, theology must see to it that its doctrine on God, and its doctrine on whatsoever theological content, genuinely facilitate the experience of God.[14]

The experience of God: the mysticism that allows one to touch God. According to Sobrino, theology must be like the glasses we wear to read the mystical letters God sends us: a filter, a lens, that give us the tools to understand what it is we're experiencing, just as much as mysticism breathes life into theology that reminds us that what we are studying is *alive* and *active* in our world: that our God is not just dusty scraps of ancient text that shall never speak new words again.

Therefore, one cannot be without the other, and in this Study, we certainly find our fill of ideas that must be sifted through, ones that must be taken apart, examined, and rebuilt, in order to better understand

---

14. Sobrino quoted in McIntosh, 27.

ourselves, our God, and the relationship between it all that causes magic to flow and miracle to ignite.

Mimi Says:

There is a time when we have felt like we are living in a spiritual desert for so long that, when something nourishing comes to rejuvenate our minds and souls, we tend to gorge and overdo it. This can look like binge or doom-scrolling, obsessing over particular texts and authors, and diving so far off one end you don't come up for air. I look back to *Discovering Christian Witchcraft*, when Sara and I were combing through scholastic texts and manuscripts, journals and articles from speeches made, and I remember one thing: that I felt incredibly and wholly overwhelmed… and then fully detached afterwards. I had to step away from the urge to just drown myself in research, and instead, let my discernment guide me to the best places to invest my mental energy and time. If I hadn't, I would've seen the vastness of available resources and end up short-circuiting.

I chalked it up to spiritual fatigue due to examining my own practices and becoming more of a figurehead in a spiritual community, because no one talks about how exhausting it is to be so open with others to guide them like a teacher and still study as if you know nothing. Because while it's true that there are a lot of books out now, my perspective on the folk magic and divine feminine was an amalgamation of near-miss publishings and a lot of Catholic influence. (It was strange to be on that side of the aisle, considering I had been raised Pentecostal and Southern Baptist.)

This point of detachment, of feeling like you've taken in too much, is actually a medical phenomenon known as cognitive overload. It's where you push yourself into mental burnout from taking in too much information in a short amount of time. When you do this with spiritual texts and TikToks and YouTube videos and blogs, you'll eventually reach the point where too much knowledge can lead to spiritual burnout, and to where the distinction between "knowing" and "believing" are blurred.

There is a scene from the movie *Constantine* (2005) that touches on this, where John and Gabriel are speaking. John asks Gabriel what

God wants from him, to which Gabriel responds with: "the usual, self-sacrifice. Belief."

John retorts, "Oh, I believe, for Christ's sake."

Gabriel hits back with, "No, no, you *know*. And there's a difference."

And there is, in fact, an incredible difference. A lot of the spiritual is based on the way we interpret signs and wonders, and an overload of information turns what was once a sign of miracle and magic into an abundance of information to hoard for later; truly, the chance to behold the awe and wonder of the moment is gone, and the sign itself is filed away to be used as a reference (eventually). Much in the same way we allow the Spirit to guide us, I spent a good bit of time in my Study to follow discernment on the tug in my gut. I didn't just pick random books that looked good; I sat with the title and text. I sampled the author's words and their background. I made sure that what I took in would nourish, not just fill. Quality over quantity. And that is where I found St. Ignatius, completely by accident.

As someone who was raised Protestant, I spent no time studying them. Not until Sara and I pooled our collective resources and experiences to write *Discovering Christian Witchcraft* and a short three month stint with an Episcopal church group, anyway. I was happy with using my imagery and signs and wonders, and even superstitions. If it was good enough for Memaw, it was good enough for me.

My first foray into the Saints was with actually with St. Francis of Assissi and St. Hildegard; I found them through Sara, who encouraged me to read their writings after bringing her the chapter on spiritual gifts and my philosophy behind "if God made it, why can't we use it?" for the first book. They are heralds of kataphatic mysticism and ones often referenced in these Christian-Witchy and folk magic spaces. I encourage a deeper look into what they taught and their understanding of the presences of God. But St. Ignatius's name seemed to *leap* out at me from the pages of *Essential Writings of Christian Mysticism* by Bernard McGinn; I recognize it as my discernment guiding me to take another look and not be put off by the dusty thoughts of dead men.

What our brains perceive as signs are often patterns in nature, scripture, and coincidences; through words, songs, colors, and everything around us, we find the patterns of divine influence. Just like our brain is built to seek out patterns to make sense of things, our brain is also built to seek out the Divine and its presence in our lives. (We see something similar with Carl Jung's theories on active imagination techniques, too.) You could consider how the spiritual meanings of birds and their presence would be a part of our understanding of the Divine, for instance. I think of it a lot when I'm getting stuck in traffic, like "God is protecting me from something up the road by telling me to slow down."

So, while St. Hildegard revealed that the influence of God is the use of imagery, St. Ignatius showed me that those things were not only to be used in the church, but a necessity everywhere, being of that kataphatic theology we discussed before. His spiritual exercises were a study in itself on taking the time to sit with nothing and meditate on Jesus and his teachings. I read his journal, now published as *The Spiritual Exercises of St. Ignatius of Loyola*, and chewed on it. And prayed on it. And listened.

Discernment comes from spiritual exercise, and as I have taken the nuggets of wisdom from such meditations and understanding the influence of inspiration (as mentioned in Ignatius' work), I realize that the Dark Night of the Senses in places like the Sitting Room and Study, and all the suffering in them, can be a point of deep spiritual understanding. The biggest point I took away from him and his story is that, no matter how much he prayed to be healed, he was shown that what he asked for was Self focused instead of Purpose focused. He was clinging to the ideas and wants of his old life, and couldn't move forward until he took that time in the darkness to understand what he was called to do.

(This is not a way to dismiss actual physical harm or pain. As someone with a debilitating genetic disease who suffers from chronic illness, I spend a lot of time in pain or in bed, feeling hopeless and helpless. It took years of pity and wallowing before I learned to take this and make the best of the good days while still allowing myself the grief of the bad days.)

Whether we have our Dark Night of the Senses from spiritual dryness, drowning, or both, after all our senses come back, we may experience ecstasies and that divine influence; truly, we learn the Divine is all around us. And in some places, we lean into our imagination and draw from it, with what we already know from study and practice, to create how we see the Divine in our world. St. Hildegard compounds this as a truth in the way of kataphatic mysticism. Sometimes, this can blend into UPG, and I'd like to say that our time spent in the Study, and all we read and learn, does actually help us to use discernment to differentiate between Divine inspiration and maladaptive daydreaming... or worse, the frayed edges of psychosis. We cultivate our discernment through the trial of the Dark Night of the *Soul* and the foundations of what we've built after deconstruction.

My favorite example is one that actually really upsets a lot of modern Christians (and some old timey ones, too): When I commune with Jesus, I refer to Him as a sassy wine aunt. I am in the thralls of worship when I sit and meditate on Him and His stories. When I pull my cards and use my scrying and discernment, I get the faintest hints of snark and sass in His answers, usually veiled in stories or lessons, just like He did in the Bible. This is a blend of both UPG testimony and scholastic understanding of who He was and is. How we interpret things like this, with study and fellowship (which St. Ignacious encourages in kataphatic theology), brings things full circle, and allows us to finally move into the realm of Illumination after the Study.

Court Recess: Occultism and Apophatic Mysticism

There's another thing that needs to be made simple now, and you might've anticipated this discussion soon enough. This is a concept called *apophatic mysticism.* If kataphatic mysticism is one that witchcraft seems to center on—one that requires images, symbols, and other such things to organize the mind and orchestrate one's energy—then apophatic mysticism is the exact opposite. It's one that works by way of negation, following a concept of *Via Negativa:* the negative way, the way of talking about what God is *not* rather than what God is, and experiencing the profound loss, the deep suffering, of having to realize that *every* single image we make of God is, in fact, an idol.

Because God is infinite. God cannot be pinned to any one idea, face, concept, thought. It seems, when we think of it this way, that we understand viscerally what God means when He says to Moses that no one can see His face and live in Exodus 33:20. Because how? How can one witness the face of all that Is, Was, and Will Be, the infinity of life itself and the infinity of its negation, and not become mentally fried like that rabbi who saw Heaven and wasted away for complete lack of interest in reality once he came back to earth? St. Augustine, in his fifty-second sermon on the New Testament, drives it home:

> So what are we to say, brothers, about God? For if you have fully grasped what you want to say, it isn't God. If you have been able to comprehend it, you have comprehended something else instead of God. If you think you have been able to comprehend, your thoughts have deceived you. So He isn't this, if this is what you have understood, but if He is this, then you haven't understood it. So what is it you want to say, seeing you haven't been able to understand it?[15]

Again, who can pin down the Infinite to finite terms? Who can explain the Ineffable, or grasp what is too big to ever be seen fully? Just as when we stand with our face inches from the base of the Eiffel Tower or some other massive structure, we can't conceive of the whole thing or physically witness it, likewise if we focus too much on any little pieces of an infinite God, we never even come close to understanding anything more about Him.

It's the tradition of the apophatic mystics, like Meister Eckhart, to peel away the many images and words and ideals we attach to God one by one, "shedding images of God until one is left with only silence, with no ideas or images at all."[16] However, something strange happens: unlike in kataphatic mysticism, which takes that more bridal approach—Communion over straight Union—in apophatic mysticism, one realizes that not only does God have no image we can attach to Him: He also has no boundary truly separating us *from* Him. "The mystic has been negated" in apophatic mysticism, after all that dark night of both soul and senses; "all traces of self or ego have been neutered. There is no trace of either the God or the mystic who began this journey," but

---

15. *The Works of St. Augustine: A Translation for the 21st Century,* ed. John E. Rotelle, Sermon 52, 57.

16. Mabry, *Growing into God,* 5.

instead the One that is both God and mystic combined in a way that shreds all preconceived separation.[17]

Mabry quotes Meister Eckhart's especially striking idea: "Our Lord says to every living soul, 'I became human for you. If you do not become God for me, you do me wrong."[18] And from this idea, Mabry parallels the very story of Jesus Himself: one who died to a world full of illusions and deceit, spent three days in the underworld, and returned as true, undoctored Divinity, with all aspects and all labels and all being (Man and Divine) resting within Him.

In witchcraft, such a thing is difficult to grasp. After all, as we discussed before, it's really *kataphatic* mysticism, with all its symbols and tools and representations, that witchcraft and ritual seem to center on—and yet, at some point, one does have to wonder if these tools are really *helping* us, or if they're *hindering* us, in our walk towards God. We've discussed the ills of commercialization of spirituality several times now, but even if we understand our tools to be just that, *tools,* not actually the source of our magic or anything we *need* to practice, we can still find ourselves hesitant to go a step further.

Let us ask you this: how attached are you to your own face? And by extension, to the limits of it? Because if you're really serious about being a Christian *or* a Witch, never mind both together, there comes a time where you have to honestly ask yourself such a question, and when, like St. Ignatius, you have to ask yourself if the things you're using your magic *for* (money, love, protection, healing, etc.) are really all that's so important in this world, or if your mental and spiritual power aren't better spent on different aims entirely. Just as sometimes we have to move away from theory and into practice, sometimes we do have to move in reverse, too: away from the workbench, away from the ritual altar, and into the deep study, the truly mystical contemplation, that contextualizes and re-centers our understanding of magic and the God that powers our own.

Apophatic mysticism, therefore, is something that unchains God from us, in that He gets loose of all the images we've wrongly tried

---

17. Ibid., 103.

18. Eckhart quoted in Mabry, 103.

to trap Him in, those idols of the modern age. Some of those ideas have people genuinely believing God is a white man, or that the Bible contains all He ever said and will say and therefore any strange Voice we may hear in our spirit is actually Satan, or that God is *good* and therefore could never be brutal or destructive (or, for some especially hurt folk, that God is *bad* and therefore could never be kind and comforting). It unchains God from us, this deletion of all images and concepts of Him, and therefore, it unchains us from ourselves, too: it removes the curse of binding we didn't realize we put on ourselves and our abilities, and on our own inheritance with Christ as something fully Human and Divine.

In our walks as Christian Witches, this style of mysticism is one that allows us to essentially see the "meta" behind the magic: we see the truth that all we're using is just symbol and metaphor, and that we don't need any of it at all. That we can access the concepts we seek without all this pomp and circumstance, and just as easily as moving our physical muscles, we can learn to flex our spiritual muscles; that muscle memory, much like riding a bike, becomes something we never lose, nor something we need to psych ourselves up into using ever again.

But the process of getting here is difficult. Agonizing, even. One that, to the outsider looking in, might not look like either faith *or* magic anymore—and yet is more deeply rooted in them than any of the *pale pretenders* we've been told is necessary for faith all this time.

Sara Says:

"That's all these are—toys."

The ritual chalice, the athame, the wand and the pentacle—all those pretty tools in the style of the Hermetic Order of the Golden Dawn's teaching—they sure did look fun like toys. They were all covered in script I couldn't read (Hebrew) and all brightly colored in reds, golds, and blues, and they certainly felt like the kind of strange and wacky tools you'd expect to see a proper ceremonial magician use to do some crazy powerful magic. After showing them to me, my good friend Fr. Kyle put them away as quickly as he'd brought them out and looked at me with a shrug.

"You don't need them to do what you need to do."

And he was right. I've come to understand that myself quite viscerally now, especially after learning about apophatic mysticism: that sometimes, the beautiful symbol that helps one's knowing can become the clumsy *thing* that eclipses one's understanding. That doesn't mean that the symbols weren't useful for a time, of course, or that I could've gotten to where I am now without them—but it did mean that, eventually, I would have to acknowledge that it was time for the shape of my magic to change. As a result, it would come to look less like "witchcraft" as seen on T.V., less like the magicians' big and elaborate rituals with all these tools and special chants, and more like just the common prayer of any other Christian, so quick and quiet that one would hardly guess that I was praying at all, breathing benedictions and maledictions alike with my eyes glazed over in focus.

Which is funny, because I guess it means that what I call "vanilla Christians" (i.e: Christians that are *not* witches) are right. Jesus (i.e: the Divine, and a relationship with the Divine) really *is* all you need in life. God is the source of all our power, and the more we realize that, the less we even have to bother with tools like crystals or herbs or what-have-you; we can just commune directly with the Source to access world-bending power and shape the currents of space and time. Fr. Kyle realized that after many years spent learning about alchemy and ceremonial magic, which had him trading those ritual robes for priestly vestments upon understanding his Source, and I realized that, too, after my every attempt to venture out into this world of gods, Saints, angels, and demons only ended with me continuously returning right back to where I started: under the shelter of my God's wings.

The only problem I have is that these vanilla Christians never seem to realize *why* they're right. This often repeated refrain of "Jesus is all you need" is little more than a platitude to most, and worse, they often miss the point of the platitude: by saying *Jesus is all you need,* many people take that to mean that *they* don't actually have to do anything except go to church and pray for what they want, and that Jesus will clap His hands and make everything better for them with no other effort on their part. Ironically, they end up thinking of and using Jesus much the same way that some more New Age people use their pretty rose quartz towers: as a tool to outsource the responsibility for the state of their life onto, and often, to blame when things don't go the way they expect.

However, along with Fr. Kyle, it was in another conversation with ceremonial magician Lucas (@thedevilsadvocate415) that had me understanding the reality behind the platitude (these ceremonial folk, I tell you! They really do put in the hard and tedious work to understand the theory behind the practice). When talking to Lucas about whether or not intention was really everything in magic, I came to understand what all this stuff, this kataphatic use of tool and symbol, was more than a tool: it was also a proof of concept.

In math proofs, for example, the whole point is to take a simple statement such as "if a < b, then a < (a - b) / 2 < b" and test it out by doing a bunch of algebra and such to show why the math works out. Likewise, going through the whole tedious process of ceremony and ritual is essentially testing out our understanding of magic, intention, the Divine, the magician, and the relationship between all these things. *Is* Jesus really all you need? *Is* intention really everything? Just like doing those long, complicated, sometimes seemingly senseless and time-wasting proofs in algebra class, one essentially has to prove these ideas to *themselves* via the practice of that ritual magic—hence how we've been saying over and over that witchcraft is something like an empirical approach to mysticism.

People forget that occultism used to be considered a science, and that this is the kind of stuff that was being grappled with. In talking to Lucas, I found much of the same concepts that I found with Fr. Kyle: that while at first, one might make a mistake in thinking that it was the magical tools themselves that caused the magic to be possible to orchestrate, the reality is that it was *us* who consecrated and made holy the magical tools to begin with. The tools were never a source, only a conductor we gave meaning to. When you understand this, you can eventually simplify your magical process much the same way you can simplify a massive math equation down to a couple little pieces as you do your proofs.

However, just reading this here in this book doesn't mean you can skip the process. Like your math teachers, God doesn't want you to just write the right answer on the test; He wants you to show your work. I had to show my work over time, too, and that's the reason I can be where I am today both theologically and magically. It all started with those proofs, and so I don't think I have a better example of proofs than a court room—nor do I have any better example of a "Court Room" with *God* than the very day I decided to confront God about witchcraft to begin with.

I was only fourteen, and yet I couldn't shake the feeling that something was *wrong* with everything I was seeing on Christian forums about how witchcraft was evil and deceptive and from "the devil." After all, I'd been playing around on the internet for a long time by that point, and since I was in fifth grade, I was having the time of my life searching online about the "chakra" system from Naruto and whatever else to bring back to the playground with my friends. When I discovered the sparkly, poorly formatted websites of the mid-to-late 2000s, you bet your back end I was all over them, learning the goofiest and zaniest spells, like how to "speed up time," for example, (which I fully intended to whip out for math class). It wasn't until later, when I picked up a copy of Judika Illes' *Pure Magic* (the only book my mom was comfortable buying for me), that I realized that a lot of the spells were for simple things, like luck or a little extra money or love or healing.

And I could not figure out what was wrong with that. Not at all. I'd gone through my First Communion, I had the most basic and simple understanding of Jesus and of Christianity and all that, and I could not square how spells for such ironically *mundane* and harmless things could ever be a problem. As I kept learning about magic, and kept stumbling upon all the forums and posts that said Christians were *not* allowed to touch all that, I looked at the picture of Mama Mary my mom had in the living room and wondered.

Then I prayed to God and asked what, exactly, His issue was with using basil or whatever else in a cloth bag to attract some money, or potatoes to heal people. I looked at Him and said, quite literally, "I don't get it; You have people healing and doing all these things all the time. You made basil and potatoes. How is it bad to use the things You made to do the things other people in the Bible do? It doesn't make any sense to me why You'd have a problem with that, and I know You can explain it, so please explain it."

No doubt every Christian on those forums would've clutched their pearls to hear me address God so bluntly and ask for answers so directly. But why not ask? If anyone could explain it to me, I figured it wouldn't be a pastor, a priest, *or* some goon on the internet; it'd be God Himself who knew better than all of them, and God Himself I trusted to guide me, so it was God Himself that I asked.

The answer didn't come right away—and even when I did get the answer, I didn't quite digest it for a long time, because I was young and more interested in Tumblr and getting into college and whatever else at that age. All I can tell you, though, was that I had the deepest conviction burning in my heart. I *did* feel like I would, and *could*, challenge God: like I could argue my case and that He would see it and help me if I were genuinely making a mistake in my reasoning. Never once was I raised to be afraid of God, or to consider this disrespectful. This was the proof of my faith from the beginning: that I could trust Him to know my heart, to hear me even if I didn't speak perfectly, and that He would answer, in one way or another. That burning in my chest, a feeling like I would get when I went to defend my friends from bullies at the time or when I knew I was right about something I had to write on or otherwise defend in school, never left; it only pushed me to keep looking, keep researching, keep reasoning, and keep gathering new materials on the topic, because that conviction, in that moment, translated to a simple fact:

There must be something more to this story. I must be missing something.

Lo and behold, there would come a day where I was out at a festival with my parents, and where I spotted something on a bookshelf far away. To this day, I don't know exactly how I spotted it; I only know that I saw a witchy looking market stall with all kinds of books, and that I recognized the shapes and colors of something that, for some reason, looked like Jesus to me sitting there on those shelves. I ran up to it to investigate, and wouldn't you know, it *was* Jesus: it was the cover of Robert Connor's book, *Magic in Christianity from Jesus to the Gnostics*. I'd had that book since high school, and while I didn't read all of it back then (again, dreaming of college, scrolling on Tumblr, and making goofy potions out of the stuff in my mom's spice rack took up all the space in my brain at that time), I did read enough of it to know explicitly that I'd been right: there *was* something more to this story. There was so much more.

To this day, I have never found that book on any shelf ever again. I've found it online, sure, but that was the only time I'd ever seen it in a bookstore or in any witchy setting. To me, this is my original question to God answered in such concrete terms; this was such a blatant, clear sign to keep going down this path. I've not only learned everything you saw Mimi and I put together for *Discovering Christian Witchcraft,* but also so much more about the Saints, about mysticism, about theology and occultism and philosophy, to the point that I realized that there are so many before us who have done the same thing, thought the same way, and pushed for the same result: a better world for all of us.

Because that's what my studying has brought me to understand. Whereas before, I might've just been flailing around with the witchy tools, doing a bunch of magical scratchwork to get familiar with all the mystical stuff I was slowly picking up, it all led to me refining my understanding of both God and Self along the way, and understanding the purpose *of* spirituality and magic: to empower us to make this world the beautiful place it should've always been. More, through my exploration of other faiths and other gods, I've also come to understand that all of humanity has been begging for exactly that all this time: a world where all are able to live in peace and harmony, with silos full of grain and fields of healthy fruits, vegetables, and livestock, with families united and festivals in full swing, with perfect contentment in the simple gift of being alive.

In fourteen years as a Christian Witch, I've discovered that, like my God, I have no edges; I was made in the image of the Imageless, the Infinite, and therefore I, too, am infinite, made of all things and unable to be represented by any one thing. This has wormed its way into my magic, too: of course I still use the color green for money spells or cinnamon to warm up my psychic power, but I know that they're really just ways to take the infinite expanse of my mind and focus it on a single theme or concept.

Honestly, the way I talk about things now, one might even think I've lost all faith entirely—that all of this is just metaphor to me, not really *real,* all just imagery and whimsy to make a point the way fairytales do. I've certainly had friends tell me that they aren't sure what I believe, because just as much as I say I believe God exists as a tangible, sentient Entity, I also say I understand God as a Force, a Framework, an Idea, a Metaphor.

In reality, it's just that there's a kernel of truth in all of these ideas, and the only way we'll know anything for sure is when we're dead. Maybe

God is an actual living, sentient Being. Maybe He's just a metaphor, a myth. Maybe He's a mask we gave to something we can't understand, so that we could at least *try* to understand it. Maybe there was never anything to understand but ourselves. I don't know for sure. I only know that, regardless of what way I view it, the result of experiencing Him and loving Him and dedicating myself to Him is the same: an organizing of my mental state into something that can affect physical change, and making sure that change aligns with the will of God.

Even if it takes a bunch of bells and whistles to convince myself I'm capable of channeling down that Divine miracle, and even if it takes a bunch of formal steps and pageantry to do what is more or less a courtship dance with the Source of that miracle, the reality is that I see that "meta": I see what I'm doing for what it is. And because I've realized what the bells and whistles are, what the point of the pageantry is—the *proofs*, the proofs of the relationship, of the connection—turns out I really don't *need* any of that anymore. Never did, in fact. I don't *need* crystals or herbs or mirrors or cauldrons or holy water or bells or candles or whatever other bullshit takes up space in one's house until they can't move in all the junk. Hell, even the books—even the books, and all those ideas, all that philosophy and theory, all that input from so many other people, even *that* feels like drinking from a firehouse sometimes. Feels like more stuff, more mind-bending noise, that distracts me from the Truth.

And that Truth is that, to do all my magic, to work wonders and channel down miracles in the name of God, I just need *God*, whatever He even really is, and I need myself—much like electricity needs two points of contact to flow through and create the current that lets there be light.

Shadow Work Prompts for The Study

- Social Media is filled with cries for deconstruction, decolonization, and anti-capitalism in spiritual spaces. What does that look like to you?

- We spoke on deconstruction in the last chapter. If you have been doing it for a while, what does that look like to you now? How deep have you gone? It can be overwhelming without anchor points while you let go of those traumas and traditions, so this is more about where you feel you have found yourself, rather than if you've started or not.

- What does decolonizing mean to you?

- How does Justice show up to you? Is it truly karma, or is there something more?

- What is one new tradition you've tucked into your practice since you started deconstructing? How has this helped you heal that trauma?

- What is a tradition you miss from your time in the church? What made it so fulfilling or special? Practice thinking outside the box to transmute that energy and make it something you enjoy again.

- What is your relationship to your own face and name?

- What does it make you feel to think of God as truly unknowable (ineffable)?

Section 3

Illumination

This is the ultimate in human knowledge of God: to know that we do not know Him.

St. Thomas Aquinas

*Questiones Dispatatiae
de Potentia Dei*

Chapter Five

The Dark Hallway

The Mystic and the Witch

*T*HE SILENCE STRETCHES ON *for so long that the Witch puts her cards down and finds herself staring out her little kitchen window. A sweet, warm breeze rushes in on occasion and sends her old curtains fluttering; birds and bees alike zip by, as well as the occasional curious wasp. All have their place out in her garden, from the smallest worm to the fattest rabbit. Though she wonders if maybe a rabbit would be worth catching for stew—*

"This next part is the worst."

With a blink, the Witch is dragged out of her thoughts of butchering the little cottontail creature outside and back to the task at hand. The Mystic stares at the Witch with such shadows under her eyes, those bruise-purple half-circles weighing her face down.

"Then get it over with," the Witch says, and she picks up her deck once more.

So, as you might imagine, Sister, in retrospect, I simply couldn't ignore the call of this Study. When I tried to pull myself away and go back to what I knew and could predict, it was as if something hooked me by the sockets of my eyes and dragged me into this new space, stuffed to the brim with everything I could ever think to learn (or unlearn).

I'd scoured book after book in this little Study, tome after tome. However, I noticed something strange after a time: every page I leafed through, every paragraph I devoured, didn't feel like it was adding anything to my understanding. No, rather, it felt like it was taking things *away*. As I settled into that comfortable little chair and set my crozier against the wall, I found that each new idea I discovered within this library was one that smashed into the previous idea, until nothing was left in my head but a storm of dust similar to whatever floated in the globes on the table. What I thought I knew, and what I enjoyed learning about in that Courtyard library, suddenly felt far too simple, and the things I was experiencing in between these pages in the Study eventually brought me to the next phase of this strange vision: feeling like I'd finally zoomed out to see a much wider picture of the whole situation I was in.

From this point, I started wondering: is any of this real? *Any* of it? Because by then, it was all starting to sound a little unbelievable, a little *insane,* even. What had I been studying this entire time, and what for? The more I added to my mind, the less any of it seems to be *true*, and the less I felt I understood what value this holds. As comfortable as the Study was, and as beautiful as everything in it looked, I eventually closed the last book I'd read and sat in a silence that reminded me all too much of the empty room I just left. This time, however, my hands were clasped in my lap out of my own will, not because I had nothing else to do—and between my fingers were not the pages of another book, but the cool beads of a rosary, smooth and comforting in my hand. Something about muttering the *Hail Mary* on each bead I touched, even if muttering it absently as my mind hummed, kept me rooted to myself and my peace for the time being.

Hail Mary, full of grace, the Lord is with thee...

What was I actually learning about? God? Magic? The world? Myself?

Blessed art thou among women...

Or was I learning about all of them at the same time? Together, as if they were never so separate to begin with?

And blessed is the fruit of thy womb, Jesus…

But here was where the thoughts sped up, and I was left awash in their torrent. After all, I'm nothing worthy of being united with God. Right? I'm just a person, and the God I've heard about all my life is *God*.

Holy Mary, Mother of God, pray for us sinners…

There could be no connection between me and Him like that because He is something Other than little old me; He is great, all powerful, all knowing, an ever present Deity in the sky—

Now and at the hour of our death.

And I am simply—

Amen.

The silence that swiftly settled after I finished my prayer wasn't in my head, I realized. It was in my heart, my soul. And all these thoughts, as I moved from bead to bead, weren't my thoughts. At least, they weren't the thoughts I really thought. I realized, sitting on a chair of roses and lilies like a child in a Mother's lap and sinking deeper into that cushioned embrace, that these were the thoughts I came here with—and that I could not leave with them. I realized these thoughts were like thorns, barbs, and that they were trying to scratch my heart and soul, to rouse some feeling in it, any feeling at all. The kinds of feelings these thoughts brought back were ones I remembered well: the smallness, the need to cower, the heart-squeezing anxiety, the hope for mercy that I've been told all my life I don't deserve, but that I get anyway from our gracious God.

And yet I felt none of that then. These thoughts came and went, like a wasp hovering in my face. Once, I might've flinched or cowered, or even panicked when it landed on me and gotten myself stung. But right then, I just watched, and I noticed how the legs of these thoughts hung down limp, and how their yellow and black stripes were the same as another familiar garden friend, yet with none of the fuzziness or softness. These thoughts were imposters of the good thoughts that came with my meditations, I knew, and they were buzzing and filling my ears with noise, hovering by my lips in search of sugar (and possibly threatening whatever may come out of it).

So I sat, never reacting, and eventually, the thoughts had no choice but to fade and search for what they wanted elsewhere. It was a victory. Yet the silence—God, that silence—it felt so strange. Still, yet not empty.

Safe, yet just a hair off from peaceful. There were more questions brimming underneath this blanket of silence resting on my heart that I simply didn't know what to do with, nor did I know where to find the answers to satisfy them. All that I did notice, as the *Hail Mary* droned from a voice that came from my mouth and yet felt so far away, was one odd book with no letters poking out of one of the bookshelves.

Eventually, I found my crozier back in my hand, and myself standing on my own two feet. As if in a dream, each blink took me closer to that unmarked book, though I never quite realized when I got up or when I moved. I reached for that book, sticking out like an outstretched hand, and I pushed it back in place, knowing that at this point, adding more ideas would not help me unravel the mystery of this silence that came over me.

Click.

As the book nestled back into its place, that *click* made me pause. Then, as the whole case of books jerked, I flinched—and I watched in awe as the outline of a door became visible around what I thought was a simple shelf built into the wall. It creaked and groaned as some invisible gears *kerchunked* away, and then, it swung back, revealing a long, dark Hallway lined with other closed doors. One grand double door stood barely defined at the very end.

There was a moment of hesitation before I entered. It reminded me entirely too much of the Sitting Room, what with how dark it was, and I didn't trust that any of these doors would open when I tried to access them. I also didn't trust that this secret door wouldn't close behind me and seal me in. Yet, for some inexplicable reason, my feet moved as if commanded by their own mind and dragged me inside. I didn't resist, thinking perhaps something deep in an untouched corner of my mind knew something I didn't and was leading me to it.

It wouldn't have been the strangest idea I'd run into by that point.

Once I cleared the door, as expected, it swung shut and sealed me in darkness. Yet I didn't panic over this, unlike last time. For some reason, I simply… accepted it. My eyes adjusted, and my crozier began to gleam with a faint golden shine, as if mirroring the warm feeling of my soul that I'd come to know: the energy, the life of it, the *magic*. Each door handle sparkled in this gentle light as if beckoning me closer, but as I reached out to rattle one, expecting to find it locked, I instead found that it swung open—and put me face to face with the most terrible beast.

It was an uncanny thing. All it was, was two pairs of eyes floating in the darkness, the whites of them round as the full moon, the big black pupil a void of nothingness. As I locked myself in a staring contest with it, something else reflected my crozier's light: dozens of tiny little teeth, glinting white and beginning to gnash. I stood frozen, terrified, and in a move almost too fast to track, a claw as dark as death caught the crozier's light; the black scales of this thing gleam for just a moment as it shot out and swiped me from throat to chest, ripping flesh with jagged talons and leaving skin and muscle flapping in tatters along my body.

It hurt. God, it *hurt,* as if I'd been bathed in liquid fire where the thing tore me open. I smacked that claw away and yanked the door closed as fast as I could, hoping to anyone or anything that could hear me that the door *stayed locked,* and I dropped to the floor from the shock of it: of the the rips and tears in my flesh that I never expected to experience in a place where Someone was watching. But as I tossed my crozier aside to clutch my wounds, I stared in ever-deepening horror as my one tool, my one comfort, melted into the shadows and *disappeared.*

True darkness set in with the absence of my crozier's light. The door handles of every door rattled as I curled into myself on that floor, with my back pressed against the wall. Some*thing* was on the other side of each and every one, and I shouted for Someone to come help me. They'd been watching the whole time, this Someone, so where were They? And what did They trap me here for? Just to let me die in some dark, secret place and rot, forgotten? I wondered if perhaps this was just what I deserved for ignoring the obvious warning of the Sitting Room. Where *was* this Someone? What were They doing while I struggled? Why did they *want* me to struggle?

And more than that, where was my *God?* The God my family and friends and the rest of my ashen little community told me would never leave me? The God that was supposed to be all seeing, all knowing, all powerful, and able to protect me with the blood of His Son? If I were a right and proper devotee, which I was—which I am!—then why, *why,* was He not coming to save me from what must've clearly been a house full of demons?

Those questions continued to echo off my skull, even as the rattling of the doors scrambled any other thoughts about Someone and their Mansion of horrors. *Where did my God go? Where is He? Did He abandon me?*

I asked that as if God was with me the whole time, even though I never directly saw any signs from Him in this house. But in fact, I knew He *was* with me, because suddenly, I was so painfully aware of that raw, gaping *absence* He left behind, as if a warm cloak had been torn off me on a frigid winter night. Even whoever owns this Mansion was gone, their presence sucked out of the air like all the moisture sucked out of a day in the desert. Someone was missing: Someone was gone. While I didn't quite understand Their presence until now, I could feel Their sudden absence even more deeply than the wounds I tried to hold together—Their absence *and* God's.

Or are their presences really so different—?

Some*thing* rattled around behind these doors, interrupting my thoughts. My eyes didn't adjust to the dark no matter how much I blinked, and I grew cold as I found that there was, in that Hallway with me, no*thing*.

And worse: No*one*.

The silence returns, this time a cocooning force, as if the house has been filled with soft cotton. The Witch shuffles her deck for a moment, reverently, knowing the energy has changed with this part of the story. She asks for clarity once more; her lips move with silent request. Only after she has asked does the Moon slip from the deck with ease.

"This is uncertainty and doubt," she says as she slides the card into the middle of the table. "The Eclipsed moon, surrounded by howling dogs, brings a disorienting energy that proves nothing is what it seems. You are now forced into the overwhelming presence of all that you've come through. You must hold onto the pain of all the things you've healed from to ensure you don't repeat the same cycles, and that these things won't impact the future. This looks like cycle-breaking, generational healing, recognizing your own limits and boundaries while the root of your fears continue to come up.

"So I think those claws that ripped you, and the darkness that lured you in, are the same thing: images of deception. They are the lies you tell yourself: 'I have everything under control,' 'I have it all planned out,' 'I can't help that I'm this way, I have these wounds from traumas,'" the Witch says in a low and mocking tone as she waves her hands around. She shakes her head and blows a lock of hair out of her face. "And those lies can bring you through doors that lead to nowhere except right back into the Hallway. That Hallway is, in itself, its own loop of confusion. You don't realize you're wandering in the darkness until you reach the pitch black of all your woes combined, and it is made manifest."

All the while, as the Witch speaks, the Mystic sits wide-eyed as if watching a terrible horse-riding accident in the streets of her monastery's city.

"I know a man who spoke of something like this once," the Mystic murmurs. "A certain St. John of the Cross. He was trapped like I was in this vision, you know; he was wrongly imprisoned by his fellows and left to die." Her hands find her throat, where her skin was made into ribbons in that vision, but of course, it's smooth and unmarked. "He called it his 'Dark Night of the Soul,' wondering where God went."

The Witch nods. She isn't done, however; her fingers twitch back towards her deck, and her brows furrow as she picks up on another thread of energy lingering in the air.

"But it doesn't stop there, your vision," she says. "I feel a pull for something more..."

She scoops the deck completely and starts to shuffle; steady at first, but after the pace quickens, a card violently flips from its place and lands face down. Her brows pinch tighter together, breath catches in her throat, and that shaking hand can already feel what lies hidden. She flips the card and snaps it down against the table, the gravity of its meaning striking viciously at the two women—viciously as the lightning that catapults two men from a high and crumbling tower depicted on it.

"Speak of the devil—or, I suppose, your St. John?" When the Mystic huffs, the Witch winks. She puts that card down and taps it with sharp clicks of her nail. "That 'Dark Night' of yours is the Tower, yes; Divinity has responded to you just now. Like your St. John, you're locked in a Tower moment, trapped with all these illusions and with no way to escape just yet. The way your world crashes down, and you feel the absolute dead weight of it all." The Witch leans closer and looks her friend square in the eye. "This is rock bottom, spiritually, *emotionally, and sometimes even mentally and physically. Do not let that diminish what you're about to experience, where the material and spiritual world collide and combust. This is not a punishment, but a natural turn of events. It is the same as the time spent crying out of frustration because you feel like there is nothing worth the pain and agony."The Witch pauses, noticing the scrunch in the Mystic's forehead and the mist of worry that crept into her gaze. Her warm hand clasped over her friend's wrist and gave a reassuring squeeze.*

"It is not a test, either," she whispers. "It is a decision. Will this energy make you leave and abandon your quest, or will you keep pushing? There is no right answer. Only what you believe you can withstand."

That makes the Mystic pause. Not a test, but a decision? Did she have any rights to make a decision when she was clearly being shown something, pushed somewhere? She didn't think so—and yet there were holy men and women of God who were given exactly that opportunity. Or did Elijah not cry out for God to end his life after experiencing such terrible things under Jezebel's rule? And when things were so hard for David, did he not make his sufferings clear in his 88th Psalm, yet persist anyway?

Even Mother Mary was given a choice as to whether or not she would carry God's Son—and whether she would one day have to sit and grieve her *Son.*

"I see," she says. The wrinkles of worry begin to fade from her head. "That makes sense to me. And makes a little of the next part make sense, too."

"The next part!" The Witch's lips twitch into a half smile. Her friend's penchant for nearly never-ending visions is something the Witch never did understand; even a fraction of this would've given her a headache, had the spirits outside tried to tell her this much. Yet those visions always fascinated her all the same, especially when Divinity asked her to help the Mystic understand what might've otherwise looked like the dreams of the possessed or the lunatics. Her chair scrapes against the floor as she stands and puts her cards down. "Well, you think about how you'll tell me that part, and I'll show you the carrots I've started growing. Come, come."

Encountering the Dark Night of the Soul

Silence is the language of God; all else is poor translation. —Rumi

You knew this was coming eventually: not the cute, quasi-existentialist mess that is the Dark Night of the Senses, but the *real* struggle that is the Dark Night of the Soul. It's a phrase that gets people all kinds of nervous, especially as they read about the many ways people suffer throughout it, because they just can't square how the God that's supposed to love them could also be the one to abandon them when they need Him most—or so it seems.

However, one of the greatest misconceptions we see about God is that if you follow Him, He will guarantee that your life will go amazingly and give you everything you ever wanted, like money and nice things and a spouse and whatever else. We've seen people say the same thing in different ways: *no, if you follow God, He should protect you! He should take care of you! He should sustain you! He should, should, should—!*

To which, we must remind you: Satan is not God's enemy, nor is he even truly ours. Satan is God's *employee,* and our *adversary.* There is a world of difference between the ideas of *enemy* and *adversary,* even if at first glance, they appear to mean the same thing. The reality is that Satan, or "the devil" that you've been told about in Christian theology from friends and family and pastors and churches, is something we're willing to bet takes on a more black and white, us vs. them quality: one that has all the good Christians pinned against this whole army of evil that's coming to reign down terror on us all, and that so long as we follow God and do everything *just so,* Satan will never be able to hurt us.

This, however, is a mindset that very clearly skipped the entire Book of Job, as well as the Book of Lamentations. The fact of the matter is that God the Father is not like humans (and that's part of the reason He had to make Jesus, His Logos, into a human to come down and meet us on our level): He doesn't see things from the same vantage point as we do, nor does He experience time the way we do. For Him, entire empires rise and fall in the blink of an eye, and the troubles of humans are ones He takes pity on us for, but still doesn't see from the same angle we see them. Nor do we see His actions from a full perspective, either, and so we can't understand why He takes action or not in this world, or how He chooses to act. We only know that God is moving—and sometimes, it feels like He's moving against us.

However, despite all of Job's suffering. there's wisdom that he professes: when his wife tells him to curse God and die for all the trouble he's had, he responds, "You are talking like a foolish woman. Shall we accept good from God, and not trouble?"[1] And later, after Job has lost everything and been afflicted with sores, his friend Eliphaz the Temanite comes with Bildad the Shuhite and Zophar the Naamathite to comfort him, and Eliphaz says:

"Blessed is the one whom God corrects; so do not despise the discipline of the Almighty. For he wounds, but he also binds up; he injures, but his hands also heal.

From six calamities he will rescue you; in seven no harm will touch you.

From this, we understand: God has duality. How could He not? An infinite being, a being of all things that stand in the light and hide in the dark–how could He only ever bless and not curse? How could He, ineffable, ever act only in ways that are easy for us to predict or understand? Even as Job questions God, wondering why God bothers to scrutinize us so hard and test us so much, the fact is that God as a Force that stitches this world together just can't be perfectly understood by any one creature on this earth. As Zophar puts it:

Can you fathom the mysteries of God? Can you probe the limits of the Almighty? They are higher than the heavens above—what can you do? They are deeper than the depths below—what can you know?

1. Job 2:10

Their measure is longer than the earth and wider than the sea.[2]

Moreover, books like Job and Lamentations are written precisely *to* process the fact that despite all of God's love and protection, bad things do still happen sometimes, and that's just life. Job spends a lot of time going back and forth, asking why evil people get good things, only for his friends to respond that the good they seem to have now surely won't last forever, and the evil that good people feel now surely won't, either. Still, the question of evil has been one plaguing people for a long time as they wonder how an all powerful God could allow such horrible things to happen in His sight, and those like scholar Thomas Jay Oord set out to find reasons for it that make sense. In doing so, however, he shatters one of the most commonly held ideas about God: that He is all powerful.

This is a terrifying thought: that the God we trust, who we are told can do anything and everything, actually does *not* have the control over the world we're told He does by those around us in our faith communities. However, in the Dark Night of the Soul, this is simply one of the many ideas that needs to be broken apart. In his book, *The Death of Omnipotence and the Birth of Amipotence,* theologian Thomas Jay Oord argues that the idea of God being all powerful, and therefore able to do all things, isn't Biblical. God can do *great* things, sure, and God can do *many* things that humans can't, but *all* things? Not quite.

Oord's book points out the many qualifications and limits the Bible sets on God (His inability to lie, His inability to deny a covenant He made and agreed to, etc.), as well as the fact that creatures with free will are not coerced by God to do anything against their wishes. Even the hardening of the Pharaoh's heart is pointed out to be something the Pharaoh did himself, too, as Oord quotes another scholar, Terence Fretheim, to note that "'an act of hardening does not make one totally or permanently impervious to outside influence; it does not turn the heart on and off like a faucet,' and 'divine hardening did not override

---

2. Job 11:7-9

Pharaoh's decision making powers.'"[3] And one especially fascinating assertion Oord makes, after analyzing the ways in which God acts in tandem with His creation *to* create or change this world, is that "God did these almighty deeds–including miracles–alongside and with the cooperation of creatures rather than by omnipotent control. Perhaps God *requires* creaturely cooperation or the conducive conditions of creation."[4]

Wouldn't you know? This concept is actually the wellspring of the Mystic's purpose: to be the hands and feet of God. Oord's book is a truly fascinating one that argues that God's power is not this absolute, coercive, and free-will-erasing force (omnipotence), but rather a force that woos, that convinces, that allures people into cooperating with God so that He, as an intangible being, can make change in a tangible world via the submission and acceptance of His creation.[5] Therefore, as Oord argues his case, he brings us to the second part of his argument: that while God is not all powerful, He *is* all loving (amipotent), and therefore He feels our pain, our anguish, and sympathizes with it; He wants to stand with us, to help us oppose the injustice that tyrants and demagogues create in this world, and the greatest testament to His wish to do so is how He suffered injustice and died with us on that cross as God the Son.

Still, though, it's understandable that one would be rattled to even consider that the God they trust in is not simply doing things that seem *unfair,* like in the Book of Job, but actively being *unable* to do certain things at all. "Why worship God at all in that case?" So some have asked us. "Why consider God the Most High if He's not all powerful?" And as they ask this, they fall away from the faith, or decide that any other god is just as good to hold near and dear as the God they left for not being "good enough" by standards humans invented in the first place. Thus they ignore the *beauty* in the idea of the Most High still needing our help: that we get to co-create with the Creator. That He loves us and

---

3. Thomas Jay Oord, *The Death of Omnipotence and the Birth of Amipotence* (USA: SacraSage Press, 2023), 33.

4. Ibid., 37.

5. Ibid., 101-103.

wants to include us in His justice and His fight *against* evil; that Creator and Creature are strongest together.

However, remember: this is just one idea out of infinite ideas of an infinite God, and ones you will have to sort through for the rest of your life. We've already begun a discussion on deconstruction earlier in this book. As we said before: there are *so many things* that you may take for granted that you know about, and every day may very well be a new day to discover some *other* concept you have to totally break down to its disparate nuts and bolts. There will never be an end to those concepts, be they spiritual or be they rooted in other areas of life, like politics (and the vast propaganda machines at work that want us to think only one way about things for the good of whoever is in power). However, it's at this point, in the Dark Night of the Soul, that a new (and, frankly, *terrifying*) type of deconstruction comes up: the deconstruction of God.

Think about that moment in the Hallway. Who even *is* God? What is God? And where in hell does He *go* when everything is crashing down around us? One of the hallmarks of this stage of the mystic journey, as we are forced to face the reality of how little we know about God, is a suffering so deep, a living hell so brutal, that it makes us wonder if God even exists in the first place. It shakes us from all of our happy associations with God and reminds us that *yes,* in fact, if God created light, then He also created darkness; if God brings good things, He also brings calamity. It also shows us that every image, idea, and association we've attached to God is a link in a chain that keeps the true magnitude of Him bound and hidden from our sight.

Something happens when we realize that: something soul rending, something painful beyond belief. We realize here, in this Dark Night of the Soul, that the God we thought we'd pinned, that we thought we knew and could predict, that we thought would always be with us exactly the way we *wanted* Him to be, could in fact never be, because that would limit Him not to the status of true Godhood, but to the status of something like a Pokemon you could call upon to fix your life at the snap of your fingers. McColman remarks, and rightfully so, that "someone once said that 'if God were small enough to understand, then

He wouldn't be big enough to worship,'" and that is precisely right.[6] In ever believing God could be so easily predictable and contained within the pages of the Bible, it would be no exaggeration to say that we have brazenly committed that very sin of idolatry: creating some image of God to clap between two covers of a Book, so we might keep Him close and burdened by our endless onslaught of wishes. We would be imagining a sanitized and palatable face for the great and ineffable Thing that very well may have never had a face to begin with.

With a realization like this, typically at a point of great suffering and a place where we feel we've been altogether abandoned by our Lord, God doesn't just change in our mind's eye. God genuinely *disappears.* He vanishes, and all our false understanding vanishes with Him, to the point where we may wonder if God was ever with us to begin with—if He ever truly existed at all. And goodness, is this a lonely, cold, and desolate place to find oneself in the inner mystical journey.

Sara Says:

It likely won't surprise you if I tell you that I've seen people say a *lot* of silly things on the internet. Once, I saw someone say that if you follow the Abrahamic God, that He should protect you always and never let anything bad happen to you. I've also seen Christians who think they know a lot more than they do tell me that they'll "never" go through a Dark Night of the Soul (because the name of it sounds really bad and spooky, and why would God ever allow such a *bad* thing to happen to them?)

But here's the thing: that's something you might expect from the Evangelical Egregore. Protection from all harm, no matter your actions or anyone else's, complete peace and bliss and shelter from all the ills of the world, all the luck and comfort in the world... it's the love bombing of a parasite that wants you to keep it around. And it always comes with a price.

Meanwhile, when you deal with the *real* God—and if I'm frank, if I'm honest, with *any* Divinity, be it Odin or Zeus or the Morrigan or

6. McColman, *The Big Book of Christian Mysticism*, 162.

whoever else—then you will not just be handed a free ride to a happy life. We already told you about Job; we don't need to get into that again, and that's not all of what I'm talking about. Another thing is just the fact that, in the many years I've spent with this God, I've noticed two things:

1. God created both light and dark, per Isaiah 45:7

2. God does not shield you from the consequences of your own actions.

But I didn't know everything I know now. If I'm honest, I didn't do much with Christian Witchcraft, either in studying it or in actually practicing it, during my teenage years. I had books, of course, but they were boring to me and often hard to understand. And I did spells now and again, too, but I was more interested in playing Skyrim or scrolling endlessly on Tumblr in those days. I don't know when the switch flipped where I would be tearing through the heavy, dense books on Christian theology, history, and philosophy, or when I would be doing regular rituals and magic, but it obviously happened eventually as I got older. In the early days, I was more like the main character of Ursula K. Le Guinn's *Earthsea* series: impatient, bratty, and just wanting to do powerful magic without developing the mental fortitude.

As a result, I also held onto a lot of silly beliefs that didn't make any sense when held up against the Bible and gave me way too much false confidence in myself. The first time I came face to face with that fact was when, in the early days of my Interviews with the Gods series, somewhere in 2022, I spoke to Apollo.

You can see exactly what I'm talking about in *Where the Gods Left Off,* where between my Apollo and Persephone interview, I very clearly made a lot of mistakes and then paid the price for it. In essence: I was highly uneducated about proper practice in ancient Greek religion, which means when I went to speak to Apollo, I didn't realize I'd done everything wrong and, as a result, didn't understand why Apollo was so difficult to talk to, or why he felt actually antagonistic. It was the first time I'd had an experience like that, and I thought when I felt Archangel Michael step in and everything go silent that God sent the angel to protect me—because why wouldn't He, right?

Well, come to find out, gods and God aren't what we're told they are. Other gods are not fallen angels or demons or whatever tripe, they are *gods,* and God does not automatically dismiss, reject, or antagonize other divinities, nor does He automatically protect His children from other gods if said children step out of line. That moment of silence between Michael and Apollo wasn't a "back off" silence, it was a "hold on, not yet" silence. In that moment, I've come to understand, God had Michael work out a deal: to not hit me right then and there, where I could've scrapped the whole interview and never let it see the light of day, but to let me brazenly and boldly display my hubris in public, where the damage would be done and unable to cover up, and where I'd get hit ten times worse not just by Apollo, but all those who love Apollo in the Hellenic polytheist community.

I learned that week, let me tell you. I still cringe thinking about the whole thing. But that week, as I was getting dog piled by a big corner of #witchtok, and the platform I'd worked so hard on and run myself so ragged to build between two other jobs was threatened for reasons I didn't understand just yet, I felt helpless. What was happening? Why was everyone refusing to understand my perspective? What had I done that was so wrong? Why couldn't people leave me alone and just scroll if they didn't like what I was doing?

If I could have a conversation with myself from that time, I'd tell her those were bratty and selfish questions. Looking back, it is really funny to think how grown up I thought I was, and how very *not* grown up I was. You'd think I'd have been more mature in my early/almost mid-twenties, but no. Still, it went on so long that I ended up just crying at my altar to Jesus, wondering what the hell I was supposed to do, and why God was silent; where He went, and why He wasn't helping me in any way. Jesus gave me a very simple solution to my problem:

Apologize. Make it right.

Jesus revealed to me that not only had God not been helping deflect the dogpile, but He'd actively helped set it up to teach me a lesson. Because while that answer seemed obvious, it was something my ego didn't want to accept just yet. I was of course trying to be professional and cordial with people, even as they were dogging me—this was my professional author account, after all—but I'd been digging my heels in on accepting my wrongdoing because to accept I was wrong means I had to accept I did harm, and to accept that I did harm was to damage my own image of myself, which is exactly where the ego is. Like any animal, the ego will not put itself in a position where it gets seriously hurt unless it has absolutely no choice.

And I didn't have a choice. The outcomes were obvious: make things right or demolish years of hard work and potentially blacklist my author name from people's minds and hearts, thus making all the work I would go on to do with my next books, like *Discovering Christian Witchcraft,* nearly impossible. But even then, the nature of this wrongdoing meant it couldn't be resolved just out of fear for myself and my platform; to apologize in the way Jesus demanded meant going beyond just a "sorry I messed up!" but truly *comprehending* exactly what, where, and why I'd done wrong.

It also meant doing the long and extended work of making it right by trying one last time to interview one of the Theoi (the Greek gods), Persephone, with a highly knowledgeable facilitator, Dagan, who became a good friend. There was no pretending to smooth things over; this was a time of stabbing straight into that ego and acknowledging I was wrong and needed to change not only my approach to these interviews, but my fundamental outlook and beliefs around gods and faiths outside Christianity. It was also time to acknowledge that God is not here to protect me from any darkness I might bring upon myself due to a callous and arrogant heart—a realization that stunned me just as much as the flood of negative attention in that week.

It was one of many ego deaths, and it was a time where all felt lost and I felt alone, and where I had a clear choice: go back to safety, to comfort, and ignore the call to grow, or press on into the darkness, into new and uncharted territory, and have the scales of my old understanding fall from my eyes to see God just a little more clearly. This was also far before I had any of the words or knowledge or understanding of mysticism to frame what was happening, but this was definitely it: a moment where the floor dropped from underneath me, and I had no choice but to go alone and face the music, because there was no comfort or protection or anything I'd associated with God my whole life waiting for me otherwise.

Maybe, like others who have made mistakes like this and posted their inevitable "ex-witch turned Christian" testimonies online, I could've tucked tail and ran. I could've quit #witchtok entirely, stuck hard to my original view of spirits, and gotten off the internet–given up everything, or pandered to a different kind of audience. But as much as it freaked me out, I knew that I'd just be lying to myself to do that. I'd already seen and learned too much to pretend none of it was true. I would've been serving a different god if I did such a thing: a false god of comfort and complacency. A parasite we know all too well. I could've never done such a thing.

However, this story is not the only way an ego death appears. As you've no doubt caught onto by now, there are many systems and styles of going through this mystic journey, and I've already told you about the Qliphoth a bit. There was one specific moment in my life here that I could consider a second ego death, this time centering more on me and the way I understood my position in the world. It was between 2022 and 2023, when I was getting more into my own work on my social platform, as well as into systems like the Qliphoth and everything else, that I was beginning to notice something rotting in my life: my stable nine-to-five job.

There are many details about this job and the circumstances that led to the point I describe that I think are better off not to share, especially as they're not necessarily important to understand this whole situation. However, in a big mess of both personal and professional factors—such as the death of my oma, a crescendo of inappropriate and hostile behavior towards me, my own distancing and disenchantment with the job environment/work, and my burning the candle from both ends trying (and failing) to maintain the quality of my work both there and on my growing social media—it all just fell apart. I was a fool, though; I told myself I would quit the job at the end of the year in 2022, only to try (and fail) to hold onto it well into 2023.

I told God I would, too. I'd been getting signs and messages that it was time to take this leap and trust Him, that it was time to let things go in peace and hope for the best. But I went back on that because I was afraid: afraid of what would happen if I gave up what was at that time my household's *only* stable income. I'd forgotten something, though.

Whoever tries to keep their life will lose it, and whoever loses their life will preserve it.[7]

Sometimes Jesus says things like this, and it doesn't make sense right away until you get slapped with a situation that really *demonstrates* the meaning to you. I made a rancid mess of things at work in my desperation to cling to my financial security despite the toxicity that came with it, only to still be on the verge of a mental breakdown anyway and having to take stress leave for it all.

I'd been stressed a lot in my life, but this was the first time I'd experienced such a thing. The nurse practitioner at the doctor's office for a stress/health check-up had to take my blood pressure twice: once while I was talking about the situation and my numbers were through the roof, and a second time after I'd calmed down. Needless to say I never went back to that job, and I found myself drifting on my own, trying desperately to cobble something together in my life and make it all work before the TDI ran out.

You know the rest. I got a job as an adjunct professor later that year, published *Where the Gods Left Off,* and my fiancé finally broke through this God awful job market himself and added yet another income to it all. After I broke down and pitched it all into God's hands, it worked out. But all of that isn't the ego death, no: the real ego was in my sense of self and worth some few months later. I heard later from others who still worked at my old job that my presence was scrubbed, and it was as if I'd never existed in that place. Six years of work, five of doing my very best and going above and beyond, and with people telling me that I was an integral part of the team and showering me with praise (I even had an e-mail folder where I saved those e-mails from top heads and my supervisor at the agency to look at when I felt like I wasn't worthy of the job), and it was all just... gone. Like I was never really that important, like my position didn't really matter.

And I suppose that was the lesson: I wasn't that important. My position didn't really matter. So there was no reason to stay anyway.

At this time, I was going through the Qliphotic sphere *Samael:* the Poison of God. In this sphere, illusions are dissolved to nothing, and the

---

7. Luke 17:33

lies one tells themselves to keep their sense of normalcy disappear. The status quo is shattered. Everything we thought we knew about ourselves and our place in this world is discarded. Everything seems dark, lost, and like there aren't even any pieces left to rebuild from in the first place. I thought I'd be able to get right up and into my Patreon and platform and all that when forty hours of my time was suddenly freed up, but I found myself curled up on the couch and doing absolutely nothing for a lot longer than I'd like to admit—and more so when I realized my childhood best friend was no longer my best friend a month after all this exploded.

What a mess. Truly, when all is said and done, it feels like the debacle with Apollo was just an appetizer ahead of the full meal of fuckery that happened later. Around this time, I felt truly lost at sea, with no land in sight: it was my lowest point, and I didn't know what it would even look like to get out of this hole I'd fallen into.

But now, after mentioning the Qliphoth a couple times, you may be wondering: "Sara, what the hell were *you* doing playing with this system? Aren't you a Christian? Aren't Christians supposed to… *not* do that?"

Yes, I'm a Christian, and I'm also a thrill seeker, one too curious for my own good, like a dog that gets very excited to rip the stuffing out of a couch or a cat that has to be nosey about something that will inevitably scare the daylights out of them in the next two seconds. I just had to know what it was all about, you know? Sure, there are aspects of the Qliphotic method of the mystic journey that are incompatible with Christianity (and I will insist that's all the Qliphoth really is: this exact same mystic journey we've been talking about for hours now, just darker and spookier to people still uncomfortable with demons).

However, that doesn't mean I was there to do those incompatible things, like "become my own god" or however it's often described in the occult tomes; I was there to still unify *with* God, which can still be done on this path; I was not there to walk *past* God into my own false sense of cosmic sovereignty. And to be completely, wholly honest with you, I just wanted to put on my spiritual fanny pack and sneakers and get to being a tourist in the ten circles of hell. As the old saying goes: "curiosity killed the cat, but *satisfaction brought it back*."

I won't bore you with all the details of the hot mess express that was my time with the demons in the Qliphoth. (That's for another time, and that time will come.) But that system of mystic initiation, along with my conversations with demons in *Where the Gods Left Off* and *When Angels & Demons Collude* (where my Qliphotic journey started to cross over with my interview series), showed me lesson after lesson that outright shattered my worldview and put me into a series of ego-death experiences. Around the third shell of the Qliphoth, Samael, the Poison of God, all I can say is that all that strife I told you about with the job and the friend and all that… it only ended when I learned to *let it all go.*

There were so many illusions clouding me before this: illusions about where my worth lies, or about what I need to flourish, or about what my life *should* look like (based on metrics set not by God, but the world). They were little facades of life I'd taken for granted, fake as the furniture in a dollhouse (but so very convincing to someone who was, at that time, living the life of a doll, unable to see the bigger picture outside the dollhouse). It was having the courage to approach the demons and experience their (sometimes sensible, sometimes downright violent) ways of weeding the spiritual fields, as well as continuing to cling tighter and tighter to my *idea* of God, that eventually made me stop and ask myself: *why does it seem like the demons are helping me become more like God tells us to be?*

Because I'd always been a reactive, anxious, insecure, and impatient person. A perfectionist who could never be good enough for my own standards, and who therefore held everyone else to impossibly cruel standards, too. And I'm not perfect even after running through the Qliphoth once, mind you; I still do have a hard time using my words instead of managing my temper. Rather than just having a short fuse, my temper is more like a land mine, completely still and silent until something happens that sets it off in one disorienting blast before letting the dust settle again. It's a learned pattern of behavior that I can only try to break down and understand so I can try not to do the same thing again—and it's only through the demons and their cat-like indifference to my vices that I could escape the perfectionist side of me that would otherwise shame and torture myself over these flaws.

It's funny, really: the angels might not (always) tell you that you're an idiot, but you can see their disappointment and frustration written in the very air around them when you make a mistake; you can see it carved on marble faces (if your mind is like mine and can translate energy into images and scenes). Demons, on the other hand, will tell you in no uncertain terms that you're pathetic and stupid, but it comes with absolutely no emotional investment, no judgement. You simply are what you are. If you don't like what you are, the demons invite you to change it, but they couldn't give a damn either way if you do or don't (and at least in my experience, when you prove them wrong about you, the small smile you get from them is just as, if not more, satisfying than the warm, sincere congratulations of the angels).

Point is, I wasn't spared from these dark times just because I love God and God loves me. You'll notice a through line in these situations: that I was the one responsible for holding the match to the gas on each one. It was my mistakes, my choices, my fears and misconceptions, that caused these to kick off in the first place. That isn't *always* the case, though, as surely I can't think of anything that St. John of the Cross, who coined the term *Dark Night of the Soul,* did to earn his torment and imprisonment (other than, you know, call for reform and more upright practices for his fellow Carmelites, which, it seems, ruffled quite a few feathers in that group).[8]

St. John of the Cross, originally St. Juan de Yepes, wrote many a poem about his spiritual experiences, and in explaining his poems on the Dark Night of the Soul, he notes that in the three nights one experiences with God, the soul goes through a process of purgation, because just as Raphael had Tobias burn up the heart of a fish to drive King Asmodeus away, "in order to enter on the road that leads to God, these [the heart's wish for the things of this world] must be burned up and purified of all created things in the fire of [God's] love."[9] This looks, and feels, like a horrible time: it's a time where the world proves false, and any and all pleasure or knowledge the soul would derive from the sense of the body are dulled and cut off, and so the soul sits there with nobody and nothing but itself, in the dark, and forced to face the truth of itself and

---

8. Bernard McGinn, ed., *The Essential Writings of Christian Mysticism* (New York: Modern Library, 2006), 72.

9. Ibid., 75.

its desires. In this darkness, though, the soul also has the chance to find out what is *actually* important to it, just like St. Ignatius did when he had nothing else to do with himself but read about God through the eyes of other Saints and pray.

Is this a punishment? Does this happen because we did something wrong, and this darkness is God judging us? Not necessarily. In the view of the Saints, this is a bitter time, but just like medicine, the bitterness isn't to spite you or punish you: it's simply part of the process to heal you. Still, though, as we sit in that empty space with no senses to rely on, the fact is that no matter how we got here, the dark times that come will have us feeling lost, abandoned, and also have us deeply questioning where God went.

In these moments, it's so easy to think that God has abandoned us, or stopped speaking to us, or even that *He* has failed *us,* rather than us simply having the uncomfortable realization that all the things we were ever told about God have only been trick mirrors that actually took *us* farther away from *Him.* That's a tough pill to swallow. However, if you don't swallow it, and it instead sticks in your throat, then you very well may end up in the exact same spot as with the Dark Night of the Senses: staring down a forking path, knowing that you can either keep running after a God you aren't even sure of anymore, or running *away,* back to every comfortable and cozy idea of God you were given by your parents, your pastor, your priest, and whoever else. Here, however, the resistance is, as St. John says, "a more obscure, dark, and terrible purgation"—one that completely rips you out of your satisfaction with the pleasures you get from this broken world.[10]

The choice is yours here. However, that doesn't mean you need to make your choice quietly, or that you need to swallow every complaint and pain in order to find God. In fact, what nobody seems to tell you is that if God is infinite, that means His capacity is infinite, too: His capacity for holding, and healing, your pain, trauma, frustration, despair, anger, and more. Some folks will tell you about the Void, the Abyss, that endless nothingness, especially in relation to working with entities like demons and walking that more dark side of spirituality, but

---

10. Ibid., 74.

the reality is that the infinity of God is much its own abyss in our flawed perception: something so expansive that it seems you could put every ounce of yourself into it and not even begin to alter its depth or fill it in any way.

Mimi Says:

The energy I found to relate to the Hallway was nothing short of a Scooby-Doo villain chase scene: Disorienting as hell, and anxiety-riddled for most of it. First, the urge to try every door and try on every entity found was exhausting, frustrating, and left me confused as to where the hell I was on this journey. I didn't want to go back to my old self, but I didn't feel like I still had a goal or purpose to move toward. I very much felt like I didn't belong *in* my life.

Please note: I did sit down with my therapist and it was confirmed that these experiences were not derealization or depersonalization. Please make sure you have ample mental health support in your spiritual journey, in any way you can.

I did it that way *twice*, once when I was younger and running from my calling and standing firm in my hubris, and the other when I was older, wiser, but still believing that I could handle it all on my own and God would just be there.

My first experience gave Seven of Cups vibes: everything, all at once, and no point of reference for anything except a light at the end of the tunnel—and that light was from The Moon. The more I meditated on the experience, the more I realized that I have had just as much of a connection to this card as the others; being constantly bombarded with spiritual noise and no real understanding of the ever-changing cycles, I remember throwing myself at whatever I found under that light. It wasn't always right and it definitely wasn't pretty. I had made a fool and a mess of myself.

I was younger, but not so young that I was innocent of the choices I made. Somewhere between being a child and being an adult, I found the appeal of all the deities and spells and magic imaginable. I can see now how I was both fooled and still foolish. I was more leaning on the belief that I would be taken care of (by whomever I worked with and worshiped, regardless of whether I was actually doing it right or if they were connected to me), no matter what, and my faith was so strong because I truly leaned on something that wasn't myself. The hubris of it all. But when the pain didn't go away, when the bad things still happened, when the consequences were bigger than my actions perceived, the cracks in that faith appeared, and continued to grow, until it shattered. Believe it or not, this is where my struggle with folk magic came in. Trying to claim an eclectic practice and ignoring responsibility past "well, this is how I learned it" would eventually have me facing the spirits of spurned ancestors and disrespected Deities.

(Have you ever pissed off a War God? How about a Goddess of Night and Magic? I don't recommend pissing off either, let's just say that.)

I mixed pantheons and practices and gave zero thought or care to the respect of a culture and the Divine. I wanted to do everything, know everything, and the ego that I had found in my own power was driving me to destruction through over-extending and not minding my own damn business. (What I let go of was something different: you can still have bad habits and be egocentric at this phase of the journey, it all depends on what you learn and how much you understand needs to be released, but that's for another part). The second experience was difficult and exhausting; I had broken cycles, deconstructed down to the last fiber of myself, and still found the weird urge to only find God in the signs and wonders. I was still setting an expectation on the Divine that was not mine to place or theirs to meet. I used my discernment... or at least, what I thought was my discernment.

Sometimes, there were lingering edges of a traumatic response or lesson that I didn't finish tying up and letting go. If you don't know the difference, the Hallway experience will wreck you and leave you on the edge of nothingness before you even know what hit you. I still demanded God to show up, prove Himself, and come show me what He can do. And He did, by leaving me at the end of the Hallway to figure it out on my own. Talk about disorienting.

The concept of Spirit stands in the energy, as we knew Him in the church, in the desert, in the woods—but in true apophatic theology, the more we try to put God in a box and pin Him down to *one* thing, the more we push Him into an idol.

And when we do this, when we limit our imaginations and try to control the concepts of the Spirit, who God really is slowly leaves the picture, and leaves us in silence in the Hallway. Except, this time, we truly are alone. This is the Dark Night of the Soul. The hardest part of this was when I found myself without hope; that is a terrifying place to be. Both times, I had faith. And both times, I found myself on the edge of suicide from being pushed so far, for so long, without having anything to support me. Or so I thought. To me, the Hallway and the Guest Bedroom afterwards are connected, and you cannot get through the former without ending up in the latter.

The Adversary Interrogates: The Wiles of the Egregore

Like with Job, the Adversary always finds more that can be taken from you. If not your cattle, then your house. If not your house, then your children. If not your children, then the very health of the skin your bones are wrapped in. Deeper and deeper can the Adversary go, darker and darker can the Night get, until you finally draw a line in the sand and make the decision to force your way forward—or turn back.

However, in this step of the journey, after we've shed what false images of God we can, we still have to deal with the splinters we haven't been willing to remove, and according to Mabry, while we've done everything we could get to the baseline of God, "now God must finish the job" of apophatic mysticism in the way only God can:

All of our images are illusions. So long as I am relating to God as an "other," as someone whom I can perceive as "here" or "not here," I am tied up in an illusion of duality. As long as I can even conceive of "God," then I am still worshipping a metaphor, an idol, no different from Baal. God needs us to move beyond images and idols, beyond subject and object, beyond dualities of light and dark. So in order for that to happen, God winks out of existence—so far as the mystic is concerned.[11]

---

11. Mabry, *Growing into God,* 89.

In this section, Mabry likens the mystic experience to that of the prophet Elijah, who hid in the desert alone after putting Ba'al's prophets to the sword and wished he could just lay down and die as he felt beyond abandoned out there while Jezebel was out hunting for his head. However, in this section, we get a notable admission from Mabry, too: one where he acknowledges that the "finger pointing, judgemental, 'you're-a-piece-of-shit' god that some minister somewhere felt morally obliged to plant in our brains" is *not the real God*.[12] That this callous creature, which we discussed and identified in *Discovering Christian Witchcraft* as the Evangelical Egregore, is but a pale imitation of the real God, and that to grasp this, we have to walk away from everything we think we know *about* God and plunge headfirst into the Abyss of God's infinity.

Let us tell you something, though: you can be sure that there are more egregores of Jesus than just the Evangelical one. Take your pick of denominations: the Mormon Jesus. The Jehovah's Witness Jesus. The Methodist, the Baptist, the Penetcostal, even the Catholic or Orthodox or Episcopal Jesus–hell, let's throw in the Muslim Jesus (Isa) while we're at it, just for fun. *All* denominations, and even those of other faiths, filter the ineffable quality of God (be it Father, Son, or Holy Spirit) through lenses they can understand, and what they can understand, they can predict, and what they can predict, they can control (or at least feel comfortable around). Nobody can feel comfortable around what they can't predict: just watch how people shy away from bugs who are sitting quietly one moment and buzzing and zooming around their face the next with no warning.

But as we've spent so long discussing: God is not something we can control, nor is He something we can trap or anticipate. Ever since God rejected the practice of idolatry and refused to let any images of Him be carved for the purpose of sealing Him into, as was custom in ancient Mesopotamia with one's household gods, He rejected our need to make accessible and controllable the essence of Divinity, and He refused our wish to treat Him like a genie in a bottle. He made it clear that if He was to come to us, it was on His terms alone. Unfortunately, for far too

---

12. Ibid., 83.

many people, still wrapped up in their expectations of what Divinity *should* be like, this refusal of Divinity to comply with our demands is infuriating and brings many to forsake Him—or to make little golden calves, those egregores, in His place.

Of course, as you might imagine, these egregores are all their own traps, like venus flytraps waiting for a bug to come sit on their sweet-smelling "mouths." Here comes the Adversary, again, poking at your ego and trying to trick you to run back to your comfort zone. Here he comes, dangling your own Personal Jesus in your face that, like in the Depeche Mode song, is only ever just a call away for comfort and forgiveness and what-have-you. And here, in the Dark Night of the Soul, that false Jesus shines brighter than ever, coaxing you to come to it and give it all the love and energy it desires in exchange for whatever wishes you want.

However, just as God told Elijah to eat some bread and stop whining about his situation, so to do we as Mystics, as Witches, know that the only way out of this is through. Mabry puts it to us clearly, our options:

> At this point, the mystic has a choice: to turn from the path, to give up, to abandon the covenant, to surrender to the hardness of the task and go back to a normal life of relative ease… or to follow God into the darkness. This is the ultimate act of trust—to turn from the world of being and form and follow God into nothing, to become nothing ourselves.[13]

And boy, is that trust difficult for people. If there was ever a time where one would see the "ex-witch turned Christian" testimony come out in full force, it was here: in a moment of *failing* that Dark Night. After all, read again what Mabry said: does that not sound like exactly what happened in all these testimonies? With all these people who talk about how they were assailed by darkness and demons, how they felt alone and afraid as they went and mucked about with powers they didn't

---

13. Ibid., 83.

understand, only to be met with the consequences and flee back to the safety of "God"—is that not precisely the test of the Adversary itself?

Yet these people, all too often, think that the answer to this test is to return to the false images of God we've invented for ourselves rather than stick it out and keep forging ahead after the true God in that darkness. They'll speak about everything that went wrong in their lives, from marital issues to wasting money on "witchy" items to feeling constantly paranoid and afraid of spiritual attack, not realizing that in these challenges, the retreat to "safety" and comfort was only *one* option, and it was the option that required no growth, no introspection, and certainly no faith in the One that was unpredictable, estranged, and ineffable.

There is a reason that the Mystics will tell you: this journey is *not* for everyone. This path is not for all. One cannot come out on the other side with the same God: that little god made of wishes and expectations, that little god that love-bombs us and goads us with earthly trinkets when we do what we're told, that little god that threatens and shames us when we question it. For some, this process of shedding these illusions is so painful, so destabilizing, so full of darkness and despair, that even the thought of trying to go through it is too much, because these folks love their idea of God more than God. However, for those who seek God above all, and whose love for God has them leaving all the earthly things on the shoreline of life to wade into that dark and murky nothingness, we discover something beyond all our expectations:

> And in this nothingness, the mystic finds themselves transformed. For when you subtract everything that is not real from God, you end up with nothing. And when we subtract everything that is not real from ourselves, we end up, once again, with nothing. When we meet God in the nothing, when we experience the *nothing that we are* and the *nothing that God is* as the same nothing, *we are transformed into God.*[14]

---

14. Ibid., 89–90.

While others who write about the journey to Union, like McColman, are quick to say that this experience does not literally make you into God and therefore His equal, what it does mean is that the line where we end and where God starts, or where God ends and we start, will simply not be found–that we will be absorbed into Him, understanding that God truly cannot *be* understood, and that He is greater than every single box we could ever try to put Him in for our convenience.

This is terrifying to think of. Horrifying, even, for so many who refuse to acknowledge the infinity of God, or our place in that infinity. Not because one doesn't want to acknowledge the full extent of God–as surely many of these folks who run from this challenge will crow all day long about how great and awesome and good God is–but because this trial forces your faith to become more than just talk. Like Job, you must grit your teeth and hold onto your love of God, your covenant with God, even for all the chaos and all the darkness you can't see in; like Elijah, you must shut up, eat your bread, and get back to work *for* God even as everything crashes down around you. And you must do this because you believe–you *know*, deep in your heart and soul–that where you are, God is, even if you cannot perceive Him in His infinity at every waking moment, and even if it seems like He's abandoned you.

He hasn't. But He is watching. Waiting. Like the Judge He is, He waits to see if you'll rise to Satan's bait, as He has with Job, with St. Antony, and with so many others. He waits to see if you truly love Him enough to know that the things you take comfort in are illusions in this world, and if you truly love Him enough to know you cannot contain or control Him–that He is that He is, and that there is no negotiating with this fact.

Here, once and for all, you must choose which master you will serve.

Shadow Work Prompts for the Dark Hallway

- What assumptions about God have shattered or are shattering now since you began your witchy journey?

- What have you wanted to say to God that you never could for fear of being "disrespectful" or "blasphemous"?

- What blame, if any, do you hold towards God? For what? For those who follow Him, what actions can you take to lay this at His feet as an offering?

- Do you lie to yourself to avoid addressing your fears and past trauma? How do you see it? (i.e., "I'm fine, that was a long time ago.")

Chapter Six

The Guest Bedroom

The Mystic and the Witch

THE MYSTIC ALWAYS FOUND carrot tops to look so much like parsley. Still, she delights in the break that the Witch forced her to take; she runs her hands over the fluffy green fronds and enjoys seeing the peek of orange from under the thin bit of soil. They look like they'll be good sized carrots, perfect for roasts and stews as the weather gets colder, and the Witch puffs with quiet pride when the Mystic tells her so.

They chatter about some other things out there in the garden, catching up on life in the city's monastery and life out in the woods as they inspect the Witch's other wares: mugwort, basil, sorrel, onions, garlic, and fat orange gourds. The tomato plants are covered in little green berries that won't get big before the weather gets too cold, and the pepper plants still have their optimistic white flowers among all their thin, reddening fruits, but it's been time to make sure the fall harvest is on the way, and the Witch's apple tree is already looking heavy with shiny round fruits.

Once back inside, they settle back down to their treats and yet another round of tea, and the Mystic sighs.

"Alright," she says, "here's what I saw after that wretched Hallway."

---◈✦◈---

Eventually, the rattling of the doors in the Hallway stopped. I sat with my back against the wall for what felt like a week, a month, a year, though honestly, I had no idea how much time had passed. All I knew was that the darkness was so thick that it felt like I was sitting in a lost pocket of the ocean, and I was beginning to think I never had the ability to see at all. There was absolutely nothing in this Hallway except the doors, the floor, and the wall, and ever since the rattling stopped, I'd nearly forgotten about the doors, too.

I forgot even about the boundaries of my own body. The tears in my throat and chest were wicked, yes, but if there was anything good about this darkness, it was that it seemed to numb my senses. I remembered the pain and the incident, but it seemed so far away, as if it happened in a dream—and in this darkness, I started to wonder where *I* ended and where the Hallway began. For a brief moment, I was convinced that *I* didn't really exist at all—that I was nothing, just as there was Nothing and No One in this sea of shadow.

Is this hell?

I wondered if the folks at home got it wrong. All the fire and brimstone and the eternal torture, I wondered if that was really the case about hell. And if people could get that wrong about hell, then maybe people got other things wrong: about heaven, about angels.

About God.

What *is* God, really? Who is He? *Is* He really a He? If so, how are women also made in His (Their?) image? Is Jesus a Man, or is He the Way, the Truth, and the Life? What does *that* mean? Is God love, like 1 John 4:8 says? Is He not love? Is He both, and neither, and more than that altogether? Does He even actually *exist?*

My thoughts had nowhere to go but in a circle in this darkness. Maybe if I got fed up enough, I could've turned around and found a way to open that secret bookshelf door I came through. After all, the doors in this Hallway didn't seem to be locked from my side of them. I could've just got up, gone to that bookshelf door, opened it somehow, and walked right out of this terrible Manor and never looked back. But

I stayed still, especially because I knew well enough that I couldn't find that bookshelf door if I tried: I forgot which way I even came in from and had no way to see.

Just like in the Sitting Room, all I could do was wait and hope that I didn't die here, and that sickened me. I raged against it at first, wondering what loving Creator would ever let this happen to me, and who this Someone even was to let me wander into a deathtrap like this. I couldn't help but wonder, again, if the folks I left behind in the greyscape were right, and if this *Someone* wasn't the damn devil himself. In that short, yet infinite span of time in that God-forsaken Hallway, I went through the entire color wheel of emotions, until all that was left was the same Black that the Hallway had me swimming in: emptiness.

I came to a state of mind so cold and square and logical that it would've scared me then, if I had any capacity left for fear. I thought: *surely I won't die here.* I didn't before in that Study, or before that in the Sitting Room, so there was no reason I should've in that Hallway either. Maybe this was a fallacy—actually, yes, it is a fallacy—but I didn't care in that moment. I had no choice but to not care, and no choice but to simply *believe* that *all shall be well, and all shall be well, and all matters of things shall be well.*[1] I would not die there, I decided. I refused to. Belief became rebellion in a way I'd never felt it be before: I could feel it crackling along where my bones used to be like the static of lightning about to strike.

I closed my eyes (though it made absolutely no difference) and I laid down on the hard floor, hoping to sleep until something happened. However, as fate would have it, I found no rest there: no dreams to distract me, no colors and sounds and images from my mind. No, this was one of those moments where you try to sleep, only to lay with your eyes closed for what feels like eternity. I was forced to face this nothingness, and I was forced to face *my* nothingness, and worst of all, I was forced to face the Nothing *of* the Noone, the Noone that used to be Someone watching me—watching over me.

---

1. Julian of Norwich's famous affirmation

If Someone is Noone, I thought, though my face was too leaden to smile at this ridiculous idea, *and Noone is Nothing, and I am nothing, then at least we're Nothing together.*

Then something squeaked, and a wave of orange flashed against my eyelids. I jolted up and scrambled away; suddenly, I was more than aware of the friction of polished wood against my palms and the stiffness in my joints as I tried to avoid whatever might be coming. Because Something was there; Something opened a door, and it took me a good minute to focus enough and understand that Something was also *not* barrelling down this Hallway to get me. But there was a single square of golden light pouring out of this new room—one all the way at the end of the Hallway, on the left side, right before that great double door. The handles of that double door gleamed a brilliant gold in the light of this other room, but the door itself remained so shadowed that I didn't even think about trying to open it. I just got up and, limping through the stiffness, went to investigate this new room and this sweet golden light.

As I turned the corner, I saw something out of a play, or a fairytale. It was an adorable little bedroom, this place: one with a small bookshelf of books, a simple full sized bed dressed in a fine blue quilt and soft white pillows with lace at their edges. The frame was cherry wood: its deep reddish-brown color complimented the little curves and swells carved into its feet and the bedposts, as well as the big sloping headboard. Blue hydrangea blossoms were painted on the headboard to match the blue of the quilt. And on that quilt, stark against the otherwise cool color, was the golden curve of my crozier.

Something flashed in the corner and made me nearly jump out of my skin. I clawed for my crozier, hoping that maybe this time, I'd be able to smack whatever beast would try to rip my throat out again—but as I swung around and prepared to strike, I paused. There was nobody there; there was only a big mirror. In it was me: scared, yet resolute, with my weapon in my hands.

Except it wasn't quite me, and I knew this deep in my bones. I wandered closer to the mirror and reached a hand out to the glass and found it cool to the touch. I studied my face in this mirror: one that still had traces of the one I've looked at all my life, the same color eyes and the same eyelashes, the same nose and jaw and brows, and even the same clothes I walked into this Manor with. However, there was something wrong; there was something very wrong.

My hair was far too long, as if I'd been in this Manor for months rather than hours. My frame was lighter, but not as if I hadn't eaten; rather, it was light in a way that suggests I'd somehow gone hollow. And the place where that beast cut across my neck and chest showed no blood, and really, not even any wounds left over: there were only soft pink, jagged lines running down from my jaw to my chest like little strokes of heat lightning. I'd been patched up somehow, and outside those faint scars, the only place that held any sign of what I'd been through was the very way I composed my face.

On this face was not the same doe-eyed, curious, somewhat fearful expression I used to see each morning when I got ready for a day in the greyscape I e-scaped. It was not the face of the person who would lower their gaze around pastors and parents and potential spouses, nor the one whose lips would wrench up to stop the thoughts that wanted to become unacceptable words.

Rather, it was the face of someone who had no reason to say anything other than the Truth.

Shoulders square. Brows set. Lips neutral. Eyes sharp. Chin up. I stared at myself for a long time, unsure of when this happened, or how. I couldn't have spent *that* long here. And yet, I knew these kinds of changes couldn't happen in just a few short hours. Something happened here, and all I wanted was to find out what—and by *Whose* wishes.

In the mirror, I saw another door, one that didn't lead into the Hallway, but one that seemed to connect this bedroom to the massive room behind those double doors. I tore myself away from my reflection and rushed to it, but I wasn't sure why I thought this would be any different: the door was locked. It was locked, and I wondered if it was capable of being *unlocked* from the other side. The keyhole in the handle suggested that to be the case. If Someone was behind that door, only They got to decide when I saw them, apparently.

Which meant this Guest Room, nice as it was, was nothing but a vestibule. A waiting area. A little holding zone, where there was little more to do except read, pray, and maybe sleep—this time in something a touch nicer than an empty Sitting Room, or a dark Hallway.

The Witch hums at the continuation; she had been waiting to see what would unfold from such a trial, and the decision that came with it. Her sure hand moves over the deck and flips over the top card: Strength. Without hesitation, she also slides the bottom card from the deck, and the Star shines from underneath it all.

"If you choose it, this journey seems to be your evolution," says the Witch. "Once you've come out of the rubble of whatever was left to be destroyed, whether that be your illusions or letting go of control, there is a sense of something new. A light is seen in the darkness.

"My friend, you have found Strength through perseverance and mastery over your fears. You know you can handle what comes your way and maintain an unshakable sense of Self in the Spirit. The battles you have gone through were hard fought and won fairly, though your old self wouldn't think so. The quiet strength that comes with a sound mind and knowing when to hold on and when to let go will transform the rest of your reality." Her fingers move to retrace the outline of the Star, and a small smile plays on her lips. "The Star is a gentle light with a simple message: you have made it through, relying on hope and faith to lead you. You have found the calm after the storm. On this journey, you find hope and clarity in what you know, understand, and trust. Sometimes, that is faith and God and the belief itself. Sometimes, that is nothingness. And then sometimes, it is the universe and mystery and only that there is a Spirit above that we cannot comprehend."

The Witch pauses to take a card from the middle, and shows the truth of life and experiences therein: The Wheel of Fortune.

"And, of course, you have learned that nothing lasts forever. What goes up, must come down, and back around again. You take that flexibility with you now, and maintain the stillness in the centrifuge of life. Being present is no longer something you have to work for, but something that you simply are."

"Huh." The Mystic can't deny the way such sweet words make her feel. "That's... nice."

For all the horror of her visions, seeing these cards make her shoulders drop from the tension she didn't realize she'd been holding. Her lungs stretch with what feels like the first full breath she'd been able to take all afternoon. It seems like there isn't such a bad ending after all, if this is what so spiritually experienced a friend is picking up on. And after feeling all she felt in that Guest Bedroom—after living that strange life, walking through those struggles—she stares into her cup of tea and sees that same resolute face staring back at her: one born of trial, of experience, of betrayal and reconciliation.

The Witch takes the three cards back and shuffles her deck. "Any more vision to tell, Sister?"

With her brow up and her smile teasing, the Mystic almost wants to say no just to throw off her friend's expectations, but she checks the impulse and nods.

"One final bit after this, yes."

Entering the Guest Bedroom with Trepidation

A certain Mechtild of Madgeburg, a mystic from around 1208 to 1294 or so and therefore active a little more than a century after the time of our well known St. Hildegard von Bingen, was a woman who spoke much of the personally destructive ways of God and His love:

> My body is tormented, and my soul is exceedingly delighted, for she has seen and embraced her Beloved. Through Him, she suffers torment. As He draws her to Himself, she gives herself to Him... She prefers He send her to Hell, if only all creatures might love Him above all things...

> Thus the body says to the soul: "Where have you been? I can't bear this anymore."

> The soul replies: "Silence, you fool! I will remain with my Love, even if you don't get over it. I am His joy, and He

is my torment." This is my torment, which I will always endure and never escape.[2]

Before going through this mystical journey, one might read her words and wonder who could ever worship the God she describes—and *after* a time in the Hallway, experiencing that Dark Night of the Soul, suddenly, it very well may click. After all, once we've done the work of *purgation,* in which God systematically plucks from us all our attachment to these distractions of the world, our innermost selves finally have a chance to get free of the trappings of the body and get a taste of what our soul has truly been longing for: its Creator.

And St. Teresa speaks of this sixth room, too, in a way that might alarm the average person still heavily stitched into this world:

> O My God, how many troubles both interior and exterior must one suffer before entering the seventh mansions! Sometimes, while pondering over this I fear that, were they known beforehand, human infirmity could scarcely bear the thought nor resolve to encounter them, however great might appear the gain. If, however, the soul has already reached the seventh mansions, it fears nothing: boldly undertaking to suffer all things for God, it gathers strength from its almost uninterrupted union with Him.[3]

Already, she's talking about entering the seventh room, even though we're just in the beginning of the chapter on the sixth room. It may seem like we're getting ahead of ourselves, but the reality is that, just like that door that snagged our attention in our imagining of this Guest Bedroom, we know this is but a vestibule, a waiting area, to get to where we're *really* trying to go. This is the barest step before something beyond all understanding, and to outsiders looking in, unable to see

---

2. Mechthild of Magdeburg, ed. Henry L. Carrigan, Jr., *Meditations from Mechthild of Magdeburg* (Paraclete Press, 1999), 6.

3. St. Teresa, *Interior Castle,* 68.

the internal transformation happening, it seems like we are but a husk, a person unfazed by suffering, unreacting. It's like seeing a cocoon of a soon-to-be butterfly twitch with movement that suggests a creature inside, only to cut it open and find nothing but some strange buggy custard that couldn't possibly be the source of that lifelike behavior. The outsider looking in at this point in our growth cannot comprehend what's going on, or how, or why.

You may find some interesting shifts within your mindset here. You may seem strange to others when you get to this point, or like you don't belong in this world anymore. What bothers you may also not be what makes sense, or what used to bother you. For instance, St. Teresa says:

> Besides this, praise pains such a soul more than blame because it recognizes clearly that any good it possesses is the gift of God and in no wise its own, seeing that but a short time ago it was weak in virtue and involved in grave sins. Therefore commendation causes it intolerable suffering, at least at first, although later on, for many reasons, the soul is comparatively indifferent to either.

> The first is that experience has shown the mind that men are as ready to speak well as ill of others, so it attaches no more importance to the one than to the other. Secondly, our Lord having granted it greater light, it perceives that no good thing in it is its own but is His gift, and becomes oblivious of self, praising God for His graces as if they were found in a third person.

> The third reason is that, realizing the benefit reaped by others from witnessing graces given it by God, such a one thinks that it is for their profit He causes them to discover in her virtues that do not exist. Fourthly, souls seeking God's honour and glory more than their own are

cured of the temptation (which usually besets beginners) of thinking that human praise will cause them the injury they have seen it do to others. Nor do these souls care much for men's contempt if only, by their means, any one should praise God at least once—come what may afterwards.[4]

How could praise ever lead to suffering? How are the gifts we possess not our own? If these ideas put forth by the mystics like St. Teresa rub you the wrong way at first, that's natural. We would all like to think ourselves worthy of more credit, more agency, more *sovereignty*. There's no way to read the words of the Saints who shed that, like St. Teresa, or even the words you're reading from us right now, without that little tendril of your ego recoiling like the tentacle of an octopus when touched by something foreign and possibly dangerous.

And this is dangerous. It's dangerous to your sense of self to reach this point. It hearkens back to how St. John of the Cross describes this Dark Night as *true darkness,* in which the "soul is like a person in a dark prison who has no knowledge of what passes on the outside beyond what he can learn by looking through the window of his cell" (the cell being the body and its sensory input): in this space, you become something like the prisoner gone mad, no longer interested by what goes on in the world denied to him and wholly absorbed in a world that even those looking *into* the cell at the mad little prisoner can't quite understand.[5]

You'll never outright kill your ego, of course, nor will you ever be entirely untethered from the world outside the cell, with all its temptations and distractions and pretty colors and things that the body longs for. There'll always be something that revives your ego and gets you too deep in your own face, your own bones, your own skin and hair and nails. When that happens, you'll naturally respond like a wounded animal when someone hurls insults or lies at your ego, or you'll radiate contentment after a gentle, soothing stroke and a good meal that feeds

---

4. Ibid., 69.

5. McGinn, *Essential Writings*, 76.

you ego. Over and over, you will learn lessons, forget them, and then learn them again in new ways. It is what it is.

But then there are times where you realize the emptiness of the Hallway never left, and that it instead lives inside your chest: a dark space, hollowed out like the glass chamber of a gas lamp. Trust that when we describe the Dark Night of the Soul in the Hallway, that that's not the *only* place, or only way, you'll encounter this; at its base, that experience is something that rattles, breaks apart, and levels some false belief in you, and we all have quite a few of those false beliefs, even if we think we don't. The more they break loose, the more you are greeted with an opportunity to leave the Manor: to walk out of the Guest Bedroom, down the Hallway, out the Study and Sitting Room, through the Foyer, into the Courtyard, and then back out the Gate.

You are close here. But you are not "safe." There is no "safe" so long as you have a body and live in the world. For as St. Teresa says, this is the moment not of spiritual *marriage,* but spiritual *espousal;* you are engaged to God here and can call it off at any time. Hell, even in the actual state of Union, which we come to later, it still has room for separation: St. Teresa describes the state as like "two wax candles, the tips of which touch each other so closely that there is but one light; or again, the wick, the wax, and the light become one, but the candle can again be separated from the other and the two candles remain distinct"; it's not the same with true spiritual marriage, which is more "like rain falling from heaven into a river or stream, becoming one and the same liquid, so that the river and rain water cannot be divided."[6] And of course, something as deep as *that* may very well only be possible in death, when there's nowhere for our soul to go, nothing for it to *do,* but rejoin with its Source.

Sara Says:

When St. Teresa said that the soul comes to hate praise because it understands every good thing doesn't come from its own merit, but from God's grace... boy, I felt that.

---

6. St. Teresa, *Interior Castle*, 121.

Because you see the opposite all the time on #witchtok: people crowing and roostering about their power. Showing off their beautiful spells, doing the aesthetic edits, all that. You see people all over the internet, be it on Instagram or on Pinterest or on their own blogs or wherever else, talking about the *power within,* that sovereignty they hold that nobody can take away from them. And as not everyone believes the same thing, obviously, that's fine for them; I'll always be happy someone found their path that makes them feel like they aren't so helpless and alone in this world. That's all a lot of people are looking for, and that's okay.

However, as I've discussed with many friends who also walk this path: if you're really serious in your spirituality, if you're doing it for more than gain and more than your own satisfaction... that will eventually change. What you look for will be much more than simply empowerment. That's why as a Christian Witch, and as someone who has hit a point of understanding just how tightly interwoven I am with God—who understands all that I am is a thread still attached to the spool of my Source—I know that all the power I have, isn't really mine at all.

And that makes it more powerful than anything, and yet more restricted than anything. Because magic is no longer a tool for me to get what I want in life. Rather, I see now that *I* am a tool for God to act in this world, and I dare not spit on the responsibilities He's given me by giving me this gift of the Spirit.

It was the ultimate hammer to the ego, to realize this: that I have nothing on my own, nothing save for what's necessary to connect with God and be His hands and feet in this world. There are hints of it, too, throughout Scripture; there are those little phrases we say without really internalizing what they mean or imply. For example, the famous Philippians 4:13 verse, "I can do all things through Christ who strengthens me"? It's not just a feel-good quote; for the magician, the occultist, the Mystic, the Witch, it means exactly what it says: Christ, God the Son, the Logos, is the Doorway to the Source of our true power, God the Father, with God the Spirit the ultimate giver of it, like a stream poured from that Source and through that Doorway.

I often like to use the analogy of a laptop charger: they come in two pieces, one that connects the power source from the wall to the adapter box, and then the cable from the adapter box to the laptop. It's not a perfect analogy, but it works. In essence, the reason it has these pieces is simple: if you plugged your laptop from the wall directly into the outlet, it wouldn't charge, or it would overheat the battery and catch the thing on fire. The adapter box throttles the raw flow of power to a level your laptop can safely use without exploding. The laptop can run for a while before it dies on its own, but when it's plugged in, it keeps running.

In this analogy, your soul is the adapter box, and the laptop is the realm of the Physical: both your world and your body. The power source from the wall, as in, the power of the entire electric grid, is God. Sure, you might have some power of your own that you can store for emergencies like defending yourself from spooky things, or doing a little bit of energy work; you can do some things just automatically or on the fly, the way a laptop can stay running for a couple hours without being plugged in. But if you want to do *big* work—if you want to do highly energy intensive things, and for a long time, or if you want to replenish yourself—you need to hook up to the greater electric grid: God. Even the power in your spiritual battery is a gift of God; you don't generate it on your own, even if you can use it autonomously. And if you can't find your electric grid, or you're cut off from it, then your spiritual power eventually withers and dries up, too.

I mean, think about it: don't you feel better after you sit down with God and spend some time talking to Him? Whether it be at church receiving the Eucharist, over a good hour of reading the Bible, talking to Him over tea and tarot, anything like that, when you spend time *resting* and experiencing the simple *presence* of God, it flows through your soul and fills your spiritual battery. It heals, comforts, and invigorates; it makes it clear why this whole analogy of marriage and partnership and *love* in the mystic walk itself exists. Because God is your rock, and God is your sword and shield, and God is your partner—a lover that never leaves.

If you stay connected to God, then you can channel down the raw, and often overwhelming, power of God into a much more manageable flow for the world. We see in the Bible that God's direct and fearsome power is often destructive or uncontainable; it causes massive issues, everything from floods to fireballs raining down from the sky to earth-quakes opening up and swallowing entire houses and families. It's brutal! It's raw, divine power in action! In these days, God seems to prefer moving a little quieter, and so come the folks like us: the mystics, the Witches, who know how to become that conduit for God's miracle and make it manifest in the world as magic. (Though, of course, some Saints sure have done some crazy miracles that were anything but quiet and mysterious.) We use the adapter box that is our soul to channel God's raw power into something more manageable for the world around us, so that we don't explode and melt and catch anything on fire.

But again, it's a great hammer to the ego to realize: your power isn't yours. It's not for you to use however you want, for your own gain at the expense of others. It's not for you to throw around and threaten people with, or to use to get all kinds of goods and riches in life so you might skip the struggle of living. To be Christian is to struggle; there's no way around this. Those who come close to God have no choice but to leave these kinds of vain wishes behind, and not even because they're told to, but because by time you hit this point of Union, you genuinely want to. I mean, ask yourself honestly: if you truly love God, and you want to follow the commandment, the *single* commandment of His Son, why... would you ever *want* to use magic to cheat and steal?

Perhaps this is what is meant when one talks about "faith" vs. "works." You'll hear that debate endlessly among the denominations: that one doesn't need to *do* anything to be saved, just have faith, while others insist that faith isn't enough if it bears no fruit, while others still insist that healthy faith is what *inspires* the works to be done at all. One might look to the letter of James and interpret for themselves:

> What good is it, my brothers and sisters, if someone claims to have faith but has no deeds? Can such faith save them? Suppose a brother or a sister is without clothes and daily food. If one of you says to them, "Go in peace; keep warm and well fed," but does nothing about their physical needs, what good is it? In the same way, faith by itself, if it is not accompanied by action, is dead.

> But someone will say, "You have faith; I have deeds."

Show me your faith without deeds, and I will show you my faith by my deeds. You believe that there is one God. Good! Even the demons believe that—and shudder.

You foolish person, do you want evidence that faith without deeds is useless? Was not our father Abraham considered righteous for what he did when he offered his son Isaac on the altar? You see that his faith and his actions were working together, and his faith was made complete by what he did. And the scripture was fulfilled that says, "Abraham believed God, and it was credited to him as righteousness," and he was called God's friend. You see that a person is considered righteous by what they do and not by faith alone.

In the same way, was not even Rahab the prostitute considered righteous for what she did when she gave lodging to the spies and sent them off in a different direction? As the body without the spirit is dead, so faith without deeds is dead.[7]

To me, it's plain and simple: do you really believe? Do you believe not just in your salvation, in the love of God for you and all creation, but the logic, the *Logos,* of His Law? The Law that says we must love Him, *and also one another?* Once you get to this point in your spiritual journey, the truth is that this love, this faith, stops your hand from using your gifts and resources–be they physical, financial, spiritual, etc.–for your own glorification or for petty revenge or selfish wishes. It's just inconceivable, that someone who has the faith they say they do could

---

7. James 2:14–26

ever then use that faith as a weapon to hurt people or let them suffer at the hands of a cruel and unjust world; that faith will instead inspire you to act for others in any way you can.

It's weird, though, you know? Sitting at the point of the Guest Bedroom, realizing how far you've come and how much you've changed, realizing what awaits you if you keep going–it's weird, even funny. I used to be the kind of person that would cringe at hearing all this talk about focusing entirely on God; I'd think it weird, stuffy, even lame and boring, how the Saints would go on and on about *God, God, God,* and I felt that way because I was thinking of how boring that modern Christianity–often a pale imitation of this mystic journey–makes it seem.

You can see it in those who are mimicking grace without understanding it: they make such a grand show of being a holy person, with posts about their "Jesus Glow Up" as they go from non-Christian to Christian (the only difference in the Before and After photos often just being a Bible in their hand), and they crow so loud about giving up simple things like "listening to worldly music" by some "conviction" of the Holy Spirit. It's especially weird when you get here, to this Guest Bedroom, with your eyes fixed on that connecting door to the Master Bedroom, and you realize that all that shit those people talk is just that: shit. Noise. Performative nonsense. You can see it in their eyes: the glaze-over, the emptiness, as they repeat platitudes and do what they think they *should,* not what they are actually moved by the Holy Spirit to do. It's uncanny, strange, and altogether misses the point.

However, just as so many mystics couldn't really explain the extent of this feeling as they tried to describe it, so too can I say that when you get to this point, you do come to that *God, God, God* state of mind–in a way that reminds me, honestly, of the Page of Swords. When I spoke to Jesus, He loved the suit of Swords, and all it represents: the logic (Logos), the ration, the clear sight and the spearheading of the charge for innovation and progress and change. One of my decks, the Weaver Tarot by Threads of Fate, describes the Page as that energetic force that simply can't stay silent in the face of the status quo anymore, that needs change, and one that can recruit others with more expertise to create a community dedicated to manifesting that change. Being here, one understands so explicitly the draw to God, because one understands God as more than any "God of the Bible" or any "white male god" or any other such things people have warped Him into.

One comes to understand what cannot be put into words—and they yearn for it more than anything else. More than life itself. And so every action, every ounce of our power, is spent spreading the knowledge, the love, the good works and the shining faith, that heals this world rather than tears it down.

As a Christian Witch, especially, I come to understand myself like a sentinel: my magic stays tucked away until I receive the call to act. My magic works to stitch me closer to God, and it is most potent when I cast my spells for the joy, comfort, and ease of *others* rather than the joy, comfort, and ease of my own life. It moves me like a happy puppet, making the call of the Spirit impossible to ignore, and it inspires me to remember the downtrodden in even things as simple as my monthly money spells, as well as get out and donate what food and resources I can, where I can, to those who don't have their daily food or their warm dress. I become wholly unconcerned with myself, reminding myself continuously of *God, God, God.*

Doesn't mean I'm perfect, though, as I've said so many times. I still get anxiety when my house is full of books that aren't selling as fast as they did a month before. I still find myself too tired, too distracted, to sit down with my tarot and talk to God some days. I still reach for my phone to doom scroll instead of read the stacks of books I want to read (and that I can feel my own soul nudging me to read). But so long as I'm trapped in this cell we call a body, there will always be room to stumble and fall short, as humans are prone to do. It doesn't mean the spiritual gifts I've received are any weaker, or the spiritual fruits I've grown are any lesser, but that I simply need to keep trying, keep pushing, and keep remembering the infinite, free-flowing grace of God that encourages my efforts to try again each day.

In the end, I am God's hands and feet, and I take that more seriously each day. Such is what it means to yearn for Him and recognize His role in giving and making me all I am.

The Judge Speaks: How Do You Plead?

Now, one might go through all this learning, all this suffering, and they might eventually (and understandably) ask: what causes this suffering, if God is so good, and if we're past the Dark Nights (or, at least, if we've gained enough experience with them enough to no longer fear them)? When one thinks of suffering, one thinks of pain, abuse, and all the sadness that comes with it—yet reading the words of mystics like St. Teresa or Mechthild or Hadewjich of Antwerp, one recognizes that suffering they speak of. It's the suffering of one whose Lover is far away, gone on some important duty, to the point that it feels like a part of us has been stolen and that we'd be willing to do anything to get it back. Listen to Hadewjich, how she expresses her desire for God, and how she speaks on that suffering she felt during an ecstatic experience she had while at a Pentecost church service:

> At that time I was so terribly unnerved with passionate love and in such pain that I imagined all my limbs breaking one by one and all my veins were separately in torturous pain... I desired to consummate my Lover completely and to confess and savor to the fullest extent—to fulfill his humanity blissfully with mine and to experience mine therein, and to be strong and perfect so that I in turn would satisfy him perfectly: to be purely and exclusively and completely virtuous in every virtue... For above all gifts I could choose, I choose that I may give satisfaction in all great sufferings. For that is what it means to satisfy completely: *to grow to being god with God.* (Emphasis ours.)[8]

It's not the suffering of an animal caught in a trap. Or the suffering of a man starved, beaten, and abandoned. It's the suffering of *longing,* of

---

8. McGinn, *Essential Writings*, 103.

desperation for one's Love, willing to do anything to get their attention on you and stay wrapped up in their embrace–and yet knowing that you don't deserve them, that you fall so short, and yet are still so loved by them anyway.

Yes, we're aware of how toxic that sounds. Our ego hates to think that we would ever become such groveling creatures in the face of our Love, and it invokes the image we've seen all too many times before: of the self-sacrificing partner that does everything, loses everything, for the sake of their spouse that causes them such pain doing whatever it is that they need or want to do. However, we see that image, feel these feelings, because we have no frame of reference on this earth for anything more: the people that surround us are just as flawed as we are, and their scope of this life is just as limited as ours.

That is not God. When you come into this space that these other mystics have with the Force that has created and now sustains all creation, it's not the same as the lover that just goes off on their own with no regard for the spouse left waiting at home. It's more that God, being this intangible Force, is forever waiting for us to join Him on His terms–in which, again, our ego will kick and thrash and say "what about *us?* What about *our terms?* What about *our boundaries/feelings/wishes?*" And that's precisely the issue that stops people from grasping the gravity of progressing past the Guest Bedroom. As Mechthild says:

> Love without knowledge is darkness to the wise soul.
> Knowledge without revelation is like the pain of Hell.
> Revelation without death cannot be endured.[9]

She also explains how one might suffer for God, and do it happily:

> God guides His followers in mysterious ways. God Him-
> self walked in a mysterious, noble, and holy way: for
> the One without sin and guilt suffered pain. The soul
> who longs for God rejoices in the nature of its Lord who

---

9. Mechthild, *Meditations of Mechthild,* 9.

through His great goodness endured much suffering. For the Father gave His beloved Son to be tormented by unbelievers and to be martyred in spite of His sinlessness. In these days, many people who appear to be spiritual torture God's children in body and torment them in soul, because God wills that His followers should be tormented in body and soul as His Son was so tormented.[10]

Many will tell you that the torment and suffering of Jesus is, in fact, another roadmap of the Mystic's journey, just as St. Teresa's manors are, just as this book lays out, just as Mabry or McColman or any other students of mysticism explain. For us to suffer and be tormented like Jesus is to inevitably rise up anew like Jesus, with fullness of understanding and transcendence of death entirely, and so this "suffering" isn't just endless beatings for no reason. Even our understanding of it as suffering, or mirroring it to Jesus's story, is often too literal for our minds to see past at first, and that's why we have to start looking not with the senses, but with the soul itself.

Therefore, in this place, our focus goes wholly somewhere else, and we have to make a decision. God is asking us now, as Judge, how we plead in this case the Adversary has pursued against us, and we must speak on the stand: will we continue this walk for our own power? Our own gratification? Our own joy and pleasure? Will we let our sense of what is "fair" and what we "deserve" take us by the hand and drag us back out of this great Mansion, out the Gate and back into our world of muffled grey? Or will we accept the proposal of God? Stay engaged? See it through?

Only you can decide that, and that is what we're here to help you decide, even if all we have to offer is what we've been offering all this time: our experiences and the experiences of those who came before us, and the explanations of those experiences by others peering in.

Mimi Says:

I talked about the importance of spiritual hygiene and balance previously, and that's because I have been there. It felt like I picked the wrong ending to a choose-your-own-adventure story. And that ending was more painful than anything I experienced in the Foyer, The Sitting Room, and the Hallway combined. The events that led to my Dark Night of the Soul, my big Tower moments, pushed me to the point of atheism, and the denial of anything spiritual pushed me to want to harm myself. I had lost all faith in all things, and with that, I felt like there was no reason to continue. What was the point of all that suffering, if not as a testimony? Why did the cruelty have to continue? Why was the absence of all things (physical *and* spiritual) so staggering and heartbreaking that I considered death?

The very first time I experienced this, I did not find my answer in anything. The air in my lungs, the sun on my face, and the way the rain felt on my skin was what I found to ground me. Slowly, the choice to stay was further anchored with every flower blossom and falling leaf. I started to dream again, to see my loved ones as I had before, and bond with my children again. The ember of faith in something returned and grew, little by little, over the years. It was my own way of healing, reborn from something tragic.

The second time I experienced this, it was the same, and yet different. I remember feeling so empty, so numb, and only managing to stare out the window most days. There was nothing to connect to, like a block just fell on every cry I shouted out.

In the middle of this, I happened to be on the phone with a dear friend who called to check in on me; she asked how I was doing with shifting my devotional work around (I was trying to organize things a little more and was struggling with connecting a few months before, I just hadn't recognized it yet). I told her, "It doesn't matter if I light the candle or not, it's just something to do on a certain day. No one is listening anymore. No one is there. God and Asherah aren't answering me anymore: no dreams, no signs, the only thing left is an ache to reach out, but nothing is there, no matter what I do." She was supportive, and encouraged me to keep trying, even through my stubbornness and *what's the point?* attitude.

This time, the ideation of leaving this world wasn't because of cruelty, but because of the absence of purpose. I had just finished writing *Discovering Christian Witchcraft*, and instead of feeling closer to the Spirit, there was nothing. All the extra work and deconstruction and examining and writing—for naught. I felt like Elijah in the cave, looking for God everywhere but finding nothing (without all the slaughter, of course). Every Hallway door was locked now and my cries for something, anything, echoed with the semblance of my well-intentioned idealism in the emptiness of the Guest Bedroom. What I found through the Dark Night of the Soul was not a checklist or a map, but my own expectation staring back at me.

The story of Elijah here is referenced in 1 Kings 19; he proved his point, killed a bunch of Ba'al's priests, and fled for his life into the wilderness after Queen Jezebel called for his death. He survived on hope and guidance from an angel, who gave him food to survive. Eventually, the angel told him to look for the Lord, as he would be passing through soon. There were great and terrible events: earthquakes and storms and fires – and Elijah expected God to be in those. He looked for God in those big and glorious but terrible things… and found God was not there. There was only silence.

In the Ecumenical Study Bible and the Torah, it says that Elijah heard nothing but silence—there is conjecture about the addition of hearing the still, small voice mentioned in the KJV and newer prints. Mabry points out that it may be because the idea of silence is too much for some to bear.[11] Still, Elijah wept when he sat in the silence because he thought he was alone. It wasn't until he accepted that silence and himself within it that God spoke to him. God was not in the noise but in the silence. I recognized this silence as well, and found that only when I let go of all expectation and continued to stay with myself in the silence did I then understand God. What did that look like for me? Crippling depression. Losing the friends I thought I had because my beliefs changed.

---

11. Mabry, *Growing into God*, 85.

For myself and for so many others, it looks like cutting off your family to hold your peace, only to feel like you're wholly isolated from everyone, always. It looks like giving up on trying to do work, on self or spiritually, on literally going into a cave and deciding that the silence is where I needed to stay, and where I could die. My spiritual connection is so much a part of me that, when I had nothing left except the chasm that remained that couldn't be filled by platitudes or names etched in mythos, I felt myself implode. I would not have made it without the handful of friends who remained on the outside of the cave, calling out to me.

Those few friends I had made and thought left me behind were simply on the other side of a healthy boundary, and kept holding that space for me to crash out (sometimes weekly), all the while giving me encouragement and sometimes some harsh truths. The real and harrowing reality of it is that support and trust, having something (or someone) to ground you and still give you space to breathe, is what keeps us alive. Without it, these experiences can lead exactly to that place I found myself.

This is where I leaned on the work I'd done, the community I found (and really, it found me), and stayed in the discipline that helped me get to this point to begin with. Even my children, who have no emotional responsibility to take care of me, still reinforced the meaning of connection to this world, and I lived because of all of this—because of that village I'd managed to build from the strangest corners of life.

I am not saying that going on this journey will make you want to see the other side of the Ether, but I am saying that you need these supports, or your mind could convince you of some very scary outcomes to what seems hopeless otherwise. But, this is where I found myself in that soul-shattering absence: I saw the hope in the silence and embraced the energy of the Wheel of Fortune. What goes up, must come down. The harshest and darkest parts do, in fact, come back to the light. It just takes a little push from the outside.

Shadow Work for the Guest Bedroom

- What expectations are you putting on the Divine?

- What is the most hurtful thing you've done to yourself?

- You are now face to face with your most toxic habits, the ones you've convinced yourself you need to cope. What are they?

- How do you project these habits or faults onto others? Onto Spirit? How can you instead acknowledge and integrate them into your self image constructively?

Section 4

Union

Not only so, but we also glory in our sufferings, because we know that suffering produces perseverance; perseverance, character; and character, hope. And hope does not put us to shame, because God's love has been poured out into our hearts through the Holy Spirit, who has been given to us.

St. Paul

Romans 5:3–5

Chapter Seven

The Master Bedroom

The Mystic and the Witch

B Y THIS POINT, THE *sunlight is beginning to grow rich and golden as the honey the Witch put out for them both. It won't be long before it disappears altogether, and the Mystic knows she needs to get back before she finds herself blind and lost in those woods. Maybe the Witch could find her way around just by the feel of dirt on her feet, but not the Mystic.*

"This is the last part now." The Mystic sits up and clears her throat, and the Witch sits ready with her cards. "Here goes."

It happened in the night hours of my vision-walking, when I thought I was near sleep: the *click* of that other door opening. After what felt like a thousand years lying there, thinking of everything that had brought me to that point, thinking of everything that I'd learned and all the choices I had to make, it was only when I'd given up on trying to keep my eyes open and let myself drift off that something changed. Still, as quiet as that *click* was, it ripped me from my sleep and made me practically shoot out of bed like a star.

In the moonlight, I saw it: the slight crack in the door. Through that crack, I could feel *Someone* watching me, though I could see no eye, no face, nothing. All was a pool of black behind that door, a blackness so thick I might reach out and touch it. The only thing my friends or family would tell me could hide in darkness like that is evil: no thing of God, or thing of goodness, hides in such thick shadows or avoids being seen like this.

Knowing this, however, didn't stop me from trying to understand exactly what it was—if it was the devil, or something else.

"Hello?" My voice croaked out of my throat: it'd been days since I used it. "Who are you?"

A beat passed before the door opened wider. Its hinges creaked and groaned as that heavy door slowly dragged along the carpet, and from inside what seemed like pure nothingness, I encountered a sense of sweet, cool air—of a wordless invitation, a hand outstretched.

This is scary. I'd never been comfortable walking into the pitch dark, after all. *Who's in there?*

But it was a silly question, I realized. In that cool nothingness was exactly what I'd come all this way to find. It invited me inside, and as I took my first step into this strange, yet familiar place, I found myself unraveling—my body pulled loose, as if I were only ever a poppet made of loosely wound thread.

Something was pulling me out of my shape, dragging me out of the face I didn't realize was a wooden mask over my soul; Someone was spooling me back to my Source, and I knew exactly who They were: They were Someone that has been with me all my life, shadowing my every step, watching over me, walking beside me. I knew who They were, finally.

They were my soul's Lover, hiding in that innermost chamber. They were my soul's Creator. They were my God—not the version my grey old church told me about, but the true God beyond all word, all sense, all description.

I had found Him. And resolved there, in that doorway, that I would never let Him go.

⊷❖⊶

The Witch nods in understanding, her own heart aching with the weight of such a blessing and a burden. It's one she knows well herself, in her own way.

"To be known is to be loved," she says. "And once you have reached this precipice, you truly understand the writings of the mystics that have come before you."

The shuffling has returned, soft and subtle, like the whispers of such a Source calling out in an earnest whisper. The Sun slips from its place and settles gently between the women, as if lazing like a lion on the table.

"You enter this Master Bedroom and are met by the Sun; here you find you have reached another level of ecstasy and understanding, where the warmth of love envelops you, and you know you have blossomed on your journey. I am feeling a pull to be closer, a longing, a blissful moment—you have reached the point where we can once again see the joy in not only the world, but the work that you do.

"All energies in the Sun show success and joy and even triumph in overcoming all odds and traversing all obstacles. The brilliance of the Sun's energy is also a reminder that things are cyclical, and while we deserve the rest, it is time to begin again, much like the rise and set of that celestial body. There is work to be done under the light and warm embrace of it."

The Mystic smiles at this. Sun, or Son? Either way, it seems to bring the same result—and with it, the same costless, yet most treasured, of life's pleasures: the simple ones. The great king Solomon knew this, and the line of his writings flits across the Mystic's mind: There is nothing better for a person than that he should eat and drink and find enjoyment in his labor.[1] *And yet the Witch is still not quite done with all her cards. Once again, she pulls the top card from its resting place as if compelled by some outside force, and then settled beside the Sun is none other than the Lovers.*

How fitting, for a Master Bedroom, *the Mystic muses.*

The Witch nods as if in answer to the Mystic's hidden ideas; they both know the Lovers have come to be seen, to be known, to be understood. The

---

1. Ecclesiastes 2:24

two figures are joined with a heavenly being behind them, an angel watching on as they hold onto one another.

"While not necessarily about romantic love, the Lovers shows us something far more," the Witch says. "You are making a commitment, swearing to be vulnerable, and even having honest communication with yourself and with Spirit. You hold yourself accountable to your actions as a way to show you are true to your word. I personally believe that you reach this point when you are capable of truly loving the Divine, loving your neighbor, and loving yourself, because you understand that to love the Divine is to love your neighbor, yourself. Because you see, my friend, as we all have the Spark of the Divine within us, loving one another is likened to loving Spirit. Going through these trials is our way of showing dedication and devotion–"

"—and is a way of preparing for marriage."

The Mystic's gaze softens as she stares at those cards. Her words hang like baubles between her and the Witch; they glimmer there, and the weight of them is notable, yet not crushing. After all, what joy is there in life quite like the union of two souls into one flesh? And what is the Church, the body of all believers, but that very bride of Christ? And what does a bride do to prepare herself for such union, other than purify herself to stand before the altar, under the sight of the Divine? With that purification through truth, that baptism by fire, the Mystic sees it: how love so much more readily flows, like water from a stream that has been pruned and cleared of debris.

"Thank you," the Mystic says to her friend. "I understand what I've seen now."

Reaching Understanding with Union

How are we supposed to put this into words? This place? Any word, any kataphatic symbol that we could put on this, falls so unbearably short. In the words of St. Teresa on this special, and unfathomable spiritual space:

> When our Lord is pleased to take pity on the suffer-
> ings, both past and present, endured through her long-
> ing for Him by this soul which He has spiritually taken
> for His bride, He, before consummating the celestial

marriage, brings her into this His mansion or presence chamber. This is the seventh Mansion, for as He has a dwelling-place in heaven, so has He in the soul, where none but He may abide and which may be termed a second heaven...

In the former favours our Lord unites the spirit to Himself and makes it both blind and dumb like St. Paul after his conversion, thus preventing its knowing whence or how it enjoys this grace, for the supreme delight of the spirit is to realize its nearness to God. During the actual moment of divine union the soul feels nothing, all its powers being entirely lost. But now He acts differently: our pitiful God removes the scales from its eyes letting it see and understand somewhat of the grace received in a strange and wonderful manner in this mansion by means of intellectual vision.

By some mysterious manifestation of the truth, the three Persons of the most Blessed Trinity reveal themselves, preceded by an illumination which shines on the spirit like a most dazzling cloud of light. The three Persons are distinct from one another; a sublime knowledge is infused into the soul, imbuing it with a certainty of the truth that the Three are of one substance, power, and knowledge and are one God. Thus that which we hold as a doctrine of faith, the soul now, so to speak, understands by sight, though it beholds the Blessed Trinity neither by the eyes of the body nor of the soul, this being no imaginary vision. All the Three Persons here communicate Themselves to the soul, speak to it and make it understand the words of our Lord in the Gospel that He and the Father and the Holy Ghost will come and make their abode with the soul which loves Him and keeps His commandments.[2]

One might imagine this is what people refer to when they say that one has "received the Holy Spirit." In this moment, there is no word that can describe what's going on, no name to the almost alien, unsettling peace that falls over you. There's just that *sense*. That understanding that you've never been alone, and you never will be, even when the world tricks you into thinking you are. This is the moment of Union: where you and God meet each other in the true bliss of mystery and join together into One Being, something like the way husband and wife become one flesh. (Don't be fooled, though: the way the Saints talk of this Union, which one might call *bridal mysticism,* doesn't mean you're actually doing anything literally explicit with God; it's just the closest metaphor one can get to touch on the intimacy and mystery and love one understands in this space.)

This sounds scary at first, and many times have we heard people say that they are *afraid* of Union: of the day that we realize that we are all stray grains of sand that make up God's great beach, or single drops of water that return to His great ocean. However, it's not like your actual sense of *you* disappears and you become some pseudo-soulless husk with no grip on reality or no sense of self actualization. At least, not while you live. Many students and teachers of mysticism will say that, *you*—the real you, not the mask you've been wearing all through this life—will never quite go away, even in Union.

McColman calls this Union more of something like *Comm*-union, "in which we are invited into communion/union with the Holy Spirit, with Christ, and through them, with the infinite mystery and the fullness of the One Triune God" and that's beautiful, and hopefully a balm for people who are scared of the idea of joining with their God and losing all sense of self.[3] McColman asserts that "you don't become identical with God," as is the impression one might get from reading Hadewjich's words earlier, "but the union you experience between creature and

2. St. Teresa, *Interior Castle,* 117-118.

3. McColman, *Big Book of Christian Mysticism,* 88.

creator is the closest that any two beings can enjoy."[4] Perhaps that's where we might understand what St. Teresa says, when she says that Union is not as all immersive as spiritual marriage, using that metaphor of two wax candles versus rain falling into a stream we mentioned in the last chapter.

One might wonder if the people who study mysticism aren't simply nervous themselves of the implications of what others like St. Teresa say. Many times, folks like Mabry and McColman may very well be selling short the full self-shattering of joining back with God; they may turn their noses up at the claim that we *are* God and suggest that there will always be that line between Creature and Creator. But what does a drop of rainwater become when it falls into the ocean, or a stream? Can you count the individual drops and source them from the clouds, remember their names and faces and lives in the water cycle? Or is it that, when we look at that churning ocean, that flowing stream, we simply see one Body of water?

There is nuance, of course. We're sure these scholars are more hoping to ward the people who read their works off from the delusion that the facet of God people hold within them is the facet of the Father: the one we normally call God in the first place. After all, in Trinitarian doctrine, even if God, Jesus, and the Holy Spirit are all (facets of) God, they are not each other. You may have seen this helpful diagram at some point in life that explains it:

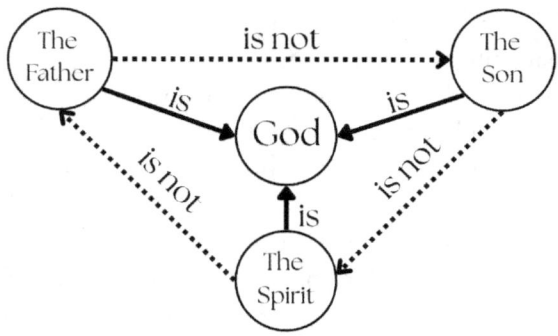

---

4. Ibid., 101.

Just as God the Son is not God the Father or God the Spirit, so too is God the Bride not God the Son, Father, or Spirit. Different facets, different parts of the great Body. However, St. Paul reminds of the folly of thinking of any of these parts as non-essential. Read, remember, and truly meditate on this passage, 1 Corinthians 12:12-27:

> There is one body, but it has many parts. But all its many parts make up one body. It is the same with Christ. We were all baptized by one Holy Spirit. And so we are formed into one body. It didn't matter whether we were Jews or Gentiles, slaves or free people. We were all given the same Spirit to drink. So the body is not made up of just one part. It has many parts.

> Suppose the foot says, "I am not a hand. So I don't belong to the body." By saying this, it cannot stop being part of the body. And suppose the ear says, "I am not an eye. So I don't belong to the body." By saying this, it cannot stop being part of the body. If the whole body were an eye, how could it hear? If the whole body were an ear, how could it smell? God has placed each part in the body just as he wanted it to be. If all the parts were the same, how could there be a body? As it is, there are many parts. But there is only one body.

> The eye can't say to the hand, "I don't need you!" The head can't say to the feet, "I don't need you!" In fact, it is just the opposite. The parts of the body that seem to be weaker are the ones we can't do without. The parts that we think are less important we treat with special honor. The private parts aren't shown. But they are treated with special care. The parts that can be shown don't need special care. But God has put together all the parts of

the body. And he has given more honor to the parts that didn't have any. In that way, the parts of the body will not take sides. All of them will take care of one another. If one part suffers, every part suffers with it. If one part is honored, every part shares in its joy.

You are the body of Christ. Each one of you is a part of it.

No matter how far we can or cannot go while in life, however, there is something to be said about how hard it is to take the physical world seriously when you encounter God enough and get the meta behind the mundane *and* the magical.

Another thing that happens here, though, is something of an ego death (yes, another one; as we said, they never really stop happening). Let us ask you this: what is the thing you want most in the world? And can you instead dedicate that thing, and the pursuit of it, to God rather than yourself?

Careful. Don't answer too fast. Let yourself sit in the discomfort that is wrestling with that ego. In fact, hold that thought and that discomfort while we continue walking together. Let us tell you individually about our own moments of Union, and our realization that made our skin feel like sackcloth, our faces like wooden masks, and our soul like fire uncontainable, climbing up our throat and flaring out our head like a crown.

Sara Says:

You know how when you were a kid, and you talked about heaven with your friends, you'd say silly things like "I bet Heaven has endless pizza" or "I bet the clouds are made of cotton candy" or something that just *thrilled* your little kid heart? Something that made you truly think of a big reward, of *paradise,* in the way only kids could conceive of?

Yeah.

My good friend Fr. Kyle and I have talked about this, and he said it well: it's not that heaven is actually like this in any way. Rather, it's that we simply don't have the means to fully grasp what it will be like to reunite with and be in full communion with God once we die and return to Him. It's beyond our comprehension. There are no words that can accurately capture it, and maybe this is why the many descriptions within Scripture and within the words of the Saints rub us the wrong way when it describes Heaven as a place where we tell God how awesome and cool He is for all eternity.

After all, that sounds like an endless church service. And while some of us might like church, you can't do it all day and night without getting bored at best, desperate to leave at worst. But that's why it's an *imperfect metaphor*, as all things are, about Heaven; the truth is, being near God (and understanding God as truly *infinite*, truly *Source*, truly the alpha and omega, the very bookends of all creation and the throughline threaded between all that is, seen and unseen), dazzles the soul. I've never died and gone to Heaven, but I have been overwhelmed by the magnitude of God, and I have definitely cried while thanking and praising Him with wild abandon for being all that He is (and not being all that He is not). That's the closest I might get, I think, to understanding that kind of ecstasy and love the Saints and prophets talk about being so infinite in Heaven—akin to enjoying the sunlight on my face from the (relative) safety of Earth instead of being right next to the sun and vaporizing myself in its infinite radiation.

Coming into this space is strange, though. It almost feels like there's something wrong with me when I sit utterly unphased at certain things that go on in the world. Sure, some things still get my goat, of course—being all *unified with God* and whatever doesn't snap the anxiety disorders and other such things away forever, and at the end of the day, it doesn't make me suddenly as perfect and holy and flawless as Christ, either, as much as I wish it might—but when I hear about the way things are going downhill in the world, or how people can be awful to each other and do terrible things, I can't explain the type of *peace* that hits.

Not peace that knows God will handle everything. Not peace that makes me feel particularly warm and fuzzy about all this. Not peace that lets me turn a blind eye to it. But the peace, or rather, the *knowing*, that humanity is simply repeating more of its awful, terrible cycles, learning the same old lessons in new variations, and that, as with the turn of the Wheel, we will all be past this terror (before being plunged into it again). When Jesus says He gives us peace, and He leaves His peace with us,[5] it really does make you squint up at Heaven and wonder what the hell kind of "peace" He's talking about—if this is it.

As you see when you read her writings, St. Teresa understands that there's an infinity to God that no amount of words will touch on—hence why apophatic mysticism becomes so important, and why *spiritual marriage* is something a touch more than the whole concept of Union, which still keeps us distinct in some way while we live out our lives on earth. When you reach this point, you, too, come to understand it, and you come to understand something even more grave: that when St. Paul says one should boast in nothing but the Lord, it's for damn good reason.

And for all your boasting and pride in your God, you learn that what He can give to you in kind is a joy almost overwhelming, the way too much sugar stings the tongue: as mystics like St. Teresa and Mechthild and Hadewjich and so many others describe, it's a love that is so unconditional and so strong that you sit in disgust with yourself for even once thinking about throwing it away, even though you know you've never loved or been loved *so* unconditionally like that outside Him. God's love is something that, like the sun on your skin after thirty minutes with no sunscreen, can go from warm and delightful to *painful* and *blistering,* and that paradox is something that takes a long time to fully accept.

In that Qliphoth, I learned a lot about myself, and by extension, I learned a lot about God: what He is, and what He is not. I'll never forget Lucifuge Rofocale telling me, there in darkest pits of Satariel, that God was not with me, and that His light could not reach me in that blackness—that I was alone, unguarded, vulnerable to any and all evil that would rip me in two in a clean second. He told me this and asked me if I was afraid, and I told him the truth: I wasn't. I'd come into that supposed Tree of Death with a radical trust, and wish to trust, these beings everyone said were so evil, and I (rather erroneously) believed

Lucifuge would never let anything happen to me, as if he were secretly bound to the same codes of protection and love one could imagine an angel was (they are not, and in fact, even angels themselves are not). I also responded with a platitude: "Where I am, God is."

He asked me if I really understood what he was saying, or what I was saying. I said yes to both. It was a twofold lie.

I don't know if I can accurately put to words the *knowing* about God that came after spending time with the demons, or the betrayal that knowing spawned. Not the betrayal some folks think they experience, where they "realize" that God is actually the "enemy" or something rote and ridiculous; no, I mean the betrayal of knowing that every second I spent in literal hell was a second spent with God, just the same as every moment I ever spent on the edge of heaven, with any Saint or angel.

Why are You here? It was the endless question I had, even if I didn't always put it to words while I was with the demons, whenever I perceived Divinity in the places I did not expect to find it. *What are You doing here?*

It's the knowing, I tell you, the *knowing* that eventually makes you go a little crazy: knowing that God truly *will* use every possible method and mode of teaching to reach us, because God *is in* every possible method and mode. That when the mystics and Saints say that to look into the eyes of another person is to see God staring back at you, it's true in the most literal and yet metaphorical of ways. That when Meister Eckhart says that every path leads to God, it's because God, in his words, *is isness.*

And even when we think we've abandoned Him, or He's abandoned us, the truth is that there is no escaping Him. He appears like a dream when we want Him, and He hounds us like a nightmare when we think we don't. No one has seen His face and lived because *He has no face.* No one has understood Him because *He cannot be understood.* Fuck, He's not even actually a He in the first place—not even canonically, within the pages of that Bible! He is *everything,* and when you are *everything,* you are also *nothing:* you are no *one* thing.

This is the Monad. This is the thing ancient Greek and Roman philosophers spoke of, that one God above even the gods of Olympus, the one that, because all things spawned from it, they believed was indirectly worshipped by the worship of its creation. The one that, according to Apollo in the Greek work, *Philosophy from Oracles,* the "holy Hebrews greatly honor,"[6] and the one that any who perceived of one Source knew: the Hindus, the Zoroastrians, anyone. Apophatic mysticism therefore tells us: every name and every face we put on this Source is not actually the Thing we desire, but the gift box we receive the Thing in. Whether it be a god-mask by the name of Hecate, Yahweh, Loki, Kokopelli, Amaterasu, Nu Wa, Ra, they are simply masks, or even doorways, that lead us up to this Infinity we cannot perceive or understand—and this Infinity baptizes us in itself, in glorious light, in *fire* that burns away all our illusions, when we encounter this Dark Night of the Soul. In that space, we realize everything we knew and thought we could expect or predict or rely on about it is wrong. We learn that we actually have no idea who God is, only some vague concept of who He presents Himself as to us.

It's enough to drive anyone to madness to think on too long. Harrowing. When I do think about it, though, as I have here, I feel it: the fiery, pepper-like, golden glitter of Something in the skin of my hands and forearms, and the mind-scrambling, somehow *loud* peace of Someone bringing me to that state that the Saints before me have called ecstasy. It makes my face feel less attached to my head, as if I could pull it off like a scab. It makes the edges of my body feel less established and the concerns the world wants me to get wrapped up in feel less real.

People have told me before: "I'm afraid of giving up who I am. I'm afraid of Union, of losing myself." But once you hit this patch of mystical grass, I tell you: you realize that "yourself" was also, like the many names of God and the many ideas we attach to Him, just another casing, another shell, that was never really *real* to begin with. Another mask and costume of a millenia-long play you're acting in. This can be hard to deal with, make no mistake; there is a fine line between a mystical knowing and a genuine mental health condition like depersonalization/derealization and dissociation, and I certainly am not talking about or advocating for the latter when I talk like this—but God, can it be hard to understand where that thin line even is between the two. It takes an iron grip on one's sanity to get here.

---

6. Robert Louis Wilken, *The Christians as the Romans Saw Them* (USA: Yale University Press, 2013), 152.

Of course, all of this doesn't mean I'm some amazing sage that is flawless and perfect and never messes up anymore. Sometimes my senses deaden again, and I fall asleep from time to time; I still get caught and snagged by illusions and get freaked out by things that don't really matter in the long run. I still find myself wanting rather than accepting, and I still find myself reacting rather than engaging. Just like with my experiences in talking to the many spirits in *Where the Gods Left Off* and *When Angels & Demons Collude,* I'll internalize a lesson so deeply, only to forget the very next day and start a cycle all over again. It is what it is. We live in a world that does everything in its power to make us forget who we are and where we come from. It's part of why this mystic cycle isn't something you accomplish once and get a certificate for; it's something that will start again and again, over and over, until you finally break free from your body in death and move on. You aren't weak or worthless for having to live these same lessons over and over again. You are simply human.

Mimi says:

For a very long time, I never thought I had reached the ideals of the Union; one where my "spirit cleaved unto God." To me, anything even remotely close to that instantly had me aligning those ideals with becoming a nun. (Thank you, black and white thinking.) And when I was young, the idea of God loving me felt warm, safe, and all the things a child looks for in comfort and love from a caregiver. God was something I thought I could trust.

The church itself has done enough damage in the name of God that, when the time came, I cut off whatever I thought was God during the beginning of my deconstruction. I kept Jesus around, though. Funnily enough, the way I still studied and talked to Jesus like a friend, it felt like I was talking to my Aunt every so often. It was parent-adjacent. And I had, in fact, kept that mindset until I was about thirty years old (because deconstruction is not an overnight thing). So to speak on Union with God, of worship and utter devotion, I... have been stumped. Just like St. Teresa, I don't know how to put this into words.

After all, I reached the energy of the Sun; I have seen the turning of the cycles with the Wheel, and yet I come up empty on what to say.

Does that mean I failed? Did I actually ever experience the energy of the Lovers? Was I just in a spiritual situationship with God? Maybe. This is going to be a little different, so bear with me. I am going to try and untangle the years of study and faith and struggle and cycles of healing while also trying to bring my UPG into clarity.

First, I do not follow the Trinitarian Doctrine, which states that God is one being who exists as three co-equal persons: the Father, the Son (Jesus), and the Holy Spirit. I came to this in my mid-twenties, when I was further deconstructing and trying to figure out why the Council of Nicea had so much to do with why we learn the Bible the way we do now.

With the research I have done (and written on in *Discovering Christian Witchcraft*), I see the Abrahamic pantheon as exactly that: a pantheon. El and Asherah are the Creator and Celestial Wife much like Osiris and Isis, Zeus and Hera, Odin and Freya, Dagda and Danu, etc. There are also a *lot* of incarnation stories from that area and time period, which led me to believe that while Jesus was the Son of God (as the incarnation of God on earth, living a human experience), Mary Magdalene was the Daughter of Asherah (with a lot of connection to historical context of how oils and perfumes worked in temples and rituals, as well as the city Magdala being a place of Goddess worship with lots of dove symbolism). Their union on this Earth created a balance between Divine Feminine and Divine Masculine.

While this may seem Esoteric, maybe even Gnostic, it isn't wholly without merit as we learn more about Caananite religion, cultural context, and further study on a larger scale. We can see it in Yin and Yang, "As Above, So Below," and so many other recognizable symbols and phrases, too. Even with the way Sara and I approach belief and write on it, you can see the split: Sara represents the Divine Masculine, and her worship of God the Father and sharp tongue and wit burn with a holy fire that many of us see reflected in male deities. On the other hand, I represent the Divine Feminine, with my worship being a focus on healing, nurturing, protecting and guiding through love and grace.

(Though please do remember that all genders can occupy all ideas here; this language is a manifestation for how we are able to perceive the balance in our lives of *all* things and how it affects us to help us understand our world. If this language doesn't work for you, that's fine.

You have a way and a calling that makes it work, and therefore, it is your own to do with as you will! I'm just calling it like I see it in my own experience and understanding, using my own *kataphatic* symbols that make sense to me.)

My relationship with God is still very much adjacent to these ideas, though I find it to be more empowering in the acknowledgement overall. My devotion is through Asherah, and I liken it to the way some followers of Greek deities would worship Hera but offer respect (not devotion) to Zeus, or the same with other deities.

Now, in particular, my relationship with the Holy Spirit, referenced as Lady Wisdom in Proverbs, Psalms, and other Old Testament books, is framed in the belief that this is the Divine Spark that makes us fully human and also divine: it is the energy we all share, spoken on through countless mediums, found in countless myths and stories, and believed by so many. If there's anywhere I might talk of Union, I feel like it could be here, in the way all these things come together in this Holy Spirit.

The energy I have found from the Lovers is shown through a commitment to maintaining balance and healing, teaching and serving through acts of stewardship to the world. The earth is my altar, prayer is my intention. The acts of service I give in love, for both man and beast, is my worship. My heart aches and pleads and finds succor in the lap of creation; the wind is my breath, the stream is my lifeblood. The grass is my skin and the trees are my fingers, ever reaching upward to Spirit; my eyes take on the flowers and my lips sing the song of insect and beast.

I do not rush to seek refuge in the woods, but rather, the seat of my soul remains in the moss and dirt, and I simply am going home. John Muir said, "And into the forest I go, to lose my mind and find my soul." This is why I am so bound with love to the Appalachian folk practice; it is as much of the Land and Spirit as I am. The way Spirit exists in everything we see, feel, hear, smell, taste, and touch – the land, the people, and the familiar tug in my heart that I know ties us all together. *That* is my Union.

The Court Declares No Guilt, But What of the Defendant?

And now, here you are, left to simmer in the truth of Union. In overcoming these trials to get to this Master Bedroom, in approaching this level of understanding, one truly begins to see the "meta" beneath the mask of mysticism and spirituality and even that fun little thing we call *witchcraft*—and that means that one cannot so easily turn from what they know and go back to the expression of spirituality one once started with.

Even if, as we have confessed, our spirituality might come to look on the surface like nothing more than the same age-old and classic Christian tradition, with prayers and church-going, hymns and Bible study, the reality is that the internal work done on a mystic path is one that can never be undone, and it is something that those in the classical Christian tradition who have *not* done will recoil from, because it looks (and feels) like hell on earth. The wisdom one gains from it, however, can never be forgotten, no matter what our path looks like in the future. Those who would turn back now, if they do, they do so not because they see this is false—but because they cannot bear the responsibility that comes with knowing it's true.

However, as many wise folk have said: this simply is not a path for everyone. If you can't seem to access this mystic path, no matter how hard you try, then perhaps the answer is to stop trying at all—especially if your understanding of what it means to succeed as Witch or Mystic is simply to have these ecstatic experiences you hear so many speak about online or in other witchy or spiritual circles. As McColman puts it:

> Mysticism is often equated with extraordinary or supernatural phenomena and, certainly, in its most dramatic forms, it is both extraordinary and supernatural. But only a very small number of Christians are destined for such dramatic experience as the presence of God, just as only a few musicians can be as great as Mozart or John Coltrane,

and only a few athletes reach the pinnacle of achievement
as Olympic gold medalists.[7]

You might read this and get discouraged, but before that sinking
feeling creeps over you, let us also remind you: "if mysticism… is only
for the chosen few, however, holiness is for everyone."[8] McColman
rightly points out that if you're only into mysticism, or witchcraft,
for the sake of those flashy experiences like St. Hildegard and others
have had—if you're only here for the rush, the thrill, of performing
miracles (spells) and manipulating the fabric of reality, hearing God
speak directly to you in some special way—then you actually miss out
on a great deal of what it means to be a mystic at all.

In fact, there are many considered mystics, contemplatives, and even
occultists who have *never* had such experiences—including the great
Agrippa! Yet look how much work he did, and how that work now
guides the many more empirically minded mystics, like magicians and
occultists and witches of the modern day. Look how many people continued, through the effort of prayer and meditation and contemplation,
to make fantastic efforts in healing the Body of Christ with their words
and civic actions, like Dietrich Bonhoeffer or Martin Luther King, Jr.

One must say this again and again for it to truly sink in: you *do not
need* to be a Witch, to be having all of these strange experiences or doing
all these supernatural works, to be united to God. You are not lacking,
nor are you powerless, nor are you unworthy. Just like some people can
see and hear spirits where the majority of us can't, just like some have
a lucky streak that seems supernatural while others have what seems
like a curse of unluckiness, just like some seem to get instant answers
from God while others can't hear Him (or recognize when He speaks),
there will always be some who are marked for different purposes (and
you may very well find yourself among the magically marked, lucky
and burdened as you are!). But that's what makes the Body of Christ so
fascinating: we don't ask the hand to see like the eye can, or the eye to
carry us places like the legs can, or the legs to feel deeply like the heart

---

7. McColman, *Big Book of Christian Mysticism*, 166

8. Ibid., 167.

can. All of us have our role, and all of us work together to manifest the love and glory of God into this broken world.

In this space of Union, in surpassing all these trials, whether as a Witch or a Mystic or simply a beloved child of God, you come to know something that, once again, can never be unlearned: you already *are* gifted, in your own unique way that doesn't need to look like anyone else's way. And while this Court finds you innocent of all charges, if you've gotten here, the Court *does not absolve you of using those gifts.* As a Witch, as a Mystic, or at least as a Contemplative, you know what you have to do. You know what is being asked of you, and to add onto McColman's insistence that holiness is for everyone, we will say: *you are expected to still work.* No one who calls themselves a friend of God can stand by while evil rolls like a cloud of miasma over our communities and threatens the health and wellbeing of our neighbors.

Just know that no matter what, no matter how you understand your gifts and skills–be they witchy and magical or concrete and tangible, or both—you have a place with God. You have a path to Him, a connection, that can't be broken unless *you* choose to break it–and even then, the difference between a *contract* and a *covenant,* as Mabry puts it, is that the covenant is never abandoned: "the party that continues [upholding the covenant] hopes that the offending party will eventually come around and the relationship can be restored."[9] Sometimes, it seems that God drops the covenant, as in the Dark Night of the Soul, when He appears to have abandoned us. Sometimes, it's us that drops the covenant, walking away from God. Always, though, *always,* is there the open door for reconciliation and restoration–for picking up like nothing ever happened and beginning the walk to God again.

So go. Pick up your covenant and walk.

Shadow Work for Union:

- Acts of forgiveness are courageous, and yet we rarely do it for ourselves. As you lean into love and peace, you may still see things you did earlier on that has left scars, proverbially or literally. What are some things you have to forgive yourself for?

- What are some ways you can show grace to yourself physically, mentally, emotionally, and spiritually?

- The other side of this is loving others as yourself. How do you feel with your new boundaries? Have you made any? Write those down, or what you think you should change/create as a boundary.

- What are some things you can do to show acts of love or devotion in your community?

Chapter Eight

The Cycle Begins Anew

The Mystic and the Witch

*I*T SEEMS LIKE THAT'S *the end of the visions and truths. The mystery is solved, for the time being; the message is decoded, and both women's spirits untangled and unburdened in the work of deciphering the Divine. The sunlight is fading fast, and so the two women know that it's time for the Mystic to leave (though, of course, with her basket emptied of her forest finds and filled anew with fresh scones and fruits and other such creations of the Witch's kitchen).*

Just as the Witch finishes tidying up and moves to put the deck back in its place, however, she notices that two cards have been left behind. Surely, it wasn't due to carelessness… No, Spirit has something else to tell the Mystic, and the Witch knows her voice is needed one last time. Before the Mystic can cross the threshold and escape back into her world of stone and dusty books and fenced off, secluded gardens, the Witch calls her and waves her back to the table to see what cards are there.

"Well," the Mystic says as she blinks at the swirling, identical designs on their backs, "alright, let's see what was left unsaid, then."

The Witch sits back down in her worn, wooden chair and dismisses its creaking with a clearing of her throat. Her fingers find the edges of the cards and flip them unceremoniously to reveal the last of the Major Arcana: Judgment and The World, the sight of which make the Mystic blink.

"This is curious, isn't it?" With a cat-like smile curling over her face, the Witch leans back and looks up at her friend. "Just as you've finished your vision, the cards speak of more—far more. In fact, they tell a story of things coming to an end, only to begin again."

All the peace the Mystic had from clarifying her strange revelation dissipates. She thinks over it all—the eventually scorching sun of the Courtyard, the bone-dry throat and eyes the Sitting Room gave her, the monsters of the Dark Hallway, and she whines, "Again?"

"Mhm." The Witch offers only one slow nod for comfort. "You must now take all that you have seen and learned and use those skills to unlock the next chapter, where you'll be challenged yet again. If I've learned anything about you, and your Lord, then I know this isn't going to be your first or last vision, my friend. You will take this journey again, until the path has worn thin with the stamping of your soles and the wind whispering through the trees speaks your name. Your triumphs are hard-fought and well won, though, and your struggles only prove your strength. Be ready, dear Mystic; be ready because you know you are ready."

A pout crops up in the Mystic's lips, and though her head sways a little, she resists the urge to huff and fully shake her frustration out. That would only send the treats in her basket onto the floor. The Witch gets up, still smiling, and offers her friend a comforting pat on the shoulder.

"Go on, now," she says, "or you'll have a hard time seeing the path home."

She kisses the Mystic's cheek, and the Mystic returns the affection. Then, in a blink, the Witch finds herself in her doorway, watching the Mystic hurry away into the woods and turning only for a moment to wave before disappearing. It's always this way between them, the Witch notices: an entire day spent talking, baking, enjoying the garden, eating—and both receiving some lesson from Spirit that neither of them expected to parse. The Witch sighs, her smile still hanging on her lips, and she goes to close her door.

Until she catches a certain energy in the air: the energy of a certain Shepherd. One whose hair is wooly white and crackles with the static of Heaven, one whose hands have holes in them and whose eyes are soft despite the fire burning within them. She tastes the electricity in the air and catches glimpses of its form every time she blinks.

"What are you still doing here?" The Witch can't help but smile wider at this energy—so rife with power, yet still sheepish, humble, like a brother that hasn't visited in far too long. She grabs a dish towel from where it's hanging on her stove and waves the damp thing through the static-y air the same way she waves troublesome chipmunks from her pea patch. "Get going and see to it that your sheep doesn't trip on a tree root on her way home."

The pink, soft glow of heat lightning from somewhere beyond illuminates the shadowing cottage for just a moment—and with what feels like a gentle laugh rolling down the Witch's spine, so too does that brotherly Shepherd's energy. Then it's gone, and the Witch looks after her friend, knowing that Someone is watching over her, ensuring her safe return home.

The Adversary Prepares for the Next Trial

Wouldn't it be nice if you only had to learn every lesson once? If all these rooms we've talked about, and all these sections of the mystical journey, were a task you could check off in your agenda as done and move on from? It sure would make life a lot simpler and easier to get through.

However, if you've ever been on a mental health journey, you know that there's no such thing as "done." There's no such thing as "perfectly healed," and there's never a risk that your old triggers won't resurface, or that you'll never have episodes again, or that you'll never regress or get your life absolutely rumbled by a long bout of executive dysfunction. The mystical journey is much the same. We will all work our hardest to be better, not out of hope for some reward from God, but simply because we know it is good to do and that God is happy to see us thrive, *and we work despite knowing that we will make mistakes anyway.* We will know viscerally what Jesus means in His parable of the prodigal son, when the father treats that lost son like royalty upon his return while the faithful brother, who never strayed, never got such treatment: that grace is freely given, not earned. That God wants to pour His love onto us just because we are alive and we are His sweet little creatures, not because we checked all the boxes of a "correct" identity and did all the right things to "prove" our faith and said all the prayers perfectly without a single stutter.

In a mystic journey like this one, there will be moments where all of our learning, all of our meditations, all of our spellwork and magic and prayer and community, will still not be enough to stop the panic and the rage and the anxiety from sprouting when the world's events rattle us to our core. There will be moments that our ego still gets snagged on the cruel words of another person, or when insecurities pressed too hard will make us lash out like a scared, wounded animal. There will be times we are tempted to give up on our values and do things we know we shouldn't because the seeming rewards smell so sweet, even though we know better. Every time, we will find ourselves wandering out of the Master Bedroom and back into any of the other rooms, or perhaps even all the way out to the Courtyard, to clean out this newly discovered wound, polish this once unnoticed spot of tarnish, that still sits on our souls.

There is nothing you can do about that. However, rather than be disheartened by this seemingly never-ending trial, think of it instead like a continuous chance to prove yourself—to learn, grow, and apply old lessons in new ways. Because that's what it is.

Sara Says:

Have you ever played an open world video game? Like *Dark Souls*, or *Elden Ring*, or *Breath of the Wild*, or anything like that? Because it's games like those, that let you go anywhere you want at any point of the game, that feel a lot the way exploring these mansions feels. You may tunnel through to nearly the end of the game, defeating monsters, growing stronger, getting better strategies together, making plans in your head… only to end up back near the start of the game, looking around for all the trinkets and side rooms and little secrets you missed when you weren't "strong" (or, rather, *comfortable*) enough to do so.

The Souls series (*Dark Souls, Bloodborne, Elden Ring*, etc.) are an especially great metaphor for this because of a little feature they have called *New Game+*, which is oddly relevant as we think of the mystic journey: it's a feature where, after you beat the whole game, you're given the option to to start over and begin the game again, but differently than before. The next time, you start with all the special items, upgraded weapons, and cool armor you collected through your first playthrough, and at first, this makes you think the second playthrough will be a breeze. It's easy to imagine that it'll be a little walk down memory lane, where all those monsters and bosses that gave you such a hard time the first go 'round are suddenly so weak and puny compared to all your actual gaming skills *and* fancy weapons and such.

Then you swing on a beginner-area soldier, and not only does he not die in one hit like you expected: he also turns around and cleaves a good quarter of your health off in one swing. That's when you realize that everything in the game got stronger with you—that all those items and skills you took with you weren't an unfair advantage, but a *necessity*. Your "walk down memory lane" has become a whole new level of struggle and frustration and, somehow, challenge–and the excitement that comes with such a challenge.

That's what it's like being on the mystic path. There's never a time where you're truly done walking through any of these mansions. To say there is would be like saying you never have to go to the kitchen in your house again because you've already been there once and made a meal in it. But a new day comes, and when you need to eat again, guess where you'll be? Whether with a sizzling, fresh meal off the stove or a little bowl of milk and soggy corn flakes, your ass will be parked in that kitchen again, munching away on whatever you found.

There's nothing wrong with this, mind you. As you go through your *life-long* journey, it's easy to feel like you've failed or that you're inept because you end up back in one of these zones you were so sure you already mastered. That's not the case, though. You can think of each time you revisit a mansion as when you have to re-wash a shirt to get a stain more faded each time, or when you wash rice and dump the water out over and over until the water is clear. Will the stain ever fully disappear in our lifetimes? Will the rice our soul is sitting in ever wash clear before we leave our bodies in the dirt?

I don't know. But what I do know is that I'm no stranger to this process, because no matter how much I think I know, and how many things I think I've learned, I find myself coming back to these "beginner" areas. So now, let me give you an example of my own repeated lessons by sharing a moment that screams *Courtyard* (yes, Courtyard, from all the way in Chapter 1!). Funnily enough, the moment happened *just* before I found it in me to write this section. It was a moment that Mimi helped me work through, and that after I'd recognized it for what it is, made me feel perfectly embarrassed to realize where I was in my spiritual journey.

After all, I'm writing a (second!) book about this stuff! *Shouldn't* I be farther along? What the hell am I doing *all the way back* in the Courtyard, being as spiritually weathered and tried as I am?

Well, that's the thing, isn't it? This spiritual journey isn't a one-and-done thing, as we've said probably a hundred times now. When you imagine that Courtyard—and the great Manor ahead with its big heavy doors, and its large Gate behind you, still open in case you want to bolt and leave—you might also imagine that there are little strings tied to you, puppet strings, that threaten to pull you back out that Gate even if you *don't* want to leave. Each string is a vice—a piece of your shadow that's been holding you back. I find one doesn't tend to realize the strings are there until they've coiled tight around the heart and begun to *squeeze* until it feels like they're about to cut through. I know many folks are familiar with that feeling.

That unease. Dread. Pure anxiety.

It's a sign that something needs to go, and it was thanks to Mimi that I figured out what. You see, I hadn't been able to make any progress writing this book for a long time. I distracted myself with other projects, told myself I'd just take a little break and get back into it. I read book after book after book, then sat there trying to organize all that information into some neatly packaged cube in my brain like I was an academic trash compactor. I made the most meticulous outlines and notes that showed *exactly* where every scrap of information I had would go, so that no one would ever doubt or question that I knew what I was talking about so that the book would be perfectly easy to understand and work through for everyone and de-mystify mysticism forever.

Hmm.

That procrastination, that promise of *I'll get to it, I'll get to it!*—it didn't make the strings tightening around my heart any lighter. My anxiety only doubled. And soon, I wasn't able to read my books anymore; I was too "burned out" to do so. I wasn't able to read, *hadn't* been able to write, was barely doing my tarot and felt like spirituality itself was becoming something of a chore when all I wanted to do was sit down and rot. And soon, there was nothing for me to do at all but maintain the status quo of my work: do my weekly duties, log off, and go pretend my problems didn't exist with some video games. The new *Fantasy Life* came out, y'know? It was self care, rest, it was what I *deserved* and *earned,* to sit there for hours and hours and play it while deadlines walked steadily my way.

But if you've read this far, you might guess what I'm about to tell you. It wasn't self care at all; it was distraction. It was refusal to face the real problem. Refusal to dig below the surface of my issues with this book. All this was made worse because I love my work! I love reading and have so many books I want to get through; I love talking with God and doing my spiritual upkeep. I love sharing new ideas with folks and experiencing new things in the spiritual world, especially if they can help others untangle some of their own dilemmas!

Yet I couldn't do it. Not just in an *I'm too tired* way, but at one point, it really felt like something was just *heavy* on me. Like I was trying to break the surface of the ocean while a twenty pound vest was holding me under the water. I kept thinking it was just the burnout, but it's clear to me now that it wasn't: it was one of these strings slowly dragging me out of the Manor, out into the Courtyard, and nearly out the Gate itself, out to a world I do not recognize and that leaves me feeling just as grey and drab and dead as the one we painted for you earlier. It wasn't until Mimi and I got together to talk and figure out the issue that we finally broke this curse; Mimi caught me in my own free-fall out of the Manor and gave me a little exercise that turned the old Courtyard into a Sandbox.

"Sara, here's what you're going to do," she said. "You're going to open a new document and you're going to write all your doubts about the book. Then you're going to go through each one and ask, 'Why?' and when you have an answer, you're going to look at that answer and ask again, 'Why?' and you're going to do that until you've gotten to the bottom of this. You can't write about shadow work if you don't do it."

After a bunch of whining and moping and groaning about it, we got off the call, and that's exactly what I did. I wrote my biggest fears about this book, and I asked myself why—and the string around my heart loosened with each response. The twenty pound weight became eighteen pounds, then fifteen, then ten, then five, then none as I sat there in the sun of the Courtyard and plunked my butt in the metaphorical dirt. I wrote out my woes with a stick in the sand, and I discovered the real problem all along: nothing but a mean case of imposter syndrome.

You see, the first book Mimi and I wrote together has been such a point of pride for me. So academic. So full of scholarly information. Such a flex of my educational muscles! This next book had to be like that, too—or so I thought. After all, who could take a book seriously that was so based on UPG and personal experience? How would a book like that be worth anything to anyone? I had to have *something* to back up everything I was saying outside myself—

Why?

—because obviously, I'm just a nobody with no real credentials. I don't have a theology degree from a fancy seminary I can hold up and point to, and that makes everything I'm saying worth less than if I *did* have that fancy degree—

Why?

—because the degree is proof, evidence, that I know what I'm talking about, and if I can't *be* that authority, then I have to have other authorities like scholars or Saints or the Bible or something that back me up; otherwise I'm nothing but a fraud—

Why?

And deeper and deeper it went, until something as innocent (and still necessary, don't get me wrong) as wanting some secondary sources to back up our arguments became revealed for what it was. Plainly, it was my attempt to cover my own shame and feelings of inadequacy over not having a stamp of approval from a man-made institution. In an age of rising anti-intellectualism, of course it's always important to know how to find and vet good quality sources, and as a teacher of rhetoric to the next generation of thinkers and leaders and workers, I'll never tell you otherwise—but I *will* tell you what I discovered here, which is that sometimes our need for credentials and accolades and titles and merit is a sign of a string tied to our souls, a string born of ego and all the lies it likes to tell us.

When I look at my astrology chart, I can tell you that I should've seen this coming. My Lilith is in Virgo in the ninth house, and one astrology website I used that I can't remember now had an interpretation that stuck with me ever since. That interpretation manifested right here, in this moment: Lilith in Virgo in the ninth house is a placement with a tendency to use their intelligence as a justification for acting holier-than-thou, and to disregard those it deems intellectually inferior.

Oops. Guilty as charged. I often have to check myself in that regard, and I don't always succeed in curbing that impulse.

But when it comes to mysticism, the true facts and figures will tell you: there *is* no "de-mystifying" mysticism (I mean, come on; just saying that out loud should've given me a hint, no?). There is no making things neat and tidy and perfectly factually accurate. There are no books that will concretely *prove* what I'm talking about, and when I think about it, I really have to ask myself: what's the difference between me running back to my sources and my academic muscle when things feel scary, uncertain, and hard to articulate, and the ex-witch that runs back to Christ when the road ahead becomes bumpy, dark, and full of terrors? From where I'm standing, not much.

I have no choice but to accept that when it comes to the inner life of the Christian Witch, the only books we have to go by besides the Bible are the ones that show us that others have been here before. Those books are the ones written by the Saints who had to figure it out for themselves, too—including our dear St. Teresa of Avila. In fact, the night before this revelation, I read another of her writings, a treatise on the four stages of prayer, and she ends it like this:

> The will must be fully occupied in loving, but it cannot understand how it loves; the intellect, if it understands, does not understand how it understands, or at least it can comprehend nothing of what it understands. It does not seem to me to be understanding, because, as I say, it doesn't understand—I really don't understand this![1]

(Me, too, girl. Me, too.)

But this is not uncommon with her. Again and again, she's asked to write books on these spiritual things, and again and again, her writings betray that really, she's not entirely sure of how to describe these things, either: only that she's been there, done that, and she's trying her best to

---

1. McGinn, *Essential Writings*, 117.

get the point across. Likewise, I realized, so am I. And I realized, in my talk with Mimi, that once upon a time, the Saints had no sources to go on, either. They had Scripture, just as you and I do, and little more—and *that did not stop them* from becoming the famous Saints we now pray to for intercession. Even though their writings became the source material for future Saints to fall back on, and for scholars to use as sources, at the time of their writing or seeing their visions, these things were what we would call UPG way back then (at least, until the other clergy around them had time to scrutinize them, such as in the case of St. Hildegard von Bingen).

This includes future Saints like you. Yes, you. And I. And Mimi. The mystic walk *is* the Saint's walk; the mystic journey is the Saint's journey (and, as you've no doubt seen now through the many tarot cards, it's also the Witch's journey). It's the journey of *anyone* on a complex spiritual walk like this, and it's important to note that they weren't *born* Saints, those holy men and women we now look back to; they didn't start knowing it all. They learned it through these exact steps we are now taking together, and we have to learn to move, perceive, and be humbled just as they were moved, just as they perceived, just as they were humbled. There is no way around it. There is no reading a book and getting a piece of paper and having a Ph.D in holiness; there is simply living it, in all our imperfection and for all our mistakes. Even the methodology, the procedural approach, of the Witch can't stave off these challenges and the lapses in our judgement as we try to overcome them.

Of course, going through this is easier said than done, and neither I nor St. Teresa are the first or the last to experience this. In fact, some four hundred years before St. Teresa, a certain St. Hildegard von Bingen experienced much the same kind of imposter syndrome and, for a very long time, refused to act on the spiritual gifts God gave her. She'd had terrible headaches, as well as extremely vivid visions, since she was a young girl, and when she got the call to share those visions, she admits in her first work, *Scivias,* that she denied the call because she didn't feel worthy:

> But I, though I saw and heard these things, refused to
> write for a long time through doubt and bad opinion and
> the diversity of human words, not with stubbornness but
> in the exercise of humility, until, laid low by the scourge
> of God, I fell upon a bed of sickness; then, compelled
> at last by many illnesses, and by the witness of a certain
> noble maiden of good conduct [the nun Richardis of
> Stade] and of that man whom I had secretly sought and
> found, as mentioned above, I set my hand to the writing.[2]

As you can see, God's response was to strike her with a sickness that
had her bedridden until she got over these feelings, got up, and got
to work. While I have no idea what her sickness entailed, that feeling
of being "struck down" and then bed rotting is certainly recognizable,
and it's because of something both St. Hildegard and I had to cut
off and leave coiled at the Gate: that imposter syndrome. St. Teresa
would've refused to write her works, too, had she not pushed herself
to be obedient to the wishes of her God and her superiors in the church
that urged her to share her knowledge—but even though she struggled
with it on the page, she still got it done, and so too did St. Hildegard
after she recovered from her illness.

Looking back on both of these holy women, these Doctors of the
Church, I see something invaluable in their experience: not only that
it happened and that they pushed through it, but that what they went
through *is* what I've gone through. That I am not alone in feeling the
way I feel or experiencing what I experience, and that this isn't a mark
of shame or a sign of my lack of faith, but rather a part of a tough, long,
and sometimes painful learning process.

In the end, that's really what this whole book is about. According to
McColman in his *Big Book of Christian Mysticism,* while one might think
of those hermits, those desert fathers like St. Antony, the reality is that
this solitude wasn't something that lasted for very long precisely because
the heart of Christianity is in community with each other; this led to

---

2. Hildegard von Bingen, *Scivias,* translated by Columba Hart and Jane Bishop with an
Introduction by Barbara J. Newman, and Preface by Caroline Walker Bynum (Paulist
Press, 1990), 60.

the start of the first monasteries, with Christians living together and understanding the function of communal contemplation and prayer.[3] The experience of the Divine, the human contact with God, is not something to be hoarded, but shared. It's not something that can live in the dark and be hidden away; it is something that touches us and makes us the *light of the world* as Jesus said. And He had a good point when it came to that light:

> You are the light of the world. A town built on a hill cannot be hidden. Neither do people light a lamp and put it under a bowl. Instead they put it on its stand, and it gives light to everyone in the house. In the same way, let your light shine before others, that they may see your good deeds and glorify your Father in heaven.[4]

That last line is a bit tricky. What does it mean to glorify God? We might've gotten a hint in the Guest Bedroom, when St. Teresa points out that if people look at our commitment to the Divine and think to praise God instead of just blowing smoke up our ass, that we've done well to achieve exactly this. But to go deeper, and to answer this more fully, we must understand what God is, which, given He's kind of infinite and ineffable and all that, is an impossible task. Still, we can at least get a rough idea, and that starts with the fact that God *is*. He just *is*. To call back to the words of Meister Eckhart, "God is is-ness." More explicitly, in Eckhart's words:

> Now the moment I flowed out from the Creator. All creatures stood up and shouted: 'Behold, here is God!'

---

3. McColman, *Big Book of Christian Mysticism*, 137-138.

4. Matthew 5:14-16

They were correct. For you ask me: 'Who is God? What is God?' I reply: 'Isness. Isness is God.' Where there is Isness, there God is. Creation is the giving of isness from God. And that is why God becomes where any creature expresses God.

Isness is so noble. No creature is so tiny that it lacks isness. If a caterpillar falls off a tree, It climbs up a wall in order to preserve its isness. So noble is isness!

What is God? God is!

Apprehend God in all things, for God is in all things. Every single creature is full of God and is a book about God. Every creature is a word of God...[5]

God exists in all things, everywhere, all the time, and He binds all things together in one Creation with His unending grace, love, and mercy, which He continuously pours out onto us. He *unifies* all things in this spirit of love, and for that reason, one can say that to glorify God is to not just shine, but specifically reflect *God's* shine, and to *help others see the way to their own shining,* their own "isness" that makes them connected *to* God. After all, according to St. Paul, we are mirrors of God when we face Him head on:

But whenever anyone turns to the Lord, the veil is taken away. Now the Lord is the Spirit, and where the Spirit

---

5. Matthew Fox, "Meister Eckhart on the Via Positiva," *Daily Meditations with Matthew Fox* (2019), https://dailymeditationswithmatthewfox.org/2019/09/11/meister-eckhart-on -the-via-positiva/.

of the Lord is, there is freedom. And we all, who with unveiled faces contemplate the Lord's glory, are being transformed into his image with ever-increasing glory, which comes from the Lord, who is the Spirit.[6]

This path was never meant to be walked alone. When one encounters something hard, something miserable, something challenging and self-rending on this path, they were not supposed to suffer alone; it was not what Christ wanted for us, not when He told us to follow Him and take up His cross, because remember: His yoke is easy, and His burden is light![7] And we are *all* part of His Body as members of the Church, therefore we are all here to support each other and keep each other functioning. When a finger is wounded on our body, the rest of the body doesn't leave it to stay wounded; it coordinates to heal that finger until it is restored, from digestion to blood flow to skin cell growth to even just easing up on using the finger until it doesn't hurt anymore. Likewise, we are here, shining, showing you that you are not, and will not, be alone in your spiritual experiences—just like the Saints showed us.

So these examples of our stories, they aren't just to talk. They aren't meant to wax poetic or to waste your time with anecdotes that go nowhere and do nothing. They're meant to give you just an example of what it might look like to go through certain trials at certain times, and how good it feels to overcome them. Because believe me, when I uncovered these bits of my shadow that had been hiding from me and slowing me down this whole time, I felt that thread burn away—literally! I was so struck with the realization that I felt a golden warmth in my hands and my feet, and a lightness in my heart that made me pause and just sit there on my couch in wonder. It was as if my shadow became a few shades lighter, and as if covered in Tinker Bells' fairy dust, I'd regained the means to fly.

About 4,000 words. That's what all this you've just read came out to, after having felt unable to truly write for months for fear of my own

---

6. 2 Corinthians 3:16-18

7. Matthew 11:28-30

seeming inadequacy. I have been taken out from under my basket. I have been raised up to the top of the lamp post; I am shining again, and I am reflecting the shine of They who owns and oversees this Manor!

But remember: this is only one of several times this has happened. It's not my first time sitting under God's light. Other times I had to leave things like this behind were just as scary and left me feeling just as anxious, just as troubled, and just as stuck in both my spiritual and physical practice. There'll always be some new worry or fear or anxiety that tries to lasso your heart and rip you back out that Gate. By the grace of God, may you always wake up before it does, and may you always find yourself not on the outside of the Gate looking in, but stopping yourself short in the warm, sunny Courtyard. May you find yourself at ease and fully aware of what you need to do to stay rooted on this journey, and may you be emboldened to begin the climb inside once more, all the way back to the Master Bedroom.

Mimi Says:

I recently wrote a Bible study for Lina's Discord group about the Parable of the Sower in Mark 4:3-20. In it, I proffered that the Sower throwing seeds isn't necessarily doing it to just anyone, as many sermons would suggest, and the latter half of the parable reads. Take it back a step, and instead of looking at the grand public, look at yourself. What if the soil where the seeds of faith are thrown is within us, and we are not ready to take it yet?

I left out an idea that I see now was meant for this book. Every year, the Sower brings seeds to plant. This is the same as the cycle of mysticism, where the hard work yields good fruit, but it's not seen while you're wrist-deep in the dirt. Every year, some seeds do not take root. Sometimes, it is because the seed is no good, and many gardeners would say "well, that's why you plant more than one seed!" You gain these ideas and inspirations of faith in many ways, not just from one single moment, one single seed. In the parable, we are met with many challenges that can keep the seed from taking root. Birds eat the seeds and sometimes your fruit, making it feel pointless in trying again. Scorching heat and choking thorns kill the seeds and stop them from taking root. But you cannot dismiss the land that you're planting on;

where we find soil that doesn't work. we don't just ignore it, we work with it, cultivate it, prune and prep until it's ready. We change it—and in the same idea, we change ourselves—to take on something new when the time comes.It is work that takes time, patience, and strength. And then, we get ready to do it again.

While a spiritual journey may not exactly be on a year's schedule, it is still a cycle. Trust me when I say that I have been exhausted by many cycles and lessons. But just as we let the soil *rest*, we also rotate crops, and use composts and fertilizers to nourish our gardens, and we must also do that with our hearts and souls. If your tomatoes don't work, don't fight the seed – make a space for them to grow. Put in the (shadow) work to prepare for the next planting. If all you're good at is growing peppers and sunflowers, then that is the (spiritual) harvest for you to share—you still have to take care of your beds and plots; feeding, watering, and all the extra that's needed.

Every cycle, I find myself cultivating something new and ending up with more than I expected. In the earlier days of this journey, I had no understanding of that, and my harvests were always weak. In the beginning, Sara asked why I became a mystic. The truth is that I didn't choose to do so, it just happened, and that is still the same. I prepared my garden beds for seeds and found that my words and work produced something that the Sower would be proud of. Winter and darkness will come again, and every time it does, I have something more I can do to prepare for it. Every season prepares for the next to be better.

Go Forth in Peace

...to love and serve the Lord.

Now, with all this said, know that we cannot stress this enough: no matter how much you struggle, no matter how many times you stumble and fall, you are not a failure for it. You don't get a limited amount of tries, nor do you have to prove yourself worthy of trying to begin with. No matter how many times you're tested, or how many battles you go through, know that you are invited to walk through the rooms again and remember who you are: God's beloved. And you are invited to do so as many times as it takes for you to truly *believe* it (and then to do so a few more times after).

Though let's also remember that you aren't the first to feel another way: frustrated that you have to walk over the hot coals of this world again and again, wishing that you could truly *see* and understand and *join with* God in all His infinity, once and for all, so nothing would ever knock you off your center again. Many have felt this way before, including dear Mechthild of Madgeburg, and what God has told her might bring you some comfort, too:

> Then the soul lamented: "Alas, Lord, You have been absent from me for too long. If only I could win You so You could find no rest except with me, then love would begin. Then You would be forced to ask me to glow with love." Then He answered:

> "Unblemished dove, let Me spare you, for the world cannot yet do without you."[8]

Wherever you are in life, whoever you are, whatever you're doing now, you're here because it's where you need to be. *The world cannot yet do without you.* So long as you are on this earth, you'll run into these trials again and again, and through them, you change the world. God, in this way, becomes like the glassblower: sometimes He heats us up to the point of burning red hot, sometimes He shapes us and tapers our edges, sometimes He cuts us and sands us and paints us, sometimes He cools us so we might hold our shape on our own, and sometimes He shatters us, so we might be re-melted into another shape we need to take. No matter what, He is our Creator, and we are His art.

And this world needs His art. It needs you. So go, go out into the world, and be the very hands and feet of God: give the will of this great Force in our universe the physical flesh and bones It needs to manifest

---

8. Mechthild, *Meditations from Mechtild of Madgeburg,* 55.

radiance and joy and love and peace, as It has been trying to do with, through, and for all Creation since the inception of all that is. Know also that we're doing it with you: that we are all part of the same Body, and that so long as this Body of God's lovers exist, you will never love Him, or suffer His love through this world, alone.

With love,

Sara Hartwell   &   *Mimi*

Shadow Work: The End is The Beginning is The End.

This book would be considered intermediate, in practicality and application. We ask you to examine yourself in ways you may not have before, to expand on your own understanding so that you (and your magic) can do more.

- We asked you, in the beginning, to write down your beginning. After making it through these chapters, what parts do you recognize your major life points are in? What part do you feel like you are in now?

- Take a bad habit you have and start writing it out with the "why" prompt, as referenced by Sara in this chapter. For every habit you do, sit with it. What would things look like if you didn't have it or do it? This could be anything from an unhealthy coping mechanism to procrastination.

- What does the energy of Judgment feel like to you?

- What does the energy of The World feel like to you?

- This, my dear friend, is not the end; like with every cycle, it must begin again. How does it make you feel to know you are never truly done? Or alone in doing?

Acknowledgements

T HIS BOOK IS THE result of so many little things lining up at just the right time. Naturally, our sisters in faith who have always had our backs and taught us so many lessons about the many ways we can love God, get our special thanks: Lina (@linathejesuswitch) and Hannah (@spirituali.tea). And more, we have to thank our allies in Christian magic and mysticism, and our allies in Christian clergy, for their help in somehow always providing the texts we need when we need them—who hear our musings and our interests, and somehow, find a way to get books (or boxes of books!) to our doorstep. Whether they're clergy we've known for a long time, like Fr. Kyle, or ones we knew only for a short time in our own churches, we are grateful for those leaders who are dedicated to learning and to providing access to wisdom wherever possible.

And of course, we couldn't have created this book without the Christian Witch community, either: your every encouragement, your every bit of excitement, your every question and comment and few moments to listen to us work through and share our learning, it all made it possible to bring one book about mysticism *by* Christian Witches, *for* Christian Witches, possible. Thank you.

May you all find your home, your peace, and your empowerment in the infinity of our Lord.

About the Authors

Sara Raztresen is fourteen years a Christian Witch, as well as an online educator, faith leader and ordained minister of the Universal Life Church. As a Slovene-American, she also has a strong grasp of Catholic folk tradition, especially in Slavic lore, with many of her mother's stories and tips to share. Her lived experience as a witch and extensive Biblical scholarship and community with other progressive Christian leaders gives her the practical and academic lens to discuss the way Christian and witchy worlds collide.

Sara is also a part of a vibrant online Christian Witch community on TikTok, with other social media channels dedicated to education on a variety of Christian witchcraft topics. Find her online via her social media:

- @srazzie97 (TikTok, Bluesky)

- @sararaztresen (Instagram)

- www.sararaztresen.com

Emyle (Mimi) D. Prata is what many would consider a hereditary witch. Her work of over 20 years to maintain the familial practice as well as lean further into apologetics and gnostic theology has helped shape her path from childhood. Immigrant grandparents and great-grands that settled in Appalachia and the Ozarks have given her a beautiful blended tapestry of magic found in God's nature. She studied at WISE Academy under Belladonna LaVeau in 2006, and took what she learned from there to sharpen her skills in nature. She has an A.S. in Applied Health studies, with her lifelong love of herbs and magic leading her into the naturopathic world.

Mimi holds hands and hearts while helping to teach others how to bring this craft to children and families in the Christian Witch community and beyond. Find her online via her social media:

- @feralsouthernhousewife (YouTube, Instagram)

- @feral_southern_housewife (TikTok)

- www.feralsouthernhousewife.wordpress.com

References and Suggested Reading

Agrippa von Netterheim, Henry Cornelius. *Invisibila Dei: A Collection of Hermetic, Mystical, and Anti-Magical Works by Heinrich Cornelius Agrippa.* Translated by Dan Attrel and Justin Sledge. USA: Esoterica Publications, 2024.

Agrippa von Netterheim, Henry Cornelius. *Three Books of Occult Philosophy.* Translated by James Freake. Edited by Donald Tyson. USA: Llewellyn Publications, 1992.

Anderson, Laura E. *When Religion Hurts You: Healing from Religious Trauma and the Impact of High-Control Religion.* Grand Rapids: Brazos Press, 2023.

Aquinas, Thomas, St. *The Summa Theologica of St. Thomas Aquinas.* 2nd. ed. USA: New Advent, 2017. https://www.newadvent.org/summa/3158.htm.

Athanasius of Alexandria, St. "Life of St. Anthony." New Advent. Accessed October 30, 2025. https://www.newadvent.org/fathers/2811.htm.

Augustine of Hippo, St. "Sermon 52." *The Works of St. Augustine, a Translation for the 21st Century: Sermons III (51-94) on the New Testament.* Translated by Edmund Hill. Edited by John E. Rotelle. Brooklyn: New City Press, 1991, 50-65.

Berline, Adele and Marc Zvi Brettler, ed. *The Jewish Study Bible.* London: Oxford University Press, 2014.

Blakney, Raymond B., translator. *Meister Eckhart: A Central Source and Inspiration of Dominant Currents in Philosophy and Theology since Aquinas with the Text of His Historic Defense Against Charges of Heresy.* New York: Harper & Row, 1941.

Dieckmann, Hans. "Shadow (Analytical Psychology)." In The International Dictionary of Psychoanalysis, ed. Ayla Michelle Demir. USA: Thomson Gale, Macmillan Reference, 2005.

Duffy, Martin. *Anathema Maranatha: Christianity and the Imprecatory Arts.* USA: Three Hands Press, 2022.

Julian of Norwich, St. *Revelations of Divine Love.* Translated by Grace Warrack. Grand Rapids: Christian Classics Ethereal Library, 1901.

Kamstra, Karla. *Deconstructing: Leaving Church, Finding Faith.* New York: St. Martin's Essentials, 2024.

Lesses, Rebecca. "Supernatural Beings," in *Jewish Annotated New Testament,* eds. Amy-Jill Levine and Marc Zvi Brettler. London: Oxford University Press, 2017. 682–688.

Mabry, John R. *Growing into God: A Beginner's Guide to Christian Mysticism.* Wheaton: Quest Books, 2012.

Matt, Daniel C. *The Essential Kabbalah: The Heart of Jewish Mysticism.* USA: HarperOne, 2009.

McIntosh, Mark A. *Mystical Theology.* Malden: Blackwell Publishers, 1998.

McClellan, Dan. *The Bible Says So: What We Get Right (and Wrong) About Scripture's Most Controversial Issues.* New York: St. Martin's Essentials, 2025.

McColman, Carl. *The Big Book of Christian Mysticism: The Essential Guide to Contemplative Spirituality.* Charlottesville: Hampton Roads Publishing Company, Inc., 2010.

McGinn, Bernard, ed. *The essential writings of Christian mysticism.* New York: Modern Library, 2006.

Mechthild of Magdeburg. *Meditations from Mechthild of Magdeburg.* Edited by Henry L. Carrigan Jr. Brewster: Paraclete Press, 1999.

Miller, Chris. "Sephora's Starter Witch Kit: Identity Construction through Social Media Protests of Commodified Religion." *Nova Re-*

ligio, vol. 25, no. 3 (2022): 87–112. https://doi.org/10.1525/nr.2022
.25.3.87.

Moltmann, Jürgen. *The Crucified God.* Minneapolis: Fortress Press,
2015.

Nixey, Catherine. *The Darkening Age: The Christian Destruction of the
Classical World.* New York: First Mariner Books, 2017.

Oord, Thomas Jay. *The Death of Omnipotence and the Birth of Amipotence.*
USA: SacraSage Press, 2023.

Stokes, Ryan E. *The Satan: How God's Executioner Became the Enemy.*
Grand Rapids: Wm. B. Eerdmans Publishing Co., 2019.

Teresa of Avila, St. *The Interior Castle or the Mansions,* 3rd ed. Edited by
Benedict Zimmerman. London: Thomas Baker, 1921, https://www
.ccel.org/ccel/teresa/castle2.html.

Throop, Prischilla (translator). *Hildegard von Bingen's Physica: The Complete English Translation of Her Classic Work on Health and Healing.*
Rochester: Healing Arts Press, 1998.

Wilken, Robert Louis. *The Christians as the Romans Saw Them.* USA:
Yale University Press, 2013.

Suggested Reading

Hayward, David. *The Lasting Supper: Letters for Deconstruction.* USA:
CreateSpace, 2016.

Herrington, Angela J. *Deconstructing Your Faith without Losing Yourself.*
USA: Eerdmans, 2024.

Kobes du Mez, Kristin. *Jesus and John Wayne: How White Evangelicals
Corrupted a Faith and Fractured a Nation.* USA: Liveright, 2020.